Developing
Personal Oracle7™
Applications

David Lockman

SAMS
PUBLISHING

201 West 103rd Street
Indianapolis, Indiana 46290

To Joanne, Josh, Michael, and Daniel

Copyright ©1995 by Sams Publishing

FIRST EDITION

International Standard Book Number: 0-672-30757-X

Library of Congress Catalog Card Number: 95-68849

98 97 96 95   4 3 2 1

Interpretation of the printing code: the rightmost double-digit number is the year of the book's printing; the rightmost single-digit, the number of the book's printing. For example, a printing code of 95-1 shows that the first printing of the book occurred in 1995.

Composed in AGaramond and MCPdigital by Macmillan Computer Publishing

Printed in the United States of America

Trademarks

Publisher	*Richard K. Swadley*
Acquisitions Manager	*Greg Wiegand*
Development Manager	*Dean Miller*
Managing Editor	*Cindy Morrow*
Marketing Manager	*Gregg Bushyeager*

Acquisitions Editor
Rosemarie Graham

Development Editor
Todd Bumbalough

Software Development Specialist
Kim Spilker

Senior Editor
Deborah Frisby

Production Editor
Kris Simmons

Copy Editor
Tonya R. Simpson

Technical Reviewers
Jeffery W. George	*Len Sterrett*
Mark Gokman	*Ed Whalen*
Scott Parker	

Editorial Coordinator
Bill Whitmer

Technical Edit Coordinator
Lynette Quinn

Formatter
Frank Sinclair

Editorial Assistants
Sharon Cox
Rhonda Tinch-Mize
Andi Richter

Cover Designer
Tim Amrhein

Book Designer
Alyssa Yesh

Production Team Supervisor
Brad Chinn

Production
Mary Ann Abramson	*Judy Everly*
Angela Bannan	*Ayanna Lacey*
Carol Bowers	*Paula Lowell*
Georgiana Briggs	*Casey Price*
Mona Brown	*Brian-Kent Proffitt*
Michael Brumitt	*Bobbi Satterfield*
Jeanne Clark	*Tina Trettin*
Terrie Deemer	*Susan Van Ness*
Cheryl Dietsch	*Mark Walchle*
Mike Dietsch	

Overview

Contents

Acknowledgments

Without the help of many people at Sams Publishing, I would not have been able to complete this book. Many thanks to Rosemarie Graham, acquisitions editor; Todd Bumbalough, development editor; Deborah Frisby, senior editor; and Kris Simmons, production editor.

Thanks to the following people for posing tough questions and accepting my technical contributions: Enrique Dagach, Barry Cooper, Anita Talbot, David Lerner, Trina Ray, Neil Toy, Irena Glazman, Ron Hungerford, Dan Zormeier, Randy Riedel, John Russo, Mark Browne, Mike Yates, Carol Sarkis, Randall Hill, Bob Nowicki, Mike Sierchio, Bill Adler, Craig Peterson, Miles Miller, James Hauge, Al Kanner, Ron Joyner, Roger Goodman, Paul Springer, and Gyan Ahluwalia.

Many thanks to John Wheeler of Oracle Corporation for providing me with a valuable opportunity and an education on the business of consulting. I am also grateful to my family and friends who offered encouragement for the past few months.

Finally, special thanks and apologies to four assistants who exhibited tremendous patience: Joanne Lockman, motivational speaker; Josh Lockman, data entry administrator; Michael Lockman, progress monitor; and Daniel Lockman, documentation specialist.

About the Author

David Lockman provides guidance to organizations on the use of Oracle products. He has participated in the design and implementation of client/server applications for a variety of industries. He also provides on-site training on the use of Oracle products and advises organizations on staff development.

At Oracle Corporation, Mr. Lockman was employed as a managing consultant where he was responsible for a group of consultants supporting a broad range of projects including the migration of large legacy databases to Oracle7, performance tuning, and applications development.

Mr. Lockman and his family live in Southern California.

He can be reached on the Internet at dlockman@earthlink.net.

Introduction

Oracle is the most popular relational database management system in the world. Its popularity is the result of several factors:

- Oracle is available on a wide range of computer systems.
- Powerful features are introduced with each new release of the product.
- The exponential growth in the quantity of data maintained by organizations requires convenient and reliable data repositories.

What This Book Is About

This book is about a new version of the Oracle relational database management system (RDBMS) called Personal Oracle7. Personal Oracle7 is a version of the Oracle product that runs on top of Microsoft Windows. Even though Personal Oracle7 is a PC-based version of the Oracle RDBMS, Personal Oracle7 provides almost all of the same features that exist in the versions of the Oracle RDBMS for large computer systems. As a result, Personal Oracle7 is an excellent tool for developers who intend to design applications for the Oracle RDBMS.

Who Should Read This Book

This book assumes that you're familiar with Microsoft Windows and that you have some experience with a database—whether relational or nonrelational.

Who will benefit from this book?

- Developers who haven't worked with Oracle but are familiar with PC databases such as dBASE, FoxPro, or Paradox.
- Oracle developers who need information on the new Database Administration Tools.
- College students interested in learning about relational databases and Structured Query Language (SQL).
- Information system professionals who must stay current with relational database technology.

Conventions Used in This Book

The following typographic conventions are used in this book:

- Code lines, statements, functions, operators, and some other special computer terms appear in a special `computer` typeface.

- When user input and computer output are shown together, the output is shown in the **`bold computer`** typeface.

- Placeholders in syntax descriptions appear in *italic* typeface. Replace the placeholder with the actual filename, parameter, or whatever element it represents.

- *Italics* highlight technical terms when they first appear in the text and are sometimes used to emphasize important points.

1

What Is Personal Oracle7 for Windows?

On January 17, 1995, Oracle Corporation announced the release of Personal Oracle, a Windows-based version of the most popular relational database in the world—Oracle7. At that time, Oracle decided to spread around a trial version of Personal Oracle to its potential customers by making Personal Oracle available for downloading via Oracle Corporation's World Wide Web (WWW) home page (`http://www.oracle.com`).

A Perspective on Relational Databases

In 1970, the *Communications of the ACM* published a paper entitled "A Relational Model of Data for Large Shared Data Banks." Authored by Dr. E. F. Codd, a member of the IBM San Jose Research Laboratory, the paper provided a theoretical and mathematical foundation for the concept of a relational database. It is difficult to point to another single article in the field of computer science that has had as great an influence on vendors, practitioners, and users as Codd's contribution.

In his paper, Codd described the elements of a relational database: relations, attributes, domains, and the relational operators. Codd's paper described a data storage system that possessed three characteristics that were sorely needed at that time. The characteristics he described are the following:

- Logical data independence: This desirable characteristic means that changes made to an attribute (column)—for example, an increase or decrease in size—have no perceivable effect on other attributes for the same relation (table). Logical data independence was attractive to data processing organizations because it could substantially reduce the cost of software maintenance.

- Referential and data integrity: Unlike other database systems, a relational database would relieve the application software of the burden of enforcing integrity constraints. Codd described two characteristics that would be maintained by a relational database—referential and data integrity, which we will discuss in detail throughout this book.

- Ad hoc query: This would provide the user the capability to indicate what data should be retrieved by the database without indicating how it should be accomplished.

Some time passed before there was an actual product that implemented some of the features of the relational database that Codd described. Today, there are several vendors of relational database management systems (RDBMS)—Oracle, Sybase, IBM, Informix, Microsoft, Computer Associates, Gupta, and many others. Of these vendors, Oracle has emerged as the leader. The Oracle RDBMS engine has been ported to more platforms than any other database product. Because of Oracle's multiplatform support, many application software vendors have made Oracle their database platform of choice. And now, Oracle Corporation has ported the same RDBMS engine to the desktop environment with its release of Personal Oracle.

> **NOTE**
>
> Today's relational databases implement a number of extremely useful features that were never mentioned in Codd's original article. However, it is interesting to observe that there is still no commercially available database that is a full implementation of Codd's twelve rules for relational databases.

Personal Oracle and the Oracle Product Line

As the world's leading vendor of relational database software, Oracle Corporation supports its flagship product, the Oracle RDBMS, on more than 90 different platforms. The release of Personal Oracle for Windows has now provided a product that is supported on the most popular desktop operating system—Microsoft Windows.

The Oracle RDBMS is available in the following three configurations:

- The *Oracle Enterprise Server* can support many users on highly scaleable platforms such as Sun, HP, Pyramid, and Sequent. The various options that are available with this configuration include the distributed option, by which several Oracle databases on separate computers can function as a single logical database. The Oracle Enterprise Server is available for a wide variety of operating systems and hardware configurations.

- The *Oracle Workgroup Server* is designed for workgroups and is available on NetWare, Windows NT, SCO UNIX, and UnixWare. The Oracle Workgroup Server is a cost-effective and low-maintenance solution for supporting small groups of users.

- *Personal Oracle* is a Windows-based version of the Oracle database engine that offers the same functionality that exists in the Oracle Enterprise Server and the Oracle Workgroup Server. Even though Personal Oracle cannot function as a database server by supporting multiple users, it still provides an excellent environment for experimentation and prototyping.

An Ideal Prototyping Environment

Personal Oracle provides almost all of the same features as the Oracle7 Server on larger platforms. As a result, you can use Personal Oracle to build a working database application that can then be ported to a multiuser version of the Oracle7 Server. You can build all of the tables, indexes, views, sequences, and other database objects that would exist in a production-quality database application. Also, Personal Oracle can be used in conjunction with application development tools such as Microsoft's Visual Basic, Powersoft's PowerBuilder, Oracle's Developer/2000, and Gupta's SQLWindows.

To use Personal Oracle, you will need a PC equipped with a 486 or Pentium and at least 16 MB of memory.

Personal Oracle and Third-Party Application Development Tools

As you'd expect, Personal Oracle works with Oracle application development tools such as Oracle Developer/2000 and Oracle Power Objects. Developer/2000 is a suite of tools that include the following:

- Oracle Forms—an enterprise tool for building robust applications for three GUI environments: Windows, Macintosh, and Motif.
- Oracle Reports—a report writer that can tackle the most complex reporting requirements and also runs in the Windows, Macintosh, and Motif environments.
- Browser—an ad hoc query tool designed for casual users.

You can also use Personal Oracle with other popular application development tools such as Visual Basic, PowerBuilder, and SQLWindows. This book contains a set of appendixes describing the use of each of these products with Personal Oracle.

Talking to Oracle with SQL: Structured Query Language

You communicate with Personal Oracle through Oracle's version of the Structured Query Language (SQL, usually pronounced *sequel*). SQL is a nonprocedural language; unlike C or COBOL, in which you must describe exactly how to access and manipulate data, SQL specifies what to do. Internally, Oracle determines how to perform the request. SQL exists as an ANSI standard as well as an industry standard. Oracle's implementation of SQL adheres to Level 2 of the ANSI X3.135-1989/ISO 9075-1989 standard with full implementation of the Integrity Enhancement Feature. As with other database vendors, Oracle provides many extensions to ANSI SQL.

In addition, Oracle's implementation of SQL adheres with the U.S. Government standard as described in the Federal Information Processing Standard Publication (FIPS PUB) 127, entitled "Database Language SQL."

The Purpose of This Book

This book is designed to serve readers who fit into the following categories:

■ You are familiar with databases such as dBASE or FoxPro but haven't worked with Oracle or other SQL-based database products.

■ You have worked with the Oracle7 Server but haven't used the new Database Administration Tools.

■ You are planning to use Personal Oracle as a prototyping tool for client/server application development.

When you have finished reading this book, you'll be familiar with the following:

■ SQL: the de facto industry and ANSI standard language for interacting with relational databases.

■ PL/SQL: Oracle's procedural language extensions to SQL used for writing database triggers and stored procedures and functions.

■ Database Administration Tools: the Windows-based tools designed to simplify the administration of Personal Oracle and the Oracle Workgroup Server.

■ Real-world development issues: database design, data loading, and the environment that exists in an upsized Oracle database running on UNIX.

Let's begin with Chapter 2, "Installing and Using Personal Oracle7."

2

Installing and Using Personal Oracle7

This chapter describes the process of installing Personal Oracle. You'll be able to follow the examples in this book more easily if you install and use the trial version of Personal Oracle on your PC. The material in this chapter—and the entire book—is based on the June 1995 release of Personal Oracle.

The CD-ROM accompanying this book contains, among other things, a 90-day trial license for Personal Oracle. You can install Personal Oracle directly from the CD. If that isn't convenient, you can download the latest version of Personal Oracle from Oracle Corporation's World Wide Web page at http://www.oracle.com.

I'll describe both methods.

Hardware and Software Requirements

To install and use Personal Oracle, your computer configuration should consist of the following:

- A PC with a 486-class, or better, CPU
- A minimum of 16 MB of RAM
- 50 MB of free disk space if installing from CD; 133 MB of free disk space if downloading from Oracle's WWW page
- MS Windows 3.1 (or 3.11) or Windows for Workgroups 3.11

> **NOTE**
>
> Oracle Corporation makes no claim that Personal Oracle will work on OS/2 or Windows NT. At press time, a production version of Windows 95 had not yet been released. When Windows 95 is available, Oracle will release a compatible version of Personal Oracle.

Downloading Personal Oracle from the Oracle WWW Page

Since January 1995, Oracle Corporation has made available a trial version of Personal Oracle on its World Wide Web page. The June 1995 version was distributed as a self-extracting .EXE file named PO7SEWIN.EXE and was 18,597,394 bytes in size. This file also includes a trial version of Oracle Objects for OLE.

Obviously, it can take quite a while to download PO7SEWIN.EXE. The time required to download the file depends on the speed of your Internet connection and the demand on the Oracle Web server.

After you've downloaded the file, place it in its own directory—I suggest c:\po7. Either exit Windows or use an MS-DOS prompt and execute the following DOS command:

```
c:\po7\po7sewin.exe -d -n
```

All of the files are extracted into three top-level directories.

```
c:\po7\gc25ptch
c:\po7\po7_win
c:\po7\win32s
```

Specific Disk Space Requirements

If you're downloading Personal Oracle from the Oracle WWW page, you really need a total of 133 MB of free disk space to perform a complete install of Personal Oracle.

- 19 MB for PO7SEWIN.EXE, a self-extracting file
- 64 MB for the unzipped files contained in the directories po7_win, gc25ptch, and win32s
- 50 MB for the directories and files installed under the Oracle home directory

Once you've installed Personal Oracle, you can free up the 64 MB of disk space consumed by the po7_win, gc25ptch, and win32s directories. You might want to save PO7SEWIN.EXE in case you decide to reinstall Personal Oracle from scratch.

Installing Win32s

Personal Oracle requires the installation of Version 1.20 of Win32s—Microsoft's 32-bit API extension for Windows. Before you begin the Personal Oracle installation, install Win32s by executing c:\po7\win32\disk1\setup.exe. You can verify that Win32s has been properly installed by running Freecell.

Using the Oracle Installer

Before you begin the Personal Oracle installation, it's a good idea to exit any open applications so that there is enough free memory to start the default Personal Oracle database.

To begin the actual installation, you'll want to execute the Oracle installer by executing ORAINST.EXE, which can be found in \po7_win\install as shown in Figure 2.1.

FIGURE 2.1.

Running ORAINST.EXE.

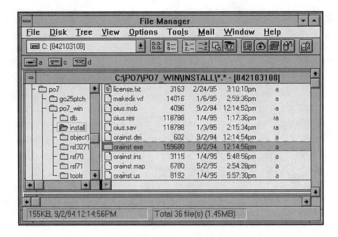

The Installer prompts you for the location to be used for the Oracle home directory (see Figure 2.2). By default, the Oracle Installer chooses to install all of the Oracle7 products into the c:\orawin directory. You can select a different drive or directory if disk space on your C drive is a concern.

FIGURE 2.2.

Choosing a directory for Oracle Home.

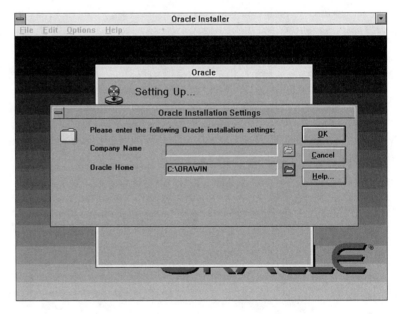

The Oracle Installer gives you three choices for your Personal Oracle installation: Complete, Minimal, and Custom (see Figure 2.3). Unless you're lacking sufficient disk space, use the Complete installation option.

FIGURE 2.3.

*Oracle instal-
lation options.*

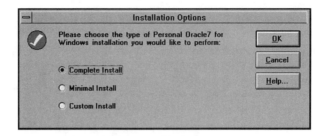

During the installation of Personal Oracle, the Oracle Installer displays a progress bar to indicate the approximate percentage of completion of the installation.

The Oracle Installer scans the directories in your DOS path to determine if there are other
copies of certain DLLs that are used by Personal Oracle. If the Installer finds another copy of
a DLL, it displays a message informing you of the situation (see Figure 2.4). You have three
choices:

■ You can allow the Installer to rename the other copy of the particular DLL with a file
extension of .OLD and proceed with the installation. If you don't choose this option,
you might have problems connecting to the Personal Oracle database from application
development tools.

■ You can choose not to rename the other copy of the DLL and instead instruct the
Installer to write the information about the duplicate DLL to a file (see Figure 2.5).

■ You can terminate the installation.

FIGURE 2.4.

*Message regarding
DLL conflicts.*

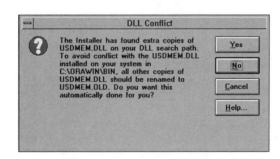

FIGURE 2.5.

*Installer message: File
describes extra DLLs.*

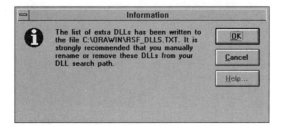

The last task performed by the Installer is the installation of a starter Personal Oracle database. When the starter database has been installed, the Installer displays a message indicating that the installation is complete (see Figure 2.6).

FIGURE 2.6.

Personal Oracle instal-
lation is complete.

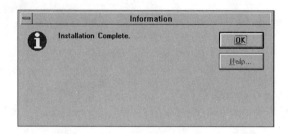

Finally, the Installer posts a message informing you that the default password for the Personal Oracle database is `oracle` and that it can be changed with the Password Manager utility (see Figure 2.7).

FIGURE 2.7.

Installer message:
Default database
password.

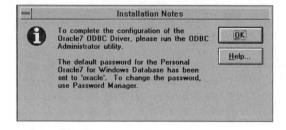

The Windows Groups

Now that you've installed Personal Oracle, let's see how the Windows desktop has changed. The Personal Oracle Installer creates the following Windows program groups:

- Personal Oracle7
- Oracle
- Oracle7 ODBC
- Oracle Objects for OLE

I'll describe the contents of each of these Windows program groups.

Personal Oracle7

The Personal Oracle7 Windows program group contains the Oracle Database Administration Tools (see Figure 2.8). If you've used the Oracle RDBMS in the past, you'll find that some of these tools are much more intuitive than using SQL*DBA or SQL*Plus to accomplish the same task. In some cases, the new tool might be easier to use by only providing a subset of the capabilities that exist in SQL*DBA or SQL*Plus. The contents of the Personal Oracle7 Windows program group include the following:

Database Manager   User Manager

Session Manager   Database Expander

Object Manager   SQL*DBA

SQL*Loader   Online Oracle7 documentation

Export   Backup Manager

Recovery Manager   Password Manager

Online help for the Database Tools   Import

FIGURE 2.8.

*The Personal Oracle7
Windows program
group.*

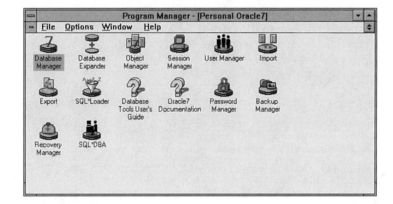

You'll find it convenient to add SQL*Plus to this program group because it saves you the trouble of having to open the Oracle program group when you want to use the program. To add SQL*Plus as an item in the Personal Oracle7 program group, select New from the Windows menu, choose Program Item, and click OK. Use Browse to select \bin\plus31.exe under the Oracle home directory.

Oracle

The Oracle Windows program group consists of the following items (see Figure 2.9):

■ Oracle Installer

■ SQL*Plus 3.1

■ Online help for installing SQL*Plus

■ A note on the installation of Windows/DOS Oracle products

■ An Oracle7 release note

FIGURE 2.9.

The Oracle Windows program group.

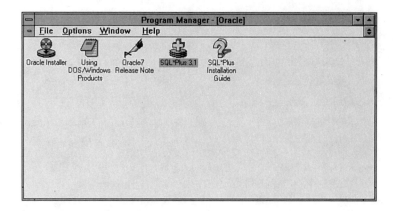

If you add SQL*Plus to the Personal Oracle7 program group, you will rarely need to use the items in the Oracle program group.

Oracle7 ODBC

The Oracle7 ODBC Windows program group contains the following items (see Figure 2.10):

- A utility for testing ODBC connections to the Personal Oracle7 database
- Release note for the Oracle ODBC driver
- The ODBC Administrator

FIGURE 2.10.

The Oracle7 ODBC Windows program group.

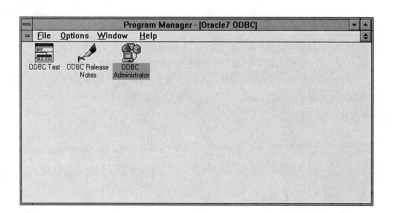

After you've created an ODBC data source for Personal Oracle, you probably won't use the items in this program group very often.

Oracle Objects for OLE

The Oracle Objects for OLE Windows program group consists of the following items (see Figure 2.11):

- Notes on Bound Controls for MFC 2.5
- Notes on Bound Controls for OWL 2.0/2.5
- Online help about the Class Library
- A Class Library Workbook
- Online help for Oracle Objects for OLE

FIGURE 2.11.

The Oracle Objects for OLE Windows program group.

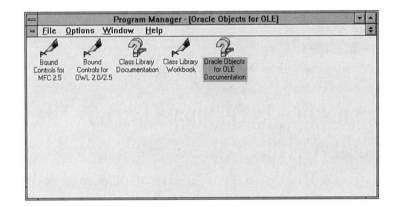

Remember that Personal Oracle and Oracle Objects for OLE are separate products. Personal Oracle doesn't depend on the installation of Oracle Objects for OLE. If you're not planning to use Oracle Objects for OLE, you can delete this program group.

Personal Oracle7, WIN.INI, and ORACLE.INI

The Oracle Installer automatically modifies the Windows initialization file, WIN.INI, by adding a section for Oracle.

```
[Oracle]
ORA_CONFIG=C:\WINDOWS\ORACLE.INI
```

The Installer creates the ORACLE.INI file in the \windows directory. The Installer uses the location that you specified for the Oracle home directory to write the following lines to ORACLE.INI:

```
[Oracle]
ORACLE_HOME=C:\ORAWIN
NLS_LANG=AMERICAN_AMERICA.WE8ISO8859P1
ORAINST=C:\ORAWIN\dbs
RDBMS71=C:\ORAWIN\RDBMS71
PRO16=C:\ORAWIN\pro16
SQLPATH=C:\ORAWIN\DBS
PLUS31=C:\ORAWIN\PLUS31
EXECUTE_SQL=PLUS31
MSHELP=C:\ORAWIN\mshelp
```

```
TOOLS_GROUP=Personal Oracle7
HELP_GROUP=Personal Oracle7
RDBMS70=C:\ORAWIN\rdbms70
PRO15=C:\ORAWIN\pro15
PRO14=C:\ORAWIN\pro14
RDBMS71_PORACLE=C:\ORAWIN\RDBMS71
RDBMS71_CONTROL=C:\ORAWIN\DBS
RDBMS71_ARCHIVE=C:\ORAWIN\RDBMS71\ARCHIVE
VS10=C:\ORAWIN\VS10
LOCAL=2:
SQLNET DBNAME oracle7=2:
PLSQL21=C:\ORAWIN\PLSQL21
```

Also, the Installer makes a copy of AUTOEXEC.BAT and places c:\orawin\bin (or the bin directory beneath your Oracle home directory) at the front of the DOS path.

Connecting to Personal Oracle7: The Oracle ODBC Driver

Personal Oracle is supplied with an Oracle7 ODBC driver that can be used by many third-party application development environments—such as PowerBuilder, SQLWindows, and Visual Basic—to communicate with a Personal Oracle database. Of course, PowerBuilder and SQLWindows can use native drivers to communicate with Personal Oracle.

To access Personal Oracle via ODBC, define the Personal Oracle database as an ODBC data source with the following procedure. In the Oracle7 ODBC program group, double-click on the ODBC Administrator icon (see Figure 2.12).

FIGURE 2.12.
The ODBC Admin-istrator.

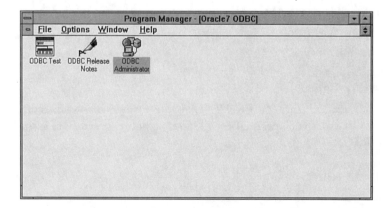

When you invoke the ODBC Administrator, it displays the Data Sources window (see Figure 2.13). Click Add to add a new data source.

The ODBC Administrator displays a list of the available ODBC drivers that you can use to create a new data source. Select the driver named Oracle71 and click OK (see Figure 2.14).

FIGURE 2.13.

The Data Sources window.

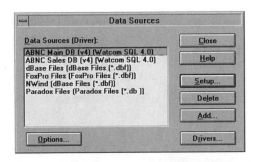

FIGURE 2.14.

The Add Data Source window.

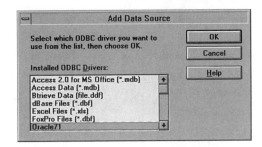

The Oracle7 ODBC Setup window appears (see Figure 2.15). In this window, specify the contents of the following three fields.

■ Data Source Name: Assign a meaningful name to the ODBC data source, such as PO7.

■ Description: Provide a description for the ODBC data source, such as Personal Oracle.

■ SQL*Net Connect String: For Personal Oracle, enter 2: to indicate that the ODBC data source is a local Oracle database.

FIGURE 2.15.

The Oracle7 ODBC Setup window.

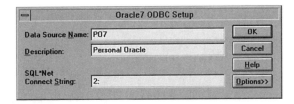

When you click OK, the ODBC Administrator records the details for the new data source, which now appears in the list of ODBC data sources (see Figure 2.16). You are now able to connect to Personal Oracle through the ODBC driver by specifying the ODBC data source name you have assigned to the Personal Oracle database.

FIGURE 2.16.

The Data Sources window with the new Personal Oracle data source.

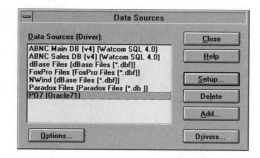

Installation Issues

The two most common installation problems are the following:

- Not enough memory to start the Personal Oracle database
- Conflicts between Personal Oracle and the Microsoft Sound System 2.0 kit

Not Enough Memory

If there isn't enough memory to start the Personal Oracle database, the Database Manager displays Oracle error ORA-09368, which can occur under the following conditions:

- Your PC doesn't have 16 MB of memory.
- One or more Windows applications are running, preventing Oracle from obtaining the memory it needs to start the Personal Oracle database. This error doesn't require a reinstallation of Personal Oracle. Just be sure that no applications are running when you start up the Personal Oracle database using Database Manager (described in Chapter 3, "Personal Oracle7 and the Database Administration Tools").

Microsoft Sound System 2.0

One known problem for Personal Oracle is Microsoft Sound System 2.0. Specifically, a driver named SNDEVNTS.DRV isn't compatible with Win32s and, as a result, can cause Personal Oracle to crash. If you must use Personal Oracle, be sure that this driver isn't loaded in your CONFIG.SYS or SYSTEM.INI. Microsoft has a patch for the driver named SEVNT022.EXE, which you can obtain from a variety of sources including the Microsoft FTP server (ftp.microsoft.com) or WWW site (www.microsoft.com).

3

Personal Oracle7 and the Database Administration Tools

Before the introduction of Personal Oracle7 and the Oracle Workgroup Server, if you managed an Oracle database, you had two choices for tools (excluding any third-party products): SQL*DBA and SQL*Plus. Both of these interfaces relied upon the user knowing what SQL and data manipulation commands to enter.

With the advent of Personal Oracle7 and the Oracle Workgroup Server, the functionality of SQL*DBA and SQL*Plus has been partitioned into the Database Administration Tools, a set of Windows-based programs that provide a friendlier interface with a familiar look and feel for PC users. In this chapter, we'll get acquainted with this toolset.

Database Manager

At this point, it's important to have a basic understanding of the Oracle architecture. You can think of the Oracle database as having three states:

- Running, available for use
- In the process of starting up or shutting down
- Shutdown, not available for use

Database Manager is a tool that simplifies the operation of a Personal Oracle7 database.

Starting Personal Oracle7

To start up the Personal Oracle7 database, double-click the Database Manager icon. Click the Startup button. A pop-up window will appear, prompting you to enter the database password. Unless you have changed it, enter the word `oracle` (see Figure 3.1).

FIGURE 3.1.

Entering the database password during database startup.

After a short time, the green light on the signal should appear, indicating that the database has been successfully started (see Figure 3.2).

FIGURE 3.2.

Database Manager screen after database startup.

Shutting Down Personal Oracle7

The process for shutting down the database is very similar. Double-click the Database Manager icon. Click the Shutdown button. Again, a pop-up window will appear for you to enter the database password. Enter the password; a screen will appear asking you to confirm that you want to shut down the database. Within a short time, the red light on the signal should appear, indicating that the database has been successfully shut down (see Figure 3.3).

FIGURE 3.3.

Database Manager screen after successful database shutdown.

> **TIP**
>
> It's a good idea to go through the shutdown process before exiting Windows or turning off your computer. This ensures that Oracle has safely closed all the database files. However, if the computer is turned off without shutting down Personal Oracle7, Oracle will perform what is called *instance recovery* the next time Personal Oracle7 is started.

Object Manager

The function of Object Manager is to create or modify database objects: tables, indexes, views, and database links. Object Manager has an intuitive interface and is quite easy to operate.

But there are times when it makes more sense to use SQL*Plus instead of Object Manager. As we all know, developing software is an iterative process. We typically write scripts and programs and continue to modify and refine them during the development process. Object Manager is a great "quick-and-dirty" tool for building database objects. It doesn't, however, have the capability to record or process scripts (see Figure 3.4).

FIGURE 3.4.

Using Object Manager to create a new table.

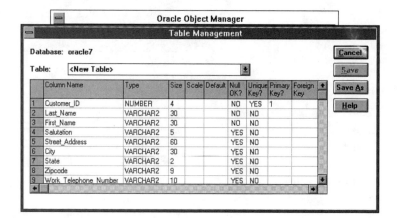

SQL*Plus

SQL*Plus is a command-line interface to the Oracle database. This tool has been used by thousands of Oracle users and programmers for many years. Even with the release of the Windows-based Database Tools, SQL*Plus will continue to be used at almost all Oracle database installations, regardless of hardware platform or operating system. It will continue to be used for two reasons:

- There are countless SQL*Plus scripts—developed by Oracle Corporation, software vendors, and end users—that are needed for the installation of products, application development, and product support.
- SQL*Plus is a common denominator among Oracle developers and users.

SQL*Plus doesn't provide a point-and-click interface. It is old-fashioned in the sense that you have to type in each SQL statement that you want Oracle to process (see Figure 3.5). SQL*Plus has a spool capability that you can use for saving the SQL statements you have entered as well as the response returned by the Oracle database.

FIGURE 3.5.

Using SQL*Plus to create the customer table.

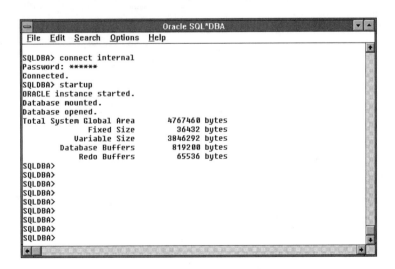

```
                              Oracle SQL*Plus                          ▼ ▲
 File   Edit   Search   Options   Help
  1   CREATE TABLE Customer
  2       (Customer_ID              NUMBER(4) NOT NULL,
  3        Last_Name                VARCHAR2(30) NULL,
  4        First_Name               VARCHAR2(30) NULL,
  5        Salutation               VARCHAR2(5) NULL,
  6        Street_Address           VARCHAR2(60) NULL,
  7        City                     VARCHAR2(30) NULL,
  8        State                    VARCHAR2(2) NULL,
  9        Zipcode                  VARCHAR2(9) NULL,
 10        Work_Telephone_Number    VARCHAR2(10) NULL,
 11        Home_Telephone_Number    VARCHAR2(10) NULL,
 12        Fax_Number               VARCHAR2(10) NULL,
 13        Earliest_Time_to_Call    DATE NULL,
 14        Latest_Time_to_Call      DATE NULL,
 15        Local_Time_Zone          VARCHAR2(3) NULL,
 16        Created_Date             DATE NULL,
 17        Created_By               VARCHAR2(30) NULL,
 18        Modified_Date            DATE NULL,
 19        Modified_By              VARCHAR2(30) NULL
 20* )
SQL> /

Table created.
```

SQL*DBA

Like SQL*Plus, SQL*DBA is a command-line interface to the Oracle database. Unlike SQL*Plus, SQL*DBA can be used to start up or shut down an Oracle database. All of the critical capabilities of SQL*DBA are now available in Database Manager (see Figure 3.6).

FIGURE 3.6.

Using SQL*DBA to start up the Oracle database.

```
                              Oracle SQL*DBA                          ▼ ▲
 File   Edit   Search   Options   Help
SQLDBA> connect internal
Password: ******
Connected.
SQLDBA> startup
ORACLE instance started.
Database mounted.
Database opened.
Total System Global Area         4767460 bytes
              Fixed Size           36432 bytes
           Variable Size         3846292 bytes
        Database Buffers          819200 bytes
            Redo Buffers           65536 bytes
SQLDBA>
SQLDBA>
SQLDBA>
SQLDBA>
SQLDBA>
SQLDBA>
SQLDBA>
SQLDBA>
SQLDBA>
```

Database Expander

At some point, it might become necessary to increase the size of a database. This occurs for a couple of reasons:

- The number of records continues to increase.
- Additional tables must be created.

Unlike some database systems, Oracle relies on preallocated files for storage. If you need to store 20 MB of records in an Oracle database, you specify the name and size of each MS-DOS file that you want Oracle to use. Increasing the size of the database really means allocating additional MS-DOS files for the database's use.

Before the release of Personal Oracle7 (and its related product, the Oracle Workgroup Server), you used SQL*DBA or SQL*Plus and entered a command to allocate additional space. With the introduction of Database Expander, this procedure has been simplified; now it's a lot harder to make a mistake than it was in the past. However, if you have existing SQL*Plus scripts, you can still expand a Personal Oracle7 database by using the CREATE TABLESPACE or ALTER TABLESPACE statement.

Shown in Figure 3.7 is an example of how you can use the Database Expander to add additional space to the default Personal Oracle7 database that's created during installation.

FIGURE 3.7.

Using Database Expander to view available space in the USER_DATA tablespace.

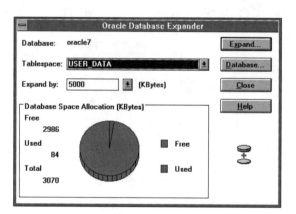

User Manager

Although Personal Oracle7 is not designed to support concurrent multiuser access, the Oracle7 database server is designed for this purpose. To support this feature, Oracle provides two database objects: the role and the user. (Roles and users aren't important to a stand-alone Oracle database, but they are very useful to a developer who is trying to learn how Oracle works in this area.)

Database Users

Throughout this book (and in other sources), the terms *Oracle user, database user, Oracle owner,* and *Oracle account* are used interchangeably. Essentially, they all refer to the same thing: an account that has been granted one or more database privileges. A number of things about Oracle accounts aren't obvious:

■ An Oracle user may represent a person or an organization.

   For instance, MGILROY could be the Oracle account for Max Gilroy, technician (see Figure 3.8). MARKETING could be the Oracle account responsible for the information of the entire marketing division.

FIGURE 3.8.

Creating database user MGILROY with User Manager.

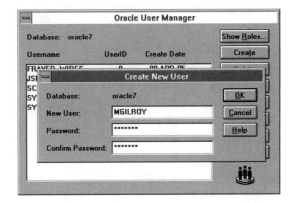

■ An Oracle account is distinct from an operating system account for the same individual.

   In a client-server environment, the Oracle server runs on a different operating system—for example, UNIX, NetWare, or Windows NT. In our example, even though MGILROY has an Oracle account, he may or may not have an operating system account. We'll discuss this further in Chapter 29, "Performance Considerations."

■ Every database object is owned by some Oracle account.

   For example, the Oracle user JSMITH may be the owner of three tables and have the ability to read the tables owned by the MARKETING account.

Database Roles

There is usually a set of well-defined roles for the individuals that compose an organization. In a marketing organization, examples of typical roles would be director, manager, analyst, and clerk. Whether or not an organization uses an automated information system, each role possesses a set of information access privileges. A director has the privilege to retrieve, add, change, or destroy any information that exists in his or her domain—whether it is found in file cabinets or on disk drives. Similarly, a clerk may make changes to information only by following a specific procedure.

Oracle supports this view by providing the database role. A *database role* is a set of privileges that serve as a template that can be assigned to individual users. For example, a database role named TECHNICIAN might have select, insert, and update privileges (the capability to read, write, and modify records) on the PRODUCT table but only the select privilege on the BUDGET table. After a database role has been defined, it can be assigned to individual users. Using database roles simplifies the work of a database administrator and reduces the odds that a hole may exist in the database's security scheme (see Figure 3.9).

FIGURE 3.9.

Creating the TECH-NICIAN database role with User Manager.

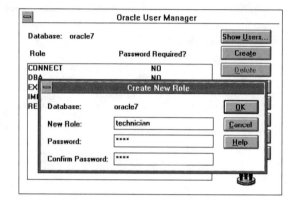

Database Privileges

Database privileges can be divided into two categories: system privileges and object privileges. An example of a *system privilege* is the right to create a table or an index. An example of an *object privilege* is the right for an Oracle user to select from or insert into a table owned by another Oracle user.

System Privileges

In Oracle Version 6, there were only three system privileges:

- CONNECT: the right to connect to the database
- RESOURCE: the right to create database objects such as tables and indexes
- DBA: all database privileges (all object privileges plus the ability to add and drop users, change passwords, and so on)

For the purpose of compatibility with Oracle Version 6, these three privileges have been transformed into three predefined roles in the Oracle7 database. In addition, Personal Oracle7 has two other predefined roles that concern the privilege to perform a full export or import (which will be discussed in Chapter 24, "Database Backup and Recovery"):

- FULL_EXP_DATABASE
- FULL_IMP_DATABASE

User Manager provides the capability to assign a subset of the system privileges to database roles (see Figure 3.10). SQL*Plus offers the full array of system and object privilege management that you would need in a multirole, multiuser environment.

FIGURE 3.10.
Granting system privileges to a role with User Manager.

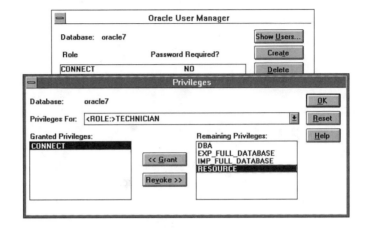

Object Privileges

The set of object privileges that can be granted to a role or a user depends upon the type of object. For example, table object privileges include the following:

Select: the capability to read records from a table

Insert: the right to add records to a table

Delete: the right to remove records from a table

Update: the right to modify existing rows in a table

Even though a database user has been granted a role, an additional database privilege can be granted to a specific user. If at all possible, you should do this sparingly; in no time at all, keeping track of who has what additional privileges can become very difficult.

Session Manager

Because the Database Administration Tools are also part of Oracle's bundle of products referred to as Workgroup/2000, some of the tools are really intended for a multiuser environment. Session Manager falls into this category.

You can have multiple tools or applications simultaneously connected to a Personal Oracle7 database. But, because MS-DOS is not a multitasking operating system, only one of these tools can be active at any given time. For instance, if you use SQL*Plus, two sessions will be displayed by Session Manager: SYS (the account that manages Personal Oracle7) and the Oracle account running SQL*Plus (see Figure 3.11).

FIGURE 3.11.

Session Manager displaying two Personal Oracle7 users.

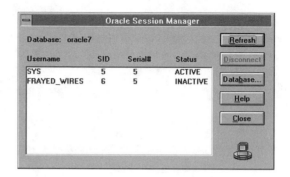

Import and Export

You've finally developed your killer Personal Oracle7 application. After much blood, sweat, and tears, you've assembled a comprehensive set of demo data that you want to distribute to other Personal Oracle7 users. Export and Import are the tools to use for this purpose.

Export and Import are used in conjunction with one another. Export is used to copy the contents of one or more tables to a binary-format MS-DOS file. Import is capable of reading an export file and loading the contents as specified by the user.

Export by Table

Export can be used to save the contents of a single table to a binary file specified by the user (see Figure 3.12). You can export a table definition without its contents. Export also offers the option of producing an export file in which the tables have been compressed.

FIGURE 3.12.

Exporting a single table.

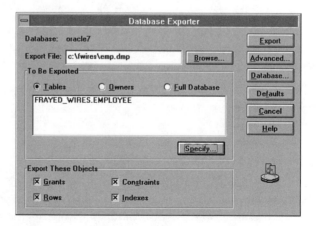

Export by Owner

Export also provides the option of saving all the database objects—tables, indexes, and others—that are owned by a specified user (see Figure 3.13).

FIGURE 3.13.

Exporting all database objects owned by a user.

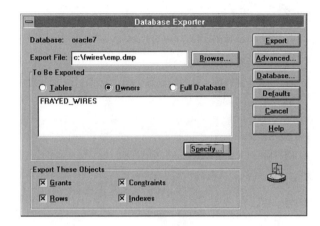

Full Export

At some point, you may want to export the entire contents of your Personal Oracle7 database—the contents of each table and its definition, all index definitions, all view definitions, and every other database object definition. Such an export is referred to as a full export (see Figure 3.14). The time required to perform a full export depends on two factors: the size of the database and the percentage of database storage that is used. A full export of a very large but mostly empty database won't take very long to complete. If it doesn't take long, a full export of your database provides the most flexibility and safety of all database backup strategies.

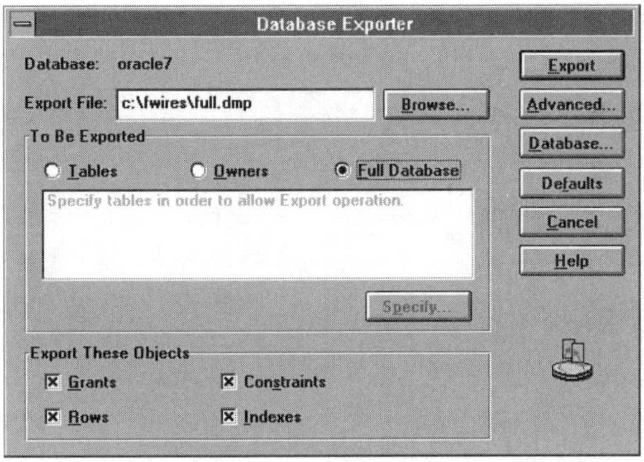

FIGURE 3.14.

Performing a full database export.

Backup Manager

In addition to the Export utility, you can use Backup Manager to safeguard your data. Backup Manager differs from Export in that it copies log files in their entirety rather than making a copy of the contents of the database (see Figure 3.15).

FIGURE 3.15.

The Backup Manager screen.

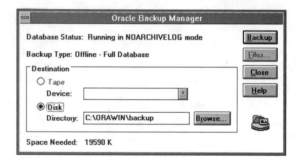

Recovery Manager

Recovery Manager works in conjunction with Backup Manager to perform database recovery (see Figure 3.16). We'll discuss the backup and recovery of a Personal Oracle7 database in Chapter 24, "Database Backup and Recovery."

FIGURE 3.16.

Invoking Recovery Manager.

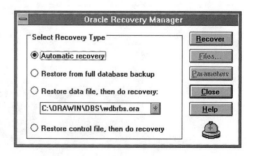

Password Manager

When you start up or shut down a Personal Oracle7 database, Oracle prompts you for a password. This password is distinct from a user password because it applies to the database as a whole. Password Manager enables you to change this password (see Figure 3.17). This is one of the first things that you should do when you install Personal Oracle7.

FIGURE 3.17.
Using Password Manager to change the database password.

NOTE

The default database password is `oracle`.

SQL*Loader

You'll want to use SQL*Loader when you have a CSV (Comma-Separated Values) file, tab-delimited file, or other flat file containing data that you want to load into an Oracle table. SQL*Loader is a sophisticated utility that enables you to describe the data and how it should be processed. Be aware that SQL*Loader is unidirectional; it isn't capable of extracting the contents of a table into a flat file.

Like SQL*DBA and SQL*Plus, SQL*Loader is a legacy tool that has been remodeled for use in a Windows environment (see Figure 3.18).

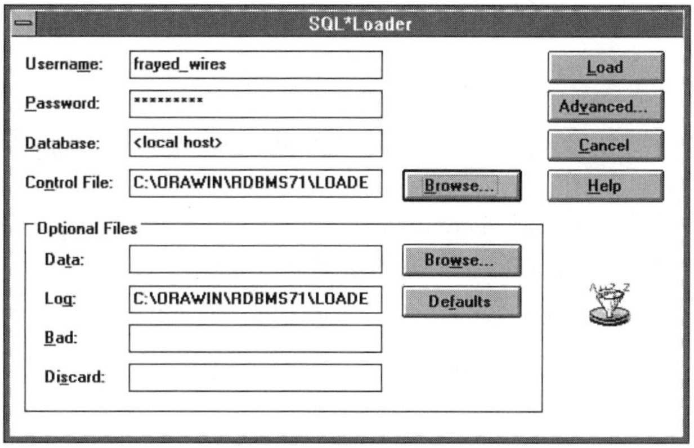

FIGURE 3.18.
*Using SQL*Loader to load customer information.*

Online Documentation

In the Personal Oracle7 Windows program group are two sets of help files: Oracle7 Documentation and Database Tools User's Guide. Both files use the Windows Help format.

The Oracle7 Documentation Help consists of the entire set of Oracle7 documentation:

- Oracle7 Server Concepts Manual
- Oracle7 Server Administrator's Guide
- Oracle7 Server Application Developer's Guide
- Oracle7 Server Migration Guide
- Oracle7 Server SQL Language Reference Manual
- Oracle7 Server Utilities User's Guide
- Oracle7 Server SQL Language Quick Reference
- Oracle7 Server Messages and Codes Manual
- Oracle7 Server Documentation Addendum
- PL/SQL User's Guide and Reference
- PL/SQL V2.1 and Precompilers V1.6 Addendum

Although it's comprehensive, the documentation is also massive—as broad and as deep as the sea. Placing it in an online format does make it more accessible.

> **TIP**
>
> You can't search a topic across manuals within the Oracle7 Documentation Help. You must select a single manual before the Search button is enabled.

Summary

This chapter focused on the following key concepts:

- Use Database Manager to start up or shut down your Personal Oracle7 database.
- Although Object Manager provides more graphical features than SQL*Plus, you'll find that you will actually rely on SQL*Plus much more because of its capability to process scripts and save results to a file.
- Use Export and Import to move Personal Oracle7 tables to another Oracle database.

4

Your First Personal Oracle7 Database

The goal of this chapter is to show how you to build a sample database with Personal Oracle7. To illustrate the concepts and techniques described throughout this book, we'll be looking at a sample database application for a repair store. Frayed Wires is a friendly neighborhood repair store specializing in the renovation of most consumer electronics. Started in 1982 by Jim Helmholtz, the business of Frayed Wires has grown over the years and is long overdue for some automation. Jim performed a thorough search of existing off-the-shelf applications for his business, but not a single one met his requirements. As a result, Helmholtz has retained you, his database consultant, to develop an Oracle database to help him manage his business.

This chapter focuses on using Personal Oracle7's Object Manager to construct the sample database. In later chapters, I'll show you how to use SQL*Plus to accomplish the same tasks.

Oracle Terminology

To understand Personal Oracle7, you need to feel comfortable with the terminology that you'll see referenced in this book, in Personal Oracle7 tools, and in Oracle documentation. In particular, let's look at two terms: *database connection* and *database user.*

Database Connection

To *connect* to Oracle means to supply a valid username and password that is accepted by the Oracle database. A user can connect to an Oracle database using any of the Database Administration Tools. A user also can establish an Oracle connection with another tool such as Oracle Forms, Visual Basic, or PowerBuilder. The terms *Oracle session, Oracle connection,* and *database connection* are often substituted for one another. They all refer to the same thing: the tasks performed by a database user from the time the user successfully connects to an Oracle database until the time the same user disconnects.

Database User

Every database connection is established on behalf of a database user. The terms *table owner, Oracle user,* and *Oracle account* are used interchangeably. A *table owner* is the database user that owns a table. A table owner is always an Oracle user, but an Oracle user may or may not own any tables of his or her own. An example should help explain this.

Let's say that the marketing department of a corporation has its own Oracle database. All of the tables are owned by an Oracle account named MKTG. Sally Jensen is the vice president of marketing and has an Oracle account named JENSENS. However, even though Jensen has access to all of the tables owned by MKTG, she owns no tables of her own.

Every table that exists in an Oracle database must have an owner. It generally makes sense to create an owner that corresponds with the organization rather than any individual in the organization. If you think about it, an organization's data—information that is created, modified, and used by the members of the organization—doesn't belong to any one person. Also, given the dynamics of an organization, people come and go but the organization remains.

In our sample application, instead of making Jim Helmholtz the owner of the Oracle tables, let's create a new user named FRAYED_WIRES and have that Oracle account own all of the tables in the application. An organization responsible for the data in the tables is sometimes referred to as the *data steward*.

As you recall, Personal Oracle7 for Windows has the same functionality that exists in its bigger brethren such as the Oracle7 Server for the UNIX operating system. Unlike its brethren, Personal Oracle7 is a single-user database, as is indicated by the first word of its name. But even though Personal Oracle7 is not designed to function as a database server, you can still define multiple users, each of whom can own a set of tables.

As a first step in setting up the sample database, we'll use User Manager to create an Oracle user, FRAYED_WIRES, which will own all of the database objects in the application database. The following section explains the steps that you need to follow.

Steps for Creating a New User with User Manager

These are the steps for creating a new user with User Manager.

1. Double-click the User Manager icon. A pop-up window, used for logging into Personal Oracle7, appears. There are three entries in this window: username, password, and database. The username should be SYSTEM, and the database should be set to oracle7. The default password for the SYSTEM account is MANAGER. Assuming that you haven't changed this password, enter MANAGER in the Password field and click the OK button.

2. You should see information about the three Oracle users that are automatically created during the installation of Personal Oracle7: SCOTT, SYS, and SYSTEM.

3. Click the Create button.

4. A pop-up window appears, asking whether you want to create a user or role. Select the User radio button and click OK.

5. A Create New User pop-up window appears. There are three fields in this window: New User, Password, and Confirm Password. Enter FRAYED_WIRES in the New User field, HELMHOLTZ in the Password field, and, once again, HELMHOLTZ in the Confirm Password field. Click the OK button (see Figure 4.1).

FIGURE 4.1.

*Adding the
FRAYED_WIRES
user.*

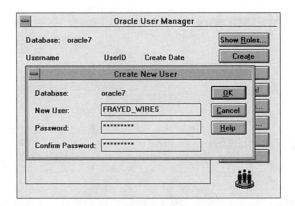

6. You should now see a list of the four Oracle users that are defined for your database: FRAYED_WIRES, SCOTT, SYS, and SYSTEM.

7. Now it's time to assign some privileges to FRAYED_WIRES. On the list of database users, click FRAYED_WIRES to highlight it. Click the Privileges button.

8. A pop-up window titled Privileges appears. You'll see two lists of privileges. The items in the list on the left are the privileges already owned by the FRAYED_WIRES Oracle account. The items in the list on the right are additional privileges that could be granted to FRAYED_WIRES. Click the privilege named RESOURCE and click the Grant button. You will now see two granted privileges for FRAYED_WIRES: CONNECT and RESOURCE. The CONNECT privilege is the privilege of connecting or logging into the Oracle database. The RESOURCE privilege is the privilege to create tables, indexes, and other database objects. Click the OK button.

You've now created the Personal Oracle7 user FRAYED_WIRES, which will be the owner of all of the database objects used in the sample application.

Creating Tables with Object Manager

You will find the Object Manager icon in the Personal Oracle7 Windows group. When invoked, Object Manager will prompt you for a username and password. After the username and password have been validated by the Personal Oracle7 database, Object Manager enables you to choose the type of database object—tables, indexes, synonyms, views, or database links—to be viewed, created, or modified. The examples that you'll see in this chapter focus on the use of Object Manager.

Object Manager and SQL*Plus

Object Manager provides a subset of the capabilities that can be found in SQL*Plus. SQL*Plus is a character-oriented command processor that accepts all valid SQL statements. Object Manager is a graphical tool that offers a more intuitive interface that simplifies the creation of tables and other database objects.

A Logical Data Model and Database Design

A *logical data model* is a representation of both the data elements used by an enterprise and the relationships between those data elements. Like any model, a logical data model is an idealization of a real system. A model is only as useful as it is accurate. Like any real enterprise, a logical data model is dynamic rather than static. It needs to evolve as the enterprise upon which it is based changes.

One of the most common methodologies used for developing a logical data model is entity-relationship modeling. *Entities* are people, places, objects, or concepts. Each entity has a set of attributes that are used to describe the entity. To his employer, an employee can be viewed as an entity described by a set of attributes, such as employee number, last name, first name, department number, and hire date. An automobile marketing manager is interested in an entirely different set of attributes for the same individual; for instance, the make, model, age, and color of the car that he currently owns. As you can see, business requirements are what drives the data model.

Entities don't exist in a vacuum—you can define relationships between entities. These relationships are used to help enforce business rules. In a repair store, a customer may bring in several items to be repaired. The information about the customer's repair can be grouped into two sets of facts. The first set consists of facts that are independent of the items to be repaired—for example, the customer's name and address—and are stored in the Repair Header table. The second set is made up of facts that are directly related to the items to be repaired—for instance, make, model, and condition—and are stored in the Repair Item table. Each repair is assigned a unique Repair ID. A relationship is defined between the Repair Header and Repair Item tables so that the Repair Item table cannot reference a Repair ID that doesn't exist in the Repair Header table.

Why bother to develop a logical data model—why not just jump right into database design? By developing a logical data model, you are forced to focus on an organization's data and how it is related without initially worrying about implementation details such as a column's datatype. You can think of the logical data model at a higher level of abstraction than the database design.

Relational Database Theory

No book that deals with relational database systems can be considered complete unless it discusses the basic concepts of relational database theory.

The Primary Key

Every entity has a set of attributes that uniquely defines an instance of that entity. This set of attributes is referred to as the primary key. The primary key may be composed of a single attribute—an employee is uniquely identified by a Social Security number—or of several attributes—a repair item is uniquely identified by the Repair ID and the item number. Sometimes, the attributes that compose the primary key are obvious, and other times they are not.

When testing your understanding of the primary key, it's necessary but not sufficient to look at existing data. You must also interview people who understand the way in which the organization operates; don't rely solely on existing data to validate your understanding of the primary key.

No Part of the Primary Key Is Null

A basic tenet of relational theory is that no part of the primary key can be null. If you think about that for a moment, it will seem intuitive. If the primary key must uniquely identify each row in an entity, it doesn't make sense if the primary key (or a part of it) is null. For instance, a repair item that has an undefined item number cannot be identified or processed in any way.

Data Integrity

According to relational theory, every entity has a set of attributes that uniquely identifies each row in that entity. Relational theory states that no duplicate rows can exist in a table. This is really just another way of saying that every table must have a primary key. This concept is referred to as *data integrity*. For example, the Social Security number for each current employee will be unique.

Referential Integrity

Tables are related to one another through foreign keys. A *foreign key* is one table column for which the set of possible values is found in the primary key of a second table. Referential integrity is achieved when the set of values in a foreign key column is restricted to the primary key that it references or the null value. Once the database designer declares primary and foreign keys, enforcing data and referential integrity is the responsibility of the database.

The Order of Rows Is Arbitrary

A key tenet of relational database theory is that a table has no implied ordering. There is no way of knowing the order in which rows will be retrieved from a table unless you specify the order. The concept of no implied order is powerful because it enables you to think abstractly about tables and, for the most part, ignore the physical implementation of a database's structures.

The Order of Columns Is Arbitrary

As with a table's rows, a table's columns have no implied ordering. If you use SQL*Plus to describe a table, SQL*Plus returns the columns in the order in which they were created. You can, however, specify any order for retrieving columns. Also, you can modify a column's definition without affecting any of the other columns. For example, you can increase the width of a column without having to modify any of your existing table definitions or SQL statements. Taking care of the physical details related to the change is the job of Personal Oracle7. A relational database is said to provide *logical data independence* because column definitions are independent from one another.

Using these concepts, let's now look closely at the sample database that we'll use throughout the remainder of the book.

The Repair Store Database

You've provided Helmholtz with your strategy: you'll use Personal Oracle7 as a prototyping tool to design a functioning database and "upsize" that database to the Oracle Workgroup Server for the actual implementation of the application.

Because he is quite meticulous, Helmholtz wants to keep track of changes to the database. Specifically, he wants to know who added or changed a record in each table and when the record was added or changed. For this reason, each table in the Frayed Wires database will contain the following information:

Created_Date: The date and time when the row was created

Created_By: The Oracle user who created the row

Modified_Date: The date and time when the row was modified

Modified_By: The Oracle user who modified the row

The Customer Table

What's a business without customers? Helmholtz values his customers and wants to maintain accurate information about them without being intrusive. The following is a list of the items he wants to track:

Customer ID

Last name

First name

Middle initial

Salutation

Street address

City

State

Zip code

Work telephone number

Home telephone number

Fax number

Earliest time to call

Latest time to call

Local time zone

As shown in Figure 4.2, you can use Object Manager to create the Customer table. In Chapter 7, "Creating and Modifying Tables," I'll cover the use of Object Manager in detail.

FIGURE 4.2.

Creating the Customer table with Object Manager.

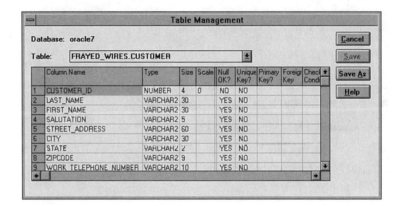

The Manufacturer Table

Frayed Wires handles repairs for all of the major consumer electronics manufacturers (and some obscure manufacturers). Helmholtz wants to be able to track the following facts about each manufacturer that his business deals with:

Manufacturer ID

Manufacturer name

Street address

City

State

Zip code

Telephone number

Fax number

As shown in Figure 4.3, you can create the Manufacturer table using Object Manager.

FIGURE 4.3.

Creating the Manufacturer table.

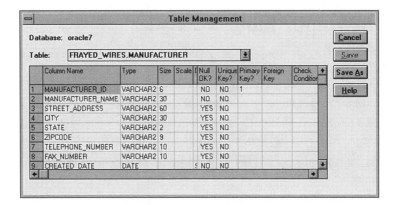

The Product Table

Because it is a repair store, Frayed Wires handles repairs on many different products. Helmholtz needs to be able to retrieve some details on these products. The following information is available for some products but not all of them:

> Product ID
>
> Product name
>
> Manufacturer ID
>
> Description
>
> Date of manufacture
>
> Initial retail value
>
> Current used value
>
> Replacement product

As shown in Figure 4.4, you can create the Product table using Object Manager.

FIGURE 4.4.

Creating the Product table.

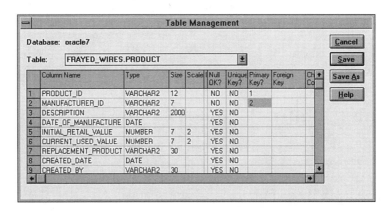

The Depot Table

Although there are four full-time technicians and two part-time technicians employed at Frayed Wires, not all repairs are done in-house. A portion of repair work is sent to several different repair depots. There are various reasons for sending repair work out. For instance, the customer's equipment may still be under warranty, and the work can be performed only by an authorized service center. Also, a repair depot may specialize in repairing older equipment—work that Helmholtz is no longer interested in performing.

After some explanation, Helmholtz indicates that he needs to keep track of the following (see Figure 4.5):

> Depot ID
>
> Company name
>
> Street address
>
> City
>
> State
>
> Zip code
>
> Telephone number
>
> Fax number
>
> Name of primary contact

FIGURE 4.5.

Creating the Depot table.

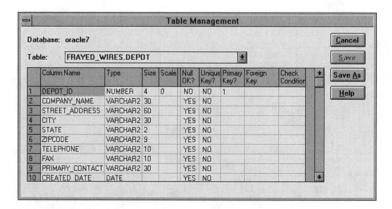

The Employee Table

As a conscientious employer, Helmholtz maintains accurate records on each employee who has worked at Frayed Wires. Each employee will be assigned a numeric code, designated as his or her employee ID. Key dates, such as the hire date and the termination date, if any, will be stored in the table. The following is a list of the information that the Employee table will contain:

Employee ID

Last name

First name

Middle initial

Street address

City

State

Zip code

Home telephone number

Social Security number

Date of birth

Hire date

Termination date

Figure 4.6 illustrates how to use Object Manager to create the Employee table.

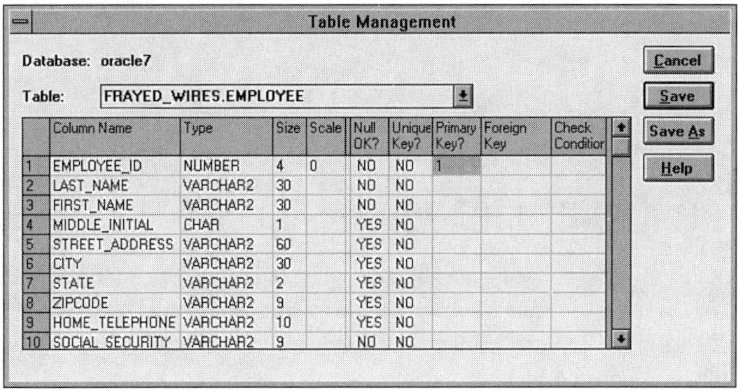

FIGURE 4.6.

Creating the Employee table.

The Business Transaction
=========================

As Helmholtz explains, the typical repair scenario is this: A customer walks through the doorway of Frayed Wires with a nonfunctioning electronic gadget cradled in his or her arms. Most customers don't want to proceed with a repair until they know what the repair will cost. Often, a technician can't quote a repair price until the broken appliance has been inspected, either in-house or at a repair depot.

Each customer may have more than one item to be repaired. Sometimes, when one appliance stops working, customers also bring in other broken appliances that they've put off having repaired.

The paper repair form (see Figure 4.7) can be represented in the database by two Oracle tables.

■ A Repair Header table, which contains information found on the upper portion of the form; for example, a unique Repair ID

■ A Repair Item table, which contains information about each item brought in for repair

FIGURE 4.7.
The paper repair form.

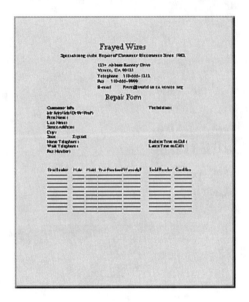

The Repair Header Table

Because there is a set of facts about a repair that is independent of the number of repair items, it makes sense to create a separate table to contain common elements related to a repair. We'll call this table Repair Header. The following data items will be stored in the Repair Header table (see Figure 4.8):

Repair ID

Customer ID

Employee ID

Deposit amount

Deposit method

Customer credit card number

Customer check number

FIGURE 4.8.

Creating the Repair Header table.

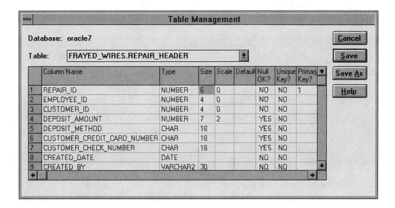

The Repair Item Table

If you look at the paper repair form currently used at Frayed Wires, you'll see there is a section that deals with each item a customer has brought in. This portion of the form is referred to as the Repair Item and consists of the following:

Repair ID

Item number

Product ID

Manufacturer ID

Condition code

Serial number

Purchase date

Warranty expiration date

Estimated cost

Estimated completion date

Customer authorization status

Customer authorization date

Item status code

Depot ID

Responsible employee ID

Item location

Figure 4.9 demonstrates how to use Object Manager to create the Repair Item table.

FIGURE 4.9.

Creating the Repair Item table.

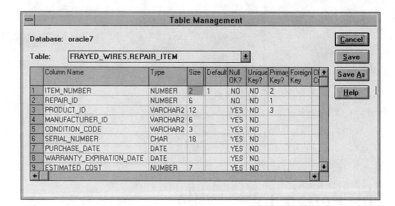

The Depot Estimate Table

When a piece of equipment is sent to a repair depot for an estimate, the depot is responsible for providing a cost and schedule estimate to Frayed Wires. When a customer brings more than one item to be repaired, each item could be repaired in-house or sent to different repair depots. To model this process, the Depot Estimate table must refer to both the Repair ID and the Item Number. The Depot Estimate table holds the following data items:

Repair ID

Item number

Depot ID

Labor cost

Parts cost

Total cost

Estimated date for completion

Technician

Telephone number

Figure 4.10 shows how to use Object Manager to create the Depot Estimate table.

FIGURE 4.10.

Creating the Depot Estimate table.

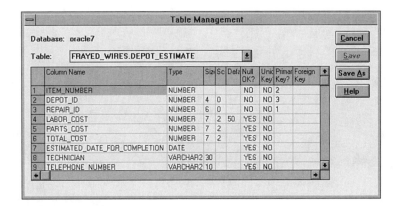

The Repair Log Table

As Jim Helmholtz has explained it to you, his business is not only labor-intensive, but also communication-intensive. By this, he means many types of communications are taking place, for example:

- Between the customer and a technician
- Between technicians regarding various repairs
- Between a technician and a repair depot

Keeping track of all of these events is incredibly error-prone and time-consuming. To provide superior customer service, Helmholtz wants to streamline this facet of the operation by recording all activity associated with each repair job. His vision is that any technician can quickly look up the activity log for an open repair account without having to interrupt another technician.

Based on everyone's input, your design for the Repair Log table consists of the following items:

Repair ID

Employee ID

Item number

Depot ID

Action code

Employee comments

Figure 4.11 outlines the creation of the Repair Log table using Object Manager.

FIGURE 4.11.

Creating the Repair Log table.

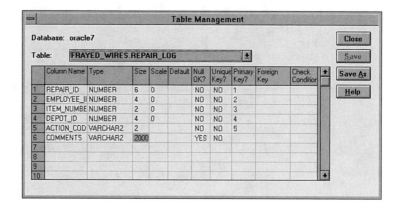

The Condition Code Table

In your effort to gather information, you've reviewed existing paper forms used at Frayed Wires. In addition, you've spoken with most of the potential users of the system that you're designing. You've discovered that when a customer brings in one or more items for repair, the lead technician assigns an initial condition code to each item. This code is used in a couple of ways. First, the technician records the fact that an item has been brought in already damaged; for instance, it's dented or scratched. Second, the lead technician can indicate what he or she thinks the problem might be—perhaps a short has damaged a component—and pass that information on to the technician assigned to the repair.

Based on your investigation, you've assembled a list of about fifteen condition codes that are frequently used. Helmholtz, the owner, mentions that these codes haven't changed in four years. Then he proceeds to tell you that he's been thinking about adding a new code related to DAT tape drives—something about the drive mechanism.

At this point, you realize that the application and database will be easier to maintain if a table is created to store each Condition code and its Description (see Figure 4.12).

FIGURE 4.12.

Creating the Condition Code table.

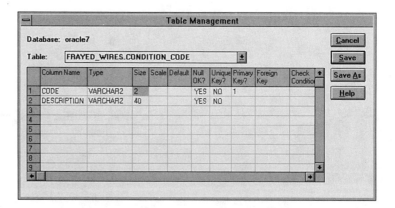

The Action Code Table

The purpose of the Action Code table is similar to that of the Condition Code table—to simplify the maintenance of the application. The Action Code table is really a lookup table that consists of these two items: Action code and Description (see Figure 4.13).

FIGURE 4.13.

Creating the Action Code table.

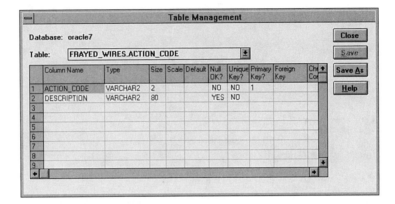

The Item Status Code Table

In addition to the other lookup tables (Condition Code and Action Code), another lookup table is used to describe the current status of each item being repaired. In the Repair Item table, a code is used to indicate the status of an item. The codes include the following:

Code	Description
DE	The item has been sent to a repair depot for an estimate.
DR	The item has been sent to a repair depot to be repaired.
WC	Waiting for customer authorization to proceed with repair.
IH	The item is being repaired in-house.
IC	In-house repair is complete.
DC	Depot repair is complete.
WP	Waiting for customer to pick up the item.

To simplify the maintenance of the application, the following items are included in your design for the Item Status Code table (see Figure 4.14): Item status code and Description.

FIGURE 4.14.
*Creating the Item
Status Code table.*

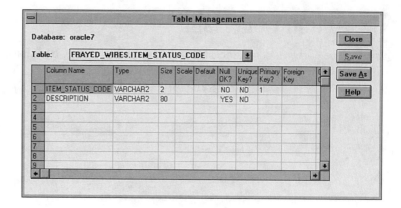

Summary

Remember the following concepts when you are designing a database:

- Begin with a logical data model.
- Identify each entity in the system that you're modeling.
- Identify a primary key for each entity.
- Determine the foreign keys you need to create.
- Remember that there is no implied ordering of rows or columns in a table.

5

The Basics of SQL

To build a Personal Oracle7 application, it's crucial that you develop a working knowledge of Structured Query Language (SQL). SQL is a powerful language that differs from traditional 3GL languages, such as C and Pascal, in several significant areas:

■ SQL is a nonprocedural language. You use SQL to inform Personal Oracle7 of what data to retrieve or modify without telling it how to do its job.

■ SQL does not provide any flow-of-control programming constructs. There are no function definitions, do-loops, or if-then-else statements available in SQL. However, as you shall see in Chapter 17, "The Basics of PL/SQL," Oracle provides procedural language extensions to SQL through the PL/SQL product.

■ SQL provides a fixed set of datatypes; you cannot define new datatypes. Unlike modern programming languages that enable you to define a datatype for a specific purpose, SQL forces you to choose from a set of predefined datatypes when you create or modify a column. In the future, you can expect Oracle to release an object-oriented database that will enable you to define datatypes specific to the application you are building.

Another similarity between SQL and a programming language is that there is usually more than one way to accomplish the same goal—particularly when retrieving information. SQL statements may achieve the same results but differ in efficiency or clarity.

A Table Is Rows and Columns

At the heart of relational theory is the concept of the table. A table consists of a set of attributes or columns and zero or more rows. Each row is a set of attribute values.

Before relational databases were available, organizations depended upon database management systems that were categorized as *hierarchical* or *network*. Both types had a major drawback: A change to an existing data element or the addition of a new data element usually involved extensive change to existing programs. Because almost 70 percent of the cost for a typical information system is incurred during the maintenance phase of its life cycle, any reduction in software maintenance costs due to database changes would save an organization time and money.

In a relational database, the effect of changing a data element—a column—is often minimal. For example, suppose the original system requirements called for a customer number that was a maximum of five digits long. As the business grows, it soon becomes obvious that a five-digit length is inadequate and that the length of the customer number needs to be eight digits. In a relational database, the increase or decrease in size of a column is independent of the other columns in the table; as far as a user is concerned, it has no effect on the other columns. Of course, it is probably necessary to change data entry screens and reports to reflect the modification to the customer number column, but the software maintenance effort is localized to the modified column.

One of the rules of relational theory is that the order of columns is unimportant. What does this statement really mean? It means that at the conceptual level, the columns of a table can be retrieved in whatever order you like. That's it. It doesn't mean that the physical storage of the data has no order; there *is* an order. The ordering information is maintained, however, at the physical level; the developer and user don't need to know about those details.

Another rule of relational theory is that the order of rows is unimportant. Again, that doesn't mean that rows aren't physically stored in some particular order, but rather that there is no implied order in the way that rows will be retrieved from a table. This is important: If you want the rows of a table returned in a particular order, you always have to specify what that order is.

Retrieving and Modifying Data

At the highest level, SQL statements can be broadly categorized in one of three areas:

- Data Manipulation Language (DML) that retrieves or modifies data
- Data Definition Language (DDL) that defines the structure of the data
- Data Control Language (DCL) that defines the privileges granted to database users

Within the category of DML, there are four basic statements:

- SELECT, which retrieves rows from a table
- INSERT, which adds rows to a table
- UPDATE, which modifies existing rows in a table
- DELETE, which removes rows from a table

SQL Grammar

Here are some facts to keep in mind when you're working with SQL.

- Every SQL statement is terminated by a semicolon (there is an exception to this rule regarding SQL*Plus that we'll discuss in Chapter 7, "Creating and Modifying Tables").
- A SQL statement can be entered on one line or split across several lines for clarity. Most of the examples shown in this book split statements into readable portions.
- SQL is not case-sensitive; you can mix uppercase and lowercase when referencing SQL keywords (such as SELECT and INSERT), table names, and column names. However, case does matter when referring to the contents of a column; if you ask for all customers whose last names begin with "a" and all customer names are stored in uppercase, you won't retrieve any rows at all.

Syntax of the *SELECT* Statement

Of the four DML statements, the SELECT statement is the one that is executed most often in a real application; this is because records are usually read more often than they are changed. A SELECT statement can also exist as a subquery in an UPDATE, INSERT, or DELETE statement, but we'll discuss that in Chapter 6, "Accessing Personal Oracle7 with SQL*Plus."

Although the SELECT statement is a tremendously powerful tool, its syntax is complicated because of the large number of ways that tables, columns, functions, and operators can be combined into legal statements. For this reason, instead of looking at the full syntax of the SELECT statement, we'll start with some basic examples of the SELECT statement on which to build.

At a minimum, a SELECT statement is composed of the following two elements:

- The SELECT list: a list of columns to be retrieved
- The FROM clause: the table from which to retrieve the rows

A Simple *SELECT* Statement

As a start, let's look at a simple SELECT statement. A query that retrieves only the Customer ID from the Customer table is shown below:

```
SQL> select Customer_ID
  2  from Customer;

CUSTOMER_ID
-----------
       1001
       1002
       1003
       1004
       1005
       1006
       1007
       1008
       1009
       6101
       6102
       6103
       6104
       6105
       2222

15 rows selected.
```

If you want to retrieve both the Customer ID and the customer's last name, simply list the columns in the desired order:

```
SQL> select Customer_ID, Last_Name
  2  from Customer;
```

```
CUSTOMER_ID LAST_NAME
----------- -----------------------------
       1001 Johnson
       1002 Martinez
       1003 Smyth
       1004 Richardson
       1005 Horace
       1006 Pareski
       1007 McClintock
       1008 Moran
       1009 Chen
       6101 Sorrel
       6102 Fleming
       6103 Kramden
       6104 Jensen
       6105 Hernandez
       2222 Fray

15 rows selected.
```

If you want to retrieve all columns in a table, SQL offers a shortcut—the *—as you see:

```
SQL> select *
  2  from Customer;


CUSTOMER_ID LAST_NAME                       FIRST_NAME                      SALUT
----------- ----------------------------- ------------------------------- -----
STREET_ADDRESS                                                CITY
------------------------------------------------------------ -------------------
ZIPCODE    WORK_TELEP HOME_TELEP FAX_NUMBER EARLIEST_ LATEST_TI LOC CREATED_D
---------- ---------- ---------- ---------- --------- --------- --- ---------
CREATED_BY                      MODIFIED_ MODIFIED_BY
------------------------------- --------- -------------------------------
       1001 Johnson                         Samuel                           Mr.
1922 Bedford Blvd.                                            Santa Margherina
91010      7145559876            7145550123


       1002 Martinez                        Steve                            Mr.
9303 Channel Drive.                                           Williamshire
12912      6025559133 6025553811 6025553833


       1003 Smyth                           Julie                            Ms.
39121 Pillar Ave.                                             Portsmith
03991      5035553843            5035551283
```

The Select List

If the select list contains multiple columns, the columns must be separated by commas. The select list can also contain valid expressions that may or may not contain columns. There is no restriction on the use of a column more than once in a select list. The following query is completely valid:

```
SQL> select Customer_ID, Customer_ID
  2  from Customer;

CUSTOMER_ID CUSTOMER_ID
----------- -----------
       1001        1001
       1002        1002
       1003        1003
       1004        1004
       1005        1005
       1006        1006
       1007        1007
       1008        1008
       1009        1009
       6101        6101
       6102        6102
       6103        6103
       6104        6104
       6105        6105
       2222        2222

15 rows selected.
```

> **TIP**
>
> You can perform arithmetic computations by selecting the problem from a utility table named DUAL, as in:
>
> ```
> select 3.14159*20 from dual;
> ```
>
> which returns
>
> ```
> 62.8318
> ```

Results Returned by a *SELECT*

The results returned by every SELECT statement constitute a temporary table. Each retrieved record is a row in this temporary table, and each element of the select list is a column. If a query doesn't return any records, the temporary table can be thought of as empty. This behavior is a fundamental principle of the relational model.

Using Expressions in the Select List

Along with specifying columns, you can also specify expressions in the select list. Expressions fall into the same datatypes as columns: character, numeric, and date. Through the use of operators, built-in functions, and constants, you can construct complex expressions to meet the needs of your application.

Keep in mind that Oracle considers each element in the select list to be a separate column, even if that expression references multiple columns.

Arithmetic Operators

The arithmetic operators used in SQL are the same as those used in C:

Description	Operator
Addition	+
Subtraction	-
Multiplication	*
Division	/

For the purpose of example, we'll use the Product table. This table provides for the storage of the current retail value and the year that the product was manufactured. Helmholtz wants a list of products in which the current used value is depreciated by 10 percent:

```
SQL> select Product_ID, Description, Current_Used_Value*0.90
  2  from Product
  3  order by Product_ID;

PRODUCT_ID
-----------
DESCRIPTION
------------------------------------------------------------------
CURRENT_USED_VALUE*0.90
-----------------------
A2001
AMPLIFIER, 100W PER CHANNEL
                225

A504
AMP 300W PER CHAN
                351

A509
AMP 600 WATTS PER CHANNEL
                607.5

A903
AMP, PROFESSIONAL 800W RMS PER CHANNEL
                742.5

B311

PRODUCT_ID
-----------
DESCRIPTION
------------------------------------------------------------------
CURRENT_USED_VALUE*0.90
-----------------------
Pre-amp, 120 W per channel
                108

B384
PREAMP, 460 W/RMS
                432
```

```
B801
PRE AMPLIFIER 150 WATTS/CHANNEL
              225
```

> **TIP**
>
> Instead of trying to remember the precedence rules for arithmetic operators used in SQL statements, you should always use parentheses if you are uncertain about the evaluation of the expression.

String Operators

One of the most important string operators in SQL is the concatenation operator ¦¦. This operator enables you to concatenate two or more strings together, as in the following:

```
SQL> select City ¦¦ ', ' ¦¦ State
  2  from Customer;

CITY¦¦','¦¦STATE
---------------------------------
Santa Margherina, CA
Williamshire, AZ
Portsmith, OR
Boston, MA
Chicago, IL
Nome, AZ
Redlawn, WA
Johnson, MI
```

Here are several reasons why you would want to concatenate strings:

- **To embed strings in the values returned by a query.** You want to address a form letter to your customers by combining a salutation, a blank, and the customer's last name:

  ```
  select Salutation ¦¦ ' ' ¦¦ Last_Name
  from Customer
  order by Last_Name;
  ```

- **To combine strings.** Your application might be required to take a substring from one column and combine it with a substring from another column for display to the user.

- **To create new values that can be assigned to a column.** In the process of implementing your application, you might need to convert existing data from one format to another.

You can use the concatenation operator with more than two strings, as shown here:

```
SQL> select Salutation ¦¦ ' ' ¦¦ First_Name ¦¦ ' ' ¦¦ Last_Name
  2  from Customer;
```

```
SALUTATION||''||FIRST_NAME||''||LAST_NAME
--------------------------------------------------------------
Mr. Samuel Johnson
Mr. Steve Martinez
Ms. Julie Smyth
Mrs. Mary Richardson
Ms. Michelle Horace
Ms. Monica Pareski
Mr. Harvey McClintock
Ms. Sarah Moran
Mrs. Laura Chen
```

Built-In Functions

Oracle provides a rich set of built-in functions that you can use to manipulate and convert different types of data. These functions can be categorized as

Character functions

Number functions

Date functions

Conversion functions

Group functions

Miscellaneous functions

We will discuss many of these functions in Chapter 10, "Manipulating Strings," Chapter 11, "Dealing with Dates," and Chapter 12, "Handling Numbers."

Specifying Criteria in the *WHERE* Clause

You usually don't want to retrieve all the rows in a table, particularly if the table has many rows. SQL provides a WHERE clause in which you specify the criteria to be used for retrieving records.

A WHERE clause consists of one or more conditions that must be satisfied for the rows that are retrieved by the query. For instance, Tesla Corp., a major consumer electronics manufacturer, has been assigned TES801 as a Manufacturer ID in the repair store database. If you want a list of the products produced by Tesla, you would specify Tesla's Manufacturer ID in the WHERE clause, as shown here:

```
SQL> select Product_ID, Description, Date_of_Manufacture
  2  from Product
  3  where
  4  Manufacturer_ID = 'TES801';
```

```
PRODUCT_ID
- - - - - - - - - - -
DESCRIPTION
- - - - - - - - - - - - - - - - - - - - - - - - - - - - - - - - - - - - - - - - - - - - - - - - - - - - - - - - - - - - - - -
DATE_OF_M
- - - - - - - - -
A2001
AMPLIFIER, 100W PER CHANNEL
01-APR-87

A903
AMP, PROFESSIONAL 800W RMS PER CHANNEL
01-APR-92

B901
Preamplifier, 200 W PER CHANNEL
01-APR-92

B311
Pre-amp, 120 W per channel
01-APR-92

B384

PRODUCT_ID
- - - - - - - - - - -
DESCRIPTION
- - - - - - - - - - - - - - - - - - - - - - - - - - - - - - - - - - - - - - - - - - - - - - - - - - - - - - - - - - - - - - -
DATE_OF_M
- - - - - - - - -
PREAMP, 460 W/RMS
01-APR-93

TR901
Tuner
01-JAN-91


6 rows selected.
```

Combining Conditions with *AND* and *OR*

If you have multiple conditions that need to be satisfied in a query, you can use the keywords AND and OR to combine them. If you wanted to see the Seny products whose descriptions include the phrase CD, you would specify both conditions in the WHERE clause, as in:

```
SQL> select Product_ID, Description, Date_of_Manufacture
  2  from Product
  3  where
  4  Manufacturer_ID = 'SEN101' and
  5  Description like '%CD%';
```

```
PRODUCT_ID
-----------
DESCRIPTION
------------------------------------------------------------
DATE_OF_M
---------
C3002
JUKEBOX, CD - 100 DISK CAPACITY
01-APR-94
```

In the preceding example, you'll see the word LIKE used. This operator is one of the most powerful tools available in SQL. The basic syntax for using the LIKE operator is this:

column_name LIKE *'pattern'*

where *column_name* is a valid column in the table referenced in the FROM clause, and *pattern* is a string pattern for which you are searching.

The % serves as a wildcard in this context; it is the equivalent of zero or more characters. The _ (underscore) is used to signify a placeholder of any single character.

Sorting Data in the *ORDER BY* Clause

The ORDER BY clause is used to designate which columns should be used to order the rows that are returned by the query. This clause is optional, but remember: The order in which rows are returned by a query is arbitrary (this is true whether or not the table has been indexed). Because of this, you'll usually want to specify an ORDER BY clause in a SELECT statement.

For example, you might want to retrieve products that are ordered first by the manufacturer ID and then by product ID, as shown:

```
SQL> select Manufacturer_ID, Product_ID
  2  from Product
  3  where
  4  Manufacturer_ID like 'TES%'
  5  order by Manufacturer_ID, Product_ID;

MANUFAC PRODUCT_ID
------- -----------
TES801  A2001
TES801  A903
TES801  B311
TES801  B384
TES801  B901
TES801  TR901

6 rows selected.
```

NOTE

You can specify columns in an ORDER BY clause even if they are not selected from the table, as in:

```
select Last_Name
from Customer
order by Customer_ID
```

You can also specify columns in the ORDER BY clause whether or not the column is part of an index on the table.

By default, Oracle orders the rows in ascending order. To order the rows in descending order, you must add the keyword DESC (for DESCENDING) after the column name. You can specify ascending columns and descending columns in the same ORDER BY clause as shown in this example:

```
SQL> select Product_ID, Manufacturer_ID
  2  from Product
  3  order by Manufacturer_ID DESC, Product_ID;

PRODUCT_ID     MANUFAC
------------   -------
fA2001          TES801
A903            TES801
B311            TES801
B384            TES801
B901            TES801
TR901           TES801
A504            SEN101
A509            SEN101
B801            SEN101
B9310           SEN101
C3002           SEN101
D301            SEN101
C2002           MIT501
C2005           MIT501

14 rows selected.
```

When You Only Want to Know How Many: Counting Rows

Occasionally, you want to know how many rows in a table satisfy the specified criteria, but you really don't need to retrieve the rows themselves. The COUNT function can be used for this purpose. When the COUNT function is used, it returns a single row which is the number of rows that satisfied the specified criteria. Here's an example:

```
SQL> select count(*)
  2  from Product
```

```
3   where
4   Description like '%CD%';
```

```
COUNT(*)
---------
        3
```

> **NOTE**
>
> COUNT is a group function (which we'll explore in greater depth in Chapter 14, "More Sophisticated Queries"). The asterisk instructs Oracle to return all rows that satisfy the criteria. Instead of the asterisk, you can specify a column name, but if you do, Oracle returns only those rows where the specified column name has been assigned a value (or are not null, in other words).

How the Subquery Is Used

A subquery is defined as a SELECT statement that appears in some other DML statement—another SELECT statement, an UPDATE statement, a DELETE statement, or an INSERT statement.

In a SELECT statement, a subquery is part of a condition in the WHERE clause. In the example below, we are selecting the product ID and description for those products whose current used value is less than or equal to the average current used value for all products:

```
select Product_ID, Description
from Product
where Current_Used_Value <=
(select avg(Current_Used_Value) from Product)
```

You should be aware of several things regarding the use of subqueries:

- ■ The subquery must be enclosed in parentheses.
- ■ The number of rows returned by the subquery must match the number of values that the function or operator expects. In the example above, the <= operator expects a single value to compare against, and the AVG function (which is a group function) returns a single value.
- ■ The ORDER BY clause is not used within a subquery.

Creating a New Table with the *SELECT* Statement

As we've already seen, Personal Oracle7 has two tools for creating a new table: Object Manager and SQL*Plus. Object Manager is easy and intuitive but doesn't offer the flexibility of SQL*Plus. An example of this flexibility is the use of the CREATE TABLE statement in conjunction with SELECT statement. Let's take a closer look.

If you wanted to experiment with the contents of a table—add, delete, and update various rows—you would be well-advised to create a copy of the table that you want to experiment with. Let's suppose that the existing table is a list of customers and contains several rows—say 100,000—but you only want a subset of those rows for your experiment. Specifically, you are only interested in those customers who live in California. You can create a table containing a subset of all customers by combining the CREATE TABLE statement with the SELECT statement:

```
SQL> create table Customer_Subset
  2    as
  3    select *
  4    from Customer
  5    where
  6    State = 'CA';
```

Table created.

Now, let's look closely at the syntax.

```
CREATE TABLE new_table_name
AS
select_stmt
```

where *new_table_name* is the name of the table to be created, and *select_stmt* is a valid SELECT statement.

The CREATE TABLE statement and the SELECT statement can be used together for another purpose. If you want to create another table that has the same structure as an existing table—all of the same column definitions—but none of the data, you can use this statement:

```
CREATE TABLE my_new_empty_table
AS
SELECT *
FROM existing_table
WHERE
1 = 2
```

Now, you're probably saying, "1 is never equal to 2." That's right. And that's why none of the rows in *existing_table* are copied into *my_new_empty_table*. The new table has the same set of column definitions as *existing_table* but no data.

Referencing Columns with an Alias

When you specify a complex expression in a select list, you can document what the expression represents by assigning an alias to it. As an example, Helmholtz, the owner of our fictitious consumer electronics repair store, Frayed Wires, wants to know the percentage of depreciation of each product by dividing its current used value by its initial retail value. Look at how this is done:

```
SQL> select Product_ID,
  2    (Current_Used_Value/Initial_Retail_Value)*100 Pct_Depreciation
  3    from Product
  4    order by Product_ID;

PRODUCT_ID   PCT_DEPRECIATION
```

```
- - - - - - - - - - -   - - - - - - - - - - - - - - -
A2001                   71.428571
A504                    66.666667
A509                    79.411765
A903                    78.571429
B311                    64.864865
B384                    64.864865
B801                    73.529412
B901                    88.372093
B9310                   76.744186
C2002                          34
C2005                   71.111111
C3002                   86.046512
D301
TR901

14 rows selected.
```

By assigning the alias `Pct_Depreciation` to the expression `Current_Used_Value/ Initial_Retail_Value*100`, you gain two benefits:

- ■ You now have a name that accurately describes the expression.
- ■ You can reference an alias in the `ORDER BY` clause.

The Concept of the Null Value

One major difference between RDBMSs and older DBMS technology is the concept of the null value. In nonrelational database systems, the absence of a value in a character or numeric field was indicated by some special value.

In a relational database, a null value for a column represents different things:

- ■ A value for this column is not applicable for the row in question.
- ■ The column has not yet been assigned a value. (For example, a customer may not have a fax machine.)

> **NOTE**
>
> In the examples that follow, the keyword NULL is all uppercase. I've done this to emphasize the word, but it isn't mandatory; you can use whatever case you choose with any of the Oracle SQL reserved words.

Finding Rows Where a Column Value Is Null

If you want to retrieve records from a table where a specific column value is not defined, you can specify the criterion in the WHERE clause. Here is a query that will retrieve those customers for whom a fax number has not been assigned:

```
SQL> select Customer_ID, Last_Name, First_Name
  2  from Customer
  3  where
  4  Fax_Number is NULL;

CUSTOMER_ID LAST_NAME                              FIRST_NAME
----------- ------------------------------------   ---------------------------
       6101 Sorrel                                 James
       6102 Fleming                                Harry
       6103 Kramden                                Ralph
       6104 Jensen                                 Rachel
       6105 Hernandez                              Ruby
       2222 Fray

6 rows selected.
```

It's important to understand the reason a value is NULL. In the case of the customer's fax number, the value may be NULL because the customer doesn't own a fax machine. However, it's also possible that Fax_Number is NULL because, even though the customer does own a fax machine, you have not yet obtained that information. To distinguish between these two situations, an additional column would need to be added to the Customer table to indicate that it is a known fact that the customer does or doesn't own a fax machine. In that case, you could query the Customer table for those customers who do own fax machines but the fax number is not known.

NOTE

This discussion of the meaning of a NULL value may sound like hair-splitting, but it really isn't. You need a thorough understanding of the meaning of your organization's data to be able to maximize its value.

You can also use the NOT operator to retrieve rows whose column values are not NULL. If you want to count the number of customers with known fax numbers, you can accomplish it with this query:

```
select count(*)
from Customer
where
Fax_Number is not NULL;
```

Searching for Rows with the *LIKE* Operator

You've already seen an example of the use of the LIKE operator. Oracle users rely on the LIKE operator to search through a table when they're not sure of the exact spelling for the item they're interested in finding.

In our fictitious electronics repair store, the store manager, Jean Smith, wants to find all the products in the Product table that are preamplifiers. Using the Description column, she constructs a SELECT statement to find these products in this way:

```
SQL> select Product_ID, Manufacturer_ID, Description
  2  from Product
  3  where
  4  Description like '%Preamplifier%';

PRODUCT_ID   MANUFAC
------------ -------
DESCRIPTION
---------------------------------------------------------------------
B901         TES801
Preamplifier, 200 W PER CHANNEL
```

Jean knows that there is more than one preamp in the Product table. She realizes that the reason the query only returned three products is that the descriptions for the other preamps do not contain the phrase Preamplifier; some of the descriptions are in uppercase, and others only contain the abbreviation Preamp or Pre-amp. After pondering this for a while, Jean submits this query to Oracle:

```
SQL> select Product_ID, Manufacturer_ID, Description
  2  from Product
  3  where
  4  upper(Description) like '%PRE%AMP%';

PRODUCT_ID   MANUFAC
------------ -------
DESCRIPTION
---------------------------------------------------------------------
B901         TES801
Preamplifier, 200 W PER CHANNEL

B801         SEN101
PRE AMPLIFIER 150 WATTS/CHANNEL

B311         TES801
Pre-amp, 120 W per channel

B9310        SEN101
Pre amp, 250 W/channel

B384         TES801
PREAMP, 460 W/RMS
```

Jean was correct. Instead of returning only one record, the query now returns five records. Let's take a close look at the WHERE clause.

By applying the UPPER function to the Description column, the distinction between the use of lowercase and uppercase letters in the Description column vanished: UPPER(Description) can be compared to all uppercase letters. The use of the additional wildcard symbol % also helps to broaden the retrieval of records. The % between PRE and AMP means that zero or more characters can exist between PRE and AMP, thereby retrieving:

    PRE-AMP

    PREAMP

    PRE_AMP

Also, by only using the phrase AMP rather than AMPLIFIER, Jean is able to retrieve products where the description is abbreviated to AMP.

Besides %, you can also use _ (underscore) as a placeholder in a string when you want to indicate that there is a single character between two other strings but you don't care (or know) what that character is. For instance, if Jean knew that all of the preamps were described as Pre:Amp or Pre-Amp or Pre Amp or Pre.Amp, she could modify her query to use the _, as in:

```
SQL> select Product_ID, Manufacturer_ID, Description
  2  from Product
  3  where
  4  upper(Description) like '%PRE_AMP%';

PRODUCT_ID    MANUFAC
-----------   -------
DESCRIPTION
------------------------------------------------------------------
B801          SEN101
PRE AMPLIFIER 150 WATTS/CHANNEL

B311          TES801
Pre-amp, 120 W per channel

B9310         SEN101
Pre amp, 250 W/channel
```

Sometimes you really want to search for a string that contains the % character. In this case, you can inform Oracle that you are using an escape character in the specified string, as in:

```
select Product_ID, Manufacturer_ID, Description
from Product
where
upper(Description) like '%POWER SUPPLY%\%SETTING%' escape '\';
```

This query uses the backslash character (\) to tell Oracle that the % that follows the \ is to be interpreted literally. The same method can be used when you want to search for an underscore (_) rather than have it represent any single character.

Here are some suggestions on using the LIKE operator in your searches:

- Apply the UPPER or LOWER function to the column that you're searching so that all characters are in the same case.

- If you are looking for records where a string occurs at the beginning of a column, don't use the wildcard character at the beginning of the pattern:
  ```
  select Product_ID, Manufacturer_ID, Description
  from Product
  where
  upper(Description) like 'TUNER%';
  ```

- Likewise, if you are looking for records where a string occurs at the end of a column, don't use the wildcard character at the end of the pattern:
  ```
  select Product_ID, Manufacturer_ID, Description
  from Product
  ```

```
where
upper(Description) like '%POWER SUPPLY';
```

Searching for Rows with the *BETWEEN* Operator

Earlier in this chapter, I explained that a SELECT statement can be structured in different ways to obtain the same result. The BETWEEN operator is a good example of this.

The BETWEEN operator is quite flexible; it works with numeric, string, and date values. For instance, to retrieve products whose current retail value is between $200 and $250, you would use:

```
select Product_ID, Manufacturer_ID, Description
from Product
where
Current_Retail_Value between 200 and 250;
```

The preceding query is really the same as:

```
select Product_ID, Manufacturer_ID, Description
from Product
where
Current_Retail_Value >= 200 and
Current_Retail_Value <= 250;
```

As you can see, the BETWEEN operator is the equivalent of two conditions that are ANDed together. When used appropriately, the BETWEEN operator simplifies a query. Of course, you can also combine the BETWEEN conditions with AND and OR operators. Here's an example of a SELECT statement that will retrieve a list of products whose value falls into two ranges—$200 to $250 and $700 to $750.

```
select Product_ID, Manufacturer_ID, Description
from Product
where
Current_Used_Value between 200 and 250 or
Current_Used_Value between 700 and 750;
```

If you wanted to assemble a list of repair depots in which the first letter of the depot name was in the range A through F, the query could be structured in this way:

```
select Depot_ID, Company_Name
from Depot
where
Company_Name between 'A' and 'F';
```

The *IN* Operator

As with the BETWEEN operator, the IN operator is used to compare the value of a column or expression with a list of possible values. The syntax for the IN operator is:

```
expression IN (expression1, expression2, ... expressionN)
```

where *expression* is a valid SQL expression, and *expression1* through *expressionN* is a list of valid SQL expressions.

The IN operator returns a Boolean value:

TRUE if the expression is equal to one of the values in the expression list

FALSE if the expression is not equal to one of the values in the expression list

Let's look at an example at how the IN operator is used. You want to retrieve only those customers whose state is one of several values. If you have a long list of possible values to check, the IN operator saves you some typing and saves Oracle's SQL statement parser some processing time. Here is an example of its use:

```
SQL> select Last_Name, First_Name, State
  2  from Customer
  3  where
  4  State IN ('CA', 'WA', 'AZ');

LAST_NAME                      FIRST_NAME                     ST
-----------------------------  -----------------------------  --
Johnson                        Samuel                         CA
Martinez                       Steve                          AZ
Pareski                        Monica                         AZ
McClintock                     Harvey                         WA
```

The alternative to the IN operator is this:

```
SQL> select Last_Name, First_Name, State
  2  from Customer
  3  where
  4  State = 'CA' or
  5  State = 'WA' or
  6  State = 'AZ';

LAST_NAME                      FIRST_NAME                     ST
-----------------------------  -----------------------------  --
Johnson                        Samuel                         CA
Martinez                       Steve                          AZ
Pareski                        Monica                         AZ
McClintock                     Harvey                         WA
```

You can combine the keyword NOT with the IN operator so that a condition is true if an expression is not equal to any of the expressions in the expression list, as in:

```
SQL> select Last_Name, First_Name, State
  2  from Customer
  3  where
  4  State NOT IN ('CA', 'WA', 'AZ');

LAST_NAME                      FIRST_NAME                     ST
-----------------------------  -----------------------------  --
Smyth                          Julie                          OR
Richardson                     Mary                           MA
Horace                         Michelle                       IL
Moran                          Sarah                          MI
Chen                           Laura                          MI
```

If you choose not to use the NOT IN operator, your WHERE clause would look like this:

```
SQL> select Last_Name, First_Name, State
  2  from Customer
  3  where
  4  State != 'CA' and
  5  State != 'WA' and
  6  State != 'AZ';
```

```
LAST_NAME                        FIRST_NAME                       ST
------------------------------   ------------------------------   --
Smyth                            Julie                            OR
Richardson                       Mary                             MA
Horace                           Michelle                         IL
Moran                            Sarah                            MI
Chen                             Laura                            MI
```

Summary

Chapter 5 dealt with the following fundamental concepts of SQL:

- Data Manipulation Language (DML) is a category of the SQL language consisting of the SELECT, INSERT, UPDATE, and DELETE statements.
- The results returned by every SELECT statement can be thought of as a temporary table.
- In developing your Personal Oracle7 application, always specify the columns to be retrieved in the SELECT statement.

6

Accessing Personal Oracle7 with SQL*Plus

SQL*Plus is a component of Personal Oracle7 that is used for executing SQL statements. SQL*Plus can also function as a rudimentary report writer with the capability to subtotal, total, and suppress repeating values.

SQL*Plus does play an important role in developing applications for Personal Oracle7. You'll use SQL*Plus to iteratively develop scripts for constructing tables, indexes, and other database objects. It's also valuable for prototyping the SQL statements that will be used by your application. After you've refined the SQL statements that your application will use, they can be incorporated into whatever application tool you're using—PowerBuilder, Oracle Forms, or Visual Basic. Another advantage of using SQL*Plus is that it works the same way in UNIX and other implementations of Oracle.

In this chapter and in the online Oracle SQL*Plus User's Guide, you'll see the use of the term *SQL*Plus session*. This term refers to commands and responses that occur from the time you connect to SQL*Plus until the time that you disconnect from SQL*Plus.

Distinguishing SQL Statements from SQL*Plus Commands

To master the use of SQL*Plus, you need to understand the difference between Oracle SQL statements and SQL*Plus commands.

SQL statements can be categorized in three ways:

- DML (Data Manipulation Language): statements that retrieve and modify the contents of Personal Oracle7 tables
- DDL (Data Definition Language): statements that create, alter, or remove database objects
- DCL (Data Control Language): statements that grant privileges to database roles and users

There are no formal categories for SQL*Plus commands. However, they can be grouped thus:

- Formatting: Commands that control the format of columns, column titles, and page numbering
- Input: Commands that enable the user to enter values
- Output: Commands that control data output
- Session: Commands that enable the user to initiate and terminate an Oracle session
- Preferences: Commands that affect the behavior of SQL*Plus
- Editing: Commands used to edit the command buffer
- Informational: Commands that provide information about database objects

> **NOTE**
>
> You can use SQL*DBA to issue SQL statements to Personal Oracle7. However, SQL*DBA doesn't recognize any SQL*Plus commands. Also, SQL*DBA doesn't have a command buffer that can be edited or saved. For these reasons, you really don't need to use SQL*DBA at all.

SQL statements differ from SQL*Plus commands in a couple of ways. SQL statements are terminated with a semicolon and don't require a continuation character at the end of each line; if a SQL*Plus command requires more than a single line of input, the hyphen character (-) must be used to inform SQL*Plus that another line of input will be provided.

SQL statements can be used in 4GLs, programs built with an Oracle precompiler, and ad hoc query tools and report writers; SQL*Plus commands cannot be used outside of SQL*Plus.

Many SQL*Plus commands remain in effect until they are overridden by new settings.

Looking at a Table Definition with *DESCRIBE*

DESCRIBE is an indispensable command that displays a table definition. The information returned by DESCRIBE includes each column name, its datatype, its length and scale, and whether or not it is mandatory.

```
SQL> desc Depot
 Name                             Null?    Type
 -------------------------------- -------- ----
 DEPOT_ID                         NOT NULL NUMBER(4)
 COMPANY_NAME                              VARCHAR2(30)
 STREET_ADDRESS                            VARCHAR2(60)
 CITY                                      VARCHAR2(30)
 STATE                                     VARCHAR2(2)
 ZIPCODE                                   VARCHAR2(9)
 TELEPHONE                                 VARCHAR2(10)
 FAX                                       VARCHAR2(10)
 PRIMARY_CONTACT_NAME                      VARCHAR2(30)
 CREATED_DATE                              DATE
 CREATED_BY                                VARCHAR2(30)
 MODIFIED_DATE                             DATE
 MODIFIED_BY                               VARCHAR2(30)
```

However, the DESCRIBE command does not indicate which columns are part of the primary key or which columns are foreign keys. In addition, the DESCRIBE command does not indicate any table or column constraints that have been defined.

The DESCRIBE command may also be used to display the calling sequence for a function, procedure, or package.

The Command Buffer

SQL*Plus maintains the current SQL statement in a command buffer. Each line in this command buffer is numbered; you can edit, invoke, and save the contents of the command buffer. The contents of the command buffer can be displayed by entering L (for LIST) at the SQL*Plus prompt.

```
SQL> list
  1  select Customer_ID, Last_Name, First_Name
  2  from Customer
  3* order by Customer_ID
SQL> l
  1  select Customer_ID, Last_Name, First_Name
  2  from Customer
  3* order by Customer_ID
```

You can edit the contents of the command buffer in three ways. You can copy and paste with the mouse and the SQL*Plus Edit menu. Second, from the SQL*Plus Edit menu item, you can invoke the Windows Notepad to edit the current contents of the command buffer. Third, you can edit the command buffer with special editing commands provided by SQL*Plus.

> **TIP**
>
> If you're trying to build a large SQL statement, use a text editor (such as Windows Notepad or Write) or word processor. The editing limitations of SQL*Plus can be quite frustrating. You'll find it easier to build your SQL statement in another tool and either copy the lines or execute them from SQL*Plus.

Copying and Pasting the Command Buffer

For new SQL*Plus users, the most intuitive method for manipulating the command buffer is through copying and pasting. For instance, you could highlight valid SQL statements from an open file in the Windows Notepad and paste the text into SQL*Plus.

To copy and paste text in SQL*Plus, do the following:

1. Highlight the text using the mouse or keyboard. Be sure to highlight only text segments that consist of valid SQL statements; do not include the SQL*Plus prompt SQL>.
2. Invoke the Copy command from the Edit menu or by entering Ctrl+Ins.
3. Paste the text by invoking the Paste command from the Edit menu or by entering Shift+Ins.

Editing the Command Buffer with an Editor

As an alternative to the copy-and-paste method, SQL*Plus furnishes an item in the Edit menu that invokes an Editor selection. Under the Editor menu item, you may either invoke the editor that's been defined or define a different editor. By default, Windows Notepad is the defined editor (see Figure 6.1).

FIGURE 6.1.

Using Notepad to edit the SQL*Plus command buffer.

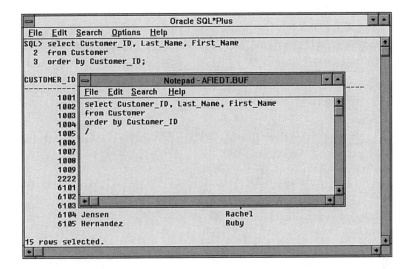

Editing the Command Buffer with Commands

A set of commands is available to you for editing the command buffer. Those of us who were SQL*Plus users before the advent of GUI interfaces were forced to rely on these commands. Although these commands are not intuitive or user-friendly, they're included here for completeness: using them is a matter of preference.

As with all editor commands, these commands are based on the concept of the current line in the command buffer.

Command	Description
L(LIST)	To list the contents of the command buffer.
N (where *N* is a number)	Make *N* the current line to be edited.
I(INSERT)	Insert a new line after the current line. The new line becomes the current line.
D(DELETE)	Delete the current line.
A(APPEND) *text*	Append *text* to the current line.
C(CHANGE)/*string1*/*string2*/	Change the first occurrence of *string1* to *string2*.

Let's look at how these commands are actually used. If you want to edit the second line, you enter a 2 at the SQL prompt.

```
SQL> l
  1  select Customer_ID, Last_Name, First_Name
  2  from Customer
  3* order by Customer_ID
SQL> 2
  2* from Customer
```

Now that line 2 is the current line, let's insert a new line.

```
SQL> 2
  2* from Customer
SQL> i
  3i where
  4i Last_Name like 'J%'
  5i
SQL> l
  1  select Customer_ID, Last_Name, First_Name
  2  from Customer
  3  where
  4  Last_Name like 'J%'
  5* order by Customer_ID
```

Now you've added a WHERE clause to the query. But you realize that you want to add an additional criterion on line 4.

```
SQL> 4
  4* Last_Name like 'J%'
SQL> a  or First_Name like '%e%'
  4* Last_Name like 'J%' or First_Name like '%e%'
```

You should notice two things about the Append command. First, if you need a space between the end of a line and what you plan to append, you'll need two spaces between the A(ppend) and whatever it is you are adding. Second, the Append command echoes the line.

Finally, you realize that you want to change the last line so that the output is ordered by Last_Name instead of Customer_ID.

```
SQL> 5
  5* order by Customer_ID
SQL> c/Customer_ID/Last_Name/
  5* order by Last_Name
```

In SQL*Plus, you can execute a SQL statement in one of three ways:

- By terminating the statement with a semicolon.

```
SQL> select Customer_ID, Last_Name, First_Name
  2  from Customer
  3  where
  4  Last_Name like 'J%' or First_Name like '%e%'
  5  order by Last_Name;
```

```
CUSTOMER_ID LAST_NAME                       FIRST_NAME
----------- ----------------------------    ----------
       1005 Horace                          Michelle
       6104 Jensen                          Rachel
       1001 Johnson                         Samuel
       1002 Martinez                        Steve
       1007 McClintock                      Harvey
       1003 Smyth                           Julie

6 rows selected.
```

■ By entering an R at the SQL*Plus prompt.

```
SQL> r
  1   select Customer_ID, Last_Name, First_Name
  2   from Customer
  3   where
  4   Last_Name like 'J%' or First_Name like '%e%'
  5*  order by Last_Name

CUSTOMER_ID LAST_NAME                       FIRST_NAME
----------- ----------------------------    ----------
       1005 Horace                          Michelle
       6104 Jensen                          Rachel
       1001 Johnson                         Samuel
       1002 Martinez                        Steve
       1007 McClintock                      Harvey
       1003 Smyth                           Julie

6 rows selected.
```

■ By entering a / at the SQL*Plus prompt.

```
SQL> /

CUSTOMER_ID LAST_NAME                       FIRST_NAME
----------- ----------------------------    ----------
       1005 Horace                          Michelle
       6104 Jensen                          Rachel
       1001 Johnson                         Samuel
       1002 Martinez                        Steve
       1007 McClintock                      Harvey
       1003 Smyth                           Julie

6 rows selected.
```

Saving SQL Statements to a File

There are two methods for saving SQL statements to an MS-DOS file. First, you can use the SAVE command; but this saves only the current contents of the command buffer to a file that you specify. Second, you can spool all output from SQL*Plus—each SQL statement and Oracle's response—to a file.

The SQL*Plus *SAVE* Command

The SAVE command stores the contents of the SQL*Plus command buffer into the specified MS-DOS file. If the file already exists, the SAVE command will not automatically override it.

```
SQL> l
  1  select Customer_ID, Last_Name, First_Name
  2  from Customer
  3  where
  4  Last_Name like 'J%' or First_Name like '%e%'
  5* order by Last_Name
SQL> save c:\fraywire\custqry
Created file c:\fraywire\custqry
```

By default, the SAVE command uses a file extension of SQL. You can override this if you specify a different file extension. If you try to save the command buffer to an existing file, SQL*Plus returns this message:

```
SQL> save c:\fraywire\custqry
File "c:\fraywire\custqry.SQL" already exists.
Use another name or "SAVE filename REPLACE".
SQL> save c:\fraywire\custqry replace
Wrote file c:\fraywire\custqry
```

Using *GET* to Obtain a SQL Statement

Presumably, you've saved a SQL statement using the SAVE command so that you can use it again. With the SQL*Plus GET command, you can retrieve the contents of the command buffer that were stored to a file with the SAVE command. In this example, we'll start with an empty command buffer, GET a file containing a valid SQL statement, and execute it by typing an R.

```
SQL> l
No lines in SQL buffer.
SQL> get c:\fraywire\custqry
  1  select Customer_ID, Last_Name, First_Name
  2  from Customer
  3  where
  4  Last_Name like 'J%' or First_Name like '%e%'
  5* order by Last_Name
SQL> r
  1  select Customer_ID, Last_Name, First_Name
  2  from Customer
  3  where
  4  Last_Name like 'J%' or First_Name like '%e%'
  5* order by Last_Name

CUSTOMER_ID LAST_NAME                          FIRST_NAME
----------- ---------------------------------- -----------------------------
       1005 Horace                             Michelle
       6104 Jensen                             Rachel
       1001 Johnson                            Samuel
       1002 Martinez                           Steve
       1007 McClintock                         Harvey
       1003 Smyth                              Julie

6 rows selected.
```

You can also use the / command to execute the contents of the command buffer. The difference between the / command and the R(un) command is that the / doesn't echo the contents of the command buffer before executing the SQL statement. Remember that if you don't specify an extension for the filename, GET assumes that it is SQL.

Saving Output to a File

The SPOOL command is used to save query results to a file. You can invoke the SPOOL command at the SQL*Plus prompt.

```
SQL> spool c:\fraywire\qry_oput
SQL> select Product_ID, Manufacturer_ID, Description
  2  from Product
  3  where
  4  Manufacturer_ID = 'SEN101'
  5  order by Product_ID;

PRODUCT_ID    MANUFA
------------  ------
DESCRIPTION
------------------------------------------------------------------

A504          SEN101
AMP 300W PER CHAN, RMS

A509          SEN101
AMP 600 WATTS PER CHANNEL, RMS

B801          SEN101
PRE AMPLIFIER 150 WATTS/CHANNEL

B9310         SEN101
Pre amp, 250 W/channel, RMS

C3002         SEN101
JUKEBOX, CD - 100 DISK CAPACITY

D301          SEN101


6 rows selected.

SQL> spool off
```

As shown in the previous example, the SQL*Plus command to stop spooling is this:

```
SQL> spool off
```

The version of SQL*Plus supplied with Personal Oracle7 also enables you to invoke the SPOOL command as a menu item (see Figure 6.2).

FIGURE 6.2.

*Invoking the SPOOL command from the SQL*Plus menu.*

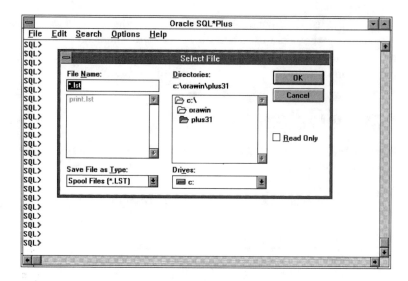

Running a Script

A SQL*Plus script consists of SQL*Plus commands and SQL statements. A SQL*Plus script can be invoked in a couple of ways:

- **From SQL*Plus itself.** While running SQL*Plus, you can execute a script by typing:

  start *script*

  or

  @*script*

  where *script* is a file named *script*.sql that is in your DOS path.

- **From a Windows program item.** You can create a Windows program item that runs a script whenever you double-click the item (see Figure 6.3).

FIGURE 6.3.

*Creating a program group item to invoke a SQL*Plus script.*

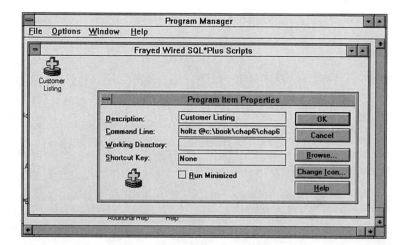

Nesting SQL*Plus Scripts

A SQL*Plus script can contain a START command to invoke another SQL*Plus script. For example, you could write a SQL*Plus script that calls four other SQL*Plus scripts in this way:

```
start c:\fraywire\cust_ca
start c:\fraywire\cust_mi
start c:\fraywire\cust_wa
start c:\fraywire\prod_sen
```

Here's the output from invoking the MASTER.SQL script.

```
SQL> start c:\fraywire\master
SQL> start c:\fraywire\cust_ca
SQL> select Customer_ID
  2  from Customer
  3  where
  4  Input truncated to 13 characters
State = 'CA';

CUSTOMER_ID
-----------
       1001

SQL> start c:\fraywire\cust_mi
SQL> select Customer_ID
  2  from Customer
  3  where
  4  Input truncated to 13 characters
State = 'MI';

CUSTOMER_ID
-----------
       1008
       1009

SQL> start c:\fraywire\cust_wa
SQL> select Customer_ID
  2  from Customer
  3  where
  4  Input truncated to 13 characters
State = 'WA';

CUSTOMER_ID
-----------
       1007

SQL> start c:\fraywire\prod_sen
SQL> select Product_ID
  2  from Product
  3  where
  4  Input truncated to 27 characters
Manufacturer_ID = 'SEN101';

PRODUCT_ID
-----------
A504
A509
```

```
B801
C3002
B9310
D301

6 rows selected.
```

Formatting Output

The formatting that you will cover in this section is achieved via SQL*Plus commands. These commands enable you to specify formats, totals, and subtotals and suppress repeating values. These commands are temporal; they remain in effect only for those SQL statements processed during the same SQL*Plus session.

Formatting a Column with the *COLUMN* Command

The COLUMN command offers many options for formatting a column's display. SQL*Plus provides default output formatting that is overridden through the use of the COLUMN command.

Specifying a Column's Format

Each column, depending on its datatype, has a format that can be specified for displaying output. For example, a numeric column used for storing price information can be formatted in many ways, including:

With a dollar sign

With negative values enclosed in parentheses

With leading zeros

In your database application, you might need to display the estimate returned by a depot in this way:

```
SQL> column Total_Cost format '$9,999'
SQL> r
  1   select Repair_ID, Item_Number, Total_Cost
  2   from Depot_Estimate
  3*  order by Repair_ID

REPAIR_ID ITEM_NUMBER TOTAL_COST
--------- ----------- ----------
     2003           1       $523
     2004           1       $316
     2005           1       $142
     2006           1       $217
     2006           2        $66
```

As you can see, the format used for the Total_Cost column didn't include a decimal point; as a result, cents aren't displayed. You can change this.

```
SQL> column Total_Cost format '$9,999.99'
SQL> r
  1  select Repair_ID, Item_Number, Total_Cost
  2  from Depot_Estimate
  3* order by Repair_ID

REPAIR_ID ITEM_NUMBER TOTAL_COST
--------- ----------- ----------
     2003           1    $522.75
     2004           1    $315.68
     2005           1    $141.94
     2006           1    $216.76
     2006           2     $65.59
```

For character columns, you can use the FORMAT option to specify the width in which a column is displayed. For the Product table, you might want a report in which the product description wraps after displaying up to 30 characters.

```
SQL> column Description format a30
SQL> r
  1  select Product_ID, Manufacturer_ID, Description
  2  from Product
  3* order by Product_ID

PRODUCT_ID   MANUFA DESCRIPTION
------------ ------ ------------------------------
A2001        TES801 AMPLIFIER, 100W PER CHANNEL, R
                    MS

A504         SEN101 AMP 300W PER CHAN, RMS
A509         SEN101 AMP 600 WATTS PER CHANNEL, RMS
A903         TES801 AMP, PROFESSIONAL 800W RMS PER
                    CHANNEL

B311         TES801 Pre-amp, 120 W per channel
B384         TES801 PREAMP, 460 W/RMS
B801         SEN101 PRE AMPLIFIER 150 WATTS/CHANNE
                    L

B901         TES801 Preamplifier, 200 W per channe
                    l, RMS

B9310        SEN101 Pre amp, 250 W/channel, RMS
C2002        MIT501 CD PLAYER, SINGLE-DISK
C2005        MIT501 5-DISK CD PLAYER
C3002        SEN101 JUKEBOX, CD - 100 DISK CAPACIT
                    Y

D301         SEN101
TR901        TES801 Tuner

14 rows selected.
```

Of course, you really don't want the description to wrap to the next line if you're in the middle of a word. To prevent this from occurring, you add the phrase WORD_WRAP to the COLUMN command in this way:

```
SQL> column Description format a30 word_wrap
SQL> r
  1  select Product_ID, Manufacturer_ID, Description
  2  from Product
  3* order by Product_ID

PRODUCT_ID   MANUFA DESCRIPTION
-----------  ------ ------------------------------
A2001        TES801 AMPLIFIER, 100W PER CHANNEL,
                    RMS

A504         SEN101 AMP 300W PER CHAN, RMS
A509         SEN101 AMP 600 WATTS PER CHANNEL, RMS
A903         TES801 AMP, PROFESSIONAL 800W RMS PER
                    CHANNEL

B311         TES801 Pre-amp, 120 W per channel
B384         TES801 PREAMP, 460 W/RMS
B801         SEN101 PRE AMPLIFIER 150
                    WATTS/CHANNEL

B901         TES801 Preamplifier, 200 W per
                    channel, RMS

B9310        SEN101 Pre amp, 250 W/channel, RMS
C2002        MIT501 CD PLAYER, SINGLE-DISK
C2005        MIT501 5-DISK CD PLAYER
C3002        SEN101 JUKEBOX, CD - 100 DISK
                    CAPACITY

D301         SEN101
TR901        TES801 Tuner

14 rows selected.
```

As an alternative to word wrapping, you can truncate the display of a column's contents by using the TRUNC option.

```
SQL> column Description format a30 trunc
SQL> select Product_ID, Manufacturer_ID, Description
  2  from Product
  3  order by Product_ID;

PRODUCT_ID   MANUFA DESCRIPTION
-----------  ------ ------------------------------
A2001        TES801 AMPLIFIER, 100W PER CHANNEL, R
A504         SEN101 AMP 300W PER CHAN, RMS
A509         SEN101 AMP 600 WATTS PER CHANNEL, RMS
A903         TES801 AMP, PROFESSIONAL 800W RMS PER
B311         TES801 Pre-amp, 120 W per channel
B384         TES801 PREAMP, 460 W/RMS
B801         SEN101 PRE AMPLIFIER 150 WATTS/CHANNE
B901         TES801 Preamplifier, 200 W per channe
```

```
B9310        SEN101 Pre amp, 250 W/channel, RMS
C2002        MIT501 CD PLAYER, SINGLE-DISK
C2005        MIT501 5-DISK CD PLAYER
C3002        SEN101 JUKEBOX, CD - 100 DISK CAPACIT
D301         SEN101
TR901        TES801 Tuner

14 rows selected.
```

> **TIP**
>
> Remember that if you set a column's format with the COLUMN command, SQL*Plus uses that format for all columns with the same name—even if they occur in different tables. You can either reissue the COLUMN command with a different format before each SELECT statement, or specify an alias so that each column name is unique.

Changing a Column's Heading

When you specify a list of columns to be displayed in a query, SQL*Plus uses the column name as the column heading. If you want to use a different column heading, you have two choices: use a column alias, or use the COLUMN command to specify a different column heading.

A column alias is specified after the column expression. In this example, we specify the alias Depreciated_Amount for the column expression Initial_Retail_Value − Current_Used_Value.

```
SQL> select Product_ID, Initial_Retail_Value - Current_Used_Value
  2  Depreciated_Amount
  3  from Product
  4  order by Product_ID;

PRODUCT_ID  DEPRECIATED_AMOUNT
----------- ------------------
A2001                      100
A504                       195
A509                       175
A903                       225
```

If you want to use more than one word as a column heading, enclose the column heading in double quotes. In this case, you aren't using an underscore (_) character between the words *Depreciated* and *Amount*.

```
SQL> r
  1  select Product_ID, Initial_Retail_Value - Current_Used_Value
  2  "Depreciated Amount"
  3  from Product
  4* order by Product_ID

PRODUCT_ID  Depreciated Amount
----------- ------------------
A2001                      100
A504                       195
A509                       175
A903                       225
```

Here's an example of how to change a column heading with the FORMAT command.

```
SQL> column Manufacturer_ID format A20 heading "Manufacturer"
SQL> r
  1   select Product_ID, Manufacturer_ID
  2   from Product
  3   where Description like '%CD%'
  4*  order by Product_ID

PRODUCT_ID   Manufacturer
----------   --------------------
C2002        MIT501
C2005        MIT501
C3002        SEN101
```

Totals and Subtotals

Personal Oracle7 provides a built-in function for computing a total—the SUM function—but
SQL*Plus also provides a command for printing summary lines including subtotals, averages,
and totals. This is accomplished through the BREAK and COMPUTE commands. Suppose you want
to display the average value of repair depot estimates along with the details of each estimate.

```
SQL> break on Depot_ID skip 1
SQL> compute avg of Total_Cost on Depot_ID
SQL> select Depot_ID, Labor_Cost, Parts_Cost, Total_Cost
  2   from Depot_Estimate
  3   order by Depot_ID;

 DEPOT_ID LABOR_COST PARTS_COST TOTAL_COST
---------- ---------- ---------- ----------
     1001        240        260    $522.75
                  83        123    $216.76
                  21         41     $65.59
********                          ----------
avg                                $268.37

     1002        183        122    $315.68
                  93         45    $141.94
                  89        139    $240.16
********                          ----------
avg                                $232.59

     1003        320        310    $657.13
                  91         93    $192.14
********                          ----------
avg                                $424.64

     1004        119        212    $349.55
                  21         46     $71.03
********                          ----------
avg                                $210.29
```

```
DEPOT_ID LABOR_COST PARTS_COST TOTAL_COST
-------- ---------- ---------- ----------

    1005         91        251    $363.96
                 55         81    $143.09
********                         ----------
avg                               $253.53
```

12 rows selected.

In the preceding example, we used the BREAK command to suppress repeating values of Depot_ID and to skip a line whenever the value of Depot_ID changes. Next, the COMPUTE command was executed to compute the average of Total_Cost for each Depot_ID.

Suppressing Repeating Values with the *BREAK* Command

The BREAK command is used to instruct SQL*Plus to suppress the display of repeating values for a column. You can specify multiple columns for suppressing repeating values.

```
SQL> break on Repair_ID on Depot_ID
SQL> select Repair_ID, Depot_ID, Item_Number, Total_Cost
  2  from Depot_Estimate
  3  order by Repair_ID, Depot_ID, Item_Number;

REPAIR_ID DEPOT_ID ITEM_NUMBER TOTAL_COST
--------- -------- ----------- ----------
     2003     1001           1     522.75
     2004     1002           1     315.68
     2005     1002           1     141.94
     2006     1001           1     216.76
                             2      65.59
     4001     1003           1     657.13
     4002     1004           1     349.55
     4003     1005           1     363.96
     4004     1004           1      71.03
     4005     1005           1     143.09
     4006     1002           1     240.16
     4007     1003           1     192.14
```

12 rows selected.

It's important to remember that the BREAK command does not affect the ordering in which the rows are returned by the SELECT statement. Use the ORDER BY clause to specify the columns to be used in ordering the query results.

Other Examples of the *COMPUTE* Command

You can compute more than one function using the COMPUTE command. In this example, we're computing the average and total of Total_Cost for each Depot_ID.

```
SQL> break on Depot_ID skip 1
SQL> compute avg sum of Total_Cost on Depot_ID
SQL> select Depot_ID, Labor_Cost, Parts_Cost, Total_Cost
  2  from Depot_Estimate
  3  order by Depot_ID;

DEPOT_ID LABOR_COST PARTS_COST TOTAL_COST
-------- ---------- ---------- ----------
    1001        240        260    $522.75
                 83        123    $216.76
                 21         41     $65.59
********                       ----------
avg                               $268.37
sum                               $805.10

    1002        183        122    $315.68
                 93         45    $141.94
                 89        139    $240.16
********                       ----------
avg                               $232.59
sum                               $697.78

    1003        320        310    $657.13
                 91         93    $192.14
********                       ----------
avg                               $424.64
sum                               $849.27

    1004        119        212    $349.55

DEPOT_ID LABOR_COST PARTS_COST TOTAL_COST
-------- ---------- ---------- ----------
    1004         21         46     $71.03
********                       ----------
avg                               $210.29
sum                               $420.58

    1005         91        251    $363.96
                 55         81    $143.09
********                       ----------
avg                               $253.53
sum                               $507.05

12 rows selected.
```

Adding Titles to SQL*Plus Output

In conjunction with its other formatting commands, SQL*Plus provides two commands for producing titles: TTITLE for specifying the title at the top of each page and BTITLE for specifying the title at the bottom of each page.

Here's an example of the use of TTITLE and BTITLE that displays a title, a date, and the current page number.

```
SQL> ttitle left 'Frayed Wires Product Report' center 'May 8, 1995' -
> right 'Page' format 99 sql.pno
SQL> btitle center 'FOR INTERNAL USE ONLY'
SQL> select Product_ID, Manufacturer_ID, Description
  2  from Product
  3  order by Product_ID, Manufacturer_ID;

Frayed Wires Product Report   May 8, 1995                     Page  1
          PRODUCT_ID MANUFACTURER_ID DESCRIPTION
--------------------- --------------- ----------------------------------
A2001               TES801          AMPLIFIER, 100W PER CHANNEL, R
A504                SEN101          AMP 300W PER CHAN, RMS
A509                SEN101          AMP 600 WATTS PER CHANNEL, RMS
A903                TES801          AMP, PROFESSIONAL 800W RMS PER
B311                TES801          Pre-amp, 120 W per channel
B384                TES801          PREAMP, 460 W/RMS
B801                SEN101          PRE AMPLIFIER 150 WATTS/CHANNE
B901                TES801          Preamplifier, 200 W per channe
B9310               SEN101          Pre amp, 250 W/channel, RMS
C2002               MIT501          CD PLAYER, SINGLE-DISK
C2005               MIT501          5-DISK CD PLAYER
C3002               SEN101          JUKEBOX, CD - 100 DISK CAPACIT
D301                SEN101
TR901               TES801          Tuner

                       FOR INTERNAL USE ONLY
```

The TTITLE command specifies three separate strings:

- The report title, Frayed Wires Product Report, which is left-justified
- The date, which is centered
- The page number, which is right-justified

The page number refers to a SQL*Plus variable named SQL.PNO. Another SQL*Plus variable that you might want to reference in a report is SQL.LNO, the current line number.

As you can see, BTITLE uses the same syntax as TTITLE.

SQL*Plus System Variables

SQL*Plus employs a number of system variables that control the characteristics of each SQL*Plus session. The SET command is used to set a system variable to a particular value; the SHOW command is used to view the current setting of a system variable.

You can also issue this command to view all system variable settings.

```
SQL> show all
feedback ON for 6 or more rows
heading ON
linesize 100
numwidth 9
spool OFF
user is "FRAYED_WIRES"
space 1
```

Developing Personal Oracle7 Applications

```
worksize DEFAULT
lines will be wrapped
pagesize 24
showmode OFF
pause is OFF
ttitle OFF and is the 1st few characters of the next SELECT statement
btitle OFF and is the 1st few characters of the next SELECT statement
define "&" (hex 26)
escape OFF
concat "." (hex 2e)
sqlprompt "SQL> "
underline "-" (hex 2d)
null ""
verify ON
message ON
sqlcode 0
tab ON
scan ON
dclsep OFF
termout ON
echo ON
sqlcase MIXED
headsep "|" (hex 7c)
maxdata 32767
time OFF
cmdsep OFF
xisql OFF
sqlterminator ";" (hex 3b)
sqlprefix "#" (hex 23)
release 1508
sqlnumber ON
autocommit OFF
newpage 1
long 80
document ON
trimout ON
timing OFF
qbidebug OFF
numformat ""
synonym OFF
suffix "SQL"
flush ON
sqlcontinue "> "
pno 2
lno 17
buffer SQL
embedded OFF
arraysize 15
crt ""
copycommit 0
compatibility version NATIVE
recsep WRAP
recsepchar " " (hex 20)
```

```
blockterminator "." (hex 2e)
copytypecheck is ON
closecursor OFF
longchunksize 80
serveroutput OFF
flagger OFF
```

As you can see, SQL*Plus has several system variables. Let's focus on some of the more important ones.

AUTOCOMMIT

AUTOCOMMIT controls how SQL*Plus commits transactions. If AUTOCOMMIT is set to ON, SQL*Plus performs a commit after each SQL statement is processed. The default setting for AUTOCOMMIT is OFF. With AUTOCOMMIT set to ON, if you accidentally delete some rows from a table, you can't rollback from the transaction. You generally want to leave AUTOCOMMIT set to OFF.

ECHO

If you don't want the SQL statements that are processed by SQL*Plus to be echoed, set ECHO to OFF. This is commonly done when preparing reports in which you only want to see the desired results.

FEEDBACK

The system variable FEEDBACK controls when and whether or not SQL*Plus indicates the number of records returned by a query. The default setting of FEEDBACK is 6. In other words, if six or more rows are retrieved by a query, SQL*Plus displays the number of retrieved rows. If the query returns less than six rows, SQL*Plus will not provide this feedback. You can set the number of rows that will trigger FEEDBACK.

HEADING

By default, SQL*Plus displays column headings. To disable the display of headings, simply set HEADING to OFF.

LINESIZE

LINESIZE controls the maximum number of characters that appear on a line of output. However, if you want to increase the LINESIZE, you'll also need to increase the width of the screen buffer (see Figure 6.4).

FIGURE 6.4.

*Changing the SQL*Plus screen buffer width.*

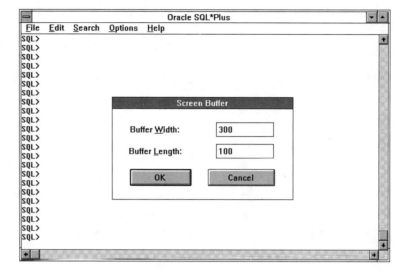

LONG

If you absolutely need to store more than 2,000 characters in a column, you'll need to define the column using Oracle's LONG datatype. Please be aware that SQL*Plus will not display more than 80 characters of a LONG column unless you increase the LONG system variable. If you need to display a large number of characters—say, up to 5,000—you'll need to set LONG to 5000. In addition, you'll probably need to reduce ARRAYSIZE to 1.

NUMWIDTH

SQL*Plus uses the value of NUMWIDTH to determine the width to use when displaying numbers. The default value of NUMWIDTH is 10. You can increase this value if your application requires it.

PAGESIZE

PAGESIZE is used to define the number of lines on a page. This number is used to determine when column headings and page titles should be displayed. If you set PAGESIZE to 0, all titles and column headings will be suppressed.

PAUSE

If you submit a query that retrieves many records, the default behavior of SQL*Plus is to send the results zipping by you on the screen. If you set PAUSE to ON or to a string, SQL*Plus waits for the Return key to be pressed before continuing with the next screen's worth of output.

```
SQL> set pause More?
SQL> select *
  2  from Customer;
More?

CUSTOMER_ID LAST_NAME                            FIRST_NAME                  SALUT
----------- -----------------------------------  -------------------------  -----
STREET_ADDRESS                                    CITY
-----------------------------------------------   --------------------
ZIPCODE    WORK_TELEP HOME_TELEP FAX_NUMBER EARLIEST_ LATEST_TI LOC CREATED_D
---------- ---------- ---------- ---------- --------- --------- --- ---------
CREATED_BY                      MODIFIED_ MODIFIED_BY
------------------------------- --------- -----------------------------
       1001 Johnson                         Samuel                        Mr.
1922 Bedford Blvd.                                   Santa Margherina
91010      7145559876            7145550123


       1002 Martinez                        Steve                         Mr.
9303 Channel Drive.                                  Williamshire
12912      6025559133 6025553811 6025553833


       1003 Smyth                           Julie                         Ms.
39121 Pillar Ave.                                    Portsmith
03991      5035553843            5035551283


More?
```

SQL*Plus prompts you to press the Return key after displaying the number of lines defined in the system variable PAGESIZE.

TIME

You can include the current time in the SQL*Plus prompt by setting TIME to ON. You may find this useful when spooling output to a file.

```
SQL> set time on
18:39:48 SQL>
```

TIMING

TIMING turns either on or off the display of timing statistics for each SQL command. If you're trying to collect performance information about Personal Oracle7, you can set TIMING on and spool the statistics to a file.

```
SQL> set timing on
SQL> select count(*) from Product;

 COUNT(*)
---------
       14

real: 1210
```

Establishing Default SQL*Plus System Variables

In the ORAWIN\PLS31 directory, you will find a file named GLOGIN.SQL. You can incorporate additional SQL*Plus commands by adding lines to this file. These system variable settings take effect for each SQL*Plus session.

Writing Flexible Queries with Substitution Variables

Within SQL*Plus, you can reference substitution variables in your SQL statements. Substitution variables enable you to rerun the same SQL statement with a different set of values. You denote a substitution variable by preceding a user variable name with a single or double ampersand (&). For instance, a query is more flexible when it references a substitution variable.

```
SQL> r
  1  select Product_ID, Manufacturer_ID, Initial_Retail_Value
  2  from Product
  3  where
  4  Initial_Retail_Value > &init_value
  5* order by Product_ID
Enter value for init_value: 500
old   4: Initial_Retail_Value > &init_value
new   4: Initial_Retail_Value > 500

PRODUCT_ID    MANUFA INITIAL_RETAIL_VALUE
------------  ------ --------------------
A504          SEN101                  585
A509          SEN101                  850
A903          TES801                 1050
B384          TES801                  740
C3002         SEN101                 2150
```

You can also embed a substitution variable inside a string like this:

```
SQL> r
  1  select Product_ID, Manufacturer_ID, Initial_Retail_Value
  2  from Product
  3  where
  4  Initial_Retail_Value > &init_value and
  5  Manufacturer_ID like '%&Manuf_ID%'
  6* order by Product_ID
Enter value for init_value: 400
old   4: Initial_Retail_Value > &init_value and
new   4: Initial_Retail_Value > 400 and
Enter value for manuf_id: SEN
old   5: Manufacturer_ID like '%&Manuf_ID%'
new   5: Manufacturer_ID like '%SEN%'

PRODUCT_ID    MANUFA INITIAL_RETAIL_VALUE
------------  ------ --------------------
A504          SEN101                  585
A509          SEN101                  850
B9310         SEN101                  430
C3002         SEN101                 2150
```

When you are prompted by SQL*Plus to supply a value for a substitution value, you must supply a value that corresponds to the appropriate datatype. For example, if you want to retrieve products whose Manufacturer_ID is like '%SEN%', you must remember to incorporate single quotes into the string.

```
SQL> r
  1  select Product_ID, Manufacturer_ID, Initial_Retail_Value
  2  from Product
  3  where
  4  Manufacturer_ID like &Manuf_ID
  5* order by Product_ID
Enter value for manuf_id: %SEN%
old   4: Manufacturer_ID like &Manuf_ID
new   4: Manufacturer_ID like %SEN%
Manufacturer_ID like %SEN%
                         *
ERROR at line 4:
ORA-00911: invalid character
```

The convenience of a substitution variable is that it enables you to rerun the same SQL statement with different values. You should use substitution variables with INSERT statements to reduce your keystrokes. Give your substitution variables meaningful names.

Passing Values to SQL*Plus Scripts with Substitution Variables

The START command invokes a specified SQL*Plus script that contains SQL statements and SQL*Plus commands. Another feature of the START command is the capability to pass values to the script that you want to run.

Suppose that you want to create a report containing customer information for customers living in a specific state. However, you want to be able to specify the state when you run the report.

Let's look at the SQL*Plus script named custstat.sql.

```
set echo off

spool c:\fraywire\custstat

select Customer_ID, Last_Name, First_Name
from Customer
where
State = '&1'
order by &2;

spool off
```

Notice that instead of having meaningful names, the substitution variables are named &1 and &2. From SQL*Plus, you invoke the custstat.sql script with the START command in this way:

```
SQL> start c:\fraywire\custstat 'MI' Last_Name
old   4: State = '&1'
new   4: State = 'MI'
old   5: order by &2
new   5: order by Last_Name
```

```
CUSTOMER_ID LAST_NAME                       FIRST_NAME
----------- ------------------------------- -------------------------------
       1009 Chen                            Laura
       1008 Moran                           Sarah
```

You probably observed that the name of each substitution variable corresponded to its order in the START command: &1 corresponded to 'MI', and &2 corresponded to Last_Name. In general, the syntax for the START command is

```
START script [sub1] [sub2] ... [subN]
```

where *script* is the filename of the SQL*Plus script to be executed, and *sub1* through *subN* are arguments to be used as values in substitution variables.

Other Ways of Setting User Variables

SQL*Plus provides two commands that can be used for setting user variables: DEFINE and ACCEPT.

With the DEFINE command, you can create a user variable and assign a character value to it.

```
SQL> define Selected_Mfgr = "SEN101"
SQL> r
  1  select Product_ID, Manufacturer_ID, Description
  2  from Product
  3  where
  4  Manufacturer_ID = '&Selected_Mfgr'
  5* order by Product_ID
old   4: Manufacturer_ID = '&Selected_Mfgr'
new   4: Manufacturer_ID = 'SEN101'

Frayed Wires Product Report    May 8, 1995                  Page   1
            PRODUCT_ID MANUFACTURER_ID DESCRIPTION
            ---------- --------------- ------------------------
A504                   SEN101          AMP 300W PER CHAN, RMS
A509                   SEN101          AMP 600 WATTS PER CHANNEL, RMS
B801                   SEN101          PRE AMPLIFIER 150 WATTS/CHANNE
B9310                  SEN101          Pre amp, 250 W/channel, RMS
C3002                  SEN101          JUKEBOX, CD - 100 DISK CAPACIT
```

The ACCEPT command specifies a user variable, its datatype, and the text to be used in a user prompt.

```
SQL> accept Descrip_Pattern char -
> prompt 'Enter Description text to search for: '
Enter Description text to search for: CD
SQL> select Product_ID, Manufacturer_ID, Description
  2  from Product
  3  where
  4  Description like '%&Descrip_Pattern%';
old   4: Description like '%&Descrip_Pattern%'
new   4: Description like '%CD%'
```

```
Frayed Wires Product Report   May 8, 1995                    Page  1
           PRODUCT_ID MANUFACTURER_ID DESCRIPTION
.............  ............... ..............................
C2002          MIT501          CD PLAYER, SINGLE-DISK
C2005          MIT501          5-DISK CD PLAYER
C3002          SEN101          JUKEBOX, CD - 100 DISK CAPACIT
```

If you want to provide multiple lines of information when prompting the user, use the PROMPT command in conjunction with ACCEPT. Here's a SQL*Plus script that contains the PROMPT and ACCEPT commands.

```
column Description format a20 trunc
set echo off

prompt Please enter the pattern to search
prompt product descriptions. You may use the percent sign
prompt as a wildcard and the underscore as a placeholder
accept Descrip_Pattern char prompt 'Pattern: '

select Product_ID, Manufacturer_ID, Description
from Product
where
Description like '&Descrip_Pattern'
order by Product_ID;
```

Here is how the SQL*Plus script behaves when invoked.

```
SQL> @c:\fraywire\accept
Please enter the pattern to search
product descriptions. You may use the percent sign
as a wildcard and the underscore as a placeholder
Pattern: %AMP%
old   4: Description like '&Descrip_Pattern'
new   4: Description like '%AMP%'

PRODUCT_ID   MANUFA DESCRIPTION
............  ...... ....................
A2001        TES801 AMPLIFIER, 100W PER
A504         SEN101 AMP 300W PER CHAN, R
A509         SEN101 AMP 600 WATTS PER CH
A903         TES801 AMP, PROFESSIONAL 80
B384         TES801 PREAMP, 460 W/RMS
B801         SEN101 PRE AMPLIFIER 150 WA

6 rows selected.
```

The SQL*Plus *COPY* Command

One SQL*Plus command that you'll find quite useful is the COPY command. At first glance, COPY seems to offer the same capability as the INSERT and CREATE TABLE statements: it copies data from an existing table to another existing table or a new table. The COPY command does have one major advantage over the INSERT statement that we'll discuss in Chapter 8, "Using SQL to Modify Data."

Summary

SQL*Plus is a Personal Oracle7 tool that offers an interactive SQL interface. It is a suitable tool for creating database objects such as tables, indexes, triggers, and stored procedures. In addition, you can use SQL*Plus for prototyping SQL statements for use in an application development tool such as PowerBuilder or Visual Basic.

SQL*Plus can process SQL statements interactively or it can invoke a script that contains SQL statements and SQL*Plus commands.

Each SQL statement is stored in a command buffer that can be repeatedly executed or modified.

7

Creating and Modifying Tables

In this chapter, you look at another subset of SQL: Data Definition Language (DDL). DDL consists of SQL statements used to create, modify, and discard database objects.

If you're involved in developing many database applications, you should definitely consider the use of a Windows-based CASE tool such as Oracle's Designer/2000, Logic Works's ERwin, or System Architect. These products enable you to graphically define a logical model and generate the correct SQL statements for creating a database.

Even if you're using a CASE tool, you should acquire a working knowledge of the Oracle toolset. There are two ways to create tables, indexes, and other database objects in Personal Oracle7. The first method is to use SQL*Plus. As you saw in Chapter 6, "Accessing Personal Oracle7 with SQL*Plus," SQL*Plus is an interactive tool that you can use to submit all SQL statements.

The other alternative is Object Manager, which was introduced with the Oracle Workgroup Server and Personal Oracle7. Object Manager is a Windows-based graphical tool that enables you to perform common database tasks. Unlike SQL*Plus, Object Manager is not command-oriented. Object Manager packages your inputs and submits them to the Oracle7 database engine. This tool is ideal for users who aren't familiar with SQL and don't have a desire to learn the language. There are limitations to using Object Manager. Nevertheless, Object Manager offers a straightforward interface for viewing and modifying database objects.

Creating a Table with Object Manager

The Object Manager icon resides in the Personal Oracle7 Windows group. Object Manager can be invoked by double-clicking on the Object Manager icon. Object Manager prompts you for an Oracle username and password to be used in connecting to the database (see Figure 7.1). We'll stick to our running example and enter FRAYED_WIRES for the username, HELMHOLTZ for the password, and click the OK button.

FIGURE 7.1.

Entering the username and password in Object Manager.

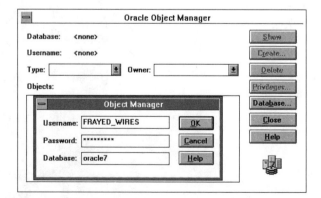

After you've successfully connected to the Personal Oracle7 database with Object Manager, you click the Type drop-down list and select Table as the database object. Object Manager then retrieves the existing tables that are owned by the Frayed_Wires Oracle account (see Figure 7.2).

FIGURE 7.2.

Object Manager displays a list of existing tables.

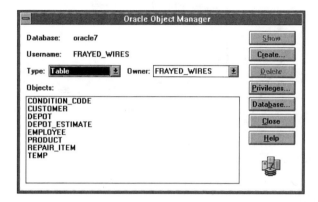

Because you're creating a new table, click the Create button. A pop-up window entitled Create New Object will appear. You'll see a group of radio buttons that are used to select the type of database object to be created (see Figure 7.3). Select the Table radio button, and click the OK button.

FIGURE 7.3.

Choosing the type of database object to be created.

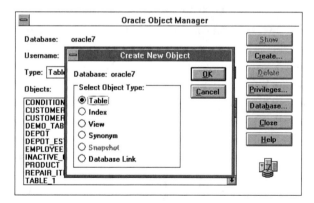

Another pop-up window entitled Table Management is displayed. This window functions much like a spreadsheet program and is initially empty (see Figure 7.4). The initial width of the Column Name column is fairly narrow. You can increase its width by moving the pointer to the line that separates the Column Name and Type columns, holding the mouse button down, and moving the pointer to the right.

FIGURE 7.4.

Empty spreadsheet displayed by Table Management.

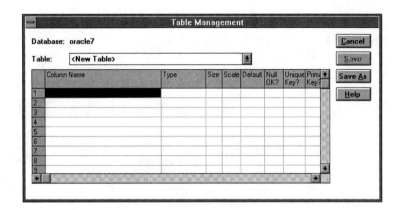

In our example, we're going to create the Manufacturer table. For each column, follow this procedure (see Figure 7.5):

1. Column Name: Enter the column name.

2. Type: Select the appropriate datatype.

3. Size: Specify the size, if appropriate. For instance, you don't need to specify a size for a DATE type.

4. Scale: Used for NUMBER and FLOAT to indicate the number of digits to the right of the decimal place that Oracle will store.

5. Default: Specify a default value that should be used for this column, if appropriate.

6. Null OK?: Indicate whether nulls are allowed. You can toggle this setting by clicking the cell.

7. Unique Key?: Set to YES if this value is unique but not if the column is part of the primary key.

8. Primary Key?: If the column is part of the primary key, click the cell. You'll learn more about primary keys later. However, you'll notice that if you do click on this cell, a 1 will be displayed to indicate that the column is part of the primary key. Object Manager would provide greater clarity if it displayed YES instead of 1.

In Figure 7.6, some of the spreadsheet columns have been resized to display the Primary Key, Foreign Key, and Check Condition columns.

After you've defined all of the columns for the Manufacturer table, click the Save button. Object Manager brings up a pop-up window entitled New Table Name. In the Table Name field, enter Manufacturer and click the OK button (see Figure 7.7).

FIGURE 7.5.

Defining a table's columns with Object Manager.

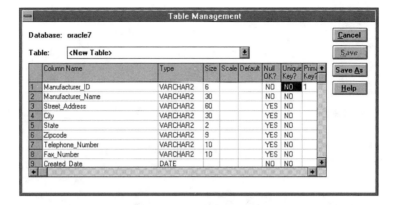

FIGURE 7.6.

Additional columns displayed in the Table Management spreadsheet.

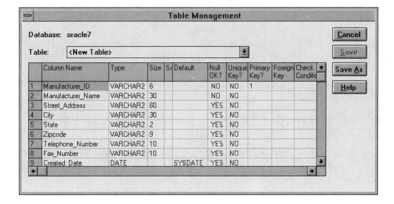

FIGURE 7.7.

Supplying a new table name to Object Manager.

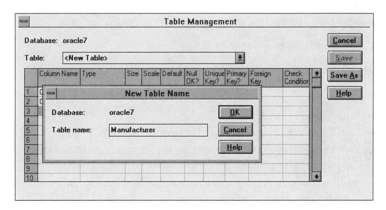

At this point, Object Manager has packaged the information entered on the spreadsheet, assembled a CREATE TABLE statement (which is hidden from the user), and submitted the statement to the Oracle7 database engine. If the table is created successfully, Object Manager displays a success message. The Table Management window then displays the new table name, as shown in Figure 7.8.

FIGURE 7.8.

The Table Management window after table creation.

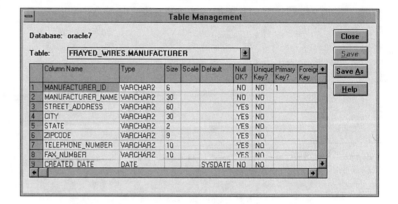

Designing a Database for Maximum Flexibility

You've seen how easy it is to create a table with Personal Oracle7. However, it's crucial that you take the time to study the optimal design for your application's database.

A facet of relational database theory comes into play in this discussion. Normalization theory is the study of relations (tables), attributes (columns), and the dependency of attributes upon one another. The goals of normalization include the following:

   Minimizing redundant data

   Avoiding update anomalies

   Reducing inconsistent data

   Designing data structures for easier maintenance

Because we're talking theory here, let's discuss some terminology. Table 7.1 shows how these terms can be placed into three categories: theoretician, analyst, and developer. As you read about databases, whether the material is academic or industry-oriented, you'll come across terms that are easily exchanged. As you read the material in this chapter, you'll see these terms used interchangeably. You can use whichever terms you prefer, as long as you use them appropriately and understand what they represent.

Table 7.1. Orientation of database terminology.

Theoretician	*Analyst*	*Developer*
Relation	Entity	Table
Column	Attribute	Column
Tuple	Row	Row/Record

Normalization theory describes the desired arrangements of tables and columns as Normal Forms. I'll present the First, Second, and Third Normal Forms, which are often cited as 1NF, 2NF, and 3NF. Although these terms sound theoretical and abstract, they are actually quite intuitive. There are other Normal Forms—Boyce-Codd, 4th, and 5th Normal Forms—that address more complex normalization issues. Those topics are beyond the scope of this book.

Normalization Rule #1: All Columns Should Contain a Single Piece of Information

An entity (table) is in First Normal Form (1NF) if all of its attributes are atomic. By *atomic* I mean that each attribute consists of a single fact about the entity. In addition, an entity should not have attributes that represent repeating values. To understand the implications of First Normal Form, let's consider the consequences of not adhering to this first normalization rule.

Suppose that you used a single table to store all customer repair information.

Suppose that the Customer table is modified so that Street_Address, City, State, and Zip Code are consolidated into a single column—Address. The Address column is defined to contain up to 80 characters. However, by consolidating several columns into a single column, we've lost the ability to control the formatting of Address. As a result, the format of a customer's address could vary from record to record.

```
SQL> select Customer_ID, Last_Name, First_Name, Address
  2  from Customer;

CUSTOMER_ID LAST_NAME     FIRST_NAME   ADDRESS
----------- ------------- ------------ ----------------------------------------
       1001 Johnson       Frank        1001 S. Elm Ave. Detroit, Michigan 01234
       1002 Richards      Mary         321 N. Main St. Jackson, MI 01235
       1003 Soule         Harold       919 Allen Circle, Flint, Mich. 01919
       1004 Golden        Marie        222 N. Michigan Ave., Chicago, IL 01933
```

Now, what happens when we want to assemble a list of those customers who live in Michigan? This query won't retrieve the complete list:

```
SELECT Customer_ID, Last_Name, First_Name
FROM Customer
WHERE
upper(Address) LIKE '%MICHIGAN%';
```

This query returns a record that doesn't belong to the set you are looking for:

```
SELECT Customer_ID, Last_Name, First_Name
FROM Customer
WHERE
upper(Address) LIKE '%MICH%';
```

To design a SELECT statement that retrieves the desired information, you must look at the entire set of data and account for all exceptions. For the non-1NF Customer table, this query returns the customers who live in Michigan:

```
SELECT Customer_ID, Last_Name, First_Name
FROM Customer
WHERE
upper(Address) LIKE '%MICHIGAN%' or
upper(address) LIKE '%,MI %' or
upper(address) LIKE '%,MICH %';
```

Normalization Rule #2: All Columns Depend Only on the Primary Key

For an entity to be in Second Normal Form (2NF), all of its columns must depend only on the primary key. Put simply, this means that a table must not contain *extraneous* information. Let's consider the example of the Depot Estimate table. Its purpose is to store an estimate received from the repair depot to repair an item brought in by a customer. The primary key consists of the Repair ID, the Item Number, and the Depot ID; all three columns are necessary to uniquely define a row in the table. If the Depot Estimate table also contained a column for storing the repair depot's address, the table would not be in 2NF; the repair depot's address depends only on the Depot ID, not the entire primary key.

Normalization Rule #3: All Columns Depend on the Primary Key and Nothing but the Primary Key

To be in Third Normal Form (3NF), a table's columns must be entirely dependent on the primary key. The key word in that last sentence is *entirely*. Each column in the table must be dependent on the entire primary key, not just a portion of it.

Again, I'll illustrate this rule with the Depot Estimate table. Suppose you were to add a column named Product ID to this table. This additional column would contain the product ID for the item for which the estimate has been prepared. But you are already storing this product ID in the Repair Item table. This information can be obtained by joining these tables by the Repair ID and Item Number columns (which will be discussed in further detail in Chapter 14, "More Sophisticated Queries"). The value of Product ID depends only upon the Repair ID and the Item Number—and not upon the Depot ID. So we can say that Product ID is dependent on part of the primary key, but it is not wholly dependent on the primary key.

You'll sometimes see this concept referred to as the derived column. In the previous example, Product ID can be derived from Repair ID and Item Number. According to relational theory, a table should not contain any derived columns. In practice, you will frequently see tables that contain derived columns.

Applying Normalization to Database Design

Normalization theory discusses normal forms beyond the Third Normal Form, but I won't delve into that here. I would like to discuss the application of normalization theory. If you read articles about relational database technology, you will encounter what can be called the Great Debate. Relational purists say that all tables must be in at least 3NF, although practitioners argue that to achieve acceptable performance, it is necessary to *denormalize* a database—in other words, reduce the database design from Third Normal Form to Second Normal Form. My position is somewhere in the middle. Here are my recommendations:

◼ Ensure that your design is in Third Normal Form.

◼ Do not make any assumptions about poor performance. Generate realistic test data and characterize the performance of your database.

◼ Try to solve performance problems with hardware improvements rather than database design compromises. Realize that, in the long run, better hardware is usually less expensive than a denormalized database design.

◼ Do not denormalize your tables unless you fully understand the tradeoffs that you are making—improved query performance for more data redundancy, more complicated update logic, and more difficulty in augmenting the database design during the application's life cycle.

Enough about theory. Let's examine how SQL is used to create and alter tables.

Basics of the *CREATE TABLE* Statement

Because of its many options and clauses, the SQL statement CREATE TABLE can be rather complex. Let's start by looking at a simplified version of its syntax:

```
CREATE TABLE table_name (
column_name1 datatype [NOT NULL],
...
column_nameN datatype [NOT NULL]);
```

where `table_name` is the name for the table; `column_name1` through `column_nameN` are valid column names; and `datatype` is a valid Oracle datatype specification.

The CREATE TABLE statement can be directly invoked from SQL*Plus (and SQL*DBA). Object Manager packages the user's entries and indirectly invokes the CREATE TABLE statement. In this section, we'll focus on the use of SQL*Plus in creating tables.

Naming a Table

Oracle has several restrictions on table names.

- Each table owned by an Oracle account must have a unique name.
- A table name cannot exceed 30 characters in length.
- A table name must begin with an alphabetic character.
- A table name can contain the letters A through Z, the digits 0 through 9, and the characters $, #, and _ (underscore).
- A table name cannot be a SQL reserved word.
- You can use uppercase and lowercase characters in naming tables; Oracle is not case sensitive.
- A table name should be descriptive. Do not use excessive abbreviations when naming tables and other database objects. Many application development tools, such as PowerBuilder or Oracle Forms 4.5, provide a point-and-click interface for selecting a table. Because no typing is involved, a long table name is just as easy to select as a short table name.

Naming a Column

Here are some considerations for naming columns.

- Within a single table, a column name must be unique. There is no restriction on using the same column name in different tables.
- Like other database objects, a column name can be up to 30 characters in length.
- The column name must begin with an alphabetic character.
- The column name can contain the letters A through Z, the digits 0 through 9, and the characters $, #, and _ (underscore).
- A column name cannot be a SQL reserved word.
- As with tables, be descriptive in naming a column. By providing descriptive column names, you actually make it easier for users to understand the definition of each column.
- An Oracle table may have up to 254 columns.

Examples of Creating Tables

To start, let's look at a simple example. We'll construct a CREATE TABLE statement to create the Depot Estimate table:

```
SQL> CREATE TABLE Depot_Estimate
  2         (Item_Number                 NUMBER(2) NOT NULL,
  3         Depot_ID                     NUMBER(4) NOT NULL,
  4         Repair_ID                    NUMBER(6) NOT NULL,
  5         Labor_Cost                   DECIMAL(7,2),
  6         Parts_Cost                   DECIMAL(7,2),
  7         Total_Cost                   DECIMAL(7,2),
  8         Estimated_Date_for_Completion DATE,
  9         Technician                   VARCHAR2(30),
 10         Telephone_Number             VARCHAR2(10),
 11         Created_Date                 DATE,
 12         Created_By                   VARCHAR2(30),
 13         Modified_Date                DATE,
 14         Modified_By                  VARCHAR2(30)
 15    );

Table created.
```

Let's examine some aspects of the statement's syntax. As you see, the list of columns are enclosed in parentheses. Mandatory columns have the phrase NOT NULL following the column's datatype specification. Where applicable, column widths are enclosed in parentheses after the datatype.

As an option, you can explicitly specify that a column is optional by specifying NULL after the datatype specification, as in:

```
SQL> CREATE TABLE Depot_Estimate
  2         (Item_Number                 NUMBER(2) NOT NULL,
  3         Depot_ID                     NUMBER(4) NOT NULL,
  4         Repair_ID                    NUMBER(6) NOT NULL,
  5         Labor_Cost                   DECIMAL(7,2) NULL,
  6         Parts_Cost                   DECIMAL(7,2) NULL,
  7         Total_Cost                   DECIMAL(7,2) NULL,
  8         Estimated_Date_for_Completion DATE NULL,
  9         Technician                   VARCHAR2(30) NULL,
 10         Telephone_Number             VARCHAR2(10) NULL,
 11         Created_Date                 DATE NULL,
 12         Created_By                   VARCHAR2(30) NULL,
 13         Modified_Date                DATE NULL,
 14         Modified_By                  VARCHAR2(30) NULL
 15    );

Table created.
```

As I mentioned, Oracle's implementation of SQL is not case sensitive (this isn't true of all vendors). Here's an example.

```
SQL> CREATE TABLE depot_ESTIMATE
  2         (ITEM_NUMBER                 NUMBER(2) NOT NULL,
  3         DEPOT_id                     NUMBER(4) NOT NULL,
  4         repair_ID                    NUMBER(6) NOT NULL,
  5         Labor_Cost                   DECIMAL(7,2),
  6         Parts_Cost                   DECIMAL(7,2),
  7         Total_Cost                   DECIMAL(7,2),
```

```
  8          Estimated_Date_for_Completion DATE,
  9          Technician            VARCHAR2(30),
 10          Telephone_Number      VARCHAR2(10),
 11          Created_Date          DATE,
 12          Created_By            VARCHAR2(30),
 13          Modified_Date         DATE,
 14          MODIFIED_BY           VARCHAR2(30)
 15   );
```

```
Table created.
```

Although Oracle SQL is not case sensitive, it's still a good idea to be consistent in your references to table and column names.

Identifying the Primary Key

A table's primary key is the set of columns that uniquely identify each row in the table. Let's take another look at the CREATE TABLE syntax:

```
CREATE TABLE table_name (
column_name1 datatype [NOT NULL],
...
column_nameN datatype [NOT NULL],
[Primary key (column_nameA, column_nameB, ... column_nameX)]);
```

where table_name is the name for the table; column_name1 through column_nameN are valid column names; column_nameA through column_nameX are the table's columns that compose the primary key; and datatype is a valid Oracle datatype specification.

Although it's an essential concept in relational database theory and practice, the primary key clause of the CREATE TABLE statement is optional. Using the Depot Estimate table again, here's how the primary key is declared.

```
SQL> CREATE TABLE Depot_Estimate
  2          (Item_Number           NUMBER(2) NOT NULL,
  3          Depot_ID               NUMBER(4) NOT NULL,
  4          Repair_ID              NUMBER(6) NOT NULL,
  5          Labor_Cost             DECIMAL(7,2),
  6          Parts_Cost             DECIMAL(7,2),
  7          Total_Cost             DECIMAL(7,2),
  8          Estimated_Date_for_Completion DATE,
  9          Technician             VARCHAR2(30),
 10          Telephone_Number       VARCHAR2(10),
 11          Created_Date           DATE,
 12          Created_By             VARCHAR2(30),
 13          Modified_Date          DATE,
 14          Modified_By            VARCHAR2(30),
 15   Primary Key (Repair_ID, Depot_ID, Item_Number));
```

```
Table created.
```

There are a couple of restrictions regarding the use of primary keys. First, a column that is part of the primary key cannot be null. Second, a column that is defined as LONG or LONG RAW cannot be part of the primary key. Third, the primary key can be composed of a maximum of

16 columns. This last restriction can be circumvented through the use of a surrogate key—an artificial value that can be guaranteed to uniquely identify all rows in a table.

Identifying Foreign Keys

Now that you know how to specify the primary key in the CREATE TABLE statement, let's see how foreign keys are declared. Here is the CREATE TABLE syntax that includes primary and foreign key declarations:

```
CREATE TABLE table_name (
column_specification1,
...
column_specificationN,
[Constraint constraint_name Foreign key (column_nameF1,...column_nameFN)
references referenced_table_name [ (column_nameP1,...column_namePN) ],]
[Constraint constraint_name Primary key (column_nameA, column_nameB, ...
column_nameX)]);
```

with the variables:

> *table_name* is the name for the table.
>
> *column_specification1* through *column_specificationN* are valid column specifications (described below in detail).
>
> *constraint_name* is the constraint name that you want to assign to a primary or foreign key.
>
> *referenced_table_name* is the name of the table referenced by the foreign key declaration.
>
> *column_nameF1* through *column_nameFN* are the columns that compose the foreign key.
>
> *column_nameP1* through *column_namePN* are the columns that compose the primary key in *referenced_table_name*.
>
> *column_nameA* through *column_nameX* are the table's columns that compose the primary key.
>
> *datatype* is a valid Oracle datatype specification.

Here is the syntax for a *column_specification*:

```
column_name datatype [DEFAULT default_value]
[CONSTRAINT constraint_name] [NULL]¦[NOT NULL]¦[UNIQUE]¦CHECK (condition)
```

with the variables:

> *column_name* is a valid Oracle column name.
>
> *datatype* is a valid Oracle datatype specification.
>
> *default_value* is a legal default value assigned to the column on an insert.
>
> *constraint_name* is a legal constraint name to be assigned to the constraint—NOT NULL, UNIQUE, or CHECK.

condition is a valid Oracle Boolean condition that must be true for a value to be assigned to a column.

For the Depot Estimate table, you actually need to declare two foreign keys:

- A reference to the Repair Item table for Repair ID and Item Number
- A reference to the Depot table for Depot ID

Therefore, you need to add two foreign keys to the CREATE TABLE statement:

```
SQL> CREATE TABLE Depot_Estimate
  2         (Item_Number              SMALLINT NOT NULL,
  3          Depot_ID                 NUMBER(4) NOT NULL,
  4          Repair_ID                NUMBER(6) NOT NULL,
  5          Labor_Cost               DECIMAL(7,2),
  6          Parts_Cost               DECIMAL(7,2),
  7          Total_Cost               DECIMAL(7,2),
  8          Estimated_Date_for_Completion DATE,
  9          Technician               VARCHAR2(30),
 10          Telephone_Number         VARCHAR2(10),
 11          Created_Date             DATE,
 12          Created_By               VARCHAR2(30),
 13          Modified_Date            DATE,
 14          Modified_By              VARCHAR2(30),
 15          Primary key (Repair_ID, Item_Number, Depot_ID),
 16          Constraint fk_repair_item
 17          Foreign key (Repair_ID, Item_Number) references
 18                  Repair_Item (Repair_ID, Item_Number),
 19          Constraint fk_depot Foreign key (Depot_ID)
 20          references Depot (Depot_ID)
 21  );

Table created.
```

> **TIP**
>
> Even though it's optional, I recommend that you use constraint names in a CHECK clause or when declaring foreign keys. If you don't explicitly declare a constraint name, Oracle automatically generates a constraint and assigns it a rather cryptic name. If you want to drop the foreign key, you'll have to look up the Oracle-generated constraint name. You'll save yourself some grief by declaring a constraint in the first place.

The columns in the referenced table must actually compose the primary key of the referenced table. If they don't, Oracle will not create the foreign key. In this example, we've dropped the primary key from the Depot table. When Oracle attempts to create the foreign key, it will determine that Depot_ID is not defined as the primary key for the Depot table; the CREATE TABLE statement will fail:

```
SQL> alter table Depot drop primary key;

Table altered.

SQL> CREATE TABLE Depot_Estimate
  2          (Item_Number                SMALLINT NOT NULL,
  3           Depot_ID                   NUMBER(4) NOT NULL,
  4           Repair_ID                  NUMBER(6) NOT NULL,
  5           Labor_Cost                 DECIMAL(7,2),
  6           Parts_Cost                 DECIMAL(7,2),
  7           Total_Cost                 DECIMAL(7,2),
  8           Estimated_Date_for_Completion DATE,
  9           Technician                 VARCHAR2(30),
 10           Telephone_Number           VARCHAR2(10),
 11           Created_Date               DATE,
 12           Created_By                 VARCHAR2(30),
 13           Modified_Date              DATE,
 14           Modified_By                VARCHAR2(30),
 15           Primary key (Repair_ID, Item_Number, Depot_ID),
 16           Constraint fk_repair_item
 17           Foreign key (Repair_ID, Item_Number) references
 18                   Repair_Item (Repair_ID, Item_Number),
 19           Constraint fk_depot Foreign key (Depot_ID)
 20             references Depot (Depot_ID)
 21   );
        Constraint fk_depot Foreign key (Depot_ID) references Depot (Depot_ID)
                                            *
ERROR at line 19:
ORA-02270: no matching unique or primary key for this column-list
```

Constraining a Column's Value with the *CHECK* Clause

A powerful feature of SQL is the capability to specify rudimentary data validation for a column during table creation. This is accomplished with an optional CHECK clause, which can be specified for each column. The CHECK clause is a Boolean condition that is either true or false. If the condition evaluates to true, the column value is accepted by Oracle; if the condition evaluates to false, Oracle will return an error code.

Here is a simple example using the Customer table. We'll modify the definition of the Customer table so that the table allows a customer's state to be only California, Illinois, or Michigan.

```
SQL> CREATE TABLE Customer
  2          (Customer_ID              NUMBER(4) NOT NULL,
  3           Last_Name                VARCHAR2(30),
  4           First_Name               VARCHAR2(30),
  5           Salutation               VARCHAR2(5),
  6           Street_Address           VARCHAR2(60),
  7           City                     VARCHAR2(30),
  8           State                    VARCHAR2(2)
  9               check (state in ('CA','IL','MI')),
```

```
10          Zipcode                   VARCHAR2(9),
11          Work_Telephone_Number     VARCHAR2(10),
12          Home_Telephone_Number     VARCHAR2(10),
13          Fax_Number                VARCHAR2(10),
14          Earliest_Time_to_Call     DATE,
15          Latest_Time_to_Call       DATE,
16          Local_Time_Zone           VARCHAR2(3),
17          Created_Date              DATE,
18          Created_By                VARCHAR2(30),
19          Modified_Date             DATE,
20          Modified_By               VARCHAR2(30)
21  );

Table created.
```

If you now attempt to insert a customer whose address isn't in California, Illinois, or Michigan, Oracle returns an error code indicating that a check constraint has been violated.

```
SQL> insert into Customer
  2  (Customer_ID, Last_Name, First_Name, State)
  3  values
  4  (6002, 'Moore', 'Les', 'HA');
insert into Customer
*
ERROR at line 1:
ORA-02290: check constraint (FRAYED_WIRES.SYS_C00419) violated
```

Establishing a Default Value for a Column

By using the DEFAULT clause when defining a column, you can establish a default value for that column. This default value is used for a column whenever a row is inserted into the table without specifying the column in the INSERT statement.

For example, suppose you wanted to be sure that if the labor cost in the Depot Estimate table wasn't specified, its default value would be $50. Here is how you would modify the CREATE TABLE statement to achieve this.

```
SQL> CREATE TABLE Depot_Estimate
  2          (Item_Number              SMALLINT NOT NULL,
  3          Depot_ID                  NUMBER(4) NOT NULL,
  4          Repair_ID                 NUMBER(6) NOT NULL,
  5          Labor_Cost                DECIMAL(7,2)
  6              DEFAULT 50.0,
  7          Parts_Cost                DECIMAL(7,2),
  8          Total_Cost                DECIMAL(7,2),
  9          Estimated_Date_for_Completion DATE,
 10          Technician                VARCHAR2(30),
 11          Telephone_Number          VARCHAR2(10),
 12          Created_Date              DATE,
 13          Created_By                VARCHAR2(30),
 14          Modified_Date             DATE,
 15          Modified_By               VARCHAR2(30)
 16  );

Table created.
```

Now that the table has been defined, let's try inserting a row without specifying a value for Labor_Cost. The SELECT statement returns a single row with Labor_Cost set to the default value of 50.0.

```
SQL> insert into Depot_Estimate
  2  (Repair_ID, Item_Number, Depot_ID)
  3  values
  4  (2002, 1, 1001);

1 row created.

SQL> select Repair_ID, Item_Number, Depot_ID, Labor_Cost
  2  from Depot_Estimate;

REPAIR_ID ITEM_NUMBER  DEPOT_ID LABOR_COST
--------- ----------- --------- ----------
     2002           1      1001         50
```

Modifying a Table with Object Manager

At this point, we'll investigate the use of Object Manager to modify an existing table. Suppose you want to modify Depot_Estimate by adding another column to record a priority code. To begin, you'll double-click the Object Manager icon and log in to Oracle as FRAYED_WIRES. Next, you'll select the table object to retrieve the tables owned by FRAYED_WIRES (see Figure 7.9).

FIGURE 7.9.
Retrieving the list of tables to modify.

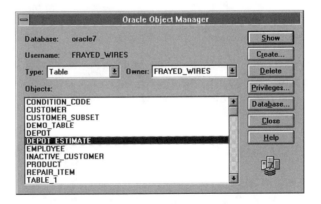

Select the Depot_Estimate table and click the Show button. A pop-up window appears showing the current definition of the Depot_Estimate table (see Figure 7.10).

After the last column, specify Priority_Code as the column name and NUMBER as the datatype. Set the width of Priority_Code to 2 (see Figure 7.11).

FIGURE 7.10.

Pop-up window showing definition of Depot_Estimate.

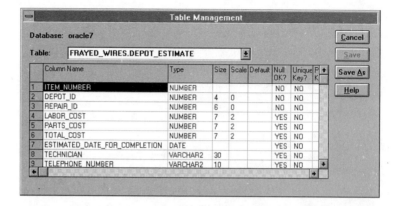

FIGURE 7.11.

Adding another column to a table.

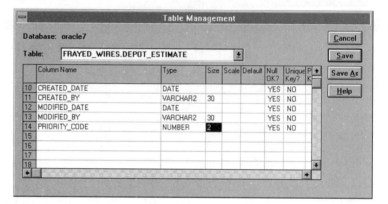

You can also use Object Manager to define the primary key for a table. In the Primary Key column of the spreadsheet, click the Repair_ID, Item_Number, and Depot_ID columns. As you click the mouse button, Object Manager places a number in the cell that is one greater than the existing primary key (see Figure 7.12).

FIGURE 7.12.

Specifying the primary key with Object Manager.

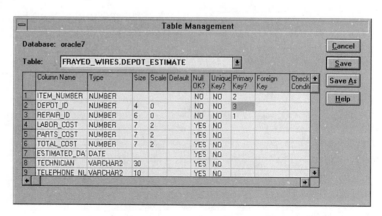

The Table Management spreadsheet also provides a Default column in which you can specify a default value for one of the table's columns. Enter `50` in this column for Labor_Cost (see Figure 7.13).

Table Management
Database: oracle7
Table: FRAYED_WIRES.DEPOT_ESTIMATE
Cancel
Save
Save As
Help
Column Name Type Size Scale Default Null OK? Unique Key? Primary Key? Foreign Key Check Condit
1 ITEM_NUMBER NUMBER NO NO
2 DEPOT_ID NUMBER 4 0 NO NO
3 REPAIR_ID NUMBER 6 0 NO NO
4 LABOR_COST NUMBER 7 2 50 YES NO
5 PARTS_COST NUMBER 7 2 YES NO
6 TOTAL_COST NUMBER 7 2 YES NO
7 ESTIMATED_DA DATE YES NO
8 TECHNICIAN VARCHAR2 30 YES NO
9 TELEPHONE_NL VARCHAR2 10 YES NO

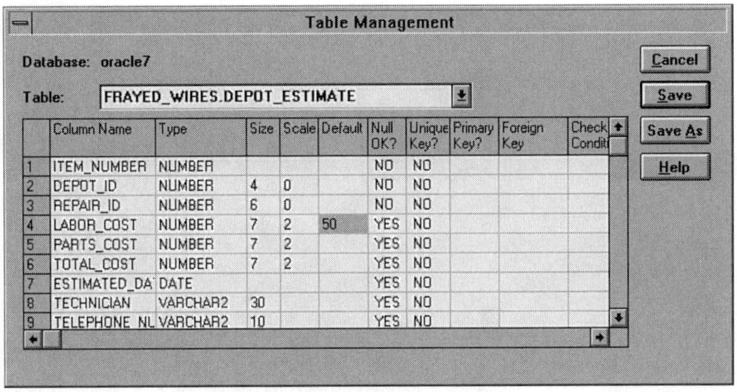

FIGURE 7.13.
Specifying a default value for a column.

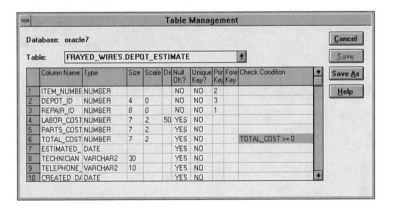

Object Manager also enables you to specify a Check Condition for a column. The Check Condition column is the rightmost column on the Table Management spreadsheet. Figure 7.14 illustrates the use of the Check Condition column by specifying that the Total_Cost column must be greater than or equal to zero.

Table Management
Database: oracle7
Table: FRAYED_WIRES.DEPOT_ESTIMATE
Cancel
Save
Save As
Help
Column Name Type Size Scale De Null OK? Unique Key? Pri Key Fore Key Check Condition
1 ITEM_NUMBE NUMBER NO NO 2
2 DEPOT_ID NUMBER 4 0 NO NO 3
3 REPAIR_ID NUMBER 6 0 NO NO 1
4 LABOR_COST NUMBER 7 2 50 YES NO
5 PARTS_COST NUMBER 7 2 YES NO
6 TOTAL_COST NUMBER 7 2 YES NO TOTAL_COST >= 0
7 ESTIMATED_ DATE YES NO
8 TECHNICIAN VARCHAR2 30 YES NO
9 TELEPHONE_ VARCHAR2 10 YES NO
10 CREATED_D DATE YES NO

FIGURE 7.14.
Specifying a Check Condition for a column.

Click the Save button to actually save the changes that you have made to the table. A pop-up window appears asking for you to confirm that the table changes should be saved (see Figure 7.15).

Finally, Oracle displays a message indicating that the table changes were made without error (see Figure 7.16).

FIGURE 7.15.

Confirming the table changes.

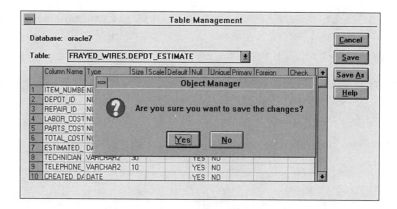

FIGURE 7.16.

Object Manager message indicating table changes were successful.

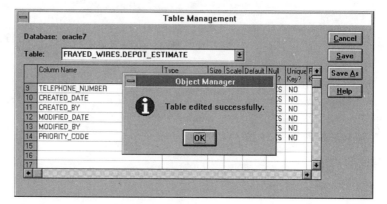

Using *ALTER TABLE* to Modify the Table Definition

At times, you'll find it necessary to modify a table's definition. The ALTER TABLE statement serves this purpose. This statement is used to change the structure of a table, not its contents. Using ALTER TABLE, the changes you can make to a table include:

- Adding a new column to an existing table
- Increasing or decreasing the width of an existing column
- Changing an existing column from mandatory to optional or vice versa
- Specifying a default value for an existing column
- Specifying other constraints for an existing column

Here are the three basic forms of the ALTER TABLE statement:

```
ALTER TABLE table_name
ADD (column_specification ¦ table_constraint ,...
     column_specification ¦ table_constraint);
```

or

```
ALTER TABLE table_name
MODIFY (column_specification ¦ table_constraint ,...
        column_specification ¦ table_constraint);
```

or

```
ALTER TABLE table_name
DROP PRIMARY KEY;
```

The first form of the statement is used for adding a column, the primary key, or a foreign key to a table.

The second form of the statement is used to modify an existing column. Among other things, you can increase a column's width or transform it from mandatory to optional.

The third form of the ALTER TABLE statement is used for dropping a table's primary key.

In the next few pages, I'll demonstrate the use of this statement with several examples.

Changing a Column Definition from *NOT NULL* to *NULL*

There are no restrictions on changing a column from mandatory to optional. You should think about why the change is necessary. Is this attribute really optional, or are you working with a test data set that isn't representative of realistic application data?

The current definition for demo_table is this:

```
SQL> desc demo_table
 Name                            Null?    Type
 ------------------------------- -------- ----
 RECORD_NO                       NOT NULL NUMBER(38)
 DESCRIPTION                              VARCHAR2(40)
 CURRENT_VALUE                   NOT NULL NUMBER
```

To change the column from mandatory to optional, you issue this command:

```
SQL> alter table demo_table modify (current_value number null);

Table altered.

SQL> desc demo_table
 Name                            Null?    Type
 ------------------------------- -------- ----
 RECORD_NO                       NOT NULL NUMBER(38)
 DESCRIPTION                              VARCHAR2(40)
 CURRENT_VALUE                            NUMBER
```

Changing a Column Definition from *NULL* to *NOT NULL*

If a table is empty, you can define a column to be NOT NULL. However, if a table isn't empty, you can't change a column to NOT NULL unless every row has a value for that particular question.

Here's how Oracle will respond if we attempt to make the current_value column mandatory.

```
SQL> alter table demo_table modify (current_value number not null);
alter table demo_table modify (current_value number not null)
                               *
ERROR at line 1:
ORA-01449: column contains NULL values; cannot alter to NOT NULL
```

However, if you ensure that current_value has a non-null value for each row in the table, you'll be able to set the current_value to NOT NULL.

```
SQL> update demo_table
  2  set current_value = record_no + 100;

4 rows updated.

SQL> select current_value from demo_table;

CURRENT_VALUE
-------------
          121
          122
          123
          124

SQL> commit;

Commit complete.

SQL> alter table demo_table modify (current_value number not null);

Table altered.
```

Increasing a Column's Width

The ALTER TABLE statement is used to increase the width of a character column. Suppose the current definition of a table is this:

```
SQL> desc demo_table
 Name                            Null?    Type
 ------------------------------- -------- ----
 RECORD_NO                       NOT NULL NUMBER(38)
 DESCRIPTION                              VARCHAR2(40)
 CURRENT_VALUE                   NOT NULL NUMBER
```

To increase the width of the description column from 40 to 50 characters, you enter this command:

```
SQL> alter table demo_table modify (description varchar2(50));

Table altered.

SQL> desc demo_table
 Name                            Null?    Type
 ------------------------------- -------- ----
 RECORD_NO                       NOT NULL NUMBER(38)
```

```
DESCRIPTION                         VARCHAR2(50)
CURRENT_VALUE            NOT NULL NUMBER
```

Increasing the width of numeric columns works in the same way:

```
SQL> desc demo_table
Name                       Null?    Type
------------------------- -------- ----
RECORD_NO                 NOT NULL NUMBER(38)
DESCRIPTION                        VARCHAR2(50)
CURRENT_VALUE             NOT NULL NUMBER
MAX_READINGS                       NUMBER(4)
```

If you want to increase the width of max_readings, you can use this statement:

```
SQL> alter table demo_table
  2  modify
  3  (max_readings number(6));

Table altered.
```

Decreasing a Column's Width

In the course of designing a database application, you may find that you erred in sizing a column: you specified a larger size for a column that is actually needed. Initially, you might think that this isn't a problem because the column will be able to accommodate the data. But it is a problem because it indicates that your data model is inaccurate. If you want to "do the right thing," you need to reduce the size of the column.

The same SQL statement—ALTER TABLE—that is used to increase a column's width is used to decrease a column's width. Let's investigate how this is done.

Look at one of the sample tables.

```
SQL> desc repair_item
Name                                Null?    Type
--------------------------------- -------- ----
ITEM_NUMBER                       NOT NULL NUMBER
REPAIR_ID                         NOT NULL NUMBER(6)
PRODUCT_ID                                 VARCHAR2(12)
MANUFACTURER_ID                            VARCHAR2(6)
CONDITION_CODE                             VARCHAR2(3)
SERIAL_NUMBER                              CHAR(18)
PURCHASE_DATE                              DATE
WARRANTY_EXPIRATION_DATE                   DATE
ESTIMATED_COST                             NUMBER(7,2)
ESTIMATED_COMPLETION_DATE                  DATE
CUSTOMER_AUTHORIZATION_STATUS              VARCHAR2(10)
CUSTOMER_AUTHORIZATION_DATE                DATE
CREATED_DATE                      NOT NULL DATE
CREATED_BY                        NOT NULL VARCHAR2(30)
MODIFIED_DATE                              DATE
MODIFIED_BY                                VARCHAR2(30)
```

While meeting with Jim Helmholtz, owner of Frayed Wires, to discuss your data model, he tells you that a two-character code is used to keep track of the customer's authorization. Therefore, you decide to "do the right thing" by decreasing the width of Customer_ Authorization_Status from 10 characters to 2 characters.

```
SQL> alter table repair_item
  2  modify
  3  (customer_authorization_status varchar2(2));
(customer_authorization_status varchar2(2))
 *
ERROR at line 3:
ORA-01441: column to be modified must be empty to decrease column length
```

As you might have suspected, Oracle will not allow you to decrease a column's width if there are column values. Let's examine the contents of the column.

```
SQL> select customer_authorization_status
  2  from repair_item;

CUSTOMER_A
----------
ON HOLD
AUTHORIZED
AUTHORIZED
ON HOLD
AUTHORIZED
ON HOLD

6 rows selected.
```

Even if you update the Repair Item table so that the Customer Authorization Status is only two characters, Oracle will still not allow you to reduce the width of the column, as you can see:

```
SQL> update repair_item
  2  set customer_authorization_status =
  3       substr(customer_authorization_status,1,2);

6 rows updated.

SQL> commit;

Commit complete.

SQL> select customer_authorization_status
  2  from repair_item;

CUSTOMER_A
----------
ON
AU
AU
ON
AU
ON
```

```
6 rows selected.

SQL> alter table repair_item
  2   modify
  3   (customer_authorization_status varchar2(2));
(customer_authorization_status varchar2(2))
 *
ERROR at line 3:
ORA-01441: column to be modified must be empty to decrease column length
```

However, if you update the table by setting the Customer_Authorization_Status to NULL, Oracle then permits the column's width to be reduced.

```
SQL> update repair_item
  2   set customer_authorization_status = null;

6 rows updated.

SQL> commit;

Commit complete.

SQL> alter table repair_item
  2   modify
  3   (customer_authorization_status varchar2(2));

Table altered.
```

Common Restrictions on Modifying a Table

During the database design phase, a developer typically experiments with an application's database structures to determine their accuracy and suitability. This can rarely be done without populating tables with sample data. If a table requires a change—for example, an additional column—it is much more convenient to alter the table than to drop the table and recreate it with its new definition. However, sometimes the necessary change cannot be made without modifying the sample data.

Changing the Primary Key

Often, changing a table's primary key without disturbing the rest of a database design is difficult. The reason is simple: Tables are usually related to one another through the declaration of foreign keys. A foreign key depends upon the existence of a primary key in another table. Therefore, if you change the primary key, the change can ripple throughout the entire database. In fact, Oracle prevents that from happening.

Changing a primary key is a two-step process: dropping the primary key and recreating it. Suppose you had originally created on the Customer table a primary key consisting of the customer's last and first names. After some thought, you realize that you have made a mistake and decide to use Customer ID as the primary key.

```
SQL> alter table Customer add
  2  (primary key (Last_Name, First_Name));

Table altered.

SQL> alter table Customer drop primary key;

Table altered.

SQL> alter table Customer add
  2  (primary key (Customer_ID));

Table altered.
```

First of all, you cannot drop a primary key that is referenced by a foreign key. In the sample database, the Repair Header table contains the Customer ID column. A foreign key is declared for the Customer ID column that references the Customer table and the Customer_ID column. If you attempt to drop the primary key of the Customer table, here's what occurs:

```
SQL> alter table Customer drop primary key;
alter table Customer drop primary key
*
ERROR at line 1:
ORA-02273: this unique/primary key is referenced by some foreign keys
```

Changing a Foreign Key

The procedure for changing a table's foreign key is slightly different from the process of changing a primary key. You can't modify an existing foreign key—you must drop the constraint associated with the foreign key and recreate it. For instance, here's how you drop a foreign key on the Repair Item table:

```
SQL> CREATE TABLE Repair_Item
  2          (Item_Number           SMALLINT NOT NULL,
  3          Repair_ID              NUMBER(6) NOT NULL,
  4          Product_ID             VARCHAR2(12),
  5          Manufacturer_ID        VARCHAR2(6),
  6          Condition_Code         VARCHAR2(3),
  7          Serial_Number          CHAR(18),
  8          Purchase_Date          DATE,
  9          Warranty_Expiration_Date DATE,
 10          Estimated_Cost         DECIMAL(7,2),
 11          Estimated_Completion_Date DATE,
 12          Customer_Authorization_Status CHAR(18),
 13          Customer_Authorization_Date CHAR(18),
 14          Created_Date           DATE NOT NULL,
 15          Created_By             VARCHAR2(30) NOT NULL,
 16          Modified_Date          DATE,
 17          Modified_By            VARCHAR2(30),
 18          Constraint fk_product
 19          foreign key (Product_ID, Manufacturer_ID) references
 20                  Product (Product_ID, Manufacturer_ID));

Table created.
```

```
SQL> alter table Repair_Item drop constraint fk_product;
```

Table altered.

Here is how you would add a foreign key to the Repair Item table:

```
SQL> alter table Repair_Item add
  2  (constraint new_fk_product
  3   foreign key (Product_ID, Manufacturer_ID) references
  4   Product (Product_ID, Manufacturer_ID));
```

Table altered.

Summary

Keep the following ideas in mind when designing your Personal Oracle7 database:

- ■ Try to ensure that the initial database design is in Third Normal Form (3NF).
- ■ Use Object Manager to quickly build tables.
- ■ Use the CREATE TABLE statement via SQL*Plus for greater control over the statement options or to process a script.
- ■ Use the ALTER TABLE statement to modify an existing table.
- ■ Define default values for columns where appropriate.
- ■ Every table should have a primary key.
- ■ Use foreign keys to enforce referential integrity.

8

Using SQL to Modify Data

Chapter 5, "The Basics of SQL," briefly talked about the Data Manipulation Language (DML) facet of SQL and delved into the use of the SELECT statement. The SELECT statement can only look at the contents of tables; it does not have the capability to create or modify data. In this chapter, we'll explore the three remaining DML statements and their use in Personal Oracle7: INSERT, UPDATE, and DELETE.

Some of the topics that are covered in this chapter are critical in multiuser database applications rather than in a single-user database like Personal Oracle7. Although it cannot function as a database server, Personal Oracle7 is an excellent platform for database developers for two reasons.

1. Personal Oracle7 provides a realistic prototyping environment because it provides the functionality of Oracle 7.1 (except for distributed database support).
2. When Personal Oracle7 is combined with a Windows-based application development tool, a database developer has an affordable and convenient stand-alone development environment.

In the course of developing an application for Personal Oracle7, you will probably be using a "front-end" tool, such as Oracle Forms, Visual Basic, or PowerBuilder, in which many INSERT, UPDATE, and DELETE statements will be internally generated by the application development environment. However, almost every application will require the development of scripts containing SQL statements.

SQL Data Manipulation Language

In Chapter 4, "Your First Personal Oracle7 Database," you learned the three perspectives of a database: the user perspective, the conceptual perspective, and the physical perspective. To fully comprehend how SQL modifies data, it's best to focus on the conceptual perspective. Think only of tables, columns, and rows, and you'll master SQL and Personal Oracle7 more quickly. Initially, don't worry about how Oracle executes SQL statements; instead, concentrate on the purpose of the SQL statement.

Here's another helpful hint for successful use of DML. When you think about the effect of a SQL statement (INSERT, UPDATE, or DELETE) visualize a set of rows being affected rather than individual rows. This is discussed in more detail later in this chapter.

The first things that many programmers and developers want to learn about Oracle are the internal operating system file formats and special codes. This is the wrong approach! Keep in mind the following:

■ The format of the Oracle database files is proprietary to Oracle Corporation.

■ These formats and codes are subject to change with each new Oracle release.

■ Your application will be easier to maintain if you rely on an industry standard such as SQL instead of any knowledge you have about the Oracle file formats. Also, you will have a much easier time porting a SQL application from Oracle to another RDBMS.

A Transaction Is a Logical Unit of Work

Another powerful concept that you need to master is the transaction. A *transaction* is defined as a logical unit of work—a set of database changes to one or more tables that accomplish a defined task. A transaction begins after a COMMIT statement, a ROLLBACK statement, or an initial Oracle connection. A transaction ends when any of the following events occur:

- ◼ A COMMIT statement is processed
- ◼ A ROLLBACK statement is processed
- ◼ The Oracle connection is terminated

For example, suppose Mishuga Electronics has just come out with an amplifier that provides twice the performance of existing amps for the same price. As a result, the market value of existing amplifiers will drop by 50 percent. If you need to keep track of the market value of Mishuga's products, you can change the market value for Mishuga's older amplifiers with a single UPDATE statement.

Saving Work with *COMMIT*

You can think of a transaction as a change you make in a document using your favorite word processor. You may make several changes and either undo them or exit the program without saving the changes. When you instruct the word processor to save the file, you are permanently changing the file stored on disk.

Committing a transaction is similar to saving a file in Microsoft Word. The COMMIT statement commits a transaction. The COMMIT statement makes permanent all the database changes made since the execution of the previous COMMIT (or ROLLBACK). You can only COMMIT the database changes that you yourself have made; the COMMIT statement that Jim Helmholtz issues has no effect on database changes made by Max Gilroy.

Undoing Changes with *ROLLBACK*

In the same way, the ROLLBACK statement does the same thing that an Undo command does in a word processor—with one major exception: the ROLLBACK statement will undo all database changes made by the user since the last committed transaction or since the beginning of the session.

Let's look at the interplay between COMMIT and ROLLBACK. To illustrate these concepts, I'll use a simple table—table_1—with a single column—table_1_col. Initially, there are four rows in table_1.

```
SQL> select * from table_1;

TABLE_1_COL
-----------
        99
        99
```

```
          99
          99
```

If you delete the rows from table_1 and then query table_1 after you delete them, you see that the table is empty.

```
SQL> delete from table_1;

4 rows deleted.

SQL> select * from table_1;

no rows selected
```

If you issue a ROLLBACK and query the table again, you see that the table is restored to the state in which it existed before you issued the DELETE statement.

```
SQL> rollback;

Rollback complete.

SQL> select * from table_1;

TABLE_1_COL
-----------
         99
         99
         99
         99
```

> **NOTE**
>
> Oracle performs an automatic commit for DDL statements such as CREATE TABLE.
> A ROLLBACK statement will not remove a table created via a CREATE TABLE statement.
> If you want to eliminate a table, you must use the DROP TABLE statement.

Savepoints

For transactions that involve the execution of multiple SQL statements, you might want to consider using *savepoints* as intermediate steps for the transaction. You can think of a savepoint as a label within a transaction that references a subset of a transaction's changes. You can establish a savepoint in the following way:

```
SQL> savepoint null_fax_numbers;

Savepoint created.
```

You use a savepoint along with a ROLLBACK statement; the savepoint gives you the option of rolling back a transaction to an intermediate point (a savepoint). The syntax for the ROLLBACK statement is

```
ROLLBACK [TO savepoint];
```

where *savepoint* is a previously named savepoint.

Consider an example. Imagine that your application has a transaction that updates three tables: table_1, table_2, and table_3. If Oracle returns an error on the update to table_2, you can rollback to the first savepoint, which is table_1_update.

```
SQL> update table_1
  2  set table_1_col = 11;

4 rows updated.

SQL> savepoint table_1_update;

Savepoint created.

SQL> delete from table_2;

3 rows deleted.

SQL> rollback to table_1_update;

Rollback complete.

SQL> select * from table_2;

TABLE_2_COL
-----------
         99
         99
         99
```

Savepoints should be used with care, because they add an additional layer of complexity to an application. Be sure that your transactions are well-defined before you decide to implement savepoints.

Adding Rows with *INSERT*

The INSERT statement is used to add rows to a table. You supply literal values or expressions to be stored as rows in the table.

INSERT Syntax

There are two forms of the INSERT statement. The first form is

```
INSERT INTO table_name
[(column_name[,column_name]...[,column_name])]
VALUES
(column_value[,column_value]...[,column_value])
```

where *table_name* is the table in which to insert the row, *column_name* is a column belonging to *table_name*, and *column_value* is a literal value or an expression whose type matches the corresponding *column_name*.

For instance, if you want to add a new depot to the Depot table, the INSERT statement might be

```
SQL> insert into Depot
  2 (Depot_ID, Company_Name)
  3 values
  4 (2001, 'Minivox Electronics');

1 row created.
```

Notice that the number of columns in the list of column names must match the number of literal values or expressions that appear in parentheses after the keyword VALUES. In the example that follows, there are three columns but only two literal values. If you specify more column names than values, Oracle returns the following:

```
SQL> insert into Depot
  2 (Depot_ID, Company_Name, Street_Address)
  3 values
  4 (3001, 'Consumer Electronic Depot');
values
*
ERROR at line 3:
ORA-00947: not enough values
```

If you specify fewer column names than values, Oracle returns the following error message:

```
SQL> insert into Depot
  2 (Depot_ID, Company_Name)
  3 values
  4 (3001, 'Consumer Electronic Depot', '2323 Main St.');
values
*
ERROR at line 3:
ORA-00913: too many values
```

If a column name referenced in an INSERT statement is misspelled, the following occurs:

```
SQL> insert into Customer
  2 (Customer_ID, Street_Adress)
  3 values
  4 (4001, '123 Main St.');
(Customer_ID, Street_Adress)
                *
ERROR at line 2:
ORA-00904: invalid column name
```

> **TIP**
>
> If you're executing an INSERT with a long list of column names and Oracle returns ORA-00947 or ORA-00913, it's up to you to do the dirty work of matching the list of column names with the list of values or expressions. After you've checked and still can't find the problem, try reducing the number of columns and values to isolate the problem.

Specifying Values in an *INSERT*

Each column value supplied in an INSERT statement must be one of the following:

- A NULL
- A literal value, such as 3.14159 or 'Radish'
- An expression containing operators and functions, such as SUBSTR(Last_Name,1,4)

In an INSERT statement, you can mix literal values with expressions. In the following example, the Initial_Retail_Value of $275.00 is increased by 10 percent:

```
SQL> insert into Product
  2  (Product_ID, Manufacturer_ID, Initial_Retail_Value)
  3  values
  4  ('D301','SEN101',275*1.10);

1 row created.
```

Column and Value Datatype Must Match

With a couple of exceptions, the datatypes for a column and its corresponding value must be identical. It doesn't make sense to insert an alphanumeric string into a numeric column as in the following example:

```
SQL> insert into Product
  2  (Product_ID, Manufacturer_ID, Initial_Retail_Value)
  3  values
  4  (1020, 'SEN101', 'Two hundred and fifty dollars');
(1020, 'SEN101', 'Two hundred and fifty dollars')
                                 *
ERROR at line 4:
ORA-01722: invalid number
```

In the preceding example, Oracle returned an error code ORA-01722 because the string 'Two hundred and fifty dollars' cannot be stored in a column defined as a number. However, if the string is a valid number, the INSERT statement will be processed successfully, as in the following example:

```
insert into Product
(Product_ID,Manufacturer_ID,Initial_Retail_Value)
values
(1020,2001,'347.42');

1 row created.
```

Another exception to this rule involves strings and dates. For example, a literal string that adheres to the Oracle default date format (DD-MON-YY) can be inserted into a date column.

```
SQL> insert into Product
  2  (Product_ID, Manufacturer_ID, Description, Date_of_Manufacture)
  3  values
  4  ('TR901','TES801','Tuner','01-JAN-91');

1 row created.
```

Using Pseudocolumns as Values

Oracle provides a set of functions called *pseudocolumns.* Oracle named these functions pseudocolumns because they appear to be columns to the uninitiated. Two commonly used pseudocolumns are

USER: The Oracle user who is currently connected to the Oracle database

SYSDATE: The current date and time

You can use pseudocolumns in an INSERT statement to assign a value to a column. For instance, USER and SYSDATE can be used to store the name of the Oracle user who created the row and the date and time when the row was inserted, as in the following example:

```
insert into Product
(Product_ID,Manufacturer_ID,Initial_Retail_Value,Created_By,Created_Date)
values
(1020,2001,275.00*1.10,USER,SYSDATE);
```

The pseudocolumn USER can be assigned only to a string column. Similarly, the pseudocolumn SYSDATE can be assigned only to a date column. You can manipulate these pseudocolumns by applying functions and operators. For example, you could insert the first four characters of the current user's name into a string column by using USER as an argument to the SUBSTR function in the following way:

```
SQL> show user
user is "FRAYED_WIRES"
SQL>
SQL> insert into Customer
  2  (Customer_ID, Last_Name)
  3  values
  4  (2222, SUBSTR(USER,1,4));

1 row created.

SQL> select Customer_ID, Last_Name
  2  from Customer
  3  where Customer_ID = 2222;

CUSTOMER_ID LAST_NAME
----------- ----------------------------
       2222 FRAY
```

Why Columns Should Be Specified in an *INSERT*

If you look carefully at the syntax diagram for the INSERT statement in the online Oracle SQL Language Reference Manual, you'll notice that the column list is an optional element. This means that if you don't specify the column names to be assigned values, Oracle will, by default, use all of the columns. In addition, the column order used by Oracle is the order in which the columns were specified when the table was created; this is the same order that you see when you DESCRIBE a table in SQL*Plus. Look at the following example:

```
insert into Depot
values
(101,'RCB ELECTRONICS SERVICE CENTER','123 Alvarado Ave.'
'San Felipe','CA','90000','2135550123','2135559876',
'RICHARD HEINZ');
```

1 row created.

On the surface, everything looks fine—the row was successfully inserted into the table. However, there are several dangers in using this syntax.

1. The table definition might change; the number of columns might decrease or increase and the INSERT will fail as a result.

2. The INSERT statement might be difficult to comprehend. The values might be indistinguishable from one another and, by accident, be transposed. Tracking down the problem without being able to visually match a column with its corresponding value is tricky.

3. The INSERT statement might succeed, but the wrong data could be entered in the table. This can occur when two adjoining values with the same datatype are accidentally transposed. This is the most dangerous scenario because Oracle might not return an error to inform you that something is wrong.

Using a Subquery with *INSERT*

Up to this point, the examples have demonstrated how each execution of an INSERT statement can add a single row to a table. We are now going to look at performing an INSERT without specifying literal values.

INSERT Syntax with Subquery

The alternative form of the INSERT statement substitutes the list of column values with a SELECT statement in the following way:

```
INSERT INTO table_name
[(column_name[,column_name]...[,column_name])]
select_statement
```

In this code, `table_name` is the table in which to insert the row, `column_name` is a column belonging to `table_name`, and `select_statement` is a valid SELECT statement.

Consider the following example. As part of a new marketing campaign, you want to insert rows from the Inactive_Customer table into the Customer table. To accomplish this, you use a subquery to select the rows from the Inactive_Customer table and insert them into the Customer table with the following statement:

```
SQL> insert into Customer
  2  (Customer_ID, Last_Name, First_Name, Salutation)
  3  select Customer_ID, Last_Name, First_Name, Salutation
  4  from Inactive_Customer;
```

5 rows created.

To use a subquery with an INSERT statement, the number of columns referenced in the INSERT statement must equal the number of items in the subquery's select list.

Generating Test Data

When you develop a database application, you need to be able to exercise the software with test data. Developing a sizeable set of test data can be a tedious task. The INSERT statement can be used to duplicate and increase the size of the test data.

You can use a subquery to copy the existing rows in a table to the same table. Let's suppose that the Product table initially contains 12 rows. If you perform an INSERT that SELECTs those 12 rows, there will be 24 rows in the table. If you perform the same INSERT once more, there will be 48 rows in the Product table. As you can see, the number of rows will double each time an INSERT is performed.

```
SQL> insert into Product
  2  (Product_ID, Manufacturer_ID, Initial_Retail_Value)
  3  select Product_ID, Manufacturer_ID, Initial_Retail_Value
  4  from Product;

12 rows created.
```

Of course, this method won't generate realistic test data: the primary key (Product_ID and Manufacturer_ID) cannot have duplicate values. But we can circumvent that problem by using an expression in the SELECT statement. As you can see in the following code, you can concatenate two substrings together to form a value for Product_ID and Manufacturer_ID that doesn't already exist in the table:

```
SQL> insert into Product
  2  (Product_ID, Manufacturer_ID, Initial_Retail_Value)
  3  select SUBSTR(Product_ID,1,3) ¦¦ SUBSTR(Product_ID,1,3),
  4  SUBSTR(Manufacturer_ID,1,3) ¦¦ SUBSTR(Manufacturer_ID,1,3),
  5  Initial_Retail_Value * 1.1
  6  from Product;

12 rows created.
```

> **NOTE**
>
> If you use the technique outlined here to generate test data, the number of rows will grow geometrically. If you start with 100 rows, after seven INSERTs are performed the table will hold 12,800 rows. If you don't perform a COMMIT after each INSERT, the rollback segments may not be able to store the uncommitted transaction and Oracle will return an error code of ORA-01653; the table space in which the rollback segments were trying to allocate more space will appear in the error message.

Modifying Data with *UPDATE*

If you want to modify existing data in your Personal Oracle7 database, you'll need to use the UPDATE statement. With this statement, you can update zero or more rows in a table.

Basic Syntax of *UPDATE*

Like the INSERT statement, the syntax of the UPDATE statement is far simpler than that of the SELECT statement. The UPDATE statement has the following syntax:

```
UPDATE table_name
SET column_name = expression [, column_name = expression] ...
                            [, column_name = expression]
[WHERE condition]
```

In this code, table_name is the table to be updated, column_name is a column in the table being updated, expression is a valid SQL expression, and condition is a valid SQL condition.

As you can see, the UPDATE statement references a single table and assigns an expression to at least one column. The WHERE clause is optional; if an UPDATE statement doesn't contain a WHERE clause, all rows in the table will have the column in question set to the specified value.

Changing the Value of More Than One Column

As the syntax for the UPDATE statement illustrates, an UPDATE statement can change the value for more than one column in a table. For example, the following UPDATE statement assigns values to two columns: Salutation and Last_Name.

```
SQL> update Inactive_Customer
  2  set
  3  Salutation = 'Mister',
  4  Last_Name = 'Johnson';

5 rows updated.
```

Think of Sets Instead of Records

To demonstrate that SQL is set-oriented, let's look at an UPDATE statement that exchanges the values between two columns. The following query shows the values for Customer_ID, Home_Telephone_Number, and Fax_Number that are currently in the Customer table.

```
SQL> select Customer_ID, Home_Telephone_Number, Fax_Number
  2  from Customer
  3  order by Customer_ID;
```

```
CUSTOMER_ID HOME_TELEP FAX_NUMBER
----------- ---------- ----------
       1001 7145550123
       1002 6025553833 6025553811
       1003 5035551283
       1004 8015558194
       1005 3015558331 3015556020
       1006 8085558183
       1007 6025551384
       1008 8105558356
       1009 8105554199 8105553535
```

9 rows selected.

Now, we'll swap the telephone and fax numbers in the Customer table with a single UPDATE statement. You do not need to store the voice and fax numbers in temporary variables as you would if you were using a programming language to swap these columns.

```
SQL> update Customer
  2  set
  3  Home_Telephone_Number = Fax_Number,
  4  Fax_Number = Home_Telephone_Number;
```

9 rows updated.

If we take another look at the Customer table, we see that the swap of the two columns was successful.

```
SQL> select Customer_ID, Home_Telephone_Number, Fax_Number
  2  from Customer
  3  order by Customer_ID;
```

```
CUSTOMER_ID HOME_TELEP FAX_NUMBER
----------- ---------- ----------
       1001            7145550123
       1002 6025553811 6025553833
       1003            5035551283
       1004            8015558194
       1005 3015556020 3015558331
       1006            8085558183
       1007            6025551384
       1008            8105558356
       1009 8105553535 8105554199
```

9 rows selected.

```
SQL> rollback;
```

Rollback complete.

Throwing Out Data with the *DELETE* Statement

The DELETE statement is used to remove rows from a table. With Personal Oracle7, you don't need to know the physical ordering of the rows in the table to perform a DELETE. Oracle uses the criteria in the WHERE clause to determine which rows to delete; the Oracle database engine will determine the internal location of the rows.

DELETE Syntax

The DELETE statement has the simplest syntax of all four DML statements, which is this:

```
DELETE FROM table_name
[WHERE condition]
```

In this syntax, table_name is the table to be updated and condition is a valid SQL condition.

If you think that the SQL syntax is inconsistent, you're correct. For example, the syntax for the UPDATE statement (UPDATE table_name) is inconsistent when compared with the DELETE statement syntax (DELETE FROM table_name). Many other idiosyncrasies can be found in SQL and they aren't going to go away soon. If you want to take advantage of the power in SQL, concentrate on learning the syntax and working through a lot of examples.

Removing All Rows with *TRUNCATE*

In designing an application, there are situations in which all of the rows in a table need to be deleted. If there are many rows in the table, using a DELETE to accomplish this can be quite time-consuming. As an alternative, you should consider using the TRUNCATE TABLE statement. The TRUNCATE TABLE statement deletes all of a table's rows without writing the deleted rows so that the deletion can be undone. As a result, the TRUNCATE TABLE statement deletes rows much faster than the DELETE statement.

The TRUNCATE TABLE statement is typically used in the following way:

```
TRUNCATE TABLE table_name
```

One caveat: the TRUNCATE TABLE statement is not a DML statement. This means that if you issue a TRUNCATE TABLE statement, you cannot change your mind and perform a rollback to recover the lost rows; the TRUNCATE TABLE statement is a "one-way trip."

Locking a Row with the *SELECT FOR UPDATE* Statement

If you're designing a database application, you want a system that will support multiple, concurrent users. To successfully implement such a system, users should not be able to simultaneously modify the same record at the same time. Oracle provides the capability to lock one or more rows via the SELECT FOR UPDATE statement.

The syntax for the SELECT FOR UPDATE statement is almost identical to that of the SELECT statement except for the keywords FOR UPDATE that are appended to the SELECT statement.

Concurrency

A significant characteristic of an information system is the capability to provide concurrent access to multiple users. Of course, you would also want to be sure that one user could not step on the changes made by another user. For instance, if Jean Smith is making changes to repair number 2013, Max Gilroy should not be able to change the status of repair number 2013 until Jean Smith has committed the changes she has made.

By the same token, the fact that Smith is changing repair number 2013 should not prevent anyone from changing a different repair number.

Read-Only Transactions

In a multiuser Oracle environment, Oracle provides what is termed "read consistency" at the SQL statement level. What this means is that a single SQL statement cannot return results that are contradictory or inconsistent. Look at an example to understand this concept.

If you want to know the initial retail value, the current used value, and the difference between the two values for all products, you would issue the following query:

```
select Initial_Retail_Value, Current_Used_Value,
       Initial_Retail_Value - Current_Used_Value
from Product;
```

Let's assume that Jean Smith is modifying the current used value for a product while the previous SELECT statement is executing. Statement level consistency means that the previous query will never return a row in which the actual difference for Initial_Retail_Value and Current_Used_Value does not equal the *returned* difference. Depending on when Jean commits her changes, you will either see the change or you won't, but you will never see a partial change manifested in a single SQL statement.

However, even though Oracle provides consistency within a single SQL statement, its default behavior doesn't guarantee read consistency during more than one statement. If you query a table twice, you may obtain different results the second time if another Oracle user has changed the same table in between your first and second queries. Of course, read consistency is only applicable to an Oracle database that is supporting multiple users, such as the Oracle Enterprise Server or the Oracle Workgroup Server.

There may be a time when you'll need more than single-statement read consistency. In fact, you may need to have read consistency across a particular transaction. For this purpose, you need to issue the following statement:

```
set transaction read only;
```

We'll explore this topic later in Chapter 16, "Defining Transactions."

Setting a Column Value to *NULL*

The following are the various ways in which a column's value is set to NULL:

■ The column is not assigned a value during an INSERT and it has no default value.

■ The column is explicitly assigned a NULL value during the INSERT.

■ The column is explicitly set to NULL in an UPDATE.

Assigning a *NULL* During an *INSERT*

You can explicitly set a column to NULL in an INSERT statement in the following way:

```
insert into Customer (
Customer_ID, Last_Name, First_Name, Fax_Number)
values
(2002, 'Smith', 'Wendy', NULL);
```

Setting a Column to *NULL* with an *UPDATE*

The UPDATE statement can be used to set a column's value to NULL in the following way:

```
update Product
set Current_Used_Value = NULL
where
Manufacturer_ID = 'TES801';
```

After you have set the current used value to NULL for the specified rows, you can verify that Personal Oracle7 has indeed made the change.

```
select Product_ID, Manufacturer_ID, Description
from Product
where
Manufacturer_ID = 'TES801' and
Current_Used_Value is NULL;
```

Default Values and *NULL*

When you create a table, you specify a column as mandatory by adding NOT NULL after you name the column's datatype. A mandatory column must be assigned a value each time a row is inserted into a table. If you try to insert a row without specifying a value for a mandatory column, Oracle returns an error message. For instance, the following INSERT statement attempts to add a row to the Product table without specifying a value for the Product_ID column, which is defined as NOT NULL.

```
SQL> insert into Product
  2  (Manufacturer_ID, Description)
  3  values
  4  ('SEN101','GPS Receiver');
insert into Product
            *
ERROR at line 1:
ORA-01400: mandatory (NOT NULL) column is missing or NULL during insert
```

Unfortunately, Oracle doesn't indicate the mandatory column (or columns) that need to be referenced in the INSERT statement. When you see an ORA-01400 error code, it's up to you to compare the column list in the INSERT statement with the table definition.

Assigning a *NULL* During an *UPDATE*

To explicitly set a column in an existing row to NULL, you must use the UPDATE statement. For example, you can set all customer's fax numbers to NULL with the following statement:

```
SQL> update Customer
  2  set Fax_Number = NULL;

9 rows updated.
```

One of the complaints about SQL is its inconsistent syntax. In the UPDATE statement, a NULL value is assigned to a column with the equal sign (=). However, in the WHERE clause of a SELECT statement, instead of using an equal sign, you use the word IS (or IS NOT) to test for a NULL value for a column. Because of this, you can wind up with UPDATE statements that look like the following:

```
SQL> update Customer
  2  set Fax_Number = NULL
  3  where
  4  Fax_Number is not NULL;

3 rows updated.
```

Summary

The contents of Personal Oracle7 tables are manipulated through the use of the following three statements:

- ■ INSERT adds rows to a table.
- ■ UPDATE modifies existing rows.
- ■ DELETE removes rows from a table.

You can also use a subquery in conjunction with these three statements.

A database transaction is a set of changes to one or more database tables that constitute a logical unit of work. You use the COMMIT statement to make the transaction permanent. Alternatively, you use the ROLLBACK statement to rescind the transaction.

9

The Oracle Datatypes

As you have seen, every column must be defined to be a valid Oracle datatype. In previous chapters, you've seen many examples of how to use SQL; you've also seen some of the fundamental datatypes: INTEGER, NUMBER, VARCHAR2, and DATE. In this chapter, you'll take a closer look at all of the Oracle datatypes and explore how they are used in applications. You'll see how columns based on these datatypes behave. In Chapters 11 through 13, you'll study the built-in Oracle functions and operators that can be used for each datatype.

Numeric Data

Oracle offers several datatypes that are used to store numeric data; each is suited for different purposes. Nevertheless, from an internal perspective, Oracle uses only the NUMBER and FLOAT datatypes for storing numeric data.

- INTEGER is used to store integers
- NUMBER is used to store general numbers
- DECIMAL is used for storing fixed point numbers and enables Oracle to be compatible with other relational databases—specifically SQL/DS and DB2
- FLOAT is used for storing floating point numbers and enables Oracle to be compatible with the ANSI FLOAT datatype

The NUMBER datatype offers the greatest flexibility for storing numeric data. It will accept positive and negative integers and real numbers, and has from 1 to 38 digits of precision. The syntax for specifying the NUMBER datatype is

```
NUMBER (precision, scale)
```

where *precision* is the maximum number of digits to be stored, and *scale* is used to indicate the position of the decimal point number of digits to the right (positive) or left (negative) of the decimal point. The scale can range from -84 to 128.

The INTEGER datatype can store an integer of up to 38 digits in size. If you try to store a real number in an INTEGER column, Oracle will round the real number to the nearest integer. The following INSERT statement shows how the value 102.501 is rounded to 103 when stored in an INTEGER column.

```
SQL> insert into integer_demo
  2  (record_no, int_value)
  3  values
  4  (101, 102.501);

1 row created.
SQL> select record_no, int_value
  2  from integer_demo;

RECORD_NO INT_VALUE
--------- ---------
      101       103
```

Numeric Precision

As was mentioned, Oracle is capable of storing from 1 to 38 digits of precision for a number. This is because Oracle doesn't convert the characters to an internal format, but actually stores each digit as a character (along with sign and exponent data).

Let's illustrate this concept with a good example. Insert a very precise number into a NUMBER column:

```
SQL> insert into number_demo
  2  (record_no, value)
  3  values
  4  (101, 1234567890.123456789012345678901234567);

1 row created.
```

If you use SQL*Plus to look at what was actually stored, you may be misled.

```
SQL> select record_no, value
  2  from number_demo;

 RECORD_NO      VALUE
---------- ----------
       101 1234567890
```

At first glance, it appears as though Oracle truncated the fractional part of the number that was inserted. However, the apparent truncation is caused by a SQL*Plus system variable—NUMWIDTH—that has a default value which isn't large enough to display the full precision of the value. To see the full precision, you can increase NUMWIDTH.

```
SQL> set numwidth 38
SQL> select record_no, value
  2  from number_demo;

                              RECORD_NO                                    VALUE
-------------------------------------- ----------------------------------------
                                   101 1234567890.123456789012345678901234567
```

If you limit the precision, Oracle will limit the values that can be stored in the column to the defined precision. For instance, suppose you define a table in the following way:

```
SQL> create table number_digits_demo (
  2  record_no int not null,
  3  value number(4));

Table created.
```

If you store values that meet and exceed the specified number of digits, the following occurs:

```
SQL> insert into number_digits_demo
  2  (record_no, value)
  3  values
  4  (101, 9999);

1 row created.
```

```
SQL> insert into number_digits_demo
  2  (record_no, value)
  3  values
  4  (101, 10000);
(101, 10000)
         *
ERROR at line 4:
ORA-01438: value larger than specified precision allows for this column
```

The following is an example on the use of scale and precision in a numeric column. The table is defined as

```
SQL> create table scale_precision_demo (
  2  record_no int not null,
  3  value number(6,2));

Table created.
```

In the number column, the precision is 6 and the scale is 2. In other words, out of a total of 6 digits of precision, Oracle will reserve 2 digits to the right of the decimal point, leaving a maximum of 4 digits to the left of the decimal point. Also, the column cannot store more than 6 digits of precision for any number.

The number 1234.5 can be stored in the number column.

```
SQL> insert into scale_precision_demo
  2  (record_no, value)
  3  values
  4  (901, 1234.5);

1 row created.
```

The number 12345.1 can't be stored because it contains five digits to the left of the decimal point.

```
SQL> insert into scale_precision_demo
  2  (record_no, value)
  3  values
  4  (901, 12345.1);
(901, 12345.1)
          *
ERROR at line 4:
ORA-01438: value larger than specified precision allows for this column
```

Again, the number 12345, even though it has only five digits of precision, can't be stored in the column because it has five digits to the left of the decimal point.

```
SQL> insert into scale_precision_demo
  2  (record_no, value)
  3  values
  4  (901, 12345);
(901, 12345)
         *
ERROR at line 4:
ORA-01438: value larger than specified precision allows for this column
```

The number 1234.56 is stored successfully.

```
SQL> insert into scale_precision_demo
  2  (record_no, value)
  3  values
  4  (901, 1234.56);

1 row created.
```

If you try to store the number 1234.567 in the column, Oracle rounds the fractional portion .567 to .57 so that it fits into the 2 digits—the specified scale for the column.

```
SQL> insert into scale_precision_demo
  2  (record_no, value)
  3  values
  4  (901, 1234.567);

1 row created.


SQL> select record_no, value
  2  from scale_precision_demo;

 RECORD_NO      VALUE
---------- ----------
       901     1234.5
       901    1234.56
       901    1234.57
```

Using the DECIMAL Datatype

The DECIMAL datatype is really just a synonym for the NUMBER datatype. In the following example, the decimal_test table is created with a column named my_decimal defined as decimal(5). If you then describe the table, you'll see that the column is defined as NUMBER(5).

```
SQL> create table decimal_test (
  2  record_no int not null,
  3  my_decimal decimal(5));

Table created.

SQL> desc decimal_test
 Name                                      Null?    Type
 ----------------------------------------- -------- ----
 RECORD_NO                                 NOT NULL NUMBER(38)
 MY_DECIMAL                                         NUMBER(5)
```

Using the FLOAT Datatype

Oracle supplies the FLOAT datatype, which is compatible with the ANSI FLOAT type. The FLOAT datatype is covered in more detail in Chapter 12, "Handling Numbers."

String and Number Conversion

You can assign to a number column a string that contains a number. To illustrate this, the following table has a NUMBER column.

```
SQL> create table number_demo (
  2   record_no int not null,
  3   value number);
```

Table created.

First, insert a single row into the table.

```
SQL> insert into number_demo
  2   (record_no, value)
  3   values
  4   (101, 2.333);
```

1 row created.

Next, update this column by setting its value to a string.

```
SQL> update number_demo
  2   set value = '33.33';
```

1 row updated.

```
SQL> select record_no, value
  2   from number_demo;

RECORD_NO      VALUE
--------- ---------
      101     33.33
```

Notice that Oracle automatically converted the string '33.33' to a value of 33.33.

In the same way, Oracle will automatically convert numeric values to strings.

```
SQL> desc number_demo
 Name                               Null?    Type
 -------------------------------- -------- ----
 RECORD_NO                        NOT NULL NUMBER(38)
 VALUE                                     NUMBER
 TEXT                                      VARCHAR2(30)

SQL> update number_demo
  2   set text = 123.44;
```

1 row updated.

```
SQL> select * from number_demo;

 RECORD_NO       VALUE TEXT
--------- --------- ------------------------------
      101  1234567890 123.44
```

Strings and dates must be enclosed in single quotes to be converted to a string value. Otherwise, Oracle tries to interpret the text as a column name or expression, as shown in the following two examples.

```
SQL> update number_demo
  2   set text = abc123;
set text = abc123
```

```
              *
ERROR at line 2:
ORA-00904: invalid column name


SQL> update number_demo
  2  set text = 123abc;
set text = 123abc
                *
ERROR at line 2:
ORA-00933: SQL command not properly ended
```

Character Data

To store character data, you can choose from several datatypes.

> CHAR
>
> VARCHAR
>
> VARCHAR2
>
> LONG

The bulk of many databases is character data, so look at some of the advantages and disadvantages of each datatype.

The CHAR datatype stores fixed-length character strings of up to 255 characters. If you do not specify a length, a CHAR column will store a single character.

You probably don't want to use the VARCHAR datatype at all. Oracle warns that the VARCHAR datatype may not be supported in future releases. The VARCHAR2 datatype was introduced with Oracle7 and is meant to replace the use of VARCHAR. If you're building a new Oracle application, there's no reason for you to use the VARCHAR datatype.

VARCHAR2 will store up to 2000 characters. If you absolutely must store more than that, you need to consider using the LONG datatype.

You can store up to 2 GB of characters in a LONG column. However, you cannot use any of Oracle's built-in functions or operators with LONG columns. It's best to think of a LONG column as a very large black box. You cannot search the contents of this box unless the box is emptied.

Follow these guidelines in choosing an appropriate datatype for a column that will store character data.

- ■ Try to use CHAR to define columns that will store a single character.
- ■ Use VARCHAR2 to store variable strings of up to 2000 characters.
- ■ Use LONG, as a last resort, to store more than 2000 characters.

If you're trying to store more than 2000 characters, don't create multiple VARCHAR2 columns to store the data. Assembling, searching, or manipulating the contents of multiple columns is impractical. This example should help explain the rationale.

Suppose you need a table that can store up to 6000 characters of text. You also want to use Oracle's built-in functions and operators, so you decide not to use a LONG column. Here is the initial table:

```
SQL> create table text_demo (
  2   record_no int not null,
  3   employee_id int not null,
  4   text1 varchar2(2000),
  5   text2 varchar2(2000),
  6   text3 varchar2(2000));

Table created.
```

Assuming that the table contains text that you're interested in searching, you submit the following query.

```
SQL> select record_no, text1, text2, text3
  2   from text_demo
  3   where
  4   text1 like '%there%' or
  5   text2 like '%there%' or
  6   text3 like '%there%';

RECORD_NO
---------
TEXT1
-------------------------------------------------------------------------
TEXT2
-------------------------------------------------------------------------
TEXT3
-------------------------------------------------------------------------
     1001
This is the most amazing story. Three pigs left their home to find their fortun
Once upon a time, in a cottage in the forest, there lived three bears - a papa
A long time ago, in a galaxy far, far away - lived three creatures named ...
```

Suppose you had to search fifty columns instead of three. The query would become quite unwieldy. Instead of using a table in which each text line was stored as a separate column, you could create a separate table so that the two tables looked like the following:

```
SQL> create table text_master (
  2   record_no int not null,
  3   employee_id int not null);

Table created.

SQL> create table text_detail (
  2   record_no int not null,
  3   line_no int,
  4   text_line varchar2(2000));

Table created.
```

Now you can reduce your query to the following:

```
SQL> select line_no, text_line
  2  from text_detail
  3  where
  4  record_no = 1001 and
  5  text_line like '%the%';

   LINE_NO
----------
TEXT_LINE
------------------------------------------------------------------------
         1
This is the most amazing story. Three pigs left their home to find their fortun

         2
Once upon a time, in a cottage in the forest, there lived three bears - a papa
```

The alternative to this approach is to use a LONG column and perform all manipulation and searching outside of SQL. For instance, if you're using PowerBuilder as a development tool, you would write an event script, in PowerScript, that stored the contents of the LONG column into a PowerBuilder BLOB variable, where it could then be manipulated using PowerScript functions and operators. The search results could then be presented to the user. Choosing between the use of a LONG column or breaking up the long text into VARCHAR2 columns can be difficult; you need to carefully evaluate the specific requirements of the application.

Using the CHAR Datatype

Because the CHAR datatype stores fixed-length columns, use it when you are defining columns that will contain a single character. Using the CHAR datatype to store larger strings isn't efficient because you will waste storage space doing so.

Using the VARCHAR2 Datatype

Because it stores variable length strings, the VARCHAR2 datatype is the preferred datatype for storing strings. It can be used to store up to 2000 characters. In Chapter 10, "Manipulating Strings," you'll analyze the many ways to use the Oracle built-in string functions and operators.

Date/Time Data

One of Oracle's strengths is its DATE datatype. The DATE datatype should really be named DATETIME because it provides storage for both date and time information. Oracle allocates a fixed 7 bytes for a DATE column. This is true even if you're using a DATE column to store date information only or time information only.

There are quite a few built-in functions provided specifically for manipulating DATE values and expressions. In Chapter 11, "Dealing with Dates," you'll look at many detailed examples of how to use these functions.

The DATE datatype enables you to store dates in the range of January 1, 4712 BC to December 31, 4712 AD. Oracle uses the default format of DD-MON-YY for entering and displaying dates.

```
SQL> create table date_demo (
  2  record_no int not null,
  3  date_of_birth date);

Table created.

SQL> insert into date_demo
  2  (record_no, date_of_birth)
  3  values
  4  (101, '09-MAY-57');

1 row created.
```

However, if you use a different format for the date without telling Oracle what the format is, the following will occur:

```
SQL> insert into date_demo
  2  (record_no, date_of_birth)
  3  values
  4  (102, 'SEP 08, 1955');
(102, 'SEP 08, 1955')
               *
ERROR at line 4:
ORA-01858: a non-numeric character was found where a numeric was expected
```

Large Strings

As was mentioned earlier, if you must store more than 2000 characters in a single column, Oracle supplies the LONG datatype. A LONG column can accommodate up to 2 GB of characters. However, there are a number of restrictions on the use of LONG columns in SQL. To investigate the use of LONG columns, use this simple table:

```
SQL> desc long_demo
 Name                            Null?     Type
 -------------------------------- -------- ----
 RECORD_NO                       NOT NULL  NUMBER(38)
 COMMENTS                                  LONG
```

Put a row in the long_demo table.

```
SQL> insert into long_demo
  2  (record_no, comments)
  3  values
  4  (100,
```

```
   5  'We will investigate the capabilities and restrictions
   6  of a LONG column by entering data into this column');
```

```
1 row created.
```

If you select the contents of this table, SQL*Plus returns the following:

```
SQL> select *
  2  from long_demo;

RECORD_NO COMMENTS
--------- -------------------------------------------------------------------
      100 We will investigate the capabilities and restrictions of a LONG colum
```

Notice that SQL*Plus has truncated the contents of the Comments column to 80 characters. SQL*Plus uses a system variable, LONG, to determine the number of characters in a LONG column to display to the user. By default, this parameter is set to 80. Increase the LONG variable to 200 and perform the query again. Also, you'll need to increase the width of the SQL*Plus screen buffer so that the results can be displayed.

```
SQL> set long 200
SQL> select *
  2  from long_demo;

RECORD_NO COMMENTS
--------- -------------------------------------------------------------------
      100 We will investigate the capabilities and restrictions of a LONG
          column by entering data into this column
```

Now you see the complete contents of the Comments column.

You can't use Oracle functions or operators to search or modify the contents of a LONG column. If you try this, the following will happen:

```
SQL> select record_no, comments
  2  from long_demo
  3  where
  4  comments like '%LONG%';
comments like '%LONG%'
       *
ERROR at line 4:
ORA-00932: inconsistent data types
```

That's right; you can't search the contents of a LONG column. Let's look at applying a function to a LONG.

```
SQL> select record_no, substr(comments,1,5)
  2  from long_demo;
select record_no, substr(comments,1,5)
                         *
ERROR at line 1:
ORA-00932: inconsistent data types
```

Again, Oracle won't enable you to apply a function to a LONG column. In a sense, you can think of a LONG column as a large container into which you can store or retrieve data—but not manipulate it.

Remember: you can have only one LONG column per table.

Storage of Binary Data

As you're probably aware, most databases provide for the storage of Binary Large Objects (BLOBs). BLOBs include documents, graphics, sound, video—actually, any type of binary file you can think of. The Oracle LONG RAW datatype is designed for BLOB storage.

When you want to associate a BLOB with a "normal" row, there are two choices available to you.

■ Store the BLOB in an operating system file (such as an MS-DOS file) and store the directory and filename in the associated table.

■ Store the BLOB itself in a LONG RAW column.

Some developers feel more comfortable with the first choice. They feel that the BLOB is more readily available if it's stored in the file system instead of in the Oracle database. They reason that there is little added benefit to storing a BLOB in a table column if it can't (or shouldn't) be manipulated by the Oracle database.

Others see an advantage in centralizing all data storage in the Oracle database. They present the argument that this approach provides greater portability; they have fewer OS-specific issues to deal with by removing references to a directory and filename.

Advantages and Disadvantages of the LONG RAW Datatype

A column defined as LONG RAW can accommodate up to 2 GB for each row. Obviously, a LONG RAW column is capable of storing extremely large BLOBs such as documents, images, sound, and even video.

Like LONG columns, LONG RAW columns have a number of limitations. For example, you cannot use any of the built-in functions with a LONG RAW column.

The RAW Datatype

Oracle also provides the RAW datatype, which can accommodate up to 255 bytes of binary data. Because of this storage restriction, a RAW column is less useful than a LONG RAW column. Nevertheless, I'll create a sample table to demonstrate the use of a RAW column.

```
SQL> create table raw_demo
  2  (record_no integer not null,
  3  byte_stream raw(255));

Table created.
```

Now that the table exists, let's put a record in it.

```
SQL> insert into raw_demo
  2  (record_no, byte_stream)
```

```
  3  values
  4  (100, 'abcd');
```

1 row created.

At first glance, it appears that a RAW column will accommodate strings and convert them into an internal binary format. Try inserting another row.

```
SQL> insert into raw_demo
  2  (record_no, byte_stream)
  3  values
  4  (101, 'xyz');
(101, 'xyz')
         *
ERROR at line 4:
ORA-01465: invalid hex number
```

As you see, you must use a valid hexadecimal number to insert a value into a RAW column. You also have the option of using a built-in function called HEXTORAW, which converts a hexadecimal number into a binary value.

The following is an example of how to select values from a RAW column:

```
SQL> select record_no, byte_stream
  2  from raw_demo;

RECORD_NO
---------
BYTE_STREAM
-----------------------------------------------------------------------------
      100
ABCD

      102
012345ABCDEF
```

As you see, Oracle displays the contents of a RAW column as hexadecimal digits.

Summary

Keep the following concepts in mind when you work with Oracle datatypes:

- Every column in a table must have an Oracle datatype.
- Use INTEGER, NUMBER, DECIMAL, and FLOAT to store numeric data.
- Use CHAR to store single characters.
- Make it a practice to use VARCHAR2 to store strings. It can store strings of up to 2000 characters, and it will support the use of Oracle built-in functions and operators.
- Use LONG when you must store very large text strings.
- Use DATE to store all date and time information.
- Use LONG RAW to store BLOBs (Binary Large Objects) of up to 2 GB.

10

Manipulating Strings

This chapter examines the techniques that Oracle provides for manipulating strings. You'll find that these techniques will prove useful in the following situations:

- Transforming strings from one form to another in a database application
- Generating reports
- Performing ad hoc queries
- Converting data from one database to another

Oracle provides an extensive set of built-in functions and operators for string manipulation. The real power of these functions and operators is realized by nesting these functions within each other. You'll see several examples of this technique in this chapter.

Finding the Length of a String

The LENGTH function is used to obtain the length of a string column. LENGTH returns a number equal to the number of characters in the argument, as the following code shows:

```
SQL> select Last_Name, length(Last_Name)
  2  from Customer
  3  order by Last_Name;

LAST_NAME                        LENGTH(LAST_NAME)
-------------------------------- -----------------
Chen                                             4
Fleming                                          7
Fray                                             4
Hernandez                                        9
Horace                                           6
Jensen                                           6
Johnson                                          7
Kramden                                          7
Martinez                                         8
Mcclintock                                      10
Moran                                            5
Pareski                                          7
Richardson                                      10
Smyth                                            5
Sorrel                                           6

15 rows selected.
```

Extracting a Substring from a String

The SUBSTR function is used to extract a substring from a string. The SUBSTR function is used in the following way:

```
SUBSTR (string, starting character, number of characters)
```

In this example, *string* is a character column or string expression, *starting character* is the starting position of the substring, and *number of characters* is the number of characters to return.

As an example, if you want to obtain the first four characters of the customer's last name, the call to the SUBSTR function looks like

```
SQL> select Last_Name, substr(Last_Name,1,4)
  2  from Customer
  3  order by Last_Name;
```

```
LAST_NAME                       SUBS
------------------------------- ----
Chen                            Chen
Fleming                         Flem
Fray                            Fray
Hernandez                       Hern
Horace                          Hora
Jensen                          Jens
Johnson                         John
Kramden                         Kram
Martinez                        Mart
Mcclintock                      Mccl
Moran                           Mora
Pareski                         Pare
Richardson                      Rich
Smyth                           Smyt
Sorrel                          Sorr
```

15 rows selected.

In addition to using literal values in the SUBSTR function, you can use a function as an argument in the SUBSTR function. For instance, suppose you want to retrieve the last three characters of the customer's last name. You would use the LENGTH function to find the last character position. To determine the correct starting character for the SUBSTR function, you subtract $n - 1$ from LENGTH, where n is the number of characters that you want to retrieve—in the following example, $3-1 = 2$:

```
SQL> select substr(Last_Name,length(Last_Name)-2,3)
  2  from Customer
  3  order by Last_Name;
```

```
SUB
---
hen
ing
ray
dez
ace
sen
son
den
nez
ock
ran
```

```
ski
son
yth
rel

15 rows selected.
```

Finding Patterns in a String

You learned how to use the LIKE operator in Chapter 5, "The Basics of SQL." As a quick review, the LIKE operator can be used to search for patterns in string expressions. With careful construction of a pattern, you can perform very specific searches.

To illustrate, if you want to retrieve all rows in which the Description column contains the pattern WATTS or RMS, you could use the LIKE function in the following query:

```
SQL> select Description
  2   from Product
  3   where
  4   Description like '%WATTS%' or
  5   Description like '%RMS%';

DESCRIPTION
------------------------------------------------------------------------
AMP 600 WATTS PER CHANNEL
AMP, PROFESSIONAL 800W RMS PER CHANNEL
PRE AMPLIFIER 150 WATTS/CHANNEL
PREAMP, 460 W/RMS
```

Replacing a Portion of a String

A common data manipulation need is the capability to transform one pattern into another in a particular column. Suppose you wanted to change the product description in the Product table so that all amplifiers were not abbreviated as AMP, but instead, spelled out as Amplifier. At the same time, you want to be careful not to transform a phrase like 50 AMPS to 50 AmplifierS.

Fortunately, Oracle provides a function, REPLACE, that is used to manipulate a column by replacing one string with another string. The syntax for the REPLACE function is

```
REPLACE (string, existing_string, [replacement_string])
```

In this example, *string* is a string expression, *existing_string* is a string that might occur in *string*, and *replacement_string* is an optional string with which to replace *existing_string*.

Look at how REPLACE can be used to change a product description in the Product table. First, display the current product descriptions.

```
SQL> select description from product;
```

```
DESCRIPTION
------------------------------------------------
AMPLIFIER, 100W PER CHANNEL, RMS
AMP 300W PER CHAN, RMS
AMP 600 WATTS PER CHANNEL, RMS
AMP, PROFESSIONAL 800W RMS PER CHANNEL
Preamplifier, 200 W per channel, RMS
PRE AMPLIFIER 150 WATTS/CHANNEL
CD PLAYER, SINGLE-DISK
5-DISK CD PLAYER
JUKEBOX, CD - 100 DISK CAPACITY
Pre-amp, 120 W per channel
Pre amp, 250 W/channel, RMS
PREAMP, 460 W/RMS

Tuner

14 rows selected.
```

Next, use an UPDATE statement to change occurrences of W per channel, RMS to W PER CHANNEL.

```
SQL> update Product
  2  set Description =
  3  replace(Description,'W per channel, RMS','W PER CHANNEL')
  4  where
  5  Description like '%W per channel%';

2 rows updated.

SQL> select Description
  2  from Product;

DESCRIPTION
-----------------------------------------------------------------
AMPLIFIER, 100W PER CHANNEL, RMS
AMP 300W PER CHAN, RMS
AMP 600 WATTS PER CHANNEL, RMS
AMP, PROFESSIONAL 800W RMS PER CHANNEL
Preamplifier, 200 W PER CHANNEL
PRE AMPLIFIER 150 WATTS/CHANNEL
CD PLAYER, SINGLE-DISK
5-DISK CD PLAYER
JUKEBOX, CD - 100 DISK CAPACITY
Pre-amp, 120 W per channel
Pre amp, 250 W/channel, RMS
PREAMP, 460 W/RMS

Tuner

14 rows selected.
```

If you don't specify a replacement string in the REPLACE function, the existing string will be removed from the column. Using the same example, the product descriptions are displayed with the following query:

```
SQL> select description from product;
```

```
DESCRIPTION
-------------------------------------------------------
AMPLIFIER, 100W PER CHANNEL, RMS
AMP 300W PER CHAN, RMS
AMP 600 WATTS PER CHANNEL, RMS
AMP, PROFESSIONAL 800W RMS PER CHANNEL
Preamplifier, 200 W PER CHANNEL
PRE AMPLIFIER 150 WATTS/CHANNEL
CD PLAYER, SINGLE-DISK
5-DISK CD PLAYER
JUKEBOX, CD - 100 DISK CAPACITY
Pre-amp, 120 W per channel
Pre amp, 250 W/channel, RMS
PREAMP, 460 W/RMS

Tuner

14 rows selected.
```

Next, the REPLACE function is used without a replacement string to eliminate all occurrences of the pattern RMS in the Description column.

```
SQL> update Product
  2  set Description =
  3  replace(Description,'RMS')
  4  ;

14 rows updated.
```

As you can see in the following query, the pattern RMS has been removed from all product descriptions.

```
SQL> select Description from Product;

DESCRIPTION
-------------------------------------------------------
AMPLIFIER, 100W PER CHANNEL
AMP 300W PER CHAN
AMP 600 WATTS PER CHANNEL
AMP, PROFESSIONAL 800W PER CHANNEL
Preamplifier, 200 W PER CHANNEL
PRE AMPLIFIER 150 WATTS/CHANNEL
CD PLAYER, SINGLE-DISK
5-DISK CD PLAYER
JUKEBOX, CD - 100 DISK CAPACITY
Pre-amp, 120 W per channel
Pre amp, 250 W/channel
PREAMP, 460 W/

Tuner

14 rows selected.
```

Trimming a String

If a character column contains leading or trailing blanks, a query based on a specified value for the column might return misleading results. To illustrate this point, modify the Product table so that the length of Manufacturer_ID is seven characters. This will enable you to add a blank to the end of a six-character Manufacturer_ID.

```
SQL> alter table product modify (manufacturer_id  varchar2(7));

Table altered.
```

Next, add a trailing blank to Manufacturer_ID where Manufacturer_ID is equal to SEN101—the code used for Seny Electronics.

```
SQL> update product
  2    set manufacturer_id = 'SEN101 '
  3    where
  4    manufacturer_id = 'SEN101';

6 rows updated.
```

Now, if you query the table for products for which the Manufacturer_ID is equal to SEN101, Oracle won't return any records because 'SEN101' isn't equal to 'SEN101'.

```
SQL> select Product_ID
  2    from Product
  3    where
  4    Manufacturer_ID = 'SEN101';

no rows selected
```

Of course, if you hadn't been aware of the trailing blank, you would have been surprised by the fact that no rows were returned by the query. To avoid misleading query results, you should remove leading and trailing blanks before or after a row has been added to a table. Trailing blanks are a far more common problem than leading blanks because they aren't as obvious.

Oracle provides two functions for trimming blanks: LTRIM and RTRIM. LTRIM removes leading blanks in a string, and RTRIM trims a string's trailing blanks.

To trim leading and trailing blanks from a string, simply embed the RTRIM function inside the LTRIM function. If there are no leading or trailing blanks, LTRIM and RTRIM won't modify the existing string. Look at the following example to see how the RTRIM function is used:

```
SQL> update Product
  2    set Manufacturer_ID = RTRIM(Manufacturer_ID)
  3    where
  4    Manufacturer_ID like '% ';

6 rows updated.
```

Notice how the WHERE clause was used to update only those rows in which the Manufacturer_ID contained a trailing blank. RTRIM will trim trailing blanks without this WHERE clause, but if you have a large table the performance of the UPDATE statement will be better.

As you can see, LTRIM and RTRIM are supplied with a single argument: the string to be trimmed. There is a second optional argument that can be specified for both functions: an alternative set of characters to be trimmed from the string argument. As an example, suppose you have a table named TEST_TRIM with a single VARCHAR2 column named MY_COL. You know that there are some rows which have some leading characters that you want to trim off: x, y, and z.

```
SQL> select my_col
  2  from test_trim;

MY_COL
------------------------------------------------------------
yzzxHello, world
zyxGoodbye, cruel world
```

Use LTRIM to remove the offending characters.

```
SQL> update test_trim
  2  set my_col = ltrim(my_col,'xyz');

2 rows updated.

SQL> select my_col from test_trim;

MY_COL
------------------------------------------------------------
Hello, world
Goodbye, cruel world
```

You can eliminate other trailing characters by employing the same technique using RTRIM.

Checking for Trailing Blanks

There are several ways to check for trailing blanks. One of the easiest methods uses the LIKE operator.

```
select Manufacturer_ID
from Product
where
Manufacturer_ID like '% ';
```

This method certainly works, but concentrate on preventing leading and trailing blanks from being stored with your data in the first place. You can do this in two ways.

- Make sure that your front-end application—whether it's Visual Basic, PowerBuilder, or Oracle Forms—trims any trailing blanks entered on a form.

- Trim all leading and trailing blanks when you load data from non-Oracle sources into your Personal Oracle7 database.

Padding a String

Undoubtedly, you've been in a situation in which you need to pad a string with leading or trailing characters. Oracle provides two functions for this purpose: LPAD and RPAD.

LPAD

To left-pad a string, use the LPAD function. The syntax is

```
LPAD (string, n, pad_string)
```

In this example, *string* is the literal string or string column to be left-padded, *n* is the total length of the string returned by LPAD, and *pad_string* is the string to left-pad onto *string*.

Let's see how this works. Use LPAD to left-pad blanks onto a column.

```
SQL> select lpad(my_col,20) from test_trim;

LPAD(MY_COL,20)
--------------------
        Hello, world
Goodbye, cruel world
```

When *pad_string* is not supplied as an argument, LPAD uses a blank to left-pad the string. You can specify a literal string that LPAD will use to left-pad the string. However, the number of characters that are padded on the string depends on the value of *n*. The following example demonstrates how you can add a fixed value to the LENGTH function as an argument to LPAD:

```
SQL> select lpad(my_col,length(my_col)+8,'You say ') from test_trim;

LPAD(MY_COL,LENGTH(MY_COL)+8,'YOUSAY')
----------------------------------------------------------------
You say Hello, world
You say Goodbye, cruel world
```

By increasing the number added to LENGTH, you can left-pad the *string* with *pad_string* more than once, as shown next.

```
SQL> select lpad(my_col,length(my_col)+16,'You say ') from test_trim;

LPAD(MY_COL,LENGTH(MY_COL)+16,'YOUSAY')
----------------------------------------------------------------
You say You say Hello, world
You say You say Goodbye, cruel world
```

You can also left-pad a string with the contents of another column. As you can see in the query that follows, my_col2 is left-padded onto my_col. The number of times that this is performed depends on the length of values in both columns. In the following example, the second argument for LPAD is 50. If My_Col is equal to California and My_Col2 is equal to Los Angeles, LPAD returns a string in which California (10 characters) is left-padded with Los Angeles (11 characters) so that Los Angeles fills 40 characters.

```
SQL> select * from test_trim;

MY_COL                           MY_COL2
-------------------------------- --------------------------------
California                       Los Angeles
Michigan                         Jackson
Washington                       Seattle
Oregon                           Portland

SQL> select lpad(my_col,50,my_col2) from test_trim;

LPAD(MY_COL,50,MY_COL2)
--------------------------------------------------
Los AngelesLos AngelesLos AngelesLos AngCalifornia
JacksonJacksonJacksonJacksonJacksonJacksonMichigan
SeattleSeattleSeattleSeattleSeattleSeattWashington
PortlandPortlandPortlandPortlandPortlandPortOregon
```

By combining these built-in functions, you can assemble elaborate expressions. In the next example, we'll use the lengths of my_col and my_col2 to be sure that we only left-pad one time:

```
SQL> select lpad (my_col, length(my_col)+length(my_col2)+2, my_col2 ¦¦ ', ')
  2  from test_trim;

LPAD(MY_COL,LENGTH(MY_COL)+LENGTH(MY_COL2)+2,MY_COL2¦¦', ')
-----------------------------------------------------------------------------
Los Angeles, California
Jackson, Michigan
Seattle, Washington
Portland, Oregon
```

Dissect the SELECT statement. LPAD's first argument is my_col. For the second argument, you add my_col's length to my_col2's length and add an additional 2 for the ', ' that will be placed between my_col and my_col2. Finally, for LPAD's third argument, you concatenate my_col2 with , .

RPAD

RPAD works just like LPAD. Use the following syntax:

```
RPAD (string, n, pad_string)
```

In this line, *string* is the literal string or string column to be right-padded, *n* is the number of times to right-pad *pad_string*, and *pad_string* is the string to right-pad onto *string*.

Changing the Case in a String

Oracle provides three functions that enable you to change the case of a string's characters:

1. INITCAP converts the first character of each word to uppercase.

2. LOWER converts all of the characters in a string to lowercase.

3. UPPER converts all characters to uppercase.

All three functions have a single argument: the string expression to be manipulated. Let's investigate the use of these functions. In the following example, the first 15 characters of the product description are selected along with the same characters converted to uppercase:

```
SQL> select substr(Description,1,15),
  2  substr(upper(description),1,15)
  3  from Product;

SUBSTR(DESCRIPT SUBSTR(UPPER(DE
--------------- ---------------
AMPLIFIER, 100W AMPLIFIER, 100W
AMP 300W PER CH AMP 300W PER CH
AMP 600 WATTS P AMP 600 WATTS P
AMP, PROFESSION AMP, PROFESSION
Preamplifier, 2 PREAMPLIFIER, 2
PRE AMPLIFIER 1 PRE AMPLIFIER 1
CD PLAYER, SING CD PLAYER, SING
5-DISK CD PLAYE 5-DISK CD PLAYE
JUKEBOX, CD - 1 JUKEBOX, CD - 1
Pre-amp, 120 W  PRE-AMP, 120 W
Pre amp, 250 W/ PRE AMP, 250 W/
PREAMP, 460 W/R PREAMP, 460 W/R

Tuner           TUNER

14 rows selected.
```

Similarly, you can use the LOWER function to convert all characters to lowercase.

```
SQL> select substr(Description,1,15),
  2  substr(lower(Description),1,15)
  3  from Product;

SUBSTR(DESCRIPT SUBSTR(LOWER(DE
--------------- ---------------
AMPLIFIER, 100W amplifier, 100w
AMP 300W PER CH amp 300w per ch
AMP 600 WATTS P amp 600 watts p
AMP, PROFESSION amp, profession
Preamplifier, 2 preamplifier, 2
PRE AMPLIFIER 1 pre amplifier 1
CD PLAYER, SING cd player, sing
5-DISK CD PLAYE 5-disk cd playe
JUKEBOX, CD - 1 jukebox, cd - 1
Pre-amp, 120 W  pre-amp, 120 w
Pre amp, 250 W/ pre amp, 250 w/
PREAMP, 460 W/R preamp, 460 w/r

Tuner           tuner

14 rows selected.
```

Finally, the INITCAP function will convert all characters to lowercase and capitalize the first letter of each word.

```
SQL> select substr(Description,1,15),
  2   substr(initcap(Description),1,15)
  3   from Product;


SUBSTR(DESCRIPT SUBSTR(INITCAP(
--------------- ---------------
AMPLIFIER, 100W Amplifier, 100w
AMP 300W PER CH Amp 300w Per Ch
AMP 600 WATTS P Amp 600 Watts P
AMP, PROFESSION Amp, Profession
Preamplifier, 2 Preamplifier, 2
PRE AMPLIFIER 1 Pre Amplifier 1
CD PLAYER, SING Cd Player, Sing
5-DISK CD PLAYE 5-Disk Cd Playe
JUKEBOX, CD - 1 Jukebox, Cd - 1
Pre-amp, 120 W  Pre-Amp, 120 W
Pre amp, 250 W/ Pre Amp, 250 W/
PREAMP, 460 W/R Preamp, 460 W/R

Tuner           Tuner

14 rows selected.
```

Using the *DECODE* Function to Return a String

Many database applications reference columns that contain encoded information. Sometimes, a database designer creates a table to store a code and its description, especially if there's a possibility that the codes may change. In other situations, the column containing the code stands alone without any additional description available in the database.

In our sample application, we created a Condition Code table that stores a condition code—a code used to describe a piece of equipment brought in for repair—and its description. But imagine for a minute that there is no Condition Code table.

If you want to create a repair report that lists the condition of each item brought in for repair, you can write a simple query. But if this report is given to someone who isn't familiar with the condition codes that are used at the repair store, that individual is going to have difficulty understanding the report without some assistance.

Fortunately, there is a function that serves this purpose: DECODE. Its syntax is

```
DECODE (expression, value1, returned_value1, ...
valueN, returned_valueN,
[default_returned_value])
```

In this code, *expression* is a valid Oracle expression, *valueN* is a possible value to which *expression* might be equal, and *returned_valueN* is the value returned by DECODE if *expression* is equal to *valueN*. *default_returned_value* is an optional value returned by DECODE if *expression* is not equal to any of the values, *value1* through *valueN*.

I will use condition code as an example. At Frayed Wires, the consumer electronics repair store, each piece of equipment brought in by a customer will be assigned a condition code by a technician (see Table 10.1). An entry is made in the REPAIR_DETAIL table for each item that a customer brings in for repair.

Table 10.1. Condition codes.

Code	Description
DS	Dents and scratches
ES	Electrical short
IP	Intermittent problem
MK	Missing knobs
MS	Missing screws, connectors
NG	No good at all
NP	No power
SC	Some scratches
X	Excellent

The following are the current contents of REPAIR_DETAIL:

```
SQL> select Repair_ID, Product_ID, Manufacturer_ID, Item_Number, Condition_Code
  2  from Repair_Item
  3  order by Repair_ID;

REPAIR_ID PRODUCT_ID   MANUFA ITEM_NUMBER CON
--------- ------------ ------ ----------- ---
      501 C2002        MIT501           1 SC
      502 D301         SEN101           1 X
      503 B311         TES801           1 MK
      504 B801         SEN101           1 NG
      505 A903         TES801           1 NP
      506 TR901        TES801           1 IP

6 rows selected.
```

You can use the DECODE function to provide a translation for the encoded value. For example, the following query uses the DECODE function to return a description for the value of Condition_Code.

```
SQL> select Repair_ID, Product_ID, Manufacturer_ID, Item_Number,
  2          decode(Condition_Code,
  3                 'DS','Dents and scratches',
  4                 'ES','Electrical short',
  5                 'IP','Intermittent problem',
  6                 'MK','Missing knobs',
  7                 'MS','Missing screws, connectors',
  8                 'NG','No good at all',
```

```
 9                'NP','No power',
10                'SC','Some scratches',
11                'X', 'Excellent',
12                'Unknown condition code')
13  from Repair_Item
14  order by Repair_ID;

REPAIR_ID PRODUCT_ID   MANUFA ITEM_NUMBER DECODE(CONDITION_CODE,'DS'
--------- ------------ ------ ----------- --------------------------
      501 C2002        MIT501           1 Some scratches
      502 D301         SEN101           1 Excellent
      503 B311         TES801           1 Missing knobs
      504 B801         SEN101           1 No good at all
      505 A903         TES801           1 No power
      506 TR901        TES801           1 Intermittent problem

6 rows selected.
```

Converting a Character to Its ASCII Numeric Value

At some point, you may want to obtain the ASCII numeric equivalent of a character in a column. The ASCII function serves this purpose. It has a single string argument. ASCII returns the ASCII numeric equivalent of the first character of its argument.

```
SQL> select ASCII(Last_Name), Last_Name
  2  from Customer
  3  order by Last_Name;

ASCII(LAST_NAME) LAST_NAME
---------------- ----------------------------
              67 Chen
              70 Fleming
              70 Fray
              72 Hernandez
              72 Horace
              74 Jensen
              74 Johnson
              75 Kramden
              77 Martinez
              77 Mcclintock
              77 Moran
              80 Pareski
              82 Richardson
              83 Smyth
              83 Sorrel

15 rows selected.
```

Finding the Occurrence of a Pattern in a String

Many of Oracle's built-in string functions are the equivalent of functions available in programming and scripting languages. A good example is the INSTR function, which indicates the position of one string inside another string. The syntax for INSTR is

```
INSTR (string1,string2,[starting_position,[occurrence_number]])
```

In this code, *string1* is the string to be searched, *string2* is the string to look for in *string1*, and *starting_position* is the position in *string1* to begin the search. *occurrence_number* is the number of the occurrence of *string2* in *string1* for which you're looking.

INSTR will return the position of *string2* in *string1* based on the supplied values for *starting_position* and *occurrence_number*. If *string2* cannot be found in *string1* based on the other arguments, INSTR returns a zero.

The following code is an example that illustrates the use of INSTR. If you want to find the first occurrence of an in my_col, you can use this query.

```
SQL> select my_col, instr(my_col,'an')
  2  from test_trim;

MY_COL                          INSTR(MY_COL,'AN')
------------------------------  ------------------
California                                       0
Michigan                                         7
Washington                                       0
Oregon                                           0
Louisiana                                        7
Illinois                                         0
Albany                                           4
Pennsylvania                                     9
Arizona                                          0
Nevada                                           0
Montana                                          5
North Dakota                                     0

12 rows selected.
```

Summary

The following are some of the string functions and operators that Personal Oracle7 offers:

- ■ SUBSTR returns a specified portion of a string.
- ■ LENGTH returns the length of a string expression.
- ■ LPAD and RPAD are used for left and right padding of strings.
- ■ LTRIM and RTRIM are used for left and right trimming of blanks and other characters.
- ■ REPLACE substitutes one string for another string.
- ■ LOWER, UPPER, and INITCAP control the use of upper- and lowercase in a string.
- ■ DECODE translates column values.
- ■ ASCII returns the ASCII numeric equivalent of a character.
- ■ INSTR provides the character position in which a pattern is found in a string.

11

Dealing with Dates

There is tremendous variation in the treatment of dates and times among database systems. Fortunately, Oracle provides a special datatype—the date—for dealing with dates and times. This datatype has its own internal format with which you needn't be concerned, other than knowing that it provides for the storage of the century, year, month, day, hour, minute, and second. As you will see, there are many advantages to using this datatype where appropriate.

The Oracle Date Datatype

The Oracle date datatype is efficient because it requires only seven bytes of storage. In addition, when you define a column as a date, you are able to use all of Oracle's built-in functions that are available for manipulating dates and times.

The Oracle date datatype is also extremely convenient for the application developer. One can argue about whether or not the algorithms used by Oracle are optimal; you may feel that there are more efficient methods for storing date and time values. But there is no question that using the Oracle date datatype can save you a significant amount of time and effort in application development.

As you will see, the advantages of this datatype are clear—you really should use the Oracle datatype whenever you need to store date or time information.

There Is More to the Date Datatype Than the Date

The Oracle date datatype also stores time information: hour, minute, and second. You can use a column defined as a date to store only date information or only time information or both.

If you choose a different datatype for storing date and time information, you will be forced to use other algorithms for manipulating the formats you have defined. You won't be able to use any of Oracle's built-in functions for manipulating dates and times. What could normally be accomplished in a single SELECT statement will require additional processing in a programming language or development environment. Let's look at an example to see the consequence of *not* using the Oracle date datatype when its use is appropriate.

Using the example of a database for a consumer electronics repair store, Frayed Wires, let's assume that you need to store the hire date for each employee and a possible termination date. Suppose you made an incorrect decision and decided to store the employee's hire date as a numeric value in the format YYMMDD. For example, the hire date for an employee hired on May 9, 1957 would be stored as 570509. Here's what the table would look like:

```
Employee_ID NUMBER
Last_Name VARCHAR2(30)
First_Name VARCHAR2(15)
Position VARCHAR2(30)
Hire_Date NUMBER(6)
```

Cleverly (or so you thought), you decided to use a format of YYMMDD so that the hire date could be ordered either in ascending or descending order. You could then use the following SELECT statement to retrieve employee information ordered by hire date:

```
select Last_Name, First_Name, Hire_Date
from Employee
Order by Hire_Date
```

But there are a few problems with this approach, namely:

- **Erroneous assumption**: When employees are hired after 1999, the preceding SELECT statement will not return the correct results. Employees hired in 2000 and beyond will show up at the beginning of the list because the format only stores the last two digits of the year in which an employee was hired.

- **More work and lower reliability**: Because you can't rely on Oracle date validation, the burden of developing an algorithm for validating a hire date is on your shoulders.

- **Limited functionality**: If you need to query a table based on date arithmetic, what could have been accomplished with a single SELECT statement incorporating built-in functions will instead require additional processing. You can't write a SELECT statement that will retrieve all employees whose hire date is less than the mean hire date.

Using the Oracle date datatype instead helps to ensure that any application you develop will be portable to a different platform.

Date formats are supported on every platform on which Oracle runs. If you are planning to support an application on a variety of operating systems, you'll find that it's easier to use the Oracle date datatype than to support a variety of date and time formats for each operating system.

Searching for Rows Within a Date Range

It's common for a user to retrieve records within a particular date range. This is accomplished easily with SQL. Let's say that you want to know all of the customers who have brought in equipment for repair between January 20 and February 14. Because this information is stored in the REPAIR_HEADER table, one possible SELECT statement to retrieve the desired rows is the following:

```
select Last_Name, First_Name, Creation_Date
from Repair_Header
where
Creation_Date >= '20-JAN-95' and
Creation_Date <= '14-FEB-95'
```

Another way to retrieve the same information uses the BETWEEN function.

```
select Last_Name, First_Name
from Repair_Header
where
Creation_Date between '20-JAN-95' and '14-FEB-95'
```

The Current Date and Time: *SYSDATE*

Oracle has a number of values called pseudocolumns that can be referenced in SQL statements. One of these is SYSDATE. Despite its name, SYSDATE also contains time information. Like the date datatype, SYSDATE is accurate to the second. SYSDATE is an extremely useful construct for timestamping rows during an insert or update operation. We'll be using SYSDATE in many of the examples in this chapter.

The Oracle Date Format Model

Because the date datatype stores the values for century, year, day, month, hour, minute, and second, each of these values can be extracted and formatted independently. Also, the date and time elements can be abbreviated or fully spelled out according to the format that you specify.

You also have the option of repeating a date or time element in different formats. For instance, you can retrieve the month as a two-digit value and as a fully spelled-out name.

```
SQL> select Last_Name, First_Name, to_char(Hire_Date,'MM MONTH') month
  2  from Employee
  3  order by Hire_Date;

LAST_NAME                       FIRST_NAME            MONTH
------------------------------  --------------------  -------------
SMITH                           JEAN                  04 APRIL
HERNANDEZ                       RANDY                 11 NOVEMBER
GLEASON                         PAUL                  04 APRIL
BARRETT                         SARAH                 01 JANUARY
HIGGINS                         BEN                   02 FEBRUARY
YEN                             CINDY                 06 JUNE
GILROY                          MAX                   09 SEPTEMBER
CARSON                          BETH                  12 DECEMBER
SWANSON                         HARRY                 05 MAY

9 rows selected.
```

Alternatively, you may use Object Manager to specify a column as a DATE.

> **NOTE**
>
> It's a good idea to use SYSDATE and the DUAL table to experiment with various date and time formats. You can select SYSDATE from the DUAL table, but don't insert any rows into the DUAL table: it must have only one row for some Oracle tools to work correctly.

Table 11.1 contains a list of the valid elements that can be utilized in the date format.

Table 11.1. List of date format elements.

Format Element	Description	Range
SS	Second	0–59
SSSSS	Seconds past midnight	0–86399
MI	Minute	0–59
HH	Hour	0–12
HH24	Military hour	0–23
DD	Day of the month	1–31 (depends on month)
DAY	Day of the week	SUNDAY–SATURDAY
D	Day of the week	1–7
DDD	Day of the year	1–366 (depends on year)
MM	Month number	1–12
MON	Abbreviated month	JAN–DEC
MONTH	Month	JANUARY–DECEMBER
YY	Last two digits of year	e.g. 96
YYYY	Full year value	e.g. 1996
YEAR	Year fully spelled	
CC	Century	e.g. 19
Q	Quarter	1–4
J	Julian day	e.g. 2448000
W	Week of the month	1–5
WW	Week of the year	1–52

Specifying a Date Column

Defining a column using the date datatype is quite simple. There is no need to specify a format model for a column during table creation or modification. Here is an example of a CREATE TABLE statement containing date columns:

```
SQL> create table Employee (
  2   employee_id        number(4) not null,
  3   last_name          varchar2(30) not null,
  4   first_name         varchar2(30) not null,
  5   middle_initial     char(1),
  6   hire_date          date not null,
  7   termination_date   date,
  8   date_of_birth      date not null);

Table created.
```

The Oracle Default Date Format

The default date format is DD-MON-YY. For instance, 01-JAN-95 is a date in accordance with Oracle's default date format. You can specify dates with this format model without using any other functions or datatype conversion. But if you need to display or specify dates in a different format, then you'll need to use a built-in function to specify the format model you want to use.

If you try to assign a string that doesn't adhere to this default format to a date column, Oracle will probably return an error. For example, if the first two digits are greater than 31, Oracle will always return the error code ORA-01847. If the abbreviation for the month is not JAN, FEB, MAR, APR, MAY, JUN, JUL, AUG, SEP, OCT, NOV, or DEC, Oracle will return error code ORA-01843. If the day of the month is not within the valid range for that particular month, Oracle will return error code ORA-01839. Table 11.2 contains a list of Oracle error codes related to the manipulation of date values.

Table 11.2. Oracle error codes related to dates.

Oracle Error Code	Description
ORA-01847	Day of month must be between 1 and last day of month
ORA-01813	Hour may only be specified once
ORA-01839	Date not valid for month specified

NOTE

We are rapidly approaching a new millennium. Because the beginning years of the 21st century will be in the same range as the days in a month, there will no doubt be some confusion between the year and the day of the month. For instance, if you want to assign the date January 2, 2003, it would be very easy to switch the digits and enter 03-JAN-02 instead of 02-JAN-03. In either case, Oracle would accept the date as valid according to the date format.

Converting Dates to Strings

It's important to remember that a date column value remains a date until you convert it to some other datatype. If, for example, you want to extract the first character of a date column value, you'll need to convert the date column value to a string using a built-in function named TO_CHAR. The format for this function is

```
TO_CHAR(date_value,date_format)
```

where *date_value* is a literal date value, a date value from a column, or a date value returned by a built-in function, and *date_format* is a valid Oracle date format.

For example, the following query uses the TO_CHAR function to return the employee hire date using the format MONTH DD, YYYY.

```
SQL> select Last_Name, First_Name,
  2  to_char(Hire_Date,'MONTH DD, YYYY') H_DATE
  3  from Employee
  4  order by Hire_Date;
```

LAST_NAME	FIRST_NAME	H_DATE
SMITH	JEAN	APRIL 10, 1982
HERNANDEZ	RANDY	NOVEMBER 18, 1983
GLEASON	PAUL	APRIL 05, 1984
BARRETT	SARAH	JANUARY 16, 1989
HIGGINS	BEN	FEBRUARY 11, 1989
YEN	CINDY	JUNE 09, 1991
GILROY	MAX	SEPTEMBER 22, 1992
CARSON	BETH	DECEMBER 12, 1992
SWANSON	HARRY	MAY 18, 1993

9 rows selected.

Once a date value has been converted to a string with the TO_CHAR function, it can then be used as an argument in other string functions. For example, you can use the function SUBSTR, which is used to extract a substring from a string. Here is an example of how to use the SUBSTR function to extract the first letter of the employee's month of hire.

```
SQL> select Last_Name, First_Name,
  2  substr(to_char(Hire_Date,'MON'),1,1) the_first_letter_of_the_month
  3  from Employee
  4  order by the_first_letter_of_the_month;
```

LAST_NAME	FIRST_NAME	T
SMITH	JEAN	A
GLEASON	PAUL	A
CARSON	BETH	D
HIGGINS	BEN	F
BARRETT	SARAH	J
YEN	CINDY	J
SWANSON	HARRY	M
HERNANDEZ	RANDY	N
GILROY	MAX	S

9 rows selected.

Let's look at some of the many ways in which dates and times can be displayed. You have a tremendous amount of flexibility in how to display and specify these values.

Displaying Dates in a Variety of Formats

Let's take a closer look at the many different formats that you can use in the date format model. Remember that each of the format models must be enclosed in single quotes within the TO_CHAR function. Let's look at how you can display date values in some commonly used formats.

To display values using the MM/DD/YY format, use the following example:

```
SQL> select Last_Name, First_Name, to_char(Hire_Date,'MM/DD/YY') H_Date
  2  from Employee
  3  order by Hire_Date;

LAST_NAME                           FIRST_NAME              H_DATE
--------------------------------    --------------------    --------------------
SMITH                               JEAN                    04/10/82
HERNANDEZ                           RANDY                   11/18/83
GLEASON                             PAUL                    04/05/84
BARRETT                             SARAH                   01/16/89
HIGGINS                             BEN                     02/11/89
YEN                                 CINDY                   06/09/91
GILROY                              MAX                     09/22/92
CARSON                              BETH                    12/12/92
SWANSON                             HARRY                   05/18/93

9 rows selected.
```

Realize that even if you choose to only display the last two digits of the year, the date value still contains the full year.

You can specify the date format model to display the day of the week fully spelled, as in:

```
SQL> select Last_Name, First_Name,
  2  to_char(Hire_Date,'DAY, MON YEAR') H_Date
  3  from Employee
  4  order by Hire_Date;

LAST_NAME         FIRST_NAME      H_DATE
---------------   -------------   -------------------------------------------
SMITH             JEAN            SATURDAY  , APR NINETEEN EIGHTY-TWO
HERNANDEZ         RANDY           FRIDAY    , NOV NINETEEN EIGHTY-THREE
GLEASON           PAUL            THURSDAY  , APR NINETEEN EIGHTY-FOUR
BARRETT           SARAH           MONDAY    , JAN NINETEEN EIGHTY-NINE
HIGGINS           BEN             SATURDAY  , FEB NINETEEN EIGHTY-NINE
YEN               CINDY           SUNDAY    , JUN NINETEEN NINETY-ONE
GILROY            MAX             TUESDAY   , SEP NINETEEN NINETY-TWO
CARSON            BETH            SATURDAY  , DEC NINETEEN NINETY-TWO
SWANSON           HARRY           TUESDAY   , MAY NINETEEN NINETY-THREE

9 rows selected.
```

To display the ordinal value for the day of the month, add the characters th after the D. In the following example, you'll see that the Oracle date format will use the proper characters for the ordinal value.

```
SQL> select Last_Name, First_Name,
  2  to_char(Hire_Date,'MONTH DDth, YYYY') H_Date
```

```
  3   from Employee
  4   order by Hire_Date;
```

LAST_NAME	FIRST_NAME	H_DATE
SMITH	JEAN	APRIL 10th, 1982
HERNANDEZ	RANDY	NOVEMBER 18th, 1983
GLEASON	PAUL	APRIL 05th, 1984
BARRETT	SARAH	JANUARY 16th, 1989
HIGGINS	BEN	FEBRUARY 11th, 1989
YEN	CINDY	JUNE 9th, 1991
GILROY	MAX	SEPTEMBER 22nd, 1992
CARSON	BETH	DECEMBER 12th, 1992
SWANSON	HARRY	MAY 18th, 1993

```
9 rows selected.
```

To display the quarter in which the date value falls, Oracle will use 1 for January through March, 2 for April through June, 3 for July through September, and 4 for October through December. Notice how a string such as QTR: can be embedded in the returned value by enclosing it in double quotes.

```
SQL> select Last_Name, First_Name,
  2   to_char(Hire_Date,'"QTR" Q, YY') H_Date
  3   from Employee
  4   order by Hire_Date;
```

LAST_NAME	FIRST_NAME	H_DATE
SMITH	JEAN	QTR 2, 82
HERNANDEZ	RANDY	QTR 4, 83
GLEASON	PAUL	QTR 2, 84
BARRETT	SARAH	QTR 1, 89
HIGGINS	BEN	QTR 1, 89
YEN	CINDY	QTR 2, 91
GILROY	MAX	QTR 3, 92
CARSON	BETH	QTR 4, 92
SWANSON	HARRY	QTR 2, 93

```
9 rows selected.
```

To retrieve the month spelled out fully, use MONTH in the format model. Notice that the name of the month is a maximum of nine characters (SEPTEMBER) and that some months will have trailing blanks so that the returned value is always nine characters in length.

```
select to_char(Hire_Date,'MONTH DD, YYYY'
from Employee
order by Hire_Date
```

The next example demonstrates that the elements of the date format model can be combined in odd ways. In the following example, we are displaying the month as a two-digit value with the day of the week and the year fully spelled out.

```
SQL> select Last_Name, First_Name,
  2   to_char(Hire_Date,'MM DAY, YEAR') H_Date
  3   from Employee
  4   order by Hire_Date;
```

```
LAST_NAME          FIRST_NAME      H_DATE
---------------    ------------    ----------------------------------------
SMITH              JEAN            04 SATURDAY  , NINETEEN EIGHTY-TWO
HERNANDEZ          RANDY           11 FRIDAY    , NINETEEN EIGHTY-THREE
GLEASON            PAUL            04 THURSDAY  , NINETEEN EIGHTY-FOUR
BARRETT            SARAH           01 MONDAY    , NINETEEN EIGHTY-NINE
HIGGINS            BEN             02 SATURDAY  , NINETEEN EIGHTY-NINE
YEN                CINDY           06 SUNDAY    , NINETEEN NINETY-ONE
GILROY             MAX             09 TUESDAY   , NINETEEN NINETY-TWO
CARSON             BETH            12 SATURDAY  , NINETEEN NINETY-TWO
SWANSON            HARRY           05 TUESDAY   , NINETEEN NINETY-THREE

9 rows selected.
```

Converting Strings to Dates

Not surprisingly, the conversion of string values to dates is similar to the conversion of dates to strings. Instead of using the TO_CHAR built-in function, we'll use the TO_DATE built-in function because our goal is to specify a date value using a legal date format. The arguments of the TO_DATE function are the reverse of the arguments of the TO_CHAR function.

```
TO_DATE (string_value, date_format)
```

For example, if you want to convert a string that doesn't use the Oracle default date format (DD-MON-YY), you would use the TO_DATE function. The following example will display the number of days that have elapsed since the American Bicentennial.

```
SQL> select SYSDATE - TO_DATE('07-04-1976','MM-DD-YYYY')
  2  from dual;

SYSDATE-TO_DATE('07-04-1976','MM-DD-YYYY')
------------------------------------------
                                 6878.9465
```

Using Dates in *INSERT, UPDATE,* and *DELETE* Statements

If you're trying to refer to a date column in an INSERT, UPDATE, or DELETE statement, you need to use the TO_DATE function to convert the string equivalent of the date or time to a valid date format, as in:

```
update Employee
set Hire_Date = TO_DATE('JAN 18, 1981','MON DD, YYYY')
where
Employee_ID = 1001
```

Dates and Time

Remember that every column defined using the date datatype contains both a date and a time value. If you are only interested in storing a time value in this column, the date value will be set to a default value. Here is a demonstration of the use of a common format for displaying times— HH:MI:SS.

```
SQL> select Employee_ID, to_char(Time_Clocked_In,'HH:MI:SS') Time_Clocked_In
  2  from Time_Clock
  3  order by Employee_ID;

EMPLOYEE_ID TIME_CLOCKED_IN
----------- --------------------------------------------------------------
       1002 09:02:03
       1003 08:51:12
       1004 08:59:33
       1005 09:22:12
```

Remember that the Oracle date datatype is capable of storing time to the nearest second.

If you wanted to use a 24-hour time format, the time format should be specified in the following way:

```
SELECT TO_CHAR(arrival_time,'HH24:MI:SS') FROM DUAL;
```

NOTE

It's very easy to confuse months and minutes in date and time formats. For instance, the following INSERT statement will be accepted by Oracle even though it really isn't what you intended:

```
INSERT INTO EMPLOYEE
(EMPLOYEE_ID, START_TIME)
VALUES
(1033,TO_CHAR('08:05','HH24:MM');
```

Oracle will interpret this statement as the start time for employee number 1033 is set to 8:00 AM and the month of May. Because MM will always be between 1 and 12, Oracle will always accept the supplied value even though it isn't what was intended.

Oracle also has a time format model that will enable you to express a time as seconds past midnight. In the following example, let's assume that the current time is 2:00 AM.

```
SELECT TO_CHAR(SYSDATE,'SSSSS') FROM DUAL;
```

```
7200     which is the equivalent of two hours
```

By using the time format model SSSSS, Oracle returns the time expressed in seconds past midnight. The time 2:00 AM represents two hours past midnight, which is equal to 7200 seconds.

If you are inserting a new row into a table and specifying a value for a date column using a time-only format model, the date value will be set to the first day of the month and year when the row was inserted.

```
insert into Customer
(Customer_ID, Last_Name, First_Name, Earliest_Time_to_Call)
values
(2001, 'KNUDSEN', 'MELANIE', to_date('09:00','HH24:MI'));
```

How to Deal with Fractions of a Second

If you need to keep track of time to a fraction of a second—say, milliseconds or microseconds—it's a good idea to continue to use the Oracle date datatype for storing hours, minutes, and seconds. You can then create a separate column in whatever units are appropriate. Let's look at an example.

Suppose you've been asked to keep track of the finish times for a group of marathon runners at your company. Because this group of runners is incredibly competitive, you need to store the time down to a resolution of a thousandth of a second. Using the advice given previously, you would add columns to the table for storing the number of milliseconds in the following way:

```
EMPLOYEE_ID             NUMBER
LAST_NAME               VARCHAR2(30)
FIRST_NAME              VARCHAR2(20)
BEST_TIME               DATE
BEST_TIME_MSEC          NUMBER
LATEST_TIME             DATE
LATEST_TIME_MSEC        NUMBER
```

This table is designed to store both the best marathon time and the latest marathon time for each runner.

Is It Morning or Afternoon: AM, PM, or a 24-Hour Format

By default, if you request to see the hours, minutes, and seconds for a date column, Oracle will return the hour without an indication of whether the hour is AM or PM. If you want to see AM or PM in dates, you need to append the time format with PM, as in:

```
TO_CHAR(order_date,'HH:MI:SS PM')
```

If you want to retrieve or specify the hour based upon a 24-hour clock, you must use HH24 in place of HH, as in:

```
TO_CHAR(order_date,'HH24:MI:SS')
```

Calculating the Differences Between Two Dates

Another advantage of using the Oracle date datatype is the date arithmetic that is available. You can add or subtract days from an existing date, as in:

```
select sysdate + 7 from dual;
```

By adding 7 to SYSDATE, we are able to obtain the date a week from the current date. In the same way, you can also subtract days from a date value to calculate an earlier date.

The following query will return a list of employee names and their respective termination dates minus one week for those employees who have been terminated; the employees in the list will be ordered in chronological order based on the employee's termination date.

```
SQL> select Last_Name, First_Name,
  2  Termination_Date, Termination_Date - 7
  3  from Employee
  4  where
  5  Termination_Date is not NULL
  6  order by Termination_Date;

LAST_NAME        FIRST_NAME       TERMINATI TERMINATI
---------------  ---------------  --------- ---------
HERNANDEZ        RANDY            25-NOV-89 18-NOV-89
BARRETT          SARAH            04-APR-91 28-MAR-91
```

To calculate the difference between two dates expressed in days, you simply subtract one date from the other. The following example demonstrates the calculation of the age, in days, of employees on the day of their termination of employment.

```
SQL> select Last_Name, First_Name,
  2  Termination_Date - Date_of_Birth Age_in_Days
  3  from Employee
  4  where
  5  Termination_Date is not NULL
  6  order by Termination_Date;

LAST_NAME        FIRST_NAME       AGE_IN_DAYS
---------------  ---------------  -----------
HERNANDEZ        RANDY                  12524
BARRETT          SARAH                  10578
```

Oracle also supplies a built-in function, MONTHS_BETWEEN, that can be used to calculate the difference between two dates in months. The function uses a 31-day month to perform the calculation and will return a fractional portion that corresponds to the fractional portion of a month, if applicable.

In conjunction with the built-in function MONTHS_BETWEEN, the function ADD_MONTHS can be used to add months to a date value. In the following example, we are using the MONTHS_BETWEEN function to return the age of an employee, in months, when they were hired and assign the value to the alias Age_When_Hired. Also, we are ordering the rows that are returned by the alias Age_When_Hired.

```
select months_between(Hire_Date,Date_of_Birth) Age_When_Hired
from Employee
order by Age_When_Hired;
```

The MONTHS_BETWEEN function will return a fractional portion if the difference between the dates is not evenly divisible by 31.

If You've Got the Time: Handling Time Zones

Retrieving records in chronological order is straightforward. Using our example, let's imagine that you want to retrieve the list of customers according to the date when the record was created. The SELECT statement is

```
select Last_Name, First_Name
from Customer
order by Creation_Date;
```

Oracle will place the customer records in chronological order based on the date and time when the record was created. Customers who were entered into the system on the same date will be sorted using the time portion of CREATION_DATE.

It is also possible to sort these records in reverse chronological order.

```
select Last_Name, First_Name
from Customer
order by Creation_Date DESC;
```

where DESC represents descending order. Oracle assumes ascending order as the default for any columns listed in the order clause. However, you can specify ascending order with the abbreviation ASC, if you think that it helps to clarify the SQL syntax, as in:

```
select Last_Name, First_Name
from Customer
order by Creation_Date ASC;
```

Dealing with Changing Time Zones

Depending on your application requirements, you may find that you need to be able to easily convert a time from one time zone to another. Fortunately, Oracle provides a built-in function, NEW_TIME, that does exactly that.

NEW_TIME requires three arguments:

- The date value to be converted
- The current time zone of the date value
- The new time zone

NEW_TIME will return the time (and possibly date) in the specified time zone.

Let's rely once again on our sample application—the repair store. Jim Helmholtz, owner of Frayed Wires, is very cautious in his dealings with customers. As you may recall, Jim has instructed you to provide a column in the CUSTOMER table to keep track of the earliest and latest times of the day to contact a customer regarding a repair. However, because Jim's store is located in Venice, California, his store is frequented by many out-of-towners, some of whom rely on Frayed Wires to have their consumer electronics repaired. Because of this, Jim also wanted to keep track of the time zone of each customer's residence.

One of Jim's customers, Randolph McPherson, lives in a small village on the coast of Newfoundland. On his customer information card, McPherson indicated that he did not want to be bothered with calls before 10:00 AM or after 8:00 PM—local time.

Assuming that daylight saving time is not yet in effect, how can you construct a SELECT statement that will provide the earliest and latest times for calling McPherson in Jim's local time zone—Pacific Standard Time?

```
select to_char(new_time(Earliest_Time_to_Call,Time_Zone,'PST'),'HH24:MI'),
to_char(new_time(Latest_Time_to_Call,Time_Zone,'PST'),'HH24:MI')
from Customer
where
Last_Name = 'MCPHERSON'

05:30           15:30
```

With a single SELECT statement, we are able to convert the earliest and latest times for contacting any customer, regardless of what time zone they're located in. You'll also notice that we've embedded the NEW_TIME function within the TO_CHAR function. Table 11.3 contains a list of time zones that work with the NEW_TIME function.

Table 11.3. List of U.S. time zones.

Time Zone	Description
AST	Atlantic Standard Time
ADT	Atlantic Daylight Saving Time
BST	Bering Standard Time
BDT	Bering Daylight Time
CST	Central Standard Time
CDT	Central Daylight Saving Time
EST	Eastern Standard Time
EDT	Eastern Daylight Saving Time
GMT	Greenwich Mean Time
HST	Alaska-Hawaii Standard Time
HDT	Alaska-Hawaii Daylight Saving Time

continues

Table 11.3. continued

Time Zone	Description
MST	Mountain Standard Time
MDT	Mountain Daylight Saving Time
NST	Newfoundland Standard Time
PST	Pacific Standard Time
PDT	Pacific Daylight Saving Time
YST	Yukon Standard Time
YDT	Yukon Daylight Saving Time

Daylight Saving Time

The discussion about time conversion brings up an important question to consider—is daylight saving time in effect or not? Unfortunately, there is no single built-in function that you can use to determine this. But you can use a series of built-in functions to determine whether or not daylight saving time is in effect.

Daylight saving time goes into effect on the first Sunday in April. If the date in question falls during the months of January, February, March, November, or December, daylight saving time is not in effect. If the date in question falls during the months of May, June, July, August, or September, daylight saving time is in effect. If the date in question falls during the month of April, we need to follow the following algorithm:

1. Determine the day of the week on which April 1 falls. We'll embed the TO_DATE function within the TO_CHAR function so that '01-APR-95' is a date value rather than a string. Let's refer to the value returned by the following query as D.

   ```
   select to_char(to_date('01-APR-95'),'D')
   from dual
   ```

   ```
   7
   ```

2. The value returned from the query (7) represents the day of the week that April 1, 1995 falls on: Saturday. We now need to calculate how many days there are from that day until Sunday.

   ```
   if D = 1 then
           April 1 falls on a Sunday
   else
           First Sunday = April 1 + (7 - D + 1) days
   ```

   For 1995, we add:

   ```
   7 - D + 1 = 7 - 7 + 1 = 1 day to April 1, 1995
   ```

   and therefore, April 2, 1995 is the first Sunday in the month of April.

3. If the date that we're interested in occurs on or after April 2, then we know that daylight saving time is in effect.

The Julian Day Format

The concept of a Julian day was developed by Joseph Scaliger in 1582. Its purpose was to create a time period of 7,980 years that would simplify the calculation of the number of days between two different dates. Essentially, the Julian day (or number, as it is sometimes called) is the number of days since January 1, 4712 B.C. The Julian day is commonly used by astronomers in a variety of calculations. In our era, the Julian day is just shy of 2.5 million days.

So, if you're not Carl Sagan or Stephen Hawking, is there any value in using a Julian day format? The answer is maybe. If you need to calculate the difference between two date and time values to the second, you may want to consider using the Julian day format. Let's see how this format works. To view the current date in the default date format and its equivalent Julian day:

```
select sysdate, to_char(sysdate,'J') from dual;
```

```
15-APR-95 2449823
```

Calculating the Difference in Seconds Between Two Dates

Using the Julian day date format, let's look at an example of how the difference between two dates, expressed in seconds, can be calculated. Suppose our fictitious store owner, Jim Helmholtz, is becoming rather compulsive. He is no longer interested in knowing the number of days that each employee has been working at his repair store, Frayed Wires. He now wants you to provide a SELECT statement that will let him know how long they have been employed to the nearest second!

Let's make some assumptions.

- Each employee began work at midnight on his or her hire date.
- We will count the elapsed time since the hire date, not just the working hours.
- Each day is composed of 86,400 seconds (24 hours/day × 60 minutes/hour × 60 seconds/minute).

```
SQL> select Last_Name, First_Name,
  2  (to_number(to_char(sysdate,'J')) -
  3   to_number(to_char(Hire_Date,'J'))) * 86400 +
  4  to_number(to_char(sysdate,'SSSSS')) Length_of_Employment
  5  from Employee
  6  order by Length_of_Employment;
```

LAST_NAME	FIRST_NAME	LENGTH_OF_EMPLOYMENT
SWANSON	HARRY	61944927
CARSON	BETH	75509727

```
GILROY        MAX                    82508127
YEN           CINDY                 123202527
HIGGINS       BEN                   196469727
BARRETT       SARAH                 198716127
GLEASON       PAUL                  349656927
HERNANDEZ     RANDY                 361666527
SMITH         JEAN                  412383327

9 rows selected.
```

Summary

This chapter covered the following issues involving date and time values:

- The Oracle date datatype stores date and time information to a resolution of a second.
- The Oracle date datatype should be used whenever possible, even when storing only date or only time information.
- SYSDATE is a pseudocolumn that will always return the current date and time down to the second.
- The default Oracle date format is DD-MON-YY—for example, 01-JAN-96 for January 1, 1996.
- The TO_CHAR function is used to convert date values to strings.
- The TO_DATE function is used to convert strings to date values.

12

Handling Numbers

In Chapter 10, "Manipulating Strings," you learned about the use of strings and string functions in Personal Oracle7. In Chapter 11, "Dealing with Dates," you explored the advantages of the date datatype and the related Oracle built-in functions. In this chapter, we'll investigate the use of numeric datatypes in Personal Oracle7.

Specifying a Numeric Column

A column's datatype is specified in the CREATE TABLE and ALTER TABLE statements. The general syntax for specifying a numeric datatype is

```
NUMBER ([precision [, scale]])
```

where *precision* is an optional argument that specifies the number of digits of precision that Oracle should store for column values, and where *scale* is an optional argument indicating the number of digits to the right of the decimal point that Oracle should store for column values.

If you don't specify *precision* or *scale*, Oracle allows a number of up to 38 digits of precision to be stored—the maximum precision that Oracle offers. When you specify a column, it's an excellent idea to limit the width of numeric values by using an appropriate precision. For example, if a column stores a patient's body temperature in degrees Fahrenheit, you would specify the column as:

```
Body_Temp_F Number(4,1)
```

A precision of 4 and a scale of 1 allows Body_Temp_F to store a total of four digits, including one digit to the right of the decimal point. As a result, Oracle accepts the following values.

```
SQL> update Patient
  2   set Body_Temp_F = 99.2
  3   where
  4   Patient_ID = 'A2002';

1 row updated.

SQL> update Patient
  2   set Body_Temp_F = 103.8
  3   where
  4   Patient_ID = 'E3893';

1 row updated.
```

The column definition prevents a bad value from accidentally being stored in the table.

```
SQL> update Patient
  2   set Body_Temp_F = 1003.8
  3   where
  4   Patient_ID = 'N3393';
set Body_Temp_F = 1003.8
                   *
ERROR at line 2:
ORA-01438: value larger than specified precision allows for this column
```

Of course, this definition for Body_Temp_F allows values up to 999.9 degrees Fahrenheit—an impossible value for humans. In addition to specifying the precision and scale, you also need to specify a CHECK constraint for this column to restrict its values to a range. I illustrate how this is done in Chapter 13, "Defining Table and Column Constraints," in a discussion of table and column constraints.

If you specify a value for *precision* but not for *scale*, Oracle truncates the fractional value of a real number before storing the value in the column. Consider the following examples.

```
SQL> create table Number_Demo (
  2  Int_Value    number(3),
  3  Real_Value   number(3,1),
  4  Num_Value    number);

Table created.

SQL> insert into Number_Demo
  2  (Int_Value)
  3  values
  4  (1234);
(1234)
 *
ERROR at line 4:
ORA-01438: value larger than specified precision allows for this column


SQL> insert into Number_Demo
  2  (Int_Value)
  3  values
  4  (12.2);

1 row created.

SQL> select Int_Value
  2  from Number_Demo;

INT_VALUE
---------
       12
```

If values for *precision* and *scale* have been furnished and you store a numeric value whose scale exceeds the column's scale, Oracle truncates the fractional value to the column's scale.

```
SQL> insert into Number_Demo
  2  (Real_Value)
  3  values
  4  (3.144);

1 row created.

SQL> select Real_Value
  2  from Number_Demo;

REAL_VALUE
----------
       3.1
```

In addition to the NUMBER datatype, Oracle accepts the following keywords that describe a numeric column.

- NUMERIC, DECIMAL, and DEC
- INTEGER, INT, and SMALLINT
- FLOAT, DOUBLE PRECISION, and REAL

These other datatypes are supported by Oracle to provide compatibility with ANSI SQL and other relational database systems such as IBM SQL/DS and DB2. The NUMERIC, DECIMAL, and DEC datatypes are identical to the NUMBER datatype. INTEGER, INT, and SMALLINT are translated to NUMBER(38). FLOAT, DOUBLE PRECISION, and REAL are all translated to NUMBER. Unless you are converting a database schema from some non-Oracle database, you should generally use the NUMBER datatype when specifying columns.

How Oracle Stores Numbers

Oracle doesn't store numbers in the manner of programming languages such as C and Fortran. A floating point variable in C requires the same amount of storage regardless of its value. In Oracle, the number of bytes used to store a number depends on the number's precision. To illustrate this fact, you can use an Oracle built-in function called VSIZE, which returns the number of bytes used by its argument. The following code fragment is a query of a table that contains a number column named Num_Value. To the right of the column value is VSIZE(Num_Value)—which returns the number of bytes used to store Num_Value. Oracle is able to store two digits of precision in one byte. Another byte is used for storing the sign and exponent.

```
SQL> select Num_Value, vsize(Num_Value)
  2  from Number_Demo;

NUM_VALUE VSIZE(NUM_VALUE)
--------- ----------------
      123                3
     1234                3
    12345                4
   123456                4
  1234567                5
 12345678                5
123456789                6
12345.679                6
```

Converting a Number to a String

You will typically want to convert a numeric value to a string value for two reasons.

- To change the display format of a number in a form or report
- To concatenate a numeric expression with a string for use in a form or report

Automatic Conversion of a Number to a String

In some situations, SQL automatically converts a number to a string. For example, if you perform an INSERT or UPDATE, Oracle converts a specified number to a character value if it is being stored in a VARCHAR2 column.

```
SQL> insert into Product
  2  (Product_ID, Manufacturer_ID, Initial_Retail_Value)
  3  values
  4  ('D1001',1001,500);

1 row created.
```

If you look at the row that was just inserted, you can see that the number 1001, which was used to specify a value for Manufacturer_ID, has been converted to a VARCHAR2 value of 1001, which is stored in the Manufacturer_ID column.

```
SQL> select Product_ID, Manufacturer_ID, Initial_Retail_Value
  2  from Product
  3  where
  4  Product_ID = '&Product_ID';
Enter value for product_id: D1001
old   4: Product_ID = '&Product_ID'
new   4: Product_ID = 'D1001'

PRODUCT_ MANUFA INITIAL_RETAIL_VALUE
-------- ------ --------------------
D1001    1001                    500
```

Using *TO_CHAR* to Convert a Number to a String

The TO_CHAR function is used to *explicitly* convert a number to a string. Its syntax is

```
TO_CHAR (number [,format])
```

where *number* is the numeric expression to be converted, and *format* is the optional format model to be used by TO_CHAR.

Here's an example of using TO_CHAR without a format. Notice that the first column—Real_Value—is right-justified by SQL*Plus, whereas the second column—to_char(Real_Value)—is left-justified by SQL*Plus because it is a character column.

```
SQL> select Real_Value, to_char(Real_Value)
  2  from Number_Demo;

REAL_VALUE TO_CHAR(REAL_VALUE)
---------- ---------------------------------------
     3.1 3.1
```

Here is an appropriate point to discuss the Oracle number format model. The following code segments show the most important format model elements—the ones that you'll rely on most often.

To specify the number of digits to display, use 9 for each digit. You also can add a comma and decimal point to the specified format.

```
SQL> select Product_ID, to_char(Initial_Retail_Value,'9,999.99')
  2  from Product
  3  order by Product_ID;

PRODUCT_ID    TO_CHAR(I
-----------   ---------
A2001            350.00
A504             585.00
A509             850.00
A903           1,050.00
B311             185.00
```

To display a number with leading zeros, use 0 at the beginning of the format.

```
SQL> select Product_ID, to_char(Initial_Retail_Value,'0,999.99')
  2  from Product
  3  order by Product_ID;

PRODUCT_ID    TO_CHAR(I
-----------   ---------
A2001          0,350.00
A504           0,585.00
A509           0,850.00
A903           1,050.00
B311           0,185.00
```

To display a leading dollar sign, begin the format with a $.

```
SQL> select Product_ID, to_char(Initial_Retail_Value,'$9,999.99')
  2  from Product
  3  order by Product_ID;

PRODUCT_ID    TO_CHAR(IN
-----------   ----------
A2001            $350.00
A504             $585.00
A509             $850.00
A903           $1,050.00
B311             $185.00
```

To have a negative value enclosed in angle brackets, add PR to the format.

```
SQL> select Symbol, to_char(Last_qtr_EPS,'$99.99PR')
  2  from Security_Price
  3  order by Symbol;

SYMBO TO_CHAR(
----- --------
ABC    <$.58>
ACME   $1.81
ZGEGE  <$.18>
```

To return the sign of each value, add S to the format.

```
SQL> select Symbol, to_char(Last_qtr_EPS,'S99.99')
  2  from Security_Price
  3  order by Symbol;

SYMBO TO_CHA
----- -------
ABC      -.58
ACME   +1.81
ZGEGE    -.18
```

Finally, if you want a number to appear in scientific notation, follow the specified precision with EEEE.

```
SQL> select Num_Value, to_char(Num_Value,'9.9999EEEE')
  2  from Number_Demo
  3  order by Num_Value;

NUM_VALUE TO_CHAR(NUM_
--------- ------------
      123   1.2300E+02
     1234   1.2340E+03
    12345   1.2345E+04
12345.679   1.2346E+04
```

Converting a String to a Number

The TO_NUMBER function is the converse of TO_CHAR: it is used to convert a character expression to a number by specifying a format. The syntax for TO_NUMBER is

TO_NUMBER (*string* [,*format*])

where *string* is the character expression to be converted, and *format* is the optional format model to be used by TO_NUMBER.

TO_NUMBER uses the same format model as TO_CHAR. As an example, here is how you would convert a string value, representing earnings per share, to a number.

```
SQL> update Security_Price
  2  set Last_Qtr_EPS = to_number('$2.81','$999.99')
  3  where
  4  Symbol = 'ZGEGE';

1 row updated.

SQL> select Symbol, Last_Qtr_EPS
  2  from Security_Price
  3  where
  4  Symbol = 'ZGEGE';

SYMBO LAST_QTR_EPS
----- ------------
ZGEGE         2.81
```

Using Statistical Built-In Functions

Oracle furnishes the following statistical functions that are actually group functions.

■ AVG(*value*), which computes the average, or mean, of its argument from the set of rows to which it is applied

■ STDDEV(*value*), which returns the standard deviation of its argument from the set of rows it operates upon

■ VARIANCE(*value*), which returns the variance of its argument from the set against which it is exercised

Because these are group functions, their use is described in detail in Chapter 14, "More Sophisticated Queries."

Rounding and Truncating Numbers

Oracle provides four built-in functions related to rounding and truncating fractional numbers.

```
ROUND(value,[scale])
TRUNC(value,[scale])
FLOOR(value)
CEIL(value)
```

where *value* is a numeric expression, and *scale* is an optional argument indicating the number of digits that the function should use for rounding or truncating (the default is 0).

Let's look at an example of how each function can be utilized.

ROUND

The ROUND function has two arguments: the numeric expression and an optional number of digits to be used for rounding. If the second argument isn't supplied, ROUND returns the value of its numeric argument rounded to the nearest integer. If the second argument is supplied, ROUND returns the value of its numeric argument rounded to the nearest fractional number with the specified number of digits to the right of the decimal point. ROUND can be used with literal values, as in the following example.

```
SQL> select round(123.2) from dual;

ROUND(123.2)
------------
         123

SQL> select round(123.27,1) from dual;

ROUND(123.27,1)
---------------
           123.3
```

```
SQL> select round(101.8) from dual;

ROUND(101.8)
------------
         102
```

The ROUND function also accepts numeric expressions.

```
SQL> select Current_Used_Value*0.87, Round(Current_Used_Value*0.87)
  2  from Product;

CURRENT_USED_VALUE*0.87 ROUND(CURRENT_USED_VALUE*0.87)
----------------------- ------------------------------
                  217.5                            218
                  339.3                            339
                 587.25                            587
                 717.75                            718
                  330.6                            331
```

TRUNC

The TRUNC function is similar to the ROUND function. However, instead of rounding to the nearest integer, TRUNC removes the fractional portion of its numeric argument. You can supply a literal number to TRUNC.

```
SQL> select trunc(123.33), trunc(123.567,2)
  2  from dual;

TRUNC(123.33)  TRUNC(123.567,2)
-------------  ----------------
          123            123.56
```

TRUNC also accepts numeric expressions.

```
SQL> select Current_Used_Value*0.87, Trunc(Current_Used_Value*0.87)
  2  from Product;

CURRENT_USED_VALUE*0.87 TRUNC(CURRENT_USED_VALUE*0.87)
----------------------- ------------------------------
                  217.5                            217
                  339.3                            339
                 587.25                            587
                 717.75                            717
                  330.6                            330
```

FLOOR

The FLOOR function is almost identical to the TRUNC function, except that FLOOR cannot truncate to a fractional number. The FLOOR function returns the integer that is less than or equal to its numeric argument.

```
SQL> select floor(128.3), floor(129.8)
  2  from dual;

FLOOR(128.3) FLOOR(129.8)
------------ ------------
         128          129
```

The argument for FLOOR can also be a numeric expression.

```
SQL> select Current_Used_Value*0.87, Floor(Current_Used_Value*0.87)
  2  from Product;

CURRENT_USED_VALUE*0.87 FLOOR(CURRENT_USED_VALUE*0.87)
----------------------- -----------------------------
                  217.5                           217
                  339.3                           339
                 587.25                           587
                 717.75                           717
                  330.6                           330
```

CEIL

The CEIL function returns a *ceiling* integer for its numeric argument—the smallest integer that is greater than or equal to its argument. CEIL can accept constants.

```
SQL> select ceil(128.3), ceil(129.8)
  2  from dual;

CEIL(128.3) CEIL(129.8)
----------- -----------
        129         130
```

CEIL's argument can also be a numeric expression.

```
SQL> select Current_Used_Value*0.87, Ceil(Current_Used_Value*0.87)
  2  from Product;

CURRENT_USED_VALUE*0.87 CEIL(CURRENT_USED_VALUE*0.87)
----------------------- ----------------------------
                  217.5                          218
                  339.3                          340
                 587.25                          588
                 717.75                          718
                  330.6                          331
```

Finding the Largest or Smallest Value

The MAX and MIN functions can be used to retrieve the largest and smallest values for a particular column in a table. Technically, MAX and MIN are group functions. However, you aren't required to specify the SELECT statement's GROUP BY clause to use these functions. As an example, here is how you would retrieve the largest and smallest estimates for labor costs from the Depot Estimate table.

```
SQL> select min(Labor_Cost), max(Labor_Cost)
  2  from Depot_Estimate;

MIN(LABOR_COST) MAX(LABOR_COST)
--------------- ---------------
             56             202
```

The preceding query retrieves the smallest and largest values for the Labor_Cost column found in the entire Depot_Estimate table. But suppose you want to compare the value of two or more columns. Specifically, let's assume that you need to find the largest cost—labor or parts. In this case, the MAX and MIN functions won't work because they each can accept only a single argument. However, there are two functions that can serve this purpose: GREATEST and LEAST. The syntax for these functions is quite simple.

```
GREATEST(expression1, ... ,expressionN)
LEAST(expression1, ... ,expressionN)
```

where *expression1* through *expressionN* are valid SQL expressions.

Using the GREATEST function, you submit the following query to retrieve whichever is larger—Labor_Cost or Parts_Cost.

```
SQL> select greatest(Labor_Cost,Parts_Cost)
  2  from Depot_Estimate;

GREATEST(LABOR_COST,PARTS_COST)
- - - - - - - - - - - - - - - - - - - - - - - - - - - - -
                            202
                            123
                            183
                            103
                            104
                            151

6 rows selected.
```

Oracle returns an error message if the datatypes of the expressions don't match.

```
SQL> select greatest(Labor_Cost,Estimated_Date_for_Completion)
  2  from Depot_Estimate;
select greatest(Labor_Cost,Estimated_Date_for_Completion)
                          *
ERROR at line 1:
ORA-00932: inconsistent datatypes
```

The GREATEST and LEAST functions don't indicate which value was largest or smallest. To obtain that information, you can use the DECODE function in conjunction with GREATEST and LEAST in the following way.

```
SQL> select decode(greatest(Labor_Cost,Parts_Cost),
  2               Labor_Cost,'Labor',
  3               Parts_Cost,'Parts'),
  4          greatest(Labor_Cost,Parts_Cost)
  5  from Depot_Estimate;

DECODE( GREATEST(LABOR_COST,PARTS_COST)
- - - - - - -  - - - - - - - - - - - - - - - - - - - - - - - - - - -
Labor                               202
Labor                               123
Parts                               183
Labor                               103
Parts                               104
Parts                               151

6 rows selected.
```

Now, let's analyze this query in detail. The first argument to the DECODE function is the expression that you want to decode—in this case, GREATEST(Labor_Cost,Parts_Cost). First, you compare the value returned by GREATEST to the value of Labor_Cost, and if the values are equal, DECODE returns the string Labor. If they're not equal, DECODE compares the value returned by GREATEST to the value of Parts_Cost, and if those two values are equal, DECODE returns the string Parts.

The next SELECT statement illustrates how to use the DECODE function to return a string value that concatenates the type of cost—Labor or Parts—with the amount.

```
SQL> select decode(greatest(Labor_Cost,Parts_Cost),
  2                 Labor_Cost,'Labor = ' || to_char(Labor_Cost),
  3                 Parts_Cost,'Parts = ' || to_char(Parts_Cost),
  4                 'Unknown')
  5  from Depot_Estimate;

DECODE(GREATEST(LABOR_COST,PARTS_COST),LABOR_COS
------------------------------------------------
Labor = 202
Labor = 123
Parts = 183
Labor = 103
Parts = 104
Parts = 151

6 rows selected.
```

The previous query is just another example of how a function can be used as the argument to another function. In this case, the TO_CHAR function, when concatenated with a literal string, is an argument to the DECODE function.

Determining If a Value Is Null

When developing an Oracle application, you are bound to encounter situations in which a screen or report will return information about a column that can be null. Sometimes, you'll want to return a specific value in place of a null value. Fortunately, Oracle furnishes the NVL function, which makes the replacement. Here is the syntax:

NVL (*column-value*, *substitute-value*)

where *column-value* is the column value to evaluate, and *substitute-value* is the value that the NVL function will return if *column-value* is null.

Consider the following situation. The Repair Header table records the amount, if any, that the customer has placed on deposit toward the repair. If you select Deposit_Amount from Repair_Header, some of the values for Deposit_Amount are blank.

```
SQL> select Repair_ID, Deposit_Amount
  2  from Repair_Header
  3  order by Repair_ID;
```

```
REPAIR_ID DEPOSIT_AMOUNT
--------- --------------
      501            125
      502
      503            120
      504
      505             85
      506

6 rows selected.
```

You can use the NVL function to return a zero instead of a null.

```
SQL> select Repair_ID, NVL(Deposit_Amount,0.0)
  2    from Repair_Header
  3    order by Repair_ID;

REPAIR_ID NVL(DEPOSIT_AMOUNT,0.0)
--------- -----------------------
      501                     125
      502                       0
      503                     120
      504                       0
      505                      85
      506                       0

6 rows selected.
```

The NVL function can be used as an argument for other Oracle built-in functions. For instance, you can query the Repair Header table for the average deposit.

```
SQL> select avg(Deposit_Amount)
  2    from Repair_Header;

AVG(DEPOSIT_AMOUNT)
-------------------
                110
```

When you embed the NVL function inside the AVG function, the result is different.

```
SQL> select avg(NVL(Deposit_Amount,0.0))
  2    from Repair_Header;

AVG(NVL(DEPOSIT_AMOUNT,0.0))
----------------------------
                         55
```

The reason for the difference is that the null values are not used by the AVG function, whereas the zero values returned by NVL are used by AVG.

Miscellaneous Numeric Functions

The following code segments show some additional built-in mathematical functions that Oracle provides. These functions can be used in all four DML statements: SELECT, INSERT, UPDATE, and DELETE.

The function EXP(*n*) returns the value of the mathematical constant *e* raised to the *n*th power.

```
SQL> select exp(2.1) from dual;

 EXP(2.1)
----------
8.1661699
```

LN(*n*) returns the natural logarithm of *n*, where *n* is greater than 0.

```
SQL> select ln(1.0), ln(2.781828) from dual;

   LN(1.0) LN(2.781828)
---------- ------------
         0    1.0231083
```

The function LOG(*m*, *n*) returns the logarithm of *n*, using a base of *m*.

```
SQL> select log(10,1), log(10,2) from dual;

LOG(10,1) LOG(10,2)
---------- ---------
         0   .30103
```

POWER(*m*, *n*) returns the value of *m* raised to the *n*th power.

```
SQL> select power(10,2), power(2,16) from dual;

POWER(10,2) POWER(2,16)
----------- -----------
        100       65536
```

The function SQRT(*n*) returns the square root of *n*. If *n* is less than zero, Oracle returns an error. Here is an example of its use:

```
SQL> select sqrt(256) from dual;

SQRT(256)
----------
        16
```

```
SQL> select sqrt(-0.001) from dual;
ERROR:
ORA-01428: argument '-.001' is out of range
```

The *MOD* Function

MOD provides the modulus function in Oracle SQL. Its syntax is

MOD(*m*, *n*)

where *m* is a number, and *n* is divided into *m*.

MOD returns the remainder of *m* divided by *n*.

```
SQL> select mod(23,5)
  2  from dual;
```

```
MOD(23,5)
---------
        3
```

The *ABS* Function

The ABS function returns the absolute value of its argument, as shown in the following example.

```
SQL> select abs(-21.34), abs(131)
  2  from dual;

ABS(-21.34)  ABS(131)
-----------  --------
      21.34       131
```

The *SIGN* Function

The SIGN function returns the location of its numeric argument relative to zero. SIGN(*value*) returns the following indicators:

- ■ -1 if *value* is less than zero
- ■ 0 if *value* is equal to zero
- ■ 1 if *value* is greater than zero

Following is an example of how SIGN works.

```
SQL> select sign(-22), sign(0), sign(7.2)
  2  from dual;

SIGN(-22)   SIGN(0) SIGN(7.2)
---------  -------- ---------
       -1         0         1
```

Converting a Number to Its ASCII Character Value

Another built-in function—CHR—converts an integer expression to its equivalent ASCII character. Here is an example:

```
SQL> select chr(60), chr(120)
  2  from dual;

C C
- -
< x
```

Trigonometric Functions

Oracle provides six built-in trigonometric functions. For each function, the argument is expressed in radians.

SIN(*value*) returns the sine of *value*.

```
SQL> select sin(3.14159/2) from dual;

SIN(3.14159/2)
--------------
             1
```

The function COS(*value*) returns the cosine of *value*.

```
SQL> select cos(0) from dual;

   COS(0)
----------
         1
```

TAN(*value*) returns the tangent of *value*.

```
SQL> select tan(3.14159/4) from dual;

TAN(3.14159/4)
--------------
     .99999867
```

The function SINH(*value*) returns the hyperbolic sine of *value*.

```
SQL> select sinh(3.14159/6) from dual;

SINH(3.14159/6)
---------------
      .54785297
```

COSH(*value*) returns the hyperbolic cosine of *value*.

```
SQL> select cosh(3.14159/6) from dual;

COSH(3.14159/6)
---------------
      1.1402381
```

The function TANH(*value*) returns the hyperbolic tangent of *value*.

```
SQL> select tanh(3.14159/6) from dual;

TANH(3.14159/6)
---------------
      .48047244
```

Summary

Keep the following concepts in mind when you are constructing SQL statements for your application.

- Specify numeric columns with the NUMBER datatype.
- You can convert a numeric expression to a string with the TO_CHAR function.
- You can convert a character expression to a number by using the TO_NUMBER function.
- MAX and MIN are group functions that will return the maximum and minimum values for a particular column from a set of rows.
- The GREATEST and LEAST functions determine the largest and smallest values from multiple numeric columns.
- Use the NVL function to return a different value—such as zero or N/A—in place of the null value.

13

Defining Table and Column Constraints

Every information system must maintain data and referential integrity. In addition, an information system must also enforce the business rules of the organization that it serves. In the past, many information systems were monolithic—an in-house developed software package accessing a single database residing on a single mainframe computer. Occasionally, third-party utilities were used to access the database, but not always.

Today, systems commonly employ a variety of off-the-shelf client tools to access and modify a database. As a result, it's critical that information is protected at the server level as well as the client level. It isn't sufficient to enforce security at the client application through menu options and other mechanisms. In this chapter, we explore the use of table and column constraints to preserve data and referential integrity and enforce business rules.

To begin, let's review the basic steps for defining primary and foreign keys.

Using a Primary Key

You should be sure to define a primary key for every table in your database. This is necessary for a few reasons. First, a primary key prevents duplicate rows from being inserted into a table; depending on the circumstances, duplicate rows can be a nuisance, or they can cause an application to crash. Second, a table must have a primary key if it is going to be referenced by a foreign key in another table.

Defining a Primary Key During Table Creation

You can define a table's primary key in the CREATE TABLE statement with the following syntax:

```
CREATE TABLE table-name
(column-definition1,
...
column-definitionN,
[CONSTRAINT constraint-name] PRIMARY KEY (column1,...,columnN))
```

The variables include the following:

> table-name is a valid Oracle table name.
>
> column-definition1 through column-definitionN are legal column declarations.
>
> constraint-name is a constraint name that is assigned to the primary key constraint.
>
> column1 through columnN are the columns that compose the primary key.

Here is how you would define a primary key on the Product table:

```
SQL>
  1  CREATE TABLE Product
  2       (Product_ID              VARCHAR2(12) NOT NULL,
  3        Manufacturer_ID         VARCHAR2(6) NOT NULL,
  4        Description             VARCHAR2(2000),
  5        Date_of_Manufacture     DATE,
```

```
6          Initial_Retail_Value      NUMBER(7,2),
7          Current_Used_Value        NUMBER(7,2),
8          Replacement_Product       VARCHAR2(30),
9          Created_Date              DATE,
10         Created_By                VARCHAR2(30),
11         Modified_Date             DATE,
12         Modified_By               VARCHAR2(30),
13         Constraint Product_PK Primary Key (Product_ID, Manufacturer_ID)
14* );
```

```
Table created.
```

The following SQL statements illustrate how the primary key prevents duplicate rows from being inserted into the table. A duplicate row is defined as a row whose primary key columns have the same values as those of another row. The following code reveals that the primary key is enforced even though the INSERT transaction hasn't been committed.

```
SQL> insert into Product
  2  (Product_ID, Manufacturer_ID, Initial_Retail_Value)
  3  values
  4  ('B101','KANIN', 500);

1 row created.

SQL> insert into Product
  2  (Product_ID, Manufacturer_ID, Initial_Retail_Value)
  3  values
  4  ('B101','KANIN',600);
insert into Product
       *
ERROR at line 1:
ORA-00001: unique constraint (FRAYED_WIRES.PRODUCT_PK) violated
```

You also have the option of defining the primary key after the table has been created.

TIP

If you don't provide a constraint name, Oracle automatically creates constraint names for each of the table and column constraints that you define. The Oracle-generated names are fairly cryptic, and you won't know what they are unless you query the Oracle data dictionary view named USER_CONSTRAINTS. In several situations, you need to know a constraint name. For example, when you want to drop a foreign key, you'll need to drop the constraint associated with the foreign key. Unless you've supplied the constraint name for the foreign key, you'll have to look up the constraint name. Therefore, it's always a good idea to provide Oracle with constraint names for primary and foreign keys. Consider naming primary key constraints as tablename_PK and foreign key constraints as tablename_column_FK, staying within the 30-character limit on Oracle object names.

Defining a Primary Key After Table Creation

To define a primary key constraint for an existing table, use the ALTER TABLE statement.

```
SQL> CREATE TABLE Product
  2         (Product_ID              VARCHAR2(12) NOT NULL,
  3          Manufacturer_ID         VARCHAR2(6) NOT NULL,
  4          Description             VARCHAR2(2000),
  5          Date_of_Manufacture     DATE,
  6          Initial_Retail_Value    NUMBER(7,2),
  7          Current_Used_Value      NUMBER(7,2),
  8          Replacement_Product     VARCHAR2(30),
  9          Created_Date            DATE,
 10          Created_By              VARCHAR2(30),
 11          Modified_Date           DATE,
 12          Modified_By             VARCHAR2(30));

Table created.
```

If the existing table contains duplicate rows, Oracle returns an error message when you attempt to define the primary key.

```
SQL> insert into Product
  2  (Product_ID, Manufacturer_ID, Initial_Retail_Value)
  3  values
  4  ('B101','KANIN', 500);

1 row created.

SQL> insert into Product
  2  (Product_ID, Manufacturer_ID, Initial_Retail_Value)
  3  values
  4  ('B101','KANIN', 500);

1 row created.

SQL> alter table Product add
  2  Constraint Product_PK Primary Key (Product_ID, Manufacturer_ID);
alter table Product add
*
ERROR at line 1:
ORA-02299: cannot add or enable constraint (FRAYED_WIRES.PRODUCT_PK)-
duplicate keys found
```

Let's review how primary and foreign keys work in concert to enforce referential integrity.

The Foreign Key and Referential Integrity

A foreign key in a table is a column, or set of columns, whose values are restricted to those of the primary key in another table. It's in your best interest to define foreign keys whenever possible. For client/server applications, the first line of defense for referential integrity is the client application software. The last line of defense for referential integrity is the primary and foreign keys that have been defined for the database.

As with a primary key, a foreign key can be declared when a table is first created.

Declaring a Foreign Key During Table Creation

To illustrate the definition of a foreign key, let's refer to the Product and Manufacturer tables in the Frayed Wires sample database. Each manufacturer is assigned a unique ID that is kept in the column Manufacturer_ID. To address the possibility that two manufacturers could use the same product ID, we'll store Manufacturer_ID in the Product table. To uniquely identify rows in the Product table, we'll declare the primary key to be Product_ID and Manufacturer_ID.

```
SQL> CREATE TABLE Manufacturer
  2        (Manufacturer_ID          VARCHAR2(6) NOT NULL,
  3         Manufacturer_Name        VARCHAR2(30) NOT NULL,
  4         Street_Address           VARCHAR2(60),
  5         City                     VARCHAR2(30),
  6         State                    VARCHAR2(2),
  7         Zipcode                  VARCHAR2(9),
  8         Telephone_Number         VARCHAR2(10),
  9         Fax_Number               VARCHAR2(10),
 10         Created_Date             DATE NOT NULL,
 11         Created_By               VARCHAR2(30) NOT NULL,
 12         Modified_Date            DATE,
 13         Modified_By              VARCHAR2(30),
 14         Constraint Manufacturer_PK Primary Key (Manufacturer_ID));

Table created.

SQL> CREATE TABLE Product
  2        (Product_ID               VARCHAR2(12) NOT NULL,
  3         Manufacturer_ID          VARCHAR2(6) NOT NULL
  4         Constraint Manufacturer_ID_FK
             References Manufacturer(Manufacturer_ID),
  5         Description              VARCHAR2(2000),
  6         Date_of_Manufacture      DATE,
  7         Initial_Retail_Value     NUMBER(7,2),
  8         Current_Used_Value       NUMBER(7,2),
  9         Replacement_Product      VARCHAR2(30),
 10         Created_Date             DATE,
 11         Created_By               VARCHAR2(30),
 12         Modified_Date            DATE,
 13         Modified_By              VARCHAR2(30),
 14         Constraint Product_PK Primary Key (Product_ID, Manufacturer_ID));

Table created.
```

After the foreign key has been defined, referential integrity is enforced.

```
SQL> insert into Product
  2  (Product_ID, Manufacturer_ID, Description)
  3  values
  4  ('X1000','SCH100','VCR, Stereo-HiFi, 4-Head');
insert into Product
            *
ERROR at line 1:
ORA-02291: integrity constraint (FRAYED_WIRES.MANUFACTURER_ID_FK)
violated - parent key not found
```

As an alternative, you can opt not to specify the datatype for a column that is a foreign key. For example, the next example doesn't include VARCHAR2(6) in the declaration of Manufacturer_ID. Instead, Oracle looks up the datatype and width for the Manufacturer_ID column in the Manufacturer table and uses those definitions when creating the Product table.

```
SQL> CREATE TABLE Product
  2          (Product_ID              VARCHAR2(12) NOT NULL,
  3           Manufacturer_ID         NOT NULL
  4           Constraint Manufacturer_ID_FK
             References Manufacturer(Manufacturer_ID),
  5           Description             VARCHAR2(2000),
  6           Date_of_Manufacture     DATE,
  7           Initial_Retail_Value    NUMBER(7,2),
  8           Current_Used_Value      NUMBER(7,2),
  9           Replacement_Product     VARCHAR2(30),
 10           Created_Date            DATE,
 11           Created_By              VARCHAR2(30),
 12           Modified_Date           DATE,
 13           Modified_By             VARCHAR2(30),
 14           Constraint Product_PK Primary Key (Product_ID, Manufacturer_ID));

Table created.

SQL> desc Product
 Name                               Null?     Type
 -------------------------------- --------- ----
 PRODUCT_ID                       NOT NULL VARCHAR2(12)
 MANUFACTURER_ID                  NOT NULL VARCHAR2(6)
 DESCRIPTION                               VARCHAR2(2000)
 DATE_OF_MANUFACTURE                       DATE
 INITIAL_RETAIL_VALUE                      NUMBER(7,2)
 CURRENT_USED_VALUE                        NUMBER(7,2)
 REPLACEMENT_PRODUCT                       VARCHAR2(30)
 CREATED_DATE                              DATE
 CREATED_BY                                VARCHAR2(30)
 MODIFIED_DATE                             DATE
 MODIFIED_BY                               VARCHAR2(30)
```

The advantage of not declaring a datatype for a foreign key column is that you are guaranteed that the foreign key column will have the same datatype definition as its primary key counterpart. The disadvantage is that you can't determine the foreign key column's datatype by examining the CREATE TABLE statement.

Declaring a Foreign Key After Table Creation

As an alternative to declaring a foreign key when you create a table, you have the option of declaring a foreign key on an existing table with the ALTER TABLE statement.

```
SQL> create table AP_Detail (
  2  Bill_Number            NUMBER(4) NOT NULL,
  3  Vendor_Invoice_Number  VARCHAR2(10) NOT NULL,
  4  Item_Number            NUMBER(3) NOT NULL,
```

```
 5  Billed_Amount            NUMBER(8,2) NOT NULL,
 6  Approved_Amount          NUMBER(8,2),
 7  Paid_Amount              NUMBER(8,2));

Table created.

SQL> alter table AP_Detail add constraint AP_Detail_Vendor_Inv_Num_FK
  2  foreign key (Vendor_Invoice_Number) references AP_Header;

Table altered.
```

Primary and Foreign Key Columns

When you define a foreign key, Oracle verifies the following:

- There is a primary key defined for the table referenced by the foreign key.

- The number of columns composing the foreign key matches the number of primary key columns.

- The datatype and width of each foreign key column matches the datatype and width of each primary key column.

As an example, suppose there are two tables: Employee and Employee Dependent. The primary key of the Employee table is Employee_ID. Of course, the Employee Dependent table also contains Employee_ID.

```
SQL> desc employee
Name                            Null?     Type
------------------------------- --------  ----
EMPLOYEE_ID                     NOT NULL  NUMBER(4)
LAST_NAME                       NOT NULL  VARCHAR2(30)
FIRST_NAME                      NOT NULL  VARCHAR2(20)
MIDDLE_INITIAL                            CHAR(1)
HIRE_DATE                       NOT NULL  DATE
TERMINATION_DATE                          DATE
DATE_OF_BIRTH                             DATE
MONTHLY_SALARY                            NUMBER(5)
MANAGER                         NOT NULL  CHAR(1)
USERNAME                                  VARCHAR2(31)

SQL> desc employee_dependent
Name                            Null?     Type
------------------------------- --------  ----
EMPLOYEE_ID                     NOT NULL  VARCHAR2(4)
LAST_NAME                                 VARCHAR2(30)
FIRST_NAME                                VARCHAR2(20)
MIDDLE_INITIAL                            CHAR(1)
RELATIONSHIP                              VARCHAR2(30)
```

Observe that the Employee table's definition for Employee_ID is NUMBER(4), but the Employee Dependent table's definition for Employee_ID is VARCHAR2(4). As a result, Oracle does not allow the foreign key to be defined for Employee_ID in Employee_Dependent, which references Employee_ID in Employee.

```
SQL> alter table Employee_Dependent add Constraint Employee_Dependent_FK1
  2              Foreign Key (Employee_ID) references Employee;
            Foreign Key (Employee_ID) references Employee
                            *
ERROR at line 2:
ORA-02256: number, type and size of referencing columns must match
referenced columns
```

Disabling and Enabling Key Constraints

As I've mentioned previously, primary and foreign key constraints enforce two crucial aspects of the relational model: data and referential integrity. For at least two tasks, it's often convenient to disable these constraints—the task of designing the database and the task of migrating the organization's legacy data.

The Process of Designing a Database

A database is usually designed for an organization that has existing information, both computer-based and paper-based. The database design process is not a one-time task; rather, it is iterative. Regardless of how simple or complex the organization's operations may be, the analysis and design process can be boiled down to these steps:

1. You develop an initial logical data model by interviewing a cross-section of organization members, analyzing the organization's business processes, and inspecting existing automated and manual forms, reports, and data.

2. You present the developed logical data model to a cross-section of users and obtain feedback from the users—to correct erroneous assumptions on your part, missing entities and attributes, and exceptions of which you weren't aware.

3. You incorporate the user feedback into the logical data model and present the refined logical data model.

During this process, you will want to look at legacy data to determine if your logical data model is appropriate. The terms *legacy system* and *legacy data* refer to the existing information system and its data. The quality of the legacy data depends on how well legacy application software has enforced data and referential integrity. The legacy data may be very *clean*; there may be no duplicate records and no illegal field values. However, this is the exception rather than the rule in the vast majority of cases. Most legacy data contains some duplicate records. Field values may not correspond to the meaning of the field—for example, an N/A in a field used to store order quantity. Referential integrity may be violated in numerous instances. As a result, it isn't feasible to load legacy data into an Oracle database in which data and referential integrity are properly enforced. Consider the following example.

Suppose you've designed a set of Oracle tables to support accounts payable operations. Two of the tables are

■ AP_Header

■ Vendor

The legacy system has files that correspond to the AP_Header and Vendor tables.

■ APMASTR

■ VENDORS

You've already loaded the contents of APMASTR and VENDORS into *intermediate* Oracle tables—tables that are structurally equivalent to the legacy files. Here are the contents of the intermediate tables:

```
SQL> select BILLNO, VENDID, VINVNO
  2  from APMASTR;

  BILLNO VENDID VINVNO
-------- ------ ----------
    1001 M202   AG7001
    1002 S501   TR2111
    1003 G309   QE03911
    1004 T703   WE09834
    9101 N/A    N/A

SQL> select VENDID, COMPNAME
  2  from VENDORS;

VEND COMPNAME
---- ----------------------------------------
M202 METATRON INDUSTRIES
S501 SOLIPSISM INC.
G309 GOLIATH BUSINESS SYSTEMS CO.
T703 TRANSWORLD STONE INC.
```

Now that the intermediate Oracle tables have been loaded, you decide to insert the rows into the *final* tables—AP_Header and Vendor.

```
SQL> insert into Vendor
  2  (Vendor_ID, Company_Name)
  3  select VENDID, COMPNAME
  4  from VENDORS;

4 rows created.

SQL> commit;

Commit complete.

SQL> insert into AP_Header
  2  (Bill_Number, Vendor_ID, Vendor_Invoice_Number)
  3  select BILLNO, VENDID, VINVNO
  4  from APMASTR;
insert into AP_Header
*
ERROR at line 1:
```

```
ORA-02291: integrity constraint (FRAYED_WIRES.AP_HEADER_VENDOR_ID_FK)
violated - parent key not found
```

When you look at the contents of APMASTR, it's evident why Oracle has rejected the records. For Bill_Number 9101, the Vendor_ID is listed as N/A—not applicable, as documented in the legacy data. However, there is no row in the Vendor table in which Vendor_ID is N/A. Accordingly, the INSERT statement violates the referential integrity constraint, and the rows aren't inserted into AP_Header.

In reality, there could be many legacy records—hundreds or thousands—that violate declared constraints. As a temporary measure, you can disable these constraints in this manner:

```
SQL> alter table AP_Header disable constraint AP_Header_Vendor_ID_FK;

Table altered.

SQL> insert into AP_Header
  2  (Bill_Number, Vendor_ID, Vendor_Invoice_Number)
  3  select BILLNO, VENDID, VINVNO
  4  from APMASTR;

5 rows created.

SQL> commit;

Commit complete.
```

After the bad data has been corrected or removed, the constraint can be enabled.

```
SQL> delete from AP_Header
  2  where Bill_Number = 9101;

1 row deleted.

SQL> alter table AP_Header enable constraint AP_Header_Vendor_ID_FK;

Table altered.

SQL> select Bill_Number, Vendor_ID, Vendor_Invoice_Number
  2  from AP_Header;

BILL_NUMBER VENDOR VENDOR_INV
----------- ------ ----------
       1001 M202   AG7001
       1002 S501   TR2111
       1003 G309   QE03911
       1004 T703   WE09834
```

Dropping a Primary Key

During the database design process, you may need to drop a table's primary key. To do this, use the ALTER TABLE statement with this syntax:

```
ALTER TABLE table-name DROP PRIMARY KEY;
```

where table-name is the table associated with the primary key.

For the sake of illustration, suppose you create a table for the storage of accounts payable data and define the primary key to be the Vendor's invoice number.

```
SQL> create table AP_Header (
  2  Bill_Number             NUMBER(4) NOT NULL,
  3  Vendor_Invoice_Number   VARCHAR2(10) NOT NULL,
  4  Vendor_ID               VARCHAR2(6)  NOT NULL,
  5  Date_Received           DATE         NOT NULL,
  6  Bill_Status             VARCHAR2(5),
  7  PRIMARY KEY (Vendor_Invoice_Number));

Table created.
```

After inspecting some data and pondering this definition, you realize that it's possible for two different vendors to supply the same invoice number. Therefore, you drop the primary key for the table.

```
SQL> alter table AP_Header drop primary key;

Table altered.
```

What if you've already declared a foreign key in the AP_Detail table that references the primary key of AP_Header? If that is the case, Oracle does not allow you to drop AP_Header's primary key.

```
SQL> create table AP_Detail (
  2  Bill_Number             NUMBER(4) NOT NULL,
  3  Vendor_Invoice_Number   VARCHAR2(10) NOT NULL,
  4  Item_Number             NUMBER(3) NOT NULL,
  5  Billed_Amount           NUMBER(8,2) NOT NULL,
  6  Approved_Amount         NUMBER(8,2),
  7  Paid_Amount             NUMBER(8,2),
  8  Constraint AP_Detail_FK Foreign Key (Vendor_Invoice_Number)
  9            References AP_Header);

Table created.

SQL> alter table AP_Header drop primary key;
alter table AP_Header drop primary key
*
ERROR at line 1:
ORA-02273: this unique/primary key is referenced by some foreign keys
```

There is an option to the DROP PRIMARY KEY clause; you can use the keyword CASCADE. Use this feature with caution! CASCADE drops the primary key as well as any foreign keys that reference it.

```
SQL> alter table AP_Header drop primary key cascade;

Table altered.
```

Dropping a Foreign Key

During the database design process, you may find that you've mistakenly defined a column as a foreign key. Dropping a foreign key is a bit different than dropping a primary key. Because a table can have more than one foreign key, the ALTER TABLE statement requires that you supply the constraint name associated with the foreign key, using this syntax:

```
ALTER TABLE table-name DROP CONSTRAINT constraint-name;
```

where *table-name* is the table associated with the primary key, and *constraint-name* is the constraint associated with the foreign key.

For instance, suppose there is an additional column in the AP_Header table named Vendor_Status, which, coincidentally, has the same datatype and width as Vendor_ID. You mistakenly create a foreign key for Vendor_Status that references the primary key of the Vendor table.

```
SQL> desc AP_Header
 Name                             Null?    Type
 -------------------------------- -------- ----
 BILL_NUMBER                      NOT NULL NUMBER(4)
 VENDOR_INVOICE_NUMBER            NOT NULL VARCHAR2(10)
 VENDOR_ID                        NOT NULL VARCHAR2(6)
 DATE_RECEIVED                    NOT NULL DATE
 BILL_STATUS                               VARCHAR2(5)
 VENDOR_STATUS                             VARCHAR2(6)

SQL> alter table AP_Header add constraint AP_Header_Vendor_Status_FK
  2                             foreign key (Vendor_Status) references Vendor;

Table altered.
```

After you try to insert a value into the Vendor_Status column, you quickly realize your error and drop the foreign key assigned to the column.

```
SQL> alter table AP_Header drop constraint AP_Header_Vendor_Status_FK;

Table altered.
```

Declaring Unique Constraints

In addition to primary and foreign keys, Oracle enables you to indicate that a column must have unique values. A unique constraint is not a substitute for a primary key constraint. As an example, most organizations assign a number to each employee—an employee number. On top of that, each employee also has a Social Security number, which is unique. But the Social Security number is an attribute of an employee, whereas the Employee_ID is used to uniquely identify rows in the Employee table.

```
SQL> create table Patient (
  2  Patient_ID              varchar2(6) primary key,
  3  Last_Name               varchar2(30) not null,
  4  First_Name              varchar2(20) not null,
  5  Middle_Name             varchar2(20),
  6  Social_Security_Number varchar2(9) unique,
  7  Insurance_Carrier_Code varchar2(4));

Table created.
```

```
SQL> insert into Patient
  2 (Patient_ID, Last_Name, First_Name)
  3 values
  4 ('A901', 'NORTON', 'ED');

1 row created.

SQL> insert into Patient
  2 (Patient_ID, Last_Name, First_Name, Social_Security_Number)
  3 values
  4 ('A902', 'KRAMDEN', 'RALPH', '123456789');

1 row created.

SQL> insert into Patient
  2 (Patient_ID, Last_Name, First_Name, Social_Security_Number)
  3 values
  4 ('A903', 'NORTON', 'TRIXIE', '123456789');
insert into Patient
            *
ERROR at line 1:
ORA-00001: unique constraint (FRAYED_WIRES.SYS_C00550) violated
```

Differences Between Primary Key and Unique Constraints

A couple of differences between primary key and unique constraints are worth noting. First, a table can have only one primary key—but it can have many unique constraints. Second, when a primary key is defined, the columns that compose the primary key are automatically mandatory. When a unique constraint is declared, the columns that compose the unique constraint are not automatically defined to be mandatory; you must also specify that the column is NOT NULL.

Table Indexes

It isn't possible to discuss primary and foreign key constraints without also discussing indexes—the topics are closely related. A table index is an Oracle object that contains the values that exist in one or more columns in a table. Let's discuss what table indexes are and how they are used by both the application developer and Oracle.

Oracle provides two types of table indexes: unique and nonunique. Unique indexes are used to enforce primary key and unique constraints. Nonunique indexes are used to improve query performance, which is discussed further in Chapter 30, "Oracle Internals." Both types of indexes are implemented internally via a B*-tree data structure. A B*-tree data structure is graphically depicted as a balanced, inverted tree in which each leaf represents an index value. It's critical that you keep the following concepts in mind when designing your application's database:

■ An ORDER BY clause in a SELECT statement can reference any column in a table—whether or not there is an existing index based on that column.

- An index cannot be composed of more than 16 columns.
- An index doesn't store NULL values.
- There is no SQL statement that will enable you to inspect the contents of an index.
- An index can only be created for a table, not a view.

Creating an Index

Here is the basic syntax to use when creating an index:

```
CREATE [UNIQUE] INDEX index-name
ON table-name (column1, ... columnN);
```

where *index-name* is the name to be given to the index (subject to Oracle database object-naming restrictions), *table-name* is the table for which the index is created, and *column1* through *columnN* are the columns to be used in creating the index.

Notice that the keyword UNIQUE is optional. If you don't include UNIQUE, the created index is nonunique. In other words, the nonunique index does not restrict the values of a set of columns in any way. If you include the keyword UNIQUE, the index prevents a duplicate set of column values from being stored in the table.

Let's take a straightforward example. The primary key of the Employee table is Employee_ID. However, you'll frequently query the Employee table based on an employee's last name. To improve the performance of those queries, you create an index.

```
SQL> create index Employee_Last_Name on Employee (Last_Name);

Index created.
```

Why You Shouldn't Create Unique Indexes

Although CREATE UNIQUE INDEX is a legal Oracle statement, you shouldn't use it; instead, declare PRIMARY KEY and UNIQUE constraints. There are two principal reasons for this:

- When you declare PRIMARY KEY and UNIQUE constraints, Oracle automatically creates the appropriate unique index to enforce the constraints.
- You won't be able to declare a FOREIGN KEY constraint unless you also declare a corresponding PRIMARY KEY constraint.

Mandatory Column Values: *NOT NULL* Constraints

When you declare a column as NOT NULL, Oracle treats the mandatory requirement as a constraint. In fact, this is the only constraint that can be seen with the SQL*Plus DESCRIBE command. Here is an illustration of this:

```
SQL> describe employee
Name                            Null?    Type
------------------------------- -------- ----
EMPLOYEE_ID                     NOT NULL NUMBER(4)
LAST_NAME                       NOT NULL VARCHAR2(30)
FIRST_NAME                      NOT NULL VARCHAR2(20)
MIDDLE_INITIAL                           CHAR(1)
HIRE_DATE                       NOT NULL DATE
TERMINATION_DATE                         DATE
DATE_OF_BIRTH                            DATE
MONTHLY_SALARY                           NUMBER(5)
MANAGER                         NOT NULL CHAR(1)
USERNAME                                 VARCHAR2(31)
```

The DESCRIBE command shows that the Employee table has five mandatory columns. This number is somewhat misleading because Employee_ID was defined as the table's primary key—which is automatically NOT NULL. You can use the Oracle data dictionary view named USER_CONSTRAINTS to see the constraints associated with a table. The columns returned by USER_CONSTRAINTS include:

- CONSTRAINT_NAME
- CONSTRAINT_TYPE
- SEARCH_CONDITION

Following are the results of a query of USER_CONSTRAINTS for all constraints associated with the Employee table. As shown, there are four NOT NULL constraints, a CHECK constraint on the Manager column, and a primary key constraint that is indicated by a value of P for Constraint_Type.

```
SQL> select constraint_name, constraint_type, search_condition
  2  from user_constraints
  3  where
  4  table_name = 'EMPLOYEE';


CONSTRAINT_NAME                 CONST SEARCH_CONDITION
------------------------------- ----- ----------------------------------------
SYS_C00517                      C     LAST_NAME IS NOT NULL
SYS_C00518                      C     FIRST_NAME IS NOT NULL
SYS_C00519                      C     HIRE_DATE IS NOT NULL
SYS_C00520                      P
SYS_C00521                      C     Manager in ('Y','N')
SYS_C00522                      C     MANAGER IS NOT NULL

6 rows selected.
```

You can provide a constraint name for a NOT NULL constraint in this manner:

```
SQL> create table demo_not_null (
  2  my_column number constraint Value_Required not null);

Table created.

SQL> select constraint_name, constraint_type, search_condition
  2  from user_constraints
  3  where
  4  table_name = 'DEMO_NOT_NULL';
```

```
CONSTRAINT_NAME                    CONST SEARCH_CONDITION
- - - - - - - - - - - - - - - - - - - - - - - - - - - - -  - - - - - - - - - - - - - - - - - - - - - - - - - - - - - - - - - - - - - -
VALUE_REQUIRED                     C     MY_COLUMN IS NOT NULL
```

Restricting Values with a Column *CHECK* Constraint

The CHECK constraint is a column-level constraint that serves at least two purposes.

■ Some columns—usually numeric values—do not have a set of discrete values that can be referenced with a foreign key. However, there is still a need to constrain the value of such a column to a particular range.

■ The legal range of a column is not constant; it must be calculated when the column value is inserted or updated.

The CHECK constraint is declared in a CREATE TABLE or ALTER_TABLE statement using this syntax:

```
column-name datatype [CONSTRAINT constraint-name] [CHECK (condition)]
```

with the variables defined in this way:

column-name is the column name.

datatype is the column's datatype, width, and scale.

constraint-name is the constraint name subject to Oracle database object-naming restrictions.

condition is a legal Oracle SQL condition that returns a boolean value.

To illustrate this concept, let's create a table that is used in a hospital database to store patient information. One of the columns in this table is the patient's body temperature in degrees Fahrenheit. It's a good idea to restrict the possible values of this column by defining it as NUMBER(4,1). But this still allows the storage of numbers from 0.0 to 999.9—including some obviously nonsensical values for body temperature. You can use a CHECK constraint to restrict the value from 60.0 (for patients suffering from hypothermia) to 110.0.

```
SQL> create table Patient (
  2  Patient_ID      varchar2(6) primary key,
  3  Body_Temp_Deg_F  number(4,1) constraint Patient_Body_Temp
  4                   Check (Body_Temp_Deg_F >= 60.0 and
  5                          Body_Temp_Deg_F <= 110.0));

Table created.

SQL> insert into Patient
  2  (Patient_ID, Body_Temp_Deg_F)
  3  values
  4  ('A1001', 98.6);

1 row created.
```

```
SQL> insert into Patient
  2 (Patient_ID, Body_Temp_Deg_F)
  3 values
  4 ('Q7777', 111.2);
('Q7777', 111.2)
             *
ERROR at line 4:
ORA-02290: check constraint (FRAYED_WIRES.PATIENT_BODY_TEMP) violated
```

You can use Oracle built-in SQL functions in a CHECK constraint. As an example, here is a CHECK constraint that verifies that a patient's insurance status is either Y or N:

```
SQL> create table Patient (
  2 Patient_ID       varchar2(6) primary key,
  3 Body_Temp_Deg_F  number(4,1) constraint Patient_Body_Temp
  4                    Check (Body_Temp_Deg_F >= 60.0 and
  5                           Body_Temp_Deg_F <= 110.0),
  6 Insurance_Status Char(1) constraint Patient_Insurance_Status
  7                    Check (Insurance_Status in ('Y','y','N','n')));

Table created.

SQL> insert into Patient
  2 (Patient_ID, Insurance_Status)
  3 values
  4 ('R4321','Y');

1 row created.

SQL> insert into Patient
  2 (Patient_ID, Insurance_Status)
  3 values
  4 ('U3030','U');
('U3030','U')
          *
ERROR at line 4:
ORA-02290: check constraint (FRAYED_WIRES.PATIENT_INSURANCE_STATUS) violated
```

A Column Can Have More Than One *CHECK* Constraint

There is no restriction on the number of CHECK constraints that can be defined for a column or a table. The following code is an example of a column—Amount_Approved—that has two constraints:

```
SQL> create table Loan_Application (
  2 Loan_Application_No     number(6) primary key,
  3 Borrower_Last_Name      varchar2(30) not null,
  4 Borrower_First_Name     varchar2(20) not null,
  5 Borrower_Middle_Name    varchar2(20),
  6 Amount_Requested        number(9,2) not null,
  7 Amount_Approved         number(9,2)
  8                         constraint Amount_Approved_Limit
  9                         check (Amount_Approved <= 1000000)
 10                         constraint Amount_Approved_Interval
 11                         check (mod(Amount_Approved,1000)=0)
 12 );

Table created.
```

```
SQL> insert into Loan_Application
  2  (Loan_Application_No, Borrower_Last_Name, Borrower_First_Name,
  3   Amount_Requested, Amount_Approved)
  4  values
  5  (2001, 'RUBRIK', 'STANLEY', 1000000, 999950);
insert into Loan_Application
                *
ERROR at line 1:
ORA-02290: check constraint (FRAYED_WIRES.AMOUNT_APPROVED_INTERVAL) violated


SQL> insert into Loan_Application
  2  (Loan_Application_No, Borrower_Last_Name, Borrower_First_Name,
  3   Amount_Requested, Amount_Approved)
  4  values
  5  (2001, 'RUBRIK', 'STANLEY', 1000000, 999000);

1 row created.

SQL> insert into Loan_Application
  2  (Loan_Application_No, Borrower_Last_Name, Borrower_First_Name,
  3   Amount_Requested, Amount_Approved)
  4  values
  5  (2001, 'RUBRIK', 'STANLEY', 1000000, 1001000);
insert into Loan_Application
                *
ERROR at line 1:
ORA-02290: check constraint (FRAYED_WIRES.AMOUNT_APPROVED_LIMIT) violated
```

In this example, there's no reason you can't combine both constraints into a single constraint. However, you should consider defining separate constraints if there might be a need to disable a single constraint while allowing other constraints to remain enabled.

Referencing Other Columns in a *CHECK* Constraint

One of the limitations of a column CHECK constraint is that it cannot reference other columns in the same table. Suppose you're responsible for defining a table for storing loan application information. In this table, Amount_Requested contains the loan amount requested by the borrower; Amount_Approved is the amount that was approved by the loan committee. The lender never approves an amount greater than that requested. However, you can't use a CHECK constraint to enforce this business rule.

```
SQL> create table Loan_Application (
  2  Loan_Application_No        number(6) primary key,
  3  Borrower_Last_Name         varchar2(30) not null,
  4  Borrower_First_Name        varchar2(20) not null,
  5  Borrower_Middle_Name       varchar2(20),
  6  Amount_Requested           number(9,2) not null,
  7  Amount_Approved            number(9,2)
  8                             constraint Amount_Approved_Limit
  9                             check (Amount_Approved <= Amount_Requested)
 10  );
)
*
```

```
ERROR at line 10:
ORA-02438: Column check constraint cannot reference other columns
```

However, you can use a table constraint to reference any column in a table. By adding a comma after the definition of Amount_Approved, the column constraint becomes a table constraint.

```
SQL> create table Loan_Application (
  2         Loan_Application_No      number(6) primary key,
  3         Borrower_Last_Name       varchar2(30) not null,
  4         Borrower_First_Name      varchar2(20) not null,
  5         Borrower_Middle_Name     varchar2(20),
  6         Amount_Requested         number(9,2) not null,
  7         Amount_Approved          number(9,2),
  8            constraint Amount_Approved_Limit
  9            check (Amount_Approved <= Amount_Requested)
 10  );

Table created.


SQL> insert into Loan_Application
  2  (Loan_Application_No, Borrower_Last_Name, Borrower_First_Name,
  3   Amount_Requested, Amount_Approved)
  4  values
  5  (2001, 'CRANDALL', 'JULIE', 300000, 310000);
insert into Loan_Application
                  *
ERROR at line 1:
ORA-02290: check constraint (FRAYED_WIRES.AMOUNT_APPROVED_LIMIT) violated


SQL> insert into Loan_Application
  2  (Loan_Application_No, Borrower_Last_Name, Borrower_First_Name,
  3   Amount_Requested, Amount_Approved)
  4  values
  5  (2001, 'CRANDALL', 'JULIE', 300000, 300000);

1 row created.
```

Using Pseudocolumns in a *CHECK* Constraint

A CHECK constraint cannot reference pseudocolumns such as SYSDATE, ROWNUM, and USER. If you need to define a business rule that refers to these pseudocolumns, rely on a database trigger to restrict column values. Chapter 22, "Enforcing Business Rules with Database Triggers," explains how database triggers are used to enforce business rules.

But What About the Children: Referential Integrity and the *UPDATE* and *DELETE* Statements

Referential integrity is enforced for all DML statements: INSERT, UPDATE, and DELETE. For instance, if you attempt to update a table so that a foreign key is set to a value that doesn't exist as a primary key in the referenced table, Oracle rejects the update.

```
SQL> update Repair_Item
  2 set
  3 Repair_ID = 509
  4 where
  5 Repair_ID = 506;
update Repair_Item
       *
ERROR at line 1:
ORA-02291: integrity constraint (FRAYED_WIRES.REPAIR_ITEM_REPAIR_ID_FK)
violated - parent key not found
```

Let's discuss the effect of UPDATE and DELETE on a primary key value.

Restricting Changes to a Primary Key

The default behavior of Oracle is to prevent changes to a primary key value if that primary key value has *children*. The children are the rows in other tables whose foreign key values refer to the primary key value to be changed. Using the repair store example, observe what happens if you try to delete Repair ID 505 from the Repair Header table.

```
SQL> set linesize 132
SQL> delete from Repair_Header
  2 where
  3 Repair_ID = 505;
delete from Repair_Header
*
ERROR at line 1:
ORA-02292: integrity constraint (FRAYED_WIRES.REPAIR_ITEM_REPAIR_ID_FK)
violated - child record found
```

Oracle rejects the DELETE statement because the Repair_Item table has one or more rows in which Repair ID is equal to 505. Similarly, Oracle also rejects an UPDATE statement that attempts to change the value of Repair ID from 505 to 999.

```
SQL> update Repair_Header
  2 set Repair_ID = 999
  3 where
  4 Repair_ID = 505;
update Repair_Header
        *
ERROR at line 1:
ORA-02292: integrity constraint (FRAYED_WIRES.REPAIR_ITEM_REPAIR_ID_FK)
violated - child record found
```

Cascading Deletes

Oracle provides an option for a foreign key constraint that causes the deletion of a primary key value to cascade to any child records that reference that value. To use the previous example, if Repair ID 505 was deleted from the Repair_Header table, the DELETE CASCADE option would cause the rows in the Repair_Item table in which Repair ID was 505 to also be deleted. The syntax for this feature is used in the following way:

```
SQL> alter table Repair_Item
  2  add constraint Repair_Item_Repair_ID_FK
  3  foreign key (Repair_ID) references Repair_Header
  4  on delete cascade;

Table altered.
```

Now, when Repair ID is deleted from Repair_Header, its child rows in Repair_Item are deleted automatically.

```
SQL> delete from Repair_Header
  2  where
  3  Repair_ID = 505;

1 row deleted.

SQL> select Repair_ID
  2  from Repair_Item
  3  where
  4  Repair_ID = 505;

no rows selected
```

Summary

Remember the following concepts when defining table and column constraints:

■ You can define a table's primary key by using the CREATE TABLE or ALTER TABLE statement.

■ You can drop a table's primary key with the ALTER_TABLE statement.

■ You can disable or enable a constraint by using the ALTER TABLE statement.

■ You can drop a constraint with the ALTER TABLE statement.

■ A table index can be defined for up to 16 columns.

■ A table index may be unique or nonunique.

■ Don't create unique indexes with the CREATE UNIQUE INDEX statement; let Oracle create them automatically by declaring primary key and unique constraints.

■ Use a CHECK constraint to restrict a column's value to a fixed or calculated range.

14

More Sophisticated Queries

Up to this point, you have seen how the SELECT statement is used to retrieve records from a single table. However, we've barely scratched the surface. In this chapter, we look at more advanced features of the SELECT statement: the GROUP BY clause, the HAVING clause, and the join operation. You'll see how powerful the SELECT statement truly is.

The syntax of the SELECT statement can be difficult to decipher; it's not feasible to understand the use of its clauses just by studying the syntax diagrams shown in the Oracle documentation. For this reason, you'll look at many examples in this chapter. I'll show you what works and what doesn't.

Built-In Group Functions

Let's begin by discussing the Oracle built-in functions that operate on groups of rows. Be warned: this topic is a good example of SQL's quirky characteristics. Even though these are group functions, they do *not* require the use of a GROUP BY clause.

- COUNT counts the number of rows that Oracle retrieves based on the supplied criteria.
- MAX and MIN return the maximum and minimum values for the specified column.
- AVG and SUM compute a column's average and total value.
- STDDEV and VARIANCE compute a column's standard deviation and variance.

Each of these functions returns a single value. Let's briefly examine some detailed examples.

The *COUNT* Function

The COUNT function comes in two flavors: COUNT(*), which counts all the rows in a table that satisfy any specified criteria, and COUNT(*column-name*), which counts all the rows in a table that have a non-null value for *column-name* and satisfy any specified criteria.

To demonstrate the use of COUNT(*), here is how you would count the number of customers who live in California.

```
SQL> select count(*)
  2  from Customer
  3  where
  4  State = 'CA';

 COUNT(*)
---------
        7
```

On the other hand, if you wanted to count the number of customers who have a fax number, you would supply Fax_Number as an argument to the COUNT function.

```
SQL> select count(Fax_Number)
  2  from Customer;
```

```
COUNT(FAX_NUMBER)
- - - - - - - - - - - - - - - -
                7
```

You can query the Customer table to verify that there really are only seven customers with fax numbers.

```
SQL> select Fax_Number
  2  from Customer;

FAX_NUMBER
- - - - - - - - - -
7145550123

5035551283
8015558194
3015558331
8085558183

8105558356
8105554199
```

```
15 rows selected.
```

The blank lines returned by the SELECT statement represent the null value returned for customer rows in which Fax_Number is NULL.

Observe that the COUNT function returns a single row—even if the count is zero.

```
SQL> select count(*)
  2  from Employee
  3  where
  4  Monthly_Salary > 100000;

COUNT(*)
- - - - - - - -
        0
```

Obtaining Maximum and Minimum Values

You can combine the MAX and MIN functions in a single SELECT statement. Here is an example of how this can be done.

```
SQL> select max(Initial_Retail_Value), min(Initial_Retail_Value)
  2  from Product;

MAX(INITIAL_RETAIL_VALUE) MIN(INITIAL_RETAIL_VALUE)
- - - - - - - - - - - - - - - - - - - - - - - - - -  - - - - - - - - - - - - - - - - - - - - - - - - -
                     2150                       185
```

You can use MAX and MIN with character values.

```
SQL> select min(Product_ID), max(Product_ID)
  2  from Product;

MIN(PRODUCT_ MAX(PRODUCT_
------------ ------------
A2001        TR901
```

You can also use MAX and MIN with date values.

```
SQL> select min(Hire_Date), max(Hire_Date)
  2  from Employee;

MIN(HIRE_ MAX(HIRE_
--------- ---------
10-APR-82 18-MAY-93
```

Using *AVG* and *SUM*

AVG and SUM work in the same way as MIN and MAX. For instance, you can retrieve the average and total of the estimated repair cost for each item brought in by customers.

```
SQL> select avg(Estimated_Cost), sum(Estimated_Cost)
  2  from Repair_Item;

AVG(ESTIMATED_COST) SUM(ESTIMATED_COST)
------------------- -------------------
              167.4                 837
```

Let's look at the data that the average calculation is based upon.

```
SQL> select Estimated_Cost
  2  from Repair_Item;

ESTIMATED_COST
--------------
           231

            83
           109
           102
           312
```

```
6 rows selected.
```

As you see, even though there are six rows in the Repair_Item table, there are only five non-null values for Estimated_Cost. The AVG function does not count null values in calculating the average: $(231+83+109+102+312)/5 = 167.4$.

Combining Group Functions with Other Columns

You cannot combine group functions and columns in the select list of a SELECT statement without using a GROUP BY clause. If you try to do this, Oracle returns the following error:

```
SQL> select max(Initial_Retail_Value), Manufacturer_ID
  2   from Product;
select max(Initial_Retail_Value), Manufacturer_ID
                                  *
ERROR at line 1:
ORA-00937: not a single-group group function
```

What is Oracle trying to tell you? It helps to think in these terms: a group function returns a single row, but Manufacturer_ID returns as many rows as exist in the table. It simply doesn't make sense to return both of these values at the same time—instead, Oracle returns an error message. However, by using a GROUP BY clause, you can combine group functions and columns in the select list. I explain the use of the GROUP BY clause in the next section.

Looking for Distinct Rows

There is an optional keyword in the SELECT statement that we haven't discussed: DISTINCT. This keyword follows SELECT and instructs Oracle to return only rows that have distinct values for the specified columns. As an example, you can obtain a list of the states in which customers live by using the following statement:

```
SQL> select distinct state from customer;

ST
--
AZ
CA
IL
MA
MI
OR
WA

7 rows selected.
```

The DISTINCT option is very useful for finding a column's set of values. It offers a method that you can use for quickly determining how values are clustered in a table.

Grouping Rows

The GROUP BY clause is another section of the SELECT statement. Although it is optional, the GROUP BY clause tells Oracle to group rows based on the distinct values that exist for the specified columns. In addition, the HAVING clause can be used in conjunction with the GROUP BY clause to further restrict the retrieved rows. Even though this topic is best explained by example, let's take a quick look at the syntax.

```
SELECT select-list
FROM table-list
[WHERE
condition [AND | OR]
```

```
...
condition]
[GROUP BY column1, column2, ..., columnN]
[HAVING condition]
[ORDER BY column1, column2, ...]
```

The variables are defined in the following ways:

> *select-list* is a set of columns and expressions from the tables listed in *table-list*.
>
> *table-list* is the tables from which rows are retrieved.
>
> *condition* is a valid Oracle SQL condition.
>
> *column1* through *columnN* are columns contained in *table-list*.

TIP

You'll find it quite easy to mix these elements into a SELECT statement that will be rejected by Oracle. In addition, you'll find that you can construct statements that Oracle processes without errors but whose results are difficult to interpret. When these things happen, it's best to go back to basics. Study your SELECT statement. If it no longer makes sense, use SQL*Plus to break it down, element by element, until it does. Analyze your use of group functions, the GROUP BY and HAVING clauses, and any join conditions.

Let's start with a simple example. Suppose you want to see a list of Manufacturer IDs found in the Product table.

```
SQL> select Manufacturer_ID
  2  from Product
  3  group by Manufacturer_ID;

MANUFAC
-------
GOL201
MIT501
SEN101
TES801
```

You can also add an ORDER BY clause to the statement so that the Manufacturer IDs are displayed in reverse alphabetic order.

```
SQL> select Manufacturer_ID
  2  from Product
  3  group by Manufacturer_ID
  4  order by Manufacturer_ID desc;

MANUFAC
-------
TES801
SEN101
MIT501
GOL201
```

If you want to count the number of rows that exist for each Manufacturer ID, you can use the following method:

```
SQL> select Manufacturer_ID, count(*)
  2  from Product
  3  group by Manufacturer_ID;

MANUFAC  COUNT(*)
-------  ---------
GOL201          1
MIT501          2
SEN101          6
TES801          6
```

Now, let's explore the use of both the GROUP BY and HAVING clauses. You can use the HAVING clause to retrieve only those Manufacturer IDs that have exactly two rows in the Product table.

```
SQL> select Manufacturer_ID, count(*)
  2  from Product
  3  group by Manufacturer_ID
  4  having count(*) = 2;

MANUFAC  COUNT(*)
-------  ---------
MIT501          2
```

Normally, group functions cannot be combined with columns in the select list—unless you use the GROUP BY clause. For instance, you can obtain the average initial retail value of products grouped by manufacturer.

```
SQL> select Manufacturer_ID, avg(Initial_Retail_Value)
  2  from Product
  3  group by Manufacturer_ID;

MANUFAC AVG(INITIAL_RETAIL_VALUE)
------- -------------------------
GOL201                        100
MIT501                        350
SEN101                     776.25
TES801                        551
```

Another use of the HAVING and GROUP BY clauses is the identification of duplicate rows. In an attempt to define a primary key for an existing table, you might find that the operation fails because there are duplicate values for the primary key columns.

```
SQL> alter table Patient add
  2  constraint Patient_PK
  3  primary key (Patient_ID);
alter table Patient add
*
ERROR at line 1:
ORA-02299: cannot add or enable constraint (FRAYED_WIRES.PATIENT_PK) -
duplicate keys found
```

By using the following query, you can identify the values of Patient_ID for which there are more than one row, identify which rows are bogus, and add the primary key.

```
SQL> select Patient_ID
  2  from Patient
  3  having count(*) > 1
  4  group by Patient_ID;

PATIEN
------
GG9999

SQL> select *
  2  from Patient
  3  where
  4  Patient_ID = 'GG9999';

PATIEN BODY_TEMP_DEG_F FEVER_CLASS
------ --------------- --------------
GG9999          107.6 LETHAL FEVER
GG9999            107

SQL> delete from Patient
  2  where Patient_ID = 'GG9999' and Body_Temp_Deg_F = 107;

1 row deleted.

SQL> alter table Patient add
  2  constraint Patient_PK
  3  primary key (Patient_ID);

Table altered.
```

Dealing with Hierarchical Information

I've included the topic of hierarchical information in this chapter—instead of one of the earlier chapters on SQL—to avoid confusion. Let me begin with an explanation of what I mean by *hierarchical information*. The classic example of relational database tables—Employee and Department (or EMP and DEPT)—is hierarchical: a department has many employees. This is actually a single-level hierarchy. A much better example of hierarchical data is a manufacturing Bill of Materials (BOM) that describes all of the parts, subassemblies, and assemblies that compose a finished product; an aircraft manufacturer might have a BOM that consists of thousands of levels and millions of parts.

Can relational databases in general and SQL in particular support this type of hierarchy? The answer: there's good news and bad news. The good news is that SQL does provide some support for hierarchical data via the CONNECT BY clause. The bad news is that the support is quite limited, and the syntax is not intuitive. Nevertheless, I'll show you an example of how to use SQL to navigate through hierarchical data.

To illustrate the use of the CONNECT BY clause, we'll use a slight variation of the Product tables that we've been using up to this point. For the moment, we'll focus on a table consisting of three columns.

■ Product_ID: The product of interest.

■ Assembly_ID: The assembly or subassembly to which the Product_ID belongs.

■ Description: The product description.

This table design is based upon the concept that every product belongs to the finished product or an assembly—except for the finished product itself. I've created some data to demonstrate this concept. A camera, the X1000, is composed of several parts and one subassembly, B200. The rows are

```
SQL> select Assembly_ID, Product_ID, Description
  2  from Product_Assembly
  3  order by Assembly_ID, Product_ID;

ASSEMBLY_ID          PRODUCT_ID    DESCRIPTION
-------------------  ------------  -------------------------------------------
B200                 I101          Titanium alloy, teflon-coated iris
B200                 S42           Variable-speed shutter, standard
B200                 W123          Manual film advance, winder
X1000                B200          Black body, stainless steel frame camera body
X1000                F100          Blue filter - standard
X1000                F55           Xenon flash unit
X1000                L100          100mm lens - standard
X1000                S04           4 foot camera strap, leather
                     X1000         Complete camera

9 rows selected.
```

Given the small quantity of data presented, you can almost *eyeball* the organization of the parts. However, the purpose of this example is to demonstrate how you can retrieve the organization of an arbitrarily large hierarchy. The SELECT statement contains two new clauses that I haven't yet presented: START WITH and CONNECT BY. The START WITH clause is used to identify the top-level row for which Oracle should retrieve subordinate rows—in this example, we're interested in finding the subordinate rows of the X1000. The CONNECT BY clause instructs Oracle on how the rows should be presented. With the PRIOR operator, we've specified that Oracle should present the rows so that each child row's Assembly_ID is equal to its parent row's Product_ID.

```
SQL> select lpad(' ',2*(level-1)) || Assembly_ID Assembly_ID,
  2  Product_ID, Description
  3  from Product_Assembly
  4  start with Product_ID = 'X1000'
  5  connect by prior Product_ID = Assembly_ID;

ASSEMBLY_ID          PRODUCT_ID    DESCRIPTION
-------------------  ------------  -------------------------------------------
                     X1000         Complete camera
  X1000              L100          100mm lens - standard
  X1000              B200          Black body, stainless steel frame camera body
    B200             S42           Variable-speed shutter, standard
    B200             I101          Titanium alloy, teflon-coated iris
    B200             W123          Manual film advance, winder
  X1000              S04           4 foot camera strap, leather
  X1000              F100          Blue filter - standard
  X1000              F55           Xenon flash unit

9 rows selected.
```

To indent each row to indicate its hierarchy level, I embedded LEVEL inside the LPAD function so that the number of blanks returned by LPAD corresponds to the hierarchy level. (LEVEL is a pseudocolumn that returns the hierarchy level for each row—from 1 for the highest level to N for the most detailed level.) LPAD is concatenated with Assembly_ID.

> **TIP**
>
> Be cautious of how you construct your data model. Be absolutely certain that you have to support hierarchical information before you employ CONNECT BY and START WITH.

To look at a particular subassembly, specify the Assembly_ID in the START WITH clause. The following SELECT statement illustrates how this is done; it also shows the value of LEVEL for each row.

```
SQL> select lpad(' ',2*(level-1)) ¦¦ Assembly_ID Assembly_ID,
  2  Product_ID, Level, Description
  3  from Product_Assembly
  4  start with Product_ID = 'B200'
  5  connect by prior Product_ID = Assembly_ID;


ASSEMBLY_ID     PRODUCT_ID  LEVEL DESCRIPTION
--------------- ----------- ----- ------------------------------------
X1000           B200          1 Black body, stainless steel frame camera body
  B200          S42           2 Variable-speed shutter, standard
  B200          I101          2 Titanium alloy, teflon-coated iris
  B200          W123          2 Manual film advance, winder
```

Using the *EXISTS* Operator

In addition to the other SQL operators, you should be familiar with another operator: the EXISTS operator. This operator operates on a subquery and returns the Boolean value:

- TRUE if the subquery returns at least one row
- FALSE if no rows are returned by the subquery

Consider the following example based on the Employee and Employee_Dependent tables. You've just received a call from your company's health insurance provider. To calculate a new rate for your company, they need a list of employees' hire dates, but only for those employees with dependents. Using the EXISTS operator, you submit this query:

```
SQL> select Last_Name, First_Name, Hire_Date
  2  from Employee E
  3  where
  4  exists
  5  (select * from Employee_Dependent D
  6  where
  7  E.Employee_ID = D.Employee_ID);
```

LAST_NAME	FIRST_NAME	HIRE_DATE
SMITH	JEAN	10-APR-82
GILROY	MAX	22-SEP-92

The EXISTS operator is useful in situations in which you're not interested in the column values returned by the subquery. Notice how table aliases were used to reduce the amount of typing (and improve the readability of the query). You can also preface the EXISTS operator with the logical operator NOT. For instance, you can change the previous query to return only the employees *without* dependents.

```
SQL> select Last_Name, First_Name, Hire_Date
  2  from Employee E
  3  where
  4  not exists
  5  (select * from Employee_Dependent D
  6  where
  7  E.Employee_ID = D.Employee_ID);
```

LAST_NAME	FIRST_NAME	HIRE_DATE
HERNANDEZ	RANDY	18-NOV-83
GLEASON	PAUL	05-APR-84
BARRETT	SARAH	16-JAN-89
HIGGINS	BEN	11-FEB-89
YEN	CINDY	09-JUN-91
CARSON	BETH	12-DEC-92
SWANSON	HARRY	18-MAY-93

```
7 rows selected.
```

Now that you have a working knowledge of SQL, it's time to delve into the world of joins. A join is used to retrieve rows from two or more tables that share a common set of values. A relational database would be of little value if it weren't for the join operation.

The Join Operation

The *join operation* is the mechanism that allows tables to be related to one another. A join operation retrieves columns from two or more tables. For instance, if you were joining two tables, the retrieval criteria would specify the condition that a column in the first table—which is defined as a foreign key—is equal to a column in the second table—which is the primary key referenced by the foreign key. A join's WHERE clause may contain additional conditions. This type of join operation is referred to as an *equi-join*. Let's look at the more general syntax for the SELECT statement that enables you to join more than two tables together.

```
SELECT select-list
FROM table1, table2, ... , tableN
WHERE table1.column1 = table2.column2 and
...
table2.column3 = tableN.columnN
...
additional-conditions
```

where the variables are defined:

> *select-list* is the set of columns and expressions from *table1* through *tableN*.
>
> *table1* through *tableN* are the tables from which column values are retrieved.
>
> *column1* through *columnN* are the columns in *table1* through *tableN* that are related.
>
> *additional-conditions* is optional query criteria.

Please note that there is no requirement that *column1* through *columnN* be referenced in the *select-list*.

To illustrate how this syntax is employed, let's look at a simple two-table join.

A Simple Two-Table Join

As you recall, the repair store database includes the Repair Header and Customer tables. The Repair Header table contains basic information about a customer's repair ID. As you'd expect, the Customer table contains customer data. If you look at the Repair Header table, you can retrieve only one piece of information about the customer: the Customer ID. By joining the Repair Header table with the Customer table based on the Customer_ID column, you can retrieve additional customer data.

```
SQL> select Repair_id, Last_Name, First_Name
  2  from Repair_Header, Customer
  3  where
  4  Repair_Header.Customer_ID = Customer.Customer_ID
  5  order by Repair_ID;

REPAIR_ID LAST_NAME                        FIRST_NAME
--------- ------------------------------   ----------------------------
      501 Martinez                         Steve
      502 Smyth                            Julie
      503 Horace                           Michelle
      504 Pareski                          Monica
      505 Moran                            Sarah
```

Let's look at each element of the SELECT statement. The select list consists of the three columns of interest: Repair_ID, Last_Name, and First_Name. The list of tables is made up of Repair_Header and Customer. The WHERE clause instructs SQL to return only rows in which Customer_ID in the Repair_Header table can be matched up with a row in the Customer table that has the same value for Customer_ID.

Oracle doesn't require that the order of the columns in the column list correspond to the order of the tables that follow FROM. For instance, it's perfectly acceptable to structure the query in this way:

```
SQL> select Last_Name, First_Name, Repair_ID
  2  from Repair_Header, Customer
  3  where
  4  Repair_Header.Customer_ID = Customer.Customer_ID
  5  order by Last_Name;
```

```
LAST_NAME                       FIRST_NAME                      REPAIR_ID
------------------------------- ------------------------------- ----------
Horace                          Michelle                              503
Martinez                        Steve                                 501
Moran                           Sarah                                 505
Pareski                         Monica                                504
Smyth                           Julie                                 502
```

The query lists Last_Name, First_Name, and Repair_ID even though Repair_Header is listed before Customer in the table list.

Ambiguous Columns

You need to keep in mind that each reference to a column in a join must be unambiguous. In this context, *unambiguous* means that if the column exists in more than one of the tables referenced in the join, the column name is qualified by the table name. Oracle returns an error message if you reference a column ambiguously.

```
SQL> select Customer_ID, Last_Name, First_Name, Repair_ID
  2  from Repair_Header, Customer
  3  where
  4  Repair_Header.Customer_ID = Customer.Customer_ID
  5  order by Last_Name;
select Customer_ID, Last_Name, First_Name, Repair_ID
       *
ERROR at line 1:
ORA-00918: column ambiguously defined
```

Oracle returns the error message because Customer_ID, which is referenced in the first line of the SELECT statement, appears in both the Repair_Header and Customer tables. To correct this, you must qualify the Customer_ID column with the table name.

```
SQL> select Customer.Customer_ID, Last_Name, First_Name, Repair_ID
  2  from Repair_Header, Customer
  3  where
  4  Repair_Header.Customer_ID = Customer.Customer_ID
  5  order by Last_Name;

CUSTOMER_ID LAST_NAME            FIRST_NAME       REPAIR_ID
----------- -------------------- ---------------- ----------
       1005 Horace               Michelle               503
       1002 Martinez             Steve                  501
       1008 Moran                Sarah                  505
       1006 Pareski              Monica                 504
       1003 Smyth                Julie                  502
```

Beware of the Cartesian Product

When you're first learning to join multiple tables, it's quite common to forget to provide a join condition in the WHERE clause. If this happens, you'll notice two things: the query takes considerably longer to execute, and the number of retrieved records is much larger than you expected. The technical term for this result is the *Cartesian product*.

Consider the example of the Repair Header and Customer tables. If you join these two tables without specifying a join condition, here's what happens:

```
SQL> select Customer.Customer_ID, Last_Name, First_Name, Repair_ID
  2  from Repair_Header, Customer
  3  order by Last_Name;
```

CUSTOMER_ID	LAST_NAME	FIRST_NAME	REPAIR_ID
1009	Chen	Laura	501
1009	Chen	Laura	502
1009	Chen	Laura	503
1009	Chen	Laura	506
1009	Chen	Laura	505
1009	Chen	Laura	504
6102	Fleming	Harry	501
6102	Fleming	Harry	502
6102	Fleming	Harry	504
6102	Fleming	Harry	503
6102	Fleming	Harry	506
6102	Fleming	Harry	505
2222	Fray		501
2222	Fray		503
2222	Fray		505
2222	Fray		506
2222	Fray		504
2222	Fray		502
6105	Hernandez	Ruby	501
.			
.			
.			
6101	Sorrel	JAMES	502
6101	Sorrel	JAMES	503
6101	Sorrel	JAMES	504
6101	Sorrel	JAMES	505
6101	Sorrel	JAMES	506

```
90 rows selected.
```

In this example, the Repair Header table has six rows, and the Customer table has fifteen rows. There is no join condition instructing Oracle to retrieve the columns from each table based on Customer_ID. As a result, Oracle returns all possible combinations of the two tables, which is six times fifteen, or ninety rows.

Multiple-Table Joins

As you see, the syntax for the SELECT statement doesn't limit the number of tables that can be joined. As an example, you can join these three tables—Repair Header, Repair Item, and Product—to retrieve a description of each repair item.

```
SQL> select R.Repair_ID, Customer_ID, Item_Number, Description
  2  from Repair_Header R, Repair_Item I, Product P
  3  where
  4  R.Repair_ID = I.Repair_ID and
  5  I.Product_ID = P.Product_ID and
```

```
6    I.Manufacturer_ID = P.Manufacturer_ID
7    order by R.Repair_ID, Item_Number;
```

```
REPAIR_ID CUSTOMER_ID ITEM_NUMBER DESCRIPTION
--------- ----------- ----------- ----------------------------------------
      501        1002           1 CD PLAYER, SINGLE-DISK
      502        1003           1 CCD Camera
      503        1005           1 Pre-amp, 120 W per channel
      504        1006           1 PRE AMPLIFIER 150 WATTS/CHANNEL
      505        1008           1 AMP, PROFESSIONAL 800W RMS PER CHANNEL
      506        1010           1 Tuner
      506        1010           2 PREAMP, 460 W/RMS
```

```
7 rows selected.
```

Notice that an alias has been specified for each of the three tables:

■ R for Repair_Header

■ I for Repair_Item

■ P for Product

Although table aliases are optional, you should use them in multiple-table joins because they reduce the size of the SELECT statement and simplify its appearance.

"Self" Joins

Another form of a two-table join is the *self-join*. This type of join is used when a table has a foreign key that references its own primary key. A good example of this is the Product_Assembly table discussed earlier in this chapter. The primary key of the Product Assembly table is Product_ID. Every product—except a complete product—belongs to an assembly. Therefore, Assembly_ID is a foreign key that references Product_ID (see Figure 14.1).

FIGURE 14.1.

Example of a table's primary key referenced by its foreign key.

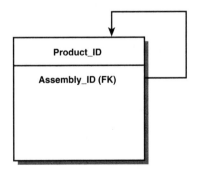

Suppose you want to retrieve the description of each product and the description of the assembly to which it belongs. This is an excellent example of the purpose of a self-join. As the example illustrates, the join statement must define an alias for both *copies* of the table. The join condition—P1.Assembly_ID = P2.Product_ID—causes Oracle to retrieve product information from P1 and assembly information from P2.

```
SQL> select P1.Description ¦¦ ' is part of ' ¦¦  P2.Description
                                              "Assembly Breakdown"
  2  from Product_Assembly P1, Product_Assembly P2
  3  where
  4  P1.Assembly_ID = P2.Product_ID
  5  order by P1.Assembly_ID, P1.Product_ID;
```

```
Assembly Breakdown
--------------------------------------------------------------------
Titanium alloy, teflon-coated iris is part of Black body, stainless steel fram
Variable-speed shutter, standard is part of Black body, stainless steel frame
Manual film advance, winder is part of Black body, stainless steel frame camer
Black body, stainless steel frame camera body is part of Complete camera
Blue filter - standard is part of Complete camera
Xenon flash unit is part of Complete camera
100mm lens - standard is part of Complete camera
4 foot camera strap, leather is part of Complete camera

8 rows selected.
```

Outer Joins

You've seen that a multiple-table join returns only columns from each table where the join conditions are met. Consider the following example. You have two tables: an Employee table and an Employee Dependent table. An employee may have zero, one, or several dependents. Accordingly, a row in Employee may have zero or more rows in Employee Dependent. Here are the contents of the tables:

```
SQL> select Employee_ID, Last_Name, First_Name
  2  from Employee
  3  order by Employee_ID;
```

```
EMPLOYEE_ID LAST_NAME                         FIRST_NAME
----------- --------------------------------- --------------------
       1001 SMITH                             JEAN
       1002 HERNANDEZ                         RANDY
       1003 GLEASON                           PAUL
       1004 BARRETT                           SARAH
       1005 HIGGINS                           BEN
       1006 YEN                               CINDY
       1007 GILROY                            MAX
       1008 CARSON                            BETH
       1009 SWANSON                           HARRY

9 rows selected.
```

```
SQL> select Employee_ID, Last_Name, First_Name, Relationship
  2  from Employee_Dependent
  3  order by Employee_ID;
```

```
EMPLOYEE_ID LAST_NAME                         FIRST_NAME           RELATIONSHIP
----------- --------------------------------- -------------------- --------------
       1001 SMITH                             JARED                CHILD
       1006 YEN                               RANDY                SPOUSE
       1007 GILROY                            ARTHUR               CHILD
```

```
        1007 GILROY                    CATHY                  SPOUSE
        1007 GILROY                    HORACE                 CHILD
```

Now, watch what happens when these two tables are joined by Employee_ID.

```
SQL> select E.Employee_ID, E.Last_Name, E.First_Name, D.Last_Name,
D.First_Name, Relationship
  2  from Employee E, Employee_Dependent D
  3  where
  4  E.Employee_ID = D.Employee_ID
  5  order by E.Employee_ID, D.Last_Name, D.First_Name;


EMPLOYEE_ID LAST_NAME      FIRST_NAME   LAST_NAME      FIRST_NAME   RELATIONSHIP
----------- -------------- ------------ -------------- ------------ ------------
       1001 SMITH          JEAN         SMITH          JARED        CHILD
       1006 YEN            CINDY        YEN            RANDY        SPOUSE
       1007 GILROY         MAX          GILROY         ARTHUR       CHILD
       1007 GILROY         MAX          GILROY         CATHY        SPOUSE
       1007 GILROY         MAX          GILROY         HORACE       CHILD
```

In the previous example, Oracle retrieves only the rows for employees with dependents. If you want to retrieve employee information regardless of whether the employee has dependents, you must use the outer join operator by appending (+) to the *optional* column in the join condition.

```
SQL> select E.Employee_ID, E.Last_Name, E.First_Name, D.Last_Name,
            D.First_Name, Relationship
  2  from Employee E, Employee_Dependent D
  3  where
  4  E.Employee_ID = D.Employee_ID (+)
  5  order by E.Employee_ID, D.Last_Name, D.First_Name;


EMPLOYEE_ID LAST_NAME      FIRST_NAME   LAST_NAME      FIRST_NAME   RELATIONSHIP
----------- -------------- ------------ -------------- ------------ ------------
       1001 SMITH          JEAN         SMITH          JARED        CHILD
       1002 HERNANDEZ      RANDY
       1003 GLEASON        PAUL
       1004 BARRETT        SARAH
       1005 HIGGINS        BEN
       1006 YEN            CINDY        YEN            RANDY        SPOUSE
       1007 GILROY         MAX          GILROY         ARTHUR       CHILD
       1007 GILROY         MAX          GILROY         CATHY        SPOUSE
       1007 GILROY         MAX          GILROY         HORACE       CHILD
       1008 CARSON         BETH
       1009 SWANSON        HARRY

11 rows selected.
```

If an employee has no dependents, Oracle returns a null for each of the columns selected from the Employee Dependent table. In fact, you can obtain a list of employees without dependents by looking for Employee Dependent rows in which Relationship is null.

```
SQL> select E.Employee_ID, E.Last_Name, E.First_Name
  2  from Employee E, Employee_Dependent D
  3  where
  4  E.Employee_ID = D.Employee_ID (+) and
```

```
5  Relationship is NULL
6  order by E.Employee_ID, D.Last_Name, D.First_Name;
```

```
EMPLOYEE_ID LAST_NAME              FIRST_NAME
----------- --------------------   --------------
       1002 HERNANDEZ              RANDY
       1003 GLEASON                PAUL
       1004 BARRETT                SARAH
       1005 HIGGINS                BEN
       1008 CARSON                 BETH
       1009 SWANSON                HARRY
```

6 rows selected.

Using Set Operators in the *SELECT* Statement

The SQL language is a partial implementation of the relational model as envisioned by Codd. As part of that implementation, Oracle's version of SQL provides three set operators: INTERSECT, UNION, and MINUS.

The *INTERSECT* Operator

The INTERSECT operator returns the rows that are common between two sets of rows. The syntax for using the INTERSECT operator is

```
select-stmt1
INTERSECT
select-stmt2
[order-by-clause]
```

where *select-stmt1* and *select-stmt2* are valid SELECT statements, and *order-by-clause* is an ORDER BY clause that references the columns by number rather than by name.

Here are some requirements and considerations for using the INTERSECT operator:

- ■ The two SELECT statements may not contain an ORDER BY clause; however, you can order the results of the entire INTERSECT operation.

- ■ The number of columns retrieved by *select-stmt1* must be equal to the number of columns retrieved by *select-stmt2*.

- ■ The datatypes of the columns retrieved by *select-stmt1* must match the datatypes of the columns retrieved by *select-stmt2*.

- ■ The *order-by-clause*—which is optional—differs from the usual ORDER BY clause in a SELECT statement because the columns used for ordering *must* be referenced by number rather than name. The reason is that there is no requirement that the column names retrieved by *select-stmt1* be identical to the column names retrieved by *select-stmt2*. Therefore, it's necessary to indicate the columns to be used in ordering results by their position in the select list.

Consider the following typical scenario for using the INTERSECT operator. You're supporting several different sales offices, each of which is using the same database tables. As you would expect, the contents of these tables differ from sales office to sales office. You have been asked to find the records that are common to both the Portland Product table and the Houston Product table. For the sake of illustration, I've reduced the contents of these tables to a comprehensible set of data.

```
SQL> select Product_ID, Manufacturer_ID
  2  from Portland_Product;

PRODUCT_ID    MANUFAC
------------  -------
C2002         MIT501
C2005         MIT501
C3002         SEN101

SQL> select Product_ID, Manufacturer_ID
  2  from Houston_Product;

PRODUCT_ID    MANUFAC
------------  -------
B901          TES801
B801          SEN101
C2002         MIT501
C2005         MIT501
C3002         SEN101
B311          TES801
B9310         SEN101
B384          TES801

8 rows selected.
```

To determine the common set of rows between the two tables, you submit the following SELECT statement to Oracle:

```
SQL> select Product_ID, Manufacturer_ID
  2  from Portland_Product
  3  INTERSECT
  4  select Product_ID, Manufacturer_ID
  5  from Houston_Product;

PRODUCT_ID    MANUFAC
------------  -------
C2002         MIT501
C2005         MIT501
C3002         SEN101
```

If you look at the rows that exist in each table, you can confirm that the two tables do indeed have three rows in common.

The *UNION* Operator (I've Paid My Dues)

Sooner or later, you'll find yourself in a situation in which you need to combine the rows from similar tables to produce a report or to create a table for analysis. Even though the tables represent similar information, they may differ considerably. To accomplish this task, you should consider using the UNION operator. The syntax for this set operator is pretty simple.

```
select-stmt1
UNION
select-stmt2
[order-by-clause]
```

where *select-stmt1* and *select-stmt2* are valid SELECT statements, and *order-by-clause* is an optional ORDER BY clause that references the columns by number rather than by name.

The UNION operator combines the rows returned by the first SELECT statement with the rows returned by the second SELECT statement. Keep the following things in mind when you use the UNION operator:

- The two SELECT statements may not contain an ORDER BY clause; however, you can order the results of the entire UNION operation.

- The number of columns retrieved by *select-stmt1* must be equal to the number of columns retrieved by *select-stmt2*.

- The datatypes of the columns retrieved by *select-stmt1* must match the datatypes of the columns retrieved by *select-stmt2*.

- The *order-by-clause*—which is optional—differs from the usual ORDER BY clause in a SELECT statement because the columns used for ordering *must* be referenced by number rather than name. The reason is that there is no requirement that the column names retrieved by *select-stmt1* be identical to the column names retrieved by *select-stmt2*.

To illustrate the use of UNION, imagine that you have been given the task of consolidating information from two different seismology labs. The first table is from the Department of Geophysics at the University of Northern South Dakota; the other table is from a private research institution, RIND. Here is the structure of the two tables:

```
SQL> desc UNSD_Event
 Name                            Null?    Type
 ------------------------------- -------- ----
 EVENT_NO                                 NUMBER
 EPICENTER_LATITUDE                       NUMBER
 EPICENTER_LONGITUDE                      NUMBER
 EVENT_MAGNITUDE                          NUMBER
 EVENT_TIME                               DATE
 EVENT_WAVE                               CHAR(1)
 INSTRUMENT_NAME                          VARCHAR2(30)


SQL> desc RIND_Event
 Name                            Null?    Type
 ------------------------------- -------- ----
 LOCATION_LAT                             NUMBER
 LOCATION_LON                             NUMBER
 RICHTER_NUMBER                           NUMBER
```

```
DATE_TIME                                    VARCHAR2(30)
WAVE_TYPE                                     CHAR(1)
```

Let's examine the similarities and differences between UNSD_Event and RIND_Event. First of all, both tables are used to store information about seismic events. UNSD_Event has two extra columns: Event_No and Instrument_Name. Both tables store the epicenter latitude and longitude, the magnitude, and the wave type (P or S). However, UNSD_Event defines Event_Time as a DATE, whereas RIND_Event uses VARCHAR2 for storing the event date and time in Date_Time. If you try to perform a UNION without converting Event_Time in UNSD_Event and Date_Time in RIND_Event to a common datatype, here is what happens:

```
SQL> select Epicenter_Latitude, Epicenter_Longitude, Event_Magnitude,
            Event_Time, Event_Wave
  2  from UNSD_Event
  3  UNION
  4  select Location_Lat, Location_Lon, Richter_Number, Date_Time, Wave_Type
  5  from RIND_Event;
select Epicenter_Latitude, Epicenter_Longitude, Event_Magnitude,
            Event_Time, Event_Wave
               *
ERROR at line 1:
ORA-01790: expression must have same datatype as corresponding expression
```

You can normalize the two columns by converting Date_Time in the RIND_Event table to a date by using the TO_DATE function.

```
SQL> select Epicenter_Latitude, Epicenter_Longitude, Event_Magnitude,
            Event_Time, Event_Wave
  2  from UNSD_Event
  3  UNION
  4  select Location_Lat, Location_Lon, Richter_Number,
            TO_DATE(Date_Time,'MM-DD-YY HH:MI:SS'), Wave_Type
  5  from RIND_Event;

EPICENTER_LATITUDE EPICENTER_LONGITUDE EVENT_MAGNITUDE EVENT_TIM E
------------------ ------------------- --------------- --------- -
            12.83              189.85             5.8 25-APR-95 P
            22.33              233.31             5.9 03-FEB-95 P
            23.33              179.11             5.3 10-JAN-95 P
            29.84              238.41             6.2 22-MAR-95 S
            31.17              208.33             6.6 19-APR-95 S
            31.84              241.21             6.1 12-MAR-95 S
            37.81              211.84             6.4 11-JAN-95 S

7 rows selected.
```

If you want to order the results by the Event_Time, simply add this line to the SQL statement:

```
SQL> select Epicenter_Latitude, Epicenter_Longitude, Event_Magnitude,
            Event_Time, Event_Wave
  2  from UNSD_Event
  3  UNION
  4  select Location_Lat, Location_Lon, Richter_Number,
            TO_DATE(Date_Time,'MM-DD-YY HH:MI:SS'), Wave_Type
  5  from RIND_Event
  6  order by 4;
```

```
EPICENTER_LATITUDE EPICENTER_LONGITUDE EVENT_MAGNITUDE EVENT_TIM E
------------------ ------------------- --------------- --------- -
            23.33              179.11             5.3 10-JAN-95 P
            37.81              211.84             6.4 11-JAN-95 S
            22.33              233.31             5.9 03-FEB-95 P
            31.84              241.21             6.1 12-MAR-95 S
            29.84              238.41             6.2 22-MAR-95 S
            31.17              208.33             6.6 19-APR-95 S
            12.83              189.85             5.8 25-APR-95 P

7 rows selected.
```

UNION Versus *UNION ALL*

Oracle's implementation of SQL supports a variant of the UNION operator called UNION ALL. The difference between UNION and UNION ALL is this: if the two tables in the union have duplicate rows between them, UNION returns only one instance of a row, regardless of the number of duplicates. UNION ALL, on the other hand, returns all duplicates that exist between the two tables. I'll illustrate this with the Houston_Product and Portland_Product tables. If you apply the UNION operator on the two tables, the results are

```
SQL> select Product_ID, Manufacturer_ID, Description
  2  from Houston_Product
  3  UNION
  4  select Product_ID, Manufacturer_ID, Description
  5  from Portland_Product
  6  order by 1;

PRODUCT_ID   MANUFAC DESCRIPTION
------------ ------- --------------------------------------------------------
B311         TES801  Pre-amp, 120 W per channel
B384         TES801  PREAMP, 460 W/RMS
B801         SEN101  PRE AMPLIFIER 150 WATTS/CHANNEL
B901         TES801  Preamplifier, 200 W PER CHANNEL
B9310        SEN101  Pre amp, 250 W/channel
C2002        MIT501  CD PLAYER, SINGLE-DISK
C2005        MIT501  5-DISK CD PLAYER
C2005        MIT501  50-DISK CD PLAYER
C3002        SEN101  JUKEBOX, CD - 100 DISK CAPACITY

9 rows selected.
```

If you use the UNION ALL operator instead of the UNION operator, two additional rows are returned. The reason is that for Product_IDs 2002 and 3002, the three specified columns—Product_ID, Manufacturer_ID, and Description—have the same values in both tables.

```
SQL> select Product_ID, Manufacturer_ID, Description
  2  from Houston_Product
  3  UNION ALL
  4  select Product_ID, Manufacturer_ID, Description
  5  from Portland_Product
  6  order by 1;
```

```
PRODUCT_ID    MANUFAC DESCRIPTION
------------  ------- -------------------------------------------------
B311          TES801  Pre-amp, 120 W per channel
B384          TES801  PREAMP, 460 W/RMS
B801          SEN101  PRE AMPLIFIER 150 WATTS/CHANNEL
B901          TES801  Preamplifier, 200 W PER CHANNEL
B9310         SEN101  Pre amp, 250 W/channel
C2002         MIT501  CD PLAYER, SINGLE-DISK
C2002         MIT501  CD PLAYER, SINGLE-DISK
C2005         MIT501  5-DISK CD PLAYER
C2005         MIT501  50-DISK CD PLAYER
C3002         SEN101  JUKEBOX, CD - 100 DISK CAPACITY
C3002         SEN101  JUKEBOX, CD - 100 DISK CAPACITY

11 rows selected.
```

The *MINUS* Operator

In addition to the INTERSECT and UNION operators, Oracle also provides the MINUS operator for comparing one set of rows against another set. The syntax for using the MINUS operator resembles that for the UNION operator.

```
select-stmt1
MINUS
select-stmt2
[order-by-clause]
```

where *select-stmt1* and *select-stmt2* are valid SELECT statements, and *order-by-clause* is an ORDER BY clause that references the columns by number rather than by name.

The requirements and considerations for using the MINUS operator are essentially the same as those for the INTERSECT and UNION operators. For illustrating the use of the MINUS operator, we'll again use two tables—a Product table as maintained in the Portland sales office and the same table as kept in the Houston sales office. You have been asked to compare the contents of a Product table from the Portland sales office with the same table from the Houston sales office. First, let's determine what Product and Manufacturer IDs exist in the Portland table but don't exist in the Houston table.

```
SQL> select Product_ID, Manufacturer_ID
  2  from Portland_Product
  3  MINUS
  4  select Product_ID, Manufacturer_ID
  5  from Houston_Product;
```

```
no rows selected
```

As expected, Oracle doesn't return any rows. Again, this is because the Product and Manufacturer IDs in Portland_Product—C2002 and MIT501, C2005 and MIT501, and C3002 and SEN101—all exist in Houston_Product. Now, let's exchange the two SELECT statements to obtain the rows that exist in Houston_Product but don't exist in Portland_Product.

```
SQL> select Product_ID, Manufacturer_ID
  2  from Houston_Product
  3  MINUS
  4  select Product_ID, Manufacturer_ID
  5  from Portland_Product;

PRODUCT_ID    MANUFAC
------------  -------
B311          TES801
B384          TES801
B801          SEN101
B901          TES801
B9310         SEN101
```

This example demonstrates that MINUS won't tell you *all* the differences between the two tables—it returns only those rows in the first set that can't be found in the second set. In fact, both tables *appear* to have information about the same Product IDs: C2002, C2005, and C3002. However, if we also retrieve the Description column from both tables, you see that there are additional differences.

```
SQL> select Product_ID, Manufacturer_ID, Description
  2  from Portland_Product
  3  where
  4  Product_ID like 'C%'
  5  MINUS
  6  select Product_ID, Manufacturer_ID, Description
  7  from Houston_Product
  8  where
  9  Product_ID like 'C%';

PRODUCT_ID    MANUFAC DESCRIPTION
------------  ------- ----------------------------------------
C2005         MIT501  50-DISK CD PLAYER


SQL> select Product_ID, Manufacturer_ID, Description
  2  from Houston_Product
  3  where
  4  Product_ID like 'C%'
  5  MINUS
  6  select Product_ID, Manufacturer_ID, Description
  7  from Portland_Product
  8  where
  9  Product_ID like 'C%';

PRODUCT_ID    MANUFAC DESCRIPTION
------------  ------- ----------------------------------------
C2005         MIT501  5-DISK CD PLAYER
```

The row in the Portland_Product table regarding Product ID C2005 describes it as a 50-DISK CD PLAYER, whereas the equivalent row's description in the Houston_Product table is 5-DISK CD PLAYER. The MINUS operator only reveals differences between the contents of selected columns of the two tables. Also, as you can see from the previous example, you can specify a WHERE clause in the SELECT statements used by the MINUS operator.

Creating a Table by Selecting from Another Table

When you're developing a new database application, you'll usually go through a phase of experimenting with various table designs. Whether you use legacy data or artificial data, it's nice to have some simple methods for experimentation. One DDL statement that you might want to use is CREATE TABLE—with a subquery. The syntax for this is

```
CREATE TABLE table-name
[(column-definition1, ... , column-definitionN)]
AS
select-statement
```

where *table-name* is the name of the new Oracle table; *column-definition1* through *column-definitionN* are optional column definitions that are used to specify different column names to be associated with the values returned by the subquery; and *select-statement* is a valid SELECT statement whose select list is used in creating the new table.

For example, the following statement is used to create a new table whose columns are a subset of an existing table:

```
SQL> create table Repair_Header_2
  2  as
  3  select Repair_ID, Customer_ID, Employee_ID, Deposit_Amount, Deposit_Method
  4  from Repair_Header;

Table created.

SQL> select count(*) from Repair_Header_2;

  COUNT(*)
--------
        6
```

Notice that Oracle doesn't tell you how many rows are inserted into the new table. In fact, you can create a new table that is empty by specifying an impossible condition.

```
SQL> create table Repair_Header_3
  2  as
  3  select Repair_ID, Customer_ID, Employee_ID, Deposit_Amount, Deposit_Method
  4  from Repair_Header
  5  where
  6  1 = 2;

Table created.

SQL> select count(*) from Repair_Header_3;

  COUNT(*)
--------
        0
```

TIP

Oracle rejects the CREATE TABLE statement if the subquery references a LONG or LONG RAW column. If you need to copy rows from a LONG column in one table to another, use the SQL*Plus COPY command. It *does* support the copying of LONG column values.

The subquery referenced in a CREATE TABLE statement can be a multiple-table join, as in:

```
SQL> create table Join_Repair_Header_and_Item
  2   as
  3   select H.Repair_ID, Customer_ID, Employee_ID, Item_Number,
  4   Product_ID, Manufacturer_ID
  5   from Repair_Header H, Repair_Item I
  6   where
  7   H.Repair_ID = I.Repair_ID;

Table created.

SQL> desc Join_Repair_Header_and_Item
 Name                             Null?     Type
 -------------------------------- --------- ----
 REPAIR_ID                        NOT NULL  NUMBER(6)
 CUSTOMER_ID                      NOT NULL  NUMBER(4)
 EMPLOYEE_ID                      NOT NULL  NUMBER(4)
 ITEM_NUMBER                      NOT NULL  NUMBER
 PRODUCT_ID                                 VARCHAR2(12)
 MANUFACTURER_ID                            VARCHAR2(6)
```

NOTE

The CREATE TABLE statement copies only one kind of table or column constraint: the NOT NULL constraint. If you want the new table to have all the existing constraints, you'll have to specify them with an ALTER TABLE statement.

Using SQL to Generate SQL Scripts

If you're willing to experiment, you'll find creative uses for SQL with SQL*Plus. One example is the use of SQL*Plus to generate SQL*Plus scripts. Suppose that you wanted a general script for counting the rows in all of your tables. Unfortunately, SQL doesn't allow the use of a wild card for specifying table names.

```
SQL> select count(*) from *;
select count(*) from *
                       *
```

```
ERROR at line 1:
RA-00903: invalid table name
```

To count the number of rows in each of your tables, you'd have to submit a SELECT statement to Oracle for each table.

```
SQL> select count(*) from Repair_Header;

  COUNT(*)
  --------
         6

SQL> select count(*) from Repair_Item;

  COUNT(*)
  --------
         6
.
.
.
SQL> select count(*) from Customer;

  COUNT(*)
  --------
        15
```

This can be quite tedious if you have many tables. If you wanted a list of your tables, you would query the Oracle data dictionary view USER_TABLES. We'll delve into some of the other Oracle data dictionary views in Chapter 30, "Oracle Internals." For now, here is the query you'd use to obtain a list of the tables:

```
SQL> select table_name from user_tables;

TABLE_NAME
-----------------------------
ACTION_CODE
CONDITION_CODE
CUSTOMER
CUSTOMER_SUBSET
DEPOT
DEPOT_ESTIMATE
EMPLOYEE
ITEM_STATUS_CODE
.
.
.
```

Now, let's concatenate three strings together—a literal string, Table_Name, and a ; to terminate the statement.

```
SQL> select 'select count(*) from ' || table_name || ';'
  2  from user_tables;

'SELECTCOUNT(*)FROM'||TABLE_NAME||';'
----------------------------------------------------
```

```
select count(*) from ACTION_CODE;
select count(*) from CONDITION_CODE;
select count(*) from CUSTOMER;
select count(*) from CUSTOMER_SUBSET;
select count(*) from DEPOT;

14 rows selected.
```

The preceding SELECT statement returns a SELECT statement for each table that the Oracle user owns. You can spool these commands to a file so that they can be executed by SQL*Plus.

```
SQL> set feedback off
SQL> set heading off
SQL> set echo off
SQL> spool c:\book\chap14\countem.sql
SQL> select 'select count(*) from ' || table_name || ';'
  2  from user_tables;

select count(*) from ACTION_CODE;
select count(*) from CONDITION_CODE;
select count(*) from CUSTOMER;
select count(*) from CUSTOMER_SUBSET;
select count(*) from DEPOT;
SQL> spool off
SQL> set feedback on
SQL> set heading on
SQL> set echo on
SQL> start count_em
SQL>
SQL> select count(*) from ACTION_CODE;

  COUNT(*)
  --------
         0

1 row selected.

SQL> select count(*) from CONDITION_CODE;

  COUNT(*)
  --------
         9

1 row selected.

SQL> select count(*) from CUSTOMER;

  COUNT(*)
  --------
        15

1 row selected.

SQL> select count(*) from CUSTOMER_SUBSET;
```

```
COUNT(*)
--------
       1
```

1 row selected.

SQL> select count(*) from DEPOT;

```
COUNT(*)
--------
       0
```

1 row selected.

This SQL*Plus script is fairly flexible. Let me explain the significance of each of the set commands. First, feedback is turned off so that the number of rows is not displayed by SQL*Plus. Next, heading is set to off so that no column headings become part of the output—we only want the SELECT statements, nothing more. Finally, we set echo to off so that the SELECT statement that generates the other SELECT statements is not captured in the output. A little experimentation with these settings will show you why they are set to these values.

After the SELECT statements are generated and spooled to a file (c:\book\chap14\count_em.sql), feedback, heading, and echo are turned back on so that each SELECT statement appears before its results.

NOTE

In the previous SQL*Plus script, the SELECT statement that appears after the spool command won't actually appear because echo has been turned off. The SQL*Plus output was presented in this way to clarify the execution of the SQL*Plus commands and the SELECT statements.

Summary

Remember the following concepts:

- Oracle provides group functions such as MAX and MIN that return a single value for an entire set of rows.
- The SELECT statement has two optional clauses—GROUP BY and HAVING—that can be used to return rows grouped by a common value for specified columns.
- Hierarchical data can be organized through the CONNECT BY clause. You must indicate a starting condition with the START WITH clause.

- A join operation is a SELECT statement whose FROM clause has two or more tables and one or more join conditions that typically equate primary and foreign keys.
- The INTERSECT operator returns the set of common rows that are found in two sets of rows.
- The UNION operator returns the distinct rows that exist in two sets of rows.
- The UNION ALL operator returns all rows that exist in two sets of rows, including duplicates.
- The MINUS operator returns the rows in one set that are not found in a second set.

15

Views, Sequences, and Synonyms

In previous chapters, we've discussed the most frequently used database objects: tables and their columns. In this chapter, we'll explore three other database objects that are available for use in Personal Oracle7.

- Views
- Sequences
- Synonyms

If you're serious about building an application based on an Oracle database, you need to understand how these objects work and when they should be used. Let's start by examining the view.

A View Is a Virtual Table

A *view* is a query of one or more tables that provides another way of presenting information. A view does not actually contain or store its own data; for this reason, you can think of a view as a virtual table. The only storage that a view actually requires is the SELECT statement that defines it.

The uses for a view include the following:

- Maintaining finer control over security
- Hiding complexity from a developer or user
- Renaming columns

As you'll see, the syntax for creating a view is really quite simple.

View Syntax

To define a view, use this syntax:

```
CREATE VIEW view-name
(column1,...,columnN)
AS
select-statement
```

where *view-name* is the name of the view (subject to the same requirements as other Oracle object names); *column1* through *columnN* are the column names of the view that correspond to the columns referenced in *select-statement*; and *select-statement* is a valid Oracle SELECT statement.

We'll look at the example of a simple view—one based on a single table. In building your repair store application for Frayed Wires, several of the users have requested a very simple way to retrieve the depreciated amount for various products. Even though you've shown them how to construct a simple query, they want you to make it even easier for them to look at this information. To please the users, you define the following view:

```
SQL> create view Product_Depreciation
  2  (Product_ID, Manufacturer_ID, Depreciated_Amount)
  3  as
  4  select Product_ID, Manufacturer_ID,
  5         Initial_Retail_Value - Current_Used_Value
  6  from Product;

View created.
```

You then show the users how to query the view.

```
SQL> select Product_ID, Depreciated_Amount
  2  from Product_Depreciation
  3  order by Product_ID;

PRODUCT_ DEPRECIATED_AMOUNT
-------- ------------------
T1000                   135
T1012                    75
T1020                   160
T1105                    85
T1800                   210
```

Restricting Data Access with a View

Oracle provides several mechanisms for restricting data access: views, database triggers, and table and column privileges that can be granted to database roles and individual users. You'll need to assess the security requirements of your application to determine which method is most appropriate.

If you use a view to restrict data access, several methods are available to you. You'll see that each method offers a different level of control over data access—from coarse to very fine. A coarse control would be when you define a view that is a subset of its base table. For example, an Employee table has a column named Salary, which you don't want to share with all users who need access to the table. Here is a view that doesn't include the Salary column:

```
SQL> create view Employee_no_salary
  2  (Employee_ID, Last_Name, First_Name, Middle_Initial,
  3   Hire_Date, Termination_Date, Date_of_Birth)
  4  as
  5  select Employee_ID, Last_Name, First_Name, Middle_Initial,
  6         Hire_Date, Termination_Date, Date_of_Birth
  7  from Employee;

View created.
```

After the view is created, you can use the SQL*Plus DESCRIBE command to display the view's definition.

```
SQL> desc Employee_no_salary
 Name                            Null?    Type
 ------------------------------- -------- -----
 EMPLOYEE_ID                     NOT NULL NUMBER(4)
 LAST_NAME                       NOT NULL VARCHAR2(30)
 FIRST_NAME                      NOT NULL VARCHAR2(20)
```

```
MIDDLE_INITIAL                        CHAR(1)
HIRE_DATE                  NOT NULL   DATE
TERMINATION_DATE                      DATE
DATE_OF_BIRTH                         DATE
```

As you see, the DESCRIBE command doesn't indicate whether the object description belongs to a table or view. Even if the user knows that the salary information is stored in the Employee table, the view can't return the column because it isn't contained in the view definition.

```
SQL> select Monthly_Salary
  2  from Employee_no_salary;
select Monthly_Salary
       *
ERROR at line 1:
ORA-00904: invalid column name
```

A Better Security View

Sometimes, limiting the columns retrieved by a view is too restrictive. Your application might require a security scheme that is *data-driven*—based on a column value in a row. As you'll see in Chapter 26, "Managing Users and Roles," this type of security scheme cannot be achieved through the use of database roles. For a finer level of security, you might need to limit access to salary data to those users who are managers. To achieve this, we'll add a column to the Employee table to indicate whether an employee is a manager. We'll also add a CHECK constraint so that the Manager column is equal to either Y or N.

```
SQL> alter table Employee
  2  add
  3  (Manager char(1) check (Manager in ('Y','N')));

Table altered.


SQL> update Employee
  2  set Manager = 'N'
  3  where
  4  Employee_ID != 1001;

8 rows updated.

SQL> update Employee
  2  set Manager = 'Y'
  3  where
  4  Employee_ID = 1001;

1 row updated.
```

Now that all rows in the Employee table have a value for the Manager column, we can again alter the table so that the Manager column is mandatory.

```
SQL> alter table Employee
  2  modify
  3  (Manager not null);

Table altered.
```

We'll also add a column for storing the employee's Oracle username. The Oracle username will be set to the first letter of the employee's first name concatenated with the last name.

```
SQL> alter table Employee
  2  add
  3  (username varchar2(31));

Table altered.

SQL> update Employee
  2  set username = substr(first_name,1,1) ¦¦ last_name;

9 rows updated.
```

We'll create a view named Restrict_Salary that performs a combination of self-join and outer-join of the Employee table.

```
SQL> create view Restrict_Salary as
  2  select e.employee_id, e.last_name, e.first_name,
  3  decode(s.manager,'Y',e.monthly_salary,null) monthly_salary
  4  from employee e, employee s
  5  where
  6  user = s.username(+);

View created.
```

An explanation is in order. First of all, one instance of the Employee table is identified with the alias e. The second instance of the Employee table is identified with the alias s. The pseudocolumn USER has the value of the Oracle user who is currently connected to the system—so its value depends on who queries the view. The outer-join condition is User equal to the value for the Username column in the Employee table. This condition is used to retrieve the value of the Manager column for the user querying the view. The DECODE function looks at the value of Manager. If it is Y, the user is a manager, and the monthly salary information is returned; if it isn't Y, the DECODE function returns a NULL.

Because Jean Smith is a manager, this is what happens when she queries the view:

```
SQL> select *
  2  from Restrict_Salary;

EMPLOYEE_ID LAST_NAME                        FIRST_NAME           MONTHLY_SALARY
----------- -------------------------------- -------------------- --------------
       1001 SMITH                            JEAN                           1500
       1002 HERNANDEZ                        RANDY                          3000
       1003 GLEASON                          PAUL                           1500
       1004 BARRETT                          SARAH                          1500
       1005 HIGGINS                          BEN                            3000
       1006 YEN                              CINDY                          1500
       1007 GILROY                           MAX                            1500
       1008 CARSON                           BETH                           3000
       1009 SWANSON                          HARRY                          2500

9 rows selected.
```

When Max Gilroy queries the view, he doesn't retrieve Monthly_Salary.

```
SQL> select *
  2  from Restrict_Salary;

EMPLOYEE_ID LAST_NAME                           FIRST_NAME              MONTHLY_SALARY
----------- ----------------------------------  ----------------------  --------------
       1001 SMITH                               JEAN
       1002 HERNANDEZ                           RANDY
       1003 GLEASON                             PAUL
       1004 BARRETT                             SARAH
       1005 HIGGINS                             BEN
       1006 YEN                                 CINDY
       1007 GILROY                              MAX
       1008 CARSON                              BETH
       1009 SWANSON                             HARRY

9 rows selected.
```

However, the preceding view might still miss the mark: you might have a requirement that some managers have more privileges than other managers. In this case, you can assign a security level to each user and to each record. You can define a view that enables a user to access only the records that have a security level less than or equal to his or her own security level.

Hiding Complexity with a View

During application development, you'll typically be dealing with developers and users who have differing organizational perspectives and a broad range of technical sophistication. As a result, you'll want to use the mechanisms that Oracle offers to customize the environment for developers and users.

I include developers in this category because, like users, their knowledge of SQL in general and Oracle in particular will vary. It's very common for a form or report to require the joining of several tables. The use of views can simplify this process because, as the application architect, *you* can define the views that developers need to be concerned with.

Views are also an excellent way to customize the database environment for end users. This is especially true for large organizations that access the same information for different purposes. Typically, each group has its own name for referring to the same piece of information. Because of the widespread use of third-party ad hoc query tools such as Andyne's GQL and Oracle's Browser, a column name should accurately describe the information it contains because that helps an end user determine which columns to query. By creating a view, you can customize the column names that will be seen by a group of users.

A view can hide the complexity that exists in a multiple-table join. By defining a view, users are freed from learning the idiosyncrasies of the SELECT statement. For instance, if you wanted to join the Report Header, Report Item, and Product tables to return a product description for each repair item, here is what the SELECT statement would look like:

```
SQL> select H.Repair_ID, I.Item_Number, P.Product_ID, P.Manufacturer_ID,
            P.Description
  2  from Repair_Header H, Repair_Item I, Product P
```

```
 3  where
 4  H.Repair_ID = I.Repair_ID and
 5  I.Product_ID = P.Product_ID and
 6  I.Manufacturer_ID = P.Manufacturer_ID
 7  order by H.Repair_ID, I.Item_Number;

REPAIR_ID ITEM_NUMBER PRODUCT_ID   MANUFA DESCRIPTION
--------- ----------- ------------ ------ ------------------------------------
      501           1 C2002        MIT501 50-CD Jukebox
      502           1 D301         SEN101 Digital rangefinder
      503           1 B311         TES801 Binary quadraphonic converter, 2000
      504           1 B801         SEN101 Binary quadraphonic filter, 20 - 200
      505           1 A903         TES801 Analog circuit transformer
      506           1 TR901        TES801 AC/DC Transformer, 300W
      506           2 B384         TES801 Bipolar resonator, digital

7 rows selected.
```

It's probably unreasonable to expect a casual user to be able to construct a statement of this complexity. But you can define a view that simplifies things for the user.

```
SQL> create view Repair_Product_View as
  2  select H.Repair_ID, I.Item_Number, P.Product_ID, P.Manufacturer_ID,
              P.Description
  3  from Repair_Header H, Repair_Item I, Product P
  4  where
  5  H.Repair_ID = I.Repair_ID and
  6  I.Product_ID = P.Product_ID and
  7  I.Manufacturer_ID = P.Manufacturer_ID;

View created.

SQL> desc Repair_Product_View
 Name                              Null?    Type
 --------------------------------- -------- ----
 REPAIR_ID                         NOT NULL NUMBER(6)
 ITEM_NUMBER                       NOT NULL NUMBER
 PRODUCT_ID                        NOT NULL VARCHAR2(12)
 MANUFACTURER_ID                   NOT NULL VARCHAR2(6)
 DESCRIPTION                                VARCHAR2(2000)
```

Using the Repair_Product_View, the user can simply select the desired columns without specifying any join conditions.

```
SQL> select Repair_ID, Item_Number, Product_ID, Manufacturer_ID, Description
  2  from Repair_Product_View
  3  order by Repair_ID, Item_Number;

REPAIR_ID ITEM_NUMBER PRODUCT_ID   MANUFA DESCRIPTION
--------- ----------- ------------ ------ ------------------------------------
      501           1 C2002        MIT501 50-CD Jukebox
      502           1 D301         SEN101 Digital rangefinder
      503           1 B311         TES801 Binary quadraphonic converter, 2000
      504           1 B801         SEN101 Binary quadraphonic filter, 20 - 200
      505           1 A903         TES801 Analog circuit transformer
      506           1 TR901        TES801 AC/DC Transformer, 300W
      506           2 B384         TES801 Bipolar resonator, digital

7 rows selected.
```

Modifying Data Through a View

The capability to modify the contents of a base table by referencing a view is called *view updatability.*

If a view is based on a single base table, Oracle updates the base table for an INSERT, UPDATE, or DELETE statement that references the view. Of course, the user must have the appropriate privileges on the base table, or Oracle will return an error message.

If a view is based on multiple base tables, Oracle does not enable you to modify the view using an UPDATE, INSERT, or DELETE statement.

```
SQL> create view nonupdatable_view
  2  (repair_id, item_number, depot_name)
  3  as
  4  select repair_id, item_number, company_name
  5  from Depot_Estimate, Depot
  6  where
  7  Depot_Estimate.Depot_ID = Depot.Depot_ID;

View created.

SQL> delete from nonupdatable_view;
delete from nonupdatable_view
                    *
ERROR at line 1:
ORA-01732: data manipulation operation not legal on this view
```

Restrictions on the Use of Views

As you might expect, the number of columns specified for a view must be equal to the number of columns contained in the SELECT statement that defines the view. If they aren't equal, the view won't be created and Oracle will return an error message.

```
SQL> create view Product_View
  2  (Product_ID, Manufacturer_ID)
  3  as
  4  select Product_ID, Manufacturer_ID,
           Initial_Retail_Value - Current_Used_Value
  5  from Product;
(Product_ID, Manufacturer_ID)
 *
ERROR at line 2:
ORA-01730: invalid number of column names specified
```

A view, like a table, can have a maximum of 254 columns. This is true even if the view is defined by several base tables. If one of a view's base tables is renamed or dropped, the view becomes invalid. Here's an example:

```
SQL> create view Product_Depreciation
  2  (Product_ID, Manufacturer_ID, Depreciated_Amount)
  3  as
  4  select Product_ID, Manufacturer_ID,
           Initial_Retail_Value - Current_Used_Value
```

```
  5  from Product;

View created.

SQL> rename Product to New_Product;

Table renamed.

SQL> select Product_ID, Depreciated_Amount
  2  from Product_Depreciation;
from Product_Depreciation
       *
ERROR at line 2:
ORA-04063: view "FRAYED_WIRES.PRODUCT_DEPRECIATION" has errors
```

Although Oracle provides an ALTER VIEW statement, it can't be used to modify the definition of the view. To change a view, you have two choices:

■ Drop the view and recreate it.

■ Use the OR REPLACE clause in the CREATE VIEW statement.

Views Based on Views

Is it possible to define a view that is based on another view? Yes, it certainly is. Let's look at an example. First, we'll create two views—one of the Employee table and one of the Dependent table. Employee_View doesn't include salary information, and Dependent_View doesn't include the dependent's date of birth.

```
SQL> create view Employee_View
  2  as
  3  select Employee_ID, Last_Name, First_Name, Middle_Initial, Hire_Date,
  4  Termination_Date
  5  from Employee;

View created.


SQL> create view Dependent_View
  2  as
  3  select Employee_ID, Last_Name, First_Name
  4  from Dependent;

View created.
```

Next, we'll create a view that is a join of Employee_View and Dependent_View.

```
SQL> create view Employee_Dependent_View
  2  (Employee_ID, Employee_Last_Name, Employee_First_Name,
     Dependent_Last_Name, Dependent_First_Name)
  3  as
  4  select E.Employee_ID, E.Last_Name, E.First_Name, D.Last_Name, D.First_Name
  5  from Employee_View E, Dependent_View D
  6  where
  7  E.Employee_ID = D.Employee_ID(+);

View created.
```

As the following SELECT statement illustrates, you can create and use a view that is actually a join of two other views.

```
SQL> select Employee_ID, Employee_Last_Name, Employee_First_Name,
            Dependent_Last_Name, Dependent_First_Name
  2  from Employee_Dependent_View
  3  order by Employee_ID;


EMPLOYEE_ID EMPLOYEE_LAST_NAME EMPLOYEE_FIRST_NAME DEPENDENT_LAST_NAME DEPENDE
----------- ------------------ ------------------- ------------------- -------
       1001 SMITH              JEAN                SMITH               BECKY
       1001 SMITH              JEAN                SMITH               RICHARD
       1002 HERNANDEZ          RANDY               GREEN               MARTIN
       1003 GLEASON            PAUL                SYLVESTER           DORIS
       1004 BARRETT            SARAH               ROBERTS             MAX
       1005 HIGGINS            BEN
       1006 YEN                CINDY
       1007 GILROY             MAX
       1008 CARSON             BETH
       1009 SWANSON            HARRY


10 rows selected.
```

In fact, Oracle imposes no limit on the number of view *layers* that you can define. However, you should avoid building views of views because of the performance penalty that can result. Let me explain why.

Let's look at views from two perspectives—conceptual and physical. (I use the word *perspective* because it would be far too confusing at this point to call them *views*.) From a conceptual perspective, a view is a convenient device with no apparent overhead with which to be concerned. From a physical perspective, each time a query is performed on a view, Oracle must create a temporary table that contains the query results. If you query a view that is based on other views, Oracle must create several temporary tables. As you can envision, Oracle might need to perform a substantial amount of work in order to produce a result. I'm not suggesting that you never define a view that is based on another view; however, you need to understand the ramifications of your design and build a prototype of the performance before you make any design commitments.

Take a Number: How Sequences Work

Organizations and individuals rely on unique, monotonically increasing numbers to identify information. Check numbers, purchase order numbers, and customer numbers are all good examples of this concept. Because of this ubiquitous need, Oracle developed another database object: the sequence.

A sequence is a set of numbers that increase or decrease at a specified increment. A good paradigm for a sequence is the paper number dispenser found in a bakery. As you pull the paper number from the dispenser, the next customer's number is guaranteed to be larger than yours.

The advantage of using an Oracle sequence is that it frees you from the headache of having to generate your own unique numbers.

Let's look at the syntax for creating a sequence.

Creating a Sequence

A sequence is created with the CREATE SEQUENCE statement. The statement contains several default values that work for most situations. The default values are

■ The sequence number is increasing.

■ The sequence number increments by 1.

■ The sequence starts with 1.

■ The maximum sequence number is 10 to the 27th power—certainly large enough for most applications.

■ The sequence will not recycle to the minimum value after it reaches the maximum value.

Most of these default values are acceptable for most applications. At a minimum, you can create a sequence with this statement:

```
CREATE SEQUENCE sequence-name
```

where *sequence-name* is the sequence name subject to the same naming restrictions as other Oracle database objects.

As an example, let's create a sequence for assigning new Customer IDs.

Using a Sequence to Assign a New Customer ID in the Repair Store

You create a sequence in this fashion:

```
SQL> create sequence Customer_ID_Seq;

Sequence created.

SQL> select Customer_ID_Seq.nextval from dual;

  NEXTVAL
---------
        1

SQL> select Customer_ID_Seq.nextval from dual;

  NEXTVAL
---------
        2
```

> **NOTE**
>
> The dual table is a special Oracle table that serves several purposes. It contains a single column, DUMMY, which is really never selected at all. The dual table contains a single row—which is its reason for existing. By having only one row, you can select pseudocolumns, such as SYSDATE and USER, and be guaranteed that only one row will be returned. As shown, you can also use dual to inspect the current and next values of a sequence. **Never** insert another row into dual. If you do, many bad things will happen; for instance, Oracle data dictionary views will no longer work, and applications that rely on a single row in dual will fail.

You can also reference the next sequence value when inserting a new row or updating an existing row.

```
SQL> insert into Customer
  2  (Customer_ID, Last_Name, First_Name)
  3  values
  4  (Customer_ID_Seq.nextval, 'Curry', 'Ronald');

1 row created.

SQL> select Customer_ID, Last_Name, First_Name
  2  from Customer
  3  where
  4  Last_Name = 'Curry';

CUSTOMER_ID LAST_NAME                      FIRST_NAME
----------- ------------------------------ ------------------------------
          3 Curry                          Ronald
```

Defining a Sequence with a Starting Number and Increment

As you saw in the previous example, a sequence will, by default, start with 1 and increment by 1. However, you might need a sequence that starts with some other number. You also might want to specify an increment other than 1. Here is the CREATE SEQUENCE syntax to accomplish this:

```
CREATE SEQUENCE sequence-name
INCREMENT BY increment-value
START WITH starting-value
```

where *sequence-name* is the sequence name subject to the same naming restrictions as other Oracle database objects; *increment-value* is the value to use when incrementing the sequence; and *starting-value* is the first value used by the sequence.

For instance, you can define a sequence that begins at 1000 and increments by 5.

```
SQL> create sequence Repair_ID_Seq
  2  increment by 5
```

```
  3   start with 1000;

Sequence created.

SQL> select Repair_ID_Seq.nextval from dual;

   NEXTVAL
---------
      1000

SQL> select Repair_ID_Seq.nextval from dual;

   NEXTVAL
---------
      1005
```

Looking at the Current Value of a Sequence

When you reference a sequence's next value, it is as though you pulled the next number from a paper number dispenser: the number automatically increments. To avoid having the number increment, you can view a sequence's current value in this manner:

```
SQL> select Repair_ID_Seq.currval from dual;

   CURRVAL
---------
      1015

SQL> select Repair_ID_Seq.currval from dual;

   CURRVAL
---------
      1015
```

As you see, currval will not increment when it is referenced. However, you cannot reference currval until you have selected at least one value from the sequence. In the following example, Oracle returns an error message when the current value of a newly created sequence is referenced. Once the next value of Employee_ID_Seq is referenced, you can select Employee_ID_Seq.currval.

```
SQL> create sequence Employee_ID_Seq
  2   start with 1001;

Sequence created.

SQL> select Employee_ID_Seq.currval from dual;
ERROR:
ORA-08002: sequence EMPLOYEE_ID_SEQ.CURRVAL is not yet defined in this session

SQL> select Employee_ID_Seq.nextval from dual;

   NEXTVAL
---------
      1001
```

```
SQL> select Employee_ID_Seq.currval from dual;

CURRVAL
---------
     1001
```

Uses for Synonyms...or in Other Words...

A synonym is another name for a table. Actually, it would be more accurate to use the term *table synonym*. Synonyms come in two flavors: private and public. A private synonym is visible only to the Oracle user who created it. A public synonym is visible to all Oracle users. Any Oracle user who has been granted the Resource role can create a private synonym. A public synonym can only be created by an Oracle user who has been granted the DBA role. I'll cover these database roles and related issues in Chapter 26.

In one way, a synonym is similar to a view: both objects enable a table to be referenced by a different name. However, a synonym doesn't enable you to restrict columns or rename them.

A synonym provides an additional name for referencing a table. It might not be feasible to rename the table because of existing applications that reference the current table name. However, a synonym that provides a more intuitive and meaningful name might be ideal for use in an ad hoc query tool.

Synonym Syntax

The syntax for creating a synonym is quite straightforward.

```
CREATE [PUBLIC] SYNONYM synonym-name
FOR owner.object-name;
```

where *synonym-name* is the synonym name and subject to Oracle database object-naming requirements; *owner* is the name of the Oracle account that owns the referenced table or view; and *object-name* is the name of the table or view referenced by the synonym.

You might want to create a synonym to reference a table whose name is inappropriate or difficult to remember. In this example, the synonym p_artifact is used to point to the table parthaginian_artifacts, which belongs to the same Oracle user.

```
SQL> create synonym p_artifact for parthaginian_artifacts;

Synonym created.
```

A private synonym can also point to a table owned by another Oracle user. Suppose Oracle user RJOHNSON has created the Project table and wants to enable Oracle user KCHOW to read the Project table. First, RJOHNSON grants the SELECT privilege on the Project table to KCHOW. However, each time KCHOW wants to look at the table, she has to remember to qualify the table name with RJOHNSON—the table owner. Consequently, she creates a private synonym that enables her to reference the table by the Project name alone.

```
SQL> select Project_Number
  2  from Project;
from Project
     *
ERROR at line 2:
ORA-00942: table or view does not exist


SQL> create synonym Project for RJOHNSON.Project;

Synonym created.

SQL> select Project_Number
  2  from Project;

PROJECT_NUMBER
- - - - - - - - - - - - -
          1201
          2143
          4310
```

Dropping Synonyms

Oracle provides a statement for eliminating a synonym—the DROP SYNONYM statement. Its syntax is

```
DROP [PUBLIC] SYNONYM synonym-name;
```

where *synonym-name* is the name of the existing synonym that you want to eliminate.

Hiding Table Ownership with Public Synonyms

Consider the following example. You've developed a project accounting application at your company. You now must support two groups of users: those users who are running Version 1.0 and those running Version 2.0. However, Version 2.0 requires some database changes; the database used by Version 1.0 cannot be used by Version 2.0. The tables used by both versions can be stored in the same Oracle database, provided that they are owned by separate Oracle accounts.

Suppose the Version 1.0 tables are owned by an Oracle account named PAV10. The Version 2.0 tables are owned by another Oracle account named PAV20. If you wanted to support a group of software testers who need to switch back and forth between the two versions, you could construct two SQL*Plus scripts. The first script drops the existing synonyms and creates synonyms that point to the Version 1.0 tables.

```
drop synonym Account_Number;
...
drop synonym Task_Header;
drop synonym Task_Detail;
...
...
```

```
create synonym Account_Number for PAV10.Account_Number;
...
create synonym Task_Header for PAV10.Task_Header;
create synonym Task_Detail for PAV10.Task_Detail;
```

The second script also drops the existing synonyms but creates synonyms that point to the Version 2.0 tables.

```
drop synonym Account_Number;
...
drop synonym Task_Header;
drop synonym Task_Detail;
...
...
create synonym Account_Number for PAV20.Account_Number;
...
create synonym Task_Header for PAV20.Task_Header;
create synonym Task_Detail for PAV20.Task_Detail;
```

With these two scripts, a user could switch back and forth between the two versions of the project accounting tables.

Summary

This chapter discussed the following important facts regarding views:

- ■ A view is a virtual table. You can think of a view as a stored query.
- ■ A view can select a subset of a table's columns.
- ■ You can use a view to provide different column names from those of the base table.
- ■ A view can hide the complexity of a join.
- ■ A view can be based on other views.
- ■ A sequence is an Oracle database object that provides a set of numbers that increase or decrease at a specified increment.
- ■ A synonym is a pointer to a table owned by either the same user or a different user.
- ■ A synonym may be private—only visible to the Oracle user who created it—or it may be public—visible to all Oracle users.

16

Defining Transactions

One of the key features provided by the Oracle relational database engine is support for transactions. As you've seen in earlier chapters, a *transaction* is a logical unit of work—a series of database changes that reflect a well-defined event in the real world. In this chapter, we'll explore the interplay between transactions and concurrency. We'll also look at the use of rollback segments in supporting transactions.

A Database Transaction

A customer transfers money from a checking account to a savings account, a patient is transferred from the Intensive Care Unit to a regular bed, a jet engine subassembly passes final inspection—these are all examples of *real* transactions or events that must be accurately represented in a database. If a bank increases the funds in a customer's savings account and, for whatever reason, the same amount is not successfully subtracted from the customer's checking account, the transaction has failed, and all database changes made on behalf of the transaction must be undone.

You can think of a database transaction as a logical unit of work. A number of changes are made to database tables. If any of these changes fails, the entire transaction is undone or *rolled back*. If all changes were successful, you can commit the transaction by invoking the SQL COMMIT statement.

Oracle defines a transaction as the set of database changes that have been made since the beginning of an Oracle session or since the last COMMIT or ROLLBACK. The changes made by a transaction are not visible to other Oracle users until the transaction is committed.

Instance Recovery

If an Oracle instance is up and running and the system in which it resides suddenly fails—for example, due to a power failure—you have *instance failure*. The next time that the instance is started, whether via Database Manager or SQL*DBA, Oracle performs *instance recovery*.

- Oracle rolls forward any transactions that were committed at the time of instance failure but whose changes didn't have a chance to be written to the database files.
- Oracle rolls back any transactions that were not committed at the time of instance failure.
- Oracle releases any table or row locks that were in effect at the time of instance failure.

Oracle automatically performs these actions whenever an Oracle instance is started, whether or not the instance had previously failed.

An Example of Concurrency

As you recall, *concurrency* is the ability of multiple users to simultaneously read and modify various database tables. Oracle maximizes concurrency by enabling multiple users to query a table even while the contents of the table are being changed. You can observe this by using SQL*Plus and SQL*DBA to modify and query the same table.

To demonstrate this concept, I'll use the table Test_Table. In SQL*Plus, a SELECT statement is issued to query Test_Table. Notice that I've set the SQL*Plus variable TIME to ON so you can observe the sequence of events. As you can see, there are seven rows in Test_Table (see Figure 16.1). I'll delete the contents of Test_Table.

FIGURE 16.1.

*Deleting the contents of a table in a SQL*Plus session.*

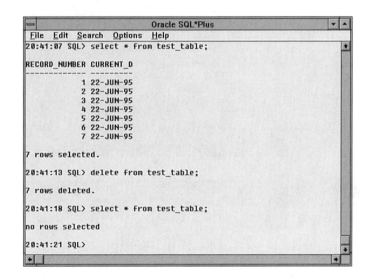

```
                        Oracle SQL*Plus
 File   Edit  Search  Options  Help
20:41:07 SQL> select * from test_table;

RECORD_NUMBER CURRENT_D
------------- ---------
            1 22-JUN-95
            2 22-JUN-95
            3 22-JUN-95
            4 22-JUN-95
            5 22-JUN-95
            6 22-JUN-95
            7 22-JUN-95

7 rows selected.

20:41:13 SQL> delete from test_table;

7 rows deleted.

20:41:18 SQL> select * from test_table;

no rows selected

20:41:21 SQL>
```

Next, I'll invoke SQL*DBA by double-clicking its icon. I'll also connect to Oracle as the user FRAYED_WIRES. Again, a query of Test_Table returns the same seven rows as seen with SQL*Plus (see Figure 16.2)—even though the rows have been deleted in the SQL*Plus session.

Switching back to the SQL*Plus window, I'll commit the transaction (see Figure 16.3).

After a COMMIT has been issued in SQL*Plus, the effect of the transaction is visible in SQL*DBA. As you can see in Figure 16.4, no rows are retrieved when Test_Table is queried. Note that the changes to the table performed by one Oracle session aren't visible to another Oracle session—even if the same Oracle user is connected to both sessions.

FIGURE 16.2.

*Retrieving rows in a SQL*DBA session.*

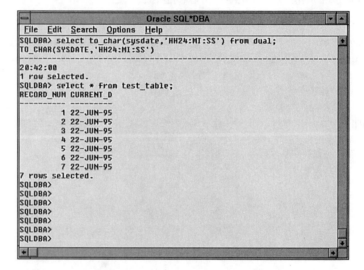

FIGURE 16.3.

*Transaction is committed in the SQL*Plus session.*

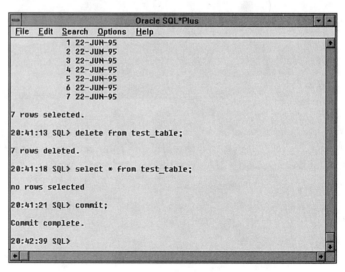

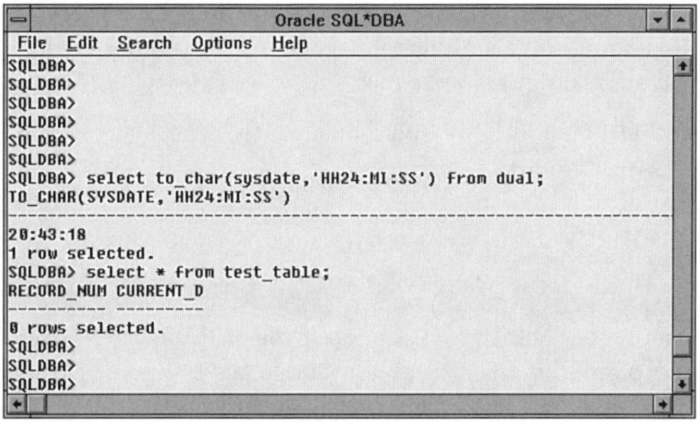

FIGURE 16.4.

Effect of transaction seen in the SQL*DBA session.

```
                    Oracle SQL*DBA                    ▼ ▲
 File  Edit  Search  Options  Help
SQLDBA>
SQLDBA>
SQLDBA>
SQLDBA>
SQLDBA>
SQLDBA>
SQLDBA> select to_char(sysdate,'HH24:MI:SS') from dual;
TO_CHAR(SYSDATE,'HH24:MI:SS')
-------------------------------------------------
20:43:18
1 row selected.
SQLDBA> select * from test_table;
RECORD_NUM CURRENT_D
---------- ---------
0 rows selected.
SQLDBA>
SQLDBA>
SQLDBA>
```

Oracle Locks

To maintain concurrency and read consistency, Oracle uses a variety of locks, depending on the submitted SQL statement (see Chapter 8, "Using SQL to Modify Data," for more information about read consistency). These locks are either *exclusive* or *share*. Exclusive locks behave as you would expect; when a user places an exclusive lock on a resource, no other user has similar access to that resource until the lock is relinquished. Share locks enable multiple users to read from the locked resource. Oracle's management of these locks is transparent to database users.

TIP

In examining the online Oracle documentation, you might stumble upon the LOCK TABLE statement, which places an exclusive lock on a table. Avoid using the LOCK TABLE statement. If you're using this statement so that users can't make any changes while you perform some table maintenance, you might be making things worse; you might forget to place a lock on all the tables that you're working on. Instead, start the database in exclusive mode via SQL*DBA.

The *SELECT FOR UPDATE* Statement

The SELECT FOR UPDATE statement is an Oracle SQL statement that is used to lock the selected rows so that they can't be modified until a COMMIT or ROLLBACK is used to release the row locks. For instance, suppose Jones and Smith are both updating patient records. Jones brings up the record for Patient ID 9191 and begins to change the billing information. Smith also brings up the record for Patient ID 9191 and starts changing the patient's insurance information. If the application software that Jones and Smith are using doesn't lock the record with a SELECT FOR UPDATE, both of them are able to make changes; however, the last person to issue an UPDATE statement actually changes the row.

To preclude this possibility, you should use the SELECT FOR UPDATE statement. The syntax for SELECT FOR UPDATE is

```
select-stmt
FOR UPDATE [NOWAIT];
```

where *select-stmt* is a valid Oracle SELECT statement that identifies the rows to be modified.

You should specify the NOWAIT option if you want Oracle to return an error code indicating that the record is already locked. Without the NOWAIT option, the statement waits until the lock is released from the row through a COMMIT or ROLLBACK issued by the Oracle user who has a lock on the row. By using the SELECT FOR UPDATE with the NOWAIT option, an application developer can take some other action when a row is locked—for example, delay five seconds and try again and notify the user after three tries that the row is currently unavailable.

For example, the record for patient ID R4321 is locked from SQL*Plus by issuing a SELECT FOR UPDATE statement (see Figure 16.5).

FIGURE 16.5.

*Locking a record from SQL*Plus.*

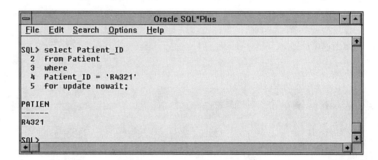

From SQL*DBA, an attempt is made to lock the same record. However, because the NOWAIT option is used with SELECT FOR UPDATE, Oracle returns an error message indicating that the resource—the row—is in use (see Figure 16.6).

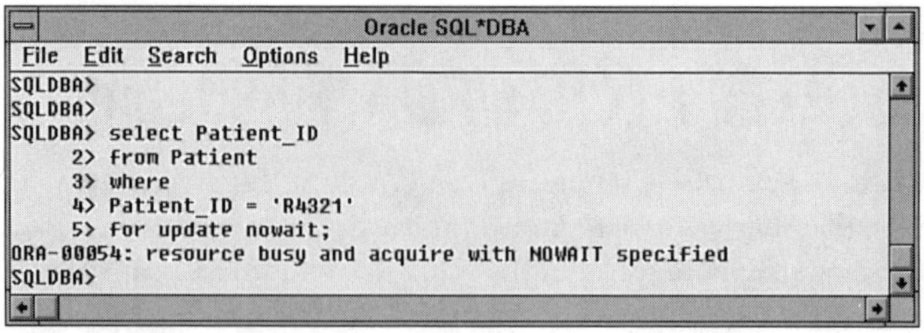

FIGURE 16.6.

*Attempting a SELECT FOR UPDATE with NOWAIT from SQL*DBA.*

Transactions and Rollback Segments

Because a database transaction can be rolled back, Oracle must have a place to write the rows that are changed by a transaction. The *rollback segment* is the database object that contains all changes that are made by a transaction. The default database installed by Personal Oracle contains four rollback segments: SYSTEM, RB_TEMP, RB1, and RB2.

With a large transaction, it's possible to exhaust the available space in the rollback segment tablespace. For example, the following anonymous PL/SQL block attempts to insert one million rows into a table.

```
SQL> declare
  2
  2    max_records constant int := 1000000;
  3    i           int := 1;
  4
  4
  4  begin
  5
  5    for i in 1..max_records loop
  6
  6      insert into XYZ
  7        (Column1, Column2)
  8      values
  9        (i, i);
 10
 10    end loop;
 11
 11    commit;
 12
 12  end;
 13  /
declare
*
ERROR at line 1:
ORA-01562: failed to extend rollback segment (id = 2)
ORA-01650: unable to extend rollback segment RB1 by 50 in
           tablespace ROLLBACK_DATA
ORA-06512: at line 6
```

If you want to delete all the rows in a table, use the TRUNCATE TABLE statement—it's faster because it doesn't write the deleted rows to a rollback segment. Don't use the TRUNCATE TABLE statement if you are deleting all rows in a table as part of a transaction.

Adding a New Rollback Segment

Whenever a transaction is started, a rollback segment is assigned to store the row changes associated with the transaction. If the transaction is very large—meaning that a large number of rows are affected by the transaction—the assigned rollback segment might have many extents allocated for storing the changed rows. It's possible to have a transaction so large that either of two events occur.

■ The number of extents allocated to the rollback segment exceeds the maximum allowed number (which is 121 by default).

■ There is not enough free space in the rollback segment tablespace—by default, ROLLBACK_DATA—to allocate another extent to the rollback segment.

To reduce the likelihood of either of these situations occurring, you should perform the following steps:

■ You should add an additional datafile to the rollback segment tablespace (which is described in detail in Chapter 25, "Managing Space").

■ You should create another rollback segment with larger initial extent and next extent sizes.

Let's look at the steps that are needed to create a new rollback segment.

Creating the New Rollback Segment

You can create a new rollback segment with the CREATE ROLLBACK SEGMENT statement with the following syntax:

```
CREATE ROLLBACK SEGMENT rollback-segment-name
[TABLESPACE tablespace-name]
[STORAGE storage-clause]
```

where *rollback-segment-name* is the name of the rollback segment to be created, and *tablespace-name* is the tablespace where *rollback-segment-name* will be stored (which should usually be set to ROLLBACK_DATA for Personal Oracle or the Oracle Workgroup Server). *storage-clause* is an optional set of storage parameters used for *rollback-segment-name* (see Chapter 25 for more information).

For example, the following code shows how you would create rollback segment RB_LARGE with larger values for the initial and next extents:

```
SQL> create rollback segment RB_LARGE
  2  tablespace ROLLBACK_DATA
  3  storage (initial 200K next 200K);

Rollback segment created.
```

Even though RB_LARGE has been successfully created, it is not yet available for use by transactions, as you can see by inspecting the data dictionary view DBA_ROLLBACK_SEGS. The status of RB_LARGE is shown as OFFLINE.

```
SQL> select segment_name, status
  2  from dba_rollback_segs;

SEGMENT_NAME                      STATUS
- - - - - - - - - - - - - - - - - - - - - - - - - - - - - -
SYSTEM                            ONLINE
RB_TEMP                           ONLINE
RB1                               ONLINE
```

```
RB2                          ONLINE
RB_LARGE                     OFFLINE
```

Modifying the Initialization Parameter

The next step in adding the new rollback segment is to modify the initialization parameter ROLLBACK_SEGMENTS to include the new rollback segment. You can accomplish this with Database Manager.

> **NOTE**
>
> Before you can modify an initialization parameter such as the list of roll back segments, you need to save the set of initialization parameters under a specific name. Please refer to "Using Database Manager to Change an initialization Parameter" in Chapter 30 for further details.

1. Invoke Database Manager by double-clicking its icon.
2. Click the Configure button.
3. Click the Advanced button.
4. Click OK when Database Manager displays the warning about editing initialization parameters.
5. Click from the drop-down list of parameters and select ROLLBACK_SEGMENTS (see Figure 16.7).
6. In the Value field, enter (RB1, RB2, RB_LARGE) and click the Set button.
7. Click the OK button.

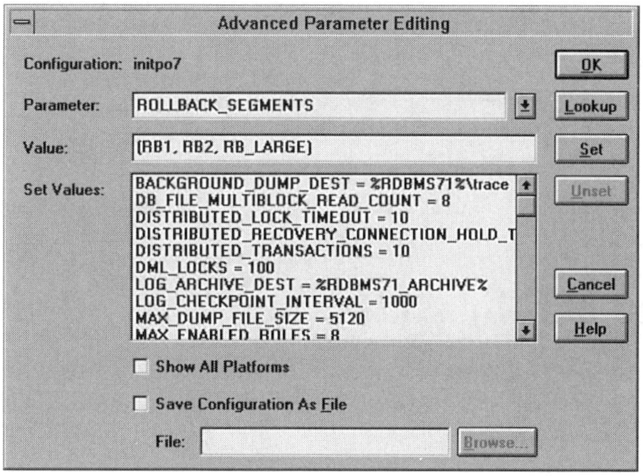

FIGURE 16.7.

Setting the value of ROLLBACK_SEGMENTS in Database Manager.

8. Database Manager displays a message informing you that the change will take effect the next time that the database is started.

Determining the Status of the New Rollback Segment

As Database Manager indicated, it is necessary to restart the database for a change to an initialization parameter to take effect. Using Database Manager, shut down Personal Oracle and restart it. Once again, query the data dictionary view DBA_ROLLBACK_SEGS. This time, you'll see that RB_LARGE is ONLINE.

```
SQL> select segment_name, status
  2  from dba_rollback_segs;

SEGMENT_NAME                      STATUS
-------------------------------   ----------------
SYSTEM                            ONLINE
RB_TEMP                           ONLINE
RB1                               ONLINE
RB2                               ONLINE
RB_LARGE                          ONLINE
```

To ensure that a transaction uses a particular rollback segment, use the SET TRANSACTION statement with the following syntax:

```
SET TRANSACTION USE ROLLBACK SEGMENT rollback-segment;
```

where `rollback-segment` is the rollback segment to be assigned to the transaction.

For example, if you issue the following statement at the beginning of a transaction, all subsequent row changes are stored in rollback segment RB_LARGE.

```
SQL> set transaction use rollback segment RB_LARGE;

Transaction set.
```

If you don't issue the SET TRANSACTION statement at the beginning of a transaction, Oracle returns the following error message:

```
SQL> set transaction use rollback segment RB_LARGE;
set transaction use rollback segment RB_LARGE
*
ERROR at line 1:
ORA-01453: SET TRANSACTION must be first statement of transaction
```

Avoid Setting *AUTOCOMMIT* to ON in SQL*Plus

One of the SQL*Plus system variables, AUTOCOMMIT, controls the transaction behavior of SQL*Plus. By default, AUTOCOMMIT is set to OFF. The effect of this setting is that SQL*Plus will only commit changes to a table in two situations.

■ When a COMMIT statement is issued

■ When SQL*Plus is exited in a normal manner

Here is an example of the effect of setting AUTOCOMMIT to ON.

```
SQL> select * from test_table;

RECORD_NUMBER CURRENT_D
------------- ---------
            1 22-JUN-95
            2 22-JUN-95
            3 22-JUN-95
            4 22-JUN-95
            5 22-JUN-95
            6 22-JUN-95
            7 22-JUN-95

7 rows selected.

SQL> set autocommit on
SQL>
SQL> delete from test_table;
Commit complete.

7 rows deleted.

SQL> rollback;

Rollback complete.

SQL> select * from test_table;

no rows selected
```

Notice that the ROLLBACK statement had no effect because the previous DELETE statement had already been committed.

Summary

This chapter included the following essential information regarding database transactions:

■ A transaction is a series of database changes that can be made permanent by issuing a COMMIT statement—or undone with the ROLLBACK statement.

■ A transaction consists of those database changes that have been performed since the beginning of an Oracle session or since the most recent COMMIT or ROLLBACK.

■ When an Oracle instance is started, Oracle automatically performs instance recovery, if needed, to roll forward any committed transactions, roll back any uncommitted transactions, and release any locks in effect at the time of instance failure.

■ Consider using the TRUNCATE TABLE statement to quickly delete all rows in a table. Don't use TRUNCATE TABLE if you need to be able to specify which rows to delete in a WHERE clause or if the deleted rows are part of a database transaction.

■ To lock a set of rows so they can't be modified by anyone else, use the SELECT FOR UPDATE statement. Other users are still able to retrieve the unmodified rows, but they can't modify them until the row locks have been released via a COMMIT or ROLLBACK statement.

17

The Basics of PL/SQL

Up to this point, I've presented SQL as a language without procedural capabilities. However, Oracle offers procedural language extensions to SQL through the PL/SQL language. PL/SQL is the basis for the following application logic elements:

- SQL*Plus script. A SQL*Plus script can incorporate PL/SQL block subprograms.
- Stored procedure or function. A stored procedure or function is a PL/SQL subprogram that can be invoked by a client application, a database trigger, or an Oracle tool application trigger.
- Database trigger. A database trigger is a PL/SQL subprogram that is used to perform some action based on the execution of a DML statement—such as INSERT, UPDATE, or DELETE—against a database table.
- Package. A set of PL/SQL procedures, functions, cursors, and other PL/SQL variables are bundled together into a package.
- Application trigger. Oracle application tools such as forms and reports are equipped with a PL/SQL engine so that developers can construct application triggers using PL/SQL.

The purpose of this chapter is to introduce the fundamental elements of PL/SQL. You should feel comfortable with the syntax and use of PL/SQL before you attempt to design stored procedures (Chapter 18, "Creating and Using Stored Procedures, Functions, and Packages") and database triggers (Chapter 22, "Enforcing Business Rules with Database Triggers"). This chapter addresses the features contained in PL/SQL Version 2.1.

TIP

Don't use SQL*Plus to type in each line of a PL/SQL script. If you make a typo, SQL*Plus won't provide any feedback until it reads the / that terminates the PL/SQL block. This is because SQL*Plus passes the entire block to the PL/SQL engine only when the block is complete. The PL/SQL engine is a component of the Oracle RDBMS. Instead, use a text editor, such as Notepad, for developing your PL/SQL scripts. You can paste the script directly into SQL*Plus or invoke it with the START or @ command.

PL/SQL Is a Block-Structured Language

PL/SQL is a block-structured language with a syntax similar to the C programming language. In addition to supporting embedded SQL statements, PL/SQL offers standard programming constructs such as procedure and function declarations, control statements such as IF and LOOP, and declared variables. A PL/SQL program consists of procedures, functions, or anonymous blocks. An anonymous block is an unnamed PL/SQL block that has no arguments and returns no value. Anonymous blocks are common in scripts that are executed in a SQL*Plus session.

From a top-level perspective, Figure 17.1 illustrates the structure of a PL/SQL block, which

FIGURE 17.1.   PL/SQL Block

Top-level structure of a
PL/SQL block.

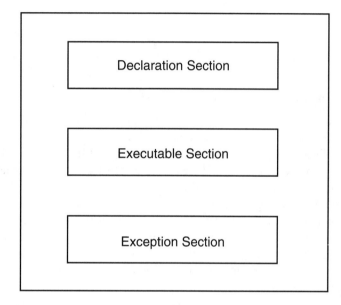

includes an optional declaration section, an executable section, and an optional section for handling PL/SQL and SQL exceptions and errors.

Let's look at a simple anonymous PL/SQL block that generates some test data. The following code, which is executed from a SQL*Plus script, inserts 100 rows into TEST_TABLE:

```
SQL> @c:\po7_book\chap17\fig1
SQL> drop table test_table;

Table dropped.

SQL>
SQL> create table test_table (
  2  record_number      int,
  3  current_date       date);

Table created.

SQL>
SQL> DECLARE
  2
  2  max_records CONSTANT int := 100;
  3  i              int := 1;
```

```
  4
  4   BEGIN
  5
  5   FOR i IN 1..max_records LOOP
  6
  6     INSERT INTO test_table
  7             (record_number, current_date)
  8     VALUES
  9             (i, SYSDATE);
 10
 10   END LOOP;
 11
 11   COMMIT;
 12   END;
/
```

```
PL/SQL procedure successfully completed.
```

Let's look at some of the elements in the previous PL/SQL script. This is an anonymous PL/SQL block because it has no name—it isn't declared as a procedure, function, or package. All the lines in this script are contained in a single SQL*Plus script. The first two SQL commands drop the TEST_TABLE and then create it. The PL/SQL block actually starts with the word DECLARE. The declaration section declares a constant, max_records, and a variable, i, which serves as a counter. The beginning of the executable portion of the block is designated by BEGIN. The block contains a single FOR LOOP that inserts a row into TEST_TABLE while i is less than or equal to max_records. When the FOR LOOP completes, the transaction is committed. The last line of the script is a /, which causes SQL*Plus to submit the PL/SQL block to the PL/SQL engine. Unless a PL/SQL compilation error occurs, the only feedback provided by SQL*Plus is a message—PL/SQL procedure successfully completed. In the next chapter, I'll discuss methods that can be used to produce diagnostics from PL/SQL that enable you to see the progress of a PL/SQL subprogram's execution.

The Declaration Section

The declaration section of a PL/SQL block is optional. However, you must declare all variables and constants that are referenced in the PL/SQL statements. To include a declaration section in a PL/SQL block, begin the PL/SQL block with the word DECLARE. Each variable or constant declaration consists of its name, datatype, and an optional default value. As with all PL/SQL statements, each variable and constant declaration is terminated with a semicolon. Here are some examples of declared variables and constants:

```
Fax_Number              VARCHAR2(10);
Current_Used_Value      NUMBER(6,2) := 100.00;
Max_Current_Used_Value        REAL := 9999.99;
State                   VARCHAR2(2) := 'CA';
```

The Executable Section

The executable section of a PL/SQL block follows the keyword BEGIN. Each PL/SQL statement is terminated by a semicolon. These statements can be categorized as

- Assignment statements
- Flow-of-control statements
- SQL statements
- Cursor statements

The Exception Section

An exception is an error condition that occurs during the execution of a PL/SQL program. An exception might be predefined—for instance, an INSERT statement attempts to add a duplicate row to a table, resulting in the DUP_VAL_ON_INDEX exception being raised. You can also define your own exceptions that are specific to your application. The exception section defines the exception handlers invoked for both predefined and user-defined exceptions. Each exception handler consists of one or more PL/SQL statements.

Declaring Variables with PL/SQL

Another capability provided by PL/SQL—but not SQL—is additional datatypes. In addition to the normal Oracle SQL datatypes, PL/SQL also enables you to declare variables with these datatypes:

- BOOLEAN: A Boolean variable can be assigned the predefined constants TRUE, FALSE, or NULL.
- BINARY_INTEGER: This type is used for manipulating signed integers in the range of −2,147,483,647 to 2,147,483,647.
- NATURAL: A subset of BINARY_INTEGER, this datatype is the set of integers from 0 to 2,147,483,647.
- POSITIVE: Another subset of BINARY_INTEGER, this datatype is the set of integers from 1 to 2,147,483,647.
- %TYPE: This designation enables you to declare a variable's datatype as being equivalent to the specified column's datatype, resulting in PL/SQL code that is easier to maintain.
- %ROWTYPE: With this datatype, you can declare a composite variable that is equivalent to a row in the specified table. The composite variable is composed of the column names and datatypes in the referenced table.

In addition, PL/SQL provides two composite datatypes: TABLE and RECORD. Chapter 19, "PL/SQL Datatypes and Variables," addresses the details of using these composite datatypes.

Using %TYPE to Declare a Variable

The syntax for declaring a variable with %TYPE is

```
variable-name    table-name.column-name%TYPE;
```

where `column-name` is a column defined in `table-name`.

For example, you declare a variable to store a repair depot technician's name in this way:

```
Tech_Name    Depot_Estimate.Technician%TYPE;
```

The benefit of using %TYPE in a variable declaration is that the PL/SQL code is dependent on the definition of the Technician column in the Depot_Estimate table.

Using %ROWTYPE to Declare a Variable

The syntax for declaring a variable with %ROWTYPE is

```
variable-name    table-name%ROWTYPE;
```

For instance, a composite variable that stores a row from the Depot_Estimate table is declared like this:

```
Depot_Est_Row    Depot_Estimate%ROWTYPE;
```

An element of `Depot_Est_Row` can be accessed in this manner:

```
Depot_Est_Row.Technician := 'RICHARDSON';
```

Some Familiar Control Structures

There are several PL/SQL statements that control the flow of execution of a PL/SQL sub-program.

- IF
- LOOP
- EXIT
- WHILE LOOP
- FOR LOOP
- GOTO
- NULL

Before you can build stored procedures and triggers, you should be familiar with the basics of PL/SQL programming. Let's explore the detailed use of these statements.

The *IF* Statement

The syntax of PL/SQL's IF statement differs somewhat from that of the C programming language.

```
IF condition THEN
   statement; ...  statement;
[ELSIF condition THEN
statement; ...  statement;]
...
[ELSIF condition THEN
statement; ...  statement;]
[ELSE
statement; ...  statement;]
END IF;
```

where *condition* is a valid PL/SQL condition, and *statement* is a valid PL/SQL statement.

Regarding the IF statement, be aware of these facts:

■ The ELSIF and ELSE clauses are optional.

■ An IF statement can have multiple ELSIF clauses but only one ELSE clause.

■ Note the spelling: ELSIF not ELSEIF.

Here's a simple example of the IF statement:

```
if MOD(i,5) = 0 then
  rec_number := 5;
elsif MOD(i,7) = 0 then
  rec_number := 7;
else
  rec_number := i;
end if;
```

The Simple *LOOP* Statement

The most basic type of loop is the LOOP statement without any additional qualifiers.

```
LOOP
   statement; ... statement;
END LOOP;
```

Obviously, this is an infinite loop. To exit this loop when a required condition is satisfied, use the EXIT statement.

The *EXIT* Statement

The EXIT statement has two forms.

■ EXIT without any other clauses—an unconditional exit

■ EXIT [*label-name*] WHEN *condition*

The first form of EXIT causes control to exit the loop that encloses the EXIT statement.

The second form of EXIT causes control to exit the enclosing loop when the specified condition is met, as in:

```
SQL> declare
  2
  2   i  positive := 1;
  3   max_loops constant positive := 100;
  4
  4   begin
  5
  5   loop
  6
  6     i := i + 1;
  7     exit when i > max_loops;
  8
  8   end loop;
  9
  9   end;
 10   /

PL/SQL procedure successfully completed.
```

The *WHILE-LOOP* Statement

The WHILE-LOOP statement adds a condition to a loop.

```
WHILE condition LOOP
  statement; ... statement;
END LOOP;
```

Here's a simple example of a WHILE-LOOP statement:

```
WHILE I < 100 LOOP
  I := I + 1;
  insert into temp_table (rec_number) values (I);
END LOOP;
```

The *FOR-LOOP* Statement

The FOR-LOOP is quite similar to the WHILE-LOOP. Here's the syntax you need to be aware of:

```
FOR loop-variable IN [REVERSE] lower-bound..upper-bound LOOP
  statement;  ...  statement;
END LOOP;
```

where *loop-variable* is an integer variable that serves as a counter, *lower-bound* is the lower bound of the increment range, and *upper-bound* is the upper bound of the increment range.

REVERSE is an optional keyword that, if used, causes the loop to decrement from *upper-bound* to *lower-bound*.

The *GOTO* Statement

Yes, PL/SQL offers the use of the potentially dangerous GOTO statement. Of course, to use GOTO, you must provide a label to which control is transferred. In PL/SQL, a statement label is defined in this way:

```
<<my_label>>
```

Here's an alternative to the EXIT statement using GOTO and a label:

```
SQL> declare
  2
  2  i  positive := 1;
  3  max_loops constant positive := 100;
  4
  4  begin
  5
  5  i := 1;
  6
  6  loop
  7
  7    i := i + 1;
  8    if i > max_loops then
  9        goto more_processing;
 10    end if;
 11
 11  end loop;
 12
 12  <<more_processing>>
 13  i := 1;
 14
 14  end;
 15  /

PL/SQL procedure successfully completed.
```

The *NULL* Statement

For certain situations, you should indicate to PL/SQL that no action is to be taken. For instance, in an exception handler, you might not want to do anything when a particular exception occurs. For the sake of clarity, use the NULL statement in an IF to indicate that no action is to be taken for a particular ELSIF clause.

Unfortunately, even though this statement has nothing to do with the null value, Oracle chose to name this statement NULL. Here's an example of how the NULL statement can be used:

```
if (mod(i,10) = 0) then
  i := i + 1;
else
    NULL;
end if;
```

The Assignment Statement

As you've already seen, PL/SQL uses `:=` to assign a value to a PL/SQL variable. You can define a constant's value or a variable's default value in the declaration section. One point is worth noting: You can't assign a NULL to a variable that was declared using the %TYPE notation when the referenced column is defined as NOT NULL.

Including Comments in a PL/SQL Subprogram

There are two ways you can document your PL/SQL code. First, you can add a comment on any line by placing a `--` followed by the comment, as shown:

```
Depot_Est_Row.Technician := Last_Tech_Name;
-- Assign the name of the last technician involved
```

You can also add comments in the *C-style*—by enclosing them within `/*` and `*/`. This method is best suited for including multiline comments:

```
j := j + 1;

/* The next section inserts a row into the Utility_Audit table
   to record the name of the current Oracle user and the
   current date and time (SYSDATE).
*/

insert into Utility_Audit
...
```

Using SQL Statements in a PL/SQL Program

You can use SQL statements in an anonymous block, procedure, or function as they are used in SQL*Plus, with a few differences. As with other PL/SQL statements, each SQL statement must be terminated by a semicolon. However, PL/SQL enables you to reference declared variables in a SQL statement, as in:

```
DECLARE

max_records CONSTANT int := 100;
i            int := 1;

BEGIN

FOR i IN 1..max_records LOOP

  if (mod(i,10) = 0) then
    INSERT INTO test_table
           (record_number, current_date)
    VALUES
           (i, SYSDATE);
  else
    NULL;
  end if;
```

```
END LOOP;

COMMIT;
END;
/
```

In this example, the INSERT statement uses the numeric variable i and the pseudocolumn SYSDATE to place values in the Record_Number and Current_Date columns.

PL/SQL and the *SELECT* Statement

In a PL/SQL subprogram, the SELECT statement employs another clause—INTO—to identify the PL/SQL variables that should receive column values. Place the INTO clause between the select list and the FROM clause. Here is an example of an anonymous PL/SQL block containing a SELECT statement:

```
SQL> set serveroutput on
SQL>
SQL> declare
  2
  2   Average_Body_Temp        Patient.Body_Temp_Deg_F%type;
  3
  3   begin
  4
  4   dbms_output.enable;
  5
  5   select avg(Body_Temp_Deg_F)
  6     into Average_Body_Temp
  7     from Patient;
  8
  8   dbms_output.put_line('Average body temp in Deg. F: ' ||
      to_char(Average_Body_Temp,'999.99'));
  9
  9   end;
 10   /
Average body temp in Deg. F:    99.80

PL/SQL procedure successfully completed.
```

PL/SQL Subprograms

PL/SQL also supports the use of subprograms—named procedures and functions. A PL/SQL procedure performs some action and can accept optional parameters. A PL/SQL function returns a value of some specified datatype and can also accept optional parameters.

Using Sub-Blocks

PL/SQL permits you to include sub-blocks within a block. For instance, this anonymous block contains another anonymous sub-block that has its own declaration section.

```
SQL> declare
  2
  2  max_i       constant int := 100;
  3  i           int := 1;
  4  rec_number  int;
  5
  5  begin
  6
  6  for i in 1..max_i loop
  7
  7    if mod(i,5) = 0 then
  8      rec_number := 5;
  9    elsif mod(i,7) = 0 then
 10      rec_number := 7;
 11    else
 12      rec_number := i;
 13    end if;
 14
 14    insert into test_table
 15      (record_number, current_date)
 16      values
 17      (rec_number, sysdate);
 18
 18  -- Here is a sub-block:
 19
 19    declare
 20    max_j constant int := 20;
 21    j int := 1;
 22
 22    begin
 23
 23      for j in 1..max_j loop
 24
 24        rec_number := rec_number * j;
 25
 25        insert into test_table
 26          (record_number, current_date)
 27          values
 28          (rec_number, sysdate);
 29
 29      end loop;
 30
 30    end;
 31
 31    commit;
 32  end loop;
 33
 33  end;
 34  /

PL/SQL procedure successfully completed.

SQL> select count(*) from test_table;

COUNT(*)
---------
     2100
```

> **TIP**
>
> Although PL/SQL supports the capability to embed blocks within one another, it's not a desirable practice for two reasons. First, it reduces the readability—and the resulting maintainability—of your code. Second, embedded blocks can't be used by other PL/SQL subprograms. It's better to design procedures and functions for improved code reuse and maintainability.

Declaring a Procedure

In addition to anonymous blocks, you can also declare PL/SQL procedures and functions. The syntax for declaring a procedure is

```
PROCEDURE procedure-name [(argument1 ... [, argumentN) ] IS
[local-variable-declarations]
BEGIN
executable-section
[exception-section]
END [procedure-name];
```

where the variables are defined in this way:

> `procedure-name` is the procedure name and subject to Oracle database object-naming restrictions.
>
> `argument1` through `argumentN` are optional argument declarations that consist of:
>
> `argument-name` [IN ¦ OUT] `datatype` [{:= ¦ DEFAULT} `value`]
>
> `local-variable-declarations` are optional declarations of variables, constants, and other procedures and functions local to `procedure-name`.
>
> `executable-section` is the PL/SQL statements that compose the procedure.
>
> `exception-section` is the optional exception-handling section of the procedure.

> **NOTE**
>
> It's important to distinguish between stored procedures and procedures that are declared and used in anonymous blocks. The procedures that are declared and called in anonymous blocks are *temporal*; when the anonymous block has completed execution, they no longer exist as far as Oracle is concerned. A stored procedure that is created with a CREATE PROCEDURE statement or contained in a package is permanent in the sense that it can be invoked by a SQL*Plus script, a PL/SQL subprogram, or a database trigger.

To illustrate this syntax, here is an example of an anonymous block that declares a procedure named Record_Patient_Temp_Deg_C. This procedure has two arguments: the patient ID and the patient's body temperature as measured in degrees Centigrade.

```
SQL> declare
  2
  2  New_Patient_ID  Patient.Patient_ID%type;
  3  High_Fever      constant real := 42.0;
  4
  4  procedure Record_Patient_Temp_Deg_C (Patient_ID varchar2,
  5                                       Body_Temp_Deg_C real) is
  6
  6  Temp_Deg_F real;
  7
  7  begin
  8
  8    Temp_Deg_F := (9.0/5.0)*Body_Temp_Deg_C + 32.0;
  9
  9    insert into Patient
 10    (Patient_ID, Body_Temp_Deg_F)
 11    values
 12    (Patient_ID, Temp_Deg_F);
 13
 13    commit;
 14  end;
 15
 15  begin
 16
 16  New_Patient_ID := 'GG9999';
 17
 17  Record_Patient_Temp_Deg_C (New_Patient_ID, High_Fever);
 18
 18  end;
 19  /

PL/SQL procedure successfully completed.

SQL> select Patient_ID, Body_Temp_Deg_F
  2  from Patient
  3  where
  4  Patient_ID = 'GG9999';

PATIEN BODY_TEMP_DEG_F
------ ---------------
GG9999            107.6
```

Notice that the variables declared within a procedure are not accessible outside of the procedure.

```
SQL> declare
  2
  2  procedure Delete_Patients is
  3
  3  Temp_Deg_F real;
  4
  4  begin
  5
```

```
  5     delete from Patient
  6     where
  7     Patient_ID = 'GG3333';
  8
  8     commit;
  9
  9   end;
 10
 10   begin
 11
 11   Temp_Deg_F := 100.0;
 12
 12   end;
 13   /
Temp_Deg_F := 100.0;
*
ERROR at line 11:
ORA-06550: line 11, column 1:
PLS-00201: identifier 'TEMP_DEG_F' must be declared
ORA-06550: line 11, column 1:
PL/SQL: Statement ignored
```

Declaring a Function

A PL/SQL function declaration is similar to a procedure declaration—except that the function returns a value of a predefined datatype. The syntax for declaring a function is

```
FUNCTION function-name [(argument1 ... [, argumentN) ]
RETURN function-datatype IS
[local-variable-declarations]
BEGIN
executable-section
[exception-section]
END [function-name];
```

where the variables are defined in this way:

> *function-name* is the function name and subject to Oracle database object-naming restrictions.
>
> *argument1* through *argumentN* are optional argument declarations that consist of:
>
> *argument-name* [IN ¦ OUT] *datatype* [{:= ¦ DEFAULT} *value*]
>
> *function-datatype* is the datatype returned by *function-name*.
>
> *local-variable-declarations* are optional declarations of variables, constants, and other procedures and functions local to *function-name*.
>
> *executable-section* is the PL/SQL statements that compose the function.
>
> *exception-section* is the optional exception-handling section of the function.

For instance, a function that returned the highest patient temperature expressed in degrees Centigrade would be declared in this way:

```
SQL> declare
  2
  2   Pat_ID      Patient.Patient_ID%type;
  3   High_Fever real;
  4   status      boolean;
  5
  5   function Highest_Fever_Temp_Deg_C (Patient_ID OUT varchar2,
  6                                      Body_Temp_Deg_C OUT real)
  7           return boolean is
  8
  8   Max_Fever_Deg_F real;
  9
  9   begin
 10
 10   select Patient_ID, Body_Temp_Deg_F
 11     into Patient_ID, Max_Fever_Deg_F
 12     from Patient
 13     where
 14     Body_Temp_Deg_F =
 15     (select max(Body_Temp_Deg_F)
 16       from Patient);
 1/
 17   Body_Temp_Deg_C := (Max_Fever_Deg_F - 32.0)*5.0/9.0;
 18
 18   return true;
 19
 19   end;
 20
 20   -- Beginning of executable section of anonymous block.
 21
 21   begin
 22
 22   dbms_output.enable;
 23
 23   status := Highest_Fever_Temp_Deg_C (Pat_ID, High_Fever);
 24
 24   dbms_output.put_line('Patient ' || Pat_ID || ' has a fever of ' ||
 25                         to_char(High_Fever,'999.9') || ' C. ');
 26
 26   end;
 27   /
Patient GG9999 has a fever of   42.0 C.

PL/SQL procedure successfully completed.
```

Procedure and Function Arguments

Each procedure and function argument can optionally be defined as one of the following:

- ■ IN. The value of the argument is passed to the procedure or function, but no value is returned to the calling PL/SQL subprogram. Within a procedure or function, you can't assign a value to an argument declared as IN; you can only reference the value of this type of argument.

■ OUT. The procedure or function doesn't use the passed value but does return a value to the calling PL/SQL subprogram. Within a procedure or function, you can't reference the value of an argument declared as OUT; you can only assign a value to this type of argument.

■ IN OUT. The value of the argument is passed to the procedure or function and is also returned to the calling PL/SQL subprogram. An argument declared as IN OUT can be referenced and assigned a value within its procedure or function.

Here's an example of how all three types of arguments are used:

```
SQL> declare
  2
  2  This_Arg1 number;
  3  This_Arg2 number;
  4  This_Arg3 number;
  5
  5  procedure Different_Arguments
  6          (arg1 IN      number,
  7           arg2 OUT     number,
  8           arg3 IN OUT number) is
  9
  9  begin
 10
 10  arg2 := arg1;
 11  arg3 := arg3 + 1;
 12
 12  end;
 13
 13  --  Beginning of executable section of anonymous block.
 14
 14  begin
 15
 15  This_Arg1 := 3.14159;
 16
 16  Different_Arguments (This_Arg1, This_Arg2, This_Arg3);
 17
 17  end;
 18  /

PL/SQL procedure successfully completed.
```

In addition, a default value can be defined for an argument.

```
procedure Different_Arguments
          (arg1 IN      number := 100,
           arg2 OUT     number,
           arg3 IN OUT number) is
```

Summary

This chapter covered the essential elements of PL/SQL.

- PL/SQL is a block-structured language in which a block consists of an optional declaration section, an executable section, and an optional exception-handling section.
- There are some additional datatypes that are available in PL/SQL's SQL extensions: BINARY_INTEGER, NATURAL, POSITIVE, %TYPE, %ROWTYPE, TABLE, and RECORD.
- Executable PL/SQL statements include IF, LOOP, EXIT, the WHILE-LOOP, the FOR-LOOP, and GOTO.
- A PL/SQL subprogram can include SQL statements that reference PL/SQL variables.
- A PL/SQL subprogram can declare its own procedures and functions.

18

Creating and Using Stored Procedures, Functions, and Packages

A stored procedure or function is a PL/SQL program stored in an Oracle database and invoked by a user, directly or indirectly. The benefits of using stored procedures and functions are

- Improved performance. In a client/server architecture, a client application issues SQL requests to a database server. As the number of users increases, so does the number of SQL requests, and the network can quickly become the performance bottleneck. The use of stored procedures offers a significant performance improvement because a single call to a stored procedure can invoke multiple SQL statements that are executed on the server, thereby reducing network traffic.

- Reusability. A PL/SQL program is written once and can be used in a variety of situations—in SQL*Plus scripts, in database triggers, and in client application logic.

- Portability. You can use a stored procedure in any Oracle7 database, regardless of platform. You don't have to deal with compatibility issues such as the operating system and compiler releases. If Oracle7 is supported by the platform, the stored procedure can be ported to it without any additional changes. Of course, if the stored procedure contains references to file and directory names, you might need to make some changes.

- Maintainability. A stored procedure is designed to perform a specific task. Such a task might be required by a database trigger, a SQL*Plus script, an application program, or another stored procedure. By calling the same stored procedure from all of these sources, you reduce the cost of software maintenance.

- Security. A stored procedure or function can provide a user with access to a table for a specific purpose.

In this chapter, you learn the essentials of using stored procedures.

Creating a Stored Procedure or Function

Using a text processor, such as Notepad or Write, to construct a stored procedure is a good idea. You can copy the stored procedure from the text processor and paste it into SQL*Plus for development and testing. The syntax for creating a stored procedure is

```
CREATE [OR REPLACE] PROCEDURE procedure-name
[(argument1 ... [, argumentN) ] IS
[local-variable-declarations]
BEGIN
executable-section
[exception-section]
END [procedure-name];
```

where the variables are defined in this way:

procedure-name is the procedure name subject to Oracle database object-naming restrictions.

argument1 through *argumentN* are optional argument declarations that consist of:

argument-name [IN ¦ OUT] *datatype* [{:= ¦ DEFAULT} *value*]

local-variable-declarations are optional declarations of variables, constants, and other procedures and functions local to *procedure-name*.

executable-section is the PL/SQL statements that compose the procedure.

exception-section is the optional exception-handling section of the procedure.

For example, the following stored procedure has a single argument that is used by the DELETE statement to determine which products to remove from the Product table.

```
SQL> create or replace procedure Delete_Specified_Product
  2          (Description_Phrase varchar2) is
  3
  3  begin
  4
  4  delete from Product
  5  where
  6  upper(Description) like Description_Phrase;
  7
  7  end;
  8  /

Procedure created.
```

The syntax for creating a stored function is very similar to that of a stored procedure. Of course, a stored function must also return a value.

```
CREATE [OR REPLACE] FUNCTION function-name
[(argument1 ... [, argumentN) ]
RETURN function-datatype IS
[local-variable-declarations]
BEGIN
executable-section
[exception-section]
RETURN function-value
END [function-name];
```

where the variables are defined in this way:

function-name is the function name subject to Oracle database object-naming restrictions.

argument1 through *argumentN* are optional argument declarations that consist of:

argument-name [IN ¦ OUT] *datatype* [{:= ¦ DEFAULT} *value*]

function-datatype is the datatype of the value returned by the function.

local-variable-declarations are optional declarations of variables, constants, and other procedures and functions local to *function-name*.

executable-section is the PL/SQL statements that compose the function.

exception-section is the optional exception-handling section of the function.

function-value is the value that the function returns to the caller.

> **NOTE**
>
> The difference between a stored procedure and a stored function is that a stored procedure does not return a value whereas a stored function does return a value. As a result, a stored function can be called in a SQL statement in the same manner as a built-in function; a stored procedure cannot. However, stored procedures and functions can both return a modified argument value if the argument was declared as IN or IN OUT.

Here is an example of a stored function that obtains a new Customer ID and stores the information about a new customer in the Customer table:

```
SQL> create or replace function Get_New_Customer_ID
  2             (Salutation      varchar2,
  3              Last_Name       varchar2,
  4              First_Name      varchar2,
  5              Street_Address  varchar2,
  6              City            varchar2,
  7              State           varchar2,
  8              Zipcode         varchar2,
  9              Home_Phone      varchar2,
 10              Work_Phone      varchar2)
 11              return number is
 12
 12  New_Customer_ID  number(4);
 13
 13  begin
 14
 14  select Customer_Sequence.nextval
 15  into New_Customer_ID
 16  from dual;
 17
 17  insert into Customer
 18  (Customer_ID, Salutation, Last_Name, First_Name,
 19   Street_Address, City, State, Zipcode, Home_Telephone_Number,
 20   Work_Telephone_Number)
 21  values
 22  (New_Customer_ID, Salutation, Last_Name, First_Name,
 23   Street_Address, City, State, Zipcode, Home_Phone, Work_Phone);
 24
 24  return New_Customer_ID;
 25
 25  end;
 26  /

Function created.
```

Obtaining Error Messages When Creating Stored Procedures

If Oracle detects errors when you create a stored PL/SQL program, it issues a nondescript message indicating that there were errors—without providing any additional details. For instance, this is what happens when you try to create a stored procedure with a syntax error:

```
SQL> CREATE OR REPLACE PROCEDURE show_inserts IS
  2
  2  max_records CONSTANT int := 100;
  3  i             int := 1;
  4
  4  BEGIN
  5
  5  dbms_output.enable;
  6
  6  FOR i IN 1..max_records LOOP
  7
  7    if (mod(i,10) = 0) then
  8      INSERT INTO test_table
  9              (record_number, current_date)
 10      VALUES
 11              (i, SYSDATE)
 12      dbms_output.put_line('The value of i is ' || to_char(i));
 13
 13    else
 14      NULL;
 15
 15    end if;
 16
 16  END LOOP;
 17
 17  END;
 18  /

Warning: Procedure created with compilation errors.
```

To view the errors resulting from the attempted compilation of the PL/SQL code, you can use the SQL*Plus command show errors, which displays the specific PL/SQL compilation errors.

```
SQL> show errors
Errors for PROCEDURE SHOW_INSERTS:

LINE/COL ERROR
-------- ---------------------------------------------------------------
12/5     PLS-00103: Encountered the symbol "DBMS_OUTPUT" when expecting
         one of the following:
         ;
         ; was inserted before "DBMS_OUTPUT" to continue.
```

When PL/SQL compiles a subprogram, the resulting compilation errors are stored in an Oracle data dictionary table. Instead of using the show errors command, you can query a data dictionary view named USER_ERRORS, which has this structure:

```
SQL> desc user_errors
 Name                             Null?    Type
 -------------------------------- -------- ----
 NAME                             NOT NULL VARCHAR2(30)
 TYPE                                      VARCHAR2(12)
 SEQUENCE                         NOT NULL NUMBER
 LINE                             NOT NULL NUMBER
 POSITION                         NOT NULL NUMBER
 TEXT                             NOT NULL VARCHAR2(2000)
```

The Name column contains the name of the stored procedure that had compilation errors. The Sequence column is the order in which the error messages should be retrieved. The Line column contains the line number of the procedure's PL/SQL statement that caused a compilation error; Position contains the column position where the error was detected.

To query USER_ERRORS to determine the cause of the warning message, use this SELECT statement:

```
SQL> select line, position, text
  2  from user_errors
  3  where
  4  name = 'SHOW_INSERTS'
  5  order by sequence;

    LINE POSITION TEXT
--------- -------- -------------------------------------------------------------
      12        5 PLS-00103: Encountered the symbol "DBMS_OUTPUT"
                  when expecting one of
                  the following:
                  ;
                  ; was inserted before "DBMS_OUTPUT" to continue.
```

Retrieving a Stored Procedure

After a stored procedure has been created, you might want to look at the source code of a PL/SQL program. However, the SQL*Plus script that was used to create the stored procedure might not be available. Even so, you can still retrieve the source code of a stored procedure by querying an Oracle data dictionary view.

The Oracle data dictionary is a group of tables that contain information about the Oracle database itself. Because these data dictionary tables are somewhat cryptic in structure, Oracle defines a set of views that provide a more coherent perspective of the data dictionary. One of these views is named USER_SOURCE.

> **TIP**
>
> By default, all of the Oracle data dictionary views are owned by the SYS account. To query any one of them, you need to specify the SYS account as the owner. However, you can run a SQL*Plus script that will create synonyms that *hide* the ownership of these views. Simply invoke this script from SQL*Plus:
>
> ```
> SQL> @c:\orawin\rdbms71\admin\catdbsyn
> ```

If you DESCRIBE USER_SOURCE, here is what you will see:

```
SQL> describe USER_SOURCE
 Name                            Null?    Type
 ------------------------------- -------- ----
 NAME                            NOT NULL VARCHAR2(30)
 TYPE                                     VARCHAR2(12)
 LINE                            NOT NULL NUMBER
 TEXT                                     VARCHAR2(2000)
```

The NAME column contains the procedure, function, package, or package body name. The TYPE column indicates whether the source belongs to a procedure, function, package, or package body. The line number of each PL/SQL source line is stored in the LINE column. Finally, TEXT contains each PL/SQL program line.

As an example, suppose that you created a stored procedure named DELETE_AMPS that consisted of the following:

```
SQL> CREATE OR REPLACE PROCEDURE DELETE_AMPS IS
  2
  2  BEGIN
  3
  3  delete from Product
  4  where
  5  upper(Description) like '%AMP%';
  6
  6  END;
  7  /

Procedure created.
```

If you want to see the source code of DELETE_AMPS, query the USER_SOURCE data dictionary view.

```
SQL> select text
  2  from User_Source
  3  where
  4  name = 'DELETE_AMPS'
  5  order by line;

TEXT
----------------------------------------------
PROCEDURE Delete_Amps IS
BEGIN
delete from Product
where
upper(Description) like '%AMP%';
END;

6 rows selected.
```

Notice that Oracle *squeezes out* the blank lines from the PL/SQL subprogram when it is stored in the database.

Obtaining a List of Procedures, Functions, Packages, and Package Bodies

You can query USER_OBJECTS to obtain a list of stored procedures, functions, packages, and package bodies owned by the Oracle account to which you are currently connected. If you wanted to see all of the objects, regardless of ownership, you would query DBA_OBJECTS rather than USER_OBJECTS. The OBJECT_TYPE column in DBA_OBJECTS indicates the type of the object: table, view, procedure, and so on.

To obtain a list of the types of database objects currently stored in the database, use the following query:

```
SQL> select distinct object_type
  2  from sys.dba_objects;

OBJECT_TYPE
------------
CLUSTER
INDEX
PACKAGE
PACKAGE BODY
PROCEDURE
SEQUENCE
SYNONYM
TABLE
TRIGGER
VIEW

10 rows selected.
```

For instance, if you wanted to see the name and owner of each package, you would submit the following query:

```
SQL> select object_name, owner
  2  from sys.dba_objects
  3  where
  4  object_type = 'PACKAGE'
  5  order by object_name;

OBJECT_NAME                        OWNER
--------------------------------   --------------------------------
DBMS_ALERT                         SYS
DBMS_DDL                           SYS
DBMS_DEFER_SYS                     SYS
DBMS_DESCRIBE                      SYS
DBMS_EXPORT_EXTENSION              SYS
DBMS_IJOB                          SYS
DBMS_IREFRESH                      SYS
DBMS_ISNAPSHOT                     SYS
DBMS_JOB                           SYS
DBMS_LOCK                          SYS
DBMS_OUTPUT                        SYS
DBMS_PIPE                          SYS
DBMS_REFRESH                       SYS
DBMS_SESSION                       SYS
```

```
DBMS_SNAPSHOT                        SYS
DBMS_SQL                             SYS
DBMS_STANDARD                        SYS
DBMS_SYS_ERROR                       SYS
DBMS_SYS_SQL                         SYS
DBMS_TRANSACTION                     SYS
DBMS_UTILITY                         SYS
DIANA                                SYS
DIUTIL                               SYS
PIDL                                 SYS
STANDARD                             SYS

25 rows selected.
```

Forward Declaration of Procedures and Functions

PL/SQL requires that any identifier—constant, variable, cursor, procedure, or function—be declared before it is used elsewhere in a PL/SQL subprogram. This requirement can cause a problem when two subprograms reference each other, as in the following code:

```
SQL> set serveroutput on
SQL>
SQL> declare
  2
  2  function Medicare_Patient (Patient_ID IN varchar2)
  3          return number is
  4
  4  status    number;
  5  Pat_ID    varchar2(6);
  6
  6  begin
  7
  7  if Insurable_Patient (Pat_ID) = 2 then
  8     status := 1;
  9  end if;
 10
 10  return status;
 11
 11  end Medicare_Patient;
 12
 12
 12  function Insurable_Patient (Patient_ID IN varchar2)
 13          return number is
 14
 14  status    number;
 15  Pat_ID    varchar2(6);
 16
 16  begin
 17
 17  if Medicare_Patient (Pat_ID) = 2 then
 18     status := 1;
 19  end if;
 20
 20  return status;
 21
 21  end Insurable_Patient;
 22
```

```
22  --   Executable portion of anonymous block.
23
23  begin
24
24  dbms_output.enable;
25
25  end;
26  /
declare
*
ERROR at line 1:
ORA-06550: line 7, column 4:
PLS-00313: 'INSURABLE_PATIENT' not declared in this scope
ORA-06550: line 7, column 1:
PL/SQL: Statement ignored
```

As you can see, PL/SQL doesn't recognize the reference to Insurable_Patient in the function Medicare_Patient because the declaration of Insurable_Patient occurs after the declaration of Medicare_Patient. To circumvent this dilemma, you include a *forward declaration* of the subprogram in the declare section. The forward declaration is a declaration of the subprogram and its arguments and return type. Here is how to specify a forward declaration for Insurable_Patient for the preceding example:

```
SQL> set serveroutput on
SQL>
SQL> declare
  2
  2   function Insurable_Patient (Patient_ID IN varchar2) return number;
  3
  3   function Medicare_Patient (Patient_ID IN varchar2)
  4          return number is
  5
  5   status    number;
  6   Pat_ID    varchar2(6);
  7
  7   begin
  8
  8   if Insurable_Patient (Pat_ID) = 2 then
  9       status := 1;
 10   end if;
 11
 11   return status;
 12
 12   end Medicare_Patient;
 13
 13
 13   function Insurable_Patient (Patient_ID IN varchar2)
 14          return number is
 15
 15   status    number;
 16   Pat_ID    varchar2(6);
 17
 17   begin
 18
 18   if Medicare_Patient (Pat_ID) = 2 then
 19       status := 1;
```

```
20   end if;
21
21   return status;
22
22   end Insurable_Patient;
23
23   -- Executable portion of anonymous block.
24
24   begin
25
25   dbms_output.enable;
26
26   end;
27   /
```

PL/SQL procedure successfully completed.

Using Stored Functions in a SQL Statement

With release 7.1 of the Oracle RDBMS, it became possible to reference a stored function within a SQL statement. This feature is enormously powerful because it extends the functionality of a single SQL statement to include the logic contained in a stored function. Here is an elementary example of how this is accomplished.

Because Oracle doesn't offer a built-in function for converting temperature from Fahrenheit to Centigrade, you create a stored function to perform the conversion.

```
SQL> create or replace function DegF_to_DegC (Deg_F IN number)
  2          return number is
  3
  3   Deg_C   number;
  4
  4   begin
  5
  5   Deg_C := (5.0/9.0)*(Deg_F - 32);
  6
  6   return Deg_C;
  7
  7   end DegF_to_DegC;
  8   /
```

Function created.

After the stored function has been successfully created, you can employ it in a SELECT statement.

```
SQL> select body_temp, degf_to_degc(body_temp)
  2   from patient;

BODY_TEMP DEGF_TO_DEGC(BODY_TEMP)
--------- -----------------------
    99.2                37.333333
   100.2                37.888889
   103.8                39.888889
```

Storing Results to a Table

Because PL/SQL doesn't have any built-in support for communicating with the user, how can you use PL/SQL to provide results to a user or another program? There are essentially two methods:

■ Write information to an intermediate table that a user or program can query.

■ Use the procedures and functions available in the Oracle-supplied package DBMS_OUTPUT.

You've already seen an example of how PL/SQL can write to an intermediate table. When compiling PL/SQL stored procedures and functions, the PL/SQL engine itself writes error messages to a data dictionary table that can be queried by the developer. If you want to provide output via SQL*Plus, using DBMS_OUTPUT is a good strategy. If you need to pass many values to a user or a program, it makes more sense to write the results to a table.

For instance, let's assume that you create a stored procedure designed to adjust the price—downward—of a specified product by some designated percentage.

```
SQL> create or replace procedure adjust_product_market_value
  2                        (Prod_ID        varchar2,
  3                         Man_ID varchar2,
  4                         Pct number) IS
  5
  5  Current_Val       number(7,2);
  6  New_Current_Val   number(7,2);
  7  Comments          varchar2(100);
  8
  8  begin
  9
  9  select Current_Used_Value
 10  into Current_Val
 11  from Product
 12  where
 13  Product_ID = Prod_ID and
 14  Manufacturer_ID = Man_ID;
 15
 15  New_Current_Val := Current_Val * (1 - Pct);
 16
 16  update Product
 17    set Current_Used_Value = New_Current_Val
 18    where
 19    Product_ID = Prod_ID and
 20    Manufacturer_ID = Man_ID;
 21
 21  Comments := 'Price adjusted from ' || to_char(Current_Val,'$99999.99')
 22                        || ' to ' || to_char(New_Current_Val,'$99999.99');
 23
 23  insert into market_value_adjustment
 24  (Product_ID, Manufacturer_ID, Comments)
 25  values
 26  (Prod_ID, Man_ID, Comments);
 27
```

```
27
27  END;
28  /
```

Procedure created.

The procedure adds a record to a table named Market_Value_Adjustment indicating the product, manufacturer, and previous and current used value.

```
SQL> execute adjust_product_market_value ('C2002', 'MIT501', 0.08);

PL/SQL procedure successfully completed.

SQL> select Product_ID, Manufacturer_ID, Comments
  2  from Market_Value_Adjustment;

PRODUCT_ID   MANUFA COMMENTS
------------ ------ ------------------------------------------------------------
C2002        MIT501 Price adjusted from    $120.00 to    $110.40
```

Displaying Results with DBMS_OUTPUT

Another way that you can present information to a user is by using an Oracle-supplied package called DBMS_OUTPUT. The procedures in DBMS_OUTPUT are intended for use with SQL*Plus. In the directory C:\ORAWIN\RDBMS71\ADMIN, you will find a series of files named DBMS*.SQL. During the installation of Personal Oracle7, each file installs a package designed for a specific purpose. DBMSOTPT.SQL is used to create the DBMS_OUTPUT package. DBMS_OUTPUT furnishes a set of procedures and functions that enable a PL/SQL program to retrieve input and display output. Remember: PL/SQL doesn't have any built-in input/output capabilities—so you can use DBMS_OUTPUT procedures and functions to perform input/output operations.

To provide output, you need to call two procedures: enable and put_line. Also, before using DBMS_OUTPUT, you need to set the SQL*Plus system variable SERVEROUTPUT to ON.

```
SQL> set serveroutput on
SQL> CREATE OR REPLACE PROCEDURE show_inserts IS
  2
  2  max_records CONSTANT int := 100;
  3  i           int := 1;
  4
  4  BEGIN
  5
  5  dbms_output.enable;
  6
  6  FOR i IN 1..max_records LOOP
  7
  7    if (mod(i,10) = 0) then
  8      INSERT INTO test_table
  9             (record_number, current_date)
 10      VALUES
 11             (i, SYSDATE);
```

```
12        dbms_output.put_line('The value of i is ' || to_char(i));
13
13   else
14     NULL;
15
15     end if;
16
16  END LOOP;
17
17  END;
18  /

Procedure created.

SQL> execute show_inserts;
The value of i is 10
The value of i is 20
The value of i is 30
The value of i is 40
The value of i is 50
The value of i is 60
The value of i is 70
The value of i is 80
The value of i is 90
The value of i is 100

PL/SQL procedure successfully completed.
```

Obtaining System Time in Hundredths of a Second

As discussed in Chapter 11, "Dealing with Dates," the Oracle date datatype is capable of storing time to the nearest second. If you need greater accuracy, there is a function in an Oracle-supplied package that you can use to obtain time to the nearest hundredth of a second. If you assign dbms_utility.get_time to a PL/SQL number variable, the result is a fairly large number. The last two digits of this number are hundredths of seconds. You can isolate the rightmost two digits by converting the PL/SQL variable to a character string with the TO_CHAR function and then using SUBSTR to obtain the rightmost two digits. Here is an example of how the function is called:

```
SQL> set serveroutput on
SQL>
SQL> declare
  2
  2  time_in_hundredths number;
  3
  3  begin
  4
  4  dbms_output.enable;
  5
  5  time_in_hundredths := dbms_utility.get_time;
  6
  6  dbms_output.put_line('Time in hundredths of a second: ' ||
                          to_char(time_in_hundredths));
  7
```

```
 7  end;
 8  /
Time in hundredths of a second: 339339033
```

Invoking a Stored Procedure

The method for invoking a stored procedure or function depends on the context.

For SQL*Plus, use the `execute` command in the following way (this is for a stored procedure that doesn't have any arguments):

```
execute show_inserts;
```

From a PL/SQL subprogram, simply reference the stored procedure or function with any required arguments.

Workarounds for Lack of Support for Stored Procedures

Some excellent application development tools, such as PowerBuilder, provide comprehensive support for the Oracle database. On the other hand, some application development tools offer only partial support for Oracle-specific features. For instance, ObjectView, produced by KnowledgeWare, does not permit a stored procedure to be invoked from its scripting language. If you've made a significant investment in application development with such a product, it might not be practical to migrate your application to another product offering greater capabilities. Instead, here's a workaround you can use to indirectly invoke a stored procedure.

Let's assume that you've created a stored procedure named Dis_Patients_Normal_Temp that is used to discharge all patients whose temperature is less than or equal to 98.6 degrees Fahrenheit. To simplify this example, the stored procedure has no arguments. Here are the statements used to create the stored procedure:

```
SQL> create or replace procedure Dis_Patients_Normal_Temp is
  2
  2  Normal_Temp    constant number := 98.6;
  3
  3  begin
  4
  4  delete from Patient
  5  where
  6  Body_Temp <= Normal_Temp;
  7
  7  end;
  8  /

Procedure created.
```

However, the client application development tool that you're using doesn't enable you to invoke Dis_Patients_Normal_Temp directly. Here's what you can do as a workaround. Create a table named Invoke_Dis_Patients with a single column.

```
SQL> create table Invoke_Dis_Patients
  2  (dummy number);

Table created.
```

Next, create a database trigger that will invoke the stored procedure, Dis_Patients_Normal_Temp, whenever a DELETE statement executes against the Invoke_Dis_Patients table. Chapter 22, "Enforcing Business Rules with Database Triggers," contains a thorough discussion of database triggers. Here is the text of the trigger:

```
SQL> create or replace trigger Delete_Invoke_Dis_Patients
  2          after delete on Invoke_Dis_Patients
  3
  3  begin
  4
  4  Dis_Patients_Normal_Temp;
  5
  5  end;
  6  /

Trigger created.
```

The first query of the Patient table returns the following five records:

```
SQL> select * from patient;

PATIEN      AGE  SYSTOLIC DYASTOLIC BODY_TEMP
------   -------- -------- --------- ---------
A2002       45      150       90      99.2
N3393       59      183      120     100.2
ER5533      33      130       80      98.3
E3893       81      173      101     103.8
UR3393      39      140       70      98.5
```

The stored procedure, Dis_Patients_Normal_Temp, is invoked by issuing a DELETE statement against the Invoke_Dis_Patients table, causing the DELETE trigger to fire, which invokes the stored procedure. As you see, the patients with a temperature below 98.6 are deleted from the Patient table.

```
SQL> delete from Invoke_Dis_Patients;

0 rows deleted.

SQL> select * from patient;

PATIEN      AGE  SYSTOLIC DYASTOLIC BODY_TEMP
------   -------- -------- --------- ---------
A2002       45      150       90      99.2
N3393       59      183      120     100.2
E3893       81      173      101     103.8
```

Packages

A *package* is a group of related PL/SQL procedures and functions. Like the Ada programming language, a PL/SQL package consists of a package specification and a package body. You can construct packages that are application specific—for instance, a package named *patient_data* would contain procedures and functions related to the manipulation and retrieval of hospital patient information. Furthermore, a package could contain procedures and functions that provide a common service, such as the conversion of location information from one coordinate system to another.

Declaring a Package

The general syntax for creating a package is

```
CREATE PACKAGE package-name IS
declaration-section
END package-name;
```

where `package-name` is the name of the package to be created and is subject to Oracle database object-naming restrictions. The `declaration-section` consists of type, variable, cursor, procedure, and function declarations.

Let's examine a simple package for the Frayed Wires consumer electronics repair store.

```
SQL> create or replace package Repair_Store_Utilities is
  2
  2  type Product_Info is record
  3       (Product_ID varchar2(12),
  4        Mfgr_ID    varchar2(6),
  5        Max_Value  number);
  6
  6  cursor Get_Max_Product_Price
  7          return Product_Info;
  8
  8  procedure Get_Max_Repair_Price
  9            (Repair_ID      OUT number,
 10             Item_Number  OUT number,
 11             Product_ID    OUT varchar2,
 12             Mfgr_ID        OUT varchar2,
 13             Max_Repair_Price OUT number);
 14
 14  function Get_New_Customer_ID
 15            (Salutation     varchar2,
 16             Last_Name      varchar2,
 17             First_Name     varchar2,
 18             Street_Address varchar2,
 19             City           varchar2,
 20             State          varchar2,
 21             Zipcode        varchar2,
 22             Home_Phone     varchar2,
 23             Work_Phone     varchar2)
 24             return number;
```

```
25
25   end Repair_Store_Utilities;
26   /
```

Package created.

The Repair_Store_Utilities package contains three items: a cursor, a procedure, and a function. The package specification begins with a type definition that is used by the cursor, which has no parameters.

> **TIP**
>
> It's best if you use the OR REPLACE clause when you create packages or package bodies. Oracle does offer the DROP PACKAGE and DROP PACKAGE BODY statements, but the OR REPLACE clause saves you the trouble of having to remember whether or not you've dropped a package before you attempt to create it.

Declaring a Package Body

A package body contains the public and private elements of a package. It hides the details of how cursors, procedures, and functions are actually implemented—details that should be hidden from developers. A package body is declared using the following syntax:

```
CREATE PACKAGE BODY package-name IS
declaration-section
procedure-bodies;
function-bodies;
initialization-section
END package-name;
```

where the variables are defined in this way:

> *package-name* is the name of the package to be created and is subject to Oracle database object-naming restrictions.
>
> *declaration-section* consists of type, variable, and cursor declarations.
>
> *procedure-bodies* consists of the executable sections of each procedure that was declared in the package specification.
>
> *function-bodies* consists of the executable sections of each function that was declared in the package specification.
>
> *initialization-section* is an optional section that is executed once when the package is first referenced.

Let's see what the Repair_Store_Utilities package body looks like.

```
SQL> create or replace package body Repair_Store_Utilities is
  2
  2   cursor Get_Max_Product_Price return Product_Info
```

```
3          is
4          select Product_ID, Manufacturer_ID, Current_Used_Value
5          from Product
6          where
7          Current_Used_Value =
8          (select max(Current_Used_Value)
9           from Product);
10
10  procedure Get_Max_Repair_Price
11          (Repair_ID      OUT number,
12           Item_Number    OUT number,
13           Product_ID     OUT varchar2,
14           Mfgr_ID        OUT varchar2,
15           Max_Repair_Price OUT number) is
16
16  begin
17
17  select Repair_ID, Item_Number, Product_ID, Manufacturer_ID,
18         Estimated_Cost
19  into   Repair_ID, Item_Number, Product_ID, Mfgr_ID,
20         Max_Repair_Price
21  from Repair_Item
22  where
23  Estimated_Cost = (select max(Estimated_Cost) from Repair_Item);
24
24  end Get_Max_Repair_Price;
25
25
25  function Get_New_Customer_ID
26          (Salutation      varchar2,
27           Last_Name       varchar2,
28           First_Name      varchar2,
29           Street_Address varchar2,
30           City            varchar2,
31           State           varchar2,
32           Zipcode         varchar2,
33           Home_Phone      varchar2,
34           Work_Phone      varchar2)
35          return number is
36
36  New_Customer_ID   number(4);
37
37  begin
38
38  select Customer_Sequence.nextval
39  into New_Customer_ID
40  from dual;
41
41  insert into Customer
42  (Customer_ID, Salutation, Last_Name, First_Name,
43  Street_Address, City, State, Zipcode, Home_Telephone_Number,
44  Work_Telephone_Number)
45  values
46  (New_Customer_ID, Salutation, Last_Name, First_Name,
47  Street_Address, City, State, Zipcode, Home_Phone, Work_Phone);
48
48  return New_Customer_ID;
49
49  end;
```

```
50
50  begin
51
51  insert into utility_audit
52  (username, timestamp)
53  values
54  (user, sysdate);
55
55  commit;
56
56  end Repair_Store_Utilities;
57  /
```

```
Package body created.
```

Now that the Repair_Store_Utilities package body has been created, you can construct an anonymous PL/SQL block that employs the procedure named Get_Max_Repair_Price in the package.

```
SQL> set serveroutput on
SQL>
SQL> declare
  2
  2  Repair_ID    Repair_Item.Repair_ID%type;
  3  Item_Number  Repair_Item.Item_Number%type;
  4  Product_ID   Repair_Item.Product_ID%type;
  5  Mfgr_ID      Repair_Item.Manufacturer_ID%type;
  6  Max_Price    Repair_Item.Estimated_Cost%type;
  7
  7
  7  begin
  8
  8  dbms_output.enable;
  9
  9  Repair_Store_Utilities.Get_Max_Repair_Price
 10    (Repair_ID, Item_Number, Product_ID, Mfgr_ID, Max_Price);
 11
 11  dbms_output.put_line('Max estimated cost is ' ||
 12                        to_char(Max_Price,'9999.99'));
 13
 13  end;
 14  /
Max estimated cost is    312.00

PL/SQL procedure successfully completed.
```

Package Initialization

A package body has an optional initialization section that executes once—the first time the package is referenced. In the Repair_Store_Utilities package, the initialization section consists of an INSERT statement that stores the current Oracle user's name and SYSDATE into the Utility_Audit table. The following anonymous PL/SQL block demonstrates how this works:

```
SQL> set serveroutput on
SQL>
```

```
SQL> delete from utility_audit;

0 rows deleted.

SQL>
SQL> commit;

Commit complete.

SQL>
SQL> declare
  2
  2   this_time    date;
  3   username     varchar2(30);
  4
  4   begin
  5
  5   dbms_output.enable;
  6
  6   if (Repair_Store_Utilities.Get_Max_Product_Price%isopen = False) or
  7      (Repair_Store_Utilities.Get_Max_Product_Price%isopen is Null) then
  8      open Repair_Store_Utilities.Get_Max_Product_Price;
  9   end if;
 10
 10   select username, timestamp
 11   into   username, this_time
 12   from utility_audit;
 13
 13   dbms_output.put_line('Username:  ' || username);
 14   dbms_output.put_line('Timestamp: ' || this_time);
 15
 15   end;
 16   /
Username:  FRAYED_WIRES
Timestamp: 04-JUN-95

PL/SQL procedure successfully completed.
```

Designing a Package for Use by Database Triggers

The procedures and functions contained in a package can be referenced from SQL*Plus scripts, PL/SQL subprograms, client application scripts (such as Oracle Forms 4.5 or PowerBuilder)—as well as database triggers. However, a database trigger cannot call any stored procedure, function, or packaged subprogram that contains a COMMIT, ROLLBACK, or SAVEPOINT statement. Therefore, if you want the flexibility of calling a package's subprograms from a database trigger, be sure that none of the procedures and functions in the package commit or roll back transactions.

Summary

This chapter focused on the following concepts:

- The Oracle DDL statements CREATE PROCEDURE and CREATE FUNCTION are used to create stored procedures and functions, respectively.

- A stored procedure or function is composed of PL/SQL declarations and executable statements that are compiled and stored in the database.

- You can define arguments for a stored procedure or function that input only, output only, or input and output.

- Oracle supplies a predefined package, DBMS_OUTPUT, which contains routines for displaying information from within a PL/SQL subprogram.

- A stored function can be referenced in an Oracle SQL statement. The datatype of each value passed to the function must match its corresponding argument.

- A package is a group of related procedures and functions. A package has a specification and a body.

- A package specification is created via the CREATE PACKAGE statement. A package body is created with the CREATE PACKAGE BODY statement.

19

PL/SQL Datatypes and Variables

In Chapter 17, "The Basics of PL/SQL," I presented some of the essentials of PL/SQL programming. As you've seen, PL/SQL supports all of the datatypes that are available in SQL. However, PL/SQL also provides the following additional datatypes that aren't available for use in ordinary SQL statements:

- BOOLEAN
- BINARY_INTEGER, NATURAL, and POSITIVE
- %TYPE
- %ROWTYPE
- The PL/SQL table (or array)
- The user-defined record

In this chapter, I'll explain the use of PL/SQL variables that are based on these additional datatypes.

The BOOLEAN Datatype

One of the additional datatypes that PL/SQL supports is BOOLEAN. The following code shows how you declare a BOOLEAN variable.

```
SQL> declare
  2  Payment_Is_Late  boolean;
  3
  3  begin
  4  Payment_Is_Late := TRUE;
  5  end;
  6  /

PL/SQL procedure successfully completed.
```

You can initialize a BOOLEAN variable to either TRUE or FALSE.

```
SQL> set serveroutput on
SQL>
SQL> declare
  2  Payment_Is_Late  boolean := TRUE;
  3
  3  begin
  4
  4  dbms_output.enable;
  5
  5  if Payment_Is_Late then
  6      dbms_output.put_line('The payment is late!');
  7  end if;
  8
  8  end;
  9  /
The payment is late!

PL/SQL procedure successfully completed.
```

Until you assign a value to it, a BOOLEAN variable has the null value. In the following example, the BOOLEAN expression `Day_of_Month > 5` is assigned to the BOOLEAN variable Payment_Is_Late:

```
SQL> set serveroutput on
SQL>
SQL> declare
  2  Payment_Is_Late  boolean;
  3  Day_of_Month     integer;
  4
  4  begin
  5
  5  dbms_output.enable;
  6
  6  select to_number(to_char(sysdate,'DD'))
  7    into Day_of_Month
  8  from dual;
  9
  9  Payment_Is_Late := Day_of_Month > 3;
 10
 10  if Payment_Is_Late then
 11     dbms_output.put_line('The payment is late!');
 12  end if;
 13
 13  end;
 14  /
The payment is late!

PL/SQL procedure successfully completed.
```

The BINARY_INTEGER Datatype

The BINARY_INTEGER datatype is used for storing signed integers in the range of -2,147,483,647 to 2,147,483,647. PL/SQL also provides two other datatypes that are subtypes of BINARY_INTEGER.

- NATURAL can store integers in the range of 0 to 2,147,483,647.
- POSITIVE can store integers in the range of 1 to 2,147,483,647.

You might want to declare variables that would never have a fractional part, such as a loop counter, with the NATURAL or POSITIVE datatype.

When you assign a real number to a variable that has been declared as BINARY_INTEGER, NATURAL, or POSITIVE, the number is truncated.

```
SQL> declare
  2  Counter            natural;
  3
  3  begin
  4
  4  dbms_output.enable;
  5
  5  Counter := 103.2;
```

```
   6
   6  dbms_output.put_line('Counter: ' || to_char(Counter,'999.999'));
   7
   7  end;
   8  /

Counter:  103.000
```

Using %TYPE

PL/SQL offers two notations for referencing Oracle table and column datatypes.

- Use %TYPE to declare a variable with the same datatype as a specified column (or previously declared variable).

- Use %ROWTYPE to declare a composite variable whose structure mirrors that of a specified table or cursor.

These two datatypes help integrate PL/SQL code with the table and column definitions that exist in the Oracle data dictionary.

To define a variable as having the same datatype as a column, use the %TYPE designation with the following syntax:

```
variable-name table-name.column-name%TYPE;
```

where *variable-name* is the PL/SQL variable being declared, and *table-name.column-name* specifies the column whose datatype should be used for *variable-name*.

The beauty of using %TYPE is that it generally reduces the amount of work needed to maintain PL/SQL code. As an example, suppose that you've defined the Patient table as follows:

```
SQL> desc Patient
 Name                            Null?    Type
 -------------------------------- -------- ----
 PATIENT_ID                      NOT NULL VARCHAR2(6)
 BODY_TEMP_DEG_F                          NUMBER(4,1)
 FEVER_CLASS                              VARCHAR2(20)
 LAST_NAME                                VARCHAR2(20)
 FIRST_NAME                               VARCHAR2(10)
```

As part of your application, you've written a PL/SQL stored procedure that displays the names of patients whose fevers exceed a specified temperature.

```
SQL> create or replace procedure Display_Feverish_Patients
  2                             (Patient_Temp in number) is
  3
  3  Patient_LName  Patient.Last_Name%TYPE;
  4  Patient_FName  Patient.First_Name%TYPE;
  5
  5  cursor Get_Patient_Names (Temp_Threshold number) is
  6  select Last_Name, First_Name
```

```
 7   from Patient
 8   where
 9   Body_Temp_Deg_F >= Temp_Threshold;
10
10   begin
11
11   dbms_output.enable;
12
12   open Get_Patient_Names (Patient_Temp);
13
13   loop
14
14     fetch Get_Patient_Names into Patient_LName, Patient_FName;
15     exit when Get_Patient_Names%NOTFOUND;
16
16     dbms_output.put_line ('Feverish patient: ' || Patient_FName || ' ' ||
17                            Patient_LName);
18
18   end loop;
19
19   end;
20   /
```

```
Procedure created.
```

```
SQL> execute Display_Feverish_Patients (101.0);
Feverish patient: HERMAN SMOLTON
Feverish patient: RED FENSTER

PL/SQL procedure successfully completed.
```

The hospital admitting manager has just notified you that two brothers, Vatadreykopswarthamurthyohm and Vatadreykopswarthamurthy Bhakavandiranian-subrumaniam, have been admitted with fevers of unknown origin. Given the length of their first and last names, you'll need to expand the length of the two columns in the Patient table by using an ALTER TABLE statement.

```
SQL> alter table Patient modify
  2  (Last_Name varchar2(30),
  3   First_Name varchar2(30));
```

```
Table altered.
```

Because you used %TYPE to declare the variables of the stored procedure Display_Feverish_Patients, you don't need to make any changes to the stored procedure, which works with the new definition for the table.

```
SQL> execute Display_Feverish_Patients (104.0);
Feverish patient: RED FENSTER
Feverish patient: VATADREYKOPSWARTHAMURTHY BHAKAVANDIRANIANSUBRUMANIAM
Feverish patient: VATADREYKOPSWARTHAMURTHYOHM BHAKAVANDIRANIANSUBRUMANIAM

PL/SQL procedure successfully completed.
```

Using %ROWTYPE

You use the %ROWTYPE designation to declare a variable—a record, really—whose structure is identical to the structure of a specified table. %ROWTYPE is used with the following syntax:

```
variable-name table-name%ROWTYPE;
```

where *variable-name* is the PL/SQL variable being declared, and *table-name* specifies the table to which *variable-name* will correspond.

For example, a record named Product_Rec is declared as Product%ROWTYPE. As a result, Product_Rec's fields have the same names and datatypes as the columns of the Product table.

```
SQL> declare
  2
  2  Product_Rec      Product%ROWTYPE;
  3
  3  begin
  4
  4  dbms_output.enable;
  5
  5  select *
  6  into Product_Rec
  7  from Product
  8  where
  9  Product_ID = 'A2001';
 10
 10  dbms_output.put_line('Product ID: ' || Product_Rec.Product_ID);
 11  dbms_output.put_line('Manufacturer ID: ' ||
 12                       Product_Rec.Manufacturer_ID);
 13  dbms_output.put_line('Initial Retail Vaue: ' ||
 14                       to_char(Product_Rec.Initial_Retail_Value,'$999.99'));
 15
 15  end;
 16  /
Product ID: A2001
Manufacturer ID: TES801
Initial Retail Value:  $350.00

PL/SQL  procedure successfully completed.
```

As you can see, the fields of a %ROWTYPE record are referenced by

```
variable-name.field-name
```

where *variable-name* is the name of the declared %ROWTYPE variable, and *field-name* is the name of a column in the table specified in *variable-name*'s declaration.

WARNING

Although you can reference a record declared using %ROWTYPE in a SELECT statement, you cannot reference the entire record with the INSERT statement. For instance,
PL/SQL rejects the following INSERT statement:

```
SQL> declare
  2   Patient_Rec   Patient%rowtype;
  3
  3   begin
  4
  4   Patient_Rec.Patient_ID       := 'HHH111';
  5   Patient_Rec.Body_Temp_Deg_F  := 102.7;
  6
  6   insert into Patient
  7   (Patient_ID, Body_Temp_Deg_F)
  8   values
  9   Patient_Rec;
 10
 10   end;
 11  /
Patient_Rec;
*
ERROR at line 9:
ORA-06550: line 9, column 1:
PLS-00103: Encountered the symbol "PATIENT_REC"
           when expecting one of the follow
an aggregate
Resuming parse at line 9, column 12.
```

You can also assign one variable to another variable if they are both declared using the
%ROWTYPE designation for the same table. The following example illustrates this concept
by assigning New_Patient to ER_Patient.

```
SQL> declare
  2
  2   New_Patient   Patient%ROWTYPE;
  3   ER_Patient    Patient%ROWTYPE;
  4
  4   begin
  5
  5   dbms_output.enable;
  6
  6   select *
  7   into New_Patient
  8   from Patient
  9   where
 10   Patient_ID = 'ZZ0123';
 11
 11   ER_Patient := New_Patient;
 12
 12   dbms_output.put_line('ER_Patient.Body_Temp_Deg_F: ' ||
```

```
13                          to_char(ER_Patient.Body_Temp_Deg_F));
14
14  end;
15   /
```

```
ER_Patient.Body_Temp_Deg_F: 98.6
```

However, you cannot assign one %ROWTYPE variable to another %ROWTYPE variable if the two variables do not point to the same database table, even if the two tables are identical.

```
SQL> create table Identical_Patient as
  2  select * from Patient;

Table created.

SQL> set serveroutput on
SQL>
SQL> declare
  2
  2  New_Patient    Patient%ROWTYPE;
  3  ER_Patient     Identical_Patient%ROWTYPE;
  4
  4  begin
  5
  5  dbms_output.enable;
  6
  6´ select *
  7  into New_Patient
  8  from Patient
  9  where
 10  Patient_ID = 'ZZ0123';
 11
 11  ER_Patient := New_Patient;
 12
 12  dbms_output.put_line('ER_Patient.Body_Temp_Deg_F: ' ||
 13                          to_char(ER_Patient.Body_Temp_Deg_F));
 14
 14  end;
 15   /
declare
*
ERROR at line 1:
ORA-06550: line 11, column 15:
PLS-00382: expression is of wrong type
ORA-06550: line 11, column 1:
PL/SQL: Statement ignored
```

More Complex Datatypes: PL/SQL Tables and Records

PL/SQL supports two additional composite datatypes: *tables* and *records*. Each of these objects are first declared as a datatype, and then the actual PL/SQL table or record is declared based upon the specified datatype.

You can think of a PL/SQL table as an array: it consists of a single field. Also, you don't declare an upper limit on the number of elements that a PL/SQL table can contain; its size is dynamic.

> **NOTE**
>
> It is unfortunate that Oracle chose to apply the label *table* to a structure that is more appropriately described as an array. A PL/SQL table, unlike a database table, is composed of a single column. As with an array, the values of a PL/SQL table are accessed by an index. Just remember that a PL/SQL table and a database table are two distinct objects with very different characteristics and uses.

A user-defined record offers more flexibility than the %ROWTYPE designation. You should consider using a user-defined record when both of the following conditions are true:

- You only need a subset of the table's columns.
- You also want to store associated or *derived* information in the record.

Let's delve into the use of PL/SQL tables.

> **TIP**
>
> If you declare a user-defined record type that is associated with a database table, use the %TYPE designation for each field that mirrors a column in the database table. It reduces the effort needed to maintain PL/SQL code in response to those inevitable database changes.

Declaring PL/SQL Tables

A type for a PL/SQL table is declared using the following syntax:

```
TYPE type-name IS TABLE OF
table-name.column-name%TYPE
INDEX BY BINARY_INTEGER;
```

where *type-name* is the name of the declared type, and *table-name.column-name* specifies the column whose datatype is the base type for *type-name*.

After you've declared a PL/SQL table type, you can then declare variables based on that type. For example, in the following anonymous PL/SQL block, Customer_ID_Tab is declared as a table of the column Customer_ID in the Customer table. A cursor FOR LOOP selects each Customer_ID from the Customer table and assigns it to an element in Customer_ID_Tab.

```
SQL> declare
  2    type Customer_ID_Type is table of Customer.Customer_ID%TYPE
  3        index by binary_integer;
```

```
4
4   Customer_ID_Tab     Customer_ID_Type;
5   i                   binary_integer := 0;
6   final_count         binary_integer;
7
7   begin
8
8   dbms_output.enable;
9
9   for Cust_ID_Rec in (select Customer_ID from Customer) loop
10
10    i := i + 1;
11    Customer_ID_Tab(i) := Cust_ID_Rec.Customer_ID;
12
12  end loop;
13
13  final_count := i;
14
14  for i in 1..final_count loop
15
15    dbms_output.put_line('Customer_ID_Tab(' || to_char(i) ||
16                          ') = ' || Customer_ID_Tab(i));
17
17  end loop;
18
18  end;
19  /
```

```
Customer_ID_Tab(1) = 1001
Customer_ID_Tab(2) = 1002
Customer_ID_Tab(3) = 1003
Customer_ID_Tab(4) = 1004
Customer_ID_Tab(5) = 1005
Customer_ID_Tab(6) = 1006
Customer_ID_Tab(7) = 1007
Customer_ID_Tab(8) = 1008
Customer_ID_Tab(9) = 1009
Customer_ID_Tab(10) = 6101
Customer_ID_Tab(11) = 6102
Customer_ID_Tab(12) = 6103
Customer_ID_Tab(13) = 6104
Customer_ID_Tab(14) = 6105
Customer_ID_Tab(15) = 2222
```

You can pass a PL/SQL table as an argument to a procedure or function. Along with the PL/SQL table, you'll also want to pass a BINARY_INTEGER variable that indicates the number of elements in the PL/SQL table. Here's an example of a procedure that returns a PL/SQL table containing Customer_IDs numbered higher than 6000.

```
SQL> declare
  2   type Customer_ID_Type is table of Customer.Customer_ID%TYPE
  3       index by binary_integer;
  4
  4   Customer_ID_Tab     Customer_ID_Type;
  5   i                   binary_integer := 0;
```

```
 6   Total_Number        binary_integer;
 7
 7
 7   procedure Get_Customer_IDs (Num_Rows out binary_integer,
 8                              Customer_ID_Table out Customer_ID_Type) is
 9
 9   i   binary_integer := 0;
10
10   begin
11
11   for Cust_ID_Rec in (select Customer_ID from Customer
         where Customer_ID > 6000) loop
12
12     i := i + 1;
13     Customer_ID_Table(i) := Cust_ID_Rec.Customer_ID;
14
14   end loop;
15
15   Num_Rows := i;
16
16   end Get_Customer_IDs;
17
17   --  Main block.
18
18   begin
19
19   dbms_output.enable;
20
20   Get_Customer_IDs (Total_Number, Customer_ID_Tab);
21
21
21   for i in 1..Total_Number loop
22
22     exit when Customer_ID_Tab(i) = NULL;
23
23     dbms_output.put_line('Customer_ID_Tab(' || to_char(i) ||
24                          ') = ' || Customer_ID_Tab(i));
25
25   end loop;
26
26   end;
27 /
Customer_ID_Tab(1) = 6101
Customer_ID_Tab(2) = 6102
Customer_ID_Tab(3) = 6103
Customer_ID_Tab(4) = 6104
Customer_ID_Tab(5) = 6105
```

NOTE

PL/SQL doesn't restrict the range of the PL/SQL table index; you could start at -100, 0, 1, or any other number that is appropriate.

Declaring User-Defined Records

The process for using a user-defined record is much like that of a PL/SQL table: you define a datatype for the record and then declare variables based on the new type. The following is the syntax for declaring a record type:

```
TYPE type-name IS RECORD
(field-name field-datatype [NOT NULL] [initial-value],
...
 field-name field-datatype [NOT NULL] [initial-value]);
```

where the variables are defined:

> *type-name* is the name of the declared record type.
>
> *field-name* is the name of the field and subject to PL/SQL variable-name restrictions.
>
> *field-datatype* is the datatype of the field, which can be a specific PL/SQL datatype (such as NUMBER or BOOLEAN) or can reference a column's datatype using the %TYPE designation.
>
> *initial-value* is an initial value that must be assigned to *field-name* if it is declared as NOT NULL.

TIP

One advantage of the user-defined record is that you can declare fields for storing derived data in a record that isn't stored in the associated database table.

The following example illustrates the declaration of a user-defined record type. In this case, we're declaring a record type named Patient_Rec_Type that is composed of three fields: Patient_ID, Body_Temp, and Bed_Number. The first two fields exist in the Patient table; however, Body_Temp has a different name—Body_Temp_Deg_F—in the table. The third field, Bed_Number, doesn't exist in the Patient table.

```
SQL> declare
  2
  2    type Patient_Rec_Type is record
  3    (Patient_ID    Patient.Patient_ID%TYPE,
  4     Body_Temp     Patient.Body_Temp_Deg_F%TYPE,
  5     Bed_Number    varchar2(4));
  6
  6    Patient_Rec   Patient_Rec_Type;
  7
  7    begin
  8
```

```
 8  dbms_output.enable;
 9
 9  Patient_Rec.Patient_ID := 'ZZ0123';
10  Patient_Rec.Body_Temp  := 98.6;
11  Patient_Rec.Bed_Number := 'A123';
12
12  dbms_output.put_line('Patient ID: ' ¦¦ Patient_Rec.Patient_ID);
13  dbms_output.put_line('Body_Temp: ' ¦¦ to_char(Patient_Rec.Body_Temp));
14  dbms_output.put_line('Bed Number: ' ¦¦ Patient_Rec.Bed_Number);
15
15  insert into Patient
16  (Patient_ID, Body_Temp_Deg_F)
17  values
18  (Patient_Rec.Patient_ID, Patient_Rec.Body_Temp);
19
19  end;
20  /

Patient ID: ZZ0123
Body_Temp: 98.6
Bed Number: A123
```

Specifying Default Values for Variables

By default, all variables are initialized to NULL whenever you enter a procedure, function, or anonymous block. There are two ways you can initialize a variable in the PL/SQL declare section:

```
variable-name    data-type   := initial-value;
```

or

```
variable-name    data-type   DEFAULT initial-value;
```

Here is an anonymous block that illustrates both methods of initializing a PL/SQL variable.

```
SQL> declare
  2
  2  i              natural := 33;
  3  my_string      varchar2(30) default 'JACKSON';
  4
  4  begin
  5
  5  dbms_output.enable;
  6
  6  end;
  7  /

PL/SQL procedure successfully completed.
```

Summary

In this chapter, you learned the following:

- PL/SQL supports several datatypes that aren't available for use in Oracle SQL statements: BOOLEAN, BINARY_INTEGER, NATURAL, and POSITIVE.

- A BOOLEAN variable can have a value of TRUE, FALSE, or NULL.

- By using %TYPE, you can declare a variable to have the same datatype as a particular column in a table.

- Use the designation %ROWTYPE to declare a record whose structure is equivalent to a specified table. You can also use %ROWTYPE to declare a record with the same structure as a cursor.

- A PL/SQL table is a user-declared datatype that you can think of as an unbounded array composed of one field. To declare a PL/SQL table, you must first declare a table datatype.

- A user-defined record consists of one or more fields. Each field's datatype is either explicitly declared using an Oracle SQL or PL/SQL datatype, or it uses the %TYPE designation to point to the datatype of a database column. A field may be declared as NOT NULL and initialized in its declaration.

20

Handling Errors and Exceptions in PL/SQL

The *Oracle Error Messages and Codes* manual lists all error codes and messages, not including operating-specific errors. Probably at some point, your application will encounter some of these errors. In PL/SQL, Oracle errors are referred to as *exceptions*. Some of the exceptions have predefined names that can be referenced in PL/SQL subprograms. In addition to these predefined Oracle exceptions, you can define application-specific exceptions in a PL/SQL subprogram.

One method for handling errors in a PL/SQL subprogram is to check for any Oracle error code after each SQL statement. The problem with that approach is that the resulting subprogram can be difficult to follow. As an alternative, PL/SQL enables you to specify what processing should take place for a particular exception. This is called the *exception section* of a PL/SQL subprogram. A predefined exception is said to be *raised* when an Oracle error occurs during the execution of a PL/SQL subprogram. You raise a user-defined exception by invoking the RAISE statement at an appropriate location in the PL/SQL code.

In this chapter, you'll learn how to define an exception handler for Oracle errors and user-defined exceptions. Also, I'll show some examples of predefined exceptions.

The Exception Section

The exception section is an optional section of a PL/SQL subprogram that instructs PL/SQL how to handle particular exceptions. The syntax for the exception section is

```
EXCEPTION
  WHEN exception-name1 THEN
    PL/SQL-statements;
  ...
  WHEN exception-nameN THEN
    PL/SQL-statements;
  ...
  [WHEN OTHERS THEN
    PL/SQL-statements;]
END;
```

where *exception-name1* through *exception-nameN* are the names of predefined and user-defined exceptions, and *PL/SQL-statements* is one or more PL/SQL statements that are executed when the exception is raised.

To illustrate, here is a PL/SQL block that contains an exception section. Notice that the exception section contains two exception handlers: one for a predefined exception—the TOO_MANY_ROWS exception—and one for all other exceptions—signified by the word OTHERS.

```
SQL> declare
  2
  2    Product_Rec    Product%ROWTYPE;
  3
  3    begin
  4
  4    dbms_output.enable;
  5
```

```
 5   select *
 6   into Product_Rec
 7   from Product;
 8
 8   exception
 9
 9     when TOO_MANY_ROWS then
10       dbms_output.put_line('TOO_MANY_ROWS Exception Raised');
11       dbms_output.put_line('Occurred in anonymous block');
12
12     when OTHERS then
13       NULL;
14
14   end;
15   /
```

```
TOO_MANY_ROWS Exception Raised
Occurred in anonymous block
```

If you remove the exception handler for OTHERS and cause an exception to be raised that does not have an exception handler, PL/SQL returns an error message. In the following example, a string of 18 characters is assigned to a variable that can store up to 5 characters, resulting in an Oracle error.

```
SQL> declare
  2
  2   xyz    varchar2(5);
  3
  3   begin
  4
  4   dbms_output.enable;
  5
  5   xyz := 'This will not fit!';
  6
  6   exception
  7
  7     when TOO_MANY_ROWS then
  8       dbms_output.put_line('TOO_MANY_ROWS Exception Raised');
  9       dbms_output.put_line('Occurred in anonymous block');
 10
 10   end;
 11   /
declare
  *
ERROR at line 1:
ORA-06502: PL/SQL: numeric or value error
ORA-06512: at line 5
```

Predefined Exceptions

All exceptions can be categorized as either predefined or user-defined. Predefined exceptions are automatically raised; for example, a SQL statement that references a table that doesn't exist results in an Oracle error. Predefined exceptions have meaningful names. Here are some predefined exceptions that you might encounter in developing an Oracle application:

- DUP_VAL_ON_INDEX
- INVALID_NUMBER
- NO_DATA_FOUND
- TOO_MANY_ROWS
- VALUE_ERROR

I'll illustrate the conditions that cause each of these predefined exceptions.

The DUP_VAL_ON_INDEX Exception

The DUP_VAL_ON_INDEX is raised when a SQL statement attempts to create a duplicate value for a unique index. To illustrate, the following PL/SQL anonymous block tries to update the product table so that all rows have the same value for Product_ID and Manufacturer_ID, thereby raising the DUP_VAL_ON_INDEX exception.

```
SQL> declare
  2
  2  begin
  3
  3  dbms_output.enable;
  4
  4  update Product
  5  set
  6  Product_ID = 'A1234',
  7  Manufacturer_ID = 'SEN101';
  8
  8  exception
  9
  9    when DUP_VAL_ON_INDEX then
 10      dbms_output.put_line('DUP_VAL_ON_INDEX exception raised');
 11
 11  end;
 12  /

DUP_VAL_ON_INDEX exception raised
```

The INVALID_NUMBER Exception

The INVALID_NUMBER exception is raised when a SQL statement specifies an invalid number. For instance, the following example attempts to update a table in which a numeric column, Initial_Retail_Value, is assigned a value that can't be converted to a legal number.

```
SQL> declare
  2
  2  Bogus_Value    varchar2(30) := 'NOT A NUMBER';
  3
  3  begin
  4
  4  dbms_output.enable;
  5
  5  update Product
```

```
 6  set
 7  Initial_Retail_Value = to_number(Bogus_Value);
 8
 8  exception
 9
 9    when INVALID_NUMBER then
10      dbms_output.put_line('INVALID_NUMBER exception raised');
11
11  end;
12  /

INVALID_NUMBER exception raised
```

The NO_DATA_FOUND Exception

The NO_DATA_FOUND exception is raised when a SELECT statement doesn't return any rows, as shown:

```
SQL> declare
  2
  2  Product_Rec    Product%ROWTYPE;
  3
  3  begin
  4
  4  dbms_output.enable;
  5
  5  select *
  6  into Product_Rec
  7  from Product
  8  where
  9  Product_ID = 'NOSUCH';
 10
 10  end;
 11  /
declare
*
ERROR at line 1:
ORA-01403: no data found
ORA-06512: at line 5
```

After you add an exception handler for NO_DATA_FOUND, PL/SQL no longer returns the error to the calling environment—in this case, SQL*Plus.

```
SQL> declare
  2
  2  Product_Rec    Product%ROWTYPE;
  3
  3  begin
  4
  4  dbms_output.enable;
  5
  5  select *
  6  into Product_Rec
  7  from Product
  8  where
  9  Product_ID = 'NOSUCH';
 10
```

```
10   exception
11
11     when NO_DATA_FOUND then
12       dbms_output.put_line('No data returned');
13
13     when OTHERS then
14       NULL;
15
15   end;
16   /
```

```
No data returned
```

The TOO_MANY_ROWS Exception

In the PL/SQL environment, a SELECT statement cannot retrieve more than one row without raising the TOO_MANY_ROWS exception. To retrieve an arbitrary number of rows from a query, you can use a cursor, which can be thought of as a window on the results returned by a query. Chapter 21, "Retrieving Data with Cursors," focuses on the use of cursors in PL/SQL. Here is an example of how an exception handler is used for the TOO_MANY_ROWS exception.

```
SQL> declare
  2
  2   Product_Rec    Product%ROWTYPE;
  3
  3   begin
  4
  4   dbms_output.enable;
  5
  5   select *
  6   into Product_Rec
  7   from Product
  8   where
  9   Manufacturer_ID = 'SEN101';
 10
 10   exception
 11
 11     when TOO_MANY_ROWS then
 12       dbms_output.put_line('TOO_MANY_ROWS raised - use a cursor');
 13
 13     when OTHERS then
 14       NULL;
 15
 15   end;
 16   /
```

```
TOO_MANY_ROWS raised - use a cursor
```

The VALUE_ERROR Exception

The VALUE_ERROR exception is raised in a number of situations related to truncation and conversion errors. For example, the following PL/SQL block attempts to assign the string More than 5 characters to a variable that has been declared as varchar2(5).

```
SQL> declare
  2
  2   xyz   varchar2(5);
  3
  3   begin
  4
  4   dbms_output.enable;
  5
  5   xyz := 'More than 5 characters';
  6
  6   exception
  7
  7     when VALUE_ERROR then
  8       dbms_output.put_line('VALUE_ERROR raised');
  9
  9     when OTHERS then
 10       NULL;
 11
 11   end;
 12   /

VALUE_ERROR raised
```

Declaring an Exception

In addition to dealing with the predefined exceptions, you can also define application-specific exceptions and declare them in the following way:

exception-name EXCEPTION;

where *exception-name* is the declared exception and subject to PL/SQL object-naming restrictions.

The following example declares an exception named Life_Threatening_Fever that is raised if a patient's body temperature exceeds 106 degrees Fahrenheit.

```
SQL> declare
  2
  2   Life_Threatening_Fever   exception;
  3   Patient_ID   Patient.Patient_ID%TYPE;
  4
  4   begin
  5
  5   dbms_output.enable;
  6
  6   for Patient_Rec in
  7     (select Patient_ID, Body_Temp_Deg_F from Patient) loop
  8
  8     if Patient_Rec.Body_Temp_Deg_F > 106.0 then
  9
  9       Patient_ID := Patient_Rec.Patient_ID;
 10       raise Life_Threatening_Fever;
 11
 11     end if;
 12   end loop;
```

```
13
13  exception
14
14    when Life_Threatening_Fever then
15      dbms_output.put_line(Patient_ID ¦¦ ' has a life ' ¦¦
16                            'threatening fever!');
17
17  end;
18  /
```

```
GG9999 has a life threatening fever!
```

Success or Failure: Inspecting SQLCODE and SQLERRM

SQLCODE is a predefined symbol that contains the Oracle error status of the previously executed PL/SQL statement. If a SQL statement executes without errors, SQLCODE is equal to 0.

SQLERRM is a PL/SQL symbol that contains the error message associated with SQLCODE. If a SQL statement executes successfully, SQLCODE is equal to 0 and SQLERRM contains the string ORA-0000: normal, successful completion, as shown:

```
SQL> declare
  2
  2  begin
  3
  3  dbms_output.enable;
  4
  4  dbms_output.put_line('SQLCODE: ' ¦¦ to_char(SQLCODE));
  5  dbms_output.put_line('SQLERRM: ' ¦¦ SQLERRM);
  6
  6  end;
  7  /
SQLCODE: 0
SQLERRM: ORA-0000: normal, successful completion
```

If an error actually occurs, SQLCODE and SQLERRM contain the applicable code and message, respectively. The following example illustrates.

```
SQL> declare
  2
  2  Product_Rec    Product%ROWTYPE;
  3
  3  begin
  4
  4  dbms_output.enable;
  5
  5  select *
  6  into Product_Rec
  7  from Product;
  8
  8  exception
```

```
  9
  9    when OTHERS then
 10      dbms_output.put_line('SQLCODE: ' ¦¦ to_char(SQLCODE));
 11      dbms_output.put_line(SQLERRM);
 12
 12  end;
 13  /

SQLCODE: -1422
ORA-01422: exact fetch returns more than requested number of rows
```

Returning Errors with RAISE_APPLICATION_ERROR

Oracle provides a procedure in the DBMS_STANDARD package named RAISE_APPLICATION_ERROR. You can use this procedure to return application-specific error messages to a caller—such as SQL*Plus, a PL/SQL subprogram, or a client application. Oracle reserves error codes in the range of -20000 to -20999 for these user-defined errors. For instance, here is a block that declares an exception named Fever_Out_of_Range. A cursor FOR LOOP reads through each row in the Patient table. If a patient's temperature exceeds 115 degrees Fahrenheit, the Fever_Out_of_Range exception is raised. In the exception section, the exception handler for Fever_Out_of_Range calls RAISE_APPLICATION_ERROR and passes it an error code of -20000 and a relevant error message.

```
SQL> declare
  2
  2  Fever_Out_of_Range exception;
  3  Patient_ID          Patient.Patient_ID%TYPE;
  4
  4  begin
  5
  5  dbms_output.enable;
  6
  6  for Patient_Rec in
  7    (select Patient_ID, Body_Temp_Deg_F from Patient) loop
  8
  8    if Patient_Rec.Body_Temp_Deg_F > 115.0 then
  9
  9      raise Fever_Out_of_Range;
 10
 10    end if;
 11
 11  end loop;
 12
 12  exception
 13
 13    when Fever_Out_of_Range then
 14      raise_application_error (-20000,
             'Fever is out of the range 65 Deg. F to 115 Deg. F');
 15
 15  end;
```

```
  16  /
declare
  *
ERROR at line 1:
ORA-20000: Fever is out of the range 65 Deg. F to 115 Deg. F
ORA-06512: at line 14
```

Summary

This chapter addressed the following important facts:

- In PL/SQL, an error or warning is called an exception.
- A number of predefined exceptions are associated with Oracle SQL errors.
- An exception handler is a series of PL/SQL statements that are executed in response to a raised exception.
- You may declare application-specific exceptions and specify exception handlers for them.
- A PL/SQL block may have an exception section that contains one or more exception handlers.
- You use the RAISE statement to raise a user-defined exception.
- Oracle provides a procedure named RAISE_APPLICATION_ERROR to return an application-specific error to the caller of a PL/SQL subprogram.

21

Retrieving Data with Cursors

When you're using SQL*Plus, you can submit a query without being concerned with the number of rows that are returned. It doesn't matter whether the query retrieves zero, one, or a thousand rows. However, this isn't true for PL/SQL subprograms. You cannot use an ordinary SELECT statement to retrieve more than one row. If a SELECT statement in a PL/SQL subprogram—whether it's an anonymous block, a stored procedure, or a trigger—retrieves more than one row, Oracle returns an error message. Obviously, the capability to retrieve more than one row is essential, and there must be a mechanism to support it. Oracle provides a resource to accomplish this: the cursor. Cursors are automatically created and used by Oracle utilities such as SQL*Plus.

Here's an example of how Oracle deals with a SELECT statement that returns more than one row:

```
SQL> declare
  2
  2    Employee_ID      Employee.Employee_ID%type;
  3    Last_Name        Employee.Last_Name%type;
  4    First_Name       Employee.First_Name%type;
  5
  5  begin
  6
  6    select Employee_ID, Last_Name, First_Name
  7    into    Employee_ID, Last_Name, First_Name
  8    from Employee
  9    order by Employee_ID;
 10
 10  end;
 11  /
declare
*
ERROR at line 1:
ORA-01422: exact fetch returns more than requested number of rows
ORA-06512: at line 6
```

A cursor can be thought of as a window into the result set of a query (see Figure 21.1). Generally, there are four steps to using a cursor:

- Declaring the cursor: The cursor is assigned a name and associated with a SELECT statement, which is parsed.

- Opening the cursor: The Oracle RDBMS executes the query associated with the cursor and determines the qualified rows (active set).

- Fetching rows from the cursor: The values for each row are returned to the PL/SQL subprogram environment.

- Closing the cursor: All resources consumed by Oracle related to the cursor are released.

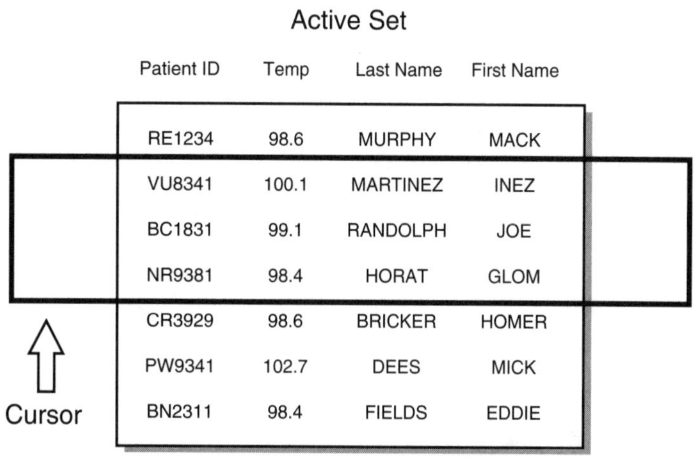

FIGURE 21.1.

Illustration of a cursor.

Active Set

Patient ID	Temp	Last Name	First Name
RE1234	98.6	MURPHY	MACK
VU8341	100.1	MARTINEZ	INEZ
BC1831	99.1	RANDOLPH	JOE
NR9381	98.4	HORAT	GLOM
CR3929	98.6	BRICKER	HOMER
PW9341	102.7	DEES	MICK
BN2311	98.4	FIELDS	EDDIE

Cursor

NOTE

In PL/SQL, a SELECT statement that returns more than one row raises the predefined exception TOO_MANY_ROWS.

This chapter focuses on the practical use of cursors in PL/SQL.

Here is a stored procedure that will return information about repair items that probably shouldn't be repaired because the market value of the item is less than the estimated repair cost. This procedure—Get_Uneconomical_Repairs—makes use of a cursor.

```
SQL> create or replace procedure Get_Uneconomical_Repairs is
  2
  2   Rep_ID        Repair_Item.Repair_ID%type;
  3   Item_No       Repair_Item.Item_Number%type;
  4   Est_Cost      Repair_Item.Estimated_Cost%type;
  5   Used_Val      Product.Current_Used_Value%type;
  6
  6   cursor get_est_cost_used_val is
  7          select Repair_ID, Item_Number, Estimated_Cost, Current_Used_Value
  8          from Repair_Item I, Product P
  9          where
 10          I.Product_ID = P.Product_ID and
 11          I.Manufacturer_ID = P.Manufacturer_ID and
 12          Estimated_Cost > Current_Used_Value
 13          order by Repair_ID, Item_Number;
 14
 14   begin
 15
 15   dbms_output.enable;
 16
 16   open get_est_cost_used_val;
 17
```

```
17  loop
18
18     fetch get_est_cost_used_val
19          into Rep_ID, Item_No, Est_Cost, Used_Val;
20     exit when get_est_cost_used_val%notfound;
21
21     dbms_output.put_line(Rep_ID || ' ' || to_char(Item_No) || ' '
22          || ' ' || to_char(Est_Cost) || ' '
23          || to_char(Used_Val));
24
24
24  end loop;
25
25  end;
26  /
```

```
Procedure created.

SQL> set serveroutput on
SQL> execute Get_Uneconomical_Repairs;
501  1    231  85
501  1    231  85

PL/SQL procedure successfully completed.
```

Let's look at each step of this cursor in detail. First, the cursor—Get_Est_Cost_Used_Val—is declared as a join between two tables—Repair_Item and Product. Next, the cursor is opened within the executable section of the stored procedure. A loop statement fetches rows from the cursor until no more rows are retrieved.

Declaring a Cursor

Every cursor must be declared before it can be used. Declaring a cursor means giving it a name and specifying the SELECT statement with which the cursor is associated. Here is the basic syntax that is used in PL/SQL to declare a cursor:

```
CURSOR cursor-name
[(parameter1 parameter1-datatype [:= default1],
...
 parameterN parameterN-datatype [:= defaultN])]
IS select-stmt;
```

where the variables are defined in this way:

> cursor-name is the name of the cursor and subject to Oracle object-naming requirements.
>
> parameter1 is the name of the first parameter to be supplied to the cursor.
>
> parameter1-datatype is the datatype for parameter1.
>
> default1 is an optional default value for parameter1.
>
> parameterN is the name of the last parameter to be supplied to the cursor.

parameterN-datatype is the datatype for *parameterN*.

defaultN is an optional default value for *parameterN*.

select-stmt is a valid SELECT statement that will be associated with the declared cursor.

For instance, here is a simple cursor declaration that doesn't specify any parameters:

```
cursor get_employees is
    select Employee_ID, Last_Name, First_Name
    from Employee
    order by Employee_ID;
```

Here is an example of a cursor declaration with three parameters:

```
2   cursor patients_with_hypertension
3          (patient_age number,
4           normal_dyastolic,
5           normal_systolic) is
6           select patient_id, age, dyastolic, systolic
7           from patient
8           where
9           dyastolic > normal_dyastolic * (age+200)/200 and
10          systolic > normal_systolic * (age+200)/200;
```

Here is the same cursor with default values specified for each of the cursor parameters:

```
2   cursor patients_with_hypertension
3          (patient_age number default 55,
4           normal_dyastolic number default 70,
5           normal_systolic  number default 130) is
6           select patient_id, age, dyastolic, systolic
7           from patient
8           where
9           dyastolic > normal_dyastolic * (age+200)/200 and
10          systolic > normal_systolic * (age+200)/200;
```

NOTE

If you use any of the Oracle precompilers—for example, Pro*C—you'll need to use a cursor to retrieve more than one row from a SELECT statement.

Opening a Cursor

Before you can fetch rows from a cursor, the cursor must be opened. When the cursor is opened, its SELECT statement is executed, and Oracle constructs a list of the qualified rows. These rows are referred to as the *active set*. If the cursor was declared without any parameters, the syntax is very simple.

```
open my_cursor;
```

If the cursor was declared with parameters, you must supply a PL/SQL variable or a literal value for each parameter when you open the cursor.

```
SQL> declare
  2
  2   cursor patients_with_hypertension
  3          (patient_age number,
  4           normal_dyastolic number) is
  5           select patient_id
  6           from patient
  7           where
  8           dyastolic > normal_dyastolic * (age+200)/200 and
  9           systolic > 180;
 10
 10   Patient_ID Patient.Patient_ID%type;
 11
 11   begin
 12
 12   open patients_with_hypertension (45, 80);
 13
 13   end;
 14   /

PL/SQL procedure successfully completed.
```

If the cursor was declared with parameters—and default values were specified for those parameters—you aren't required to furnish a PL/SQL variable or a literal value for each parameter.

```
SQL> declare
  2
  2   cursor patients_with_hypertension
  3          (patient_age number default 55,
  4           normal_dyastolic number default 70,
  5           normal_systolic  number default 130) is
  6           select patient_id
  7           from patient
  8           where
  9           dyastolic > normal_dyastolic * (age+200)/200 and
 10           systolic > normal_systolic * (age+200)/200;
 11
 11   Patient_ID Patient.Patient_ID%type;
 12
 12   begin
 13
 13   dbms_output.enable;
 14
 14   open patients_with_hypertension;
 15
 15   loop
 16
 16      fetch patients_with_hypertension
 17           into Patient_ID;
 18      exit when patients_with_hypertension%notfound;
 19
 19      dbms_output.put_line(patient_record.patient_id);
 20
 20   end loop;
```

```
 21
 21   end;
 22    /

N3393

PL/SQL procedure successfully completed.
```

If the cursor was declared with parameters—but no default values were specified for those parameters—you must supply a PL/SQL variable or a literal value for each parameter. Otherwise, Oracle will reject the open cursor statement.

```
SQL> declare
  2
  2   cursor patients_with_hypertension
  3          (patient_age number,
  4           normal_dyastolic number,
  5           normal_systolic number) is
  6           select patient_id
  7           from patient
  8           where
  9           dyastolic > normal_dyastolic * (age+200)/200 and
 10           systolic > 180;
 11
 11   Patient_ID Patient.Patient_ID%type;
 12
 12   begin
 13
 13   open patients_with_hypertension;
 14
 14   end;
 15    /
declare
 *
ERROR at line 1:
ORA-06550: line 13, column 1:
PLS-00306: wrong number or types of arguments
          in call to 'PATIENTS_WITH_HYPERTENSION'
ORA-06550: line 13, column 1:
PL/SQL: SQL Statement ignored
```

Fetching Rows from a Cursor

Once the cursor has been opened, the query has been executed and the qualified rows have been identified. To retrieve the rows, you must execute the FETCH statement, which retrieves the value of each column specified in the cursor's SELECT statement and places it in a PL/SQL variable. In general, you'll want to fetch rows within a loop. To illustrate, here is an anonymous PL/SQL block that fetches rows from the Employee table:

```
SQL> declare
  2
  2   Employee_ID      Employee.Employee_ID%type;
  3   Last_Name        Employee.Last_Name%type;
  4   First_Name       Employee.First_Name%type;
```

```
  5
  5   cursor get_employees is
  6           select Employee_ID, Last_Name, First_Name
  7           from Employee
  8           order by Employee_ID;
  9
  9   begin
 10
 10   dbms_output.enable;
 11
 11   open get_employees;
 12
 12   loop
 13
 13      fetch get_employees
 14         into
 15         Employee_ID, Last_Name, First_Name;
 16
 16      exit when get_employees%notfound;
 17
 17      dbms_output.put_line(to_char(Employee_ID));
 18
 18   end loop;
 19
 19   end;
 20   /
1001
1002
1003
1004
1005
1006
1007
1008
1009
```

```
PL/SQL procedure successfully completed.
```

Never make any assumptions about how many rows will be fetched from a cursor. Instead, you should use the EXIT statement to exit the loop when all rows have been fetched from the cursor. The syntax to use is

```
EXIT [label] [WHEN condition]
```

where *label* is an optional label name that specifies which loop should be exited, and *condition* is a PL/SQL condition that returns a Boolean value.

Four specific attributes are associated with declared cursors: %ROWCOUNT, %FOUND, %NOTFOUND, and %ISOPEN. These attributes are referenced by placing them after a cursor's name. To terminate a loop with the EXIT statement, reference a cursor's %NOTFOUND attribute in this way:

```
exit when get_employees%notfound;
```

Closing a Cursor

There are two reasons for closing a cursor. First, you must close a cursor if you want to reopen it with a different set of parameter values. The second reason to close a cursor is to release the resources consumed by the cursor. If a PL/SQL program doesn't close a cursor, Oracle closes the cursor when the subprogram disconnects from the Oracle database, either by terminating or by performing a DISCONNECT. Closing a cursor is straightforward.

```
close get_employees;
```

Let's see how you can supply a different set of parameter values to a cursor by closing the cursor, changing the parameter values, and reopening the cursor. We'll use the patients_with_hypertension cursor to illustrate this. First, the cursor is opened with age set to 50 and normal_dyastolic set to 80. The rows are fetched in a loop, and the cursor is closed. Next, the cursor is reopened with age equal to 40 and normal_dyastolic set at 70. The rows are fetched in a loop with different results.

```
SQL> declare
  2
  2    Patient_ID    Patient.Patient_ID%type;
  3    Age           Patient.Age%type;
  4    Dyastolic     Patient.Dyastolic%type;
  5
  5    cursor patients_with_hypertension
  6          (patient_age number,
  7           normal_dyastolic number) is
  8           select patient_id, age, dyastolic
  9           from patient
 10           where
 11           dyastolic > normal_dyastolic * (age+200)/200;
 12
 12  begin
 13
 13    dbms_output.enable;
 14
 14    open patients_with_hypertension (50, 80);
 15
 15    loop
 16
 16       fetch patients_with_hypertension
 17             into Patient_ID, Age, Dyastolic;
 18       exit when patients_with_hypertension%notfound;
 19
 19       dbms_output.put_line('With age=50, dyas=80: ' || Patient_ID);
 20
 20    end loop;
 21
 21    close patients_with_hypertension;
 22
 22    open patients_with_hypertension (40, 70);
 23
 23    loop
 24
```

```
24      fetch patients_with_hypertension
25              into Patient_ID, Age, Dyastolic;
26      exit when patients_with_hypertension%notfound;
27
27      dbms_output.put_line('With age=40, dyas=70: ' || Patient_ID);
28
28  end loop;
29
29  close patients_with_hypertension;
30
30  end;
31  /
With age=50, dyas=80: N3393
With age=40, dyas=70: A2002
With age=40, dyas=70: N3393
With age=40, dyas=70: E3893

PL/SQL procedure successfully completed.
```

Working with Cursor *FOR* Loops

As an alternative to opening, fetching, and closing a cursor, Oracle furnishes another approach—the cursor FOR loop. With the cursor FOR loop, Oracle implicitly declares a variable—the loop index—that is of the same record type as the cursor's *record*.

```
SQL> declare
  2
  2  cursor Get_Unecon_Repairs is
  3          select Repair_ID, Item_Number, Estimated_Cost, Current_Used_Value
  4          from Repair_Item I, Product P
  5          where
  6          I.Product_ID = P.Product_ID and
  7          I.Manufacturer_ID = P.Manufacturer_ID and
  8          Estimated_Cost > Current_Used_Value
  9          order by Repair_ID, Item_Number;
 10
 10  begin
 11
 11  dbms_output.enable;
 12
 12  for Get_Unecon_Repairs_Rec in Get_Unecon_Repairs loop
 13
 13     dbms_output.put_line ('Repair ID: ' ||
 14                             Get_Unecon_Repairs_Rec.Repair_ID);
 15
 15  end loop;
 16
 16  end;
 17  /
Repair ID: 501

PL/SQL procedure successfully completed.
```

The name that follows FOR is the loop index that is implicitly declared. However, you can't reference the loop index outside of the loop statement.

```
SQL> declare
  2
  2   cursor Get_Unecon_Repairs is
  3           select Repair_ID, Item_Number, Estimated_Cost, Current_Used_Value
  4           from Repair_Item I, Product P
  5           where
  6           I.Product_ID = P.Product_ID and
  7           I.Manufacturer_ID = P.Manufacturer_ID and
  8           Estimated_Cost > Current_Used_Value
  9           order by Repair_ID, Item_Number;
 10
 10   begin
 11
 11   dbms_output.enable;
 12
 12   for Get_Unecon_Repairs_Rec in Get_Unecon_Repairs loop
 13
 13      dbms_output.put_line ('Repair ID: ' ||
 14                           Get_Unecon_Repairs_Rec.Repair_ID);
 15
 15   end loop;
 16
 16   Get_Unecon_Repairs_Rec.Manufacturer_ID := 'XYZ';
 17
 17   end;
 18   /
declare
  *
ERROR at line 1:
ORA-06550: line 16, column 24:
PLS-00201: identifier 'GET_UNECON_REPAIRS_REC.MANUFACTURER_ID' must be declared
ORA-06550: line 16, column 1:
PL/SQL: Statement ignored
```

Was It %FOUND or %NOTFOUND?

In previous examples, you've already seen how the %NOTFOUND attribute is used to determine whether a FETCH statement retrieved a row. When all of the rows in the active set have been fetched and the last FETCH statement fails to retrieve a row, %NOTFOUND evaluates to TRUE.

NOTE

Before the FETCH statement has been invoked, %NOTFOUND returns a NULL. If your PL/SQL program has a loop in which the FETCH statement might not be called, you should consider testing for the condition of %NOTFOUND evaluating to NULL.

Getting the Number of Rows with %ROWCOUNT

You don't need a counter to keep track of the number of rows that are fetched from a cursor. Instead, reference the cursor's %ROWCOUNT attribute. %ROWCOUNT returns the *running* count of the rows that have been fetched. Here's an example:

```
SQL> declare
  2
  2   Employee_ID      Employee.Employee_ID%type;
  3   Last_Name        Employee.Last_Name%type;
  4   First_Name       Employee.First_Name%type;
  5
  5   cursor get_employees is
  6          select Employee_ID, Last_Name, First_Name
  7          from Employee
  8          order by Employee_ID;
  9
  9   begin
 10
 10   dbms_output.enable;
 11
 11   open get_employees;
 12
 12   loop
 13
 13      fetch get_employees
 14         into
 15         Employee_ID, Last_Name, First_Name;
 16
 16      exit when get_employees%notfound;
 17
 17      dbms_output.put_line ('Rowcount: ' || get_employees%rowcount);
 18
 18   end loop;
 19
 19   end;
 20   /
Rowcount: 1
Rowcount: 2
Rowcount: 3
Rowcount: 4
Rowcount: 5
Rowcount: 6
Rowcount: 7
Rowcount: 8
Rowcount: 9

PL/SQL procedure successfully completed.
```

Instead of exiting a loop when there are no more rows in the cursor, you can specify an exit condition when a specified %ROWCOUNT is achieved.

```
SQL> declare
  2
  2   Employee_ID      Employee.Employee_ID%type;
  3   Last_Name        Employee.Last_Name%type;
```

```
 4  First_Name        Employee.First_Name%type;
 5
 5  cursor get_employees is
 6          select Employee_ID, Last_Name, First_Name
 7          from Employee
 8          order by Employee_ID;
 9
 9  begin
10
10  dbms_output.enable;
11
11  open get_employees;
12
12  loop
13
13     fetch get_employees
14         into
15         Employee_ID, Last_Name, First_Name;
16
16     exit when get_employees%rowcount >= 5;
17
17     dbms_output.put_line ('Rowcount: ' || get_employees%rowcount);
18
18  end loop;
19
19  end;
20  /
Rowcount: 1
Rowcount: 2
Rowcount: 3
Rowcount: 4

PL/SQL procedure successfully completed.
```

The Cursor %ISOPEN

A PL/SQL subprogram can have multiple cursors open simultaneously. The program logic of a PL/SQL subprogram might be quite complex; during the subprogram's execution, you might need to determine whether a particular cursor is open. The %ISOPEN attribute can be associated with any cursor and returns TRUE if the cursor is open and FALSE if the cursor is not open.

```
SQL> declare
 2
 2  Employee_ID       Employee.Employee_ID%type;
 3  Last_Name         Employee.Last_Name%type;
 4  First_Name        Employee.First_Name%type;
 5
 5  cursor get_employees is
 6          select Employee_ID, Last_Name, First_Name
 7          from Employee
 8          order by Employee_ID;
 9
 9  begin
10
10  dbms_output.enable;
```

```
11
11   open get_employees;
12
12   loop
13
13      fetch get_employees
14         into
15         Employee_ID, Last_Name, First_Name;
16
16      exit when get_employees%rowcount >= 5;
17
17      if get_employees%isopen then
18        dbms_output.put_line ('The get_employees cursor is open.');
19      else
20        dbms_output.put_line ('The get_employees cursor is closed.');
21      end if;
22
22   end loop;
23
23   close get_employees;
24
24   if get_employees%isopen then
25     dbms_output.put_line ('The get_employees cursor is open.');
26   else
27     dbms_output.put_line ('The get_employees cursor is closed.');
28   end if;
29
29   end;
30   /
The get_employees cursor is open.
The get_employees cursor is open.
The get_employees cursor is open.
The get_employees cursor is open.
The get_employees cursor is closed.

PL/SQL procedure successfully completed.
```

Using Multiple Cursors

It's possible to declare cursors based on very complex SELECT statements—for example, multiple-table joins or UNIONs. However, some calculations involve multiple steps that simply can't be performed in a single SELECT. In this case, one cursor can be *nested* inside another cursor to implement the processing logic.

I'll illustrate this concept with an example from the repair store application. Using the Repair Header and Repair Item tables, suppose that you wanted to retrieve each repair header, analyze the related customer information, and—depending on the results of the customer analysis—retrieve information on each repair item for that repair. This is achieved by defining two cursors: get_repair_header_info and get_repair_item_info. The second cursor is defined with an argument: Repair_ID. Here's what the block looks like:

```
SQL> declare
  2
```

```
 2   Rep_ID              Repair_Header.Repair_ID%type;
 3   Customer_ID         Repair_Header.Customer_ID%type;
 4   Item_Number         Repair_Item.Item_Number%type;
 5   Product_ID          Repair_Item.Product_ID%type;
 6   Manufacturer_ID     Repair_Item.Manufacturer_ID%type;
 7
 7   cursor get_repair_header_info is
 8           select Repair_ID, Customer_ID
 9           from Repair_Header
10           order by Repair_ID;
11
11   cursor get_repair_item_info (This_Repair_ID number) is
12           select Item_Number, Product_ID, Manufacturer_ID
13           from Repair_Item
14           where
15           Repair_ID = This_Repair_ID
16           order by Item_Number;
17
17   begin
18
18   dbms_output.enable;
19
19   open get_repair_header_info;
20
20   loop
21
21      fetch get_repair_header_info
22              into Rep_ID, Customer_ID;
23      exit when get_repair_header_info%notfound;
24
24      dbms_output.put_line('Repair_ID: ' || Rep_ID);
25
25      open get_repair_item_info (Rep_ID);
26
26   -- Additional statements for customer analysis
27   -- appear here.
28
28      loop
29
29         fetch get_repair_item_info
30                 into Item_Number, Product_ID, Manufacturer_ID;
31         exit when get_repair_item_info%notfound;
32
32         dbms_output.put_line('   Item_Number:     ' || to_char(Item_Number));
33         dbms_output.put_line('   Product_ID:      ' || Product_ID);
34         dbms_output.put_line('   Manufacturer_ID: ' || Manufacturer_ID);
35
35      end loop;
36
36      close get_repair_item_info;
37
37   end loop;
38
38   close get_repair_header_info;
39
39   end;
40   /
```

```
Repair_ID: 501
Item_Number:     1
Product_ID:      C2002
Manufacturer_ID: MIT501
Repair_ID: 502
Item_Number:     1
Product_ID:      D301
Manufacturer_ID: SEN101
Repair_ID: 503
Item_Number:     1
Product_ID:      B311
Manufacturer_ID: TES801
Repair_ID: 504
Item_Number:     1
Product_ID:      B801
Manufacturer_ID: SEN101
Repair_ID: 505
Item_Number:     1
Product_ID:      A903
Manufacturer_ID: TES801
Repair_ID: 506
Item_Number:     1
Product_ID:      TR901
Manufacturer_ID: TES801

PL/SQL procedure successfully completed.
```

Summary

In this chapter, we covered the following concepts:

- A cursor must be used if a query might return more than one row.
- A cursor is a window into the set of rows retrieved by a query.
- Every explicit cursor must be declared in the declaration section of a PL/SQL subprogram.
- A cursor can be declared with parameters with optional default values. The value of each parameter may be specified when the cursor is opened.
- The query associated with a cursor is executed when the cursor is opened.
- You obtain the results of a query by fetching rows from a cursor.
- Every cursor has four attributes: %NOTFOUND, %FOUND, %ISOPEN, and %ROWCOUNT.
- A PL/SQL subprogram can have multiple cursors open simultaneously.

22

Enforcing Business Rules with Database Triggers

In a traditional information system, the business rules of the organization served by the system are implemented in application software. For instance, one business rule might be that if the inventory on hand for a part falls below the stocking level for that part, an order for the required quantity is entered into the system. You would commonly enforce this rule by writing a routine in COBOL or some other programming language that was invoked at an appropriate point in the application. There are several problems with this method:

- The rule is only enforced if an application program or tool invokes the routine. If some other tool is used to modify records in the database, the rule isn't enforced.

- It isn't easy to obtain a list of the algorithms that are used to enforce business rules. You have to rely on documentation (which might not be entirely accurate) or face the drudgery of reviewing application software.

Oracle, along with other modern RDBMSs, provides a mechanism—the database trigger—that eases the task of implementing an organization's business rules. A *database trigger* is a block of PL/SQL statements that are executed when a SQL statement—a DELETE, UPDATE, or INSERT statement—is applied to a table. You can use a database trigger to perform the following tasks:

- Enforce a sophisticated security policy

- Change a column value based on the value of other columns in the same table or a different table

- Perform complex validation of column values—for instance, you might need to compare a column value to some aggregate column value from a different table

- Document changes to a record by writing modified values to another table

This chapter focuses on the details of creating triggers for a variety of purposes.

Creating a Trigger

You'll want to use a text editor to write your triggers. The Oracle statement CREATE TRIGGER creates (or replaces) a trigger that is fired when a specified event occurs on a table. The syntax for the CREATE TRIGGER statement is

```
CREATE [OR REPLACE] TRIGGER trigger-name {BEFORE ¦ AFTER}
triggering-event ON table-name
[FOR EACH ROW]
[WHEN (condition)]
PL/SQL-block
```

where the variables are defined:

trigger-name is the name of the trigger to create and is subject to Oracle object-naming restrictions.

triggering-event is either INSERT, UPDATE, or DELETE corresponding to the three DML statements.

table-name is the name of the table with which the trigger is associated.

FOR EACH ROW is an optional clause that, when used, causes the trigger to fire for each affected row.

condition is an optional Oracle boolean condition that, when TRUE, enables the trigger to fire.

PL/SQL-block is the PL/SQL block that is executed when the trigger fires—referred to as the *trigger body*.

Let's examine how these elements of the CREATE TRIGGER statement are employed.

Statement-Level and Row-Level Triggers

A database trigger fits in one of the following two classifications:

- *Statement-level* triggers do not include the clause FOR EACH ROW in the CREATE TRIGGER statement.
- *Row-level* triggers do include the clause FOR EACH ROW in the CREATE TRIGGER statement.

A statement-level trigger fires only once for the triggering event and does not have access to the column values of each row that is affected by the trigger. A row-level trigger fires for each row that is affected by the trigger and can access the original and new column values processed by the SQL statement.

You generally use a statement-level trigger to process information about the SQL statement that caused the trigger to fire—for instance, who executed it and when. You typically use a row-level trigger when you need to know the column values of a row to implement a business rule.

Referencing Column Values in the Trigger Body

Within the trigger body, a row-level trigger can reference the column values of the row that existed when the trigger was fired. These values depend on which SQL statement caused the trigger to fire.

- For an INSERT statement, the values that will be inserted are contained in :new.*column-name*, where *column-name* is a column in the table.
- For an UPDATE statement, the original value for a column is contained in :old.*column-name*; the new value for a column is contained in :new.*column-name*.
- For a DELETE statement, the column values of the row being deleted are contained in :old.*column-name*.

Triggering Events

When you create a trigger, you specify what event will cause the trigger to fire. The three possible events are

■ The insertion of a new row in the table through an INSERT statement

■ The modification of a set of rows (or no rows) via an UPDATE statement

■ The deletion of a set of rows (or no rows) with a DELETE statement

In addition, you can combine these triggering events so that a trigger fires whenever a DELETE or INSERT or UPDATE statement is executed, as shown in the following code:

```
SQL> create or replace trigger Block_Trade_After_All After
  2  insert or update or delete on Tab1
  3  for each row
  4
  4  declare
  5
  5  begin
  6
  6  insert into Tab11
  7  (col11)
  8  values
  9  (11);
 10
 10  end;
 11  /

Trigger created.
```

BEFORE and AFTER Triggers

A BEFORE row-level trigger is fired before the triggering event is executed. As a result, you can use a BEFORE row-level trigger to modify a row's column values. An AFTER row-level trigger fires after the triggering event has occurred. You can't modify column values with an AFTER trigger.

Possible Triggers for a Table

Based on all of the permutations you can use in the CREATE TRIGGER statement, a single table can have up to twelve types of triggers.

■ Six row-level triggers for BEFORE DELETE, BEFORE INSERT, BEFORE UPDATE, AFTER DELETE, AFTER INSERT, AFTER UPDATE

■ Six statement-level triggers for BEFORE DELETE, BEFORE INSERT, BEFORE UPDATE, AFTER DELETE, AFTER INSERT, AFTER UPDATE

> **TIP**
>
> If you're considering the use of an entity-relationship modeling tool for database design—which you should—you'll find that most of them will automatically generate database triggers based on the primary and foreign key relationships you define. Some tools, such as Logic Works' ERwin, will either create the triggers directly via an Oracle connection or store the triggers in a script file. If you choose the latter method, you can modify the trigger creation script by adding application-specific business rules to any triggers that have been generated.

Just because you can create all twelve types of triggers for a table doesn't mean that you must! In fact, you should be judicious in creating triggers for your tables.

> **NOTE**
>
> With the release of Oracle 7.1, Oracle now enables you to create multiple triggers of the same type on the same table. In Oracle 7.0, Oracle installations that used snapshots couldn't create AFTER ROW triggers for the master table because the snapshot logs used AFTER ROW triggers on the same table. The restriction was removed for Oracle 7.1. However, unless you're planning to use an AFTER ROW trigger for a table referenced by a snapshot, you should avoid defining multiple triggers of the same type for a given table—the potential for design error and confusion is too great.

Let's explore some uses for database triggers.

Validating Column Values with a Trigger

As the DBA for a credit card company, you are responsible for implementing credit policy via database triggers. Company research has shown that the probability of credit card fraud is greater than 80 percent when more than $1000.00 in credit charges have accumulated on a single account within three days. The director of operations has requested that any account that meets this criteria be recorded in a separate table where it can be investigated in detail.

To accomplish this, you create a trigger on the Credit_Charge_Log table that fires before a row is inserted. The trigger looks at the total amount of charges for the specified card number for the past three days, and if the total exceeds $1000, it performs an INSERT in the Credit_Charge_Attempt_Log table where it will be investigated by credit agents. Here is the CREATE TRIGGER statement for this trigger:

```
SQL> create or replace trigger Credit_Charge_Log_Ins_Before before
  2  insert on Credit_Charge_Log
  3  for each row
```

```
4
4   declare
5
5   total_for_past_3_days  number;
6
6   begin
7
7   --  Check the credit charges for the past 3 days.
8   --  If they total more than $1000.00, log this entry
9   --  in the Credit_Charge_Attempt_Log for further handling.
10
10  select sum(amount)
11  into total_for_past_3_days
12  from Credit_Charge_Log
13  where
14  Card_Number = :new.Card_Number and
15  Transaction_Date >= sysdate-3;
16
16  if total_for_past_3_days > 1000.00 then
17
17      insert into Credit_Charge_Attempt_Log
18         (Card_Number, Amount, Vendor_ID, Transaction_Date)
19         values
20         (:new.Card_Number, :new.Amount,
            :new.Vendor_ID, :new.Transaction_Date);
21
21  end if;
22
22  end;
23  /
```

```
Trigger created.
```

To set up the trigger so that it will fire, I've initialized the contents of the Credit_Charge_Log table with several rows.

```
SQL> select * from credit_charge_log;

CARD_NUMBER          AMOUNT VENDOR_I TRANSACTI
----------------- -------- -------- ---------
8343124443239383    128.33 12345678 19-JUN-95
9453128834232243     83.12 98765432 18-JUN-95
4644732212887321     431.1 18181818 19-JUN-95
0944583312453477    211.94 09090909 18-JUN-95
0944583312453477    413.81 08080808 18-JUN-95
0944583312453477    455.31 91919191 19-JUN-95
0944583312453477       225 12341234 20-JUN-95
0944583312453477    512.22 12341234 20-JUN-95

8 rows selected.
```

Before a row is inserted into the table for card number 0944583312453477, the trigger is fired and it queries the table to see if the charges for that card number for the past three days exceed $1000. If they do, a row is added to the Credit_Charge_Attempt_Log table, as you can observe:

```
SQL> insert into Credit_Charge_Log
```

```
2  (Card_Number, Amount, Vendor_ID, Transaction_Date)
3  values
4  ('0944583312453477', 128.28, '43214321', '20-JUN-95');
```

```
1 row created.
```

As you see, because there have been more than $1000 in charges for the account in the past three days, the trigger inserts a row into Credit_Charge_Attempt_Log.

```
SQL> select * from Credit_Charge_Attempt_Log;

CARD_NUMBER         AMOUNT VENDOR_I TRANSACTI
----------------- -------- -------- ---------
0944583312453477    128.28 43214321 20-JUN-95

SQL> commit;

Commit complete.
```

Enforcing Security with a Trigger

Here's an example of how a database trigger can be used to enforce a security policy. Acme Corporation's database is designed so that a row must be inserted into the Shipment table for an actual shipment to be made. The Shipment table has a column, Manual_Check, that indicates whether a shipping clerk should verify by phone the accuracy of the shipping request. To reduce the likelihood of fraud, corporate policy is that a shipping clerk should check any shipping request that has been entered after normal working hours—5:00 PM.

As the DBA, it is your responsibility to implement this policy. You create a trigger, Shipment_Ins_Before, that will fire before the execution of an INSERT statement on the Shipment table. The trigger body consists of a single PL/SQL statement—the assignment of Y to the column Manual_Check. In addition, you decide to use a WHEN clause so that the trigger only fires after 5:00 PM (or 17:00 using a 24-hour clock).

```
SQL> create or replace trigger Shipment_Ins_Before before
  2  insert on Shipment
  3  for each row
  4  when (to_number(to_char(sysdate,'HH24')) > 17)
  5
  5  declare
  6
  6  begin
  7
  7  :new.Manual_Check := 'Y';
  8
  8  end;
  9  /

Trigger created.
```

Now that the trigger has been created, let's test it out. As you can see in the following code, it is sometime after 7:00 PM.

```
SQL> select to_char(sysdate,'HH24') from dual;

TO_CHAR(SYSDATE,'HH24')
----------------------------------------------------------------
19
```

When a row is inserted into the Shipment table, the Manual_Check column is set to Y as intended.

```
SQL> insert into Shipment
  2  (Shipment_ID, Product_Code, Quantity, Customer_ID)
  3  values
  4  ('SHIP1001', 'PROD123', 100, 'CUST999');

1 row created.

SQL> select * from Shipment;

SHIPMENT_ID  PRODUCT_CODE   QUANTITY CUSTOMER_ID  M ENTERED_BY
-----------  -------------  -------- ------------ - --------------------
SHIP1001     PROD123             100 CUST999      Y
```

Setting Column Values with a Trigger

Another use for a trigger is to set a column to a particular value before a SQL statement takes effect. The following scenario demonstrates how this is done. Suppose a table named Block_Trade_Log is used to record block trading on the NASDAQ. The table contains the following: the stock symbol, the trading price, the number of blocks that were traded, when the trade occurred, whether the blocks were bought or sold, and the three-day running average for the stock. When a row is inserted into the table, a trigger is used to set the value for Running_Avg_3_Days. Here is the statement that creates the trigger:

```
create or replace trigger Block_Trade_Log_Ins_Before before
insert on Block_Trade_Log
for each row

declare

Running_Avg number;

begin

select avg(price)
into Running_Avg
from Block_Trade_Log
where
Stock_Symbol = :new.Stock_Symbol and
Timestamp >= SYSDATE-3;

:new.Running_Avg_3_Days := Running_Avg;
end;
/
```

Notice that the value of Running_Avg_3_Days is set by assigning the value to :new.Running_Avg_3_Days. Remember: if the triggering event is an INSERT, the column values that will actually be stored in the table are referenced with :new.

Let's look at the current contents of Block_Trade_Log. Notice that there are two rows for stock symbol QQQQQ: one at $102.125 and the other at $103.5.

```
SQL> select * from block_trade_log;

STOCK_      PRICE BLOCKS_TRADED B RUNNING_AVG_3_DAYS TIMESTAMP
------   -------- ------------- - ------------------ ---------
QQQQQ    102.125           100 B                     19-JUN-95
QQQQQ      103.5           100 S                     19-JUN-95
VVVVV      55.75          3000 S                     19-JUN-95
VVVVV       55.5          1000 B                     20-JUN-95
```

When another row for stock symbol QQQQQ is inserted into Block_Trade_Log, the trigger fires and computes the three-day running average for that security—102.8125—and assigns it to the column Running_Avg_3_Days, as shown in the following code.

```
SQL> insert into block_trade_log
  2 (Stock_Symbol, Price, Blocks_Traded, Bought_Sold, Timestamp)
  3 values
  4 ('&stock',&price,&numblocks,'&BS','&date')
  5 ;
Enter value for stock: QQQQQ
Enter value for price: 104.25
Enter value for numblocks: 300
Enter value for bs: B
Enter value for date: 20-JUN-95
old   4: ('&stock',&price,&numblocks,'&BS','&date')
new   4: ('QQQQQ',104.25,300,'B','20-JUN-95')

1 row created.


SQL> select * from block_trade_log;

STOCK_      PRICE BLOCKS_TRADED B RUNNING_AVG_3_DAYS TIMESTAMP
------   -------- ------------- - ------------------ ---------
QQQQQ    102.125           100 B                     19-JUN-95
QQQQQ      103.5           100 S                     19-JUN-95
VVVVV      55.75          3000 S                     19-JUN-95
VVVVV       55.5          1000 B                     20-JUN-95
QQQQQ     104.25           300 B           102.8125  20-JUN-95
```

NOTE

You can see the effect of a trigger before the transaction that caused the trigger to fire is committed. The following example will illustrate. The trigger Repair_Header_Delete_After is invoked when Repair ID 506 is deleted from the Repair_Header table. As you can see in the following code, a row is inserted into the Repair_Header_Log table before any COMMIT is issued:

```
SQL> delete from Repair_Header
  2   where
  3   Repair_ID = 506;

1 row deleted.

SQL> select * from Repair_Header_Log;

REPAIR_ID CUSTOMER_ID DATE_DELE USER_DELETING
--------- ----------- --------- -----------------------------
      506        1010 20-JUN-95 FRAYED_WIRES
```

Cascading Triggers

The interaction of triggers can be quite complex. For instance, you can create a trigger that, when fired, causes another trigger to fire. Triggers that behave in this way are called *cascading triggers*. To illustrate the concept of cascading triggers, I'll create three simple tables.

```
create table tab1
(col1     number);

create table tab2
(col2     number);

create table tab3
(col3     number);
```

To initialize the three tables, I'll insert a single row in each table.

```
SQL> select * from tab1;

     COL1
---------
        7

SQL> select * from tab2;

     COL2
---------
       10

SQL> select * from tab3;

     COL3
---------
       13
```

For table tab1, I'll create a row-level BEFORE UPDATE trigger that will insert the old value of the col1 column from tab1 into tab2.

```
SQL> create or replace trigger tab1_Update_Before before
  2  update on tab1
  3  for each row
  4
  4  declare
  5
  5  begin
  6
  6  insert into tab2
  7  (col2)
  8  values
  9  (:old.col1);
 10
 10  end;
 11  /
```

Trigger created.

For table tab2, I'll create a row-level BEFORE INSERT trigger that updates table tab3 and sets the value of col3 to the new value of col2.

```
SQL> create or replace trigger tab2_Insert_Before before
  2  insert on tab2
  3  for each row
  4
  4  declare
  5
  5  begin
  6
  6  update tab3
  7  set
  8  col3 = :new.col2;
  9
  9  end;
 10  /
```

Trigger created.

NOTE

A table is *mutating* when its contents are being changed by a INSERT, UPDATE, or DELETE statement that has not yet committed. A row-level trigger cannot read or modify the contents of a mutating table because a mutating table is in a state of flux. The only exception to this rule is that a BEFORE INSERT row-level trigger for a table with a foreign key may modify columns in the table containing the primary key. For more information about mutating tables, please refer to Chapter 8 of the Oracle7 Server Application Developer's Guide, available online.

Finally, for table tab3, I'll create a statement-level AFTER UPDATE trigger that inserts a row into tab3 with the value of col3 equal to 27.

```
SQL> create or replace trigger tab3_Update_After after
  2   update on tab3
  3
  3   declare
  4
  4   begin
  5
  5   insert into tab3
  6   (col3)
  7   values
  8   (27);
  9
  9   end;
 10   /
```

```
Trigger created.
```

Now, the moment of truth—let's see what happens when a row in tab1 is updated.

```
SQL> update tab1
  2   set col1 = 8;
```

```
1 row updated.
```

```
SQL> select * from tab1;

     COL1
---------
        8
```

```
SQL> select * from tab2;

     COL2
---------
       10
        7
```

```
SQL> select * from tab3;

     COL3
---------
        7
       27
```

As you can see in the preceding code, the following changes have taken place:

- In tab1, the value of col1 was updated to 8.
- In tab2, trigger Tab1_Update_Before inserted a new row with the old value of col1: 7.
- In tab3, trigger Tab2_Insert_Before fired as a result of the new row in tab2 and set the value of col3 to be the same as the value that was inserted into tab2: 7. When tab3 was updated, trigger Tab3_Update_Before inserted another row into tab3 with the value 27.

> **TIP**
>
> By default, the number of cascaded triggers that can fire is limited to 32. That number is controlled by the Oracle initialization parameter max_open_cursors, which can be changed. However, keep this in mind—your ability to understand the ramifications of an INSERT, UPDATE, or DELETE statement is inversely proportional to the number of cascading triggers associated with that SQL statement. In other words, keep it straight-forward.

COMMIT and *ROLLBACK* Cannot Be Used in Triggers

You cannot execute a COMMIT or ROLLBACK statement in a database trigger. Also, a trigger may not call a stored procedure, function, or package subprogram that performs a COMMIT or ROLLBACK. Oracle maintains this restriction for a good reason. If a trigger encounters an error, all database changes that have been propagated by the trigger should be rolled back; but if the trigger committed some portion of those database changes, Oracle would not be able to roll back the entire transaction. Here is an example of the error that Oracle returns if a trigger contains a COMMIT:

```
SQL> create or replace trigger Shipment_Upd_After before
  2  Update on Shipment
  3  for each row
  4
  4  declare
  5
  5  begin
  6
  6  :new.Manual_Check := 'N';
  7
  7  commit;
  8
  8  end;
  9  /

Trigger created.

SQL> update Shipment
  2  set Quantity = 100;
update Shipment
       *
ERROR at line 1:
ORA-04092: cannot COMMIT in a trigger
ORA-06512: at line 2
ORA-04088: error during execution of trigger 'FRAYED_WIRES.SHIPMENT_UPD_AFTER'
```

Calling Stored Procedures from a Trigger

You can call a stored procedure or function, whether stand-alone or part of a package, from the PL/SQL body of a database trigger. As an example, I've rewritten the trigger Block_Trade_Log_Ins_Before so that it calls the stored function Get_3_Day_Running_Avg. The trigger is based on the Block_Trade_Log table previously discussed in this chapter. Here is the stored function that the trigger will reference:

```
SQL> create or replace function Get_3_Day_Running_Avg
  2                      (Stock_Symb in varchar2)
  3                      return number is
  4
  4    Running_Avg    number;
  5
  5    begin
  6
  6    select avg(price)
  7    into Running_Avg
  8    from Block_Trade_Log
  9    where
 10    Stock_Symbol = Stock_Symb and
 11    Timestamp >= SYSDATE-3;
 12
 12    return Running_Avg;
 13
 13    end;
 14    /

Function created.
```

Here is the modified version of Block_Trade_Log_Ins_Before that calls the stored function Get_3_Day_Running_Avg.

```
SQL> create or replace trigger Block_Trade_Log_Ins_Before before
  2    insert on Block_Trade_Log
  3    for each row
  4
  4    declare
  5
  5    Running_Avg    number;
  6
  6    begin
  7
  7    :new.Running_Avg_3_Days := Get_3_Day_Running_Avg (:new.Stock_Symbol);
  8
  8    end;
  9    /

Trigger created.
```

Raising an Exception in a Trigger

Another use for a trigger is to disallow a SQL statement or transaction by raising an exception. In this example, I create a row-level AFTER INSERT trigger and declare the exception

Too_Many_Blocks. If the value of Blocks_Traded in the inserted row is greater than one million, the exception is raised. In the exception section, an exception handler for the user-defined exception passes back an Oracle error and message.

```
SQL> create or replace trigger Block_Trade_Log_Ins_After after
  2  insert on Block_Trade_Log
  3  for each row
  4
  4  declare
  5
  5  Too_Many_Blocks    exception;
  6
  6  begin
  7
  7  if :new.Blocks_Traded > 1000000 then
  8     raise Too_Many_Blocks;
  9  end if;
 10
 10
 10  exception
 11
 11    when Too_Many_Blocks then
 12      raise_application_error (-20001,
                'You cannot trade more than one million blocks');
 13
 13  end;
 14  /

Trigger created.
```

For example, if you insert a row into Block_Trade_Log in which Blocks_Traded is equal to 1000, the row is inserted successfully.

```
SQL> insert into Block_Trade_Log
  2  (Stock_Symbol, Price, Blocks_Traded, Timestamp)
  3  values
  4  ('AXAXA', 104.25, 1000, SYSDATE);

1 row created.
```

However, if you try to insert a row into Block_Trade_Log in which Blocks_Traded is equal to 1,000,001, the exception is raised and the Oracle error returned to the caller—in this case, SQL*Plus.

```
SQL> insert into Block_Trade_Log
  2  (Stock_Symbol, Price, Blocks_Traded, Timestamp)
  3  values
  4  ('AXAXA', 103.25, 1000001, SYSDATE);
insert into Block_Trade_Log
            *
ERROR at line 1:
ORA-20001: You cannot trade more than one million blocks
ORA-06512: at line 9
ORA-04088: error during execution of trigger
          'FRAYED_WIRES.BLOCK_TRADE_LOG_INS_AFTER'
```

Dropping, Enabling, and Disabling Triggers

If you've decided that you absolutely don't want a particular trigger, you can drop it with the following statement:

```
DROP TRIGGER trigger-name;
```

where *trigger-name* is the name of the trigger to be dropped.

For example, to drop the DELETE AFTER trigger on the Repair Header table, issue the following statement via SQL*Plus.

```
SQL> drop trigger Repair_Header_Delete_After;

Trigger dropped.
```

Sometimes, dropping a trigger is too drastic. Instead, you might want to temporarily deactivate a trigger. You can disable a trigger until it makes sense to enable it. To do this, use the following ALTER TRIGGER statement.

```
ALTER TRIGGER trigger-name DISABLE;
```

where *trigger-name* is the trigger to disable.

The following example disables the trigger Repair_Header_Delete_After.

```
SQL> alter trigger Repair_Header_Delete_After disable;

Trigger altered.
```

To enable a disabled trigger, use the following statement:

```
ALTER TRIGGER trigger-name ENABLE;
```

where *trigger-name* is the trigger to enable.

For instance, you can enable Repair_Header_Delete_After by issuing the following command:

```
SQL> alter trigger Repair_Header_Delete_After enable;

Trigger altered.
```

Looking at Triggers Through DBA_TRIGGERS

Oracle provides a data dictionary view named DBA_TRIGGERS that you can query to obtain information about any existing database triggers. DBA_TRIGGERS consists of the following columns:

```
SQL> desc dba_triggers
 Name                            Null?    Type
 ------------------------------- -------- ----
 OWNER                           NOT NULL VARCHAR2(30)
 TRIGGER_NAME                    NOT NULL VARCHAR2(30)
```

```
TRIGGER_TYPE                       VARCHAR2(16)
TRIGGERING_EVENT                   VARCHAR2(26)
TABLE_OWNER               NOT NULL VARCHAR2(30)
TABLE_NAME                NOT NULL VARCHAR2(30)
REFERENCING_NAMES                  VARCHAR2(87)
WHEN_CLAUSE                        VARCHAR2(2000)
STATUS                             VARCHAR2(8)
DESCRIPTION                        VARCHAR2(2000)
TRIGGER_BODY                       LONG
```

For example, if you wanted to see all of the triggers that were created by Oracle user FRAYED_WIRES, you could use the following query:

```
SQL> select trigger_name, trigger_type, triggering_event, status
  2  from dba_triggers
  3  where
  4  owner = 'FRAYED_WIRES'
  5  order by trigger_name, triggering_event, trigger_type;
```

TRIGGER_NAME	TRIGGER_TYPE	TRIGGERING_EVENT	STATUS
BLOCK_TRADE_LOG_INS_BEFORE	BEFORE EACH ROW	INSERT	ENABLED
REPAIR_HEADER_DELETE_AFTER	AFTER EACH ROW	DELETE	ENABLED
SHIPMENT_INS_BEFORE	BEFORE EACH ROW	INSERT	ENABLED
SHIPMENT_UPD_AFTER	BEFORE EACH ROW	UPDATE	ENABLED
TAB1_UPDATE_BEFORE	BEFORE EACH ROW	UPDATE	ENABLED
TAB2_INSERT_BEFORE	BEFORE EACH ROW	INSERT	ENABLED
TAB3_UPDATE_BEFORE	AFTER STATEMENT	UPDATE	ENABLED

You can also query DBA_TRIGGERS to see the actual trigger body that executes when the trigger fires.

```
SQL> select trigger_body
  2  from dba_triggers
  3  where
  4  trigger_name = 'BLOCK_TRADE_LOG_INS_BEFORE';

TRIGGER_BODY
----------------------------------------------------------------
declare
Running_Avg number := 0;
begin
select avg(price)
into Running_Avg
from Block_Trade_Log
where
Stock_Symbol = :new.Stock_Symbol and
Timestamp >= SYSDATE-3;
:new.Running_Avg_3_Days := Running_Avg;
end;
```

Summary

The main ideas discussed in this chapter include the following:

- A database trigger is a PL/SQL block that executes when a triggering event—INSERT, UPDATE, or DELETE—occurs.

- You define a trigger with the CREATE TRIGGER statement, which can be issued from SQL*Plus.

- You can use a trigger for a variety of purposes that include enforcing a security policy, performing complex validation of column values, and calculating the default column values.

- A row-level trigger fires for each row that is affected by a trigger. A row's column values can be inspected or modified with a row-level trigger.

- A statement-level trigger is fired only once by the triggering event. A statement-level trigger cannot access the column values of any row.

- A BEFORE trigger fires before its triggering event. An AFTER trigger fires after its triggering event.

- A trigger may have an optional clause that specifies a condition which must be true for the trigger to fire.

- You can drop a trigger with the DROP TRIGGER statement.

- You can enable or disable a trigger by using the ALTER TRIGGER statement.

- A trigger body cannot contain a COMMIT or ROLLBACK statement.

- You can invoke a stored procedure or function from within the trigger body.

- You can obtain a list of each trigger and associated information by querying the data dictionary view DBA_TRIGGERS.

23

Saving and Loading Data

It goes without saying that a database is useless without data. This chapter focuses on two aspects of Personal Oracle7: saving existing data so that no data loss occurs and loading data from external sources into a Personal Oracle7 database. To save and restore Personal Oracle7 data, Oracle provides the Export and Import programs. The Export utility writes to a binary file, and the Import utility reads a file produced by the Export utility. As an Oracle application developer, you'll want to be proficient in using both programs.

In addition to Export and Import, Oracle supplies a utility program, SQL*Loader, that loads records from *flat* files into one or more Oracle tables. I'll demonstrate how SQL*Loader is used to load fixed and variable length records into a Personal Oracle database.

Using the Export Program

Export and Import work in conjunction with one another to perform the following tasks:

- Save Personal Oracle7 structures and table contents to a binary file
- Move Oracle database structures to another Oracle database
- Restore data from an "old" export file to an existing table

Whenever you use Export or Import, you must connect to the Oracle database by supplying a valid Oracle username and password. Export offers three modes of saving Oracle data and structures:

- Table: A list of specified tables
- Owner: All objects and their contents owned by a specified user
- Full: An export of all database objects in an Oracle database

The Export program icon is in the Personal Oracle7 program group. Double-click the Export icon. A dialog box will appear, prompting you for the Oracle username and password. To use Export (and Import), the Personal Oracle7 database must be available and running. We'll use the username and password from the repair store example—FRAYED_WIRES and HELMHOLTZ.

After you've successfully connected to the Oracle database, Export provides three principal choices for export mode. We'll start by designating the tables to be exported. On the Database Exporter screen, a section labeled Export These Objects contains four checkboxes.

- Grants: If this box is checked, Export saves any object privileges that exist for the exported database objects.
- Rows: If this box is checked, Export writes the contents of exported tables to the export file. If you don't want to save the contents of tables—only their definitions— make sure this box is unchecked.
- Constraints: If this box is checked, Export saves all constraints that belong to the exported tables.

■ Indexes: If this box is checked, Export writes all the definitions of all indexes for exported tables. Export *never* writes the contents of an index to the export file. Depending on user options, indexes are recreated when Import is invoked.

Unless otherwise indicated, leave the previous options as is when working with the examples in this chapter.

Exporting Designated Tables

By default, Export uses the same name for the export file that was used in the previous export session. Let's change the name to 4TABLE.DMP. Click the Table radio button. Click the Specify button to designate the tables to be exported.

> **NOTE**
>
> By default, the export file has an extension of .DMP. Unfortunately, other programs sometimes produce diagnostic or dump files with the same extension. Avoid confusion—be sure to name your Oracle export files with meaningful names and store them in an appropriate directory where they won't be mistaken as dump files.

After you've pressed the Specify button, Export presents a dialog box that displays the tables owned by the user you've used to connect to Oracle—FRAYED_WIRES. These are the tables that can be exported (see Figure 23.1).

FIGURE 23.1.

Export displays tables that can be exported.

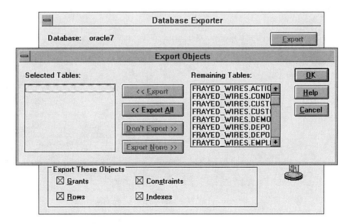

To indicate that a table should be exported, click the table in the list of Remaining Tables. You have the option of exporting all the tables by clicking the Export All button. The first time that you click a table in the list of Remaining Tables, the Export button will be enabled (see Figure 23.2). After you've highlighted a table for export, press the Export button to move the table to the Tables to Export list. After you've selected the tables that you want to export, click the OK button to return to the Database Exporter screen.

FIGURE 23.2.

Designating tables to be exported.

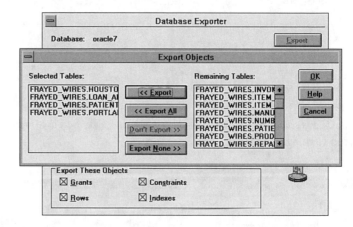

At this point, you can begin the export process by clicking the Export button. The Export Status window will appear; a box on this screen displays the progress of the database export (see Figure 23.3). When all of the tables have been exported, Export displays the following message:

```
Export terminated successfully without warnings.
```

In addition, the Close button on the Export Status window will be enabled; click it to return to the Database Exporter screen.

FIGURE 23.3.

Export Status window showing exported tables.

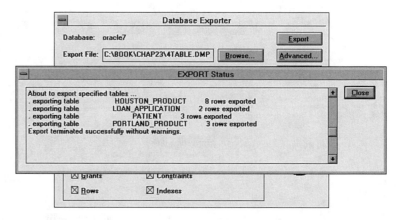

If you want to save the contents of the Export Status window, you have two choices. Your first choice is to copy the contents of the box and then paste them to an editor. As an alternative, you can specify an Export Log file by performing the following steps:

1. Click the Advanced button on the Database Exporter screen.

2. At the bottom of the Advanced Export Options screen, you'll see a field for specifying the name of the Export Log. Enter the directory and filename you want, and click the OK button (see Figure 23.4).

FIGURE 23.4.

*Specifying the Export
Log filename.*

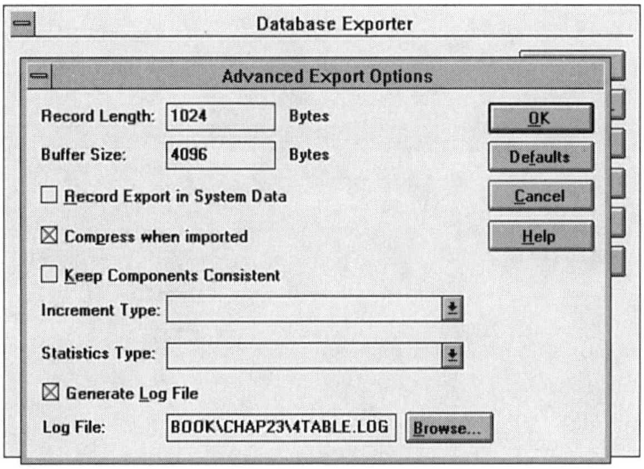

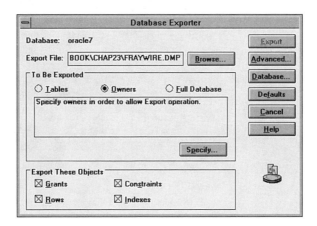

Exporting Objects Owned by a Designated User

The second export mode is to export all objects owned by a designated Oracle user. To start from the beginning, click the Export icon and provide a valid Oracle username and password to connect to the Personal Oracle7 database. Once again, we'll use FRAYED_WIRES and HELMHOLTZ, respectively, for Oracle username and password. In the To Be Exported section of the screen, click the Owners radio button. As in other cases, the word Owners is synonymous with Oracle user and Oracle account. To designate the Oracle user whose database objects are to be exported, click on the Specify... button.

FIGURE 23.5.

*Specifying an Export by
owner.*

The Export program will display an Export Objects screen. On this screen, you'll see two lists: Selected Owners and Remaining Owners. Selected Owners displays a list of the Oracle owners whose objects should be exported—yes, you *can* specify more than one Oracle account to export. In addition, four buttons are visible—Export, Export All, Don't Export, and Export None (see Figure 23.6).

FIGURE 23.6.

The Export Objects screen.

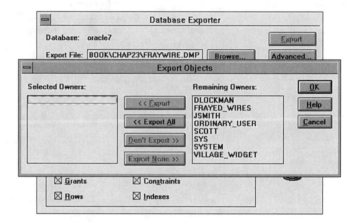

Entries in the Remaining Owners list are highlighted with a mouse click; each highlighted owner can be exported by pressing the Export button. When you press the Export button, the owner is removed from the Remaining Owners list and placed on the Selected Owners list (see Figure 23.7). All owners can be exported by clicking the Export All button.

FIGURE 23.7.

Specifying an owner to be exported.

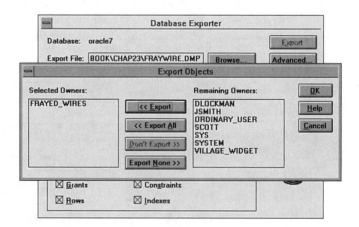

If you want to prevent a selected owner from being exported, highlight the owner in the Selected Owners list and press the Don't Export button. If you want to deselect all owners from being exported, press the Export None button. Click the OK button to return to the Database Exporter screen. Start the export process by clicking the Export button.

Performing a Full Export

The final export option is the full export. This option exports all database users and their objects. This is the most thorough method of exporting an Oracle database, but this method is also the most time-consuming.

To perform a full export, click the Export icon and provide a valid Oracle username and password to connect to the Personal Oracle7 database. Again, we'll use FRAYED_WIRES and HELMHOLTZ, respectively, for Oracle username and password. In the To Be Exported section of the screen, click the Full radio button (see Figure 23.8). There are no other options to specify; when you press the Export button, the Export Status window will appear, and the full export will begin. When the full export is completed, you can close the Export Status window.

FIGURE 23.8.

Performing a full export.

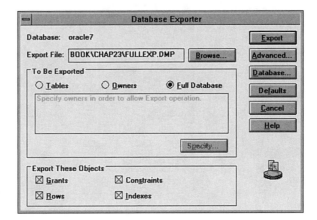

Using the Import Program

The Import program, in concert with the Export program, offers a method for loading Oracle database objects—tables, views, and others—and table data into a Personal Oracle7 database. Import relies on the file created by Export—a .DMP file.

Import has three primary modes of operation.

- Importing a list of designated tables
- Importing database objects owned by an Oracle user into the same Oracle account— or another Oracle user's account
- Performing a full import—by processing the entire contents of an export file

To invoke the Import program, double-click the Import icon in the Personal Oracle7 program group. A dialog box will appear, prompting you for the Oracle username and password. Remember, the Personal Oracle7 database must be available and running before you can use the Import utility. Again, we'll use the username and password from the repair store example— FRAYED_WIRES and HELMHOLTZ.

To start, let's go through the steps of importing a set of tables.

Importing Tables

After you've established a connection to Oracle via Import, enter the name of the export file in the Import File field on the screen. You'll see a group of radio buttons on the Database Importer screen labeled Import Mode. Click the Table radio button (see Figure 23.9).

FIGURE 23.9.

Entering the export file to use for importing tables.

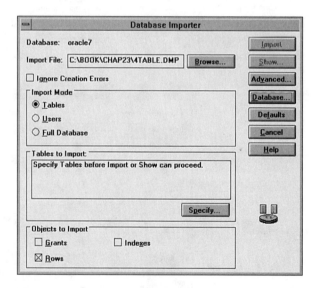

To indicate which tables should be imported, press the Specify button. Import will display a dialog box that displays the tables contained in the export file. These are the tables that can be imported (see Figure 23.10).

To indicate that a table should be imported, click the table in the list of Remaining Tables (see Figure 23.11). You have the option of importing all of the tables by clicking the Import All button. When you click a table in the list of Remaining Tables, the Import button is enabled. After you've highlighted a table for import, press the Import button to move the table to the Tables to Import list. When you've selected the tables that you want to import, click the OK button to return to the Database Importer screen.

FIGURE 23.10.

Display of tables that can be imported.

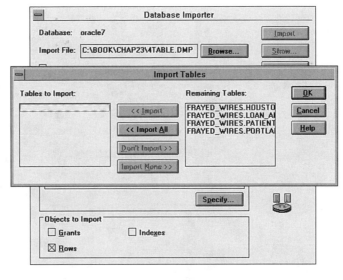

FIGURE 23.11.

Designating tables to be imported.

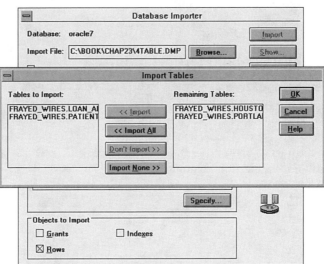

You are now ready to begin the import by clicking the Import button. The Import Status window will appear; a box on this screen displays the progress of the database import (see Figure 23.12). When all of the tables have been imported, Import displays the following message:

```
Import terminated successfully without warnings.
```

FIGURE 23.12.

Import Status window showing imported tables.

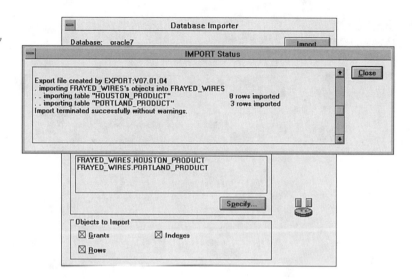

Also, the Close button on the Import Status window will be enabled; click it to return to the Database Importer screen.

The Ignore Creation Errors Option

On the Database Importer screen is a checkbox labeled Ignore Creation Errors. The default setting for this option is unchecked. If a table is imported into an Oracle account and the table already exists in that Oracle account, Import will not import the table and will display an error to the user (see Figure 23.13). If you enable the Ignore Creation Errors option, Import attempts to add the rows from the export file into the existing table. Oracle will enforce any constraints defined for the table or its columns.

FIGURE 23.13.

Import displays an object creation error.

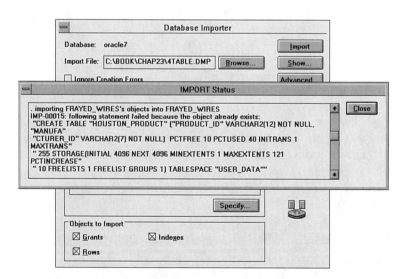

Figure 23.14 illustrates how the table's rows can be imported once Ignore Creation Errors is enabled.

FIGURE 23.14.

Enabling the Ignore Creation Errors mode.

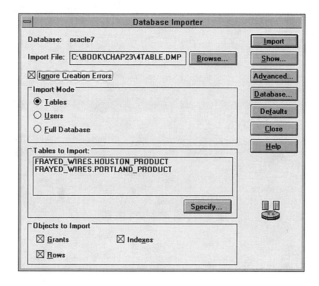

Importing an Owner's Objects

The second method of importing database objects is by owner. Each object referenced in an export file is associated with an owner. You can import all Oracle objects owned by a specified Oracle user that are contained in an export file. For example, let's assume that Jean Smith, manager of the Frayed Wires electronics repair store, has an Oracle account with DBA privileges. As an experiment, she decides that she wants to import some tables that were exported from the FRAYED_WIRES Oracle account. Jean invokes Import and connects to her Oracle account in the Personal Oracle database. She then clicks the Users button to indicate the Import Mode and enters the name of the export file (see Figure 23.15).

Next, Jean clicks the Specify button to identify the user whose Oracle objects will be imported into her Oracle account.

Import will display an Import Users screen. On this screen, you'll see two drop-down lists: Import This User and To This User. Import This User displays a list of the Oracle owners with objects in the export file. To This User displays a list of all Oracle accounts that exist in the Personal Oracle database (see Figure 23.16).

FIGURE 23.15.

Specifying the Import Mode as Users.

FIGURE 23.16.

Selecting the user to import.

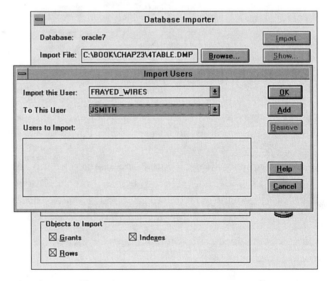

Jean clicks FRAYED_WIRES in the Import This User list and selects her own account—JSMITH—in the To This User list. She then clicks the OK button, and the Database Importer screen has the input focus. In the Users to Import list box, a single line is shown: FROM FRAYED_WIRES TO JSMITH (see Figure 23.17).

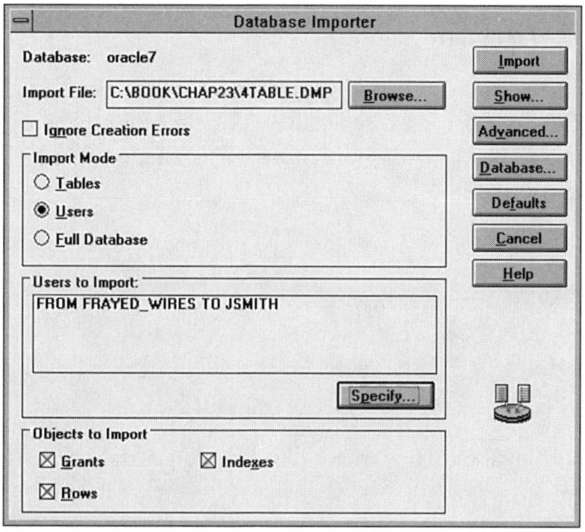

FIGURE 23.17.

Database Importer displaying the users to import.

Jean starts the import by clicking the Import button. The Import Status window appears; a box on this screen will display the progress of the database import. When all of the tables have been imported, Import will display the following message:

```
Import terminated successfully without warnings.
```

The Close button on the Import Status window will be enabled; Jean clicks it to return to the Database Importer screen.

Performing a Full Import

The third operational mode offered by Import is the full import. If you select this mode, the Import program will attempt to import all of the database objects contained in the export file. I don't recommend using this option with one exception—when you're trying to reconstruct a database from scratch. I'll discuss this further in Chapter 24, "Database Backup and Recovery."

> **CAUTION**
>
> Do not import objects owned by the SYS account. The SYS account owns all of the Oracle7 data dictionary tables. By adding rows to existing data dictionary tables, you might inadvertently corrupt the Oracle data dictionary with potentially disastrous results. The only exception to this is the AUD$ table, which is optionally used to store Oracle7 auditing data.

SQL*Loader

SQL*Loader is an Oracle utility program designed to load data into Oracle tables from external files. SQL*Loader is a very flexible utility; it offers many options and settings to deal with a wide variety of data loading situations. SQL*Loader uses the following files during the loading process:

- Control
- Data
- Bad
- Discard
- Log

Figure 23.18 illustrates how these files function with SQL*Loader.

FIGURE 23.18.

*Relationship between files used by SQL*Loader.*

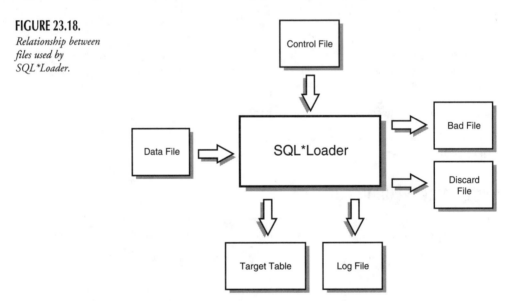

The SQL*Loader Control File

The control file contains a description of the records in the data file, the Oracle table to be loaded, special processing options to be used, and other SQL*Loader settings. Also, the name of the control file, unless indicated otherwise, is used for naming the discard, bad, and log files. For instance, if the control file is named itemmast.ctl, the other filenames default to the following:

Discard file:	itemmast.dsc
Bad file:	itemmast.bad
Log file:	itemmast.log

The SQL*Loader Data File

The data file is the external file that is read by SQL*Loader. This file may consist of fixed length records, variable length records, and records whose data fields are delimited by specific characters. The data file is referred to as an external file because it is external to the Oracle database.

The SQL*Loader Bad File

When SQL*Loader is unable to process a record, it places the record in the bad file. For instance, let's assume that the control file specifies that the first six characters of each record is a date in the format MMDDYY. SQL*Loader will reject records if the first two characters are not in the set 01, 02, 03... through 12. When SQL*Loader finishes, the rejected records in the bad file can be reviewed, corrected, and reloaded, or remain unloaded.

The SQL*Loader Discard File

You can optionally configure the SQL*Loader control file to discard records that do not meet specific criteria into a discard file. For example, if you were only interested in loading records from the ITEMMAST file where the creation date of the records was greater than or equal to 01-JAN-84, you would add a line to the control file to enforce this constraint. Any records whose creation date was earlier than 01-JAN-84 would be placed in the discard file.

The SQL*Loader Log File

SQL*Loader records a summary of its activity in the log file. This summary includes the number of successfully loaded records, the number of discarded records, and the number of rejected records. Also, the log file will contain the SQL error associated with each rejected record.

Using SQL*Loader

As with the other Personal Oracle database administration tools, SQL*Loader is found in the Personal Oracle7 program group. To invoke SQL*Loader, double-click the SQL*Loader program icon. As with Import and Export, the use of SQL*Loader requires that the Oracle database be running and available.

The syntax for the SQL*Loader control file can get fairly complex, depending on the data loading requirements. I'll present two common examples in this chapter: loading fixed length records and loading variable length records. For the sake of clarity, some of the details that you would see in a real-world situation have been left out.

Once you've invoked SQL*Loader, a screen will appear, containing several fields. In the username and password, I'll enter the Oracle username and password that I've created for this example—VILLAGE_WIDGET and VILLAGE, respectively.

Using SQL*Loader to Load Fixed Format Records

Let's assume that your company, Village Widget Corporation, is rightsizing the computerized manufacturing system that was developed in-house. Your task is to load and convert all of the legacy data to the new Oracle tables.

As a first step, you select the ITEMMAST file, which contains basic information about each item that has been purchased by Village Widget. The fixed field records in the ITEMMAST file will be loaded into the Item_Master Oracle table. The record structure for the ITEMMAST file is illustrated in Table 23.1.

Table 23.1. Record structure of the ITEMMAST file.

Field Number	Field Name	Datatype	Length
1	ITEM_NO	Alphanumeric	60
2	DESCRIP	Text	80
3	VENDID	Alphanumeric	6
4	LSTPRICE	Numeric	8
5	CREADATE	Numeric	6
6	CREAUSER	Alphanumeric	6
7	MODDATE	Numeric	6
8	MODUSER	Alphanumeric	6

Also, the record structure for the associated VENDMAST file is shown in Table 23.2.

Table 23.2. Record structure of the VENDMAST file.

Field Number	Field Name	Datatype	Length
1	VEND_NO	Alphanumeric	6
2	NAME	Text	80

The Item_Master and Vendor_Master tables are created with the following SQL statements:

```
CREATE TABLE VENDOR_MASTER (
VENDOR_ID        VARCHAR2(12),
VENDOR_NAME      VARCHAR2(60) NOT NULL,PRIMARY KEY (VENDOR_ID));
```

```
CREATE TABLE ITEM_MASTER (
ITEM_NO          VARCHAR2(12),
DESCRIPTION      VARCHAR2(2000),
VENDOR_ID        VARCHAR2(12),
RECENT_PRICE     DECIMAL(12,4),
CREATED_DATE     DATE NOT NULL,
CREATED_BY       VARCHAR2(32) NOT NULL,
DATE_MODIFIED    DATE,
MODIFIED_BY      VARCHAR2(32),
PRIMARY KEY (ITEM_NO),
FOREIGN KEY (VENDOR_ID) REFERENCES VENDOR_MASTER (VENDOR_ID));

CREATE TABLE VENDOR_MASTER (
VENDOR_ID        VARCHAR2(12),
VENDOR_NAME      VARCHAR2(60) NOT NULL, PRIMARY KEY (VENDOR_ID));

CREATE TABLE ITEM_MASTER (
ITEM_NO          VARCHAR2(12),
DESCRIPTION      VARCHAR2(2000),
VENDOR_ID        VARCHAR2(12),
RECENT_PRICE     DECIMAL(12,4),
CREATED_DATE     DATE NOT NULL,
CREATED_BY       VARCHAR2(32) NOT NULL, DATE_MODIFIED    DATE,
MODIFIED_BY      VARCHAR2(32),
PRIMARY KEY (ITEM_NO),
FOREIGN KEY (VENDOR_ID) REFERENCES VENDOR_MASTER (VENDOR_ID);
```

Because you realize that the Item_Master table is dependent on the Vendor_Master table, you decide to load the Vendor_Master table first. If you tried to load Item_Master before loading the Vendor_Master, SQL*Loader would reject all of the Item_Master records because they violate a referential integrity constraint.

Contents of the Control File

Using a text editor, you create a control file for loading the VENDMAST file into the Vendor_Master table.

```
load data
infile vendmast.dat
into table VENDOR_MASTER
(VENDOR_ID       POSITION(01:06) CHAR,
VENDOR_NAME      POSITION(07:86) CHAR)
```

Running SQL*Loader

To run SQL*Loader, click the SQL*Loader program icon, which can be found in the Personal Oracle7 program group. SQL*Loader will display a window into which you enter the username, password, and the control file to be used for loading data. To load records from the VENDMAST file, enter the values shown in Figure 23.19 and click the Load button to start the loading process. SQL*Loader will display another window that shows the loading progress. When SQL*Loader has finished processing the data file, the Close button on this window will be enabled. Click the Close button to return to the SQL*Loader window.

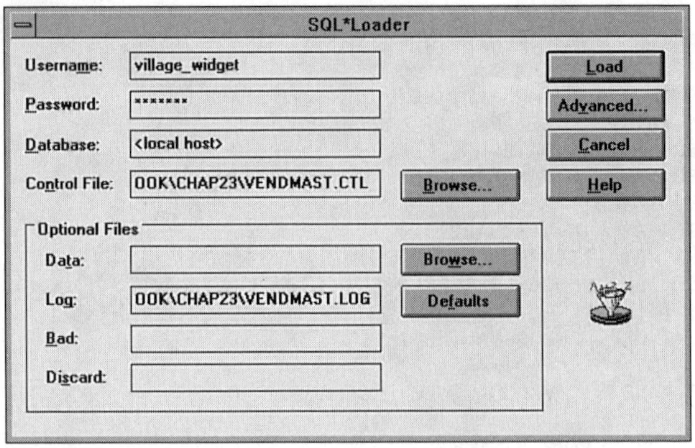

FIGURE 23.19.

*Loading VENDMAST data with SQL*Loader.*

Contents of the Log File

After SQL*Loader has finished processing, you'll find that the log file, vendmast.log, contains:

```
SQL*Loader: Release 7.1.4.0.2 - Production on Sat Jun 03 23:38:15 1995

Copyright (c) Oracle Corporation 1979, 1994.  All rights reserved.

Control File:   C:\BOOK\CHAP23\VENDMAST.CTL
Data File:      vendmast.dat
  Bad File:     C:\BOOK\CHAP23\vendmast.bad
  Discard File: C:\BOOK\CHAP23\vendmast.dsc
 (Allow all discards)

Number to load: ALL
Number to skip: 0
Errors allowed: 50
Bind array:     64 rows, maximum of 65024 bytes
Continuation:    none specified
Path used:      Conventional

Table VENDOR_MASTER, loaded from every logical record.
Insert option in effect for this table: INSERT

    Column Name             Position   Len  Term Encl Datatype
------------------------- ---------- ----- ---- ---- --------------------
VENDOR_ID                        1:6     6           CHARACTER
VENDOR_NAME                      7:86    80           CHARACTER


Table VENDOR_MASTER:
  5 Rows successfully loaded.
  0 Rows not loaded due to data errors.
  0 Rows not loaded because all WHEN clauses were failed.
  0 Rows not loaded because all fields were null.


Space allocated for bind array:                  5760 bytes(64 rows)
Space allocated for memory besides bind array:   46227 bytes
```

```
Total logical records skipped:        0
Total logical records read:           5
Total logical records rejected:       0
Total logical records discarded:      0

Run began on Sat Jun 03 23:38:15 1995
Run ended on Sat Jun 03 23:38:19 1995

Elapsed time was:      00:00:04.23
CPU time was:          00:00:00.00    (May not include ORACLE CPU time)
```

Now that you've loaded the Vendor_Master table, you're ready to begin loading the Item_Master table. Construct a control file, itemmas1.ctl, for loading records from the ITEMMAST file.

```
load data
infile itemmast.dat
into table ITEM_MASTER
(ITEM_NO POSITION(01:06) CHAR,
 DESCRIPTION POSITION(07:86) CHAR,
 VENDOR_ID POSITION(87:92) CHAR,
 RECENT_PRICE POSITION(93:100) DECIMAL EXTERNAL,
 CREATED_DATE POSITION(101:106) DATE,
 CREATED_BY POSITION(107:112) CHAR,
 DATE_MODIFIED POSITION(113:118) DATE,
 MODIFIED_BY POSITION(119:124) CHAR)
```

Running SQL*Loader

Click the SQL*Loader program icon. To load records from the ITEMMAST file, enter the following values:

- ■ Username: Village_Widget
- ■ Password: Village
- ■ Control File: itemmas1.ctl

Click the Load button to start the loading process. SQL*Loader will display another window that shows the loading progress. When SQL*Loader has finished processing the data file, the Close button on this window will be enabled. Click the Close button to return to the SQL*Loader window.

Contents of the Log File

After SQL*Loader has finished processing, the log file, itemmast.log, will contain:

```
SQL*Loader: Release 7.1.4.0.2 - Production on Mon Jun 05 23:13:19 1995

Copyright (c) Oracle Corporation 1979, 1994.  All rights reserved.

Control File:  C:\BOOK\CHAP23\ITEMMAS1.CTL
Data File:     itemmast.dat
  Bad File:    C:\BOOK\CHAP23\itemmast.bad
  Discard File: C:\BOOK\CHAP23\itemmast.dsc
 (Allow all discards)
```

```
Number to load: ALL
Number to skip: 0
Errors allowed: 50
Bind array:     64 rows, maximum of 65024 bytes
Continuation:    none specified
Path used:      Conventional

Table ITEM_MASTER, loaded from every logical record.
Insert option in effect for this table: INSERT

    Column Name                  Position   Len  Term Encl Datatype
    ------------------------     ---------- ----- ---- ---- --------------------
ITEM_NO                               1:6    6              CHARACTER
DESCRIPTION                           7:86   80             CHARACTER
VENDOR_ID                            87:92   6              CHARACTER
RECENT_PRICE                         93:100  8              CHARACTER
CREATED_DATE                        101:106  6              DATE DD-MON-YY
CREATED_BY                          107:112  6              CHARACTER
DATE_MODIFIED                       113:118  6              DATE DD-MON-YY
MODIFIED_BY                         119:124  6              CHARACTER

Record 1: Rejected - Error on table ITEM_MASTER, column CREATED_DATE.
ORA-01843: not a valid month

Record 2: Rejected - Error on table ITEM_MASTER, column CREATED_DATE.
ORA-01843: not a valid month


Table ITEM_MASTER:
  0 Rows successfully loaded.
  2 Rows not loaded due to data errors.
  0 Rows not loaded because all WHEN clauses were failed.
  0 Rows not loaded because all fields were null.


Space allocated for bind array:                8960 bytes(64 rows)
Space allocated for memory besides bind array:  57016 bytes

Total logical records skipped:         0
Total logical records read:            2
Total logical records rejected:        2
Total logical records discarded:       0

Run began on Mon Jun 05 23:13:19 1995
Run ended on Mon Jun 05 23:13:23 1995

Elapsed time was:      00:00:03.79
CPU time was:          00:00:00.00    (May not include ORACLE CPU time)
```

According to the contents of the log file, none of the records were loaded into the table.

Contents of the Bad File—What Went Wrong

If you look at the error messages in the log file, you see that Oracle returned an error code of –1843, which indicates a problem with the processing of date values. SQL*Loader returned this error because the format of the date in CREATED_DATE and DATE_MODIFIED is

MMDDYY; Oracle's default date format is DD-MON-YY. SQL*Loader has now created a bad file that contains the rejected records. For SQL*Loader to interpret the date fields correctly, you must add the date format within single quotes after the keyword DATE, as shown in the following corrected control file (itemmas2.ctl):

```
load data
infile itemmast.dat
into table ITEM_MASTER
(ITEM_NO POSITION(01:06) CHAR,
 DESCRIPTION POSITION(07:86) CHAR,
 VENDOR_ID POSITION(87:92) CHAR,
 RECENT_PRICE POSITION(93:100) DECIMAL EXTERNAL,
 CREATED_DATE POSITION(101:106) DATE 'MMDDYY',
 CREATED_BY POSITION(107:112) CHAR,
 DATE_MODIFIED POSITION(113:118) DATE 'MMDDYY',
 MODIFIED_BY POSITION(119:124) CHAR)
```

Rerunning SQL*Loader

Click the SQL*Loader program icon. To successfully load records from the ITEMMAST file, enter the following values (see Figure 23.20):

- Username: Village_Widget
- Password: Village
- Control File: itemmas2.ctl

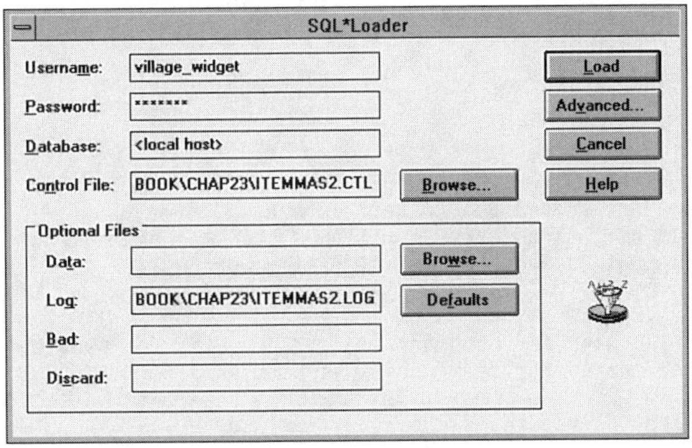

FIGURE 23.20.

*Loading ITEMMAST data with a corrected control file via SQL*Loader.*

The itemmas2.ctl control file correctly converts the date column fields in the ITEMMAST file. Click the Load button to start the loading process. SQL*Loader displays another window that shows the loading progress. When SQL*Loader has finished processing the data file, the Close button on this window will be enabled. Click the Close button to return to the SQL*Loader window.

Contents of the Log File

Now you'll see that SQL*Loader has processed the records as intended.

```
SQL*Loader: Release 7.1.4.0.2 - Production on Mon Jun 05 23:14:00 1995

Copyright (c) Oracle Corporation 1979, 1994.  All rights reserved.

Control File:   C:\BOOK\CHAP23\ITEMMAS2.CTL
Data File:      itemmast.dat
  Bad File:     C:\BOOK\CHAP23\itemmast.bad
  Discard File: C:\BOOK\CHAP23\itemmast.dsc
 (Allow all discards)

Number to load: ALL
Number to skip: 0
Errors allowed: 50
Bind array:     64 rows, maximum of 65024 bytes
Continuation:   none specified
Path used:      Conventional

Table ITEM_MASTER, loaded from every logical record.
Insert option in effect for this table: INSERT

    Column Name                     Position   Len  Term Encl Datatype
--------------------------------  ----------  -----  ---- ---- --------------------
ITEM_NO                                  1:6      6              CHARACTER
DESCRIPTION                             7:86     80              CHARACTER
VENDOR_ID                              87:92      6              CHARACTER
RECENT_PRICE                          93:100      8              CHARACTER
CREATED_DATE                         101:106      6              DATE MMDDYY
CREATED_BY                           107:112      6              CHARACTER
DATE_MODIFIED                        113:118      6              DATE MMDDYY
MODIFIED_BY                          119:124      6              CHARACTER


Table ITEM_MASTER:
  2 Rows successfully loaded.
  0 Rows not loaded due to data errors.
  0 Rows not loaded because all WHEN clauses were failed.
  0 Rows not loaded because all fields were null.


Space allocated for bind array:                     8960 bytes(64 rows)
Space allocated for memory besides bind array:      57524 bytes

Total logical records skipped:          0
Total logical records read:             2
Total logical records rejected:         0
Total logical records discarded:        0

Run began on Mon Jun 05 23:14:00 1995
Run ended on Mon Jun 05 23:14:03 1995

Elapsed time was:     00:00:03.30
CPU time was:         00:00:00.00    (May not include ORACLE CPU time)
```

Not only are you able to specify the format of date values, but also you can utilize Oracle built-in functions for modifying a field value from the data file. For instance, if you wanted to modify the item description so that the first letter of each word was capitalized, you would apply the INITCAP function to the Description column.

```
load data
infile itemmast.dat
into table ITEM_MASTER
(ITEM_NO POSITION(01:06) CHAR,
 DESCRIPTION POSITION(07:86) CHAR "INITCAP(:DESCRIPTION)",
 VENDOR_ID POSITION(87:92) CHAR,
 RECENT_PRICE POSITION(93:100) DECIMAL EXTERNAL,
 CREATED_DATE POSITION(101:106) DATE 'MMDDYY',
 CREATED_BY POSITION(107:112) CHAR,
 DATE_MODIFIED POSITION(113:118) DATE 'MMDDYY',
 MODIFIED_BY POSITION(119:124) CHAR)
```

Loading Free Format, Delimited Records into a Table

We've successfully loaded the Item_Master and Vendor_Master tables. As it turns out, one of the data files—dealing with vendor quality—that we need to load was maintained in a separate system. The structure of the VENDQUAL file is shown in Table 23.3.

Table 23.3. Record structure of the VENDQUAL file.

Field Number	Field Name	Datatype	Length
1	VENDID	Alphanumeric	6
2	VENDNAME	Text	40
3	QUALRATE	Alphanumeric	2
4	RATEDATE	Numeric	8
5	RATEUSER	Alphanumeric	6

However, the VENDQUAL file has been unloaded to a file containing variable length records with each field delimited by double quotes.

```
"G01001","GREBNITZ NUTRITIONAL PRODUCTS, INC.","A+","101889","GGOMEZ"
"L02001","LOS ANGELES METALWORKING SYSTEMS, LTD.","B+","021291","RSMITH"
"R00912","RADIO STEAMERS, INC.","B","040491","CJONES"
"K01234","KENTUCKY FRIED WRENCHES, CO.","B-","080992","RSMITH"
"H12431","HOLLERITH HAMMERS, LTD.","C+","091192","GGOMEZ"
```

Contents of the Control File

Create a control file for loading the VENDQUAL file into the VENDOR_QUALITY table.

```
load data
infile 'vendqual.dat'
into table VENDOR_QUALITY
FIELDS TERMINATED BY "," OPTIONALLY ENCLOSED BY '"'
(vendor_id, vendor_name, quality_rating,
 rating_date DATE(6) "MMDDYY",
 user_id)
```

The fourth line in the control file instructs SQL*Loader on how to parse each data record.

Running SQL*Loader

Click the SQL*Loader program icon to invoke SQL*Loader. Enter the username, password, and the control file to be used for loading data. To load records from the VENDQUAL file, enter the values shown in Figure 23.21 and click the Load button to start the loading process. SQL*Loader will display another window that shows the loading progress. When SQL*Loader has finished processing the data file, the Close button on this window will be enabled. Click the Close button to return to the SQL*Loader window.

FIGURE 23.21.

*Loading VENDQUAL
data with SQL*Loader.*

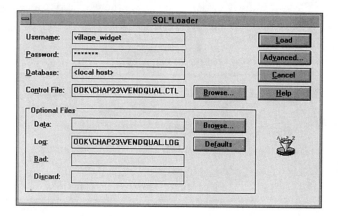

Contents of the Log File

After SQL*Loader has finished processing, you'll find that the log file, vendqual.log, contains:

```
SQL*Loader: Release 7.1.4.0.2 - Production on Sun Jun 04 00:17:45 1995

Copyright (c) Oracle Corporation 1979, 1994.  All rights reserved.

Control File:   C:\BOOK\CHAP23\VENDQUAL.CTL
Data File:      vendqual.dat
  Bad File:     C:\BOOK\CHAP23\vendqual.bad
  Discard File: C:\BOOK\CHAP23\vendqual.dsc
 (Allow all discards)
```

```
Number to load: ALL
Number to skip: 0
Errors allowed: 50
Bind array:     64 rows, maximum of 65024 bytes
Continuation:   none specified
Path used:      Conventional


Table VENDOR_QUALITY, loaded from every logical record.
Insert option in effect for this table: INSERT

    Column Name                  Position   Len  Term Encl Datatype
------------------------------- ---------- ----- ---- ---- --------------------
VENDOR_ID                        FIRST       *    ,  O(") CHARACTER
VENDOR_NAME                      NEXT        *    ,  O(") CHARACTER
QUALITY_RATING                   NEXT        *    ,  O(") CHARACTER
RATING_DATE                      NEXT        6    ,  O(") DATE MMDDYY
USER_ID                          NEXT        *    ,  O(") CHARACTER


Table VENDOR_QUALITY:
   5 Rows successfully loaded.
   0 Rows not loaded due to data errors.
   0 Rows not loaded because all WHEN clauses were failed.
   0 Rows not loaded because all fields were null.


Space allocated for bind array:                  64976 bytes(62 rows)
Space allocated for memory besides bind array:   107565 bytes

Total logical records skipped:        0
Total logical records read:           5
Total logical records rejected:       0
Total logical records discarded:      0

Run began on Sun Jun 04 00:17:45 1995
Run ended on Sun Jun 04 00:17:48 1995

Elapsed time was:      00:00:03.73
CPU time was:          00:00:00.00    (May not include ORACLE CPU time)
```

Loading Data to an Intermediate Table with SQL*Loader

As we discovered earlier, sometimes a legacy field has been used to store special values. This can occur when the legacy field stores its data as a string rather than a more restrictive datatype, such as an integer.

For example, suppose the LSTPRICE field in the ITEMMAST legacy data file had three special values:

- UNK for unknown
- SAME for the same price as the previous order
- CHECK for check with the buyer before ordering

When SQL*Loader tries to load a record that contains either of these three values, the record will be rejected and placed in the bad file because the RECENT_PRICE field is not numeric. Here are some methods of dealing with this situation:

■ Correct the rejected records in the bad file and continue.

■ Iteratively, you can go through the cycle of load, correct, load some more, correct some more—until you're finished loading. Imagine that there were 92 bad records in a file of 10,000 records. During your first iteration, you would successfully load 9,908 records. The bad file would contain the 92 rejected records. Let's assume that you correct 68 of the rejected records. You can modify the control file so that it uses the bad file as input. There would now be 24 records that still haven't been loaded (see Figure 23.22).

FIGURE 23.22.

Using the bad file to iteratively load data.

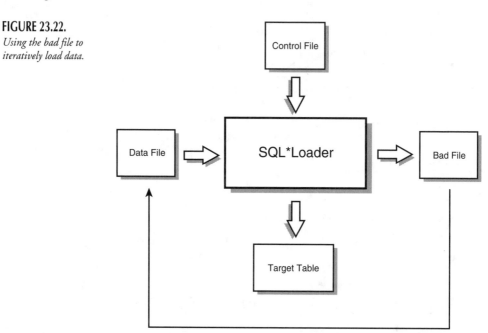

Records are corrected and bad file is used as new data file.

■ Use SQL built-in functions to translate the value. If you know that the LSTPRICE field could contain an actual price, the string N/A, or the string UNK, you could use the DECODE function in the SQL*Loader control file to translate the N/A and UNK to null values.

```
load data
infile itemmast.dat
into table ITEM_MASTER
(ITEM_NO POSITION(01:06) CHAR,
 DESCRIPTION POSITION(07:86) CHAR "INITCAP(:DESCRIPTION)",
```

```
VENDOR_ID POSITION(87:92) CHAR,
RECENT_PRICE POSITION(93:100) DECIMAL EXTERNAL
"DECODE(:RECENT_PRICE,'N/A',NULL,'UNK',NULL,
:RECENT_PRICE)",
CREATED_DATE POSITION(101:106) DATE 'MMDDYY',
CREATED_BY POSITION(107:112) CHAR,
DATE_MODIFIED POSITION(113:118) DATE 'MMDDYY',
MODIFIED_BY POSITION(119:124) CHAR)
```

■ Load the records into an intermediate table in which all fields are defined as VARCHAR2. Figure 23.23 illustrates the process of using SQL*Loader to load data to an intermediate table.

FIGURE 23.23.

Using an intermediate table in the loading process.

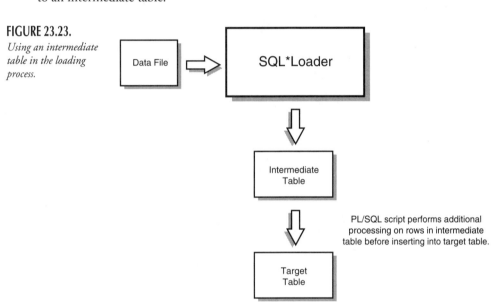

Dealing with Constraints

In the preceding example, we loaded the tables so that the foreign key constraint of the Item_Master table wasn't violated. In other words, the tables were loaded in proper order so that the SQL*Loader wouldn't reject any records due to constraint violations. Suppose we needed to reload the Vendor_Master table because we had forgotten to load a field. If we tried to reload the Vendor_Master table, the deletion of the vendor records would fail because the constraint would be violated.

Frankly, table constraints can often interfere with the task of loading many related tables. Generally, it's far easier to drop (or disable) table constraints until the more fundamental goals of data loading have been achieved. The suggestion to drop (or disable) constraints is based on a major assumption: that the tables to be loaded are not in use by anyone else. A software developer should be provided with a separate copy of the tables to work with during the data loading phase.

Summary

This chapter presented the following significant topics:

- The Import and Export programs use a binary file that has a filename extension of .DMP.

- Export can be used to save the structure of database objects and the contents of specified tables.

- Import loads designated tables from an export file into an Oracle account.

- SQL*Loader loads fixed and variable length records from a flat file into Oracle tables.

- The SQL*Loader process is directed by a control file, which specifies the structure of the flat file. The control file also defines any preprocessing of field data required before the data is loaded into an Oracle table.

24

Database Backup and Recovery

As a Personal Oracle developer, you need to understand how to properly back up your Personal Oracle database. Personal Oracle furnishes two tools for this purpose: Backup Manager and Recovery Manager. You can find both programs' icons in the Personal Oracle7 program group.

There is only one reason for backing up an Oracle database—to protect against the loss of data. An Oracle database is composed of several different files: at least one control file, at least two redo log files, and a default set of four datafiles. A datafile is associated with a tablespace, which I discuss in further detail in Chapter 25, "Managing Space." If even one of these files is lost due to accidental deletion or a disk drive failure, you won't be able to restart the Oracle database. For this reason, it's essential that you back up all of the Oracle database files.

A Consistent Backup

I highly recommend that you use only Backup Manager to safely back up your Personal Oracle database. You can use Microsoft Backup instead, but there's a risk involved. If you don't back up all of the database files, including any files that have been added with Database Expander or SQL*DBA, you won't capture a consistent backup of the database. If you ever needed to restore the database backup, you wouldn't be able to start it. Backup Manager can accurately determine the files that must be backed up for a consistent backup; Microsoft Backup has no knowledge of which files should be backed up—it's your responsibility to indicate which files should be backed up.

Backing Up a Database with Backup Manager

Backup Manager can perform a backup of a Personal Oracle database in one of the following modes:

- When the Personal Oracle database is not running
- When the Personal Oracle database is running
- When the Personal Oracle database is running with the Support Recovery option

I'll discuss each of these modes in more detail.

Using Backup Manager When the Oracle Database Is Shut Down

Backup Manager is one of the only Oracle Database Administration Tools that can be used when the Personal Oracle database isn't running. First, be sure that Oracle isn't running. Double-click the Backup Manager icon. Backup Manager displays a message informing you that it might not have complete information about all of the database files because the Personal Oracle database isn't running (see Figure 24.1). The first time that you run Backup Manager while the Oracle database isn't running, Backup Manager will use the default database files for its backup.

FIGURE 24.1.

Backup Manager message about incomplete database file information.

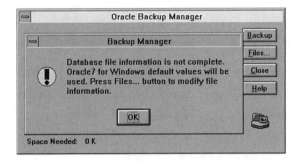

Click the OK button on the warning message. Backup Manager displays a screen showing which database files will be backed up. Backup Manager backs up the database either to the \backup directory within ORACLE_HOME (c:\orawin by default) or to a tape device, if installed (see Figure 24.2).

FIGURE 24.2.

Using Backup Manager when an Oracle instance isn't running.

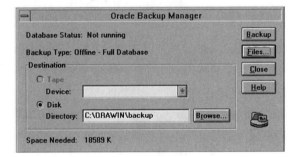

Using Backup Manager When the Oracle Database Is Running

If you invoke Backup Manager when the Personal Oracle database is running, Backup Manager displays a dialog box prompting you for the database password (see Figure 24.3). Enter `oracle` or the actual database password, and click OK.

FIGURE 24.3.

Connecting to Oracle with Backup Manager.

Backup Manager displays a screen with three backup options. A message on this screen indicates that the Oracle instance is running with NOARCHIVELOG—meaning that Archive Logging is not enabled. Archive Logging is the process by which Oracle makes a copy of a redo log file when it has filled to capacity with changed data blocks. Click the Backup button to initiate the full backup of the database (see Figure 24.4). When the backup has finished, Backup Manager displays a message (see Figure 24.5).

FIGURE 24.4.

Using Backup Manager when an Oracle instance is running without Archive Logging.

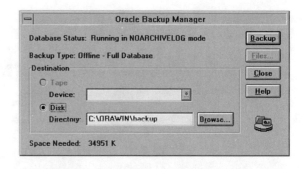

FIGURE 24.5.

Backup Manager displays successful completion message.

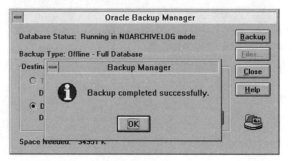

When Backup Manager has performed a full backup of a running Personal Oracle database, it obtains a complete and accurate list of all files that are part of the database. For instance, Figure 24.6 shows the list of database files, including c:\orawin\dbs\wdbfray.ora. This datafile belongs to the FRAYED_WIRES tablespace, which isn't part of the default Personal Oracle database.

FIGURE 24.6.

Backup Manager displays correct information about database files.

Enabling Database Support Recovery

By default, the Personal Oracle database is created with two redo log files. As you may recall, a redo log file contains data blocks that have changed as a result of committed transactions.

Oracle writes the changed blocks to the redo log files in round-robin fashion. It writes changed blocks to the first redo log file until the file is full, at which time it switches to the second redo log file and writes the changed data blocks to it. When the second redo log file is filled, Oracle switches back to the first redo log file. These archived redo log files are stored in c:\orawin\rdbms71\archive (see Figure 24.7).

FIGURE 24.7.

File Manager displaying archived redo log files.

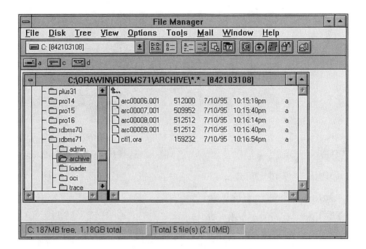

What, you might ask, does any of this have to do with backup and recovery? Quite a bit. Oracle provides a mechanism called *archive logging* (or Support Recovery for Personal Oracle) that makes a copy of a redo log file when it has filled. If you've enabled Support Recovery, you have the potential to recover transactions that have been committed since the last database backup. I use the word *potential* because you have to take some precautions to recover the committed transactions.

Here are some suggestions on using Support Recovery:

■ Perform a full database backup and save it to tape or other media.

■ To reduce the chances of failure, place the archived redo log files on a separate disk from the disk containing the database files; the likelihood of both disks crashing simultaneously is much lower that the likelihood of either disk crashing.

■ Periodically back up the archived redo log files to tape or other media.

To enable Support Recovery, invoke Database Manager and click Configure. The Configure Initialization Parameters window appears. To set up Support Recovery, click on the checkbox (see Figure 24.8). The next time the Personal Oracle database is started, Support Recovery will be enabled.

FIGURE 24.8.

Enabling Support Recovery with Database Manager.

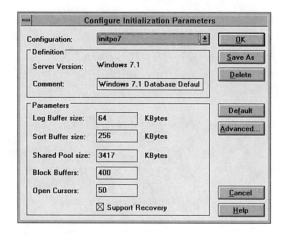

Backup Manager offers the following three options for backing up a running instance:

- Offline – Full Database
- Online – Selected Tablespace
- Online – Control File Only

Let's look at what each backup provides and how it's performed.

Backup Manager: Offline – Full Database

If you select the radio button labeled Offline – Full Database, Backup Manager shuts down the database, performs a backup of all database files to the specified destination, and restarts the database (see Figure 24.9). Click Backup to begin the full database backup. Backup Manager stores the backup files in c:\orawin\backup (see Figure 24.10). If the directory doesn't exist, Backup Manager creates it.

FIGURE 24.9.

Performing an offline backup with Backup Manager.

FIGURE 24.10.
File Manager displays the backup files.

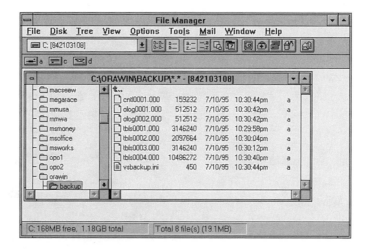

Backup Manager: Online – Selected Tablespace

Backup Manager enables you to back up a specific tablespace while the database is running (see Figure 24.11). Highlight the tablespace you want to back up and select the radio button labeled Online – Selected Tablespace. Click Backup to start the backup process.

FIGURE 24.11.
Performing an online backup of a tablespace.

Backup Manager: Online – Control File Only

If you want to back up a copy of the database control file, select the radio button labeled Online – Control File Only and then click Backup (see Figure 24.12).

FIGURE 24.12.
Performing an online backup of a control file.

Recovering from Media Failure with Recovery Manager

Invoke Recovery Manager by double-clicking its icon in the Personal Oracle7 program group. Recovery Manager prompts you for the database password; enter it and click OK (see Figure 24.13).

FIGURE 24.13.
Connecting to Personal Oracle with Recovery Manager.

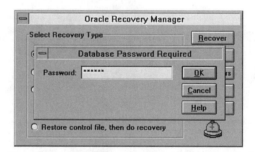

To simulate the loss of a database file, I'll delete c:\orawin\dbs\wdbuser.ora. This datafile belongs to the USER_DATA tablespace. When you try to start the database, Database Manager returns an error message indicating that it cannot find the datafile (see Figure 24.14).

FIGURE 24.14.

Database Manager detects a missing datafile.

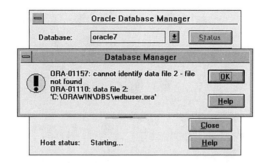

To recover the lost file, invoke Recovery Manager by double-clicking its icon in the Personal Oracle7 program group. Recovery Manager provides four options from which to choose; for this example, I'll use Automatic Recovery. Be sure that the Automatic Recovery radio button is selected and click Recover (see Figure 24.15).

FIGURE 24.15.

Recovery Manager.

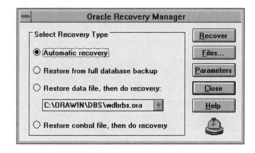

Recovery Manager displays a window in which you specify the source of the database backup. If a tape device is available, the option to recover from tape is enabled. By default, Recovery Manager uses c:\orawin\backup as the backup source (see Figure 24.16). Click OK to begin the recovery process.

FIGURE 24.16.

Recovery Manager performing automatic recovery.

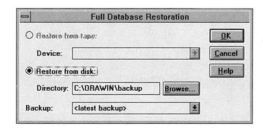

Recovery Manager restores the lost file from the backup files. Once all of the lost files have been restored, Recovery Manager automatically starts the database (see Figure 24.17).

FIGURE 24.17.
*Recovery Manager
restores and starts the
database.*

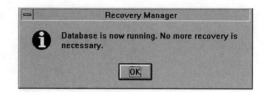

Backup Manager Versus Export

It's worth noting that in certain circumstances, a database export can be performed in less time than a database backup. This is true if the database is large but mostly empty (please refer to Chapter 25 for a detailed discussion about Oracle space management). In that case, Backup Manager spends its time copying large, sparse files whereas Export copies the database objects and their contents. It's difficult to quantify when performing an export is more efficient. If your database is large but mostly empty, you can experiment with both tools to see which is most appropriate. For the Oracle Workgroup Server or Enterprise Server, you can use Export to move data from a development database to a production database.

Summary

This chapter concentrated on the following Personal Oracle backup and recovery issues:

- Backup Manager is a Windows-based Database Administration Tool for making a backup copy of Personal Oracle database files.

- Backup Manager can back up a Personal Oracle database to tape or disk. By default, it backs up all files to a directory named \backup within the Oracle home directory.

- You can back up an Oracle database whether or not it is running. If it isn't running, Backup Manager might not have a complete list of the files that make up the database.

- Backup Manager can back up a database while it's running. In one mode, Backup Manager shuts down the database, performs the full backup, and restarts the database.

- As an option, you can enable Support Recovery for the Personal Oracle database by using the Configure option within Database Manager. Support Recovery makes a copy of a redo log file when it is filled to capacity with modified data blocks. The copy is referred to as an archived redo log file. These files are stored in c:\orawin\rdbms71\archive.

- By default, Support Recovery is disabled. If you enable it, you have the potential to recover all committed transactions.

25

Managing Space

In Chapter 7, "Creating and Modifying Tables," you learned the essential steps of creating tables. For the sake of clarity, there was no discussion of how Oracle uses physical storage for table and index data. This chapter focuses on that topic.

The installation procedures for Personal Oracle7 and the Oracle Workgroup Server were designed to fulfill the operational requirements for a broad range of Oracle users. That was a lofty goal, and, to a large extent, it was achieved. However, to attain better organization and efficiency, especially if you plan on upsizing your database, you'll want to follow the guidelines described in this chapter.

The Oracle Storage Hierarchy

The manner in which Oracle stores data can be imagined as a hierarchy (see Figure 25.1).

FIGURE 25.1.
Diagram of the Oracle storage hierarchy.

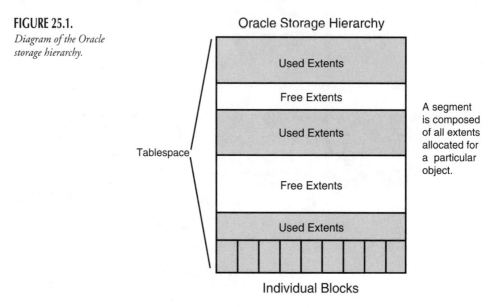

At the bottom of the hierarchy is the Oracle *block*, which forms the basis for storing all Oracle database objects. Two or more contiguous Oracle blocks are grouped into an entity called an *extent*. Multiple extents that have been allocated for a particular object—say, a table or index—are referenced as a *segment*. A *tablespace* is composed of one or more operating system files called *datafiles*. All the extents for a particular object must be stored in the same tablespace.

Oracle Blocks

The Oracle block is the basic storage building block of every Oracle database. Oracle developed the concept of an Oracle block to simplify the porting of the product to a variety of operating systems. An Oracle block is a multiple of the block size of the operating system (OS) file system in which Oracle resides. The default block size for most Oracle installations is 2048 bytes, which is also true for Personal Oracle7.

Extents

An extent is a group of contiguous blocks that are allocated to an Oracle database object such as a table or index. When a table is created, the blocks allocated to that table are referred to as the *initial* extent. As rows are added to the table, they are stored in the extent's blocks. When a user inserts a row into the table but there is no space left in the extent's blocks, Oracle allocates the *next* extent for the table—another set of contiguous Oracle blocks that may or may not be the same size as the *initial* extent.

Segments

A segment is the set of extents that have been allocated to a particular database object. If you inspect the DBA_SEGMENTS data dictionary view, you'll find a variety of segment types.

```
SQL> select distinct segment_type
  2  from dba_segments;

SEGMENT_TYPE
- - - - - - - - - - - - - - - -
CACHE
CLUSTER
INDEX
ROLLBACK
TABLE
```

Tablespaces

When you create a table or index, you have the option of specifying the tablespace in which it is created. A tablespace is a logical structure. Its purpose is to link the storage of Oracle tables, indexes, and other objects with the files of the operating system where Oracle is running. Every Personal Oracle7 tablespace is associated with one or more DOS files.

Personal Oracle7 manages the contents of these DOS files for table and index storage. Oracle refers to these files as *datafiles*. These datafiles are preallocated; as a developer or DBA, you are responsible for specifying the size of these files or allocating additional files to the Personal Oracle7 database. Without your direction, Oracle has no way of obtaining more storage space.

Predefined Tablespaces

When you install Personal Oracle7, a starter database is installed—unless you choose not to install it. The following tablespaces are contained in the starter database:

- SYSTEM
- ROLLBACK_DATA
- TEMPORARY_DATA
- USER_DATA

Let's examine the purpose of each of these tablespaces.

SYSTEM

Every Oracle database must have a SYSTEM tablespace. The primary constituent of the SYSTEM tablespace is the Oracle data dictionary. You should store application objects—tables and indexes—in a tablespace other than the SYSTEM tablespace for two reasons.

- Your Oracle database will be more organized if you store each application's database objects in a separate tablespace.
- The most critical objects in an Oracle database are the data dictionary tables. If application database tables and indexes are stored in the SYSTEM tablespace, they will consume space that might be needed by a data dictionary table. When you store application tables and indexes in a separate tablespace, the space consumed by these tables has no effect on the SYSTEM tablespace.

ROLLBACK_DATA

In Chapter 16, "Defining Transactions," I discussed the relationship between transactions and Oracle rollback segments. A rollback segment is a database object that stores a transaction's changes before they are committed. Rollback segments also support concurrency—user A can modify a row in a table while user B reads the same row. You can retrieve the default rollback segments created during Personal Oracle7 installation by selecting from the DBA_ROLLBACK_SEGS data dictionary view.

```
SQL> select segment_name, tablespace_name
  2  from dba_rollback_segs;

SEGMENT_NAME                         TABLESPACE_NAME
- - - - - - - - - - - - - - - - - -  - - - - - - - - - - - - - - - - - - -
SYSTEM                               SYSTEM
RB_TEMP                              SYSTEM
RB1                                  ROLLBACK_DATA
RB2                                  ROLLBACK_DATA
```

TEMPORARY_DATA

Occasionally, Oracle needs to create a temporary segment to process a SQL statement. For instance, if you use the UNION operator on two tables, Oracle creates a temporary segment to construct the query results. The TEMPORARY_DATA tablespace exists for the storage of these temporary segments.

USER_DATA

The USER_DATA tablespace is intended to store all user-created tables and indexes. When you create a new user with User Manager, any tables created by that user are stored in the USER_DATA tablespace by default.

Organizing Storage with Tablespaces

By creating an additional tablespace for each application or logical group of users, you maintain the organization of your database. This isn't mandatory, but it makes your life as an Oracle developer or DBA much easier. For instance, if you're building a database to support two different groups of users—the marketing team for Fuzzy Wuzzy and the engineering team for the RT100 Remote Echidna Detector—you'd probably want to create a tablespace for each group: FUZZY_WUZZY and RT100_RED. Then, the default tablespace for each user can be set to the appropriate tablespace. (Chapter 26, "Managing Users and Roles," explains how this is done.)

Using the Database Expander to Expand a Tablespace

The Database Expander is one of Oracle's Database Administration Tools. Its program icon can be found in the Personal Oracle7 program group. The Database Expander has two functions:

- ■ To determine the availability of free space in a tablespace
- ■ To add more space to existing tablespaces

Here are the steps for adding space to a tablespace with Database Expander. First, Database Expander will display a dialog box confirming that you want to connect to the Personal Oracle7 database (see Figure 25.2). Click the OK button.

Database Expander will display another dialog box in which you need to enter the database password—by default, oracle. Enter the password and click the OK button (see Figure 25.3).

The Oracle Database Expander screen has a drop-down list of tablespaces. Click the down arrow and select one of the tablespaces. Database Expander will query the database to determine the total amount of space in the tablespace and the used and free portions (see Figure 25.4).

FIGURE 25.2.
Select the oracle7 database.

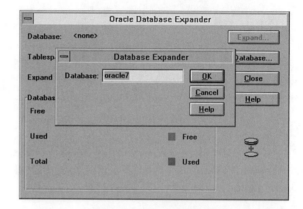

FIGURE 25.3.
Connecting to Oracle with Database Expander.

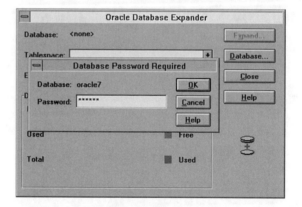

FIGURE 25.4.
Adding 5 MB to the USER_DATA tablespace.

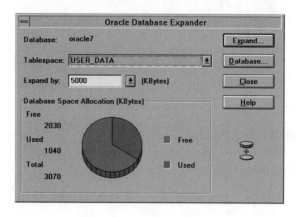

Database Expander gives you three sizes to choose from when adding a datafile to a tablespace.

- 1 MB
- 5 MB
- 10 MB

Click the down arrow of the Expand by drop-down list to select one of these values. Then, click the Expand button.

Database Expander displays a message to confirm that you really want to expand the tablespace by the specified amount (see Figure 25.5). Expanding a tablespace cannot be reversed. Click the OK button.

FIGURE 25.5.

Confirming the tablespace expansion.

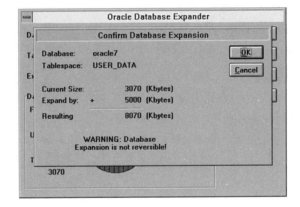

After the space has been added to the tablespace, Database Expander updates the storage information displayed for the tablespace (see Figure 25.6).

FIGURE 25.6.

Database Expander updates tablespace information.

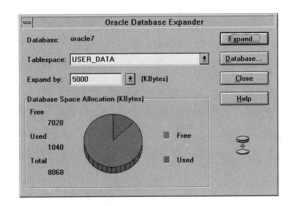

Unfortunately, one of the things that Database Expander can't do is create a new tablespace. However, you can use SQL*Plus to accomplish this.

Creating a Tablespace with SQL*Plus

You can create a new tablespace by issuing the CREATE TABLESPACE statement via SQL*Plus with the following syntax:

```
CREATE TABLESPACE tablespace-name
DATAFILE 'datafile-name'
SIZE datafile-size
DEFAULT STORAGE
(INITIAL initial-extent-size NEXT next-extent-size
MINEXTENTS minimum-number-of-extents
MAXEXTENTS maximum-number-of-extents
PCTINCREASE growth-rate)
```

where the variables are defined:

tablespace-name is the name of the tablespace to be created.

datafile-name is the directory and filename of the DOS file to be created for use by the tablespace.

datafile-size is the size to be used in creating *datafile-name*. (You can append a K or M to this number to indicate the size is expressed in kilobytes or megabytes, respectively.)

initial-extent-size is the size of the first extent allocated for the table, expressed in bytes.

next-extent-size is the size of the next extent to be allocated for the table, expressed in bytes.

minimum-number-of-extents is the minimum number of extents to be allocated for the table.

maximum-number-of-extents is the maximum number of extents to be allocated for the table.

growth-rate is the percentage increase in the extent size for each extent allocation.

As an example, let's create a new tablespace named FRAYED_WIRES that will become the default tablespace for all tables and indexes used in the repair store application.

```
SQL> create tablespace frayed_wires
  2  datafile 'c:\orawin\dbs\wdbfray.ora'
  3  size 10M
  4  default storage
  5  (initial 50k next 50k
  6   minextents 1 maxextents 121 pctincrease 15);

Tablespace created.
```

For instance, if a user creates a table in this tablespace without specifying any storage parameters, Oracle allocates an initial extent of 50 KB for the table.

Using SQL*Plus to Expand a Tablespace

As an alternative to executing Database Expander, you can use the ALTER TABLESPACE statement from SQL*Plus to expand a tablespace. You can also use the same statement to modify the default storage parameters with the following syntax:

```
ALTER TABLESPACE tablespace-name
[ADD DATAFILE 'datafile-name'
SIZE datafile-size]
DEFAULT STORAGE
(INITIAL initial-extent-size NEXT next-extent-size
MINEXTENTS minimum-number-of-extents
MAXEXTENTS maximum-number-of-extents
PCTINCREASE growth-rate)
```

where the variables are defined:

> *tablespace-name* is the name of the tablespace to be created.

> *datafile-name* is the directory and filename of the DOS file to be created for use by the tablespace.

> *datafile-size* is the size to be used in creating *datafile-name*. (You can append a K or M to this number to indicate the size is expressed in kilobytes or megabytes, respectively.)

> *initial-extent-size* is the size of the first extent allocated for the table, expressed in bytes.

> *next-extent-size* is the size of the next extent to be allocated for the table, expressed in bytes.

> *minimum-number-of-extents* is the minimum number of extents to be allocated for the table.

> *maximum-number-of-extents* is the maximum number of extents to be allocated for the table.

> *growth-rate* is the percentage increase in the extent size for each extent allocation.

As an example, you can add another datafile to the FRAYED_WIRES tablespace with the following statement:

```
SQL> alter tablespace frayed_wires
  2   add datafile 'c:\orawin\dbs\wdbfray2.ora'
  3   size 5m;

Tablespace altered.
```

You can change the size of the initial extent for the FRAYED_WIRES tablespace in this way:

```
SQL> alter tablespace frayed_wires
  2   default storage
  3   (initial 75k next 50k
  4    minextents 1 maxextents 121 pctincrease 15);

Tablespace altered.
```

> **TIP**
>
> When you create or alter a tablespace for a Personal Oracle7 database, it's a good idea to keep all of the datafiles in the same directory—C:\ORAWIN\DBS—and to use the same datafile-naming convention. Each datafile is named wdbTS.ora where TS is a five-character abbreviation for the tablespace. If you're adding another datafile to an existing tablespace, add a digit to the datafile name to indicate the number of datafiles in the tablespace.

Finding Free Space in a Tablespace

As you might expect, there are a couple of ways to determine how much free space exists in a tablespace.

- With Database Expander, you can look at free versus used space for a given tablespace.
- With SQL*Plus, you can examine detailed information about a tablespace's free space by querying the DBA_FREE_SPACE data dictionary table.

The major difference between these two methods is this—Database Expander provides *summary* information about free space, whereas the data dictionary view provides *detailed* information about each free extent in a tablespace.

I've demonstrated how Database Expander can be used to display a tablespace's used and free space. Let's see how the same thing can be accomplished through SQL*Plus.

Using SQL*Plus to Determine Tablespace Usage

Through SQL*Plus, you can query the DBA_FREE_SPACE data dictionary view to determine a tablespace's free space. You must connect to Oracle as a user who has been granted the DBA role. The columns of the view are

```
SQL> desc sys.dba_free_space
 Name                                Null?    Type
 ----------------------------------- -------- ----
 TABLESPACE_NAME                     NOT NULL VARCHAR2(30)
 FILE_ID                             NOT NULL NUMBER
 BLOCK_ID                            NOT NULL NUMBER
 BYTES                                        NUMBER
 BLOCKS                              NOT NULL NUMBER
```

The only columns in DBA_FREE_SPACE that we're really interested in are Tablespace_Name and Bytes. To see the same information that Database Expander displays for a tablespace, use the following query:

```
SQL> select sum(bytes)
  2  from dba_free_space
```

```
  3   where
  4   tablespace_name = 'USER_DATA';
```

```
SUM(BYTES)
----------
   2783232
```

Given the results of this query, you might think that you can create a table with an initial extent of 2,700,000 bytes because that is less than 2,783,232 bytes—the available space in USER_DATA. However, the previous query of DBA_FREE_SPACE summed the bytes in each free extent in a tablespace. An important piece of information is missing—the number of extents that the sum represents. You have no way of knowing whether the free space exists as a single large extent or a hundred small extents. This can be crucial information if you have a table that requires a large next extent. To determine the composition of the free space—how few or how many extents—you can modify the query to be

```
SQL> select bytes
  2   from dba_free_space
  3   where
  4   tablespace_name = 'USER_DATA';
```

```
     BYTES
----------
   2570240
      8192
    204800
```

As you can see from the results of this query, the free space in USER_DATA is actually composed of three extents. The largest extent is only 2,570,240—smaller than the initial extent that you specified when trying to create the table.

> **NOTE**
>
> When you drop a table or index, its space is returned to the list of free extents. One nice feature of Oracle's storage management is that Oracle will coalesce multiple free extents that adjoin one another, thereby creating one larger free extent.

Specifying Table Storage Parameters

In Chapter 7, I described the elementary steps needed to create a table. One aspect I didn't cover was an optional clause of the CREATE TABLE statement: the STORAGE clause. You use the STORAGE clause to provide detailed instructions to Oracle regarding the manner in which the table's storage should be allocated. Along with the STORAGE clause, you may also specify the tablespace in which the new table should reside. The syntax of a table's STORAGE clause is

```
CREATE TABLE table-name
(column-specification, ...
 column-specification, ...
```

```
  constraint-declaration, ...
  constraint-declaration)
  [PCTFREE pct-block-free]
  [PCTUSED pct-block-used]
  [TABLESPACE tablespace-name]
[STORAGE (
  INITIAL initial-extent-size
  [NEXT next-extent-size]
  [MINEXTENTS minimum-number-of-extents]
  [MAXEXTENTS maximum-number-of-extents]
  [PCTINCREASE growth-rate]
  )
```

where the variables are defined thus:

> `table-name`, `column-specification`, and `constraint-declaration` have the same definitions as shown in Chapter 7 and Chapter 13, "Defining Table and Column Contraints."
>
> `pct-block-free` is a number from 0 to 99 indicating the percentage of each block that should remain available if a row in the block needs additional storage.
>
> `pct-block-used` is a number from 1 to 99 indicating the percentage of each block that should be used for storage.
>
> `tablespace-name` is the name of the tablespace where the table data is stored.
>
> `initial-extent-size` is the size of the first extent allocated for the table, expressed in bytes.
>
> `next-extent-size` is the size of the next extent to be allocated for the table, expressed in bytes.
>
> `minimum-number-of-extents` is the minimum number of extents to be allocated for the table.
>
> `maximum-number-of-extents` is the maximum number of extents to be allocated for the table.
>
> `growth-rate` is the percentage increase in the extent size for each extent allocation.

Here's an example that illustrates how to specify a table's storage parameters. We'll create a table named XYZ and assign it to the FRAYED_WIRES tablespace.

```
SQL> create table XYZ
  2  (Dummy number)
  3  tablespace FRAYED_WIRES
  4  storage (initial 20k next 50k
  5  minextents 1 maxextents 121);

Table created.

SQL> select tablespace_name, pct_free, pct_used,
  2  initial_extent, next_extent, min_extents, max_extents
  3  from user_tables
```

```
4  where
5  table_name = 'XYZ';
```

TABLESPACE_NAME	PCT_FREE	PCT_USED	INITIAL_EXTENT	NEXT_EXTENT	MIN_EXT	MAX_EXT
FRAYED_WIRES	10	40	20480	51200	1	121

Changing the Storage Parameters of a Table

After a table has been created, you might want to change its storage parameters. For instance, you might want to change the value for PCTINCREASE. To do this, use the ALTER TABLE statement with the following syntax:

```
ALTER TABLE table-name
(column-specification, ...
column-specification, ...
constraint-declaration, ...
constraint-declaration)
[PCTFREE pct-block-free]
[PCTUSED pct-block-used]
[STORAGE (
[INITIAL initial-extent-size]
[NEXT next-extent-size]
[MINEXTENTS minimum-number-of-extents]
[MAXEXTENTS maximum-number-of-extents]
[PCTINCREASE growth-rate]
)]
```

where the variables are defined thus:

table-name, *column-specification*, and *constraint-declaration* have the same definitions as shown in Chapters 7 and 13.

pct-block-free is a number from 0 to 99 indicating the percentage of each block that should remain available if a row in the block needs additional storage.

pct-block-used is a number from 1 to 99 indicating the percentage of each block that should be used for storage.

initial-extent-size is the size of the first extent allocated for the table, expressed in bytes.

next-extent-size is the size of the next extent to be allocated for the table, expressed in bytes.

minimum-number-of-extents is the minimum number of extents to be allocated for the table.

maximum-number-of-extents is the maximum number of extents to be allocated for the table.

growth-rate is the percentage increase in the extent size for each extent allocation.

> **NOTE**
>
> After you've created a table, you can't change its tablespace. You can, however, create another table in a different tablespace and copy the contents of the original table, either with the CREATE TABLE ... AS statement or the SQL*Plus COPY command.

The following example illustrates how to use the ALTER TABLE statement. By default, the value of PCTINCREASE is 50 as the following query shows:

```
SQL> select segment_name, segment_type, tablespace_name, pct_increase
  2  from user_segments
  3  where
  4  segment_name = 'XYZ';
```

SEGMENT_NAME	SEGMENT_TYPE	TABLESPACE_NAME	PCT_INCREASE
XYZ	TABLE	USER_DATA	20

You can change the value of PCTINCREASE for additional extents allocated to table XYZ in the following manner.

```
SQL> alter table xyz
  2  storage (pctincrease 20);
```

```
Table altered.
```

By querying USER_SEGMENTS once more, you can see that PCTINCREASE has been changed.

```
SQL> select segment_name, segment_type, tablespace_name, pct_increase
  2  from user_segments
  3  where
  4  segment_name = 'XYZ';
```

SEGMENT_NAME	SEGMENT_TYPE	TABLESPACE_NAME	PCT_INCREASE
XYZ	TABLE	USER_DATA	20

Default Values for Table Storage

If not specified, a table's storage parameters are assigned the default values that exist for the tablespace in which it resides.

Here are the default values that have been defined for the tablespaces in Personal Oracle7's starter database:

```
SQL> select *
  2  from dba_tablespaces;
```

TABLESPACE_NAME	INITIAL_EXTENT	NEXT_EXTENT	MIN_EXT	MAX_EXT	PCT_INCREASE	STATUS
SYSTEM	4096	4096	1	121	10	ONLINE

```
USER_DATA             4096        4096        1     121        10 ONLINE
ROLLBACK_DATA       102400      102400        2     121        50 ONLINE
TEMPORARY_DATA        4096        4096        1     121        10 ONLINE
```

As you'll see in more detail in Chapter 26, a default tablespace may be—and should be—assigned to an Oracle user. The default tablespace is where table and index storage is allocated if a tablespace is not specified when the table or index is created.

Specifying PCTFREE and PCTUSED

The storage parameters, PCTFREE and PCTUSED, control how Oracle uses space for each data block in a table. Every data block contains a block header, which is approximately 100 bytes in size (see Figure 25.7). Another portion of each data block, called a *table directory*, contains information about the table whose rows are contained in the block. The *row directory* is an area of the block describing the rows that are stored in the block. Finally, there is an area of free space where rows can be added to the block.

FIGURE 25.7.

Diagram of a data block.

Diagram of an Oracle Block

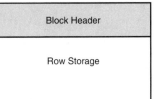

When a row is inserted in a block, Oracle looks at the free space remaining in the block. If the percentage of free space is less than that specified by the value for PCTFREE, Oracle doesn't insert the row in the block and instead uses a different block for storing the row. There is a purpose to setting aside a portion of each row as free space. When a row is first inserted in a block, many of its columns may be null. As information becomes available, the row is updated and a column that was previously null is set to some value. By keeping this updated row information in the same block as the originally inserted row, Oracle has to read only one data block to retrieve the entire row.

As rows are deleted from a block, the space that they consumed is returned to the block's free space. When the amount of free space drops to the value specified by PCTUSED or less, Oracle will once again begin inserting rows into the block. For Personal Oracle7, the default values for PCTFREE and PCTUSED are 10 and 40 percent, respectively.

PCTFREE and PCTUSED must always be less than or equal to 100. You can change these values for an existing table; however, the new values for PCTFREE or PCTUSED will only affect extents that are allocated after PCTFREE or PCTUSED have been changed.

TIP

For a table whose rows are rarely updated, it might be reasonable to set PCTFREE to just 2 or 3 percent. By reducing the value of PCTFREE, you increase the amount of data in each block and generally reduce the time needed to process a query.

Specifying Index Storage Parameters

An index consumes space in almost the same fashion as a table. An index may reside in the same tablespace as its table, or you may assign it to a different tablespace. The syntax for an index's STORAGE clause is similar to the STORAGE clause used for a table. Here is the syntax that is used with the CREATE INDEX statement to specify an index's storage parameters:

```
CREATE INDEX index-name
ON table-name (column-name, ..., column-name)
[PCTFREE pct-block-free]
[TABLESPACE tablespace-name]
[STORAGE (
[INITIAL initial-extent-size]
[NEXT next-extent-size]
[MINEXTENTS minimum-number-of-extents]
[MAXEXTENTS maximum-number-of-extents]
[PCTINCREASE growth-rate]
)]
```

where the variables are defined thus:

> *index-name* is the name of the index to create.
>
> *table-name* is the name of an existing table for which the *index-name* is to be created.
>
> *column-name* is a column in *table-name* to be used in creating the index.
>
> *pct-block-free* is a number from 0 to 99 indicating the percentage of each block that should remain available.
>
> *tablespace-name* is the name of the tablespace where the index data is stored.
>
> *initial-extent-size* is the size of the first extent allocated for the index, expressed in bytes.
>
> *next-extent-size* is the size of the next extent to be allocated for the index, expressed in bytes.

minimum-number-of-extents is the minimum number of extents to be allocated for the index.

maximum-number-of-extents is the maximum number of extents to be allocated for the index.

growth-rate is the percentage increase in the extent size for each extent allocation.

To illustrate, I'll create an index on the Shipment table.

```
SQL> create index Shipment_Perf_1
  2  on Shipment (Shipment_ID, Product_Code)
  3  tablespace User_Data
  4  storage (initial 30K next 50K pctincrease 15);

Index created.
```

Changing the Storage Parameters of an Index

You can use the ALTER INDEX statement to modify the storage parameters for an existing index.

```
ALTER INDEX index-name
[STORAGE (
[INITIAL initial-extent-size]
[NEXT next-extent-size]
[MINEXTENTS minimum-number-of-extents]
[MAXEXTENTS maximum-number-of-extents]
[PCTINCREASE growth-rate]
)]
```

where the variables are defined thus:

index-name is the name of the index to alter.

initial-extent-size is the size of the first extent allocated for the index, expressed in bytes.

next-extent-size is the size of the next extent to be allocated for the index, expressed in bytes.

minimum-number-of-extents is the minimum number of extents to be allocated for the index.

maximum-number-of-extents is the maximum number of extents to be allocated for the index.

growth-rate is the percentage increase in the extent size for each extent allocation.

Here is a demonstration of how to use the ALTER INDEX statement to change a storage parameter for an existing index. I'll modify the previously created index by increasing the value of PCTINCREASE.

```
SQL> alter index Shipment_Perf_1
  2  storage (pctincrease 25);

Index altered.
```

Summary

The following are some of the highlights of this chapter:

- The objects used for storing information in an Oracle database can be imagined as a hierarchy; starting from the lowest level, Oracle uses data blocks, extents, segments, and tablespaces as containers for data.

- An Oracle data block is generally 2048 bytes in size. It is always a multiple of the operating system block size. You can specify a different data block size when creating an Oracle database; you can't change the data block size after a database has been created.

- An extent is a contiguous set of two or more data blocks. Extents are allocated for tables, indexes, and other database objects.

- A segment is a collection of extents that have been allocated for a specific object.

- Use Database Expander to view the usage of space in a tablespace. You can also use Database Expander to add a datafile to a tablespace.

- Use SQL*Plus to create a new tablespace with the CREATE TABLESPACE statement. You can also add another datafile to an existing tablespace with the ALTER TABLESPACE statement.

- You can obtain detailed information about a tablespace's free space by querying the DBA_FREE_SPACE data dictionary view.

- Use the STORAGE clause of the CREATE TABLE statement to specify a table's storage parameters; use the ALTER TABLE statement to modify the storage parameters of an existing table.

- Use the STORAGE clause of the CREATE INDEX statement to specify an index's storage parameters; use the ALTER INDEX statement to modify the storage parameters of an existing index.

26

Managing Users and Roles

If you're interested in building only a Personal Oracle application, learning the ins and outs of Oracle user administration isn't essential. However, a basic assumption of this book is that many Personal Oracle developers intend to upsize their applications to Oracle servers, which support many simultaneous users. Even so, Personal Oracle has all the user administration functionality of its bigger brethren—the Oracle Workgroup Server and the Oracle Enterprise Server. Even though Personal Oracle cannot be used as a server—providing database services for users on other computers—you can define an account for each user you'd like to support. In other words, a single computer running Personal Oracle can be used by more than one person but, obviously, not at the same time.

Personal Oracle enables you to create a database *role*—a set of Oracle privileges that are designed to match a functional role in an organization. For example, a data entry clerk might need the capability to insert and update rows in a table but should not be enabled to delete any rows. To enforce this security scheme, you would create a database role named DATA_ENTRY, which would possess these object privileges. The data entry manager might have these same privileges but also require the capability to delete rows in the tables. A separate role named DATA_ENTRY_MANAGER would be created to implement this security policy. Once a database role is created, it can be granted to an individual user. Not only do database roles help ensure appropriate security, but they also simplify the administration of database users.

Working with User Manager

Personal Oracle is equipped with a Database Administration Tool—User Manager—that can create new users and assign database roles to them. Although User Manager is a Windows-based tool and is easy to use, you'll find it more convenient to use SQL*Plus to manage users, roles, and their privileges. It's easier to manage a significant number of Oracle users through the use of SQL*Plus scripts; managing a lot of users and roles in an interactive mode can be tedious. Later in this chapter, I'll describe the SQL commands used to create and modify database users, roles, and privileges.

To understand the concepts in this chapter, imagine that you are the database designer, application developer, database administrator, and all-around guru for St. Somewhere, a public hospital in the Northeast. To simplify the administration of the Oracle database, you've created a separate user named ST_SOMEWHERE that is the owner of the database tables used for storing patient information. In addition, you've created a set of public synonyms that point to ST_SOMEWHERE's tables, thereby hiding the ownership of the tables and simplifying the task of managing users and roles, as in:

```
SQL> create public synonym Patient
  2  for St_Somewhere.Patient;

Synonym created.
```

Let's begin by looking at how User Manager can create a new Oracle user.

Creating a New User with User Manager

Creating a new Oracle user with User Manager is very simple. Double-click the User Manager icon, which resides in the Personal Oracle7 program group. The first thing you'll need to do is connect to Oracle. User Manager displays a dialog box in which you enter your Oracle username and password (see Figure 26.1). If you're creating an Oracle user for the first time, enter SYSTEM for the username and MANAGER for the password. If you've already created an Oracle user with the DBA role, enter that username and password.

FIGURE 26.1.

Connecting to Oracle with User Manager.

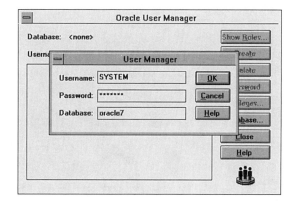

Next, click the Create button. User Manager displays a dialog box that contains two radio buttons, one for User and the other for Role. Select the User button and click OK (see Figure 26.2).

FIGURE 26.2.

Creating a new user.

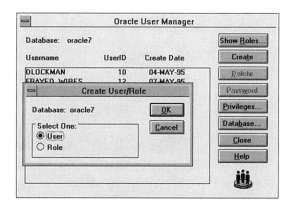

User Manager displays another screen on which you enter the user's name, the password, and a confirmation of the password. Enter the username as SDALI, and the password and its confirmation as LINCOLN (see Figure 26.3).

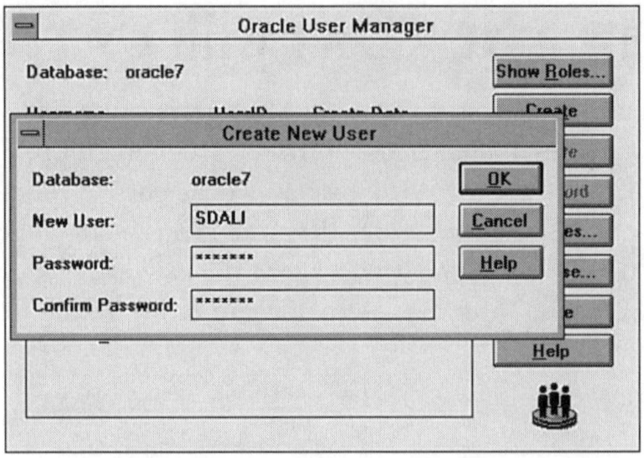

FIGURE 26.3.

*Entering the new
username, password,
and password
confirmation.*

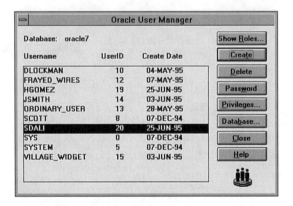

After you click the OK button, User Manager creates the new user and redisplays the User
Manager screen, showing the new user on the list of existing Oracle users (see Figure 26.4).

FIGURE 26.4.

*Displaying the new
user.*

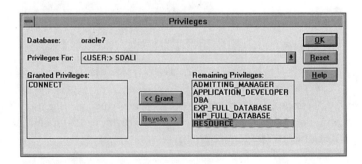

When you create a new user with User Manager, the new user automatically receives the
CONNECT privilege (it's actually a role, which I'll explain later in this chapter). To grant
another privilege to SDALI, click the Privileges button. User Manager displays a screen showing all privileges that can be granted to SDALI (see Figure 26.5).

FIGURE 26.5.

*Displaying available
privileges.*

Select the RESOURCE privilege by clicking it. Once the privilege has been selected, the Grant button is enabled. Click the Grant button to grant SDALI the privilege of creating tables, views, indexes, and other database objects. After you click the Grant button, you see the privilege on the left side of the screen (see Figure 26.6).

FIGURE 26.6.

Granting a privilege to the new user.

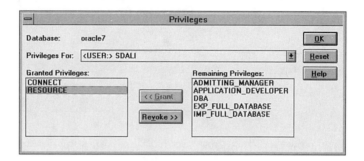

Defining a New Database Role with User Manager

Creating a new database role with User Manager is straightforward. Let's assume that User Manager is already connected to Personal Oracle. Click the Create button. User Manager displays a dialog box that contains two radio buttons, one for User and the other for Role. Select the Role button and click OK (see Figure 26.7).

FIGURE 26.7.

Creating a new role.

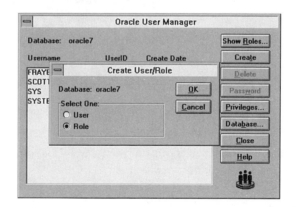

User Manager displays another screen on which you enter the name of the new database role and its password. It isn't mandatory for a database role to have a password. Enter PURCHASING_AGENT for the new role, and leave the password and its confirmation empty (see Figure 26.8).

FIGURE 26.8.

*Entering the name of
the new role.*

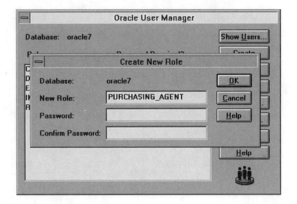

After you click the OK button, User Manager creates the new role and redisplays the User
Manager screen, showing the new role on the list of existing database roles (see Figure 26.9).

FIGURE 26.9.

*Displaying the new
role.*

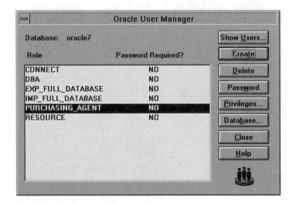

Creating a New User with SQL*Plus

Aside from using User Manager, you can also use SQL*Plus or SQL*DBA to create a new Oracle
user. The syntax for creating a new user is

```
CREATE USER user-name IDENTIFIED BY password
[DEFAULT TABLESPACE default-tablespace-name]
[TEMPORARY TABLESPACE temporary-tablespace-name]
[QUOTA disk-quota ON tablespace-name]
[PROFILE profile-name]
```

where the variables are defined:

> *user-name* is the name of the new user.
>
> *password* is the new user's password.
>
> *default-tablespace-name* is the default tablespace to be used for storing tables and
> indexes created by *user-name*.

temporary-tablespace-name is the tablespace that will be used for storing temporary tables created by Oracle on behalf of *user-name*.

disk-quota is an optional quota on the disk space used in *tablespace-name* (for example, 100K, 2M, or UNLIMITED).

profile-name is an optional resource profile to be assigned to *user-name*.

To illustrate the use of the CREATE USER statement, here is how you would create a new Oracle account for Mary Gordon, a software developer.

```
SQL> create user MGordon identified by Marys_password
  2  default tablespace User_Data
  3  temporary tablespace Temporary_Data
  4  quota unlimited on User_Data;

User created.
```

When you use the CREATE USER statement, you can set a user's default tablespace to a tablespace other than USER_DATA. Choosing your own default tablespace is one advantage of using SQL*Plus to create a new user instead of utilizing User Manager.

Restricting a User's Disk Space

In addition to providing a quota on the use of storage in a tablespace, Oracle also provides other system-level quotas that can be established for a user. These quotas include the following:

- CONNECT_TIME: The number of elapsed minutes since the user has connected to an Oracle database.
- IDLE_TIME: The number of elapsed minutes since the user last performed an action resulting in an Oracle call.
- LOGICAL_READS_PER_CALL: The number of Oracle blocks read from memory or disk to satisfy an Oracle call.

The mechanism that you use for specifying these quotas is the *profile*. For example, you might want to create a profile for a casual user that limits his or her connect time to two hours or less. In addition, you might also want to limit a casual user's idle time to 10 minutes. On top of that, you might also fear that a casual user—particularly, one who has access to an ad hoc query tool—could inadvertently construct queries that produce a Cartesian product of several tables. By setting a fairly high limit on LOGICAL_READS_PER_CALL, you can prevent the user's query from consuming memory and CPU time needed by other users. With the CREATE PROFILE statement, you would issue the following statement to define the profile:

```
SQL> create profile Casual_User
  2  limit
  3  connect_time 120
  4  idle_time 10
  5  logical_reads_per_call 10000;

Profile created.
```

Defining a New Database Role with SQL*Plus

You can create a new role by issuing the following SQL command with SQL*Plus:

```
CREATE ROLE role-name;
```

where `role-name` is the database role to be created.

As the DBA for the St. Somewhere patient information system, you create a new role—via SQL*Plus—for the hospital admitting manager.

```
SQL> create role Admitting_Manager;

Role created.
```

After you've created the new role via SQL*Plus, the role is part of the list of roles displayed by User Manager (see Figure 26.10).

FIGURE 26.10.

User Manager displays a new role.

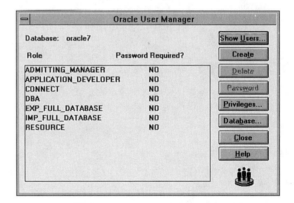

Predefined Database Roles

Personal Oracle is installed with the following three predefined roles:

- CONNECT has the capability to connect to the Personal Oracle database (via the system privilege CREATE SESSION).
- RESOURCE has the capability to create tables, indexes, views, and other Oracle objects.
- DBA consists of all system privileges needed to create, alter, or drop users and manage the database objects that they own.

These predefined roles can be seen on the User Manager screen.

> **NOTE**
>
> The historical reason for these predefined roles is that Oracle Version 6 had only three privileges: CONNECT, RESOURCE, and DBA. Because Oracle redefined these privileges as roles in Oracle7, SQL*Plus scripts developed for Oracle Version 6 can be processed in Oracle7.

Granting Privileges to a Database Role

A role isn't useful unless it has been granted at least one privilege. Oracle privileges are categorized in one of two ways.

- *System* privileges give an Oracle user the capability to execute statements such as CREATE TABLE, CREATE USER, or ALTER INDEX.
- *Object* privileges are associated with a particular operation (such as SELECT or UPDATE) on a specified database object (such as a table or index).

You can grant many different system privileges to a role or user—in fact, there are more than 80. One system privilege that almost every Oracle user needs is CREATE SESSION—the capability to establish an Oracle session.

The syntax for granting a system privilege to a role is

```
GRANT system-privilege TO role-name;
```

where `system-privilege` is a system privilege such as CREATE SESSION or ALTER USER, and `role-name` is the database role receiving the privilege.

For example, you can grant the following system privileges to an Application_Developer role.

```
SQL> grant Create Session, Create Table, Create Procedure, Create View
  2  to Application_Developer;

Grant succeeded.
```

Similarly, the syntax for granting an object privilege to a role is

```
GRANT object-privilege ON [owner.]object-name TO role-name;
```

in which the variables are defined:

> `object-privilege` is an object privilege such as SELECT or DELETE.
>
> `object-name` is the object of interest such as a table or view.
>
> `owner` is the Oracle account that owns `object-name`.
>
> `role-name` is the database role receiving the privilege.

For instance, to give the database role Admitting_Manager the capability to select, insert, update, and delete rows from the Patient table, you would use the following Oracle SQL statement:

```
SQL> grant select, insert, update, delete on Patient
  2  to Admitting_Manager;
```

Grant succeeded.

To grant a role to a user, use the following syntax:

```
GRANT role-name TO user-name;
```

where `role-name` is the database role to be granted, and `user-name` is the Oracle user receiving the granted role.

For instance, you grant the role of Admitting_Manager to Henrietta Gomez in the following way:

```
SQL> grant Admitting_Manager to HGomez;
```

Grant succeeded.

NOTE

Suppose an Oracle user has no object privileges for a table owned by another Oracle account. If the user tries to reference that table in a SQL statement, Oracle returns an error indicating that the table doesn't exist. The user can't determine whether the table exists or whether he simply doesn't have any privileges to access the table. However, if the user has at least one privilege—say the SELECT privilege—and submits a SQL statement for which he doesn't have the necessary privilege, Oracle returns an error message informing the user that he doesn't have the necessary privilege.

Granting a Database Role to a User with User Manager

At this point, you might be asking, "What good are database roles?" For a system environment in which there are many tables (more than seven), many users (more than seven), and distinct functional roles, the implementation and maintenance of a security scheme is a major task. If you, as an Oracle DBA, grant privileges directly to individual users, there's a good chance you'll make a mistake: you might forget to give some people a privilege they need to do their work, or you might give others a superfluous privilege. Also, if a change to the database application requires that the users' privileges also change, you have your work cut out for you with propagating the new privileges to each user.

By defining a database role for each functional role that exists in the organization that the database serves, you significantly reduce the task of managing users and their privileges. For instance, suppose there are ten database users—three belong to the marketing department and the other seven are in the engineering department. You would create two database roles, Marketer and Engineer, and grant the appropriate privileges to each role; the Marketer role needs access to one set of tables whereas the Engineer role requires access to a different set. You would then grant the appropriate role to each user. If the database changes—for instance, the addition of a table—you simply update the privileges of the role, not the user.

Revoking Privileges from a Role

Sometimes, it's necessary to revoke a privilege from a database role. For example, a change in the corporate security policy might reduce the functional roles that are enabled to update a particular category of information. To revoke a privilege from a database role, use the following syntax:

```
REVOKE privilege from role-name;
```

where *privilege* is the privilege to be revoked, and *role-name* is the name of the database role for which *privilege* is being revoked.

For example, to revoke the delete privilege for the Patient table from the Admitting_Manager role, you could issue the following statement in SQL*Plus:

```
SQL> revoke Delete on Patient
  2  from Admitting_Manager;
```

```
Revoke succeeded.
```

However, if you try to revoke a privilege that hasn't been granted, Oracle returns an error message.

```
SQL> revoke Alter on Patient
  2  from Admitting_Manager;
revoke Alter on Patient
      *
ERROR at line 1:
ORA-01927: cannot REVOKE privileges you did not grant
```

Revoking Roles from a User

You can also use the REVOKE statement to revoke a database role that had been granted to an Oracle user. Here's the syntax:

```
REVOKE role-name from user-name;
```

where *role-name* is the database role to be revoked, and *user-name* is the user for whom the role is revoked.

For instance, if Henrietta Gomez is reassigned to a different position at St. Somewhere, you should revoke the database role of Admitting_Manager from her Oracle account.

```
SQL> revoke Admitting_Manager from HGomez;

Revoke succeeded.
```

Special Users: SYS and SYSTEM

Every Oracle database, including Personal Oracle, has two special users: SYS and SYSTEM. The SYS account owns the Oracle data dictionary tables and associated database objects. The SYSTEM user owns tables that are used by Oracle application development tools such as Oracle Forms or Reports. You should not create any application objects such as tables or indexes while connected as SYS or SYSTEM.

TIP

After you've installed an Oracle database, the passwords for the SYS and SYSTEM accounts remain as CHANGE_ON_INSTALL and MANAGER, respectively. For two reasons, I urge you to change these passwords after the Oracle database installation is complete. First, these passwords are widely known. Second, both of these accounts have been granted the DBA role and anyone who can connect as SYS or SYSTEM has full access to the Oracle database.

Change the passwords by using the ALTER USER statement.

```
ALTER USER SYSTEM IDENTIFIED BY new_password;
```

Who's Connected to Personal Oracle: Using Session Manager

Session Manager is an Oracle Database Administration Tool for viewing the users who are connected to an Oracle database. It is really designed to be used for an Oracle instance that supports multiple concurrent users. Even so, you can see how Session Manager functions with Personal Oracle. Figure 26.11 shows the Session Manager screen, which indicates that there are two users: SCOTT, who is connected via SQL*Plus, and FRAYED_WIRES, who is connected via SQL*DBA. Also, the SYS user, who is running Session Manager, is shown as the active user; the other two users are inactive.

FIGURE 26.11.

Looking at connected users with Session Manager.

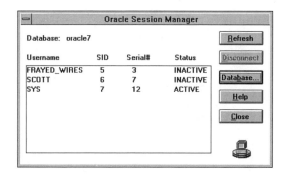

If you click FRAYED_WIRES, the user is highlighted and the Disconnect button is enabled (see Figure 26.12).

FIGURE 26.12.

Selecting a user to disconnect.

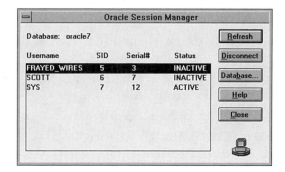

If you click the Disconnect button, Session Manager displays a dialog box to confirm that you really want to disconnect the selected Oracle user (see Figure 26.13).

FIGURE 26.13.

Confirming that a user should be disconnected.

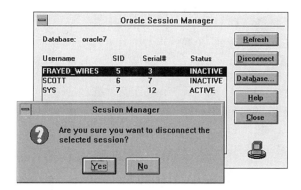

If you click the Yes button, Session Manager displays the list of connected users without Frayed_Wires (see Figure 26.14).

FIGURE 26.14.

Session Manager successfully disconnects user.

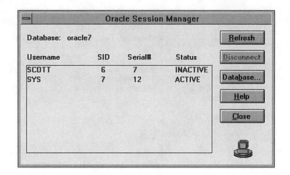

Summary

This chapter covered the following principles regarding the management of Oracle users, database roles, and privileges:

- You can use the Database Administration Tool User Manager to create a new Oracle user.
- You can use User Manager to grant a database role to an Oracle user. You can also revoke a role from a user with User Manager.
- Alternatively, the REVOKE statement revokes privileges from a role or a user.
- The CREATE USER statement creates a new Oracle user. You can specify the default tablespace to be used for storing a user's tables and indexes.
- You create a new role by issuing the CREATE ROLE statement in SQL*Plus.
- Once you've created a new role, you can grant privileges to that role with the GRANT statement.
- Remember to change the passwords for the SYS and SYSTEM Oracle accounts.
- A profile is a set of system-level quotas that can be levied on a user or role. These quotas include the amount of idle time and the number of logical reads performed for a single query.

27

From There to Here: Database Migration

The world is filled with legacy database applications that need to be rightsized for a number of reasons. Mainframe-based applications are often downsized to provide greater functionality, lower connectivity costs, and lower maintenance costs. Small applications that support a small number of users—or even a single user—are upsized so that more users can benefit from the features that they offer. It's important to recognize that there's no end in sight for this activity. When 90 percent of the legacy applications that were implemented in the early 1970s have been rightsized, we'll face the task of migrating legacy applications from the late 70s. Of course, unless your own money is funding the migration of an application, you must build a solid business case that justifies a return on the investment; the availability of a faster CPU or a glitzier user interface is not a sufficient reason for making the significant investment that is required to rightsize an information system.

The intent of this chapter is to focus on the issues that pertain to migrating an application to an Oracle database. There is no recipe for accomplishing this; every migration is somewhat unique. Instead of a recipe, I'll outline the major tasks that you'll face regardless of the application.

What Is Migration

When I use the term *migration*, I am referring to the process of converting a database application to the Oracle database. Obviously, I'm assuming that the application is using some other database for information storage. This database might fit one of the following categories:

- Desktop-based such as dBASE or Access
- Server-based such as Informix or Sybase
- A mainframe-based nonrelational database such as IMS
- A proprietary file management system

For greater efficiency, you'll want to have plenty of free disk space on your target platform and a network connection between the legacy platform and the target platform.

Migrating an application to an Oracle database consists of three main tasks.

- Migrating the database structures
- Transferring the data into the Oracle structures
- Reengineering the application logic

Let's look at each subtask in greater detail.

Migrating Database Structures

It's critical that you realize that there are really two tasks to be accomplished: migration and reengineering. Migration consists of creating an Oracle table that is equivalent in structure to each legacy table or file. I will refer to these Oracle tables as the *migrated* tables. The role of the migrated tables is that of an *intermediary*—these tables will store the legacy data before it is cleaned up and restructured.

Reengineering consists of the following tasks:

■ Developing a thorough understanding of the legacy data model: This is the starting point for migrating a database application. Without a complete grasp of the legacy data model, you will have difficulty identifying any opportunities for restructuring the data model.

■ Restructuring the legacy data model so that it is in Third Normal Form (3NF): It's quite common for a legacy field to be composed of several pieces of information or a legacy file containing a repeating field.

■ Changing the datatypes used by the migrated tables: For instance, a legacy file or table might use a character field for storing date or time information. The reengineered table would use a DATE column for storing the same information.

Figure 27.1 provides a graphical representation of the migration and reengineering tasks.

FIGURE 27.1.

The migration and reengineering tasks.

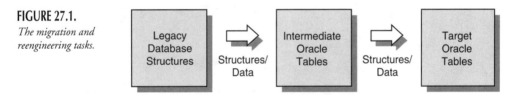

The legacy database structures that must be migrated depend on the type of database.

■ File management system: records and fields
■ Desktop database: records and fields
■ Relational database: tables, columns, primary/foreign keys, views, and indexes

I highly recommend the use of a data modeling tool for the migration of a legacy database. You'll want a tool that offers broad support for desktop and server databases, particularly if you're working with a variety of database products. The cost of purchasing a data modeling tool is quickly recouped in the improved productivity you will realize. You can think of a data modeling tool as "light" CASE. In other words, a data modeling tool provides valuable support during the analysis phase of a project without forcing you to make a commitment to an entire CASE life cycle.

As an example, I'll demonstrate how ERwin, produced by Logic Works, can support the task of database migration. There are many similar products available, but I've found ERwin to be particularly useful.

Migrating Database Structures Using ERwin ER Data Modeler

ERwin is a Windows-based tool and supports the IDEF1X data modeling standard. In IDEF1X, the logical view of a data model consists of entities, attributes, primary and foreign keys, relationships, and rolenames. The physical view consists of the tables, columns, and datatypes. ERwin enables you to define domains that can then be shared by several columns. You can switch between the logical and physical views of the data model. Based on both the logical and physical models, ERwin can generate a schema for the target database. The generated schema can be stored to a file or processed directly by the target database.

ERwin provides support for both reverse and forward engineering. *Reverse engineering* is the process of connecting to a database, capturing data dictionary information, and constructing a graphical representation of the data model. *Forward engineering* is the process of developing a data model and generating a schema for the target database.

To begin with, you identify the target server by selecting the appropriate radio button (see Figure 27.2). To illustrate this process, I'll select one of the sample Watcom databases that is supplied with PowerBuilder.

FIGURE 27.2.

Selecting the target server.

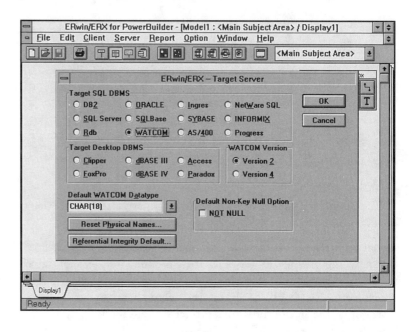

Once you've identified the target server, ERwin must connect to that database. Select Watcom Connection from the Server menu. ERwin displays a dialog box in which you specify the username, password, and database (see Figure 27.3).

FIGURE 27.3.

Connecting to the target server.

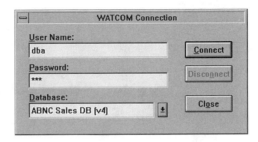

FIGURE 27.4.

Synchronizing ERwin with the WATCOM tables.

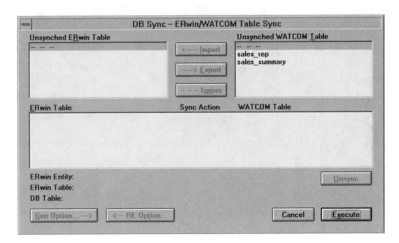

Once ERwin is connected to the target server, synchronization may begin. Synchronization is the term used by ERwin to refer to the process of aligning the ERwin data model with that of the target server. The default option is to synchronize ERwin with the target server. Select Synchronize ERwin with Watcom from the Server menu. On the right-hand side of the window that appears is a list of unsynched Watcom tables (see Figure 27.4).

Highlight both tables—sales_rep and sales_summary—and click Import. The tables appear in the listbox on the bottom of the window (see Figure 27.5). Click Execute to begin synchronization.

ERwin automatically generates a graphical layout of the target server's tables. Any relationships that exist in the target server are also captured. Figure 27.6 illustrates how the sales_rep and sales_summary tables are related by the sales rep ID.

FIGURE 27.5.

Selecting the tables to reverse engineer.

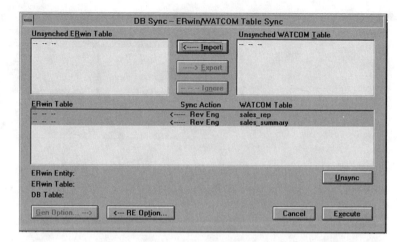

FIGURE 27.6.

Reverse engineering layout of data model.

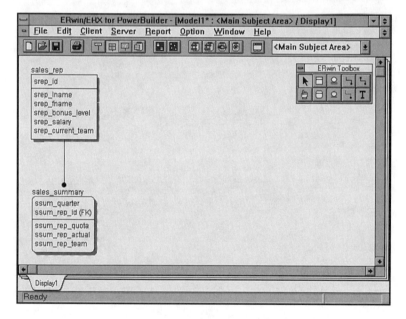

Now that you've captured the data model from the Watcom database, you may begin the process of generating the schema for Personal Oracle. Select Target Server from the Server menu. This time, select Oracle as the target server (see Figure 27.7).

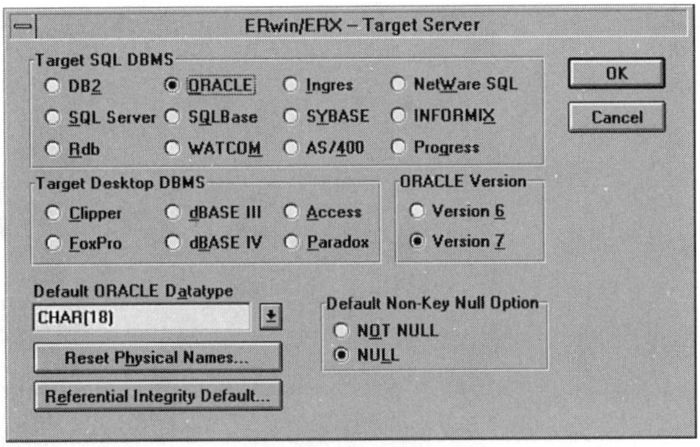

FIGURE 27.7.

Selecting Oracle as the target server.

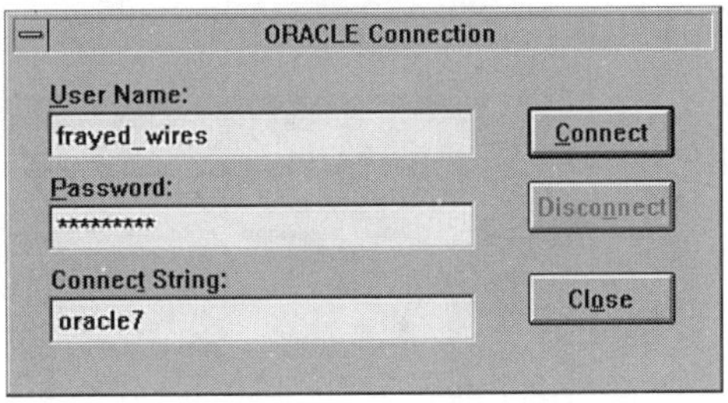

FIGURE 27.8.

Connecting to Personal Oracle.

To connect to Personal Oracle, select Oracle Connection from the Server menu. ERwin displays a dialog box in which you specify the username, password, and database (see Figure 27.8). For database, remember to specify oracle7.

To generate the schema, select Oracle Schema Generation from the Server menu. ERwin displays a window containing many options for schema generation. Using the default settings, click Execute to begin creating the sales_rep and sales_summary tables for Personal Oracle (see Figure 27.9).

ERwin displays each SQL statement submitted to Personal Oracle for execution. When it has finished generating the schema, ERwin displays the total number of statements that were processed successfully (see Figure 27.10).

FIGURE 27.9.

Selecting the schema generation options.

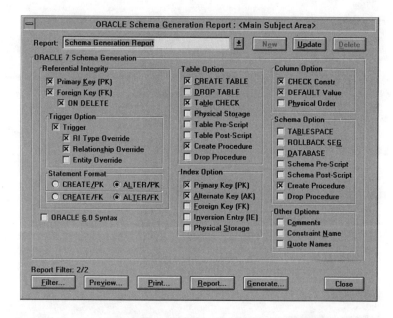

FIGURE 27.10.

Personal Oracle schema is successfully generated.

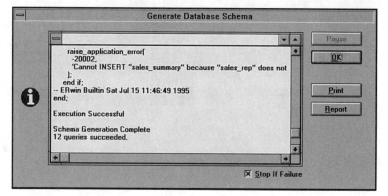

Moving the Data

Once you've migrated the database structures, the task of data conversion begins. This activity is typically a two-step process. First, you transfer the contents of the legacy to the migrated Oracle tables. Second, you copy the contents of the migrated Oracle tables to the target Oracle tables. You will rarely find that this is a straightforward process. Along the way, you'll discover erroneous data, illegal values, foreign keys whose values don't exist as primary key values—in short, it's a messy job, but somebody has to do it!

There are many ways to move the data. I'll present three different methods with the following tools:

- SQL*Loader
- PowerBuilder's Data Pipeline
- Excel

Using SQL*Loader

Chapter 23, "Saving and Loading Data," contains a discussion regarding SQL*Loader. As you recall, SQL*Loader is one of the Database Administration Tools that loads the contents of *flat* or ASCII files into an Oracle database. To use SQL*Loader for data migration, here is a procedure you can follow.

1. Unload the data from the legacy database into one or more flat files using whatever legacy tools are at your disposal. Remember that the flat files might require a considerable amount of disk storage.

2. Transfer the flat files to a location that is accessible to SQL*Loader. One option is to store the files on a network file server.

3. Using SQL*Loader, load the contents of each file into the Personal Oracle database.

Using the Data Pipeline in PowerBuilder 4.0

The data pipeline tool, which was introduced in Version 4.0 of PowerBuilder, is flexible and intuitive. Because the data pipeline is a PowerBuilder system object, it has its own attributes, events, and functions; in other words, you can control the creation and execution of a data pipeline from a PowerBuilder application.

To create a data pipeline, click the Data Pipeline icon; it looks like two aqua cylinders connected by a pipe. A window appears from which you can select an existing data pipeline (see Figure 27.11). Instead, click New.

Using its existing database profiles, PowerBuilder displays two lists: a list of source databases and a list of destination databases. Because you're interested in transferring data from the Watcom database to Personal Oracle, select ABNC Sales DB (v4) as the Source Connection and PO7 as the Destination Connection, and click OK (see Figure 27.12).

Another window appears with a list of the tables that exist in the Source Connection. Highlight the sales_rep table and click Open (see Figure 27.13).

FIGURE 27.11.
PowerBuilder: Creating a new data pipeline.

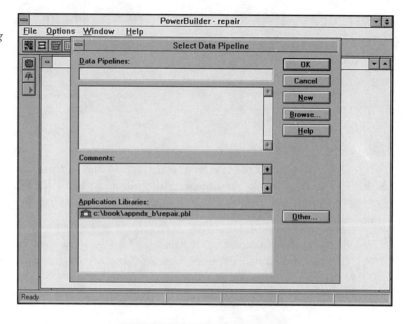

FIGURE 27.12.
Choosing the source and destination database profiles.

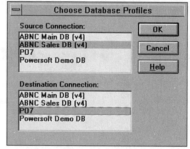

FIGURE 27.13.
Selecting a table for the data pipeline.

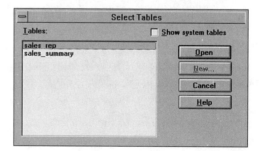

PowerBuilder displays a box containing the columns belonging to the sales_rep table (see Figure 27.14). By default, none of the columns are selected for the data pipeline. Click each column to select it; the column name appears at the top of the window in the Selection List (see Figure 27.15).

FIGURE 27.14.

The table structure is displayed.

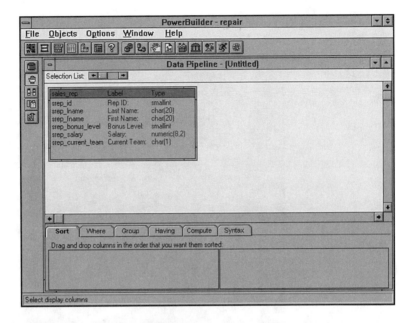

FIGURE 27.15.

Choosing the columns to be included.

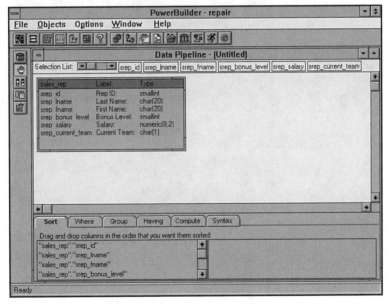

Select Design from the File menu. A window appears containing the data pipeline description along with execution parameters (see Figure 27.16). For example, the Commit field contains the value 100, signifying that a SQL Commit will be performed for every 100 rows that are inserted. To execute the data pipeline, select Execute from the Options menu. When the data pipeline execution has finished, PowerBuilder displays the execution statistics at the bottom of the window (see Figure 27.17).

FIGURE 27.16.

The data pipeline options are displayed.

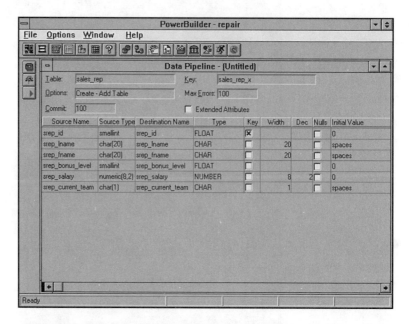

FIGURE 27.17.

The pipeline transfer is finished.

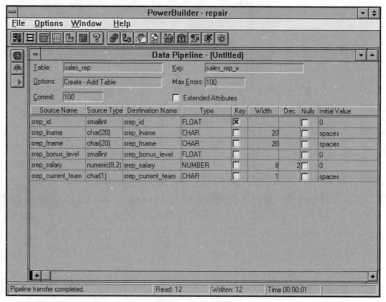

Using Excel as an Intermediate Migration Step

If you are migrating from a desktop database such as FoxPro or Paradox to Personal Oracle, you might want to use Excel as an intermediate database. This approach is worth considering if the following conditions apply:

■ The ODBC driver for the desktop database is available.

■ The desktop database isn't too large.

You can use Microsoft Query to define a query of an ODBC data source. To do this, refer to the directions in the Microsoft Help that accompanies the product.

Transforming the Application Logic

There is no silver bullet that you can buy or build that will automatically and flawlessly translate the legacy application into a client/server application. True, some specialized tools address a specific category of legacy environments, but they can be very expensive; in addition, these tools might impose a methodology that doesn't match the needs of your development environment.

If you merely translate the legacy application logic to the target application development environment, you will have missed an important opportunity to reengineer the application. To provide a simple example, consider a legacy information system that can produce 90 different management reports. Instead of blindly converting each of these reports in the new development environment, spend some time to investigate how many of these reports are actually read. The number could be much lower than you expect. In addition, some of the reports that are used might need to be reengineered to be more useful for the system's users.

Obviously, the first step in migrating the legacy application logic is to become thoroughly familiar with it. Identify the business rules of the legacy application and, where appropriate, use PL/SQL to implement these rules in the form of database triggers and stored programs.

Migrating from Another Oracle Database to Personal Oracle

Migrating from another Oracle database—whether it's from the Oracle Enterprise Server or Oracle Workgroup Server—is a fairly straightforward process. Use the Export tool to extract the database objects that you want to migrate, and use the Import tool to load those database objects into the Personal Oracle database. Be aware that because Personal Oracle doesn't support distributed database operations (except for the Enterprise Edition), you won't be able to use objects such as database links or snapshots in Personal Oracle.

Application Development Environments: Making an Appropriate Choice

I'm not suggesting that only the tools described in this book are worthy of consideration; there are other excellent products that should be evaluated. However, the viability of a development tool—the quality of each new release, its compatibility with new releases of operating systems and databases, and the existence of add-on products from third-party vendors—depends greatly on its acceptance by the market.

You should consider the following factors in choosing an application development environment:

- **Support for other server and desktop databases**: If you need to support other databases in addition to Oracle, you should probably consider using PowerBuilder, SQLWindows, Oracle Developer/2000, Oracle Power Objects, or Visual Basic. This list is by no means exhaustive. Oracle Developer/2000 is able to access non-Oracle data sources via ODBC. An optional component, Oracle Client Adapter, also works with Developer/2000 to access non-Oracle database servers. Oracle Power Objects supports access to DB2, SQL Server, Sybase, and ODBC data sources.

- **PL/SQL support**: Not surprisingly, the best support for PL/SQL is offered by the components of Oracle Developer/2000. Oracle Forms and Reports both have built-in PL/SQL engines (however, the current release of Developer/2000 components doesn't use the same version of PL/SQL that is used in the Oracle7 Server—PL/SQL Version 2.1). This means that you use the same scripting language for both the client and server. The runners-up for this category are PowerBuilder and SQLWindows. Although neither tool has a built-in PL/SQL engine, they are able to invoke Oracle stored procedures.

- **Object-oriented programming**: Of all of the products mentioned in this book, SQLWindows offers the most comprehensive object-oriented environment. PowerBuilder provides good support for creating classes, user-defined events, and inheritance. Oracle Power Objects provides object-oriented features similar to those of PowerBuilder. Developer/2000 also offers some object-oriented capabilities. However, if you compare the scripting languages of SQLWindows, PowerBuilder, and Developer/2000—SAL (SQLWindows Application Language), PowerScript, and PL/SQL, respectively—PL/SQL is quite limited in its capability to handle more than primitive datatypes. Nevertheless, Developer/2000 has many other features that you should consider when you evaluate application development environments.

- **Support for multiple platforms**: Oracle's Developer/2000 is the only development environment that currently offers production versions for the Macintosh and Motif environments. In July 1995, Oracle released a Macintosh version of Oracle Power Objects. Powersoft is also planning to release a Macintosh and Motif version of PowerBuilder in the near future.

■ **Availability of third-party add-on products**: The clear winner in this category is Visual Basic. There are a tremendous number of reasonably priced add-on products for Visual Basic. You can find trial versions of many products on the Internet. There are also a substantial number of add-on products for PowerBuilder, mostly in the form of class libraries. PowerBuilder may also use Visual Basic level 1 VBXs.

Summary

The focus of this chapter was database migration. The following pertinent ideas were presented:

■ Database migration consists of three principal subtasks: migrating the database structures, moving the data, and transforming the application logic.

■ The use of a data modeling tool, such as Logic Works's ERwin, supports the task of migrating the legacy data model to an Oracle database.

■ There are several methods you can use for moving the legacy data into an Oracle database. SQL*Loader can load legacy data from flat files into Oracle tables. PowerBuilder provides a data pipeline tool that copies data from a source database to a destination database.

28

Upsizing Considerations

A major premise of this book is that application developers will use Personal Oracle as a tool for prototyping Oracle applications. The purpose of this chapter is to discuss the things you need to consider in upsizing your Personal Oracle prototype to a client/server architecture. For an Oracle database server, you can choose between the Oracle Workgroup Server and the Oracle7 Enterprise Server. I'll present the distinguishing features in both products.

The World of Client/Server Applications

Ten years ago, most database applications were *terminal-based*—a database resided on a single computer to which some number of CRTs were attached. Sometimes, a terminal controller served as an intermediary between the central computer and a large number of CRTs. In either case, the computer was responsible for almost everything—painting each user's screen, navigating each user through a screen, validating data entry, and updating the database.

Recently, many applications have been transitioning to an entirely different architecture: client/server. The client/server architecture consists of three principal elements (see Figure 28.1).

- The client is a PC, Macintosh, UNIX workstation, or CRT. The client is generally responsible for controlling the user interface and validating entered data at some level. If the client is a CRT, the user interface control and data validation are performed by a terminal server, occasionally termed an *application server*.
- The server is a single or multiprocessor computer where the relational database resides.
- The network is a combination of local area network (LAN) and wide area network (WAN) that enables the client machines to communicate with the server. The network traffic is primarily composed of client requests to the server and data returned from the server to the clients to fulfill those requests.

FIGURE 28.1.

Diagram of a typical client/server architecture.

Client/Server Architecture

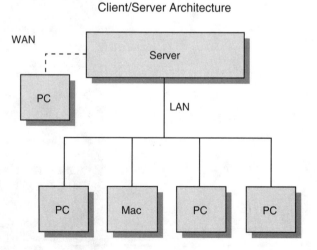

The transition to the client/server architecture has been driven by several factors.

- Scalability: When an information system is first implemented, the number of supported users may be quite small. As word spreads about the system's capabilities, the number of users grows. For the system to maintain the same level of performance, additional hardware is often added to the server. The client/server architecture supports this expansion rather well. You can add additional disk drives to the server to provide more storage space for the database. You can augment the server with additional CPUs to accommodate more transactions per second. You can add more memory to increase the size of the database cache and thereby decrease the number of I/O requests needed to accomplish the same amount of work.

- Data access: The days when a data processing center reigned over data have passed. Users demand the capability to extract portions of their data for use in spreadsheets, reports, and graphs. The individual users decide what tools they want to use. Client/server applications help satisfy this need by providing client tools that can exchange data with other PC-based software via mechanisms such as DDE, DLL, and OLE.

- Ease of use: Today, both casual and sophisticated users expect a graphical user interface (GUI) in their applications. They are accustomed to graphical elements such as buttons, scrollbars, resizable windows, and the integration of text with graphics. With a beefy PC, Macintosh, or UNIX workstation as a client machine, it's practical to supply the user with a quality GUI.

- Interoperability: Today, it is quite rare for a single vendor to supply all the hardware and software components for an information system. Instead, most information systems are constructed with a mix of vendors' products that support open standards such as SQL, TCP/IP, and Ethernet. The attribute of a client/server architecture that makes this feasible is the *decoupling* of the three main elements: client, server, and network. For instance, the choice of server platform—Solaris, HP-UX, or AIX—has little impact on the functionality of a client application.

- Affordability: Due to the realities of interoperability, competition in the hardware and software marketplace is much greater today than it was fifteen years ago. Today, it is unusual for any vendor—whether hardware or software—to have a lock on a particular solution.

- Integrity and security: Because a client/server architecture permits the use of third-party software tools, it's essential that the database server incorporate data integrity and security controls.

The client machine in a client/server architecture doesn't have to be either a PC or a Macintosh. The client could just as easily be a CRT managed by an application server (see Figure 28.2). As lovers of the latest technology, we sometimes forget that an information system exists to satisfy a business or organizational requirement. It might make perfect business sense to supply 200 data entry clerks with CRTs rather than PCs.

FIGURE 28.2.

*Using an application
server in a client/server
architecture.*

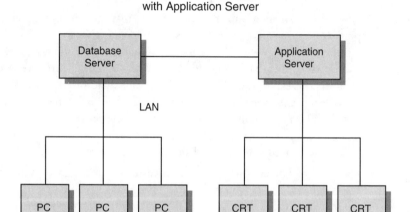

Client/Server Architecture
with Application Server

Middleware

Middleware is the software layer that enables a client application to communicate with a data-base server. For an Oracle database, there are two choices for middleware: SQL*Net Version 1 or SQL*Net Version 2.

SQL*Net Version 1

SQL*Net V1 is a software component that enables a client machine to establish a remote con-nection with a server machine running an Oracle database. SQL*Net V1 uses a listener process called *orasrv* to wait for connection requests. When a connection request is validated, orasrv creates a process on the server that is dedicated to routing the remote Oracle user's SQL re-quests to the Oracle server. SQL*Net V1 has a different version for each popular communica-tion protocol such as TCP/IP, Named Pipes, IPX/SPX, and DECNet.

SQL*Net Version 2

SQL*Net V2 serves the same purpose as SQL*Net V1—to facilitate remote connections to an Oracle database. However, SQL*Net V2 provides some additional capabilities, which include the following:

■ Capability to work with the MultiThreaded Server: Without the MultiThreaded Server (MTS), each remote connection requires its own server process on the server; if there are ten remote connections, ten server processes are needed to service those connections. For improved scalability, MTS enables multiple remote connections to share a single server process. SQL*Net V1 doesn't support the use of MTS; SQL*Net V2 does.

■ More flexible configuration of remote databases: SQL*Net V2 uses connect descriptors and service names to identify Oracle databases.

■ Support for multiple communication protocols via MultiProtocol Interchange: For a variety of reasons, one Oracle server in an organization might be using TCP/IP to support its users whereas another Oracle server in the same organization might be running DECNet. The MultiProtocol Interchange handles the conversion from one protocol to another between the Oracle servers. Only SQL*Net V2 supports the use of the MultiProtocol Interchange.

TIP

If your application is serving a small number of users who all use the same communications protocol, SQL*Net V1 probably meets your needs. However, if you're going to support many users who use different communications protocols, you need to implement SQL*Net V2.

Moving to the Oracle Workgroup Server

The Oracle Workgroup Server is a repackaging of the Oracle7 Server. It is intended for sites that won't be needing support for distributed database operations or parallel query capability. Accordingly, it doesn't include the distributed or parallel options. The Oracle Workgroup Server includes the same Windows-based Database Administration Tools that are used with Personal Oracle. Presently, the Oracle Workgroup Server is available on the following platforms:

■ NetWare Version 3.1 or 4.1

■ Microsoft Windows NT Version 3.1 or higher

■ UnixWare 2.0

■ SCO UNIX 3.0

■ Solaris x86 2.4

■ OS/2 2.1

Choosing one of these operating systems involves considerations that have little to do with Oracle. One factor you should consider is whether the operating system is capable of using multiple CPUs. As an installation option, the Workgroup Server will install a default database that is configured to meet the processing requirements of most small workgroups. Of course, you can change the initialization parameters or restructure the default database to meet your specific needs. Once you've developed a database with Personal Oracle, you can upsize to the Oracle Workgroup Server using the following strategy:

1. Perform a full export of your Personal Oracle database.
2. Using Import, connect to the Oracle Workgroup Server. Import the Oracle account that owns the application tables.
3. Using SQL*Plus, connect to the Oracle Workgroup Server. Run any SQL*Plus scripts that you've created for Personal Oracle7 for building stored procedures, functions, or packages. Run any SQL*Plus scripts that build database triggers.

Establishing a Client Connection to the Oracle Workgroup Server

To establish a connection to the Oracle Workgroup Server—or any Oracle7 Server—you need to specify three parameters:

- The Oracle user
- The password for the Oracle user
- The name of the database identified by a connect string or alias

Figure 28.3 demonstrates how SQL*Plus is used to establish a remote connection to an Oracle Workgroup Server (see Chapter 6, "Accessing Personal Oracle7 with SQL*Plus," for more information on using SQL*Plus).

FIGURE 28.3.

*Establishing a connection to the Oracle Workgroup Server using SQL*Plus.*

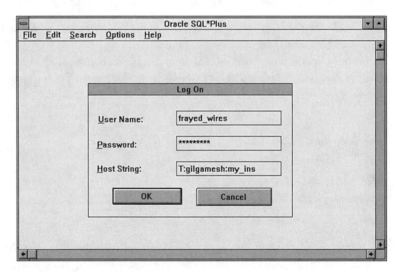

A *connect string* is used to identify the database to which a connection should be made. A connect string consists of the following:

- A protocol identifier such as T for TCP/IP or D for DECNet
- A host name or protocol address such as gilgamesh (as defined in the host's file) or 128.193.192.199
- An instance name

An example of a connect string is

```
T:137.138.139.140:my_inst
```

If you're using SQL*Net V1, you can define an alias for a database by creating a line in the file c:/windows/oracle.ini with the following format:

```
SQLNET DBNAME alias=connect-string
```

where *alias* is the alias that you wish to use for the database, and *connect-string* is a SQL*Net V1 connect string that identifies the database.

Moving to the Oracle7 Server for UNIX

The Oracle7 Server isn't restricted to UNIX. The ports of the Oracle7 Server include DEC VMS, HP MPE, and IBM MVS. However, the Oracle7 Server for UNIX—regardless of version—has the largest number of installed sites. Accordingly, it's worth discussing some of the issues that you should be aware of when migrating from Personal Oracle to the Oracle7 Server for UNIX. Of course, for full details, refer to the *Oracle Installation and Configuration Guide* that accompanies the Oracle software for your system.

Shell Environment Variables

To log in to a UNIX account on the server and access an Oracle database, you'll need to define at least four environment variables in your UNIX account .cshrc file:

- `ORACLE_BASE`: The base directory for all versions of the Oracle products.

- `ORACLE_HOME`: The home directory for the version of Oracle software that you're using. `ORACLE_HOME` is always found beneath `ORACLE_BASE` on the directory tree.

- `ORACLE_TERM`: The type of terminal (or terminal emulation) you're using with Oracle tools such as SQL*Plus.

- `ORACLE_SID`: The Oracle System Identifier (SID) or instance name. Be sure that the instance name has the correct case; UNIX, whether you like it or not, is case-sensitive.

Here's an example of how these environment variables might be set for an actual installation:

```
ORACLE_BASE=/u2/oracle
ORACLE_HOME=/u2/oracle/product/7.1.4
ORACLE_TERM=vt220
ORACLE_SID=prod
```

In addition, you need to add `$ORACLE_HOME/bin` to the `set path` statement in .cshrc if you want to use any Oracle programs, such as SQL*Plus, to access the Oracle database.

The *oracle* User and *dba* Group

To properly install Oracle, have the UNIX system administrator create a new user named `oracle` and a new group named `dba`. The `oracle` UNIX account owns the Oracle software and database files. The `dba` group is used to specify those UNIX users who have the right to start up and shut down an Oracle instance.

Implementing SQL*Net V1

Here are some guidelines on implementing SQL*Net V1 for the Oracle7 Server for UNIX. I'll assume that you'll be using TCP/IP as the communications protocol.

You'll need to add a line to the services file, which can usually be found in the /etc directory.

```
orasrv    1525/tcp
```

The SQL*Net V1 listener process is orasrv. Its role is to listen on the port specified in the services file for a request to establish an Oracle connection. When it receives this request, orasrv creates a dedicated server process. The line shown above reserves port 1525 for use by orasrv.

Oracle supplies a utility named *tcpctl*, which controls the orasrv process. From the `oracle` UNIX account, start the orasrv process by issuing the `tcpctl start` command.

```
myhost:<4> tcpctl start
tcpctl: log file is /u4/oracle/product/7.1.4/tcp/log/orasrv.log
tcpctl: SID mapping file is /var/opt/oracle/oratab
tcpctl: server will be run under oracle
tcpctl: logging mode is on

orasrv: Release 1.2.7.8.1 - Production on Tue Jun 20 08:22:18 1995

Copyright (c) Oracle Corporation 1979, 1994.  All rights reserved.


Starting server on port 1525.
tcpctl: server has been started
```

You can also determine the status of the orasrv process by issuing the command `tcpctl status`.

```
myhost<2> tcpctl status
tcputl: Status summary follows
Server is running:
  Started            : 19-JUN-95 11:13:40
  Last connection    : 19-JUN-95 11:34:33
  Total connections  : 10
  Total rejections   : 0
  Active subprocesses : 0
  ORACLE SIDs        : prod
  Default SID        : (null)
Logging mode is ENABLED.
DBA logins are DISABLED.
OPS$ logins are ENABLED.
```

```
OPS$ROOT logins are DISABLED.
Orasrv is detached from the terminal.
Break mode = OUT OF BAND.
Debug level = 1
No timeout (on orasrv handshaking).
Length of listen queue = 10
Orasrv logfile = /u4/oracle/product/7.1.4/tcp/log/orasrv.log
Orasrv mapfile = /var/opt/oracle/oratab
```

Starting a Database During System Startup

Oracle uses a file named /etc/oratab for specifying which Oracle instances should be automatically started when the system is started. Edit oratab with vi so that each line consists of the following:

```
instance-name:Oracle-home-directory:startup-option
```

where *instance-name* is the Oracle instance to be started; *Oracle-home-directory* is the directory for *instance-name*'s Oracle home directory; and *startup-option* is either Y or N.

For example, to automatically start up the prod instance, oratab would contain the following line:

```
prod:/u2/oracle/product/7.1.4:Y
```

An Oracle utility named dbstart reads the contents of oratab at system startup. Follow the directions contained in your copy of the *Oracle Installation and Configuration Guide* that describe how to edit the system startup file so that dbstart is executed when the operating system is started.

The Distributed Option

The distributed option is available only with the Oracle Enterprise Server—not Personal Oracle or the Oracle Workgroup Server. The mechanisms that are available with the distributed option include the following:

- Database links
- Distributed queries
- Distributed transactions
- Snapshots

I'll explain the function of each of these capabilities.

Database Links

A *database link* can be thought of as a pointer to an Oracle connection—it points to an Oracle database using a connect string. In addition, a database link identifies the Oracle user and password to be used for the database connection. For instance, as the database administrator for the Planetary Hospital Corporation, Al Hitchcock defines two database links.

```
SQL> create database link hobart_tasmania_facility
  2  connect to ahitchcock identified by vertigo
  3  using 'T:137.138.139.140:patient';
```

Database link created.

```
SQL> create database link antananarivo_madagasc_facility
  2  connect to ahitchcock identified by n_by_nw
  3  using 'T:231.232.233.234:patient';
```

Database link created.

Once these database links have been defined, you can use them in distributed queries and transactions.

Distributed Queries

A *distributed query* is a join of two or more tables that reside in two or more different databases. Each table in a distributed query may reference each table by using a *database link*. For instance, you construct a list of the patients in both the Chicago hospital and the Detroit hospital who have fevers higher than 103 degrees Fahrenheit with the following:

```
select Patient_ID, Body_Temp_Deg_F, Last_Name, First_Name
from Patient@Chicago
where Body_Temp_Deg_F > 103.0
union
select Patient_ID, Body_Temp_Deg_F, Last_Name, First_Name
from Patient@Detroit
where Body_Temp_Deg_F > 103.0;
```

where Chicago and Detroit are database links.

Distributed Transactions

A *distributed transaction* is a series of database changes that affect two or more databases which reside on two or more machines. You must set the Oracle initialization parameter distributed_transactions to 1 for an Oracle database to support distributed transactions. Once again using the example of the Planetary Hospital Corporation, imagine that a patient in the Kansas City, Kansas hospital was being transferred to the Kansas City, Missouri hospital. Recording the transfer requires that the Patient table in each hospital's database be updated to reflect the patient discharge in the Kansas City, Kansas hospital and the same patient's admission in the Kansas City, Missouri hospital.

```
SQL> delete from Patient@Kansas_City_Kansas
  2  where
  3  Patient_ID = 9876;
```

1 row updated.

```
SQL> insert into Patient@Kansas_City_Missouri
  2  (Patient_ID, Last_Name, First_Name, ...
  3  values
  4  (9876, ...

1 row inserted.

SQL> commit;

Commit complete.
```

Oracle uses a mechanism called a *two-phase commit* to ensure that the transaction is successfully committed in each affected database. For example, if the inserted row is rejected from the Kansas City, Missouri database for whatever reason, the entire transaction is rolled back; Patient ID 9876 will not be deleted from the Kansas City, Kansas database. An Oracle background process named RECO (an abbreviation for Recoverer) is responsible for helping each Oracle database to recover from a failed distributed transaction.

Snapshots

A *snapshot* is a mechanism for replicating a table from a remote database. The replicated table is *read-only*—it can't be modified. You can refresh the snapshot at a regular interval, or you can perform a manual refresh when it's needed. Snapshots are used for a couple of reasons. First, a snapshot reduces the need to perform a distributed query by making available a local copy of the table. Second, by using snapshots, you reduce the risk that others in an organization are creating and modifying their own copy of a table; by providing them with a read-only copy of the data, any data changes are made only to the master table.

For example, a corporate database contains a status code table that is updated at a regular interval. The corporate DBA creates a snapshot of this status code table in the local database in each field office. Whenever she makes a change to the status code table, the DBA remembers to perform a manual refresh of each snapshot (see Figure 28.4).

FIGURE 28.4.

Diagram of a snapshot.

Snapshot

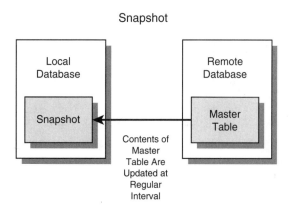

The Oracle Parallel Server

A basic Oracle installation consists of a single database that is accessed by a single Oracle instance. However, with the parallel server, multiple instances can access the same database files simultaneously. The parallel server can provide improved performance by using additional CPU resources to process SQL requests. To address the possibility of two or more instances attempting to modify the same information simultaneously, Oracle uses up to ten additional background processes, named LCK0 through LCK9, to lock a resource in use by an instance.

The Oracle Parallel Query Option

With release 7.1 of the Oracle7 Server, a new capability was introduced—the parallel query option. The parallel query option is distinct from the Oracle parallel server; to use the parallel query option, you do not need to have the parallel server. The parallel query option enables an Oracle database to take advantage of a multiprocessor machine in the following areas:

- Queries: Rather than using a single process to perform a query, the parallel query option divides a query's subtasks into separate processes that can then be assigned to separate CPUs for improved performance.

- Index creation: Creating an index for a very large table can be a time-consuming task. This option uses multiple query servers to parallelize the subtasks required for index creation—the single task of creating an index is decomposed into subtasks that can be performed in parallel. Each subtask can be allocated to its own processor for improved performance.

- Data loading: An additional clause—PARALLEL—is set to TRUE to enable SQL*Loader to execute simultaneous direct path loads on the same table. For instance, suppose there are three datafiles to be loaded, each 100 MB in size. Three separate SQL*Loader sessions—one for each datafile—can be initiated at the same time using the direct path load.

Running Multiple Oracle Instances

An Oracle instance consists of the Oracle database files, the Oracle background processes, and the System Global Area (SGA). The difference between an Oracle instance and an Oracle database is that the instance is comprised of the Oracle background processes, SGA, and database files whereas the database consists solely of the database files. When you use Database Manager to start Personal Oracle7, you are actually starting a Personal Oracle7 instance. It is possible for a system to have more than one instance running simultaneously. Both the Oracle Workgroup Server and the Oracle7 Server for UNIX support the use of multiple instances. If you're supporting a production Oracle application, you should avail yourself of this capability. In addition to your production Oracle instance, you might want to create the following two additional instances.

- A *test* instance for testing new versions of user applications, database triggers, and other PL/SQL code.

- A *model* instance for experimenting with changes to the data model.

You can create separate aliases for the production, test, and model instances by adding the following lines to c:\windows\oracle.ini on a client PC:

```
SQLNET DBNAME prod=T:amarcord:PROD
SQLNET DBNAME test=T:amarcord:TEST
SQLNET DBNAME model=T:amarcord:MODEL
```

Summary

This chapter focused on the following key ideas:

- The client/server architecture consists of three elements: the client machine, the database server, and the network that enables the client and server to communicate with each other.

- Middleware is a software layer that enables a client application to communicate with a database server. Oracle provides two different versions of SQL*Net for use as middleware: SQL*Net Version 1 and SQL*Net Version 2.

- SQL*Net Version 1 is best suited for application environments in which a single communications protocol is used.

- SQL*Net Version 2 is the best choice for supporting large groups of users. If you want to take advantage of the Oracle7 MultiThreaded Server to reduce the number of server processes, use SQL*Net Version 2.

- For SQL*Net Version 1, you use a connect string to specify the parameters of a remote connection. The string consists of a letter identifying the communications protocol, a host name or protocol address, and the name of the Oracle instance to which the connection should be made.

29

Performance
Considerations

The purpose of this chapter is to address performance issues related to Personal Oracle and, more importantly, an upsized implementation of a Personal Oracle database prototype. The material in this chapter is certainly not exhaustive. My intent is to provide some guidelines on performance improvement. In general, consider the following issues regarding overall system performance:

- Don't denormalize a logical database design without establishing, through prototyping and testing, that query performance will be inadequate.
- Try to improve performance by buying more and better hardware instead of designing and coding more complex client and server logic.
- You can never have too many disks or too much memory.
- Pick the appropriate platform—both hardware and operating system—for the application's requirements. The fact that Oracle will run on so many operating systems provides you with tremendous flexibility in considering other factors, such as hardware support and network connectivity, to select an operating system.

With these guidelines in mind, let's examine some of the performance characteristics of the elements of an Oracle client/server environment.

Where's the Bottleneck

The performance of an information system is judged best by its users. Users measure performance in terms of response time, report turnaround time, and data transfer speed. A very inefficient system may be perceived by users as providing excellent turnaround time. Conversely, a group of users might consider the performance of a very efficient information system to be inadequate. Ignore the perception of the users at your peril. Let's examine what steps should be taken to analyze a system that is the object of complaints about lackluster performance.

The four elements of a client/server architecture that should be examined are

- The network
- The Oracle database
- The client
- The server

Your goal in performance tuning should be to make the biggest immediate improvement with the least amount of disruption to existing software, hardware, and procedures. We'll look at each of the four elements in some detail.

Network

The network used in a client/server architecture may be a LAN, WAN, or a combination of both. Seek the help of a networking expert to determine the saturation level of the network. Characterize the network demands of a single client. If the network appears to be the performance bottleneck, investigate the client application software to discover whether the number of SQL requests to the server can be reduced. Changing the client application software has a huge impact; this should be your last resort!

If you're just beginning to design an application, you can reduce the network traffic by identifying functionality that can be implemented with stored procedures and functions in the database (see Chapter 18, "Creating and Using Stored Procedures, Functions, and Packages").

Database

Oracle performance-tuning efforts can be classified in three ways:

- Efforts that are application independent. For example, you don't have to modify or rebuild any software to tune the System Global Area or the MultiThreaded Server. For more information on these topics, please refer to Chapter 30, "Oracle Internals."

- Efforts that are mostly application independent. For instance, by inspecting an application's queries, you may identify indexes that you should create to improve query performance.

- Efforts that affect the application software. You might discover that the underlying database design is inefficient or that the application software makes unnecessary SQL requests. Making such changes is very expensive in terms of budget and schedule. It's very difficult to re-architect a structure after it's been constructed!

Let's focus on tuning efforts that have a minimal effect on the existing application.

Tuning the System Global Area (SGA)

Among its other uses, the SGA functions as Oracle's cache. If you increase the number of data block buffers in the SGA, there is a higher probability that a SQL statement will find the block that it needs in memory—thereby reducing the number of disk reads needed to locate a block. However, be sure that the SGA isn't so large that it's swapped out of memory by the operating system.

Here's an exercise in how to increase the number of database buffers for Personal Oracle. Invoke Database Manager by double-clicking its icon. Click the Configure button. Database Manager will display a screen titled Configure Initialization Parameters. Before you can modify any of these parameters, you must save the configuration by pressing the Save As button and assigning a name to the configuration. On this screen, one of the parameters is named Block Buffers and is set to 400 (see Figure 29.1).

FIGURE 29.1.

Viewing the initialization parameters with Database Manager.

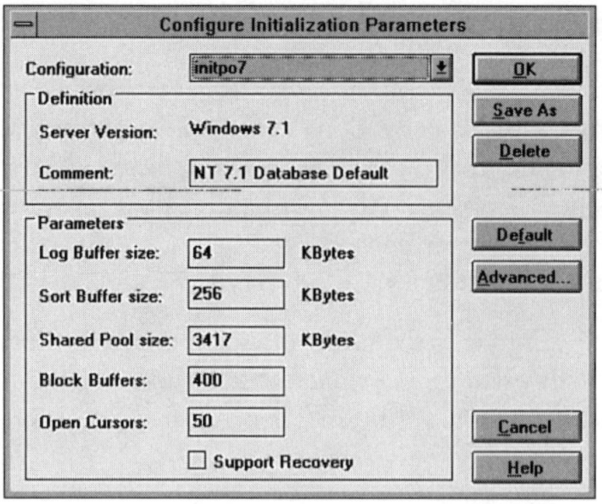

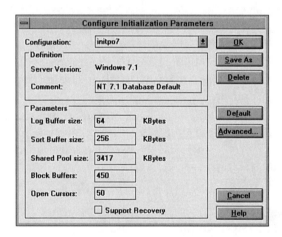

Change the value of Block Buffers from 400 to 450 (see Figure 29.2). Click the OK button.

FIGURE 29.2.

Increasing the number of block buffers.

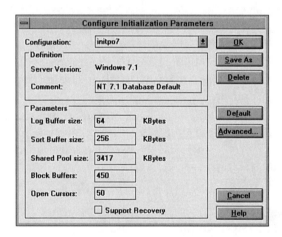

Database Manager informs you that the change will not take effect until the next time the database is started (see Figure 29.3).

FIGURE 29.3.

Database Manager displays notice.

If you wish, you can then use Database Manager to shut down and then start up the Personal Oracle database. You can leave the value of Block Buffers at 450 or set it to its original value of 400.

Tuning the MultiThreaded Server

If your Oracle server is supporting many users and the server process count is very high, consider switching from SQL*Net V1 to SQL*Net V2. By switching to SQL*Net V2, you'll be able to use Oracle's MultiThreaded Server, which will enable several remote users to share the same server process. The net result will be a reduction in the number of server processes and a reduction in server CPU utilization. Also, SQL*Net V2 is slightly more efficient than SQL*Net V1 in its network usage.

If you're already using SQL*Net V2 and the MultiThreaded Server, experiment with the number of dispatchers and the number of remote connections that can share a single server process.

Reducing Data Segment Fragmentation

In Chapter 25, "Managing Space," I explained how Oracle manages the storage of tables and indexes. As you recall, when a table is created, Oracle allocates an initial extent for the table. As more rows are inserted into the table and the free space in the initial extent is exhausted, Oracle allocates another extent for the table. Index storage works in the same way. The extents may be dispersed across a datafile—or even *across* datafiles. As the number of extents increases, a couple of problems might occur.

- Oracle might need to read more disk blocks to retrieve the qualified rows.
- The remaining free space could also be fragmented, increasing the chance that Oracle might not be able to allocate a large extent for an existing table.

To determine the level of fragmentation of a table, query the USER_EXTENTS data dictionary view. For instance, if you wanted to see the number of extents allocated to My_Table, you would issue the following query:

```
SQL> select bytes
  2  from user_extents
  3  where
  4  segment_name = 'MY_TABLE';

    BYTES
---------
    10240
    10240
    10240
    10240
    10240
    10240
    10240
    10240
    10240
    10240
    10240
    10240
    10240
```

```
10240
10240
10240
```

```
16 rows selected.
```

As you can see, the value of PCTINCREASE for My_Table is 0 because the size of each extent is the same. To store all of My_Table's rows in its initial extent, you have two choices.

- You can create a copy of My_Table with an appropriate size for the initial extent.
- You can export My_Table using Export, which will determine the optimal size for the initial extent by default. Drop the table and use Import to load it back into the database.

Ideally, the contents of every table and index should be contained within its initial extent. This minimizes the number of disk reads needed to retrieve the rows to satisfy a query.

Client

To achieve acceptable performance on the client machine, the design of the client application should invoke Oracle stored procedures and functions where appropriate. There are very few performance bandages that can be applied to a poorly designed application; performance must be designed into the application. Even with a good design, the client platform must have adequate RAM and disk space to support the application.

Server

The performance of the server and the Oracle database are tightly coupled. For instance, if the Oracle database processes many queries with each query returning a large number of rows, the server will be handling many disk I/O requests. To improve server performance, focus on tuning disk I/O and CPU utilization.

Tuning Disk I/O

To tune disk I/O, you must first determine if disk I/O requests are balanced across all the server's disk drives. Use operating system commands and utilities to identify the average number of I/O requests serviced by each disk drive. Your objectives should include the following:

- Lower the overall number of disk I/O requests by adding more memory to the server. By adding more RAM, you'll be able to increase the size of the Oracle SGA and thereby reduce overall disk I/O, assuming no other changes are made to the database.
- Lower the average number of I/O requests per drive by adding disk drives to the server. You can then relocate a tablespace's datafiles to a new disk drive by using the ALTER TABLESPACE statement with the RENAME option.

■ Lower the average number of I/O requests per disk controller by adding another disk controller to the server.

■ Balance disk I/O requests so that each drive is servicing the same number of I/O requests. This requires both analysis and experimentation to determine the optimal distribution of Oracle datafiles and redo log files.

Tuning CPU Utilization

The server's CPU utilization depends a lot on the use of the database that the server is supporting. If the database is processing many small transactions, CPU utilization might be very high. If this is true, here are options to ponder:

■ If the Oracle database is servicing many remote connections, use SQL*Net V2 and the MultiThreaded Server to reduce the process count and the related CPU activity.

■ If the operating system provides SMP (Symmetric Multiprocessor) support, add another processor to reduce overall CPU utilization.

Creating Indexes to Improve Performance

A significant portion of database activity consists of SELECT statements. Accordingly, improving query performance results in better overall application performance. A query generally is processed more quickly if it uses an index to access the qualified rows. A *full table scan* is a query in which all of a table's rows are read to find the qualified rows. To determine whether a query performs a full table scan, you must obtain the query's *execution plan*. When an execution plan indicates that a full table scan is being performed, consider creating an index that the query can use.

Be aware that it is possible to *overindex* a table. Remember that Oracle automatically maintains a table's indexes whenever the contents of the table change due to an INSERT, UPDATE, or DELETE statement. Your goal should be to optimize the most frequent queries without forcing Oracle to maintain an inordinate number of indexes.

Rule-Based and Cost-Based Optimization

Oracle furnishes two optimizers: the rule-based optimizer and the cost-based optimizer. Both optimizers are concerned with maximizing the performance of queries. The *rule-based optimizer* looks at the structure of the SQL statement to be optimized, determines what indexes exist for the table, and constructs an execution plan; it doesn't use any information about the contents of the table to be queried or its index values. The *cost-based optimizer* looks at statistics regarding the table, its columns, and its indexes and calculates an execution plan based on the lowest cost path—the number of database blocks that must be read to retrieve the query results. These statistics are stored in the data dictionary tables whenever an analysis of the tables and indexes are performed—which I'll explain shortly.

The choice between the rule-based and cost-based optimizer is controlled by an initialization parameter named OPTIMIZER_MODE, which has three possible values:

- CHOOSE: If there are no table or index statistics in the data dictionary, Oracle chooses to use the rule-based optimizer. However, if table and index statistics are available, Oracle will use the cost-based optimizer. This is the default value for OPTIMIZER_MODE.
- RULE: Oracle will always use the rule-based optimizer.
- COST: Oracle will always use the cost-based optimizer.

NOTE

Measuring the performance of a query is not as simple as it sounds. If you perform the same query twice against a large table, the second query will probably retrieve the results more quickly because the database blocks that the query needs to read are already contained in the SGA. Fewer disk reads are needed so the second query takes less time to complete.

Determining the Execution Plan for a SQL Statement with *EXPLAIN PLAN*

If you don't analyze tables and indexes, Oracle will use the rule-based optimizer to determine the best execution plan for each query. You can employ the EXPLAIN PLAN statement to obtain the execution plan for a query. The syntax for EXPLAIN PLAN is

```
EXPLAIN PLAN FOR sql-statement
```

where *sql-statement* is the SQL statement for which an execution plan is to be generated.

Before you use the EXPLAIN PLAN statement, you'll need to run a script from SQL*Plus that creates the PLAN_TABLE in your Oracle account.

```
SQL> @c:\orawin\rdbms71\admin\utlxplan.sql

Table created.

SQL> desc plan_table
 Name                            Null?    Type
 ------------------------------- -------- ----
 STATEMENT_ID                             VARCHAR2(30)
 TIMESTAMP                                DATE
 REMARKS                                  VARCHAR2(80)
 OPERATION                                VARCHAR2(30)
 OPTIONS                                  VARCHAR2(30)
 OBJECT_NODE                              VARCHAR2(128)
 OBJECT_OWNER                             VARCHAR2(30)
```

```
OBJECT_NAME                          VARCHAR2(30)
OBJECT_INSTANCE                      NUMBER(38)
OBJECT_TYPE                          VARCHAR2(30)
OPTIMIZER                            VARCHAR2(255)
SEARCH_COLUMNS                       NUMBER(38)
ID                                   NUMBER(38)
PARENT_ID                            NUMBER(38)
POSITION                             NUMBER(38)
OTHER                                LONG
```

After the PLAN_TABLE has been created, you can begin using the EXPLAIN PLAN statement. Whenever the EXPLAIN PLAN statement is executed, Oracle inserts rows into the PLAN_TABLE; as a result, you need to delete the contents of PLAN_TABLE before each use of EXPLAIN PLAN. For example, suppose you create a table that records the day of the year and the maximum temperature in degrees Fahrenheit for each day. As a developer, you want to determine the efficiency of a query's execution plan.

```
SQL> delete from plan_table;

0 rows deleted.

SQL> explain plan for
  2  select day_number, temp_deg_f
  3  from day_temp
  4  where day_number = 100;

Explained.

SQL> select operation, options, object_name, id, parent_id, position
  2  from plan_table
  3  order by id;
```

OPERATION	OPTIONS	OBJECT_NAME	ID	PARENT_ID	POSITION
SELECT STATEMENT			0		
TABLE ACCESS	FULL	DAY_TEMP	1	0	1

What you're looking for when using EXPLAIN_PLAN is the word FULL that appears in the OP-TIONS column in conjunction with the TABLE ACCESS operation. This signifies that the query performs a full table scan to retrieve the data. If a query involving Day_Number is a fairly common operation, it generally makes sense to add an index on the Day_Number column. Let's create the index and rerun EXPLAIN_PLAN.

```
SQL> create index day_temp_day_number_ck
  2  on day_temp (day_number);

Index created.

SQL> delete from plan_table;

2 rows deleted.

SQL> explain plan for
  2  select day_number, temp_deg_f
  3  from day_temp
  4  where day_number = 100;
```

```
Explained.

SQL> select operation, options, object_name, id, parent_id, position
  2  from plan_table
  3  order by id;

OPERATION            OPTIONS       OBJECT_NAME               ID PARENT_ID  POSITION
-------------------- ------------- -------------------      ---- ---------- ---------
SELECT STATEMENT                                             0
TABLE ACCESS         BY ROWID      DAY_TEMP                   1         0          1
INDEX                RANGE SCAN    DAY_TEMP_DAY_NUMBER_CK     2         1          1
```

As you can see, by creating the index, you've changed the optimizer's execution plan for the query. Instead of performing a full table scan, the optimizer will perform an index range scan, which is almost always a more efficient operation (although this isn't true for a table with a small number of rows). Even though the EXPLAIN PLAN statement supplies useful information about the methods used by the optimizer, it doesn't provide any hard performance numbers. To retrieve performance data, you'll want to use the TKPROF utility.

The TKPROF Utility

> **WARNING**
>
> In the current version of Personal Oracle7 (6/95), the TKPROF utility is not functional. This will undoubtedly be addressed in a future release of Personal Oracle7.

In the directory c:\orawin\bin, you'll find an executable file named tkprof.exe. During its installation, Personal Oracle doesn't create a program item for this utility. However, you should consider adding a new program item to the Personal Oracle7 program group to run this executable file.

TKPROF processes Oracle trace files to produce a text file that describes the SQL activity that occurred during a particular Oracle session. A trace file is extremely useful for performance analysis and tuning because:

■ It contains the exact SQL statements that were executed by a given user during a particular Oracle session.

■ If TIMED_STATISTICS is enabled, the trace file will contain statistical information about the execution of each SQL statement.

After you double-click the TKPROF icon, TKPROF will display a screen in which you can specify the trace file. Use the Browse button to identify the trace file that you want to analyze. Click the Default button so that TKPROF will use appropriate file extensions. In the Explain group, enter the Oracle user, password, and the table name PLAN_TABLE for an Oracle account in which the PLAN_TABLE has been created (see Figure 29.4). Click the OK button.

FIGURE 29.4.

Analyzing a trace file with TKPROF.

```
┌─────────────────────────────────────────────────────────────┐
│  ─                        TKPROF                             │
│                                                              │
│  Trace File   │c:\orawin\rdbms71\trace\ora06583.trc│  Browse  │
│                                                              │
│  Output File  │c:\orawin\rdbms71\trace\ora06583.ou │  Default │
│                                                              │
│  Insert       │c:\orawin\rdbms71\trace\ora06583.sql│   OK     │
│                                                              │
│  Record       │c:\orawin\rdbms71\trace\ora06583.re │  Cancel  │
│                                                              │
│                                                   About       │
│  ┌─Explain────────────────────────────┐  ┌─Sort──────┐       │
│  │ User Name  │frayed_wires      │     │  │ execnt  ▲ │       │
│  │                                │     │  │ execpu    │       │
│  │ Password   │helmholtz         │     │  │ execu     │       │
│  │                                │     │  │ exedsk    │       │
│  │ Table      │plan_table        │     │  │ exeela    │       │
│  │                                │     │  │ exemis    │       │
│  └────────────────────────────────┘     │  │ exeqry    │       │
│  ┌─Sys─────────────────────────────┐    │  │ exerow    │       │
│  │           ○ Yes      Print │   │ │    │  │ fchcnt    │       │
│  │           ◉ No               │    │  │ fchcpu    │       │
│  │                                 │    │  │ fchcu   ▼ │       │
│  └─────────────────────────────────┘    └───────────┘       │
└─────────────────────────────────────────────────────────────┘
```

By default, Personal Oracle won't produce trace files. The two methods you can use to produce trace files include the following:

■ To produce a trace file for every Oracle session, set `SQL_TRACE` and `TIMED_STATISTICS` to `TRUE` and restart the Oracle instance. (Chapter 30 covers this procedure in detail.)

■ To produce a trace file for a particular Oracle session, use the `ALTER SESSION` statement to set `SQL TRACE`. The only disadvantage of this approach is that it will not cause Oracle to collect statistics about the execution of each SQL statement.

To enable a trace file for an Oracle session, issue the following command:

```
SQL> alter session set sql_trace true;

Session altered.
```

Oracle stores trace files in c:\orawin\rdbms71\trace. Figure 29.5 is an example of the location and name of a trace file.

FIGURE 29.5.

File Manager displays the location of a trace file.

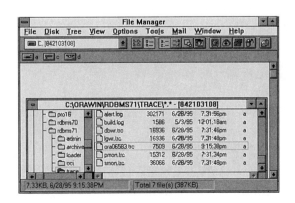

Analyzing Tables and Indexes

Oracle collects table, column, and index statistics through the execution of the ANALYZE TABLE and ANALYZE INDEX statements. The syntax for the ANALYZE_TABLE statement is

```
ANALYZE TABLE table-name COMPUTE STATISTICS
```

where *table-name* is the name of the table to be analyzed.

Here's an example of the results produced by the ANALYZE TABLE statement. I'll create a table named TEST_TABLE and put 1000 rows into it.

```
SQL> create table Test_Table (
  2    Record_Number integer,
  3    Current_Date  date);

Table created.

SQL>
SQL> declare
  2
  2    max_records constant int := 1000;
  3    i             int := 1;
  4
  4  begin
  5
  5    for i in 1..max_records loop
  6
  6      insert into Test_Table
  7        (record_number, current_date)
  8      values
  9        (i, SYSDATE);
 10
 10    end loop;
 11
 11  end;
 12  /

PL/SQL procedure successfully completed.
```

If you inspect the row in the data dictionary view USER_TABLES, which contains information about TEST_TABLE, you'll see that the relevant columns are either null or zero.

```
SQL> select num_rows, blocks, empty_blocks, avg_space, chain_cnt, avg_row_len
  2  from user_tables
  3  where
  4  table_name = 'TEST_TABLE';
```

NUM_ROWS	BLOCKS	EMPTY_BLOCKS	AVG_SPACE	CHAIN_CNT	AVG_ROW_LEN
		0	0	0	0

However, once you analyze the table, the statistics related to TEST_TABLE are populated.

```
SQL> analyze table test_table compute statistics;

Table analyzed.
```

```
SQL> select num_rows, blocks, empty_blocks, avg_space, chain_cnt, avg_row_len
  2  from user_tables
  3  where
  4  table_name = 'TEST_TABLE';

  NUM_ROWS    BLOCKS EMPTY_BLOCKS AVG_SPACE CHAIN_CNT AVG_ROW_LEN
---------- --------- ------------ --------- --------- -----------
      1000        14            5       196         0          15
```

Besides filling in values in USER_TABLES, the ANALYZE TABLE statement also updates related information in USER_TAB_COLUMNS.

```
SQL> select column_name, num_distinct, low_value, high_value, density
  2  from user_tab_columns
  3  where
  4  table_name = 'TEST_TABLE'
  5  order by column_name;

COLUMN_NAME      NUM_DISTINCT LOW_VALUE          HIGH_VALUE            DENSITY
---------------- ------------ ----------------- -------------------- ---------
CURRENT_DATE                5 77C3060C101D32    77C3060C101D36        .02631579
RECORD_NUMBER            1000 C102              C20B                  .001
```

If a table contains a very large number of rows, you may want to consider an alternate form of the statement, which will sample a percentage of the rows.

ANALYZE TABLE *table-name* ESTIMATE STATISTICS SAMPLE *percentage* PERCENT

where *table-name* is the table to be analyzed, and *percentage* is the percentage of the table's rows to be analyzed.

You can also remove the statistics for the table of interest with the following statement:

ANALYZE TABLE *table-name* DELETE STATISTICS

where *table-name* is the table whose statistics are to be eliminated.

Using the previous table as an example, you can analyze TEST_TABLE by sampling a portion of the rows.

```
SQL> analyze table Test_Table delete statistics;

Table analyzed.

SQL> analyze table Test_Table estimate statistics sample 10 percent;

Table analyzed.

SQL> select num_rows, blocks, empty_blocks, avg_space, chain_cnt, avg_row_len
  2  from user_tables
  3  where
  4  table_name = 'TEST_TABLE';

  NUM_ROWS    BLOCKS EMPTY_BLOCKS AVG_SPACE CHAIN_CNT AVG_ROW_LEN
---------- --------- ------------ --------- --------- -----------
      1000        14            5       196         0          15
```

For the cost-based optimizer to work well, the indexes that belong to the table being queried must also be analyzed. The syntax for the ANALYZE INDEX statement is almost identical to that of the ANALYZE TABLE statement.

```
ANALYZE INDEX index-name COMPUTE STATISTICS
```

where *index-name* is the name of an index on the queried table.

To illustrate how the ANALYZE INDEX statement updates index statistics in the data dictionary, here is an example that uses the unique index PK_MANUFACTURER, which enforces the primary key for the Manufacturer table.

```
SQL> select index_name, blevel, leaf_blocks, distinct_keys,
avg_leaf_blocks_per_key,
  2          avg_data_blocks_per_key
  3  from user_indexes
  4  where
  5  index_name = 'PK_MANUFACTURER';

INDEX_NAME              BLEVEL LEAF_BLOCKS DISTINCT_KEYS
                            AVG_LEAF_BLOCKS_PER_KEY AVG_DATA_BLOCKS_PER_KEY
-------------------- ---------- ----------- -------------
                             ---------------------- ----------------------
PK_MANUFACTURER
```

Next, we'll analyze the index and then query USER_INDEXES once more.

```
SQL> analyze index pk_manufacturer compute statistics;

Index analyzed.

SQL> select index_name, blevel, leaf_blocks, distinct_keys,
avg_leaf_blocks_per_key,
  2          avg_data_blocks_per_key
  3  from user_indexes
  4  where
  5  index_name = 'PK_MANUFACTURER';

INDEX_NAME              BLEVEL LEAF_BLOCKS DISTINCT_KEYS
                            AVG_LEAF_BLOCKS_PER_KEY AVG_DATA_BLOCKS_PER_KEY
-------------------- ---------- ----------- -------------
                             ---------------------- ----------------------
PK_MANUFACTURER              0           1            10
                                                   1                       1
```

As you can see, the index statistics have been updated by executing the ANALYZE INDEX statement.

Summary

This chapter examined the following aspects of Oracle client/server performance tuning:

- To maximize network performance before implementing an application: plan to use stored procedures and functions in the database to reduce the number of SQL requests on the network, minimize superfluous SQL requests from the client application, and consider switching to SQL*Net V2.

- To improve Oracle database performance: tune the SGA, tune the MultiThreaded Server, reduce data segment fragmentation, and add nonunique indexes where appropriate.

- To improve the server's performance: add memory so that more data block buffers can be added to the SGA, and add more disk drives to reduce the average number of I/O requests per disk drive.

- Oracle uses two optimizers: the rule-based optimizer and the cost-based optimizer.

- The rule-based optimizer looks at a query's syntax and the existence of indexes to determine the most efficient method for retrieving the qualified rows.

- The cost-based optimizer looks at a query's syntax, the existence of indexes, and the table and index statistics to determine the most efficient method for retrieving the qualified rows.

- To use the cost-based optimizer, obtain table and index statistics by executing the ANALYZE TABLE and ANALYZE INDEX statements.

- Use the EXPLAIN_PLAN statement to determine a query's execution plan.

- You can generate a trace file for a specific Oracle session by executing ALTER SESSION SET SQL_TRACE TRUE when the Oracle session begins.

- TKPROF is a utility that converts a binary Oracle trace file to a listing file containing each SQL statement executed during an Oracle session.

30

Oracle Internals

No book on Personal Oracle would be complete without discussing some of the internal aspects of the product. In this chapter, I'll describe the architectural elements of the Oracle database such as the System Global Area, data dictionary, and initialization parameters. Whether you're building Oracle database applications with Personal Oracle, the Oracle Workgroup Server, or the Oracle Enterprise Server, you'll benefit from the information contained in this chapter.

The Architecture of the Oracle7 RDBMS

You can conceive of an Oracle database as composed of several types of different *materials*: operating system files, memory structures, and processes. Before an Oracle database is running, the database exists as a set of disk files. After the Oracle database has been started, a memory structure—the System Global Area—is allocated, and at least four background processes are activated to help Oracle perform its work. These background processes are discussed later in this chapter.

Let's take a closer look at the files used by Oracle.

Oracle Database Files

The files that Oracle uses for storing data are referred to as *datafiles*. These are the operating system files—in the case of Personal Oracle, MS-DOS files—assigned to a tablespace. In addition to using datafiles, Oracle also uses two other types of operating system files.

- Redo log files: Every Oracle database has at least two redo log files. A redo log file contains the Oracle blocks that have been changed by a transaction. Oracle writes to the redo log files in a round-robin fashion. Changed blocks are written to redo log file #1 until it is filled; at that point, Oracle switches to writing changed blocks to redo log file #2. After redo log file #2 is filled, Oracle switches back to redo log file #1. The event of switching redo log files is referred to as a *log switch*. The redo log files serve another purpose: after a system crash, Oracle reads the redo log files to roll forward any committed transactions and roll back any uncommitted transactions. For Personal Oracle, the two redo log files are named wdblog1.ora and wdblog2.ora.

- Control file: The control file is a small binary file that contains a list of all of the operating system files in the Oracle database. In addition, the control file records a Sequence Control Number (SCN), which is also stored in each of the database files. When you install Personal Oracle7, it creates a control file named ctl1.ora.

Don't confuse the database control file with a SQL*Loader control file. The database control file is a binary file whereas a SQL*Loader control file is a text file. The file extension for a Personal Oracle control file is .ora, and the file extension for a SQL*Loader control file is .ctl.

The System Global Area

The System Global Area—or SGA—is a shared memory structure that is allocated when an Oracle database is started. For Personal Oracle, the default size of the SGA is approximately 4 MB.

Three important components of the SGA are

- Data block buffers: The largest constituent of the SGA is the data blocks that are cached in the SGA. Oracle uses a Least Recently Used (LRU) algorithm to determine which blocks to throw out of the SGA. When a block is read, Oracle looks to see which data block's last usage is oldest; that block gets replaced with a fresh block.

- Shared and private SQL areas: The shared SQL area contains parsed SQL statements that have been submitted by more than one Oracle user. Each SQL statement issued by an Oracle user is parsed and stored in a private SQL area.

- Dictionary cache: This is an area of the SGA where data dictionary information— such as the table of tables or table of columns—is stored. Every time Oracle parses a SQL statement, it must obtain information about the tables, columns, and other objects referenced in the SQL statement. The dictionary cache increases the likelihood that Oracle will find the dictionary information it needs to parse each SQL statement.

Oracle Background Processes

As you know, Personal Oracle requires the installation of Microsoft's Win32 API. This layer provides Personal Oracle with the resources it needs to perform pseudo-multitasking. At a minimum, an Oracle database uses four processes.

- DBWR (Database Writer) writes blocks to the database files.
- LGWR (Log Writer) writes changed blocks to the redo log files.
- SMON (System Monitor) performs instance recovery at instance startup and monitors the health of the other Oracle background processes.
- PMON (Process Monitor) works on behalf of an Oracle user whose connection, for whatever reason, has been abruptly terminated. PMON releases any resources that were in use by the terminated Oracle session.

The Oracle Data Dictionary

Oracle maintains information about the database and its operations in a set of tables called the data dictionary. All of these tables are owned by a special Oracle user named SYS. You can look at the structure and content of these tables by submitting the following query:

```
SQL> select table_name
  2  from dba_tables
  3  where
  4  owner = 'SYS';

TABLE_NAME
------------------------------
ACCESS$
ARGUMENT$
AUD$
AUDIT$
AUDIT_ACTIONS
BOOTSTRAP$
CCOL$
CDEF$
CLU$
COL$
COM$
CON$
DBMS_ALERT_INFO
DBMS_LOCK_ALLOCATED
DEF$_CALL
DEF$_CALLDEST
DEF$_DEFAULTDEST
DEF$_ERROR
DEF$_SCHEDULE
DEF$_TRAN
DEF$_TRANDEST
DEFROLE$
DEPENDENCY$
DUAL
DUC$
ERROR$
EXPACT$
FET$
FILE$
HISTOGRAM$
ICOL$
IDL_CHAR$
IDL_SB4$
IDL_UB1$
IDL_UB2$
INCEXP
INCFIL
INCVID
IND$
JOB$
LAB$
LINK$
MLOG$
```

```
OBJ$
OBJAUTH$
PENDING_SESSIONS$
PENDING_SUB_SESSIONS$
PENDING_TRANS$
PROCEDURE$
PRODUCT_PROFILE
PROFILE$
PROFNAME$
PROPS$
PSTUBTBL
RESOURCE_COST$
RESOURCE_MAP
RGCHILD$
RGROUP$
SEG$
SEQ$
SLOG$
SNAP$
SOURCE$
STMT_AUDIT_OPTION_MAP
SYN$
SYSAUTH$
SYSTEM_PRIVILEGE_MAP
TAB$
TABLE_PRIVILEGE_MAP
TRIGGER$
TRIGGERCOL$
TS$
TSQ$
UET$
UNDO$
USER$
USER_PROFILE
VIEW$
_default_auditing_options_

79 rows selected.
```

WARNING

Never, never, never modify—or even try to modify—the contents or structure of any of the data dictionary tables. If you do, there's a very good chance that you'll corrupt the Oracle database. The contents of the data dictionary tables are modified when you use Oracle statements such as CREATE TABLE and CREATE VIEW. Directly modifying the information in a data dictionary table is akin to modifying an MS-DOS FAT (File Allocation Table) instead of simply issuing a DOS command to create or delete a table.

If you describe one of these tables—for instance, TAB$, which happens to be the table of tables—you'll see that the columns are mostly numeric.

```
SQL> desc sys.tab$
 Name                           Null?    Type
 ------------------------------ -------- ----
 OBJ#                           NOT NULL NUMBER
 TS#                            NOT NULL NUMBER
 FILE#                          NOT NULL NUMBER
 BLOCK#                         NOT NULL NUMBER
 CLU#                                    NUMBER
 TAB#                                    NUMBER
 COLS                           NOT NULL NUMBER
 CLUCOLS                                 NUMBER
 PCTFREE$                       NOT NULL NUMBER
 PCTUSED$                       NOT NULL NUMBER
 INITRANS                       NOT NULL NUMBER
 MAXTRANS                       NOT NULL NUMBER
 MODIFIED                       NOT NULL NUMBER
 AUDIT$                         NOT NULL VARCHAR2(32)
 ROWCNT                                  NUMBER
 BLKCNT                                  NUMBER
 EMPCNT                                  NUMBER
 AVGSPC                                  NUMBER
 CHNCNT                                  NUMBER
 AVGRLN                                  NUMBER
 SPARE1                                  NUMBER
 SPARE2                                  NUMBER
```

You can't really find anything useful by looking solely at TAB$; you must join TAB$ with several other tables to comprehend the table information. To simplify this operation, Oracle supplies a number of views, called data dictionary views, which join the relevant tables and return the retrieved values to appropriately named columns. There are over 150 data dictionary views, many of which fall into the following three categories:

- Those that return information about objects owned by the current Oracle user (named USER_...)

- Those that return information about objects that are accessible to the current Oracle user (named ALL_...)

- Those that return information about all objects, regardless of ownership (named DBA_...)

I'll present some of the views that you'll find quite useful during the development and administration of an Oracle database. The following views are listed in logical, rather than alphabetical, order.

DBA_OBJECTS

DBA_OBJECTS contains primary information about all database objects such as tables and indexes. To see the types of objects that exist in the database, use the following query:

```
SQL> select distinct object_type
  2  from dba_objects;

OBJECT_TYPE
-------------
CLUSTER
FUNCTION
INDEX
PACKAGE
PACKAGE BODY
PROCEDURE
SEQUENCE
SYNONYM
TABLE
TRIGGER
VIEW
```

You can retrieve all the indexes owned by a particular user—for instance, SYS.

```
SQL> select object_name
  2  from dba_objects
  3  where
  4  owner = 'SYS' and
  5  object_type = 'INDEX'
  6  order by object_name;

OBJECT_NAME
---------------------------------------------------------
DEF$_CALLS_PRIMARY
DEF$_DEFALUTDEST_PRIMARY
DEF$_ERROR_PRIMARY
DEF$_SCHEDULE_PRIMARY
DFRPC$_TRAN_PRIMARY
I_ARGUMENT1
I_AUD1
I_AUDIT
.
.
.
I_USER#
I_USER1
I_VIEW1
SYS_C00317
SYS_C00318

72 rows selected.
```

DBA_TABLES

DBA_TABLES supplies information about all of the tables in an Oracle database in a form that is more usable than that of TAB$. Its structure is

```
SQL> desc dba_tables
 Name                             Null?    Type
 -------------------------------- -------- ----
 OWNER                            NOT NULL VARCHAR2(30)
 TABLE_NAME                       NOT NULL VARCHAR2(30)
```

```
TABLESPACE_NAME                    NOT NULL VARCHAR2(30)
CLUSTER_NAME                                VARCHAR2(30)
PCT_FREE                           NOT NULL NUMBER
PCT_USED                           NOT NULL NUMBER
INI_TRANS                          NOT NULL NUMBER
MAX_TRANS                          NOT NULL NUMBER
INITIAL_EXTENT                              NUMBER
NEXT_EXTENT                                 NUMBER
MIN_EXTENTS                                 NUMBER
MAX_EXTENTS                                 NUMBER
PCT_INCREASE                                NUMBER
BACKED_UP                                   VARCHAR2(1)
NUM_ROWS                                    NUMBER
BLOCKS                                      NUMBER
EMPTY_BLOCKS                                NUMBER
AVG_SPACE                                   NUMBER
CHAIN_CNT                                   NUMBER
AVG_ROW_LEN                                 NUMBER
DEGREE                                      VARCHAR2(10)
INSTANCES                                   VARCHAR2(10)
CACHE                                       VARCHAR2(5)
```

Several of the columns in DBA_TABLES return data that is computed by an ANALYZE TABLE statement (which concerns the use of the Oracle cost-based optimizer, discussed in Chapter 29, "Performance Considerations"). The columns that you would typically select from this view are OWNER, TABLE_NAME, TABLESPACE_NAME, and other columns containing the table's storage parameters.

If you wanted to see all the tables whose names contained the pattern PROD, the following query will retrieve the information you want.

```
SQL> select owner, table_name
  2  from dba_tables
  3  where
  4  table_name like '%PROD%'
  5  order by owner, table_name;
```

```
OWNER                              TABLE_NAME
------------------------------     ------------------------------
DLOCKMAN                           PRODUCT
FRAYED_WIRES                       HOUSTON_PRODUCT
FRAYED_WIRES                       PORTLAND_PRODUCT
FRAYED_WIRES                       PRODUCT
FRAYED_WIRES                       SAVE_HOUSTON_PRODUCT
FRAYED_WIRES                       SAVE_PORTLAND_PRODUCT
SCOTT                              PRODUCT
SYS                                PRODUCT_PROFILE

8 rows selected.
```

DBA_TAB_COLUMNS

As you might have noticed, DBA_TABLES doesn't provide any information about a table's columns; as a separate view, DBA_TAB_COLUMNS presents a table's structure by returning the following values:

```
SQL> desc dba_tab_columns
 Name                             Null?    Type
 ------------------------------   --------  ----
 OWNER                            NOT NULL VARCHAR2(30)
 TABLE_NAME                       NOT NULL VARCHAR2(30)
 COLUMN_NAME                      NOT NULL VARCHAR2(30)
 DATA_TYPE                                 VARCHAR2(9)
 DATA_LENGTH                      NOT NULL NUMBER
 DATA_PRECISION                            NUMBER
 DATA_SCALE                                NUMBER
 NULLABLE                                  VARCHAR2(1)
 COLUMN_ID                        NOT NULL NUMBER
 DEFAULT_LENGTH                            NUMBER
 DATA_DEFAULT                              LONG
 NUM_DISTINCT                              NUMBER
 LOW_VALUE                                 RAW(32)
 HIGH_VALUE                                RAW(32)
 DENSITY                                   NUMBER
```

DBA_TABLESPACES

To obtain a list of each tablespace in a database and its default storage parameters, submit the following SQL statement:

```
SQL> select *
  2  from dba_tablespaces;

TABLESPACE_NAME   INITIAL_EXTENT NEXT_EXTENT MIN_EXT MAX_EXT PCT_INCR  STATUS
---------------   -------------- ----------- ------- ------- --------- ------
SYSTEM                     4096         4096       1     121        10 ONLINE
USER_DATA                  4096         4096       1     121        10 ONLINE
ROLLBACK_DATA            102400       102400       2     121        50 ONLINE
TEMPORARY_DATA             4096         4096       1     121        10 ONLINE
FRAYED_WIRES              77824        51200       1     121        15 ONLINE
```

DBA_DATA_FILES

The DBA_DATA_FILES data dictionary view will return the name of each datafile, its size, and its associated tablespace.

```
SQL> select file_name, bytes, tablespace_name
  2  from dba_data_files;

FILE_NAME                                              BYTES TABLESPACE_NAME
---------------------------------------------------- --------- ---------------
C:\ORAWIN\DBS\wdbrbs.ora                            3145728 ROLLBACK_DATA
C:\ORAWIN\DBS\wdbtemp.ora                           2097152 TEMPORARY_DATA
C:\ORAWIN\DBS\wdbuser.ora                           3145728 USER_DATA
C:\ORAWIN\DBS\wdbsys.ora                           10485760 SYSTEM
c:\orawin\dbs\wdbfray.ora                          10485760 FRAYED_WIRES
c:\orawin\dbs\wdbfray2.ora                          5242880 FRAYED_WIRES

6 rows selected.
```

DBA_EXTENTS

The DBA_EXTENTS view returns information about every extent that has been allocated in a database. This information includes the following:

```
SQL> desc dba_extents
 Name                            Null?    Type
 ------------------------------- -------- ----
 OWNER                                    VARCHAR2(30)
 SEGMENT_NAME                             VARCHAR2(81)
 SEGMENT_TYPE                             VARCHAR2(17)
 TABLESPACE_NAME                          VARCHAR2(30)
 EXTENT_ID                       NOT NULL NUMBER
 FILE_ID                         NOT NULL NUMBER
 BLOCK_ID                        NOT NULL NUMBER
 BYTES                                    NUMBER
 BLOCKS                          NOT NULL NUMBER
```

For example, suppose the Oracle account FRAYED_WIRES owns a table named XYZ that was created with an initial extent of 10,240 bytes. Once you've added so many rows that the first extent is filled, Oracle allocates another extent of 10,240 bytes. The additional extents can be seen by querying the DBA_EXTENTS view.

```
SQL> select segment_type, bytes
  2  from sys.dba_extents
  3  where
  4  segment_name = 'XYZ';

SEGMENT_TYPE          BYTES
----------------- ---------
TABLE                 10240
TABLE                 10240
```

DBA_SEGMENTS

In a sense, the DBA_SEGMENTS view provides a summary of the data contained in DBA_EXTENTS. Using the previous example, two rows were returned when you queried the DBA_EXTENTS view to see what extents were allocated for table XYZ. If you query the DBA_SEGMENTS view, a single row returns data about the allocation of storage for table XYZ. Notice that the value of Bytes is the sum of the bytes returned by DBA_EXTENTS for the same segment name.

```
SQL> select segment_name, segment_type, tablespace_name, bytes
  2  from dba_segments
  3  where
  4  segment_name = 'XYZ';


SEGMENT_NAME    SEGMENT_TYPE    TABLESPACE_NAME                      BYTES
--------------- --------------- ------------------------------- ---------
XYZ             TABLE           FRAYED_WIRES                        20480
```

DBA_FREE_SPACE

As discussed in Chapter 26, "Managing Users and Roles," you can obtain information about the free space in a tablespace by querying DBA_FREE_SPACE. You can get the total number of free bytes in a tablespace with the following query:

```
SQL> select sum(bytes)
  2  from dba_free_space
  3  where
  4  tablespace_name = 'USER_DATA';

SUM(BYTES)
----------
   2809856
```

You can retrieve the size of each free extent by issuing the following statement:

```
SQL> select bytes
  2  from dba_free_space
  3  where
  4  tablespace_name = 'USER_DATA';

    BYTES
---------
  2801664
     8192
```

DBA_TRIGGERS

The DBA_TRIGGERS view provides information about each database trigger that exists in the database. You can retrieve information about all DELETE triggers with the following query:

```
SQL> select trigger_name, trigger_type, table_name
  2  from dba_triggers
  3  where
  4  triggering_event = 'DELETE';

TRIGGER_NAME                      TRIGGER_TYPE      TABLE_NAME
--------------------------------  ----------------  ----------------------------
DELETE_INVOKE_DIS_PATIENTS        AFTER STATEMENT   INVOKE_DIS_PATIENTS
```

The PL/SQL statements that compose a trigger can be viewed by selecting the Trigger_Body column from DBA_TRIGGERS. Notice that the SQL*Plus variable long has been increased to a large number so that the entire trigger body is displayed.

```
SQL> set long 5000
SQL> set arraysize 1
SQL> select trigger_body
  2  from dba_triggers
  3  where
  4  trigger_name = 'DELETE_INVOKE_DIS_PATIENTS';

TRIGGER_BODY
----------------------------------------------------------------
begin
Dis_Patients_Normal_Temp;
end;
```

DBA_USERS

The DBA_USERS view contains basic information about every Oracle user. Oracle assigns each user a user ID when it's created. You'll see this user ID referenced in other data dictionary tables and views. Here is a simple query of DBA_USERS that returns each Oracle user (or account) and its associated user ID.

```
SQL> select username, user_id
  2  from dba_users;

USERNAME                          USER_ID
------------------------------- ---------
SYS                                     0
SYSTEM                                  5
SCOTT                                   8
FRAYED_WIRES                           12
DLOCKMAN                               10
ORDINARY_USER                          13
JSMITH                                 14
VILLAGE_WIDGET                         15
```

DBA_VIEWS

If you want to see the definition of a view, you can retrieve the text of the view's query with the following SQL statement. Notice that I've set the SQL*Plus variable long to 5000 and reduced another SQL*Plus variable arraysize to 1 so that the buffer overflow error doesn't occur.

```
SQL> set long 5000
SQL> set arraysize 1
SQL> select text
  2  from dba_views
  3  where
  4  view_name = 'DBA_VIEWS';

TEXT
----------------------------------------------------------------
select u.name, o.name, v.textlength, v.text
from sys.obj$ o, sys.view$ v, sys.user$ u
where o.obj# = v.obj#
and o.owner# = u.user#
```

Dynamic Performance Tables

More than fifty virtual Oracle tables provide configuration and performance information about an Oracle database. By *virtual*, I mean that these tables don't actually use disk space to store their contents. They are born when the database is started and then die when the database is shut down. All of these tables begin with V$. I'll focus on the tables that you'll find most useful.

V$LOGFILE: Information About the Redo Log Files

The only way to use a SQL statement to retrieve information about a database's redo log files is by referencing V$LOGFILE. To illustrate, the following query returns the two redo log files that exist for the Personal Oracle starter database.

```
SQL> select *
  2  from v$logfile;

   GROUP# STATUS  MEMBER
--------- ------- -------------------------------------------------------
        2         C:\ORAWIN\DBS\wdblog2.ora
        1 STALE   C:\ORAWIN\DBS\wdblog1.ora
```

V$PARAMETER: The Initialization Parameter Value

V$PARAMETER can be quite useful. It provides the names and current values for all Oracle initialization parameters as shown:

```
SQL> select name, value
  2  from v$parameter
  3  order by name;

NAME                                        VALUE
------------------------------------------- -----------------------------
audit_trail                                 NONE
background_dump_dest                        %RDBMS71%\trace
blank_trimming                              FALSE
cache_size_threshold                        40
checkpoint_process                          FALSE
cleanup_rollback_entries                    20
close_cached_open_cursors                   FALSE
commit_point_strength                       1
compatible
compatible_no_recovery
control_files                               %RDBMS71_CONTROL%\ctl1.ora,
                                            %RDBMS71_ARCHIVE%\ctl1.ora
cursor_space_for_time                       FALSE
db_block_buffers                            400
db_block_checkpoint_batch                   8
db_block_lru_extended_statistics            0
db_block_lru_statistics                     FALSE
db_block_size                               2048
db_domain                                   WORLD
db_file_multiblock_read_count               8
db_file_simultaneous_writes                 4
db_files                                    32
db_name                                     oracle
dblink_encrypt_login                        FALSE
discrete_transactions_enabled               FALSE
distributed_lock_timeout                    10
distributed_recovery_connection_hold_time   0
distributed_transactions                    10
dml_locks                                   100
enqueue_resources                           155
```

```
event
fixed_date
gc_rollback_segments                     20
gc_segments                              10
gc_tablespaces                           5
global_names                             FALSE
ifile
job_queue_interval                       60
job_queue_keep_connections               FALSE
job_queue_processes                      0
license_max_sessions                     25
license_max_users                        0
license_sessions_warning                 0
log_archive_buffer_size                  127
log_archive_buffers                      4
log_archive_dest                         %RDBMS71_ARCHIVE%
log_archive_format                       ARC%S.%T
log_archive_start                        FALSE
log_buffer                               65596
log_checkpoint_interval                  1000
log_checkpoint_timeout                   0
log_checkpoints_to_alert                 FALSE
log_files                                255
log_simultaneous_copies                  0
log_small_entry_max_size                 800
max_commit_propagation_delay             90000
max_dump_file_size                       5120
max_enabled_roles                        8
max_rollback_segments                    30
mts_dispatchers
mts_listener_address                     (address=(protocol=ipc)(key=%s))
mts_max_dispatchers                      0
mts_max_servers                          0
mts_servers                              0
mts_service
nls_currency
nls_date_format
nls_date_language
nls_iso_currency
nls_language                             AMERICAN
nls_numeric_characters
nls_sort
nls_territory                            AMERICA
open_cursors                             50
open_links                               20
optimizer_comp_weight                    0
optimizer_mode                           CHOOSE
os_authent_prefix                        OPS$
os_roles                                 FALSE
parallel_default_max_instances           0
parallel_default_max_scans               0
parallel_default_scansize                100
parallel_max_servers                     5
parallel_min_servers                     0
parallel_server_idle_time                5
pre_page_sga                             FALSE
processes                                50
recovery_parallelism                     0
remote_login_passwordfile                EXCLUSIVE
```

```
remote_os_authent                          FALSE
remote_os_roles                            FALSE
resource_limit                             FALSE
rollback_segments
row_cache_cursors                          10
row_locking                                ALWAYS
sequence_cache_entries                     10
sequence_cache_hash_buckets                10
serializable                               FALSE
session_cached_cursors                     0
sessions                                   60
shared_pool_size                           3500000
single_process                             FALSE
snapshot_refresh_interval                  60
snapshot_refresh_keep_connections          FALSE
snapshot_refresh_processes                 0
sort_area_retained_size                    262144
sort_area_size                             262144
sort_mts_buffer_for_fetch_size             0
sort_read_fac                              20
sort_spacemap_size                         512
sql92_security                             FALSE
sql_trace                                  FALSE
temporary_table_locks                      60
thread                                     0
timed_statistics                           FALSE
transactions                               66
transactions_per_rollback_segment          16
user_dump_dest                             %RDBMS71%\trace

117 rows selected.
```

V$SGA: Information About the SGA

The performance table V$SGA will display rudimentary data about the SGA's size, which is the same information that SQL*DBA displays when it is used to start an Oracle instance.

```
SQL> select *
  2  from v$sga;

NAME                    VALUE
-------------------     ---------
Fixed Size                 36432
Variable Size            3846292
Database Buffers          819200
Redo Buffers               65596
```

The *ROWID*

Like SYSDATE and USER, ROWID is a pseudocolumn that returns a unique internal storage location for a table's rows. You can select ROWID from any table. Its format is

block-number.row-number.file_number

where *block-number* is an 8-digit hexadecimal number that represents the relative block number in the datafile referenced by *file-number*; *row-number* is the number of the row within its block, beginning with 1; and *file_number* is the database file number in which *block-number* resides.

To illustrate, here's how you can retrieve the ROWID for the rows in the Product table:

```
SQL> select rowid, Product_ID, Manufacturer_ID
  2  from Product;

ROWID                PRODUCT_ID    MANUFAC
-------------------  ------------  -------
00000043.0000.0002   A2001         TES801
00000043.0001.0002   A504          SEN101
00000043.0002.0002   A509          SEN101
00000043.0003.0002   A903          TES801
00000043.0004.0002   B901          TES801
00000043.0005.0002   B801          SEN101
00000043.0006.0002   C2002         MIT501
00000043.0007.0002   C2005         MIT501
00000043.0008.0002   C3002         SEN101
00000043.0009.0002   B311          TES801
00000043.000A.0002   B9310         SEN101
00000043.000B.0002   B384          TES801
00000043.000C.0002   D301          SEN101
00000043.000D.0002   TR901         TES801
00000043.000E.0002   X1000         GOL201

15 rows selected.
```

One way to distinguish between two rows that have identical values for every column is by retrieving each row's ROWID. Suppose there is a table named XYZ that has two columns, Column1 and Column2, which are both declared as numbers. We'll insert 1,000 rows into XYZ by running the following PL/SQL script:

```
SQL> create table XYZ (
  2  Column1    number,
  3  Column2    number);

Table created.

SQL>
SQL> declare
  2
  2  max_records constant int := 1000;
  3  i           int := 1;
  4
  4
  4  begin
  5
  5  for i in 1..max_records loop
  6
  6    insert into XYZ
  7      (Column1, Column2)
  8    values
  9      (i, i);
```

```
10
10  end loop;
11
11  commit;
12
12  end;
13  /

PL/SQL procedure successfully completed.

SQL> select count(*)
  2  from XYZ;

 COUNT(*)
---------
     1000
```

Now, let's add a duplicate row to XYZ to represent a bad row that you've inherited from some legacy data.

```
SQL> insert into XYZ
  2  (Column1, Column2)
  3  values
  4  (1000, 1000);

1 row created.

SQL> commit;

Commit complete.
```

Finding the duplicate rows in the table is simple.

```
SQL> select Column1, Column2
  2  from XYZ
  3  having count(*) > 1
  4  group by Column1, Column2;

  COLUMN1    COLUMN2
---------  ---------
     1000       1000

SQL> select Column1, Column2
  2  from XYZ
  3  where
  4  Column1 = 1000 and
  5  Column2 = 1000;

  COLUMN1    COLUMN2
---------  ---------
     1000       1000
     1000       1000
```

What can you do about these duplicate rows? Please ignore the fact that this table has only two columns for simplicity; in a real situation, you could encounter this problem with a table having over 100 columns. You can't delete one row without deleting the other because there isn't a way to distinguish between them—after all, they are duplicates. You can't update one of the rows to distinguish it from the other. You can identify these duplicate rows by their ROWIDs.

```
SQL> select ROWID, Column1, Column2
  2  from XYZ
  3  where
  4  Column1 = 1000 and
  5  Column2 = 1000;

ROWID               COLUMN1   COLUMN2
------------------  --------- ---------
000000E1.0020.0006    1000      1000
000000E1.0021.0006    1000      1000
```

You can delete one of the rows by referencing its ROWID in this manner:

```
SQL> delete from XYZ
  2  where
  3  rowid = '000000E1.0020.0006';

1 row deleted.

SQL> select rowid, Column1, Column2
  2  from XYZ
  3  where
  4  Column1 = 1000 and
  5  Column2 = 11000;

ROWID               COLUMN1   COLUMN2
------------------  --------- ---------
000000E1.0021.0006    1000      1000
```

STORING ROWID VALUES

In their hunger for the secrets of Oracle, some developers are elated when they learn about the ROWID pseudocolumn. The developers think they've learned a shortcut when they encounter Chapter 13 of the *Oracle7 Server Concepts* manual dealing with the rule-based optimizer and read that the fastest way to access a single row is by ROWID. "Great," the clever developer thinks. "I'll add a column to all of my tables to store ROWID and then I'll select the ROWID of each row and store the value in my new column. I'll have the fastest Oracle database on my block." There's just one problem: there is no guarantee that a row's ROWID will never change. For example, if you export the contents of a table, delete its rows, and import those rows back into the table, each row will probably have a different ROWID from what it had before. The only way you could be sure that you had the correct ROWIDs before using them would be to select every row's ROWID and use those ROWIDs in your query. If you did that, you'd be performing an additional query every time you wanted to retrieve a row! That's not counting the layer of ugly complexity you'd be adding to the database. If you remember only one thing from this book, remember this: never store ROWID as a column in a table.

Oracle Initialization Parameters

As with other components of Personal Oracle, the Oracle initialization parameters as supplied are designed to work for the majority of Personal Oracle applications. If you change the value of an initialization parameter, the change takes effect the next time the Oracle database is started. Changing an initialization parameter won't affect a database that is running. Let's look at the procedure for changing an initialization parameter.

Using Database Manager to Change an Initialization Parameter

Let me explain how you can change an Oracle initialization parameter. As an example, I'll set two parameters—SQL_TRACE and TIMED_STATISTICS—to TRUE. When enabled, these parameters create for each Oracle session a trace file that contains each SQL statement processed during that session. If you do set these parameters to TRUE, you will see some decrease in the performance of the database due to the extra processing associated with the trace files.

When you invoke Database Manager by double-clicking its icon in the Personal Oracle program group, you'll see a set of buttons on the right-hand side of the screen. One of these buttons is labeled Config. When you click the Config button, Database Manager brings up a screen titled Configure Initialization Parameters (see Figure 30.1).

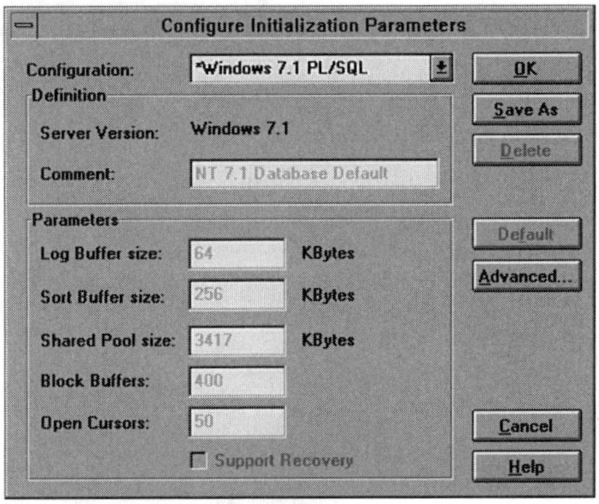

FIGURE 30.1.

The Configure Initialization Parameters screen.

You need to provide a configuration name so that you can save any modified initialization parameters. Click the Save As button and enter `initpo7` (see Figure 30.2).

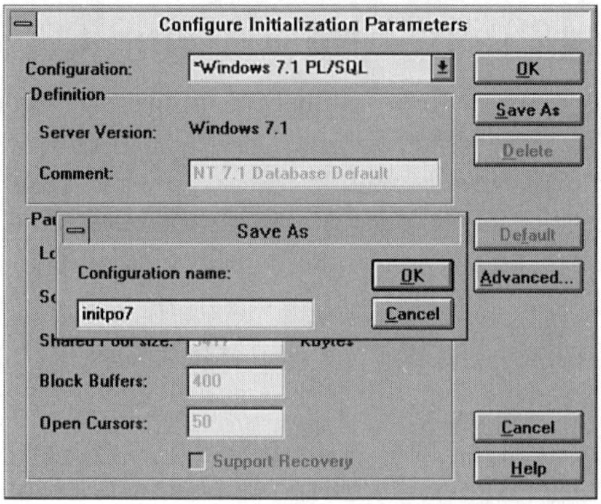

FIGURE 30.2.

Naming and saving a configuration.

When you click the OK button to save the configuration, Database Manager displays a message to inform you that any changes to the initialization parameters won't take effect until the next time the database is started (see Figure 30.3).

FIGURE 30.3.

The Database Manager message about parameter editing.

Once more, the Configure Initialization Parameters screen appears. However, this time, the configuration name is initpo7 (see Figure 30.4).

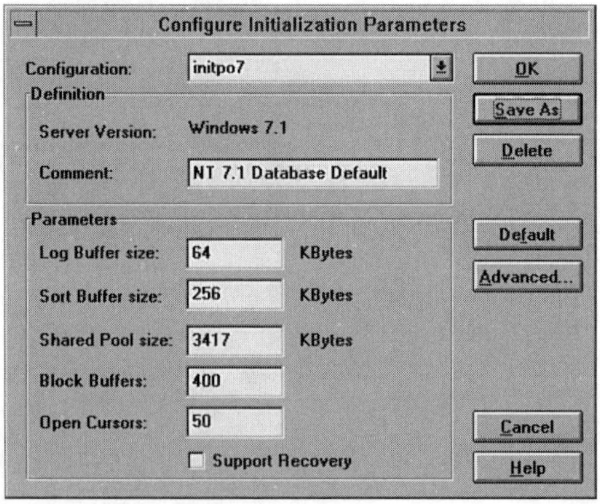

FIGURE 30.4.

Database Manager displays the configuration name.

Click the Advanced button to modify individual initialization parameters. Database Manager will display a warning message that indicates that changing the value of an initialization parameter can cause the database to cease to function (see Figure 30.5). Please take this message to heart—it's quite accurate. If you're willing to experiment, the worst thing that might happen is that you'll need to reinstall the starter database. Be sure to export your tables before you begin experimenting.

FIGURE 30.5.

Warning message about the danger of editing parameters.

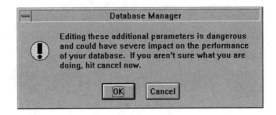

Database Manager brings up the Advanced Parameter Editing screen (see Figure 30.6). Click the down arrow on the Parameter drop-down list to display a list of all parameters. Click the SQL_TRACE parameter (see Figure 30.7).

FIGURE 30.6.

The Advanced Parameter Editing screen.

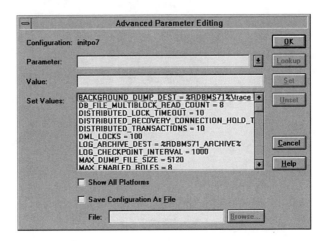

In the Value field, enter the value TRUE. Click the Set button and then the OK button (see Figure 30.8).

FIGURE 30.7.

Displaying the value of SQL_TRACE.

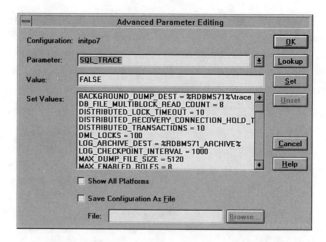

FIGURE 30.8.

Setting SQL_TRACE to TRUE.

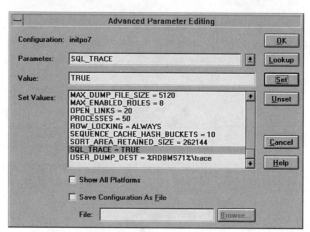

Set the TIMED_STATISTICS parameter to TRUE by following the preceding steps. Click the Set button (see Figure 30.9). The next time that the Oracle instance is started, SQL_TRACE and TIMED_STATISTICS will be set to TRUE.

At this point, you should shut down the instance and restart it for the modified initialization parameters to take effect. Once you've had practice making these changes, I recommend that you set SQL_TRACE and TIMED_STATISTICS back to FALSE if you're not interested in generating trace files for each Oracle session.

FIGURE 30.9.

*Setting
TIMED_STATISTICS
to TRUE.*

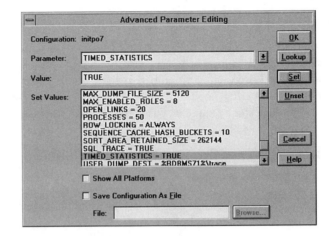

AUDIT_TRAIL

Oracle has the capability to audit a user's database activity. Events that can be audited are classified into three categories.

- ▪ Privilege level: These events are independent of a particular database object, such as establishing an Oracle connection or creating a table.
- ▪ Object level: These events pertain to a specific database object, such as the insertion of a row into table ABC.
- ▪ Statement level: These events deal with the execution of a specified SQL statement.

SQL_TRACE and TIMED_STATISTICS

If you want to be able to see the SQL statements that were processed during an Oracle session, both the SQL_TRACE and TIMED_STATISTICS parameters should be set to TRUE. By default, both of these parameters are FALSE. Setting these parameters to TRUE causes Oracle to generate a trace file for each Oracle session, which can then be processed by TKPROF, an Oracle utility. This utility is described in detail in Chapter 29.

ROLLBACK_SEGMENTS

The ROLLBACK_SEGMENTS parameter contains the names of existing rollback segments, if any, that should be activated during the startup of the Oracle database. See Chapter 25, "Managing Space," for more information on creating rollback segments.

CONTROL_FILES

If you have created a copy of the control file when the database was *cold* (not running), the only way for Oracle to use the new control file—the copy you made—is by referencing it with the CONTROL_FILES initialization parameter. The reason for having multiple control files is to protect against a single point of failure. By having another control file on a different disk drive, you've added some redundancy to the database.

Initialization Parameters That Have No Effect After Database Creation

DB_BLOCK_SIZE and DB_FILES are two Oracle initialization parameters whose values can't be changed after a database has been created.

DB_BLOCK_SIZE

The size of an Oracle block is determined by DB_BLOCK_SIZE. By default, DB_BLOCK_SIZE is set to 2048 bytes. Increasing the size of an Oracle block generally reduces the disk blocks that must be read to process a query; when the block is bigger, the header portion of each Oracle block represents a smaller percentage of the block. If you decide to create an Oracle database with a larger block size, remember to decrease the number of block buffers so that the overall size of the SGA is not too large for the available memory on your PC.

DB_FILES

MAXDATAFILES specifies the maximum number of datafiles that can exist in a database. It is specified in the CREATE DATABASE statement that creates an Oracle database (see the Oracle7 Server SQL Language Reference Manual, which can be accessed online via the Oracle7 Documentation icon in the Personal Oracle7 program group). If MAXDATAFILES isn't specified in the CREATE DATABASE statement, the initialization parameter DB_FILES is used to determine the maximum number of datafiles that can ever exist in the database. By default, DB_FILES is set to 20. When you install the Personal Oracle database, it automatically creates four datafiles, which means that you can only add another 16 files to the database. Accordingly, unless you want to recreate the database with a larger number for MAXDATAFILES, be judicious in expanding a tablespace with Database Expander or the ALTER TABLESPACE ADD statement. When you add a datafile to an existing tablespace or create a new tablespace, always add more space than you think you'll need.

Initialization Parameters That Can Be Ignored

A number of initialization parameters have no effect on a Personal Oracle database and can therefore be ignored. These include any parameter whose name begins with the following:

- SNAPSHOT_....: These parameters are concerned with snapshots, which are not supported in Personal Oracle.
- DISTRIBUTED_...: These parameters deal with the distributed database option, which isn't available in Personal Oracle.
- REMOTE_...: These parameters involve the use of the Oracle RDBMS as a server, which is not supported in Personal Oracle.
- MTS_...: These parameters are associated with the MultiThreaded Server, which cannot be used in Personal Oracle.
- PARALLEL_...: These parameters are tied to the Parallel Option, which is irrelevant for Personal Oracle because MS-DOS does not provide support for multiple processors.

Summary

In this introduction to Oracle internals, you learned the following:

- An Oracle database is composed of disk files, memory structures, and background processes.
- Besides datafiles, Oracle also uses two other types of files: a control file, which contains synchronization information about the other database files, and the redo log files, which contain Oracle blocks that have changed as a result of committed transactions.
- The System Global Area (SGA) is a large area of shared memory that serves as a cache for database blocks that have been read to satisfy SQL requests.
- Oracle maintains a set of data dictionary tables that contain information about the database objects. The preferred way to access this information is via the data dictionary views.
- When an Oracle instance is started, a set of dynamic performance tables are created to provide information about such items as the current size of the SGA.
- Another pseudocolumn provided by Oracle is ROWID. Every row can be identified by its ROWID, which contains the datafile number, relative block number, and the number of the row within its block.
- Using Database Manager, you can change the value of an initialization parameter. The change will not take effect until the next time the database is started.

31

Troubleshooting

By using examples, this chapter explains some of the Oracle errors that you might encounter when designing an Oracle database and prototyping an application. By no means is this list exhaustive. Sometimes, it is difficult to determine what error in a SQL statement or PL/SQL subprogram causes a particular Oracle error. The Oracle errors are listed in ascending order according to the Oracle error code number.

ORA-00054: resource busy and acquire with NOWAIT specified

If one Oracle user has locked a row with a SELECT FOR UPDATE and another Oracle user attempts to lock the same row with a SELECT FOR UPDATE with the NOWAIT clause, Oracle returns the ORA-00054 error message to the second user.

ORA-00901: invalid CREATE command

If Oracle cannot identify the keyword following CREATE, it returns the ORA-00901 error message. Here is an example:

```
SQL> create tablespce abc
  2  datafile 'C:\ORAWIN\DBS\wdbabc.ora'
  3  size 10m;
create tablespce abc
       *
ERROR at line 1:
ORA-00901: invalid CREATE command
```

ORA-00902: invalid datatype

For example, the following SQL statement attempts to create a column with an illegal datatype.

```
SQL> create table XYZ (
  2  record_no    number(4) primary key,
  3  time_of_day  time);
time_of_day  time)
             *
ERROR at line 3:
ORA-00902: invalid datatype
```

ORA-00903: invalid table name

Oracle returns an error when a table name does not satisfy Oracle object-naming requirements. For instance, the first letter of a table name must be a letter. Please refer to Chapter 7, "Creating and Modifying Tables," for details on Oracle's object-naming rules.

```
SQL> create table 21_day_orders (
  2  order_no    number(4),
  3  cust_no     number(4),
  4  amount      number(7,2));
create table 21_day_orders (
              *
ERROR at line 1:
ORA-00903: invalid table name
```

ORA-00904: invalid column name

Oracle returns an error when a column name does not satisfy Oracle object-naming requirements. For instance, the first letter of a column name must be a letter.

```
SQL> create table analgesic (
  2  123_compound    varchar2(30),
  3  active_ingredient  varchar2(60));
123_compound    varchar2(30),
*
ERROR at line 2:
ORA-00904: invalid column name
```

Oracle also returns this error if the specified column is not part of the table.

```
SQL> select Product_IDD from Product;
select Product_IDD from Product
              *
ERROR at line 1:
ORA-00904: invalid column name
```

ORA-00906: missing left parenthesis

If Oracle doesn't detect the left parenthesis that it expects in a SQL statement, it returns an
error message.

```
SQL> insert into Product
  2  (Product_ID, Manufacturer_ID)
  3  values
  4  'ABC999', 'MMM000');
'ABC999', 'MMM000')
*
ERROR at line 4:
ORA-00906: missing left parenthesis
```

Sometimes, Oracle returns a different error message for a missing left parenthesis. If the column list is very long, spotting the real error can be difficult. The following example is missing
a left parenthesis before Product_ID, but Oracle returns the ORA-00926 message instead:

```
SQL> insert into Product
  2  Product_ID, Manufacturer_ID)
  3  values
  4  ('ABC999', 'MMM000');
Product_ID, Manufacturer_ID)
*
ERROR at line 2:
ORA-00926: missing VALUES keyword
```

ORA-00907: missing right parenthesis

If Oracle doesn't detect the right parenthesis that it expects in a SQL statement, it returns an
error message.

```
SQL> select to_char(sysdate,'MM-DD-YY' from dual;
select to_char(sysdate,'MM-DD-YY' from dual
```

```
                                    *
ERROR at line 1:
ORA-00907: missing right parenthesis
```

In some situations you expect Oracle to report the ORA-00907 error, but it reports a different error message instead.

```
SQL> insert into Product
  2  (Product_ID, Manufacturer_ID)
  3  values
  4  ('ABC123','MMM999';
('ABC123','MMM999'
                  *
ERROR at line 4:
ORA-00917: missing comma
```

ORA-00910: specified length too long for its datatype

If the length of a particular datatype exceeds its allowed maximum length, Oracle returns an error. Here is an example:

```
SQL> create table Never_Created
  2  (Lots_of_Text varchar2(2001));
(Lots_of_Text varchar2(2001))
                           *
ERROR at line 2:
ORA-00910: specified length too long for its datatype
```

ORA-00911: invalid character

The ORA-00911 error occurs when Oracle encounters what it considers to be an invalid character. Often, the real problem is a missing character. In the following example, the error occurs due to a missing single quote.

```
SQL> select segment_name
  2  from dba_extents
  3  where
  4  segment_name like %TTT%';
segment_name like %TTT%'
                  *
ERROR at line 4:
ORA-00911: invalid character
```

ORA-00913: too many values

The ORA-00913 error can occur when the number of columns specified in an INSERT statement is less than the number of column values, as shown in this example:

```
SQL> insert into Product
  2  (Product_ID, Manufacturer_ID, Date_of_Manufacture)
  3  values
  4  ('A2003', 'SEN101', '21-JUN-91', 100.2);
values
*
```

```
ERROR at line 3:
ORA-00913: too many values
```

ORA-00917: missing comma

If Oracle is expecting a comma in a SQL statement where there isn't one, it returns the following error message:

```
SQL> insert into Product
  2  (Product_ID Manufacturer_ID)
  3  values
  4  ('BBB222', 'MNM123');
(Product_ID Manufacturer_ID)
            *
ERROR at line 2:
ORA-00917: missing comma
```

Sometimes, Oracle could return a more appropriate error message but instead returns an ORA-00917. For the following query, it would be more accurate if Oracle returned an ORA-00907 indicating that a right parenthesis is missing.

```
SQL> insert into Product
  2  (Product_ID, Manufacturer_ID)
  3  values
  4  ('ABC123','MMM999';
('ABC123','MMM999'
                 *
ERROR at line 4:
ORA-00917: missing comma
```

ORA-00918: column ambiguously defined

The ORA-00918 error occurs when two or more tables are referenced in a SQL statement. If a column that exists in more than one of the specified tables is referenced in the SQL statement without qualifying the column with its table, the column is said to be ambiguous.

```
SQL> select Employee_ID, Hire_Date, Relationship
  2  from Employee, Employee_Dependent
  3  where
  4  Employee.Employee_ID = Employee_Dependent.Employee_ID;
select Employee_ID, Hire_Date, Relationship
       *
ERROR at line 1:
ORA-00918: column ambiguously defined
```

To correct the error, qualify the column name with the assumed table name.

```
SQL> select Employee.Employee_ID, Hire_Date, Relationship
  2  from Employee, Employee_Dependent
  3  where
  4  Employee.Employee_ID = Employee_Dependent.Employee_ID;

EMPLOYEE_ID HIRE_DATE RELATIONSHIP
----------- --------- ------------------------------
       1001 10-APR-82 SPOUSE
```

```
1001 10-APR-82 CHILD
1007 22-SEP-92 SPOUSE
1007 22-SEP-92 CHILD
1007 22-SEP-92 CHILD
```

ORA-00920: invalid relational operator

If Oracle cannot identify a relational operator in a SQL statement, it issues the following message:

```
SQL> select segment_name
  2  from dba_extents
  3  where
  4  segment_name lke '%TTT%';
segment_name lke '%TTT%'
              *
ERROR at line 4:
ORA-00920: invalid relational operator
```

ORA-00921: unexpected end of SQL command

As you'd expect, Oracle returns the ORA-00921 error when you submit an incomplete SQL statement.

```
SQL> select Patient_ID, Body_Temp_Deg_F
  2  from Patient
  3  where
  4  Body_Temp_Deg_F >;
Body_Temp_Deg_F >
                 *
ERROR at line 4:
ORA-00921: unexpected end of SQL command
```

However, Oracle won't always return the ORA-00921 error for an incomplete SQL statement; it depends on where the statement terminates. For example, the following query is rejected with a different error message:

```
SQL> select Patient_ID, Body_Temp_Deg_F
  2  from Patient
  3  where
  4  Body_Temp_Deg_F ;
Body_Temp_Deg_F
               *
ERROR at line 4:
ORA-00920: invalid relational operator
```

ORA-00932: inconsistent datatypes

Oracle returns the ORA-00932 error if you apply an operator on a column whose datatype cannot be used with the operator. For example, the following query tries to apply the LIKE operator against a LONG column. What you get is a somewhat misleading error message—you might expect that Oracle would return ORA-00997: illegal use of LONG datatype.

```
SQL> create table table_with_long   (
  2  record_no     number(4),
  3  description   long);

Table created.

SQL> select record_no
  2  from table_with_long
  3  where
  4  description like '%ABC%';
description like '%ABC%'
*
ERROR at line 4:
ORA-00932: inconsistent datatypes
```

ORA-00934: group function is not allowed here

A query cannot reference a group function in the WHERE or GROUP BY clause, or else Oracle will return the following error message:

```
SQL> select Product_ID
  2  from Portland_Product
  3  where
  4  Initial_Retail_Value > Avg(Initial_Retail_Value);
Initial_Retail_Value > Avg(Initial_Retail_Value)
                       *
ERROR at line 4:
ORA-00934: group function is not allowed here
```

To compare a column value with a group function, you can use a group function in a subquery as shown:

```
SQL> select Product_ID
  2  from Portland_Product
  3  where
  4  Initial_Retail_Value > (select Avg(Initial_Retail_Value)
     from Portland_Product);

PRODUCT_ID
------------
C3002
```

ORA-00936: missing expression

The ORA-00936 error occurs when Oracle expects to see an expression. In this query, a comma follows the description column, but no more columns or expressions are in the select list.

```
SQL> select product_id, manufacturer_id, description,
  2  from product;
from product
*
ERROR at line 2:
ORA-00936: missing expression
```

In a way, the ORA-00936 error is sometimes the opposite of ORA-00917: missing comma—too many commas.

ORA-00937: not a single-group group function

A query's select list cannot contain a column and a group function unless the column is referenced in the GROUP BY clause. The following query illustrates the problem:

```
SQL> select Product_ID, Avg(Current_Used_Value)
  2  from Product;
select Product_ID, Avg(Current_Used_Value)
       *
ERROR at line 1:
ORA-00937: not a single-group group function
```

If you include the column in the GROUP BY clause, Oracle processes the query.

```
SQL> select Product_ID, Avg(Current_Used_Value)
  2  from Product
  3  group by Product_ID;

PRODUCT_ID   AVG(CURRENT_USED_VALUE)
------------ -----------------------
A903
B311
B384
B801
C2002                         110.4
D301
TR901

7 rows selected.
```

ORA-00938: not enough arguments for function

Oracle returns the ORA-00938 error when a SQL statement calls a function with an insufficient number of arguments. For instance, the DECODE function requires at least three arguments.

```
SQL> select decode('ABC')
  2  from user_tables;
select decode('ABC')
       *
ERROR at line 1:
ORA-00938: not enough arguments for function
```

ORA-00942: table or view does not exist

The ORA-00942 error usually occurs because the table or view has been misspelled. Oracle also returns this error if the table or view exists but the user has no object privileges for the table or view.

ORA-00947: not enough values

The ORA-00947 error can occur when the number of columns specified in an INSERT statement is greater than the number of column values, as shown in the following example:

```
SQL> insert into Product
  2  (Product_ID, Manufacturer_ID, Date_of_Manufacture)
  3  values
  4  ('A2003', 'SEN101');
values
*
ERROR at line 3:
ORA-00947: not enough values
```

ORA-00979: not a GROUP BY expression

Oracle returns the ORA-00979 error if a column in a query's select list is contained in a GROUP BY clause and another column in the select list is not.

```
SQL> select Product_ID, Current_Used_Value
  2  from Product
  3  Group by Product_ID;
select Product_ID, Current_Used_Value
                   *
ERROR at line 1:
ORA-00979: not a GROUP BY expression
```

Once all columns in the select list also appear in the GROUP BY clause, Oracle processes the query.

```
SQL> select Product_ID, Current_Used_Value
  2  from Product
  3  Group by Product_ID, Current_Used_Value;

PRODUCT_ID    CURRENT_USED_VALUE
------------  ------------------
A903
B311
B384
B801
C2002                      110.4
D301
TR901

7 rows selected.
```

ORA-00997: illegal use of LONG datatype

Certain operations cannot be performed on a column whose datatype is LONG. One example is the use of a subquery with the INSERT statement in which a column in the select list is a LONG column.

```
SQL> desc Table_With_Long
 Name                              Null?    Type
 -------------------------------- -------- ----
```

```
RECORD_NO                               NUMBER(4)
DESCRIPTION                             LONG

SQL> desc Another_Table_With_Long
 Name                           Null?    Type
 ------------------------------ -------- ----
 REC_NO                                  NUMBER(4)
 COMMENTS                                LONG

SQL> insert into Another_Table_With_Long
  2  (Rec_No, Comments)
  3  select Record_No, Description
  4  from Table_With_Long;
select Record_No, Description
                *
ERROR at line 3:
ORA-00997: illegal use of LONG datatype
```

ORA-01031: insufficient privileges

The ORA-01031 error occurs when a user has been granted at least one object privilege associated with a table or view but has not been granted the privilege specified in the SQL statement. To illustrate, Oracle user FRAYED_WIRES grants the select privilege on the Security_Price table to Oracle user HGOMEZ. When HGOMEZ tries to update the Security_Price table, Oracle returns the error.

```
SQL> grant select on security_price to hgomez;

Grant succeeded.

SQL> connect hgomez/hgomez
Connected.
SQL> select * from frayed_wires.security_price;

COMPANY             SYMBO LAST_QTR_EPS
------------------- ----- ------------
                    ABC          -.58
                    ACME         1.81
                    ZGEGE        2.81

SQL> update frayed_wires.security_price
  2  set
  3  last_qtr_eps = 2.22
  4  where
  5  symbol = 'ABC';
update frayed_wires.security_price
              *
ERROR at line 1:
ORA-01031: insufficient privileges
```

Once the select privilege on the Security_Price table has been revoked from HGOMEZ, Oracle returns an ORA-00942, preventing HGOMEZ from determining whether the table exists or he has no object privileges for the table.

```
SQL> revoke select on security_price from hgomez;
```

```
Revoke succeeded.

SQL> connect hgomez/hgomez
Connected.
SQL> select * from frayed_wires.security_price;
select * from frayed_wires.security_price
                           *
ERROR at line 1:
ORA-00942: table or view does not exist
```

ORA-01400: primary key or mandatory (NOT NULL) column is missing or NULL during insert

You get the ORA-01400 error when inserting a row if you don't supply a value for a mandatory column.

```
SQL> insert into Vendor
  2  (Company_Name, Street_Address)
  3  values
  4  ('ACME CO.','123 MAIN ST.');
insert into Vendor
            *
ERROR at line 1:
ORA-01400: mandatory (NOT NULL) column is missing or NULL during insert
```

ORA-01401: inserted value too large for column

If you try to assign a character string—whether it is a constant or column expression—and its length exceeds the targeted column, Oracle returns an error message.

```
SQL> insert into Portland_Product
  2  (Product_ID, Manufacturer_ID, Replacement_Product)
  3  values
  4  ('ABC100','MMM233','Preamplifier manufactured by Bovine Products, 1993');
insert into Portland_Product
            *
ERROR at line 1:
ORA-01401: inserted value too large for column
```

ORA-01403: no data found

The ORA-01403 message really isn't an error at all. Instead, you can consider it an informative message that is equivalent to the predefined PL/SQL exception NO_MORE_DATA.

ORA-01407: cannot update mandatory (NOT NULL) column to NULL

The ORA-01407 error occurs if an UPDATE statement tries to set the value of a mandatory column to NULL.

```
SQL> update Product
  2    set
  3    Product_ID = NULL
  4    where
  5    Current_Used_Value is NULL;
update Product
       *
ERROR at line 1:
ORA-01407: cannot update mandatory (NOT NULL) column to NULL
```

ORA-01408: such column list already indexed

If you try to create an index on a table that already has an index based on the same list of columns, Oracle returns an error. Here is an example:

```
SQL> create index Portfolio_SS_SIC_Code
  2    on Portfolio (Stock_Symbol, SIC_Code);

Index created.

SQL> create index Portfolio_Another_Index
  2    on Portfolio (Stock_Symbol, SIC_Code);
on Portfolio (Stock_Symbol, SIC_Code)
                  *
ERROR at line 2:
ORA-01408: such column list already indexed
```

However, Oracle creates another index if an additional column is added to the index's column list, as shown:

```
SQL> create index Portfolio_Different_Index
  2    on Portfolio (Stock_Symbol, SIC_Code, Price);

Index created.
```

ORA-01410: invalid ROWID

If you don't specify a ROWID in the proper format, Oracle returns the ORA-01410 error message. Here is an example:

```
SQL> select Product_ID
  2    from Product
  3    where rowid = '0.00010C3.0004.0001';
ERROR:
ORA-01410: invalid ROWID
```

Even if you specify the correct format for a ROWID but there is no row with the specified ROWID, Oracle returns the same error message.

```
SQL> select Product_ID
  2    from Product
  3    where rowid = '000010C3.0004.0002';
ERROR:
ORA-01410: invalid ROWID
```

```
no rows selected

SQL> select Product_ID
  2  from Product
  3  where rowid = '000010C3.0004.0001';

PRODUCT_ID
------------
A903
```

ORA-01449: column contains NULL values; cannot alter to NOT NULL

The ORA-01449 error occurs when you try to alter a table to make a column mandatory but at least one row in the table has a null value for that column.

```
SQL> alter table Product
  2  modify
  3  (Replacement_Product varchar2(30) not null);
(Replacement_Product varchar2(30) not null)
 *
ERROR at line 3:
ORA-01449: column contains NULL values; cannot alter to NOT NULL
```

Once each row has a value for Replacement_Product, the column can be altered to be mandatory.

```
SQL> update Product
  2  set Replacement_Product = 'X1000';

7 rows updated.

SQL> alter table Product
  2  modify
  3  (Replacement_Product varchar2(30) not null);

Table altered.
```

ORA-01452: cannot CREATE UNIQUE INDEX; duplicate keys found

Oracle return the ORA-01452 error if you attempt to create a unique index on a set of columns whose values aren't unique.

```
SQL> select * from Dup_Patient;

PATIEN BODY_TEMP_DEG_F I
------ --------------- -
R4321              104 Y
GG9999           107.6
AB1234             116
AB1234           102.2

SQL> create unique index Dup_Patient_PK
```

```
 2  on Dup_Patient (Patient_ID);
on Dup_Patient (Patient_ID)
    *
ERROR at line 2:
ORA-01452: cannot CREATE UNIQUE INDEX; duplicate keys found
```

ORA-01453: SET TRANSACTION must be first statement of transaction

The ORA-01453 error occurs when you issue the SET TRANSACTION statement after some other SQL statement, for instance:

```
SQL> rollback;

Rollback complete.

SQL> select sysdate from dual;

SYSDATE
---------
30-JUN-95

SQL> set transaction read only;
set transaction read only
*
ERROR at line 1:
ORA-01453: SET TRANSACTION must be first statement of transaction
```

If you issue the SET TRANSACTION statement directly after a commit, rollback, or new Oracle session, it will be successfully processed.

```
SQL> rollback;

Rollback complete.

SQL> set transaction read only;

Transaction set.
```

ORA-01481: invalid number format model

Oracle returns the ORA-01481 error when a number format model contains undefined characters. For instance, the following query uses the TO_CHAR function to convert Initial_Retail_Value to a character string. However, the number format model accidentally contains an F.

```
SQL> select to_char(Initial_Retail_Value, '$9F9.99')
 2  from Product;
ERROR:
ORA-01481: invalid number format model
```

ORA-01722: invalid number

Oracle issues the ORA-01722 error when a numeric value is illegal—whether it's a literal or a column value. Here is an example:

```
SQL> select * from Inventory;

MODEL_NO    RETAIL_PRICE OLD_RETAIL
----------  ------------ ----------
SOFABED                  350.00
COUCH                    740
END TABLE                2A2.00

SQL> update Inventory
  2  set
  3  Retail_Price = to_number(Old_Retail_Price);
Retail_Price = to_number(Old_Retail_Price)
                    *
ERROR at line 3:
ORA-01722: invalid number
```

Once you correct the bad value, the UPDATE statement is successfully processed.

```
SQL> update Inventory
  2  set
  3  Old_Retail_Price = '252.00'
  4  where
  5  Old_Retail_Price = '2A2.00';

1 row updated.

SQL> update Inventory
  2  set
  3  Retail_Price = to_number(Old_Retail_Price);

3 rows updated.
```

ORA-04091: table name is mutating, trigger/function may not see it

The ORA-04091 error typically occurs when a database trigger issues a query against a table that was modified within the transaction. For example, trigger tab1_Update_Before is fired when an UPDATE is executed against tab; in the trigger body, a row is inserted into table tab2. The INSERT causes trigger tab2_Insert_Before to fire; within its trigger body, an UPDATE statement contains a subquery that selects from tab1. However, tab1 is a mutating table, and the UPDATE statement fails with error ORA-04091.

```
SQL> create or replace trigger tab1_Update_Before before
  2  update on tab1
  3  for each row
  4
  4  declare
  5
  5  begin
  6
  6  insert into tab2
```

```
 7  (col2)
 8  values
 9  (:old.col1);
10
10  end;
11  /
```

Trigger created.

```
SQL>
SQL> create or replace trigger tab2_Insert_Before before
  2  insert on tab2
  3  for each row
  4
  4  declare
  5
  5  begin
  6
  6  update tab2
  7  set
  8  col2 = 27
  9  where
 10  col2 in (select col1 from tab1);
 11
 11  end;
 12  /
```

Trigger created.

```
SQL> update tab1
  2  set
  3  col1 = 22;
update tab1
        *
ERROR at line 1:
ORA-04091: table FRAYED_WIRES.TAB1 is mutating, trigger/function may not see it
ORA-06512: at line 3
ORA-04088: error during execution of trigger 'FRAYED_WIRES.TAB2_INSERT_BEFORE'
ORA-06512: at line 3
ORA-04088: error during execution of trigger 'FRAYED_WIRES.TAB1_UPDATE_BEFORE'
```

ORA-04092: cannot COMMIT or ROLLBACK in a trigger

Oracle issues the ORA-04092 message if a trigger tries to execute a COMMIT or ROLLBACK. Notice that Oracle issues the error message when the trigger fires, not when it is created.

```
SQL> create or replace trigger Shipment_Ins_Before before
  2  insert on Shipment
  3  for each row
  4  declare
  5
  5  begin
  6
  6  :new.Manual_Check := 'Y';
  7
  7  commit;
```

```
8
8  end;
9  /
```

Trigger created.

```
SQL> insert into Shipment
  2  (Shipment_ID)
  3  values
  4  ('ABCD1000');
insert into Shipment
*
ERROR at line 1:
ORA-04092: cannot COMMIT in a trigger
ORA-06512: at line 2
ORA-04088: error during execution of trigger 'FRAYED_WIRES.SHIPMENT_INS_BEFORE'
```

Oracle also returns the ORA-04092 error if a trigger calls a stored procedure, function, or package subprogram in which a COMMIT or ROLLBACK is issued.

ORA-04093: references to columns of type LONG are not allowed in triggers

You cannot reference a LONG column in a database trigger. This restriction is just one of several restrictions regarding the use of LONG columns in SQL. Please refer to Chapter 9, "The Oracle Datatypes," for more details on the use of the LONG datatype.

```
SQL> create or replace trigger Table_With_Long_Ins_Before before
  2  insert on Table_With_Long
  3  for each row
  4
  4  declare
  5
  5  begin
  6
  6  :new.Description := 'This is a string literal assigned to a LONG column.';
  7
  7  end;
  8  /
create or replace trigger Table_With_Long_Ins_Before before
                                      *
ERROR at line 1:
ORA-04093: references to columns of type LONG are not allowed in triggers
```

A

Glossary

Active set   The set of rows that satisfy a cursor's query. The active set is assembled when the OPEN CURSOR statement is executed.

Archive logging   The process of making a copy of a redo log file when it has filled with changed blocks.

Attribute   A characteristic or quality associated with an entity. Attributes are defined in a logical data model and implemented as columns.

Auditing   The recording of a user's database activity into the AUD$ table. Auditing is controlled with the AUDIT ON statement and enabled by setting the AUDIT_TRAIL initialization parameter to TRUE.

BLOB   A Binary Large Object. BLOBs can be stored in a column that is declared as a LONG RAW.

Block   The basic building block of an Oracle database. By default, the size of a block is 2048 bytes. The block size can't be changed once a database has been created.

Built-in function   One of the predefined functions supplied by Oracle that can be referenced in SQL statements.

CLOSE CURSOR   The action of closing a cursor and releasing any resources associated with the cursor.

Cluster   A group of two or more tables whose rows are stored together based on the common column values by which the tables are related.

Column   An attribute or characteristic of the entity on which a table is based.

Commit   The SQL statement that permanently records row changes to the database file. Once a transaction is committed, all users can see the changes resulting from the transaction.

Concurrency   The capability of the Oracle database to support the activity of multiple users. Oracle provides concurrency by enabling one user to view the contents of a table while another user is modifying the contents of the same table.

Constraint   A mechanism that ensures that the values of a column or set of columns satisfy a declared condition.

Control file   A small binary file that contains the names of the database files. The control file also maintains a sequence control number that synchronizes the database files.

Correlated subquery   A query that is referenced in the WHERE clause of a SELECT statement.

Cost-based optimizer   An Oracle software component that uses statistical information about the contents of a table and related indexes to determine the lowest cost plan for retrieving rows for a query.

CURRVAL   The current value of a sequence.

Cursor   A window into the rows returned by a query.

Data dictionary   The set of tables that Oracle uses to maintain information about database objects such as tables, indexes, columns, views, extents, segments, tablespaces, and so on.

Data dictionary table   A table used by Oracle to maintain information about its own database objects.

Data dictionary view   A view that presents data dictionary information in a more comprehensible format.

Database Expander   A Windows-based Database Administration Tool that displays the usage of space in a tablespace and allows a tablespace to be expanded by some increment.

Database file   An operating system file whose internal structure is managed by Oracle and in which Oracle objects are stored.

Database link   An Oracle object used to point to a specific Oracle user in a remote Oracle database.

Database Manager   A Windows-based Database Administration Tool that is used to start up and shut down an Oracle instance. Database Manager can also be used to change the value of an initialization parameter.

Database shutdown   The process of shutting down an Oracle instance in an orderly manner, terminating the Oracle background processes, and releasing other resources such as the SGA.

Database startup   The process of starting an Oracle instance by initiating the Oracle background processes and allocating memory for the SGA.

Datafile   An operating system file that is dedicated to a tablespace for storing table, index, and cluster data.

DATE   An Oracle datatype that stores date and time information in an internal format. A DATE column uses seven bytes of storage. Oracle provides several built-in functions for manipulating and converting DATE columns and expressions. A DATE column contains a value for century, year, month, day, hour, minute, and second.

DECLARE CURSOR   A SQL statement that is used to declare a cursor using a SELECT statement. The DECLARE CURSOR statement must be executed before an OPEN CURSOR statement.

DELETE   A SQL statement that is used to delete selected rows from a table based on any specified criteria.

Distributed database   A database whose tables are contained in more than one Oracle instance running on separate machines.

Distributed option   An optional component of the Oracle RDBMS that supports the use of distributed queries, distributed transactions, snapshots, and replicated tables.

Domain   The underlying type associated with an attribute. Many attributes may belong to the same domain. For example, the attributes Distance_Between_Cities and Distance_Travelled could belong to the same domain—Distance_Km.

Dynamic performance table   A table that is created when an Oracle instance is started. Because it is dynamic, this table doesn't use any permanent storage. Dynamic performance tables provide statistics on the current performance of an Oracle instance, such as the names of connected users, values for initialization parameters, and many other measures.

Export   A Windows-based Database Administration Tool that copies tables to a proprietary, binary file. Export files work in conjunction with the Import tool.

Entity   A person, place, thing, or concept that possesses a set of characteristics.

Entity-relationship model   A data modeling methodology in which an entity (a relation or table) is related to another entity via a foreign key/primary key relationship.

Exception handler   The set of PL/SQL statements that are executed when a specified exception is raised.

Extent   A group of contiguous data blocks that are allocated for table, index, or cluster storage.

FETCH   The SQL statement that retrieves rows from a cursor's active set.

Foreign key   An attribute whose value, if not null, must exist as the primary key value for another entity.

Hash cluster   A mechanism for storing table data based on a cluster key value. A hash function is used to quickly access rows whose cluster key is a specified value.

Import   A Windows-based Database Administration Tool that reads the contents of an export file. The Import program can load tables and other database objects previously exported with the Export utility.

Index   A database object used to improve query performance. An index consists of one or more of a table's columns that are organized as a B*-tree. A unique index is used to enforce a primary key or unique constraint. A nonunique index is only used for performance purposes.

Initialization parameter   A parameter whose value is read when an Oracle instance is started. Initialization parameters affect the performance of an Oracle instance and the resources it requires.

INSERT   The SQL statement that creates a new row in a table.

INTERSECT   A SQL operator that returns the rows that are common between two sets of rows.

JOIN   A query in which column values are retrieved from more than one table.

Lexicon   The pool of legal values associated with a domain. For example, the lexicon for the domain Days_of_the_Week is Sunday through Saturday.

Lock   A mechanism that reserves an Oracle resource for the sole use of a transaction or operation. Most locks are automatically issued by the Oracle RDBMS in response to SQL statements. It is possible to explicitly lock a set of rows using the SELECT FOR UPDATE statement.

LONG   A column datatype that can store up to 2 GB of characters. There are several restrictions on the use of LONG columns. A table can have only a single LONG column. You can't use any of Oracle's built-in functions with a LONG column.

LONG RAW   A column datatype that can store up to 2 GB of binary data. The LONG RAW datatype has the same restrictions as the LONG datatype. A LONG RAW column is commonly used for storing BLOBs.

Mandatory column   A column for which the NOT NULL constraint is defined. A mandatory column may never have a null value assigned to it.

MINUS   A SQL operator that returns the rows that exist in one set of rows but not in a second set of rows.

Mutating table   A table whose contents are modified by the execution of a database trigger.

NEXTVAL   A pseudocolumn that is used to retrieve the next value of a sequence.

Null   A keyword used to describe a value that is unknown or not applicable.

Object Manager   A Windows-based Database Administration Tool used to create and modify tables. Object Manager uses a spreadsheet; each row of the spreadsheet is used to specify a table's column.

Object privilege   The set of privileges that can be granted on a table, view, and other database objects. The object privileges that can be granted to a role or user depend upon the object type. For example, the object privileges for a table are SELECT, INSERT, UPDATE, DELETE, ALTER, INDEX, and REFERENCES.

OPEN CURSOR   The PL/SQL statement that parses the query associated with the cursor and executes it. The qualified rows are referred to as the active set.

Optimizer   A component of the Oracle RDBMS that calculates the most efficient execution plan for a query. There are two types of optimizers—a rule-based optimizer and a cost-based optimizer.

Oracle instance   A set of background processes and SGA executing against a set of Oracle database files.

Outer join   A variation of a table join. If the outer join operator is applied to a column, any rows that don't satisfy the join condition are returned with null values.

Package   A set of related procedures, functions, and other structures that are stored in an Oracle database. A package consists of an interface specification that is visible to a caller and a package body whose statements are not visible to a caller.

Package body   The PL/SQL statements that implement the logic of a package specification.

Parallel query option   An Oracle RDBMS option that breaks a query into subtasks, which are allocated to separate processors.

Parallel server   An Oracle RDBMS option that allows multiple Oracle instances to access the same database files.

Password Manager   The Personal Oracle utility used to change the database password.

PL/SQL   A set of procedural language extensions to the Oracle SQL language. Database triggers, procedures, functions, and packages are written in PL/SQL.

PL/SQL block   A PL/SQL program unit consisting of a declaration section, block, and an optional exception section.

Precompiler   An Oracle product that enables a developer to embed SQL statements in a 3GL program such as COBOL or C. An Oracle precompiler for the specific language translates the embedded SQL statements into Oracle library calls so that the precompiled program can be compiled and linked into an executable program.

Primary key   The set of attributes that uniquely identify a row.

Profile   A set of resource limits that can be assigned to a database role or user.

Pseudocolumn   A built-in value (or function without arguments) that returns a specific piece of information by querying a table—usually DUAL. For instance, SYSDATE returns the current date and time, regardless of the specified table.

Read consistency   The Oracle RDBMS will always return a set of data that is consistent within a single statement. For example, suppose a table contains three columns: Product_ID, Quantity_Sold, Quantity_Returned. If you query the table to retrieve Quantity_Sold, Quantity_Returned, and Quantity_Sold + Quantity_Returned, read consistency guarantees that Quantity_Sold + Quantity_Returned is equal to Quantity_Sold added to Quantity_Returned—for every row.

Read-only transaction   A transaction that guarantees read consistency for more than one SQL statement.

Redo log file   A file that contains any data blocks that have been modified as a result of database transactions. Every Oracle database has at least two redo log files. Oracle writes to the redo log files in a round-robin fashion.

Relation   The theoretical term for a table. A relation consists of attributes (columns) and tuples (rows).

Rollback   The act of undoing the changes that have been made by a transaction.

Rollback segment   A storage element that contains any table changes that have been made before a transaction has been committed.

ROWID   A row identifier. Every row has a unique ROWID that corresponds to the block number, file number, and relative row number.

ROWNUM   A pseudocolumn that indicates the order of the retrieved row. The ROWNUM for the first returned row is 1. ROWNUM can be used to limit the number of rows that are returned by a query.

Rule-based optimizer   The Oracle optimizer that uses the query syntax and the existence of indexes to determine the best execution plan for a query.

Savepoint   An interim point in a transaction. A complex transaction may break down the changes made by the transaction into subtasks. A subtask can be denoted by the declaration of a savepoint. If a subtask is unsuccessful, the transaction can be rolled back to a previous savepoint without losing all of the changes made by the transaction.

Segment   The set of extents that have been allocated to a particular Oracle object. Segment types include data, index, cluster, hash, and rollback.

SELECT   The SQL statement that retrieves rows from a table or view. The SELECT statement has several clauses that enable the user to specify the query criteria. SELECT statements may also be combined with operators such as INTERSECT, MINUS, and UNION.

SELECT FOR UPDATE   A SQL statement that applies a share-row lock on the rows identified by the SELECT statement. SELECT FOR UPDATE is used to prevent two users from changing the same row at the same time.

Sequence   A database object that provides a unique, monotonically increasing (or decreasing) number. A sequence is useful for creating customer IDs and other unique identifiers.

Session   The activities that are performed by an Oracle user from the time an Oracle connection is established until the user disconnects, or logs off, from the database.

Session Manager   A Windows-based Database Administration Tool that displays the names of each Oracle user who is currently connected to an Oracle instance.

SGA   See **System Global Area**.

Shared pool   The area of the SGA that contains the data dictionary cache and shared parsed SQL statements.

Snapshot   A mechanism in which a local copy of a table is periodically updated from a master table residing in a remote database. A snapshot may be refreshed at a specified interval.

SQLCODE   A built-in PL/SQL variable that contains the Oracle error code that resulted from the last executable statement. If SQLCODE is equal to 0, the previous statement was successfully executed.

SQLERRM   A built-in PL/SQL variable that contains the error message corresponding to SQLCODE.

SQL*DBA   A Windows-based Database Administration Tool that can be used to start up or shut down an Oracle database. All SQL statements can be issued through SQL*DBA. SQL*DBA can also be used to create a new database.

SQL*Loader   A Windows-based Database Administration Tool that loads data from flat files into one or more tables. SQL*Loader can load data from fixed or variable-length records. It can apply SQL functions to modify loaded data or restrict loading to records that satisfy specific criteria.

SQL*Net   An Oracle component that allows a client application to establish a remote connection with an Oracle database server. There are two versions of SQL*Net—V1 and V2.

SQL*Plus   A Windows-based Database Administration Tool that interactively processes SQL statements. SQL*Plus can process a script containing a set of SQL statements.

Stored function   A PL/SQL function that is parsed and stored in the Oracle database. A stored function can be called from a PL/SQL subprogram.

Stored procedure   A PL/SQL procedure that is parsed and stored in an Oracle database. A stored procedure can be called from SQL*Plus, a PL/SQL subprogram, and a client application (depending on the client application development tool).

Subquery   A SELECT statement that is referenced in an INSERT, UPDATE, or DELETE statement. A SELECT statement may also contain a correlated subquery.

Synonym   A pointer to an Oracle user and table or view. A synonym may either be private or public. A private synonym is only seen by its owner. A public synonym is seen by all Oracle users.

SYS user   The Oracle account that owns the Oracle data dictionary.

SYSDATE   A predefined value or pseudocolumn that always contains the current date and time to the nearest second. SYSDATE can be assigned to any column whose datatype is DATE.

System Global Area   The System Global Area (SGA) is a shared memory structure that includes data block buffers that function as a cache, a shared SQL area for storing parsed SQL statements, and a data dictionary cache.

System privilege   A privilege granted to a role or user that gives the grantee the ability to execute a particular SQL statement. An example of a system privilege is the CREATE ANY TABLE privilege, which gives the recipient the ability to create a table.

SYSTEM user   An Oracle account that owns tables and other database objects used by Oracle application development tools such as forms and reports. Unlike the SYS user, the SYSTEM user doesn't own any of the data dictionary tables.

Table   The fundamental element of a relational database. Every table has a name and set of one or more columns. Each column has a name and datatype. Once a table has been created, rows may be inserted into it.

Tablespace   A logical construct that consists of one or more operating system files referred to as datafiles. When a table, index, cluster, or rollback segment is created, its storage is assigned to a tablespace.

TKPROF   An Oracle utility program that interprets trace files to produce a list of the SQL statements and related statistics that were processed during an Oracle session.

Transaction   A set of database changes that represent some external event. A transaction consists of those changes that have been made either since the beginning of an Oracle session or since the last COMMIT or ROLLBACK was issued.

Trigger   A PL/SQL block that executes when a SQL statement—INSERT, UPDATE, or DELETE—is executed against a table.

TRUNCATE   An Oracle SQL statement that deletes the entire contents of a table. Because it doesn't write any changes to a rollback segment, the TRUNCATE TABLE statement cannot be rolled back.

Two-phase commit   The mechanism for performing distributed transactions in which the transaction is committed in two phases. Each node commits its changes. If each node has acknowledged that its commit was successful, the distributed transaction is committed on all nodes.

UNION   A SQL operator that returns the distinct rows from two or more sets of rows.

UNION ALL   A SQL operator that returns the rows, including duplicates, from two or more sets of rows.

UPDATE   A SQL statement that modifies the column values of a set of rows in a table based on specified criteria.

User Manager   A Windows-based Database Administration Tool that creates a new Oracle user, alters an existing user by granting or revoking roles to that user, and drops an existing user.

VARCHAR2   An Oracle datatype that stores character data. A column defined as VARCHAR2 may store up to 2000 characters.

View   A stored query or virtual table that is based upon one or more base tables.

B

Using Personal Oracle7 and Oracle Developer/2000

This appendix demonstrates how the components of Oracle Developer/2000 work with Personal Oracle7 as a self-contained development environment. I will illustrate the use of the principal Developer/2000 tools:

- Forms 4.5—a client application development tool that is deployed on Windows, Macintosh, and Motif.
- Reports 2.5—an industrial-strength report writer that also is deployed on Windows, Macintosh, and Motif. Reports 2.5 also contains a PL/SQL engine for building sophisticated report triggers.
- Procedure Builder—a tool for creating and managing database stored procedures and functions.
- Browser—an ad hoc query tool for casual Oracle users.

Forms 4.5

Forms 4.5 is the best choice as an Oracle applications development tool if your requirements include the following:

- Support for multiple client platforms: PCs, Macs, and UNIX workstations
- Support for Oracle Designer/2000 CASE tools
- Integration with other Developer/2000 tools such as Reports and Browser
- Tight integration with the Oracle database via packages and stored procedures and functions
- Exclusive use with Oracle databases
- Natural upgrade path for existing library of previous Oracle forms applications (SQL*Forms 2.3/3.0)

To demonstrate some of the basic capabilities of the Forms 4.5 Designer, we'll walk through the steps involved in building a simple form.

When you invoke the Forms 4.5 Designer, it displays the Object Navigator (see Figure B.1). This graphical tool simplifies the process of locating an object to view or modify its parameters.

Before you can do anything useful with the Designer, you must connect to an Oracle database. In this example, you'll connect to Personal Oracle7. In the File menu, select the Connect option. The Designer displays a Connect dialog box (see Figure B.2). Enter a valid Oracle username and password but leave the Database field blank. Click the Connect button to establish the connection to Personal Oracle7.

FIGURE B.1.
The Object Navigator.

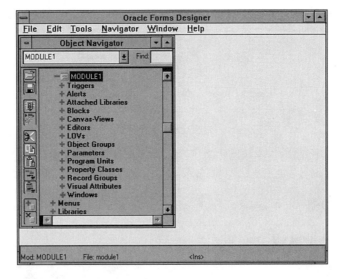

FIGURE B.2.
Connecting to Personal Oracle7.

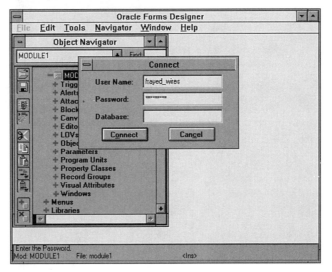

After the Oracle connection has been established, select the New Block option from the Tools menu. The Designer displays a window with four tabbed folders—General, Items, Layout, and Master/Detail. On the General folder, the Base Table is set to <NONE> (see Figure B.3). Click the Select button to the right of <NONE> to choose a base table for the block.

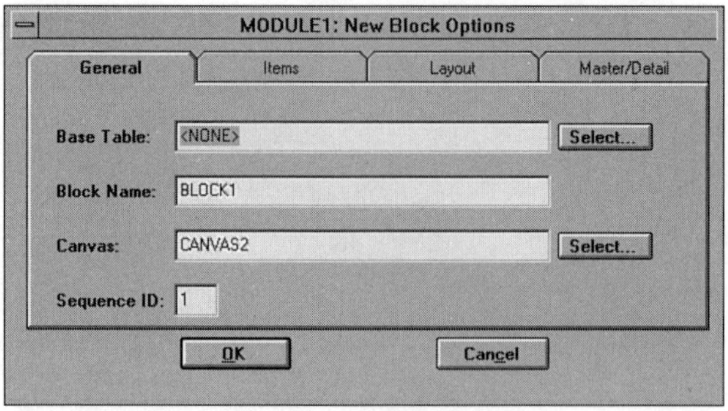

FIGURE B.3.

Creating a new block.

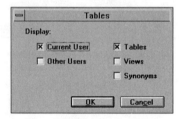

The Designer displays a Tables window in which you can choose whether all tables will be displayed or only those owned by the current user (see Figure B.4). Use the default settings and click the OK button.

FIGURE B.4.

Choosing options for displayed tables.

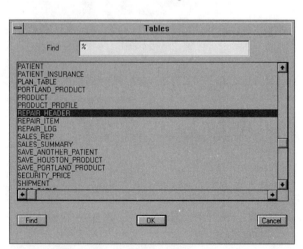

In our example, the list shows all of the tables owned by FRAYED_WIRES. Scroll down to the desired table, highlight it, and click the OK button (see Figure B.5).

FIGURE B.5.

Selecting a new block's base table.

After you've selected a base table, the Forms 4.5 Designer displays the new block's base table. Also, the name of the block is automatically set to the base table name (see Figure B.6).

FIGURE B.6.

New block options with base table.

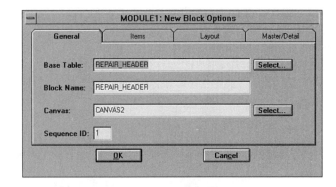

Once you've chosen a base table, you can select the columns that will be included on the block. Click the Items tab and click the Select Columns button (see Figure B.7).

FIGURE B.7.

Using the Items page for new block options.

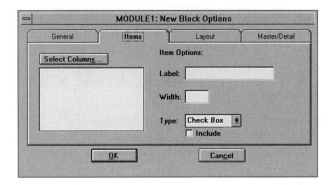

The Designer displays a scrollable list of all of the columns in the Repair_Header table. By default, all of the columns are included in the block. To prevent a column from being included in the generated block, simply click the column in the list (see Figure B.8). The + to the left of the column name changes to a –.

FIGURE B.8.

Selecting columns for a new block.

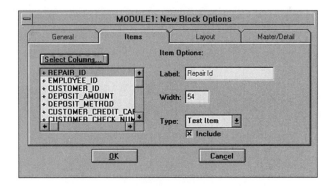

When you click the OK button on the New Block Options window, the Designer generates the new block. The Object Navigator appears and displays the new generated block (see Figure B.9).

FIGURE B.9.

The Object Navigator displays the new block.

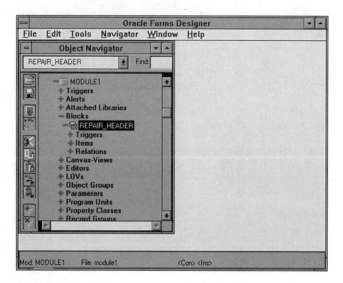

To run the generated form, select Run from the File menu. The Designer displays a Working… message in the lower-left corner of the window. The generated form appears with a menu bar (see Figure B.10). Notice that the form is empty; by default, a generated block does not perform an automatic query of its base table (as does Oracle Power Objects—see Appendix G for more information).

FIGURE B.10.

Running the generated form.

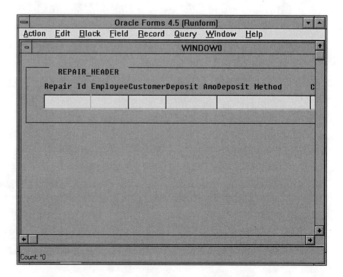

To query the base table (Repair_Header), select eXecute from the Query menu. You see the first row in the table (see Figure B.11). To navigate through the retrieved records, select Next or Previous from the Record menu. To return to the Forms 4.5 Designer, select Exit from the Action menu.

FIGURE B.11.
Querying the base table.

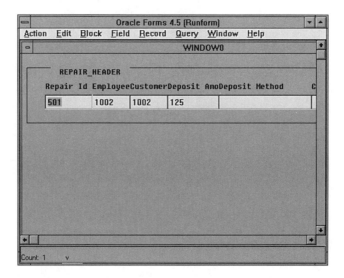

Let's see how to construct a simple master-detail form. Create another block by selecting New Block from the Designer Tools menu. For the new block, select Repair_Item as the base table and select the columns from Repair_Item that you want to appear in the detail block. To establish the relationship between the two blocks, click the Master/Detail tab. Click the Select button to choose the Repair_Header as the Master Block (see Figure B.12).

FIGURE B.12.
Choosing the master block.

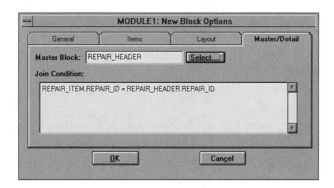

Click the OK button to return to the Object Navigator. The Object Navigator now displays both blocks: Repair_Header and Repair_Item (see Figure B.13).

FIGURE B.13.

Object Navigator displays both blocks.

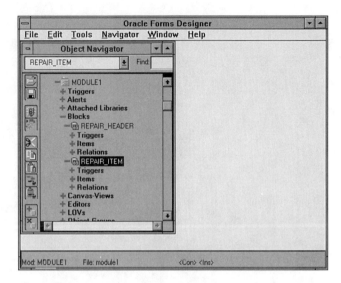

Run the generated form by selecting Run from the File menu. The Designer displays a Working… message in the lower-left corner of the window. You see the generated form, now containing two blocks (see Figure B.14).

FIGURE B.14.

Running the master-detail form.

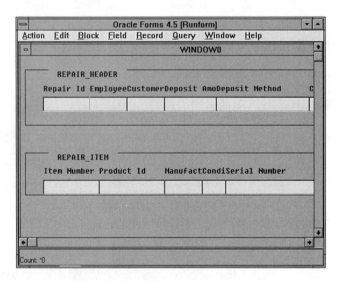

To query both blocks, select eXecute from the Query menu. You see the first row in the Repair_Header table along with its detailed records from the Repair_Item table (see Figure B.15). To navigate through the retrieved records, select Next or Previous from the Record menu. To return to the Forms 4.5 Designer, select Exit from the Action menu.

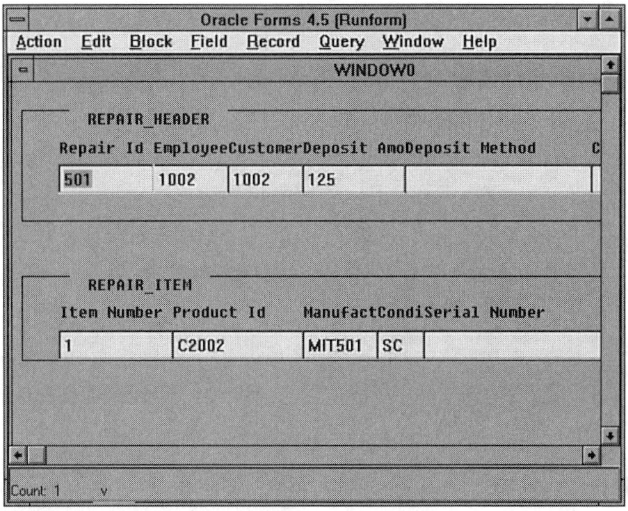

FIGURE B.15.

Querying the master-detail form.

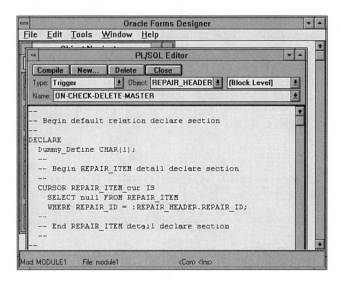

As I mentioned, Forms 4.5 and Reports 2.5 are both equipped with a built-in PL/SQL engine. When you generate a form, the Forms 4.5 Designer creates several *application* triggers to control the behavior of the form. Figure B.16 shows an example of one of the triggers that has been generated. You can create, modify, or drop these triggers with the PL/SQL Editor.

FIGURE B.16.

Viewing a trigger with the PL/SQL Editor.

Browser

Oracle Browser is an ad hoc query tool designed for casual Oracle users. It enables a user to define a query without having any knowledge of SQL. Once a query has been created, it can be stored for later use. The query can be used to produce simple reports. Also, a retrieved data set can be exported as an Excel or 1-2-3 spreadsheet.

As with the other Developer/2000 components, Browser runs in three environments: Windows, Macintosh, and Motif. Here's an example of how to connect Browser to a Personal Oracle7 database and execute a query.

To begin, invoke the Browser 2.0 User utility. You see a Connect dialog box. Enter the Oracle username and password but leave the Connect field empty (see Figure B.17). Click Connect to establish the connection to Personal Oracle7.

FIGURE B.17.

Establishing the connection to Personal Oracle7.

Next, Browser displays a radio button group with three choices. The default choice is for Browser to create a new query (see Figure B.18). Click OK for the default choice.

FIGURE B.18.

Choosing to create a new query.

A window appears with a list of tables that you can select. Highlight the table you wish to query and click Include (see Figure B.19). You see an hourglass while Browser constructs a list of the columns in the selected table. When the hourglass disappears, click Close to choose the columns.

The untitled query appears in a window with each column and a graphical representation of its datatype (see Figure B.20).

FIGURE B.19.

Selecting a table.

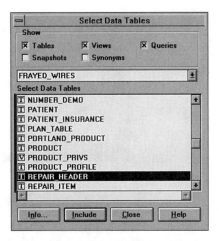

FIGURE B.20.

The table's columns are displayed.

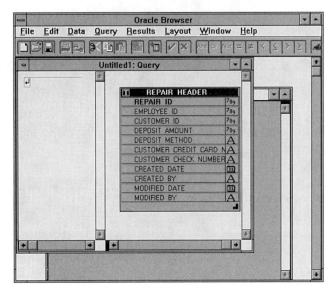

To proceed, you should save the query. Select Save As under the File menu. The Designer will display a window for specifying the manner in which the query should be saved. Specify filesystem and press OK. Specify the directory and filename to be used for saving the query (see Figure B.21). By default, a Browser query is stored with a file extension of .brw.

After the query is saved, select the columns to be displayed by selecting Display from the Results menu. You see a window containing two lists (see Figure B.22). On the left is the selected table's columns. On the right is a list of columns that will be retrieved by the query. To select a column for retrieval, simply highlight it from the list on the left and click the Copy button. When you're finished choosing the columns to retrieve, click Close. To see the query results, click Execute.

FIGURE B.21.

Saving a query.

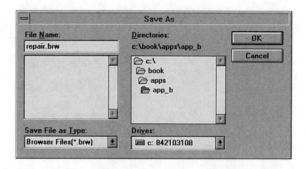

FIGURE B.22.

Choosing the columns to retrieve.

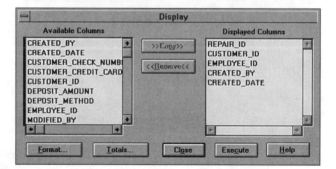

Finally, Browser executes the query and displays the results in a Results window (see Figure B.23).

FIGURE B.23.

The query results are shown.

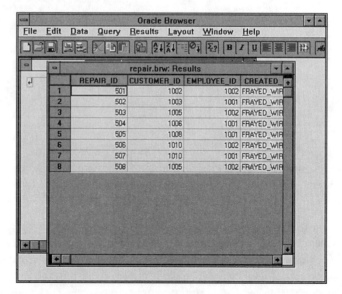

Procedure Builder

Procedure Builder is a handy tool for creating and maintaining stored procedures and functions. As with the other pieces of Developer/2000, Procedure Builder works well with Personal Oracle7. When you invoke Procedure Builder, a window entitled PL/SQL Interpreter appears (see Figure B.24).

FIGURE B.24.

The PL/SQL Interpreter window.

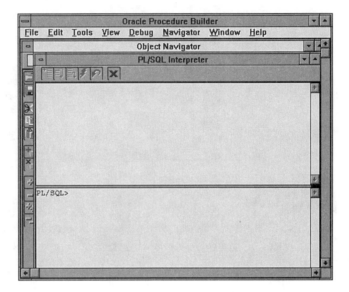

To connect to Personal Oracle7, choose Connect from the File menu. Enter the Oracle username and password but leave the Database field empty (see Figure B.25). Click Connect to establish the connection to the Personal Oracle7 instance.

FIGURE B.25.

Connecting to Personal Oracle7.

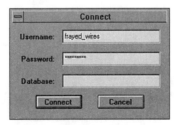

To view a stored procedure or function in the Personal Oracle7 database, select Stored Program Unit Editor from the Tools menu. Procedure Builder queries Personal Oracle7 to retrieve any stored procedures or functions. Figure B.26 is an example of a stored function retrieved and displayed by Procedure Builder.

FIGURE B.26.

Displaying a stored function.

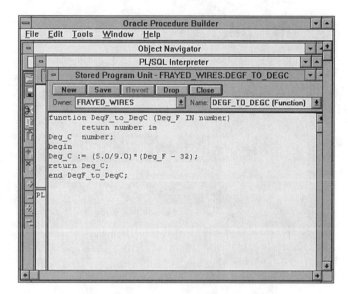

Reports 2.5

Reports 2.5 is a full-featured report writer that can be used in the Windows, Macintosh, or Motif environment. With all of its features, Reports 2.5 is capable of building complex reports. As with Forms 4.5, it has a built-in PL/SQL engine for creating report triggers that are invoked at execution time.

Let's look at building a simple report from the Personal Oracle7 database. When the Reports 2.5 Designer is invoked, you see the Object Navigator (see Figure B.27).

FIGURE B.27.

The Object Navigator.

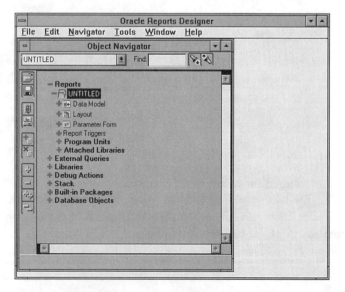

To connect to Personal Oracle7, choose Connect from the File menu. Enter the Oracle username and password but leave the Database field blank (see Figure B.28). Click Connect to establish the connection to the Personal Oracle7 instance.

FIGURE B.28.

Connecting to Personal Oracle7.

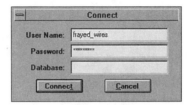

For Reports 2.5, the first step in building a report is to create a data model—a graphical representation of the tables to be queried and their relationships. Select Data Model Editor from the Tools menu. The Data Model Editor window displays an empty screen. To create a query, click the SQL icon from the Data Model Editor toolbox and draw the query on the screen (see Figure B.29).

FIGURE B.29.

Creating a query.

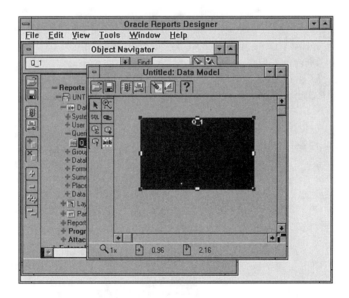

Double-click the Q_1 rounded rectangle. The Reports Designer displays a tabbed folder (see Figure B.30). Click Tables/Columns to select a table for the query.

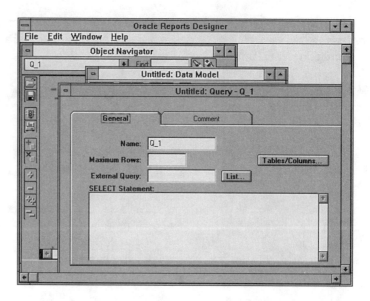

The Table and Column Names window appears (see Figure B.31). Scroll down to the Repair_Header table and select it by clicking the mouse. The Reports Designer retrieves the Repair_Header table's columns and displays them in the list of columns (see Figure B.32). Highlight the * to indicate that all of the Repair_Header columns should be included in the query and click Select-from and Close.

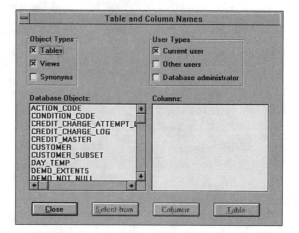

FIGURE B.32.
Choosing the columns.

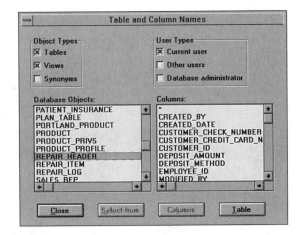

The Reports Designer constructs the SELECT statement as shown in Figure B.33. Click OK to continue.

FIGURE B.33.
The constructed SELECT statement.

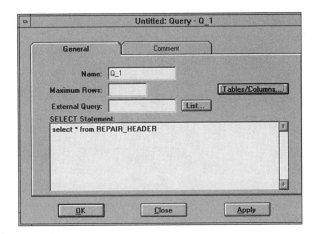

The Data Model now displays the query and its associated report group G_1, which consists of all columns in the Repair_Header table (see Figure B.34).

FIGURE B.34.
The generated report group.

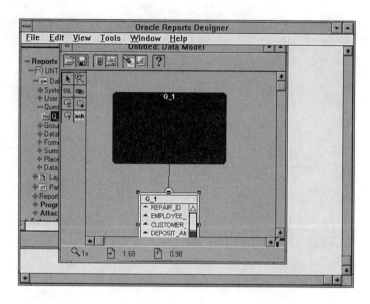

To select a default layout for the report, click the default layout icon from the Data Model Editor toolbar—it's a green drafting triangle. The Default Layout window appears (see Figure B.35). Use the default Tabular layout.

FIGURE B.35.
The Default Layout window.

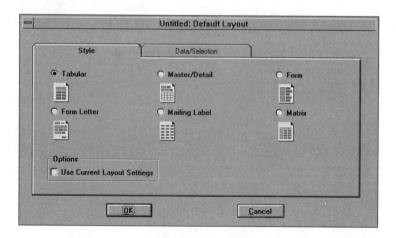

You can view the report group by clicking the Data/Selection tab. Each column, its label, and its width and height can be viewed or modified (see Figure B.36). Click OK to continue.

FIGURE B.36.

Viewing the report group.

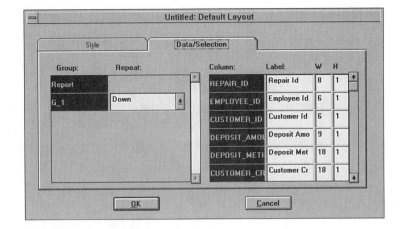

The Reports Designer displays the default layout (see Figure B.37).

FIGURE B.37.

The generated default layout.

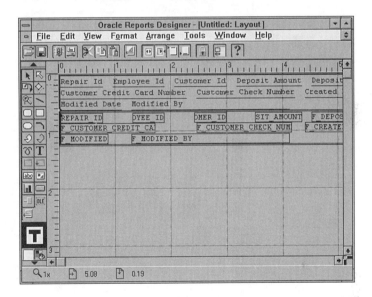

To run the report, click the green signal light icon. Before the report actually appears, you see a Runtime Parameter Form (see Figure B.38). On this form, you can direct the report to the screen, printer, or other destinations.

FIGURE B.38.

*The Runtime
Parameter Form.*

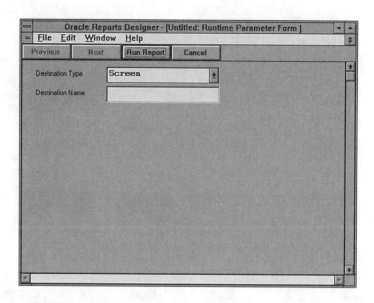

To view the generated report on the screen, click the Run Report button. You might have some trouble finding the Previewer window. To find it, select Previewer from the Window menu. Figure B.39 contains the first page of the generated report.

FIGURE B.39.

*Page 1 of the generated
report.*

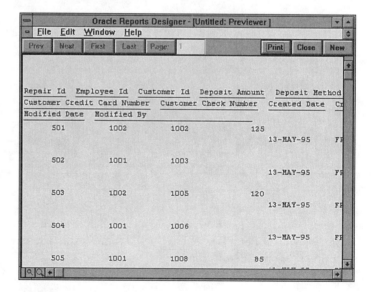

C

Using Personal Oracle7 and PowerBuilder 4.0

This appendix demonstrates how you can use PowerBuilder with a Personal Oracle database. PowerBuilder is the principal product of Powersoft, which was acquired by Sybase in late 1994. The version used for the examples in this appendix is PowerBuilder 4.0, Enterprise Edition. PowerBuilder's strengths include the following features:

- The DataWindow object: a flexible and intuitive mechanism for mapping to a database table, which is the heart of the PowerBuilder development environment.
- Support for most desktop and server databases including Oracle, Sybase, Microsoft SQL Server, Informix, DB2, and others.
- Excellent integration with Microsoft Windows via DDE and OLE support.
- Support for classes and inheritance.

PowerBuilder has a variety of objects that include the following:

- DataWindows
- Windows
- Menus
- Fields such as SingleLineEdits, MultiLineEdits, List Boxes, and DropDown List Boxes
- Buttons such as CommandButtons, PictureButtons, Radio Buttons, and Check Boxes
- User-defined objects
- Graphs
- OLE 2.0 objects
- Pictures
- Static text

As with other application development environments described in these appendixes, PowerBuilder uses a scripting language named PowerScript for event-driven programming. Each object has a set of predefined events for which a script can be written. You can define additional events for an object. PowerBuilder also includes a comprehensive set of built-in functions that can be invoked from an event script.

Using Database Painter to Set Up a Database Profile

The first step in using PowerBuilder with Personal Oracle is using the Database Painter to set up a database profile. When PowerBuilder is first installed, three database profiles are defined (see Figure C.1).

FIGURE C.1.

Using the Database Painter to set up a database profile.

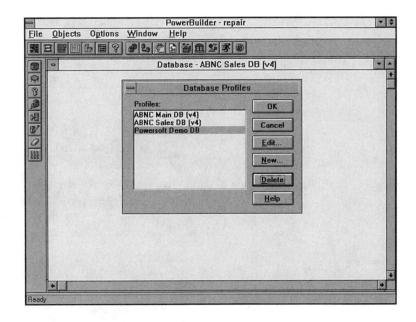

To add a profile for Personal Oracle, click New on the Database Profiles screen. A Database Profile Setup screen appears (see Figure C.2).

FIGURE C.2.

The Database Profile Setup screen.

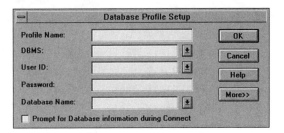

We'll use the Oracle ODBC driver to connect PowerBuilder to Personal Oracle. Click More on the Database Profile Setup screen to display the additional profile fields. Enter PO7 for the Profile Name, ODBC for the DBMS, 2: for the Server Name, FRAYED_WIRES for the Login ID, HELMHOLTZ for the Login Password, and ConnectString='DSN=PO7;DSQ=2:; UID=FRAYED_WIRES;PWD=HELMHOLTZ' for DBPARM (see Figure C.3).

After you click OK, the Database Profiles screen displays the new database profile PO7 (see Figure C.4).

FIGURE C.3.

Setting up a database profile for Personal Oracle.

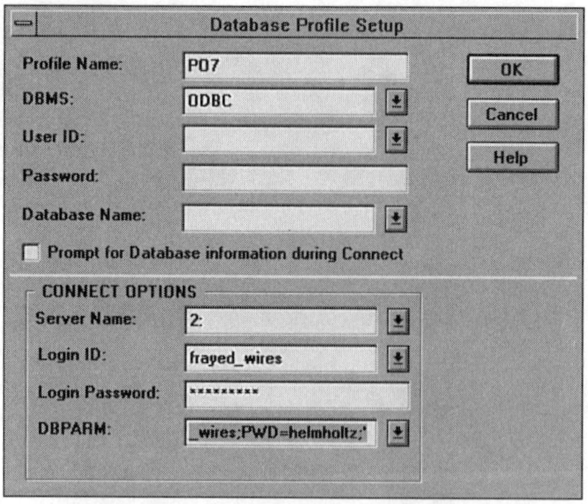

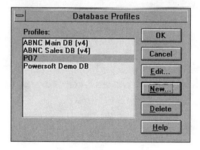

FIGURE C.4.

The Personal Oracle database profile is created.

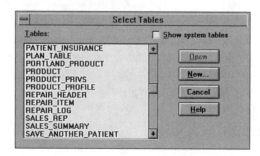

Click OK. Once the connection to Personal Oracle has been established, the Database Painter displays the tables owned by the connected Oracle user FRAYED_WIRES. Highlight the Repair_Header table and click Open (see Figure C.5). You will then see the columns of the selected table (see Figure C.6).

FIGURE C.5.

Database Painter displays available tables.

FIGURE C.6.
Database Painter displays the selected table's columns.

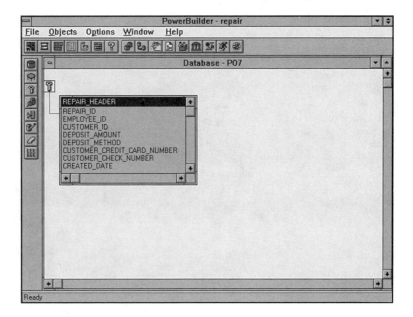

Creating a DataWindow

To further illustrate how PowerBuilder works with Personal Oracle, we'll create a datawindow. If you had to describe the PowerBuilder product with one word, it would be *datawindow*. A PowerBuilder window is usually built around an instance of a datawindow termed a *datawindow control*. When the DataWindow Painter is invoked, it displays a screen from which you can select an existing datawindow or choose to create a new datawindow (see Figure C.7). Click New to create a new datawindow.

FIGURE C.7.
Creating a new datawindow.

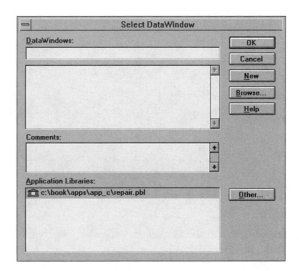

The New DataWindow screen appears (see Figure C.8). You must make two choices for the new datawindow—its Data Source and Presentation Style. Choose SQL Select for Data Source and Tabular for Presentation Style and click OK.

FIGURE C.8.

Choosing the data source and presentation style for the new datawindow.

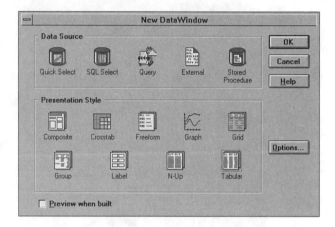

A list of the tables owned by FRAYED_WIRES appears. Scroll down to the Repair_Header table, highlight it, and click Open (see Figure C.9).

FIGURE C.9.

Choosing a table for the new datawindow.

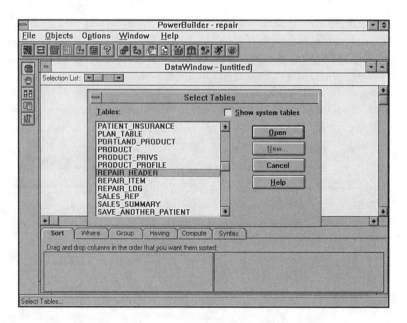

Next, you see a list of the columns from Repair_Header (see Figure C.10). To add a column to the new datawindow, simply click on the column name. Figure C.11 shows that three columns have been chosen for the datawindow—Repair_ID, Employee_ID, and Customer_ID.

FIGURE C.10.

Selecting columns for the datawindow.

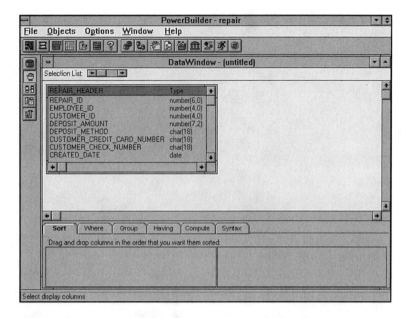

FIGURE C.11.

Three columns are selected for the datawindow.

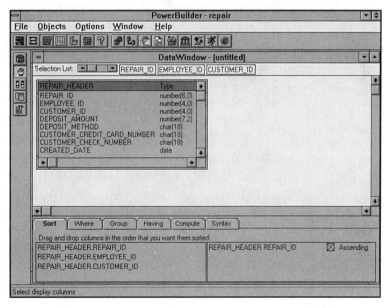

Under the File menu, choose Design to continue defining the new datawindow. Figure C.12 shows the generated datawindow. With a little work, you can modify the appearance of the datawindow by adding 3D borders, changing the background color, repositioning fields, and changing the text size (see Figure C.13).

FIGURE C.12.
The generated datawindow.

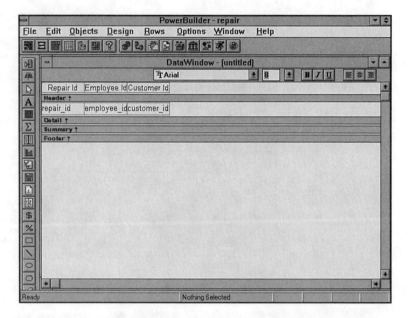

FIGURE C.13.
The modified datawindow.

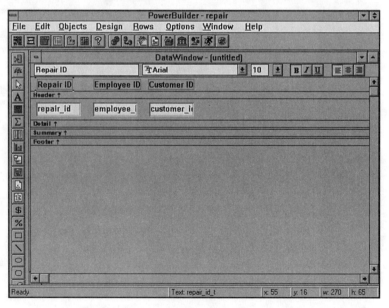

At this point, you're ready to test your datawindow. Select Preview from the Design menu. The DataWindow Painter retrieves rows from Repair_Header and displays the results in the datawindow (see Figure C.14). You can use the tools in Preview mode to review the contents of the table, modify values, or insert new rows into the table.

FIGURE C.14.

Previewing the datawindow.

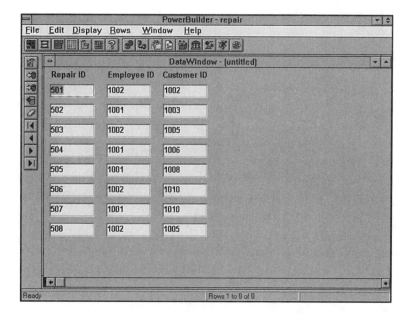

Return to design made by selecting <u>D</u>esign from the Display menu. To save the datawindow, select Save As from the File menu. A Save DataWindow window appears in which you can specify a name for the new datawindow (see Figure C.15). PowerBuilder stores objects in a library file with an extension of .PBL. As a result, object names aren't limited to eight characters because they are not stored as DOS files.

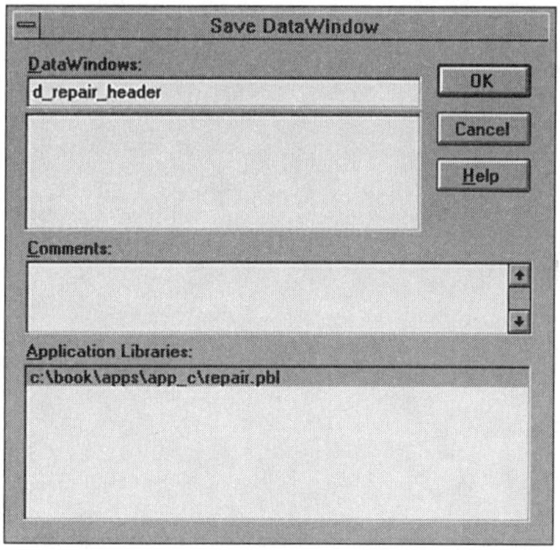

FIGURE C.15.

Saving the datawindow.

D

Using Personal Oracle7 and Visual Basic

This appendix illustrates how you can use Visual Basic with Personal Oracle. As you probably know, Visual Basic is a very popular tool for developing Windows applications. Unlike the tools described in the other appendixes, Visual Basic is not intended for use only as a client/server development tool.

The strengths of Visual Basic include the following:

■ Its support for a variety of database products via ODBC

■ The availability of many third-party add-on products in the form of VBX controls

■ Its excellent integration with Windows

Although Visual Basic is a popular tool, the example in this appendix illustrates that some of the features found in tools such as PowerBuilder, SQLWindows, and Oracle Power Objects are missing from Visual Basic. Visual Basic's shortcomings as a tool for building database applications include the following:

■ Little integration with database data dictionary

■ No support for inheritance

■ No cross-platform support

To demonstrate the use of Visual Basic with Personal Oracle, I'll present how a Visual Basic data control accesses the Repair_Header table. As you can see, even though no coding is required to access the table, Visual Basic is not able to generate a default form from a table definition; PowerBuilder, SQLWindows, Oracle Forms, and Oracle Power Objects are able to generate a default form. Figure D.1 illustrates the appearance of the Visual Basic environment when the program first starts.

FIGURE D.1.

Visual Basic: the initial form.

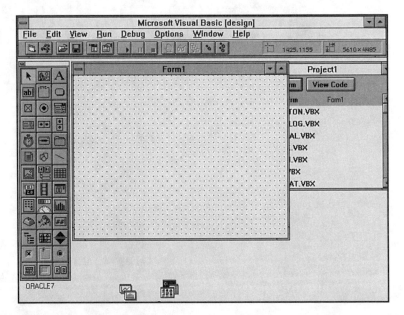

To add a data control to the form, select the data control icon from the VB toolbox (it's in the right-hand column of icons, second from the bottom). Size the data control to your liking. To use an ODBC data source with the data control, set the Connect property to `ODBC;DSN=PO7;UID=FRAYED_WIRES;PWD=HELMHOLTZ;` (see Figure D.2). Set the Caption property to Repair_Header.

FIGURE D.2.

Adding a data control to the form.

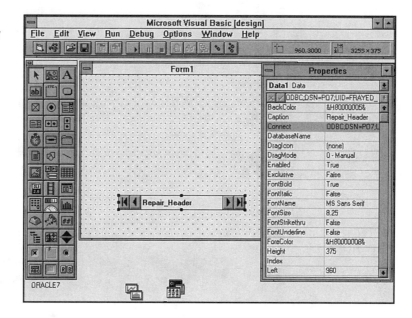

Scroll down the list of properties. Set the RecordSource to Repair_Header (see Figure D.3); this is the Personal Oracle table to which the data control will be attached. Set the Name of the data control to Repair_Header.

Now, let's add four text fields and four labels to the form (see Figure D.4). Each text field corresponds to a column in the Repair_Header table.

FIGURE D.3.
Modifying data control properties.

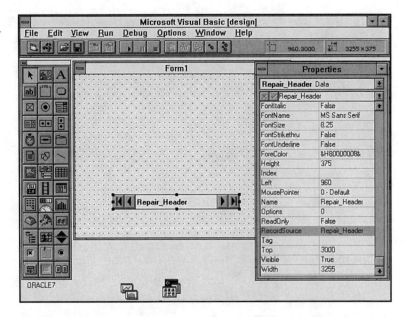

FIGURE D.4.
Adding text fields to the form.

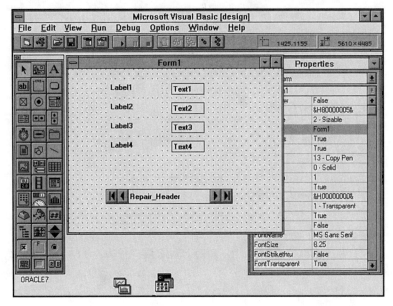

Let's set the caption of each label to correspond to its adjoining text field (see Figure D.5). After all the labels have been modified, we set the properties of each text field (see Figure D.6).

FIGURE D.5.
Modifying the labels.

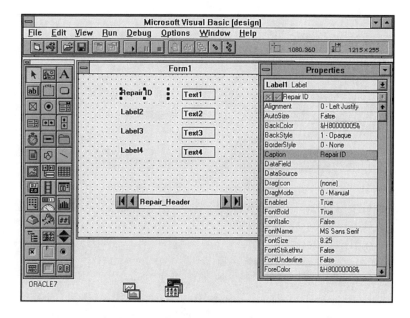

FIGURE D.6.
Setting the properties of the text fields.

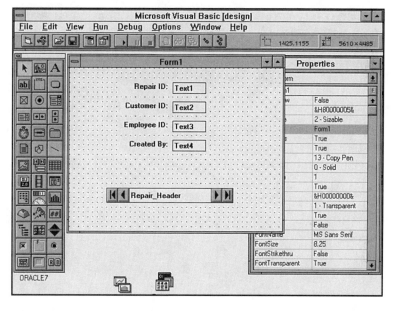

The DataSource property for all of the text fields should be set to the same data control—Repair_Header—so that each text field is bound to the data control. You can set the DataSource by simply clicking the DataSource field on the Properties window. For each text field, set the DataField to the column that you want to display in the field. Figure D.7 shows how the DataField property for the Repair_ID text field is set to Repair_ID.

FIGURE D.7.
Setting the DataField property for a text field.

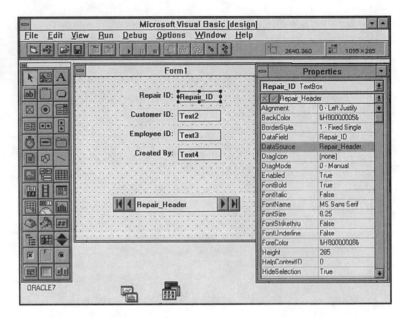

To run the form, select Run or press F5. To navigate through the records in the table, click the first, previous, next, or last control on the Repair_Header data control (see Figure D.8).

FIGURE D.8.
Running the form.

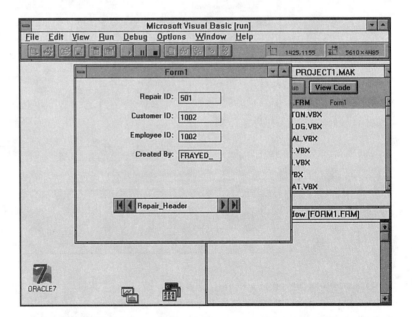

E

Using Personal Oracle7 and SQLWindows

SQLWindows is another popular third-party application development tool that you can use with Personal Oracle. Produced by Gupta Corporation, SQLWindows is equipped with a stand-alone version of Gupta's database engine, SQLBase. Like PowerBuilder, SQLWindows is a complete development environment for building client/server applications that work with the major database products—Oracle, Sybase, Informix, DB2, and, of course, SQLBase.

SQLWindows uses a *message* paradigm to describe the events that can occur in a client application. Of all the products described in this book, SQLWindows provides the most support for object-oriented development.

The examples in this appendix were produced with the Corporate Edition of SQLWindows 5.0. The purpose of this example is to illustrate the steps in developing a simple form using the SQLWindows Designer.

When you first start the SQLWindows Designer, you see a window that enables you to choose between using QuickForms, using the Custom Form Designer, or opening an existing application (see Figure E.1). We'll use QuickForms for this example.

FIGURE E.1.

SQLWindows Designer: Choosing QuickForms.

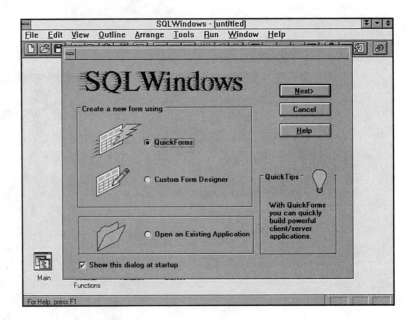

QuickForms consists of a series of screens that guide you through the process of building a form. We'll use the MDI Window Type for the form (see Figure E.2).

FIGURE E.2.
QuickForms options.

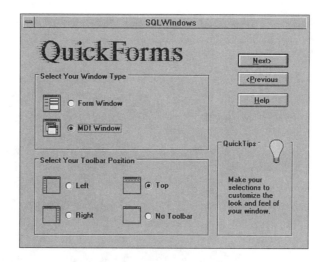

Next, the SQLWindows Designer prompts you for the database, user, and password (see Figure E.3). For the Database field, specify the name of an ODBC data source—in this case, po7.

FIGURE E.3.

*Connecting
SQLWindows Designer
to Personal Oracle.*

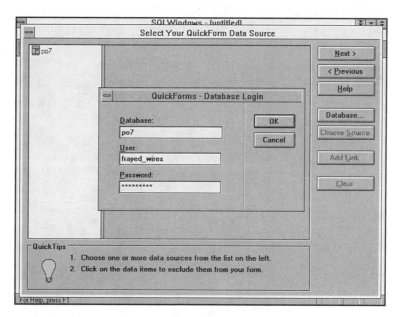

After you've established the connection to the Personal Oracle database, you see a scrolling list of all tables owned by the Oracle user FRAYED_WIRES (see Figure E.4).

FIGURE E.4.

Selecting a QuickForm data source.

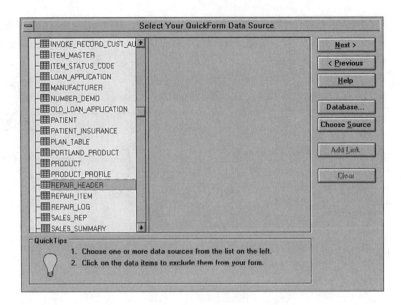

Scroll down to the Repair_Header table and double-click it. You see a list of the Repair_Header columns (see Figure E.5). By default, all of the columns appear in the generated form; you can deselect a column by clicking it.

FIGURE E.5.

Choosing the table's columns.

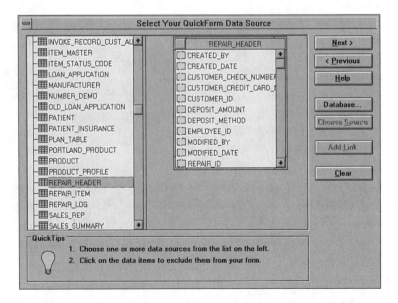

When you click the Next button, the SQLWindows Designer generates the MDI form (see Figure E.6). Included on the generated form are the basic buttons that are needed for navigating through a table: First, Previous, Next, Last, and Retrieve.

FIGURE E.6.

The generated MDI form.

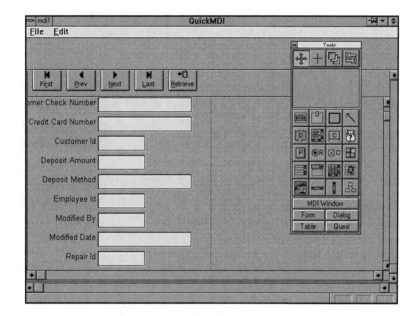

To run the generated MDI form, select User Mode from the Run menu on the SQLWindows Designer Main window (see Figure E.7). You can use the basic navigational buttons to wander through the Repair_Header table. You can also resize the generated MDI form.

One of SQLWindows's major strengths is its scripting environment. SQLWindows uses a language called SAL—SQLWindows Application Language—for describing the actions to be performed when a message is received (see Figure E.8).

FIGURE E.7.
Running the generated MDI form.

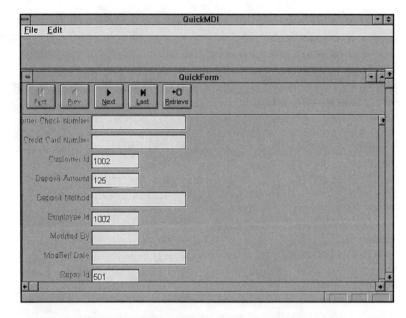

FIGURE E.8.
The SQLWindows Designer Main window.

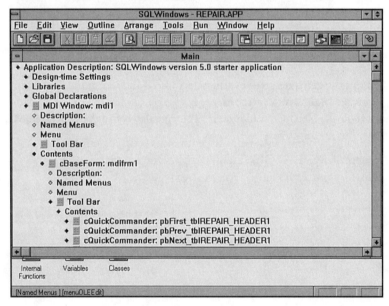

As shown in Figure E.9, the SQLWindows Designer uses an *outline* paradigm for developing the SAL script that runs a SQLWindows application. To expand the SAL code for an object, you simply click the object. In the example shown, the Quick Commander object pbRetrieve_tblREPAIR_HEADER has been clicked, causing the empty Message Actions section to appear. The Message Actions section is used to describe the processing to be performed when the object receives an event message. In the lower-left corner of the window, the SQLWindows Designer displays a list of all of the possible event messages for the object class.

FIGURE E.9.

Selecting a SQLWindows application message.

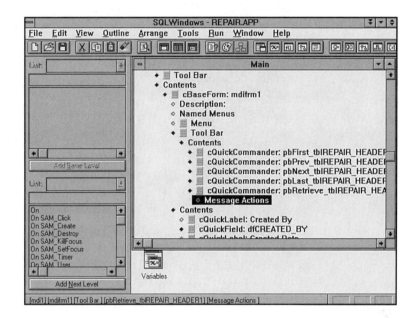

If you double-click the event message On SAM_SetFocus, the line of SAL code is added to the Main window. A list of possible SAL statements is then displayed in the lower-left corner of the window. If you choose the If statement, the If statement is added to the Main window, and the SQLWindows Designer displays two lists: a list of SAL and user-defined functions and a list of constants (see Figure E.10). The point of this example is to demonstrate the scripting environment of the SQLWindows Designer. The SQLWindows Designer development environment is called *point-and-click.* It is almost unnecessary to touch the keyboard because the Designer presents a list of the possible choices at the appropriate time—whether it's a list of functions, variables, statements, or objects.

FIGURE E.10.

Example of point-and-click coding.

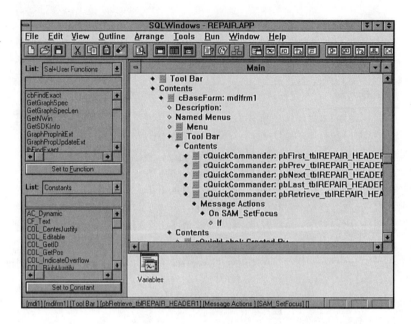

F

Using Personal Oracle7 and Oracle Objects for OLE

If you download Personal Oracle from the Oracle WWW page, you also receive a trial version of Oracle Objects for OLE, which is actually a separate product. Oracle Objects for OLE consists of an assortment of Visual Basic add-ons and a set of class libraries for the Microsoft and Borland C++ compilers. The Visual Basic-related add-ons consist of the following:

- The Oracle Data Control is a level 3 Visual Basic custom control that is installed as c:\windows\system\oradc.vbx.
- The Oracle Object Server is an OLE In-Process server that provides access to a group of programmable objects for a local or remote Oracle database.

The objects manipulated by the Oracle Data Control include the following:

- OraClient: A workstation is associated with a single OraClient.
- OraSession: An OraClient may possess multiple OraSessions.
- OraConnection: An OraSession may have more than one OraConnection.
- OraDatabase: More than one OraDatabase may be associated with a single OraSession and OraConnection.
- OraDynaset: Each OraDatabase may have multiple OraDynasets.
- OraField: Each OraDynaset may possess more than one OraField.
- OraParameter: Each OraDatabase may have more than one OraParameter.

Refer to Oracle for Objects OLE documentation for further details on these objects, properties, and methods. In this appendix, I'll focus on the use of the Oracle Data Control VBX.

I'll use the Login sample program to illustrate how Oracle Objects for OLE VB accesses the Personal Oracle database. From Visual Basic, open the Login project contained in c:\orawin\oo4o\vb\samples. Figure F.1 shows the Login form and its Properties window.

To add the Oracle data control to a project, select Add File from the File menu. In the Add File dialog box, select oradc.vbx, which is stored in c:\windows\system (see Figure F.2).

FIGURE F.1.

The Oracle Objects for OLE Login sample.

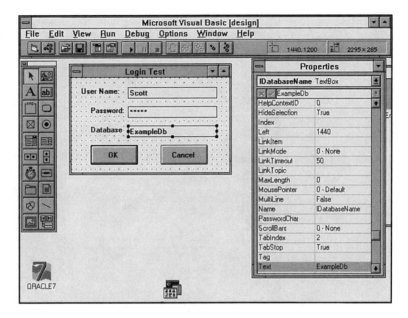

FIGURE F.2.

Adding the Oracle data control to a project.

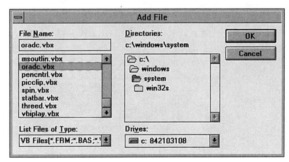

After you've added oradc.vbx to a project, the Visual Basic toolbox displays the Oracle data control as the last icon on the left side of the toolbox (see Figure F.3).

FIGURE F.3.

The VB toolbox with the Oracle data control icon.

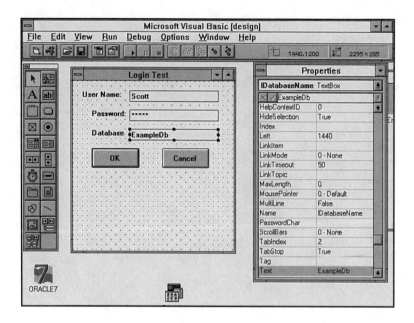

To add an Oracle data control (as opposed to an ordinary data control) to a form, simply click the icon and place it at the desired location on the form. Figure F.4 shows the new Oracle data control and its Properties sheet.

FIGURE F.4.

Adding an Oracle data control to a form.

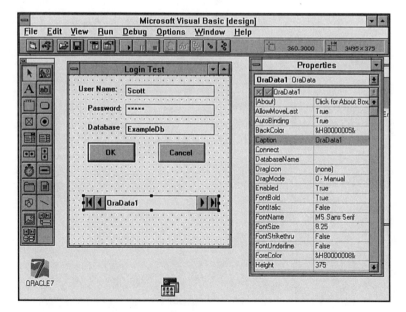

The Login sample included with Oracle Objects for OLE consists of an Oracle username, the associated password, and a database. The Login sample has the database name set to ExampleDb (see Figure F.5).

FIGURE F.5.

The database name as specified in the Login sample form.

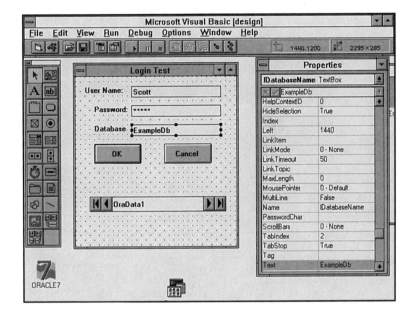

Instead of ExampleDb, I'll set the Text property for the DatabaseName to be `oracle7`—the name used to reference the Personal Oracle instance (see Figure F.6). The Oracle data control doesn't use the ODBC driver to establish an Oracle connection. Remember: in ORACLE.INI, `oracle7` translates to `2:`, the local Oracle instance—Personal Oracle.

In addition, I'll set the Text properties of the User Name and Password to the familiar strings `frayed_wires` and `helmholtz` (see Figure F.7).

To test the modified form, select Start from the Run menu. Figure F.8 shows the Login Test window.

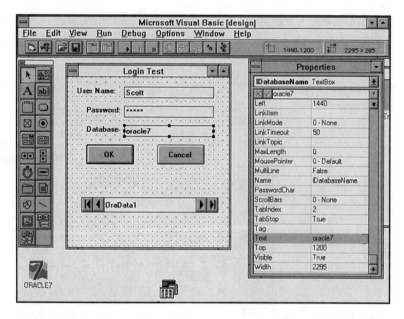

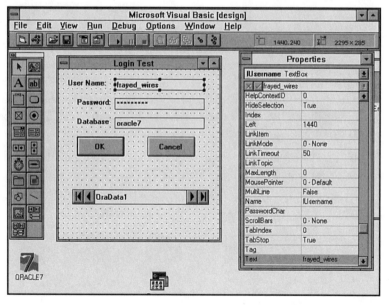

FIGURE F.8.

Running the modified Login sample form.

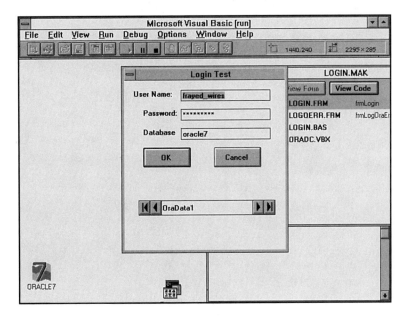

When you click OK, the Visual Basic code behind the button's click method establishes a connection with the Personal Oracle instance. Figure F.9 shows the message returned by the form indicating a successful connection.

FIGURE F.9.

Successfully connected to Personal Oracle.

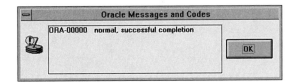

G

Using Personal Oracle7 and Oracle Power Objects

Oracle Power Objects is an object-oriented database application development environment that works with Oracle7, a stand-alone database named Blaze, and SQL Server. Oracle Power Objects is the first Oracle application tool that you can use with a non-Oracle database.

This appendix is based on Oracle Power Objects Version 1.0, which became available in July 1995.

Installing Oracle Power Objects

You can download Version 1.0 of Oracle Power Objects from Oracle Corporation's WWW page at http://www.oracle.com. The product is a self-extracting executable file named opov10.exe (see Figure G.1). I recommend creating a directory named c:\opo for storing the extracted contents; move opov10.exe to this directory. To extract its contents, use File Manager and double-click opov10.exe (see Figure G.2).

FIGURE G.1.

The file opov10.exe contains Oracle Power Objects Developer's Release 2.

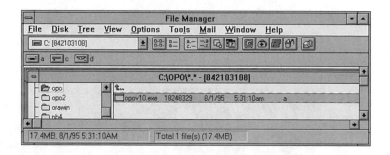

FIGURE G.2.

Files extracted from opov10.exe.

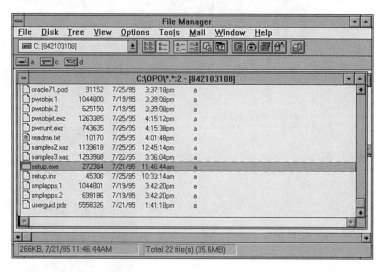

After you've extracted the contents of opov10.exe, you can begin the installation of Oracle Power Objects. Click setup.exe as shown in Figure G.2. The Oracle Power Objects Installer displays three installation options: Full Install, Custom Install, or Minimum Install (see Figure G.3). The Full Install requires approximately 30 MB of disk space; if you can afford the disk space, select the Full Install.

FIGURE G.3.

Oracle Power Objects installation options.

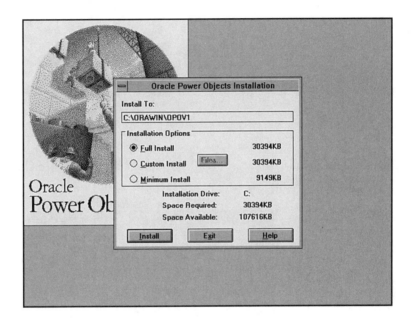

During the installation process, a message informs you that SHARE must be installed in your autoexec.bat file (see Figure G.4). However, if you're using Windows for Workgroups, do not install SHARE.

FIGURE G.4.

Message about SHARE installation.

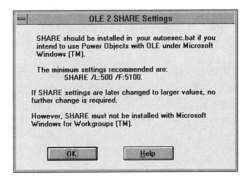

During the Oracle Power Objects installation, a progress bar shows the percentage of its completion. When installation is complete, you see a message showing all the Oracle Power Objects components that have been installed (see Figure G.5).

FIGURE G.5.

Message displaying the installed Oracle Power Objects components.

As part of the installation process, a Windows program group named Oracle Power Objects is created (see Figure G.6).

FIGURE G.6.

Oracle Power Objects program group.

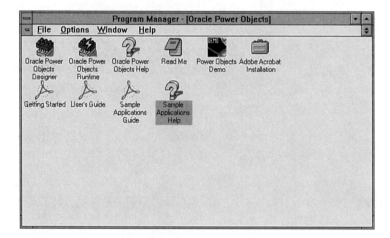

Oracle Power Objects comes with Adobe's Acrobat Reader. Oracle Power Objects's documentation is written in Adobe's PDF format, which you can view on Windows, Macintosh, and UNIX. To install Acrobat, double-click the Adobe Acrobat Installation icon in the Oracle Power Objects program group. By default, Acrobat is installed in c:\acroread.

The following three Acrobat documents are supplied with Power Objects:

- Getting Started
- User's Guide
- Sample Applications Guide

Using Oracle Power Objects Designer

To build an application with Power Objects, double-click the Power Objects Designer. The Power Objects Designer displays a message indicating that this is a trial license version of the product (see Figure G.7).

FIGURE G.7.

Message displayed by Oracle Power Objects Designer.

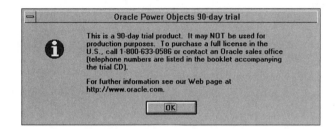

After you click the OK button on the message box, the Designer opens the Main window and reads any applications, libraries, and database sessions that were opened during the previous Designer session (see Figure G.8). The Main window shows a number of sample applications.

FIGURE G.8.

Main window of Power Objects Designer.

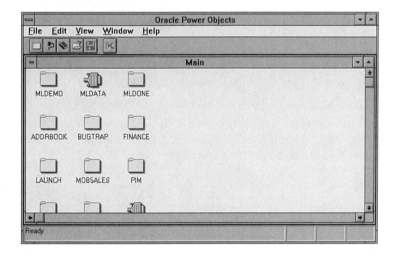

Power Objects supports the following three primary object types:

■ Database Session: If a database session is not connected to its source, the icon appears as an unconnected electrical plug. You establish the connection by double-clicking the icon. When you save a database session, Power Objects (for Windows) uses a file extension of .pos.

■ Application: An application contains application objects such as forms, reports, classes, bitmaps, and OLE objects. For the Windows version of Power Objects, an application is given an extension of .poa.

■ Library: Power Objects uses the library to implement the object-oriented features of the product. A library stores classes and bitmaps that can be shared by more than one application. For the Windows version of Power Objects, a library is given an extension of .pol.

Creating a Database Session

On the toolbar is an icon of an electrical plug. To create a database session, click this icon. The Designer displays a dialog box with two fields: Database and Connect String (see Figure G.9). By default, the Database field is set to Oracle. To connect to Personal Oracle, set the Connect String to the Oracle user and password; in this example, we're connecting to frayed_wires/ helmholtz. Of course, the Personal Oracle database must be running if you want to establish a database session.

FIGURE G.9.

Creating a database session.

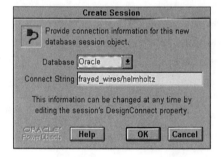

Once you've created a database session, you can save it by clicking the disk icon on the De-signer toolbar. The Designer will open the Create as window and prompt you for the directory and filename to use for saving the current database session (see Figure G.10). Don't save your Power Objects objects in the Oracle Power Objects directory tree.

FIGURE G.10.

Saving a database session as a file.

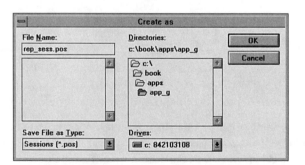

TIP

Sometimes, it is difficult to determine an object's type by looking at the Power Objects window. Unless you're displaying an object's property sheet, you might have trouble distinguishing an application from a session from a library—if they all have the same name. This is also true if you're trying to switch to a different window under the Window menu. As a result, I recommend that you add an appropriate phrase to an object's filename: APP for an application, SES for a database session, and LIB for a library. I hope such a designation won't be necessary in future releases of Power Objects.

After you save a database session, the Designer displays the database session as a disconnected electrical plug in a window labeled with the name of the database session. The database session property sheet is also displayed (see Figure G.11).

FIGURE G.11.

Database session icon and property sheet.

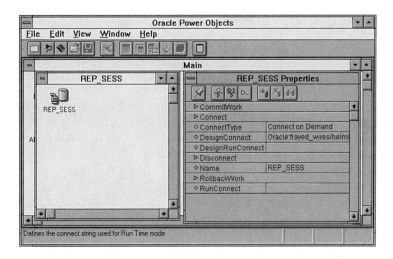

To connect to Personal Oracle through the database session, simply double-click the database session icon—the disconnected electrical plug. The database session uses the connect string to establish a connection—in this case, to Personal Oracle. The database session window displays the database session as a connected electrical plug along with all of the database objects that are visible to the specified Oracle user (see Figure G.12).

FIGURE G.12.

Connecting to Personal Oracle with the database session.

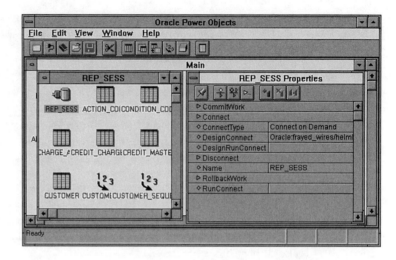

Creating an Application

To create a new Power Objects application, click the folder icon on the Designer toolbar. A dialog window appears in which you specify the new application's filename and directory (see Figure G.13). For this example, I'll name the application rep_app.poa.

FIGURE G.13.

Creating and saving a Power Objects application.

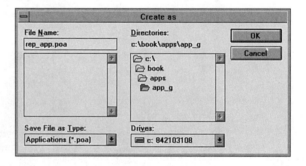

After you specify a filename and directory for the new application, the Designer displays an empty window labeled as REP_APP and the application's property sheet (see Figure G.14).

FIGURE G.14.

Power Objects application and property sheet.

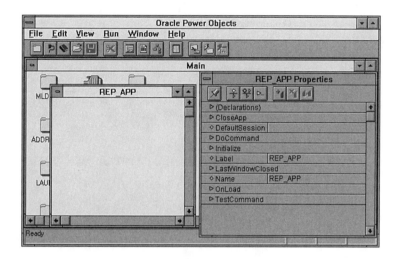

Of course, to do anything meaningful with the application, you first need to select a table. To select a table, set the Designer's focus on REP_SESS, the database session. You can do this by selecting REP_SESS from the Window menu. Scroll down through the REP_SESS window until you see the Repair_Header table (see Figure G.15).

FIGURE G.15.

Selecting a table with the database session.

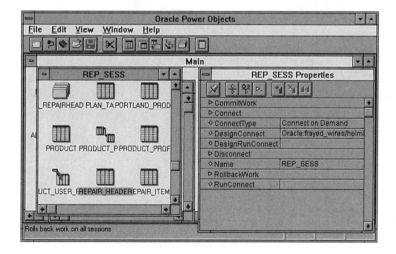

Double-click the Repair_Header table. The Table Editor window appears with the columns from the Repair_Header table (see Figure G.16).

FIGURE G.16.

Using the Power Objects Table Editor.

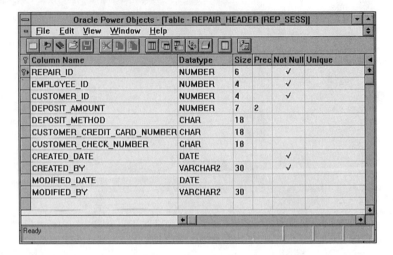

If you click the rightmost button on the toolbar (which looks like a lightning bolt), the Table Browser window appears (see Figure G.17). When invoked, the Table Browser retrieves the rows from the selected table.

FIGURE G.17.

Modifying a table's contents with the Table Browser.

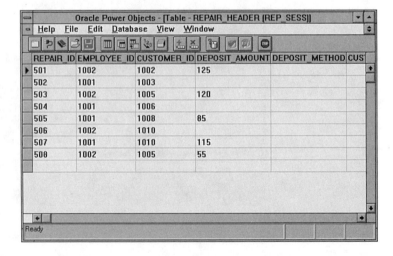

While in the Table Browser, you can peruse the retrieved rows by using the scrollbar. You can add a new row by clicking the first column of the empty row after the last retrieved row. Figure G.18 illustrates how Power Objects locks a new row by displaying a lock icon to the left of the row.

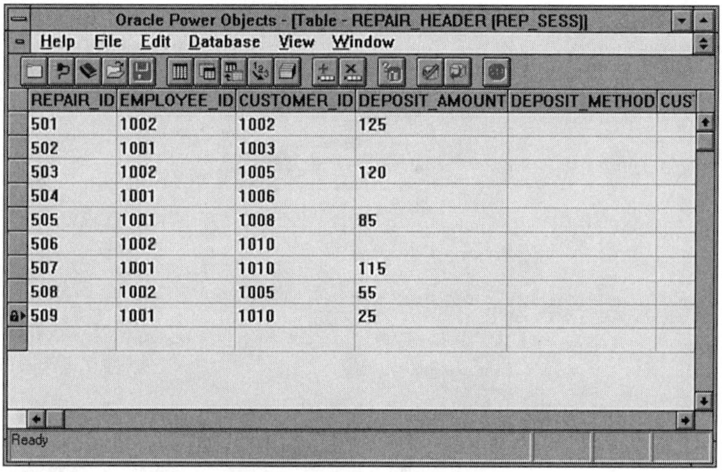

FIGURE G.18.

*Using the Table
Browser to insert a row.*

REPAIR_ID	EMPLOYEE_ID	CUSTOMER_ID	DEPOSIT_AMOUNT	DEPOSIT_METHOD	CUS
501	1002	1002	125		
502	1001	1003			
503	1002	1005	120		
504	1001	1006			
505	1001	1008	85		
506	1002	1010			
507	1001	1010	115		
508	1002	1005	55		
509	1001	1010	25		

When you're finished viewing or changing the contents of the selected table, close the Table Browser by clicking the Stop icon on the toolbar. To bring back the REP_APP application, select the REP_APP entry under the Window menu. When the REP_APP window is visible, create a new form by either selecting New Form under the File menu or clicking the New Form icon on the toolbar, which is to the right of the Scissors icon (see Figure G.19).

FIGURE G.19.

*Creating a Power
Objects form.*

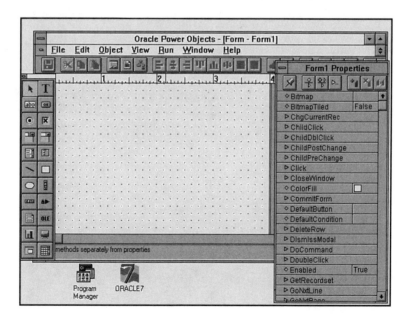

When the new form is created, its property sheet appears. The new form is named Form1; to change its name, scroll down the list of properties until you see Name. Click the field to the right of Name and enter `frmRepairHeader` (see Figure G.20).

FIGURE G.20.

Specifying the form's name on the property sheet.

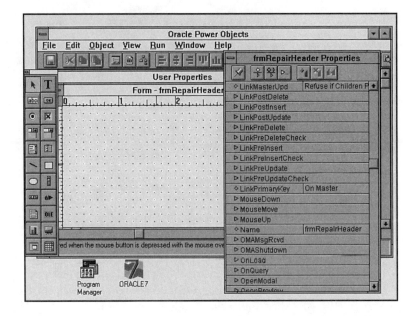

To change the form's label, scroll up to the Label property. Enter Repair Header in the field to the right of Label (see Figure G.21). Keep in mind that you must save your work by either clicking the Save icon or selecting the Save option under the File menu.

FIGURE G.21.

Specify the form's label on the property sheet.

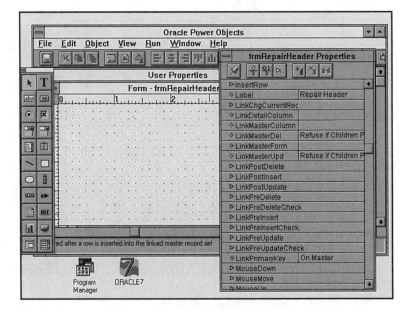

To bind the form to the table, set the Designer's focus on the Table Browser. Select each column that you want to incorporate in the form by clicking on the box to the left of the column name. When you've selected all of the columns that you want to include, drag the columns and drop them on the form. The Power Objects Designer automatically creates a label for each column (see Figure G.22).

FIGURE G.22.

The form generated by the Power Objects Designer.

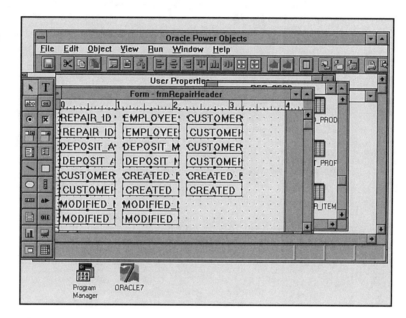

You'll almost certainly want to modify the generated form. It's easy to improve the appearance of the form by rearranging the fields and resizing the labels (see Figure G.23).

FIGURE G.23.

Editing the generated form.

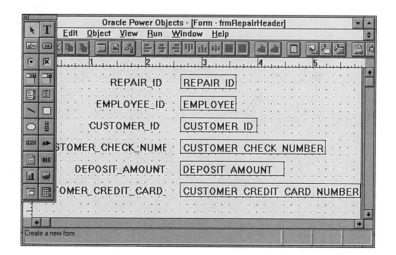

Now, add a scrollbar control for navigating through the data. Select the scrollbar, either horizontal or vertical, from the toolbox and drop it on the form (see Figure G.24).

FIGURE G.24.

Adding a scrollbar control to a form.

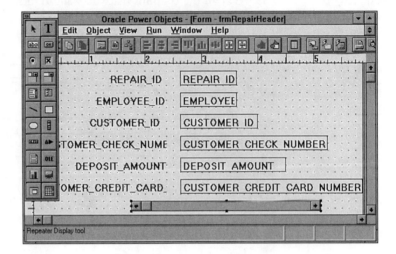

When you're happy with the form's appearance, test the form by clicking the rightmost button on the toolbar (the lightning bolt on a form). When the form is executed, it retrieves the first row and displays it (see Figure G.25). You can scroll through the data with the scrollbar control.

FIGURE G.25.

Running the form.

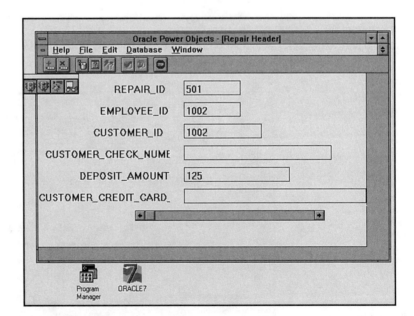

When you're finished testing the form, click the Stop icon. Let's see how we can change the form's property. On the Repair Header property sheet, scroll down to the OrderBy property. Specify Employee_ID for the OrderBy property (see Figure G.26). Try running the form again and verify that the rows are retrieved in order by the Employee_ID.

FIGURE G.26.

Changing the form's OrderBy property.

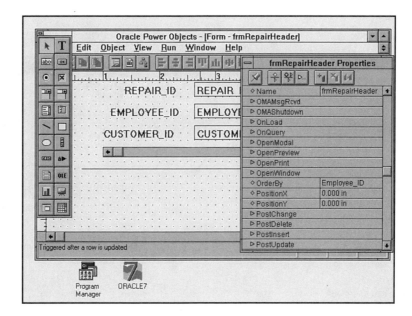

Power Objects makes it very simple to implement a master-detail relationship on a form. The repeater object is used for the detail portion of the form. Select the repeater control from the toolbox—it's the last icon at the bottom of the right-hand row. Drop it on the bottom of the form (see Figure G.27).

FIGURE G.27.

Adding a repeater to the form.

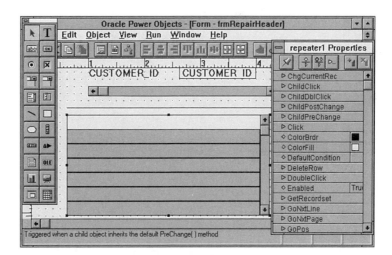

To bind the repeater to the detail table, select the REP_SESS database session by choosing it from the Window menu. Click the Repair_Item table. The Table Browser displays the columns from the Repair_Item table. Select the columns that you want to appear in the detail portion of the form. Drag the selected columns onto the repeater and drop them (see Figure G.28).

FIGURE G.28.

Dragging the detail columns to the repeater.

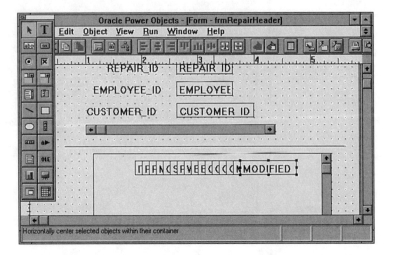

Oracle Power Objects automatically places the fields in the repeater. You'll want to improve the appearance of the detail fields by rearranging them within the repeater. To connect the master and detail portions of the form, return to the repeater's property sheet. Scroll down to the LinkDetailColumn property and set it to Repair_ID. Set the LinkMasterColumn property to Repair_ID. This column is a foreign key in the Repair_Item table and a primary key in the Repair_Header table. Set the LinkMasterForm property to frmRepairHeader (see Figure G.29). Again, try running the form and verify that the master-detail relationship is functioning properly (see Figure G.30).

FIGURE G.29.

Specifying properties for a master-detail relationship.

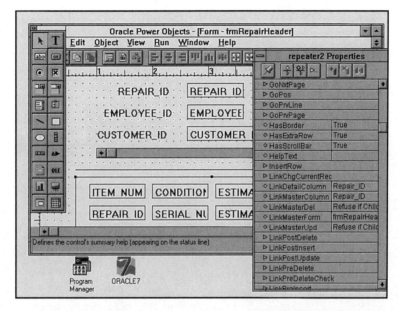

FIGURE G.30.

Running the master-detail form.

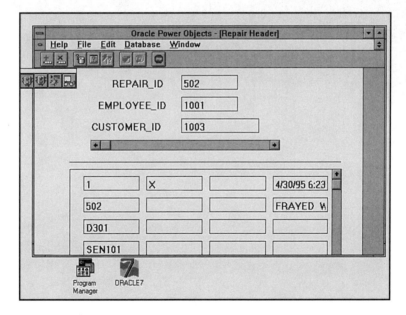

Index

G-H

I

Add to Your Sams Library Today with the Best Books for Programming, Operating Systems, and New Technologies

The easiest way to order is to pick up the phone and call
1-800-428-5331
between 9:00 a.m. and 5:00 p.m. EST.
For faster service please have your credit card available.

ISBN	Quantity	Description of Item	Unit Cost	Total Cost
0-672-30873-8		Essential Oracle7	$25.00	
0-672-30855-X		Teach Yourself SQL in 14 Days	$29.99	
0-672-30474-0		Windows 95 Unleashed (Book/CD-ROM)	$35.00	
0-672-30602-6		Programming Windows 95 Unleashed (Book/CD)	$49.99	
0-672-30717-0		Tricks of the DOOM Programming Gurus (Book/CD-ROM)	$39.99	
0-672-30714-6		Internet Unleashed, 2E (Book/3 CD-ROMs)	$39.99	
0-672-30737-5		World Wide Web Unleashed (Book/CD)	$39.99	
0-672-30669-7		Plug-n-Play Internet (Book/Disk)	$35.00	
0-672-30537-2		TWG UNIX Communications and the Internet	$35.00	
0-672-30676-X		Teach Yourself PowerBuilder 4 in 14 Days	$25.00	
0-672-30695-6		Developing PowerBuilder 4 Applications, 3E (Book/CD-ROM)	$45.00	
0-672-30685-9		Windows NT 3.5 Unleashed, 2E	$39.99	
0-672-30561-5		C Programming: Just the FAQs	$25.00	
0-672-30705-7		Linux Unleashed (Book/CD-ROM)	$49.99	

❏ 3 ½" Disk
❏ 5 ¼" Disk

Shipping and Handling: See information below.	
TOTAL	

Shipping and Handling: $4.00 for the first book, and $1.75 for each additional book. Floppy disk: add $1.75 for shipping and handling. If you need to have it NOW, we can ship product to you in 24 hours for an additional charge of approximately $18.00, and you will receive your item overnight or in two days. Overseas shipping and handling adds $2.00 per book and $8.00 for up to three disks. Prices subject to change. Call for availability and pricing information on latest editions.

201 W. 103rd Street, Indianapolis, Indiana 46290

1-800-428-5331 — Orders   1-800-835-3202 — FAX   1-800-858-7674 — Customer Service

Book ISBN 0-672-30757-X

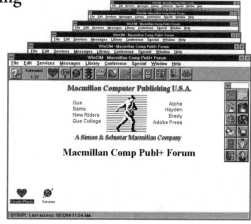